MIRRORING CHINA'S PAST

吉金鑒古

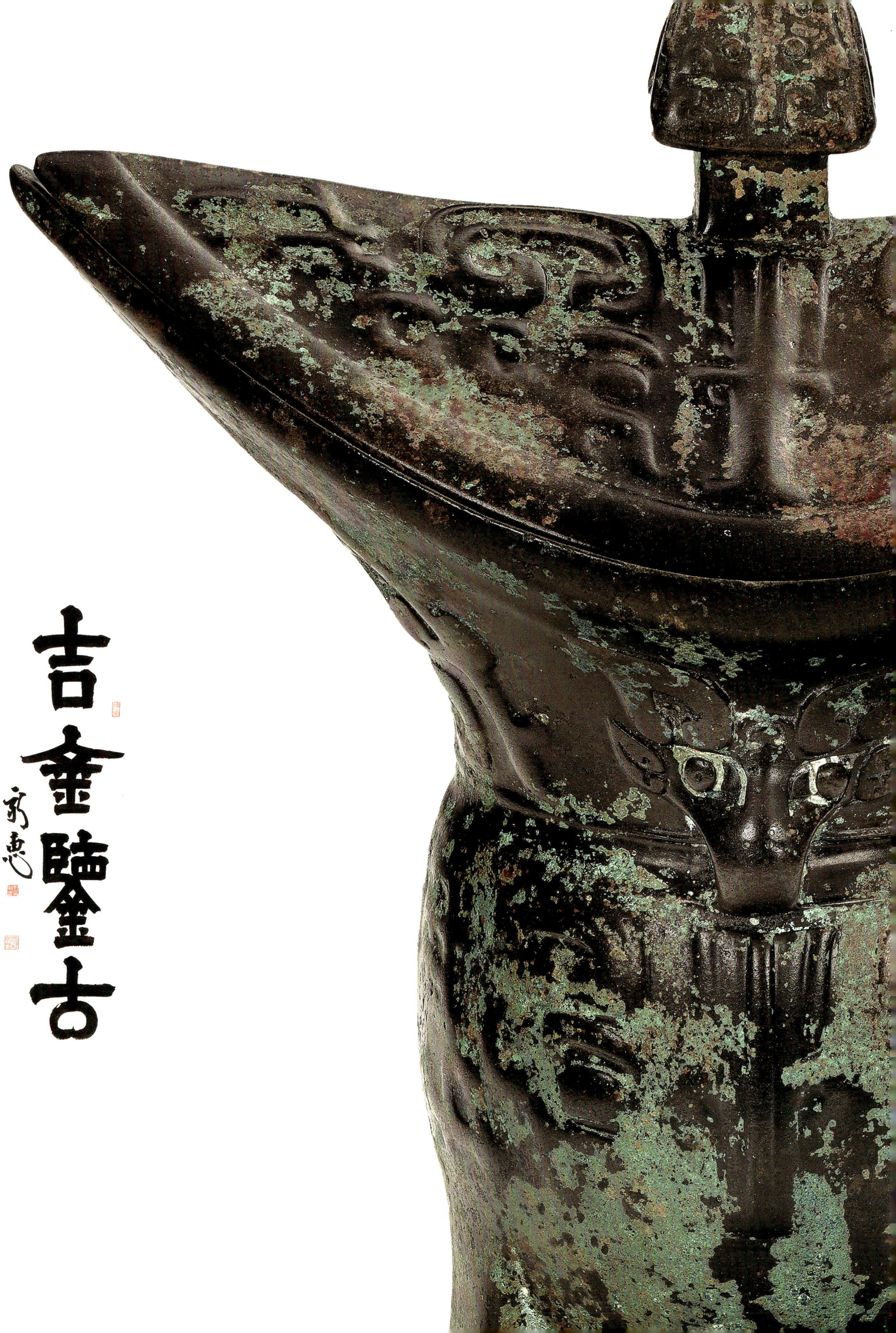

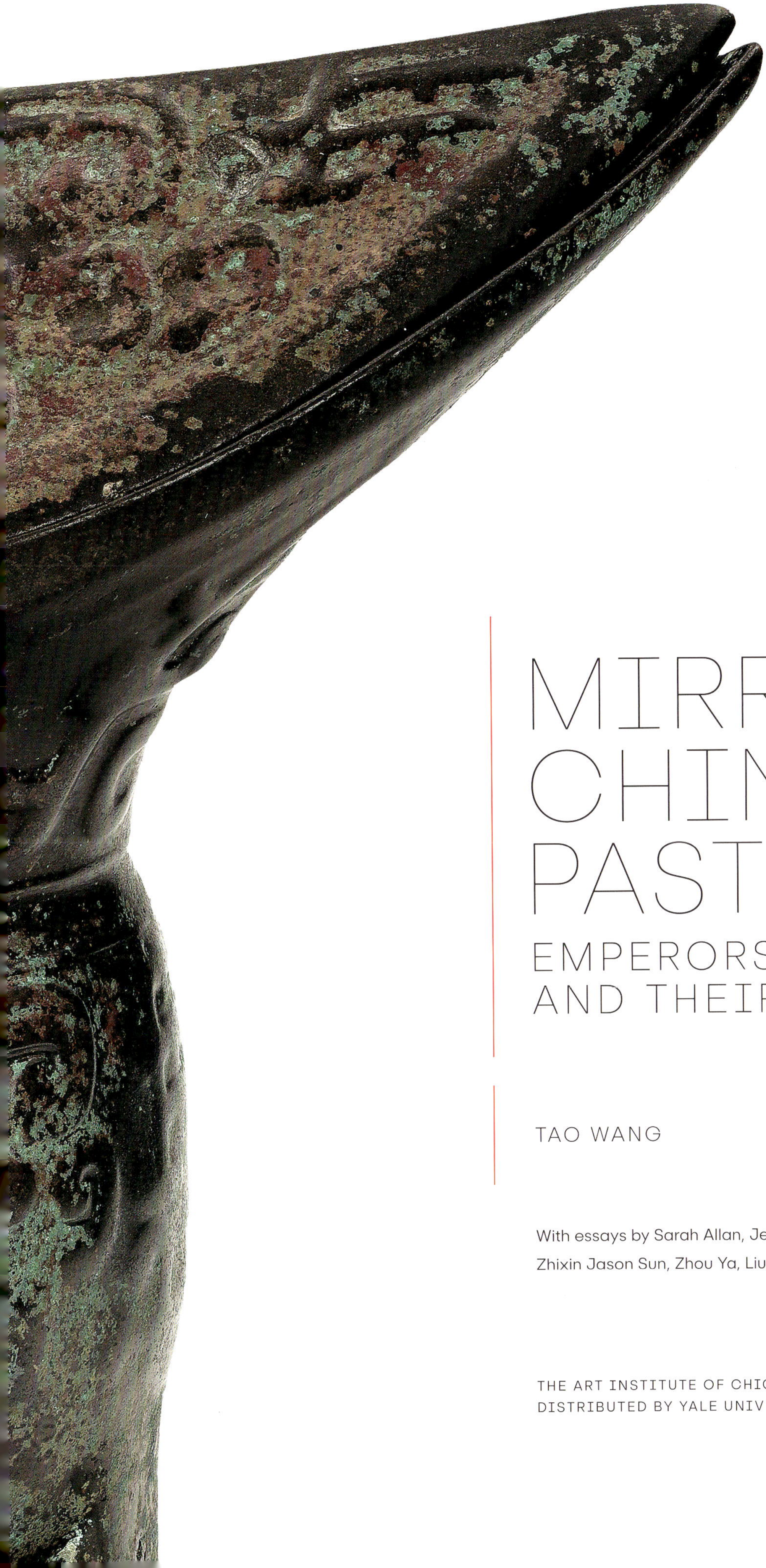

MIRRORING CHINA'S PAST

EMPERORS, SCHOLARS, AND THEIR BRONZES

TAO WANG

With essays by Sarah Allan, Jeffrey Moser, Su Rongyu, Edward L. Shaughnessy, Zhixin Jason Sun, Zhou Ya, Liu Yu, and Lu Zhang

THE ART INSTITUTE OF CHICAGO
DISTRIBUTED BY YALE UNIVERSITY PRESS, NEW HAVEN AND LONDON

Mirroring China's Past: Emperors, Scholars, and Their Bronzes is published in conjunction with an exhibition of the same name held at the Art Institute of Chicago, February 25–May 13, 2018.

Lead support for *Mirroring China's Past: Emperors, Scholars, and Their Bronzes* is generously provided by Debra and Leon Black.

Major support is provided by the Fred Eychaner Fund, The Chauncey and Marion D. McCormick Family Foundation, and The MacLean Foundation.

Additional funding is contributed by Jianming Lv, Terry and William Carey, Honghong Chen, Giuseppe Eskenazi and Daniel Eskenazi, Winnie and Michael Feng, Virginia B. Sonnenschein and the Sonnenschein Exhibition Endowment Fund for Asian and Ancient Art, Robert Tsao and Vivian Chen, and Charles H. Mottier and Philip J. Vidal.

Annual support for Art Institute exhibitions is provided by the Exhibitions Trust: Neil Bluhm and the Bluhm Family Charitable Foundation; Jay Franke and David Herro; Kenneth Griffin; Caryn and King Harris, The Harris Family Foundation; Liz and Eric Lefkofsky; Robert M. and Diane v.S. Levy; Ann and Samuel M. Mencoff; Usha and Lakshmi N. Mittal; Sylvia Neil and Dan Fischel; Thomas and Margot Pritzker; Anne and Chris Reyes; Betsy Bergman Rosenfield and Andrew M. Rosenfield; Cari and Michael J. Sacks; and the Earl and Brenda Shapiro Foundation.

Corporate Exhibition Sponsor

中国银行 BANK OF CHINA

Official Airline of the Art Institute of Chicago

UNITED

Liu Yu's essay, "Emperor Qianlong's Four Catalogues on Bronzes," was translated by Lu Zhang.

Su Rongyu's essay, "Bronze-Casting Technology in the Late Shang Dynasty," and Zhou Ya's essay, "The Hezi *You* Vessels: A Case Study in Authenticity and Forgery," were translated by David Lebovitz.

Zhixin Jason Sun's essay, "A Legend Retold: The Duanfang Bronzes' Journey to the Metropolitan Museum of Art," is an expanded version of an essay originally published in Chinese as "Duanfang, Mogen, Fukaisen: Xi Zhou Qingtong jin rucang daduhui bowuguan de yiduan chuanqi" in *Zhou ye lu min* [Noble Life of the Zhou: Bronzes Unearthed from the Cemetery of the Western Zhou Aristocrats at Shigushan of Baoji], exh. cat. (Shanghai: Shanghai shuhua chubanshe, 2014), 41–50. It was translated by Anne Feng and Thomas Kelly.

First edition

Printed in Canada

Hardcover ISBN: 978-0-300-22863-2
Softcover ISBN: 978-0-86559-298-8

Library of Congress Cataloging-in-Publication Data
Names: Wang, Tao, 1962– | Art Institute of Chicago, organizer, host institution.
Title: Mirroring China's past : emperors, scholars, and their bronzes / Tao Wang ; with essays by Sarah Allan, Jeffrey Moser, Su Rongyu, Edward L. Shaughnessy, Zhixin Jason Sun, Zhou Ya, Liu Yu, and Lu Zhang.
Description: Chicago, Illinois : The Art Institute of Chicago, 2018. | Published in conjunction with an exhibition of the same name held at the Art Institute of Chicago, February 25–May 13, 2018. | Includes bibliographical references and index.
Identifiers: LCCN 2017057170 | ISBN 9780300228632 (hardback) | ISBN 9780865592988 (softcover)
Subjects: LCSH: Bronzes, Chinese—To 221 B.C.—Exhibitions. | Bronzes, Chinese—Collectors and collecting—China—Exhibitions. | China—Kings and rulers—Art patronage—Exhibitions. | Art and society—China—Exhibitions. | China—Intellectual life—Exhibitions. | BISAC: ART / Asian. | ANTIQUES & COLLECTIBLES / Silver, Gold & Other Metals. | HISTORY / Asia / China. | HISTORY / Ancient / General. | ART / Collections, Catalogs, Exhibitions / Group Shows.
Classification: LCC NK7983.22 .M57 2018 | DDC 739.5/120951—dc23
LC record available at https://lccn.loc.gov/2017057170

Published by
The Art Institute of Chicago
111 South Michigan Avenue
Chicago, Illinois 60603-6404
www.artic.edu

Distributed by
Yale University Press
302 Temple Street
P.O. Box 209040
New Haven, Connecticut 06520-9040
www.yalebooks.com/art

Produced by the Department of Publishing at the Art Institute of Chicago

Gregory Nosan, Executive Director

Edited by Amy R. Peltz and Elissa Park

Production by Lauren Makholm, Joseph Mohan, and Rachel Edsill

Photography research by Katie Levi

Cartography by Mapping Specialists Limited

Proofreading by Kristina Youso

Indexing by Scott Smiley

Unless otherwise noted, photography of works of art is by Robert Hashimoto, Christopher Gallagher, Jonathan Mathias, Aidan Fitzpatrick, and Craig Stillwell, with postproduction by Jonathan Mathias and Shelby Silvernell, Department of Imaging, the Art Institute of Chicago.

Designed and typeset in Publica Sans by The Grillo Group, Inc., Chicago, Illinois

Separations by Professional Graphics, Rockford, Illinois

Printing and binding by Friesens, Altona, Manitoba

Front cover: Ewer (*he*), Warring States period (475–221 BC) (detail; pl.101); back cover: Tai Xiangzhou (Chinese, born 1968), *Painting of the "Bucket of Minister Xi,"* 2017 (detail; pl.171).

Details: pp. 2–3: *Goblet of Father Ding* (*Fu Ding Jue*), Western Zhou dynasty (1046–771 BC) (pl. 30); p. 8: Jar (*hu* or *zhong*), Western Han dynasty (206 BC–AD 9) (pl. 21); p. 10: Artists unknown, *One or Two? (Shiyi Shier Tu)*, Mental Cultivation Hall (*Yangxindian*) version, Qing dynasty (1644–1911), Qianlong reign (1735–96) (pl. 138); p. 16: *Bucket of Fu Cheng* (*Fu Cheng You*), late Shang dynasty (c. 1250–1046 BC) (pl. 12); p. 84: Qiu Ying (Chinese, 1494–1552), *Appreciating Antiquities in the Bamboo Garden* (*Zhuyan Pingui*), Ming dynasty (1368–1644) (pl. 162); p. 126: Vessel in the form of an ancient bronze jar (*hu*), Qing dynasty (1644–1911), Qianlong reign (1735–96) (pl. 132); p. 186: *Pedestaled Tureen of Duke Ju* (*Bo Ju Gui*), Western Zhou dynasty (1046–771 BC) (pl. 13); p. 230: Flask (*bianhu*), Warring States period (475–221 BC) (pl. 103).

The calligraphy on the title page is by Liu Xinhiu.

This book was made using paper and materials certified by the Forest Stewardship Council, which ensures responsible forest management.

FSC www.fsc.org MIX Paper from responsible sources FSC® C016245

CONTENTS

Lead support is generously provided by Debra and Leon Black.

Major support is provided by the Fred Eychaner Fund, The Chauncey and Marion D. McCormick Family Foundation, and The MacLean Foundation.

Additional funding is contributed by Jianming Lv, Terry and William Carey, Honghong Chen, Giuseppe Eskenazi and Daniel Eskenazi, Winnie and Michael Feng, Virginia B. Sonnenschein and the Sonnenschein Exhibition Endowment Fund for Asian and Ancient Art, Robert Tsao and Vivian Chen, and Charles H. Mottier and Philip J. Vidal.

Annual support for Art Institute exhibitions is provided by the Exhibitions Trust: Neil Bluhm and the Bluhm Family Charitable Foundation; Jay Franke and David Herro; Kenneth Griffin; Caryn and King Harris, The Harris Family Foundation; Liz and Eric Lefkofsky; Robert M. and Diane v.S. Levy; Ann and Samuel M. Mencoff; Usha and Lakshmi N. Mittal; Sylvia Neil and Dan Fischel; Thomas and Margot Pritzker; Anne and Chris Reyes; Betsy Bergman Rosenfield and Andrew M. Rosenfield; Cari and Michael J. Sacks; and the Earl and Brenda Shapiro Foundation.

Corporate Exhibition Sponsor

中国银行 BANK OF CHINA

Official Airline of the Art Institute of Chicago

UNITED

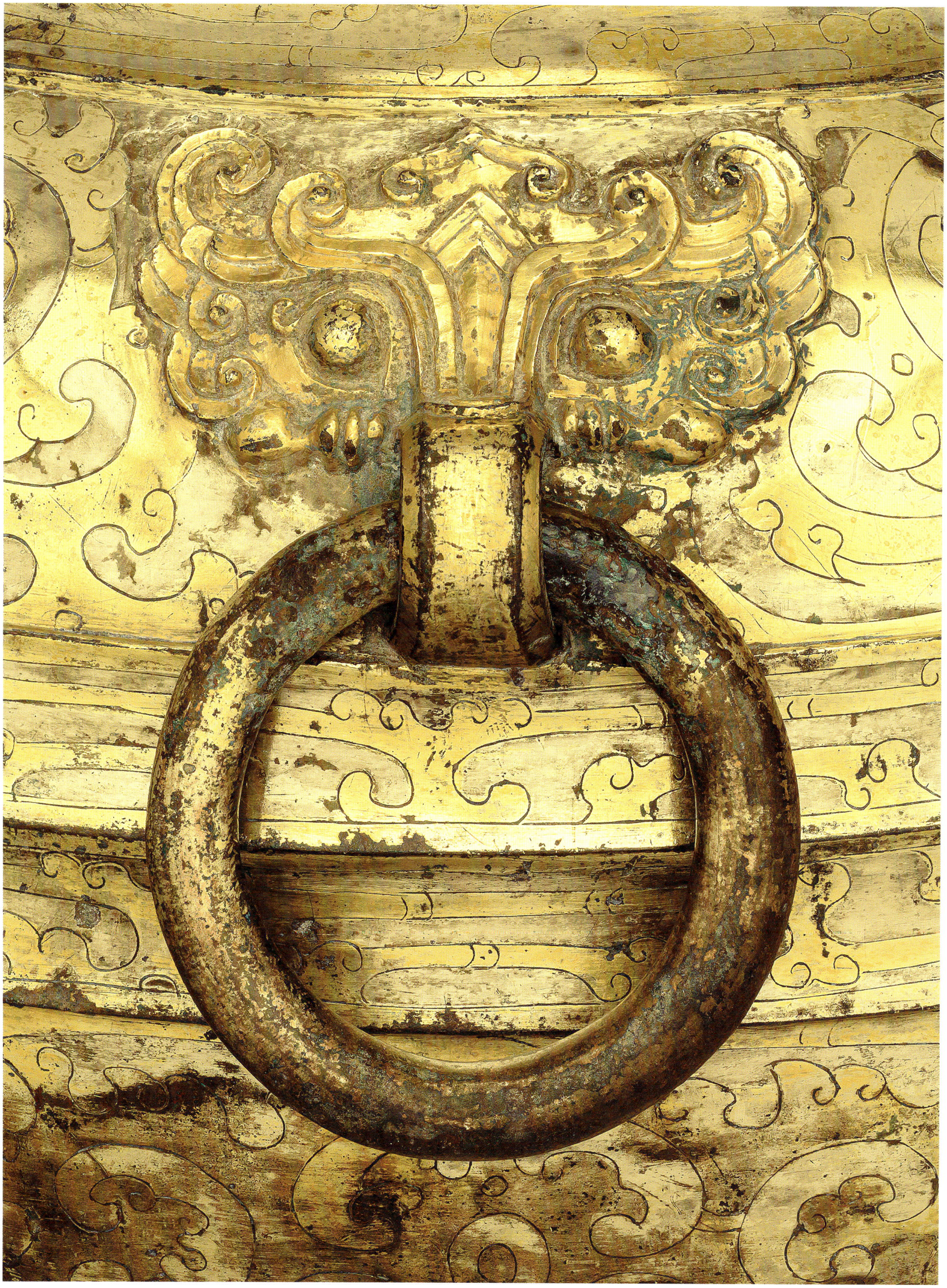

FOREWORD

Mirroring China's Past: Emperors, Scholars, and Their Bronzes celebrates Chinese bronzes and the tradition of collecting and study that developed around them over the course of centuries. This focus on collecting is fitting for an exhibition generated by the Art Institute of Chicago, which in some sense can be understood as a collection of collections. Indeed, the museum's own ancient bronzes were, before their donation, assembled by Kate S. Buckingham, one of our earliest and most generous supporters. Previous examinations of these objects explored the archaeological context of their discovery. This exhibition and catalogue illuminate how such works—some of the most distinctive achievements in the history of art—were created and originally used. They also examine how they were collected, classified, and understood, particularly from the twelfth through the early twentieth centuries. People variously approached bronzes as ritual implements, instruments of power, aesthetic objects, and historical documents. The cultural practices surrounding bronzes, with their focus on antiquity and rulership, have strongly influenced individuals and society in China through the ages.

Mirroring China's Past is organized under the leadership of Tao Wang, Pritzker Chair of Asian Art and Curator of Chinese Art and Executive Director of Initiatives in Asia, a new role at the Art Institute. His expertise has been vital to our efforts to form and strengthen partnerships with museums and other institutions around the world. *Mirroring China's Past* exemplifies the fruits of such cooperation. It features more than 170 works of art and, although a number come from the Art Institute's own strong holdings, the majority has been generously loaned by the Palace Museum in Beijing and the Shanghai Museum, with the rest coming from museums and private collections in the United States. This exhibition marks the first time many of these bronzes will be shown together after hundreds of years of separation, and it includes pieces that can be traced back to the collections amassed by China's emperors and eminent scholars. *Mirroring China's Past* not only presents works of exceptional quality, it also constitutes the largest exhibition of Chinese bronzes ever seen outside of China.

Most objects in the exhibition are bronze vessels that were created through a unique method using clay models and piece molds. Made for the ritual preparation and consumption of food and wine and found primarily in tombs, these bronzes were originally used in sacrifices to ancestors, to accompany the deceased to the underworld, and to commemorate ancestors and lineages in public ceremonies. When later rediscovered by Chinese emperors, bronzes—especially tripod cauldrons—acquired symbolic meaning as auspicious omens and manifestations of divine power that bestowed a heavenly mandate to rule. Scholars and artists also collected and studied these objects, often focusing on their inscriptions, using them as sources for historical research, and exchanging them as tokens of friendship. The exhibition includes many artworks in other forms and materials that inspired, and were inspired by, bronzes.

We acknowledge the generosity of the donors who made this project possible. Debra and Leon Black generously provided lead support. Major support was provided by the Fred Eychaner Fund, The Chauncey and Marion D. McCormick Family Foundation, and The MacLean Foundation. Additional funding was contributed by Jianming Lv, Terry and William Carey, Honghong Chen, Giuseppe Eskenazi and Daniel Eskenazi, Winnie and Michael Feng, Virginia B. Sonnenschein and the Sonnenschein Exhibition Endowment Fund for Asian and Ancient Art, Robert Tsao and Vivian Chen, and Charles H. Mottier and Philip J. Vidal. Annual support for Art Institute exhibitions is provided by the Exhibitions Trust: Neil Bluhm and the Bluhm Family Charitable Foundation; Jay Franke and David Herro; Kenneth Griffin; Caryn and King Harris, The Harris Family Foundation; Liz and Eric Lefkofsky; Robert M. and Diane v.S. Levy; Ann and Samuel M. Mencoff; Usha and Lakshmi N. Mittal; Sylvia Neil and Dan Fischel; Thomas and Margot Pritzker; Anne and Chris Reyes; Betsy Bergman Rosenfield and Andrew M. Rosenfield; Cari and Michael J. Sacks; and the Earl and Brenda Shapiro Foundation. The Bank of China generously sponsored the exhibition. United Airlines also provided valuable support.

I congratulate Tao Wang for his extraordinary work on this ambitious project and for creating an exhibition and catalogue that beautifully highlight new scholarship and celebrate the fascinating dialogue of artists, collectors, and objects across centuries. In surveying the different meanings bronzes have held for their varied audiences in previous eras, *Mirroring China's Past* encourages us to make connections—with the art, with other viewers, and with other global institutions—in the present.

JAMES RONDEAU
President and Eloise W. Martin Director
The Art Institute of Chicago

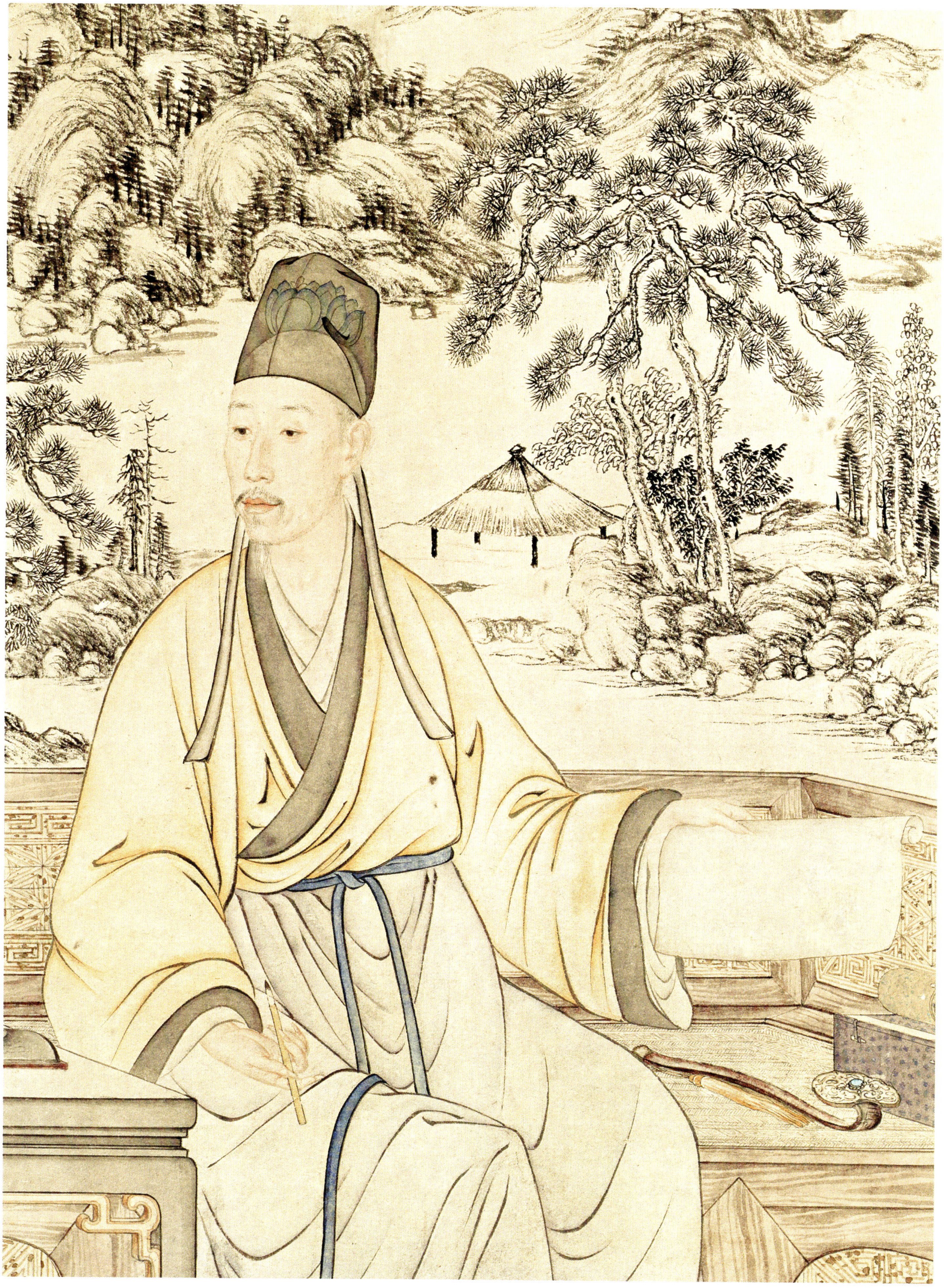

ACKNOWLEDGMENTS

Three years ago, Douglas Druick, then president and director of the Art Institute of Chicago, invited me to conceive and mount an exhibition on Chinese art in 2018. I had joined the museum only a few months before as Pritzker Chair of Asian Art and was still acclimating to Chicago and familiarizing myself with the museum's wonderful collections. That the subject of the exhibition should be Chinese bronzes seemed obvious. I had spent the past ten years researching them and had made some exciting findings that I wanted to share with a wider public. Moreover, the Art Institute had recently signed a collaborative agreement with the Palace Museum, Beijing, which holds many significant bronzes. It is an honor and privilege to curate a special exhibition of this scope and ambition so soon after my arrival, and one that so perfectly meshes with my additional role as executive director of initiatives in Asia. First and foremost, I am deeply grateful to Douglas for his unwavering trust as I developed the project, and to his successor, James Rondeau, for wholeheartedly supporting its completion.

Mirroring China's Past was also the work of Lu Zhang, Assistant Curator of Chinese Art at the Art Institute. Lu not only assisted in the negotiation of the loans, conducted valuable research, and contributed an essay to the catalogue, but she also tirelessly teamed with the Departments of Exhibition Project Management, Learning and Public Engagement, Publishing, and Digital Experience to coordinate all aspects of the show. I thank Lu for the critical role she has played.

I am immensely grateful as well to the primary lenders to the exhibition, the Palace Museum and the Shanghai Museum, who have both lent some of their most treasured pieces. The Palace Museum's collection of bronzes derives largely from the old imperial collections of the Qing dynasty, and these important objects are rarely displayed beyond the Forbidden City. The Shanghai Museum also has one of the best collections of Chinese bronzes in the world, and these as well have rarely been seen in the context of the history of collecting. For their tremendous support for the exhibition, I thank Shan Qixiang, director, and Feng Nai'en and Lou Wei, vice-directors, of the Palace Museum, and Yang Zhigang and Li Zhongmou, director and vice director of the Shanghai Museum. I also thank my colleagues at these two institutions, listed here in alphabetical order. I am especially grateful to my fellow curators Ding Meng, He Lin, Li Huan, Li Mijia, Lü Chenglong, Song Yongji, Yu Hui, and Zhang Zhen at the Palace Museum, and Ge Liang, Ling Lizhong, Ma Jinhong, and Zhou Ya at the Shanghai Museum. The staff of the Palace Museum's Foreign Affairs Department—Li Shaoyi, Luo Mengdan, Yu Jialiu, and Yuan Hong—was extremely helpful, as was the staff of the Shanghai Museum's Cultural Exchange Office—Liang Wei, Xu Liyi, and Zhou Yanqun. Photographers Hu Chui, Jin Yueping, Li Fan, Liu Mingjie, Liu Zhigang, Tian Mingjie, Wang Jin, Yu Ningchuan, and Zhao Shan of the Palace Museum as well as photographer Zhang Xudong of the Shanghai Museum contributed many of the stunning images reproduced here. Our museums' partnership and energetic spirit of collaboration were key to the success of the endeavor.

I am also very appreciative of the other lending museums, and in particular their directors and curators who share my passion for Chinese bronzes: the Metropolitan Museum of Art, New York, and Brooke Russell Astor Curator of Chinese Art Jason Zhixin Sun; the Museum of Fine Arts, Boston, and Wu Tung Curator of Chinese Art Nancy Berliner; the Harvard University Art Museums/Arthur M. Sackler Museum and Alan J. Dworsky Associate Curator of Chinese Art Melissa Moy; the Minneapolis Institute of Art and Curator of Chinese Art and Head of the Department of Asian Art Liu Yang; the Nelson-Atkins Museum of Art, Kansas City, and Senior Curator of Early Chinese Art Colin Mackenzie; the Asian Art Museum, San Francisco, and Director and Chief Executive Officer Jay Xu, and Senior Associate Curator of Chinese Art Fan Jeremy Zhang. Several distinguished private collections also generously lent several significant pieces, and I particularly wish to acknowledge the Xiling Collection and Richard A. Pegg of the Maclean Collection for their enthusiastic support. Gay-Young Cho and Christopher Chiu, and Wu Hung and Judith Zeitlin have also shared items from their splendid collections, enabling us to offer a more complete account of Chinese bronzes than ever before.

Although I wrote the main chapters of this catalogue, it would not be complete without the outstanding contributions of Researcher Su Rongyu, the Institute for the History of Natural Sciences, Chinese Academy of Sciences, Beijing; Burlington Northern Foundation Professor of Asian Studies Sarah Allan, Dartmouth College; Lorraine J. and Herrlee G. Creel Distinguished Service Professor in Early Chinese Studies Edward Shaughnessy, University of Chicago;

Assistant Professor of History of Art and Architecture Jeffrey Moser, Brown University; Researcher Liu Yu, Palace Museum, Beijing; and Curator of Ancient Bronzes Zhou Ya, Shanghai Museum; as well as those of Jason Zhixin Sun at the Metropolitan Museum of Art and Lu Zhang at the Art Institute. I truly appreciate their expertise and friendship. David Lebovitz translated the essays by Su Rongyu and Zhou Ya, Anne Feng and Thomas Kelly translated the essay by Jason Zhixin Sun, and Lu Zhang translated Liu Yu's essay. My friend the renowned artist Liu Xinhui wrote the calligraphy that graces the title page. For the expertly produced film documenting how bronzes were used in ancient rituals, I thank Johnson Chang and his team, in particular Peng Lin, Jeffery Shaw, and Paul Nichola.

At the Art Institute, I am fortunate to work with a group of talented colleagues. This catalogue would not have been possible without the dedicated skill of the team in Publishing: Gregory Nosan, Jessica Applebee, Sara Carminati, Rachel Edsill, Katie Levi, Lauren Makholm, Lisa Meyerowitz, Joseph Mohan, Elissa Park, Amy Peltz, interns Kenneth Guay and Shelby Ragsdale, and freelancers Kristina Youso and Scott Smiley. Maria Grillo and Kristin Cullen of The Grillo Group provided the elegant, contemporary design. The skilled staff in Imaging—Christopher Gallagher, Robert Hashimoto, Robert Lifson, Jonathan Mathias, Shelby Silvernell, and Craig Stillwell—produced much of the beautiful photography featured here.

Led by Eve Coffee Jeffers, Development, including James Allan, Elizabeth Dolan Wright, Anne-Marie Gwynn-Sackson, Jonathan Kinkley, Erika R. Lowe, George J. Martin, Jennifer A. Moran, and Jennifer Oatess ensured that the project had the resources it needed to succeed. In Project Management, Sara E. Urizar, Jennifer Paoletti, Zahra Bahia, Leticia Pardo, and Yau-mu Huang ably shepherded the exhibition to completion and conceived and executed its evocative design. Former colleague Jennifer Draffen, Darrell Green in Registration, and Suzanne R. Schnepp and Rachel K. Freeman in Conservation attended to the objects with care. In Legal, Maria Simon brought her expertise to complex loan agreements. Susanna Kim Vitayaudom and Salvador Cruz in Graphic Design helped make the exhibition plan a reality. Emily Lew Fry, Nenette Luarca-Shoaf, Wilson McBee, and Fawn A. Ring in Learning and Public Engagement, led by Jacqueline Terrassa, made the exhibition accessible and exciting to visitors. Michael Neault, Jennifer Snyder, Kelly McHugh, and Kyle Obriot in Digital Experience provided videos that enhanced that endeavor. In Marketing and Public Affairs, Amanda Hicks, Nora A. Gainer, and Julie P. White generated excitement about an unfamiliar subject. In Museum Facilities, Joseph Vatinno and his staff helped make the exhibition a success. In the Director's Office, I again extend warm appreciation to James Rondeau and Sarah Guernsey.

Special thanks go to my colleagues in the Asian Art Department, in particular Annette Gaspers, Charles P. Pietraszewski, and Chi Hoang Nguyen, as well as former colleague Elinor Pearlstein and volunteers Han Zhang, Xi Zhang, Anne Feng, Wenjing Wang, Yin Wu, and Zhiwei Zhou. Their support and commitment were vital to the exhibition's success. I have enjoyed working with them at every step of the process.

Last but most definitely not least, I offer my heartfelt appreciation to the sponsors of this exhibition, many of whom are close personal friends, in particular Christopher Hunt of The Chauncey and Marion D. McCormick Family Foundation; Xu Chen, Cheng Yifei, Vincent Zhao, and Xu Kefei of The Bank of China; Jimmy Lv; Bill Carey; Honghong Chen; Giuseppe Eskenazi and Daniel Eskenazi; Winnie and Michael Feng; and Tara Cederholm. Without their trust and generosity, this project would never have materialized. As they did for Chinese scholars of the eighteenth century, bronzes have once again served as a vehicle for intellectual and cultivating friendships. I dedicate this project to you all—friends of bronze and stone (*jinshi zhijiao*).

TAO WANG
Executive Director of Initiatives in Asia and
Pritzker Chair of Asian Art and Curator of Chinese Art
The Art Institute of Chicago

NOTE TO THE READER

Chinese words and phrases have been romanized according to the Hanyu Pinyin system. For the most part, Chinese names have been standardized following the Chinese convention of putting the surname first. We have, however, retained the Western format of given name first for contemporary scholars who have themselves adopted this convention.

Titles of artworks and books appear first in English, followed by Pinyin in parentheses. Subsequent mentions of a work within the same essay use the English only.

The plate sections are organized primarily thematically, according to the topics of the chapters they follow.

Until the end of Shang dynasty (1046 BC), all date ranges for cultures and dynasties are approximate. Beginning with the Zhou dynasty, date ranges for dynasties and reigns are exact, although they may vary from those employed in other publications depending on what event is used to mark the start of the reign. The following conventions are used for dates:

1911 | in 1911

c. 1911 | sometime around 1911

c. 1600–1046 BC | from within or around 1600 to within or around 1046

1644–1911 | from 1644 to 1911

AD and BC are noted only in cases of change of century or other instances where there could be confusion.

The dimensions of objects are given in as complete a form as possible. As different lenders follow different conventions regarding dimensions, some variation exists. Unless otherwise noted, height precedes width precedes depth, and height and/or width precede diameter.

The checklist employs conventional abbreviations for a selected list of historical catalogues that appears at the beginning of that section; the abbreviations are based on the works' Chinese titles. Elsewhere, citations appear in full on first mention. If an object bears an inscription, it is illustrated in the checklist or, in a few cases, elsewhere in the book, as noted in the checklist.

Unless otherwise noted, translations are by the author of the essay in which they appear, or of the translator of the essay in which they appear.

CHRONOLOGY OF ANCIENT CHINA

Bronze Age

NORTHWEST

Majiayao culture, c. 3100–2700 BC

Qijia culture, c. 2050–1700 BC

Longshan culture, c. 2500–2000 BC

Siba culture, c. 2000–1600 BC

Siwa culture, c. 1350–1000 BC

Xindian culture, c. 1000 BC

NORTHEAST

Zhukaigou culture, c. 2000–1400 BC

Lijiaya culture, c. 1200–1000 BC

SOUTHEAST

Wucheng culture, c. 1500–1000 BC

SOUTHWEST

Sanxingdui culture, c. 1400–1000 BC

CENTRAL PLAINS

Erlitou culture, c. 1900–1600 BC

Erligang culture, c. 1600–1400 BC

Shang dynasty, c. 1600–1046 BC
- Early Shang, c. 1600–1400 BC
- Middle Shang, c. 1400–1250 BC
- Late Shang, c. 1250–1046 BC

Zhou dynasty, 1046–256 BC
- Western Zhou, 1046–771 BC
  - Early Western Zhou, 1046–927 BC
  - Mid-Western Zhou, 927–850 BC
  - Late Western Zhou, 850–771 BC

Eastern Zhou period, 770–221 BC

Spring and Autumn period, 770–476 BC

Warring States period, 475–221 BC

Empires and Dynasties

Qin dynasty, 221–206 BC

Han dynasty, 206 BC–AD 220
- Western Han, 206 BC–AD 9
- Wang-Mang interregnum, 9–23
- Eastern Han, 25–220

Six Dynasties, 220–589
- Three Kingdoms, 220–280
- Jin, 265–420
- Southern and Northern Dynasties, 420–589

Sui dynasty, 581–618

Tang dynasty, 618–907

Five Dynasties, 907–960

Song dynasty, 960–1279
- Northern Song, 960–1127
- Southern Song, 1127–1279

Liao dynasty, 907–1125

Jin dynasty, 1115–1234

Xixia (Western Xia) dynasty, 1038–1227

Yuan dynasty, 1271–1368

Ming dynasty, 1368–1644

Qing dynasty, 1644–1911

EMPERORS OF THE SONG, YUAN, MING, AND QING DYNASTIES

Emperors are identified by their temple names, which were given posthumously for the purpose of rites and sacrifices. Those who did not receive temple names are designated by their reign titles or personal names and are given in parentheses. For emperors of the Ming and Qing dynasties, their commonly known reign titles follow their temple names, separated by a slash.

Song dynasty, 960–1279

NORTHERN SONG, 960–1127

Taizu, 960–76

Taizong, 977–97

Zhenzong, 998–1022

Renzong, 1023–63

Yingzong, 1064–67

Shenzong, 1068–85

Zhezong, 1086–1100

Huizong, 1100–1126

Qinzong, 1126–27

SOUTHERN SONG, (1127–1279)

Gaozong, 1127–62

Xiaozong, 1163–89

Guangzong, 1190–94

Ningzong, 1195–1224

Lizong, 1225–64

Duzong, 1265–74

Gongzong, 1275

Duanzong, 1276–77

(Di, Bing), 1278–79

Yuan dynasty, 1271–1368

Shizu, 1260–94

Chengzong, 1295–1307

Wuzong, 1308–11

Renzong, 1312–20

Yingzong, 1321–23

(Taidingdi), 1324–28

Wenzong, 1328–29

Mingzong, 1329

Ningzong, 1332

(Shundi), 1333–68

Ming dynasty, 1368–1644

Taizu/Hongwu, 1368–98

Huidi/Jianwen, 1399–1402

Chengzu/Yongle, 1403–24

Renzong/Hongxi, 1425

Xuanzong/Xuande, 1426–35

Yingzong/Zhengtong, 1436–49

Daizong/Jingtai, 1450–56

Yingzong/Tianshun, 1457–64

Xianzong/Chenghua, 1465–87

Xiaozong/Hongzhi, 1488–1505

Wuzong/Zhengde, 1506–21

Shizong/Jiajing, 1522–66

Muzong/Longqing, 1567–72

Shenzong/Wanli, 1573–1620

Guangzong/Taichang, 1620

Xizong/Tianqi, 1621–27

Sizong/Chongzhen, 1628–44

Qing dynasty, 1644–1911

Shizu/Shunzhi, 1644–61

Shengzu/Kangxi, 1662–1722

Shizong/Yongzheng, 1723–35

Gaozong/Qianlong, 1735–96

Renzong/Jiaqing, 1796–1820

Xuanzong/Daoguang, 1821–50

Wenzong/Xianfeng, 1851–61

Muzong/Tongzhi, 1862–74

Dezong/Guangxu, 1875–1908

(Puyi)/Xuantong, 1909–11

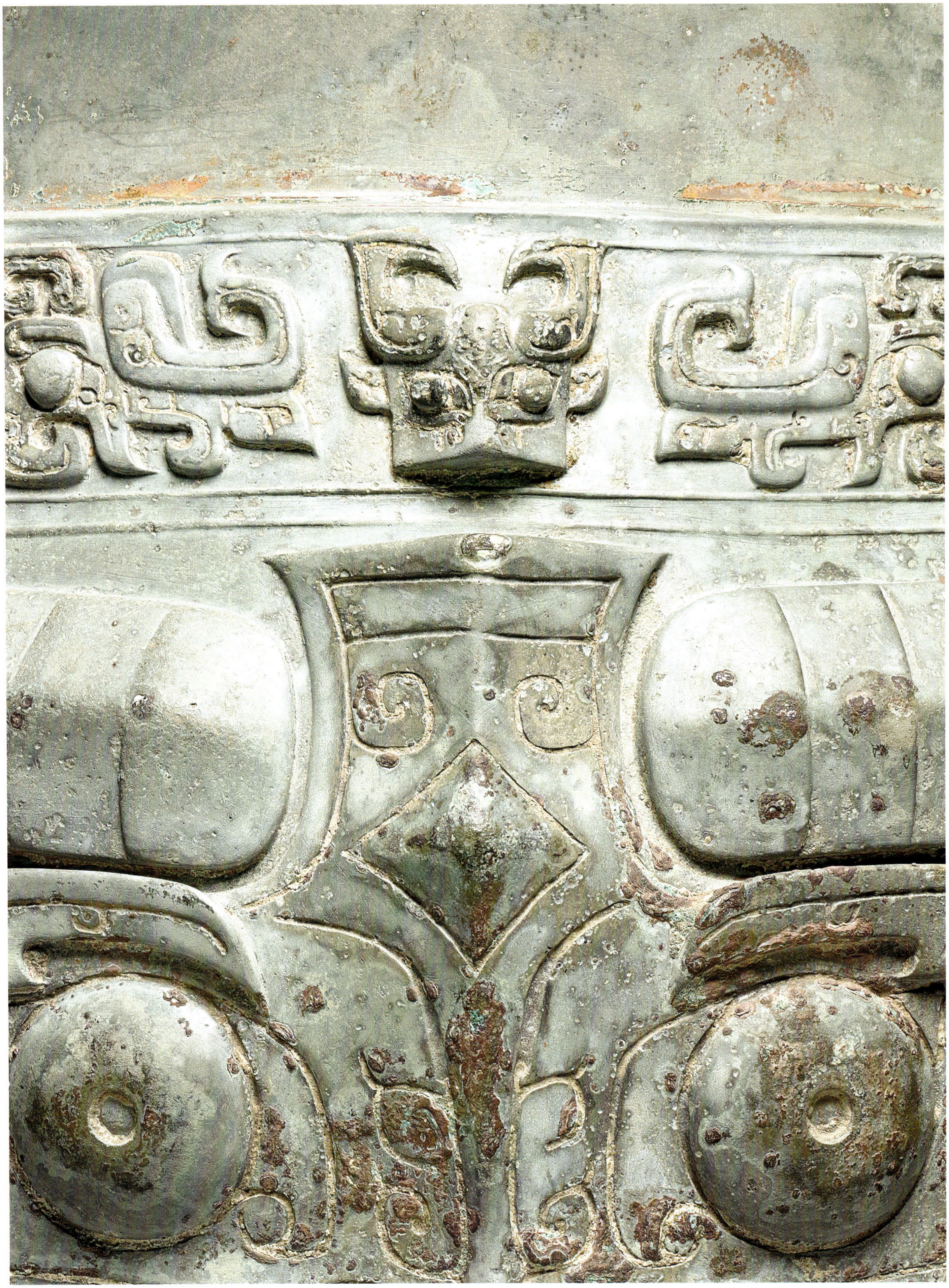

物意

MATTER OF THINGS

HOW TO READ ANCIENT CHINESE BRONZES

TAO WANG

Bronze as History

China's splendid past seems inevitably associated with the Three Dynasties (*sandai*): the Xia (c. 2100–1600 BC), the Shang (c. 1600–1046 BC), and the Zhou (traditionally understood as the Western Zhou, 1046–771 BC), when purportedly sage kings ruled the country, people lived in harmony, and society was regulated by the codified ritual system known as *li*.[1] It was during this period that the basic characteristics of Chinese civilization developed. When later historians looked at the past, they saw the Three Dynasties as a golden age, whose institutions, philosophy, and artifacts served as a model and inspiration for later generations.[2]

Materially, the Three Dynasties are marked by the invention and increasingly sophisticated use of bronze—the Bronze Age as defined by Western historians and archeologists. The invention of bronze was a technological breakthrough in human history. An alloy made mainly of tin and copper, bronze was a substance that was harder and more enduring than anything that had ever been created. Its use to structure. The Bronze Age seems to have advanced first in western and central Asia around the third millennium BC, more than a thousand years earlier than in central China.[3] The origin of the Bronze Age in China is still controversial; indeed, some scholars challenge its definition and question whether the Three Age system (Stone-Bronze-Iron) is applicable to China.[4] The obsession to determine "Who was the first to use bronze?" and "Was its development dependent or indigenous?" has abated, and now historians and archaeologists are much more interested in understanding the dynamics of bronze metallurgy and its bearing on societies in which it was used.

In Bronze Age China (see fig. 1) the earliest bronze objects are the knives and chisels found at the Majiayao culture (c. 3100–2700 BC) and Qijia culture (c. 2050–1700 BC) sites in northwestern Gansu. At the Taosi site (in Shanxi), a bronze fragment found in the 1980s has been dated to circa 2000 BC. These discoveries offer clues for investigating the beginning of bronze use in early China, but these are small and limited finds. Evidence of an independent tradition of bronze metallurgy is first seen with the arrival of the Erlitou culture (c. 1900–1600 BC) in central Henan, which provides unequivocal proof of an independent tradition of bronze metallurgy. Bronze axes, daggers, knives, plaques, small bells, and vessels—such as cauldrons, containers, and goblets—were retrieved from tombs and the residential area. Although some bronze objects may have been imported from the steppes, the majority of the bronze pieces found at Erlitou were of local manufacture. As the Erlitou culture falls within the traditional chronology of the Xia dynasty, some scholars have attributed the archaeological remains to the first dynastic rule in Chinese history.[5] However, since no contemporary written record of the Xia or the Erlitou is extant, and later records are somewhat confusing, many scholars have adopted a more cautious position. For example, Sarah Allan argues that, in writings transmitted from the Zhou

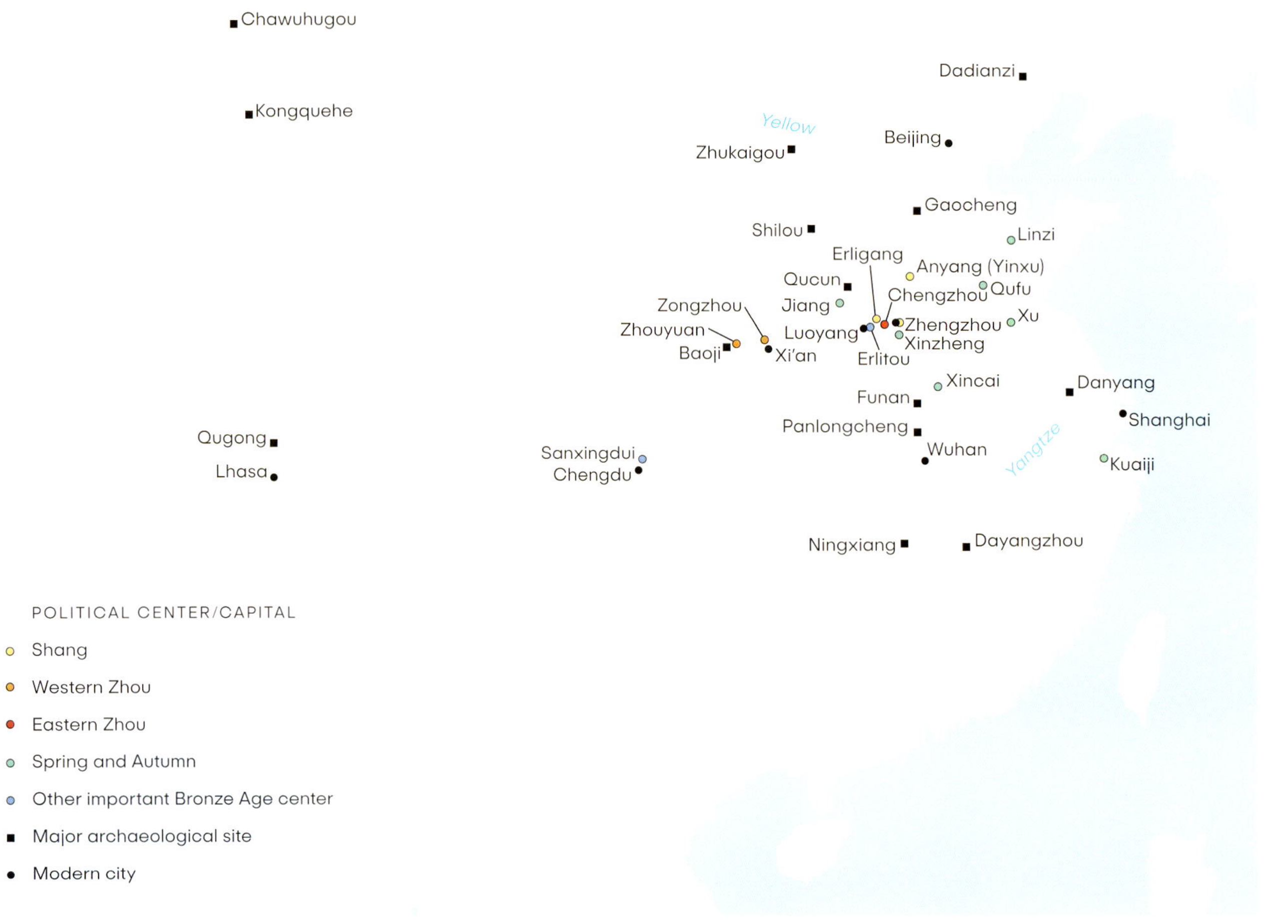

1 | Map of Bronze Age China showing important archaeological sites of bronze culture and the Shang and Western Zhou dynasties, c. 1200–700 BC.

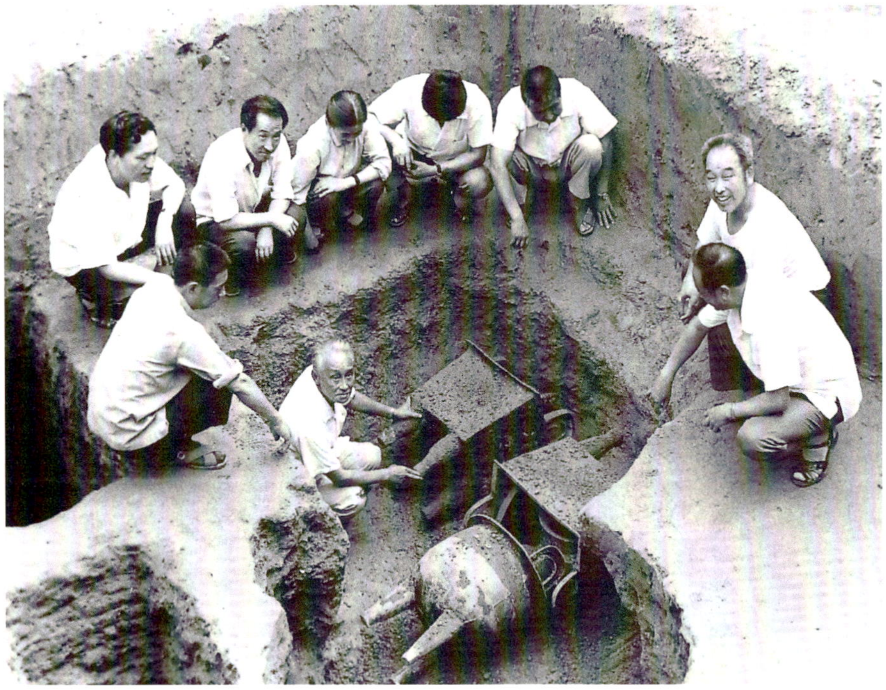

2 | Excavation at Zhengzhou, Henan province, in the 1950s.

period, the Xia is on par with the Shang, which reflects with the mythmaking of that time.[6]

By the fifteenth century BC, a more distinctive bronze culture had emerged, termed the Erligang culture (c. 1600–1400 BC) after discovery of a large site at Erligang, in Zhengzhou, in the 1950s. The correlation of the archaeological evidence with the historical Shang dynasty is widely accepted. Here, we see some of the principal features of an early state: construction of a city with defensive walls and public buildings, craft production, and the use of writing. The casting and employment of bronze are clearly associated with the political power and wealth of a social elite. The finds at Erligang added a number of new types of bronze vessels to the existing inventory, such as the ring-foot container (*zun* or *lei*) and the swinging-handle bucket (*you*). Most of the bronzes were unearthed from tombs. But several large cauldrons, all square shaped with four legs, were found in caches near the city walls (see fig. 2). Across China—from the Central Plains to south of the Yangzi River and north of the Taihang Mountains—archaeologists have excavated a number of sites, including the important Panlongcheng site (Hubei). In the process, they have revealed a significant expansion of urban life and diffusion of bronze metallurgy. The influence of the Shang people, marked by their distinctive style of bronze vessels, seems to have reached across a wide territory, sometimes referred to as the Erligang Horizon.[7]

The most important Bronze Age site is Yinxu in Anyang (Henan) (see fig. 3), which has been identified as the capital of the late Shang dynasty, dating roughly from the fourteenth century to the middle of the eleventh century BC. Controlled excavation began in the 1920s, conducted by archaeologists from Academia Sinica and, subsequently, the Chinese Academy of Social Sciences after the 1950s, when Academia Sinica moved with the Nationalist Government to Taiwan.[8] Finds include a large quantity of bronzes, jades, and chariots, as well as over one hundred thousand fragments of inscribed animal bones (*jiaguwen*), known in the west as oracle bone inscriptions, which are the earliest divinatory records of the Shang royal houses. The oracle bone inscriptions provide little direct reference to bronze casting but give useful information about the general contexts in which the bronzes were used.[9] The bronzes found at Yinxu are of the highest quality in terms of both technology and artistic rendering. Several foundries were excavated at Yinxu, providing further evidence regarding the process and organization of bronze metallurgy in the Shang dynasty.

In 1046 BC the Zhou, who swept down from the northwest and rapidly established political control across China, conquered the Shang. Because the Zhou had originally been a tribute state under the Shang, the Shang heavily influenced Zhou culture, including its technological and artistic traditions.

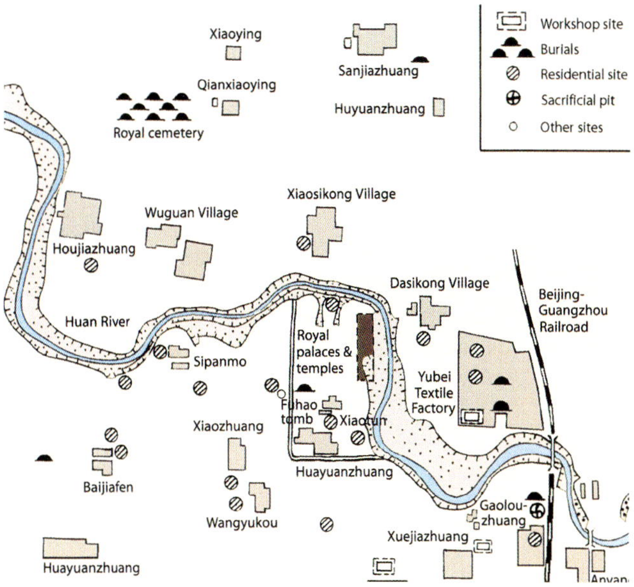

3 | Distribution of sites at Yinxu, the late Shang dynasty capital (c. 1300–1046 BC), at Anyang, Henan province.

For an initial period, the Zhou made bronzes in a very similar way to the Shang. But, gradually, changes began to take place. In the middle of the tenth century BC, a noticeable shift occurred in the forms of the major bronze vessels, as well as in the composition of sets of bronzes. This was probably caused by changes in production but was perhaps more closely associated with the ritual reforms carried out by the Zhou royal court at that time. A significant change appears also in the inscriptions found on bronzes. Unlike the ancestral names and short dedications seen on Shang bronzes, the inscriptions on Zhou bronzes are longer and more informative, containing historical information and details of royal activities. In the Zhou dynasty, bronzes played a major role in gift exchange between the royal court and aristocrats, and among the aristocracy themselves. They bear important witness to the social and political history of the time.

One of the most recent advances in Chinese archaeology is the broadened discussion of regional cultures and their role in the development of China's Bronze Age.[10] As mentioned earlier, during the Erligang period, bronze metallurgy spread to regions beyond the Central Plains; in many cases the direction was not always one way from the center to the periphery. At the same time, many regions developed their own traditions, which in turn influenced the metropolitan centers in Zhengzhou and Anyang. For example, the Sanxingdui culture in Sichuan (c. 1400–1000 BC), and bronzes from Xingan Dayangzhou in Jiangxi, represented independent or semi-independent traditions (see figs. 4 and 5). After the eighth century BC, as the Zhou royal house's authority waned, each regional state began to assert its political power and new artistic expression. Bronzes were still used at rituals and ceremonies but were made increasingly for utilitarian purposes: for domestic use and for trade.

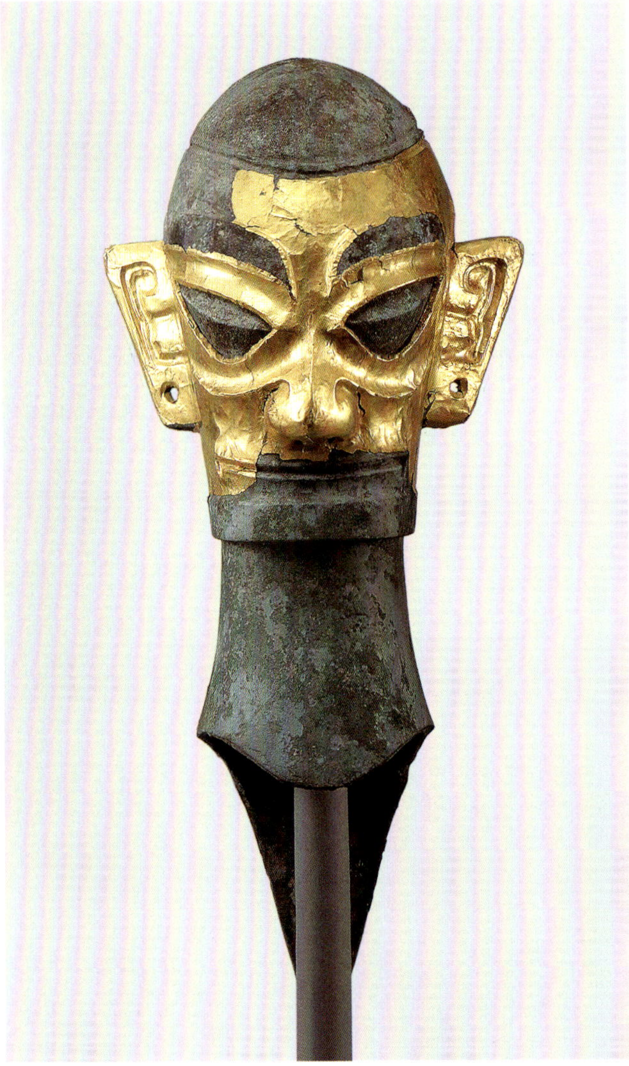

4 | Head with mask, Sanxingdui culture (c. 1400–1000 BC). Bronze and gold; h. 48.5 cm (14 3/4 in.). From pit 2 at Sanxingdui, Guanghan, Sichuan province. Sanxingdui Museum, Guanghan, Sichuan province.

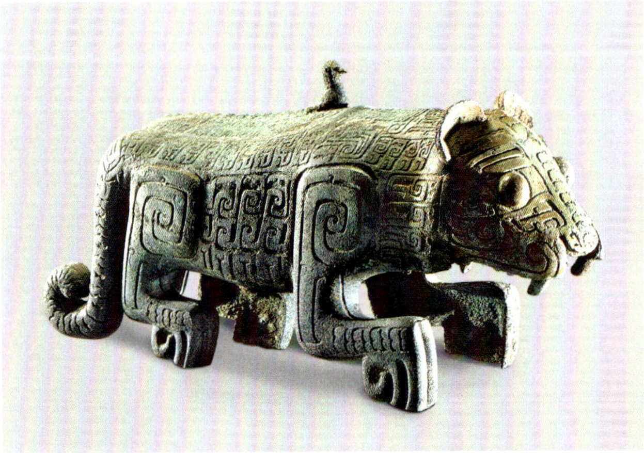

5 | Tiger, late Shang period (c. 12th–11th century BC). Bronze; 25.5 × 53.5 cm (10 × 21 1/8 in). From Dayangzhou, Xin'gan, Jiangxi province. Jiangxi Provincial Museum, Nanchang.

In addition, their form and design also reflected the frequent exchange between the central states and the nomadic peoples of the north and south, in particular the steppes.[11] For example, two pictorial bronzes included in this exhibition show stylized representations of, respectively, hunting and a landscape scene (see figs. 6a and 6b and pl. 53, and pl. 54).

From the sixth century BC, the use of iron became popular and was widespread. Many historians thus regard this period as the emergence of the Iron Age in China.[12] However, the arrival of iron did not replace the use of bronze. Instead, bronze was continuously treated as a prestigious material, and the technology involved with bronze making became even more complicated. Bronze was used together with inlays of iron, gold, silver, and other precious materials. The lost-wax method (*cire perdue*) was used in conjunction with traditional piece-mold casting. In other words, the Bronze Age in China never ended. Even when Qin Shihuangdi, the First Emperor of Qin, unified the country in 221 BC, the standard measurements and weights used for collecting taxes were made of bronze and carved with a long inscription of an imperial edict, as on a bronze weight (*quan*) in the exhibition (pl. 55). Its inscription reads:

> In the twenty-sixth year of his reign, the emperor amalgamated all lords under the heaven, and common people were pacified. He then adopted the title of Huangdi [august sovereign], and ordered his chancelors Zhuang and Wan to regulate the system of measurements. For those who had used various measurements and were confused, they now can be all clear about this unified system.

Throughout the history of China, bronze was held in the highest regard not only as a representation of spiritual power but also as a historical inspiration.

Bronze as Ritual Art

When the word *bronze* is mentioned in art historical contexts, we often immediately think of classical Greek and Roman sculptures of humans or animals. However, compared with those of other cultures around the world, early Chinese bronzes have some very distinctive characteristics. First, they were made using piece-molds rather than by hammering or the lost wax methods that were popular in western and central Asia. This innovative method usually, although not always, relied on sophisticated technology, and involved ceramic models, sectioned molds, and clay cores.[13] Second, from the very beginning, bronze was employed for a different purpose. Whereas in the West, bronze was largely limited to weapons and tools, in ancient China—with perhaps the exception of a few weapons and musical instruments—it was mainly

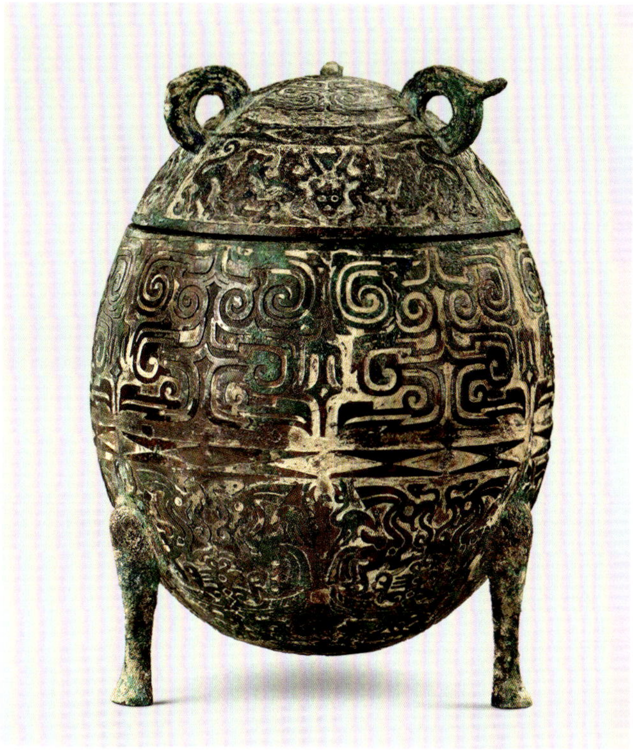

6a | Bipartite hemispherical bowl (*dui*), Eastern Zhou dynasty, Spring and Autumn period (770–476 BC). Bronze; h. 16.2 cm (6 3/8 in.); diam. of rim: 12.1 cm (4 3/4 in.). Private collection. See pl. 53.

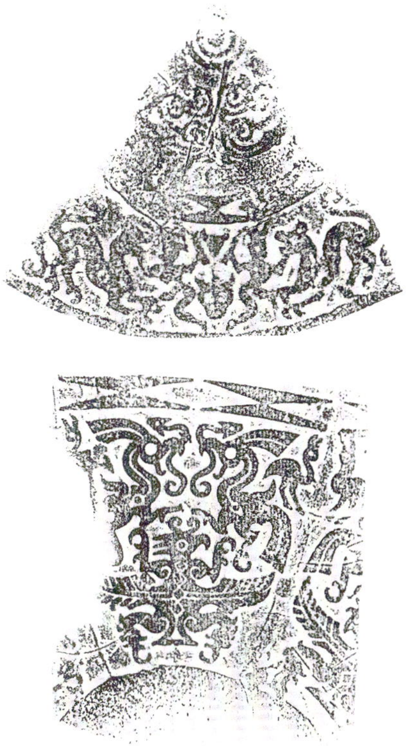

6b | Rubbing of fig. 6a.

used for cooking, drinking, and serving vessels. This raises the questions: Why did ancient Chinese invest so much in making vessels, and how were they used?

It is not easy to explain why there are so many different forms of bronzes in the Shang and Zhou periods. From a cultural-technical point of view, bronze metallurgy in China was closely associated with earlier pottery traditions.[14] Neolithic potters were highly skilled in shaping and firing a wide range of vessels, including bowls, cups, ewers, jars, and tripods, which served as the prototypes for bronzes. Based on the physical forms of these early bronzes, we can group them into round, square, and animal-shaped vessels, and then describe them in more detail: tall, low footed, decorated, plain, with or without handles, and so on. This stylistic analysis not only gives us a useful way to record newly unearthed artifacts but also proves to be informative regarding the social context of their making. Just as developments in ceramic production in the late Neolithic period reflect social change—for instance, its diversification in the Shandong Longshan culture (c. 2500–2000 BC) suggests increased social complexity—bronze vessels indicate developments within Bronze Age Chinese society.[15]

We must perceive the bronzes in their original ritual context. First, the vessels' forms and generic names offer clues that lead to a deeper understanding of their functions. Thus, the majority of scholars and archaeologists prefer to use the traditional classification system that was first developed by Song-dynasty antiquarian scholars in the eleventh and twelfth centuries, which categorizes bronze vessels as being used for food, wine, or water. The individual forms have distinct names, such as *ding*, *dou*, *gui*, *hu*, *jia*, *jue*, *you*, and *zun*, which we know from textual records that also provide explanations of how the vessels were employed in early rituals.[16] For example, in *Zhouli* (Rites of Zhou), the *ding* (a bronze cauldron) is described as a container for meat and the *dou* for meat sauces and pickled vegetables. Other ritual texts such as *Yili* (Book of Rites) and *Liji* (Notes on Rites) also contain rich information about the ways in which the ritual vessels were used. However, the textual records cannot be easily verified by Shang written sources such as oracle bone inscriptions (see fig. 7).[17] We must be cautious with this information: in many cases, the details may be prescriptive views of how vessels should be used rather than descriptions of how they were actually used.[18]

It is striking that the majority of bronzes have been found in tombs of the elite. A popular perception is that the bronze vessels were intended to accompany the deceased to the underworld where they could continue to make sacrifices to the ancestors. But close examination of the burial context reveals that the bronze vessels were probably also used in the burial ritual of the deceased.[19] Furthermore, the number, type, and combination of bronzes may reflect the status of the tomb's occupant. For example, in the tomb of Lady Hao, a consort of the Shang king Wuding (r. c. 1250–1192 BC), there were more than four hundred bronzes, including over two hundred vessels, one hundred thirty weapons, twenty-three bells, forty-four implements, four mirrors, four tigers, and more than twenty other unidentified objects.[20] In later texts, the number of bronze *ding* cauldrons was prescribed according to the rank and status of the deceased. Although such strict codes may not have been observed each time, there is, however, a discernible pattern in the use of bronzes in different tombs.[21]

Modern scholarship on Shang oracle bone inscriptions has shed much light on the religious practices in which bronze production was developed to an unprecedented extent. Ancestral worship was the most dominant feature of Bronze Age China. Society was organized on a lineage structure, and sacrifices were offered on a daily basis to the ancestors (both direct and mythical), who in return would protect the interests of their descendants. Shared ancestral worship would have brought the people psychologically close together and would have served, according to David Keightley, "as affirmation of holy kinship."[22]

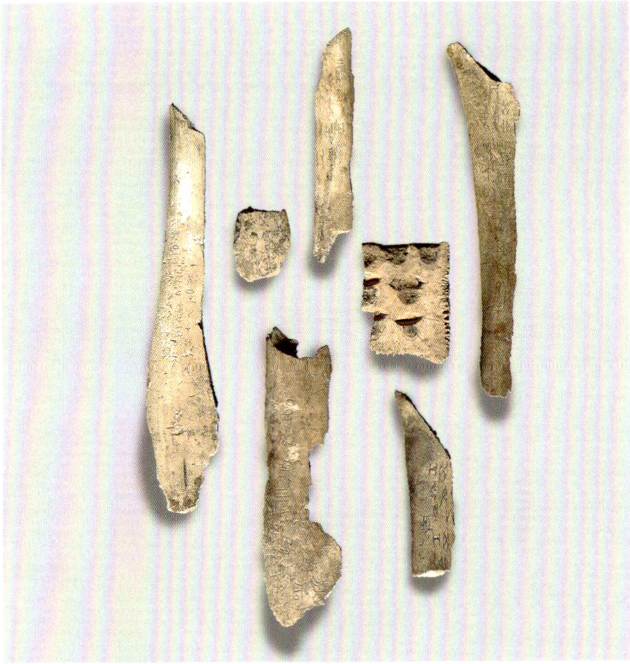

7 | Inscribed oracle bones, late Shang dynasty (c. 1250–1046 BC). Segments of turtle plastrons and bones of oxen; polished, burned, and carved with inscriptions; dimensions variable. The Art Institute of Chicago, Alyce and Edwin DeCosta and the Walter E. Heller Foundation, Frederick W. and Nathalie C. Gookin Endowment, and Frederick W. Renshaw Acquisition Funds, 2008.65.1–76.

Although the exact practices of early Shang rituals are extremely difficult to verify, we know from contemporary records that they were richly varied and included slaughtering, holocaust, libation, and exorcism. The nature of the sacrifices in ancestral cults was also wide-ranging: the most common offerings were wine and food, followed by domestic animals such as oxen, pigs, sheep, and dogs. Wild boars, deer, tigers, birds, and other wild creatures caught in hunting were also frequently offered. Human sacrifice featured heavily. There can be no doubt that for the Shang people, performing rituals and making sacrifices were of enormous importance. The majority of divination records are about how these were to be undertaken, what the offerings were, and to whom they were addressed.

At ancestral rituals, sacrifices were prepared and displayed in temples and halls built for the ancestors, with the exception of holocausts, which took place in the open air. The animals and human victims were slaughtered and dismembered (using bronze axes and knives) and then cooked and offered to the ancestors in different bronze tripods. Similarly, cooked grains and vegetables were placed in bronze *gui* containers, and fragrant wine was brought in bronze *you* jars and served in *jue* and *jia* goblets. This is why these vessels are also known as "ritual bronzes." When these objects were being produced, the idea of making something specifically for worshipping the deities and ancestors was embedded with magic and divinity, and the manufacturing process was accompanied by ritual actions such as smearing blood onto the newly produced bronzes.[23] As a consequence, the vessels became living things that acted as the most powerful agents linking Bronze Age man with the spiritual world. Those who made or owned them were thus viewed not only as politically superior but also morally superior and powerful.

Such works were often arranged in sets. Each vessel served a particular purpose, and sometimes more than one vessel would serve the same function. As Jessica Rawson has suggested, different vessels were employed in the most complex rituals for particular movements and "clear definition of shape probably made it possible to select quickly the vessels in the sequence required for the proper performance of the rituals."[24] In her view, the shape and ornamentation of bronzes also indicate the social status of the owner.[25]

The power attributed to these vessels lies not only in their forms and functions but also in their ornamentation. The intricate and varied decorations found on Shang and Zhou bronzes have been a focus of art historical inquiry. They are mainly geometric as well zoomorphic, including depictions of birds, cicadas, deer, elephants, fish, owls, rabbits, snails, snakes, tigers, toads, and turtles, as well as some highly imaginary animals such as dragons.[26] In addition, a small number are made in the shape of animals such as a bird, an ox, and a ram. The human figure was also sometimes used but played a minor role on regional bronzes.[27] Yet the most prominent motif bronzes is the two-eyed mask known as the *taotie* (see pls. 9–12). Although the *taotie* is not the only key to understanding Shang bronzes, its unique position in the iconography and its complexity as a motif demand special treatment.[28]

Because of the cultural prominence and technological development of bronzes, we can argue that bronze making was perceived as an important art in ancient China. The virtuosity of their technical perfection, originality of form, and complexity of decoration have not been equaled in later history. However, ancient bronze making cannot be easily assimilated to modern definitions of art. The bronzes were not expressions of individual artists or craftsmen, but a collective work. As Max Loehr has pointed out,

> Participating in their production were designers, modelers and mold-makers (of whom the latter two must have been master potters), together with smelters, furnace builders, bellow makers, and casters: the foundry gang, in a word, under the direction of a master craftsman. Changes of form and style, however, do not take place automatically, nor are they the result of group endeavor; they presuppose an intense concern for minutiae of design on the part of the responsible master, whether he be called craftsman or artist.[29]

Treating the decoration as a pure graphic development, Loehr assigned five styles to Shang ritual bronzes, ranging from a simple geometric pattern to a more sophisticated rendering of motifs; he was dismissive toward any assignment of religious, cosmological, or mythological meaning. For him, typical Shang and Zhou bronzes could not be described as representational art; once the decoration became pictorial, which happened in the late Eastern Zhou period (770–221 BC), the day of the bronze vessel was over.[30]

Contrary to Loehr's theory, Bernhard Karlgren argued that the ornamentation of early bronzes followed strict conventions and a "curious mechanization," evolving from a more realistic representation to a dissolved geometric style; he also recognized that different styles could have coexisted side by side.[31] Any definitive explanation of the mysterious decoration on early ritual bronzes remains elusive but clearly emerged from its own graphic tradition and the ritual context in which they were used. This is well argued by Harrie Vanderstappen in his discussion of Shang bronze decor: "The visual vocabulary resembles the cracks on oracle bones, which are in need of shamanistic interpretation or at least confirmation. And maybe there is a parallel between the extremely well-prepared and controlled lines of the cracks on oracle bones and the patterns on the bronze decor. In both cases, the forms confirm that the power invoked is in agreement with the proposed rituals."[32] In echoing Vanderstappen's words, Martin Powers asserts, "Manipulations of visual form could have direct and rather drastic effects on the allocation of resources. For this reason, the craft officers and ceremonial officers who attended to such matters needed a more complex understanding of ornaments than the notion that beauty confers importance."[33]

Bronzes as Things

To understand the significance of ancient bronzes in Chinese culture, we need to formulate an interpretative framework in which the multiple meanings of a category or a particular object can be investigated. But, instead of presenting a theoretical overload of various interpretations, let us start with a well known story that is found in one of the classics, the *Zuozhuan* (Zuo Commentaries)—an early narrative chronicle compiled in the fourth century BC:

> In the spring of the third year of Duke Xuan [605 BC], on his military expedition against the Luhun nomads in the northern zone, the Viscount of Chu reached the capital Luoyang where he stationed and inspected his troops at the border of Zhou territory. King Ding sent his minister Wangsun Man to greet the Viscount of Chu, and the viscount then inquired about the size and weight of the bronze cauldrons at the Zhou court. Wangsun replied: "Your question should not be about the cauldron itself but its power. In ancient times when the Xia dynasty possessed power, states of distant regions made pictures of things and sent [them] in together with metals as tributes from the nine provinces. The cauldron was cast in the forms of those things; and hundreds of things thus prepared the people to recognize spirits and demons. Therefore, when people went into rivers, marshes, hills, and forests, evil could be averted and monstrous spirits of rivers and mountains would be avoided. The cauldron is used to harmonize the upper and the lower, and for receiving heavenly blessing. When the Xia king Jie's power was befuddled, the cauldron was removed to the Shang dynasty, and for six hundred years the Shang ruled. But once the Shang king Zhou became oppressive and cruel, the cauldron was then removed to the Zhou dynasty. When power is commendable and brilliant, the cauldron, though small, will be heavy. But, if power is wicked and diminished, even if the cauldron is big, its weight will be light. Heaven grants brilliant power, and stops and rests on it. When King Cheng first settled the cauldron at Jiaru, divinations predicted that the Zhou royal house would have thirty generations of kings and last over seven hundred years. This is the Mandate from Heaven. The power of Zhou is declining, but the Mandate of Heaven has not yet changed. You cannot ask about the weight of the cauldron!"[34]

Wangsun was obviously not offering a historical narrative here, but a theorization of the ideas and perceptions of an important cultural relic of the past. In this paragraph, one intriguing point is the multiple uses of *wu* or "thing." The casting of bronze vessels is all about the object, the thing, we see "Distant regions made pictures of things" (*yuanfang tu wu*); "The cauldron was cast in the forms of those things" (*zhu ding xiang wu*). Although the character *wu* has previously been translated into English as "creature," "object," and "material," my preference here is to translate it as "thing," or more precisely "living thing," since this provides an interpretive framework for our discussion.

In classical Chinese, *wu* was originally a basic color term. It meant "color" or "colored," in contrast to "plain" or "colorless." It could also be used as a verb meaning "to select (by color)," and it was probably for that reason that it became a general word referring to categorization and classification. Even today Chinese speakers use terms such as "divine thing" (*shenwu*), "play thing" (*wanwu*), and "cultural thing" (*wenwu*) to denote objects transmitted from the past. They reflect different perceptions of antiquity. The study of "thingness" or materiality is now a serious academic inquiry.[35] In Western thought, there is also a double ambiguity of the word "thing" as, according to Bill Brown, "it denotes massive generality as well as particularities."[36] The description in the *Zuozhuan* passage reveals two intriguing aspects of the bronze cauldron. It was made in the form of "things," with form and color, and an ability "to harmonize the upper and the lower, and for receiving heavenly blessing." Thus, the cauldron was not merely a material thing but also a "divine thing" (*shenwu*), the idea being that the complex concept of power (*de*), sometimes translated as "virtue," is embodied in the bronze vessel; the two cannot be separated. Wangsun was explicit that the concern should not be with the physical properties of the object but with its metaphysical veracity. To borrow from cognitive linguistics, the bronze in this circumstance turns into a conceptual metaphor on which our understanding and experience of the past is based.

Ancient bronzes are living things. In Wu Hung's description, they are metamorphic, always in a state of transmutation and reconfiguration that evokes strong visual and cognitive reactions from viewers.[37] He quotes a description in the *Huainanzi*—a book written by the Han prince Liu An and his scholars in the second century BC, that reads:

> The grand ceremonial bells and *ding* tripods, there are beautiful *qi* of extraordinary importance. They are engraved with elaborate birds of intertwining bodies, crouching rhinoceros, stealthy tigers, and coiling dragons whose interlocking forms resemble a textile design. Their shining color dazzles people's eyes; ablaze with lights, they radiate even more brilliantly. Flexible and intricate, their spiral decoration comprises complex patterns. Further inlaid with tin and iron, they change their appearance as if the sky were now darkened, now brightened.[38]

Indeed, the surface decoration, in particular the color of bronzes, plays an important part in peoples' perceptions of them. Today we see ancient vessels covered with incrustations of green malachite, red cuprite, and blue azurite, a result of long periods of exposure to minerals underground. Originally the works would have looked polished and shiny, either golden or silvery. Many are inlaid with materials including turquoise, copper, silver, gold, and glass. When new, they must have had a dazzling appearance. Their color and surface patina can be—and often were—controlled or even artificially induced to match the taste of connoisseurs and collectors for a sense of mystery and age based on particular ideas about antiquity.[39]

In his interpretation of the nine cauldrons story, Wu argues that the bronzes belong to the general category of an "intentional monument," that they "not only commemorated a past event but also legitimated and consolidated the consequence of the event."[40] Of course, we cannot be sure to what degree the story recorded in the *Zuozhuan* reflects the ideas of the Shang and Zhou periods, but it shows that in the Spring and Autumn period (770–476 BC) of the Eastern Zhou dynasty, ancient bronzes and their discovery were regarded as omens of dynastic change. We read in the *Yijing* (Book of Changes), compiled between the ninth and fifth centuries BC, that the cauldron *ding* was a means of divination, full of signs and portents. Throughout Chinese history, the bronzes of the Three Dynasties played a significant role in conceptualizing the moral and political legitimacy of the government. We find that the story of the cauldrons is delineated on stone reliefs of the Han dynasty (206 BC–AD 220; see fig. 8). However, this is not to say that we can take such statements for granted; the meaning and symbolism of ancient objects were not subject to straightforward coding and decoding, but were often played out in an intricate religious and social trajectory, as Eugene Wong has argued.[41]

The Han dynasty emperor Wudi (r. 140–87 BC) was the first emperor in Chinese history to formally adopt the reign-name system (*nianhao*), and he changed his reign-name eleven times during his rule.[42] Each change was inspired or determined by some event that the emperor regarded as auspicious, such as the capture of a rare animal or the discovery of an ancient bronze. There is a story recorded in the *Shiji* (Records of the Grand Historian; 109–84 BC), written by Sima Qian. It goes like this:

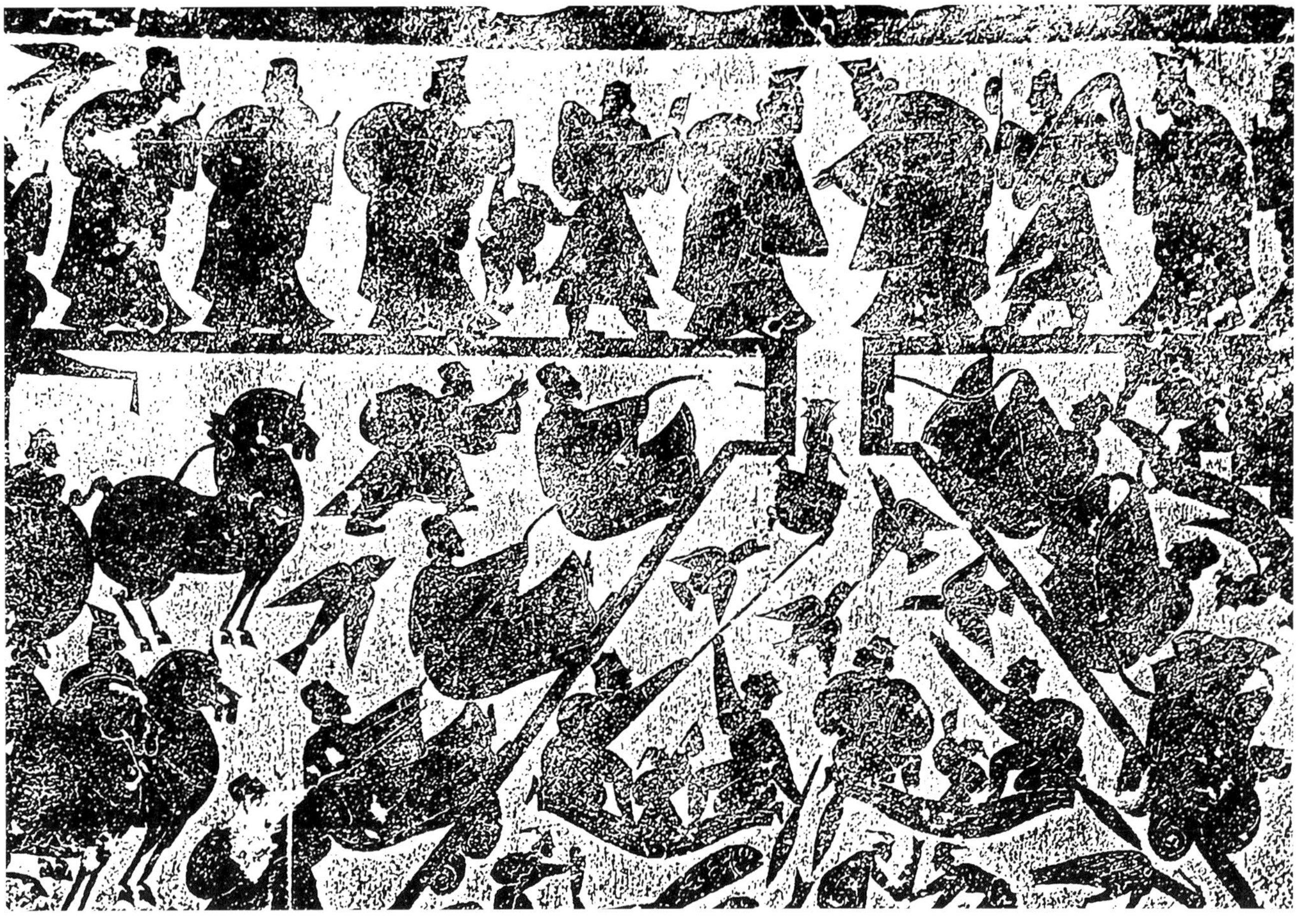

8 | Rubbing showing the first emperor's unsuccessful search for the divine tripod on the Wu family shrine, late Eastern Han dynasty (25–220), 2nd half of 2nd century AD, in Jiaxiang, Shandong province.

In the summer, during the sixth month of this year [113 BC], the shaman Jin of Fenyin was performing a sacrifice for the sake of the common people to the Earth Lord at the Rump Hill altar in the region of Wei, when he noticed an object shaped like a hook sticking up out of the ground at the side of the altar. Digging up the soil around it, he unearthed a cauldron. It was much larger than any ordinary cauldron and had a pattern incised on it, but no inscription. Much struck by his find, he reported it to the officials, who in turn informed Sheng, the governor of Hedong province. The governor having relayed intelligence of the affair to the throne, the emperor dispatched an envoy to question the shaman on how he had come into possession of the cauldron. The envoy, finding no evidence of fraud or deceit, sacrificed with full ceremony at the altar and bore the cauldron back with him to the Palace of Sweet Springs, where the emperor determined to take it along with him on one of this journeys and offer it to the spirits of Heaven. For this purpose he made a trip to the mountains, whereupon the sun shone forth with a bright, warm glow and a yellow cloud came and stood over the place where the cauldron was. Just then a large deer passed by the imperial party, which the emperor shot down in person and used as a sacrifice.

When the emperor and his party returned to Chang'an, the ministers and high officials all gathered in conference and requested that due honor be shown to the precious cauldron. The emperor announced, "Recently the Yellow River overflowed its banks and for several years the harvests were poor. Therefore I journeyed about the empire and performed sacrifices to the Earth Lord, praying for the sake of the common people that the grain might grow well. This year, though the harvest has been rich and plentiful, I have not yet returned thanks for this blessing. Why then should this cauldron appear?"

To this the officials all replied, "We have heard that in ancient times the Great Emperor Fu Xi made a single sacred cauldron. The number one symbolizes the unification of heaven and earth,

> showing that all things of creation were brought together. The Yellow Emperor made three precious cauldrons, symbolizing heaven, earth, and man, while Emperor Yu collected metal from the nine ancient provinces and cast nine cauldrons. All of them used the cauldrons to boil offerings and present them to the Lord on High and the other spirits. Only when a sage ruler appeared on the throne were these cauldrons made. The cauldrons were handed down during the successive dynasties of the Xia and Shang, but later, when the virtue of the Zhou rulers declined and the altars of the soil of the state of Song, ruled by the descendants of the Shang kings, were destroyed, the cauldrons sank into the waters and disappeared from sight. The temple hymn in the *Book of Odes* [Shijing] reads:
>
> > From hall to gatehouse,
> > From ram to bull he moves,
> > With great cauldron and small [. . .]
> > Neither contentious nor proud,
> > Beautiful shall be the blessing
> > of long life for him!
>
> Now this cauldron was brought to the Palace of Sweet Springs and a radiance burst forth, shimmering like a dragon. Boundless beauty was received from on high when it was carried among the mountains. A cloud of yellow and white descended to cover it and an omen in the form of a beast appeared. With the great bow and a set of four arrows, the beast was captured and placed at the foot of the altar, a sacrifice of thanksgiving accepted with great favour on high. Only an emperor who has received the Mandate of Heaven can understand the meaning of these signs, and he alone possesses the virtue needed to answer them. The cauldron should therefore be presented in the temple of the ancestors and stored away in the imperial court in accordance with these bright omens!" The emperor gave his consent to this.[43]

Here, the narrative is so vivid and full of details that it requires little explication. The ministers at the Han court clearly used the legend of the nine cauldrons to support their rhetoric, which led the Emperor Wudi to change his reign name to "first cauldron" (*yuanding*). But, it cannot be denied that this bronze cauldron, presumably of Shang or Zhou date, was made in the first place as a ritual vessel to sacrifice to the ancestors and deities. The sage kings of the Three Dynasties made the ritual bronze vessels, and their significance could only be communicated to the emperors who received the Mandate of Heaven (*tianming*). Thus, the proper place for bronzes should be first and foremost the temples, and after their discovery, they could be stored away in the imperial courts.

Bronze as Collectible

Collecting is a universal activity. We collect: objects, paintings, books, stamps—old or new, and sometimes even broken or fragmented—to forge a relation with the world we live in. There are many discussions on collecting, mostly from a perspective of social psychology.[44] But, though collecting is seen mainly as a personal activity, emerging from different motivations, it is also an extension of one's identity that is culturally constructed.[45] Through accumulating objects from the past, a collector tries to reconnect with particular times in history or imagined history.

The word *collection* does not simply imply that something collected has come from the past; it also implies something that makes sense in a large cultural system. Taking a semiotic approach, Krzysztof Pomian points out: "The collection is thus a unique domain, whose history cannot be consigned to the narrow confines of the histories of art, the sciences or history itself. It is, or rather should be, a history in its own right concentrating on 'semiophores,' or objects bearing meaning, on their production, their circulation and their 'consumption' which generally takes the form of mere viewing and does not, as such, involve any physical destruction."[46] Art collecting evolved independently in China, as Joseph Alsop argues, as in Greece. In a sense, art collecting is not merely a "by-product of the art," but rather is itself an intentional engagement with the past.[47] Collections should also be viewed as multifaceted phenomena.

There are many historical accounts, such as the one cited above from the *Shiji*, that show that bronze collecting was an activity with a long history.[48] Recent archaeological discoveries seem to support such records. For instance, from the tomb of the Duke of Haihun of the Han dynasty, excavated in 2016 in Jiangxi, archaeologists retrieved a bronze *you* vessel of the Western Zhou period (see fig. 9). It is difficult to determine in what circumstances this piece ended up in a tomb more than eight hundred years after it was made. Whether it was the result of a chance discovery, or had been passed down from earlier generations, we can probably call this kind of object a collected piece.

Scholars have long recognized that there is a pattern of collecting and deployment of the past in Chinese history, defined by some scholars by comparison with its counterpart, "antiquarianism," in the West.[49] Although many factors remain unknown, it seems that in China and Europe antiquarianism shared certain characteristics: collectors passionately

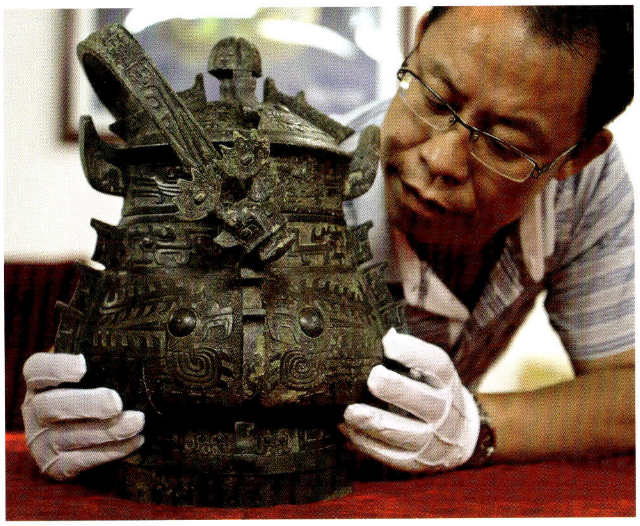

9 | A 2016 China News Agency report on the excavation of a Western Zhou bronze you from the tomb of the Duke of Haihun (92–59 BC).

sought ancient items, in particular those that bore inscriptions, as they realized the complicated relationship between objects and texts. The collectors found great pleasure in securing certain things and sometimes became obsessive about obtaining them. In his comparative study of world antiquarianism, Alain Schnapp has observed that all ancient civilizations, including Egypt, Mesopotamia, and China, deployed different strategies to engage and express their connections to the past. Egyptian pharaohs built indestructible stone monuments. Mesopotamian sovereigns carefully buried inscribed brick tablets in the foundations of their palaces and temples. Chinese rulers aimed to possess ancient bronze vessels used in rituals. As Schnapp says, "The search for bronzes was a topos of the Chinese historical tradition. In order to find vessels, it was necessary to obtain them from a collector or to discover them through excavation."[50]

In Chinese history, there were two main types of collectors who distinguished themselves with their holdings of ancient bronzes: emperors and the social elite who were usually educated officials (*shidafu*); here, we will call the latter scholar-collectors.[51] For the emperor-collectors, as discussed above, ancient bronzes were perceived as the Mandate of Heaven—an embodiment or symbol of moral and political authority. Their collecting activity would not be considered as that of a mere individual, but to a large degree as the representation of state power. Indeed, emperors frequently demanded that government offices pursue antiquities in the name of the state and often received them as tribute. For them, collecting ancient art, in particular ritual bronzes, had a political and cultural function, and such activity was often used as an instrument of cultural policy.

We can see this in later emperors: Emperor Huizong (r. 1101–1126) of the Song dynasty (960–1279) and Emperor Qianlong (r. 1735–95) of the Qing dynasty (1644–1911) are excellent examples. Huizong, known as the artist-emperor, was the first to take art collecting as a serious national endeavor and systematically formed imperial collections. Qianlong, one of the greatest collectors in world history, assembled an art collection containing hundreds of thousands of objects, including almost five thousand bronzes. Huizong and Qianlong both acquired an enormous number of ancient bronzes, and they also replicated them for the purpose of court ceremonies. This was all closely related to the reinstitution of the ritual system of the imperial courts during their reigns. Through collecting, cataloguing, and reproducing ancient bronzes, the emperors attempted to establish a new political order in the society they ruled over by referring to one that no longer existed. Of course, this is not to say that they did not derive any aesthetic enjoyment from the art they amassed or that they paid no attention to the study of epigraphy—but at this highest level, to a large degree their efforts were more about rulership than scholarship. As Lothar Ledderose points out, "By selecting some objects and by rejecting others the imperial collectors could deliberately influence the history of art." Moreover, he views the art collection kept in the imperial palaces as some kind of "spiritual treasure" (*lingbao*)—"a tally of a contract that Heaven concludes with the ruler, and secondly, these treasures are preserved in the palace like the vital force in a human body." At a certain point, a transition from palace collections of antiquity to an imperial art collection occurred, and in that process, magical objects such as ancient bronzes came to be regarded as art objects that were seen as a guarantee of legitimate political and cultural tradition. Whenever an art collection was lost or dispersed from a palace, it generally marked the decline of imperial power, both in terms of political influence and ideological control.[52]

Compared to emperor-collectors, private collectors had a different relationship with objects in their possession. On one hand, their collecting could not draw on public resources but was based on their own means. The collector would experience the pain of seduction, suffered willingly or unwillingly—from the temptation of profound pleasure and the desire to possess what some might call "playthings" (*wanwu*). Writing an essay on his friend Wang Shen's collection, the famous Song scholar and calligrapher Su Shi (also known as Su Dongpo) described vividly the internal paradox of the collector:

> A gentleman may temporarily lodge his mind in external things, but he may not let his mind dwell permanently on them. If he temporarily lodges his mind in things, then trivial ones will be sufficient to bring him pleasure, and enticing ones will be unable to afflict him. If, however, he lets his mind dwell permanently on things, then trivial ones

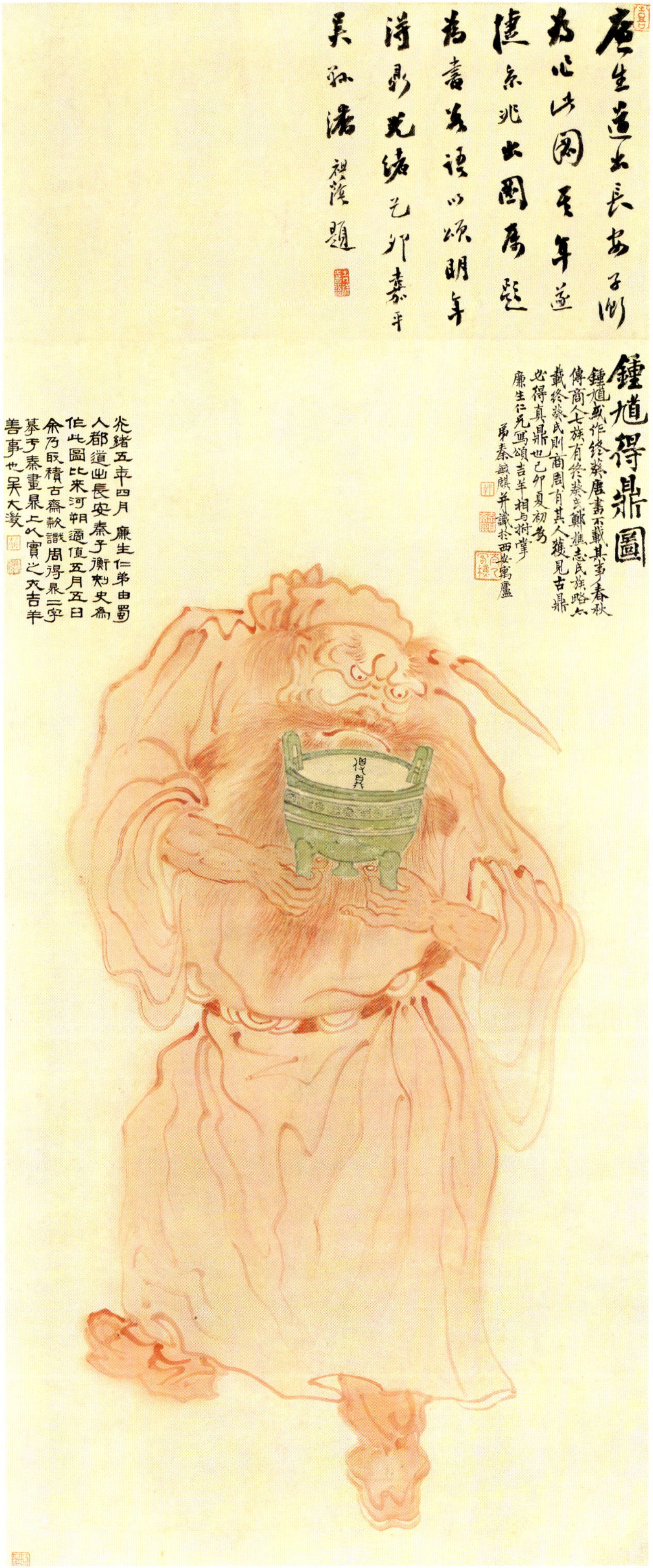

10 | Painted by Qin Yuqi (active late 19th century). Inscription written by Pan Zuyin (1830–1930) and Wu Dacheng (1835–1902). Detail of *Zhong Kui Obtaining a Cauldron*, Qing dynasty (1644–1911), 1879. Hanging scroll, ink on paper; 119.5 × 51.5 cm (47 1⁄16 × 20 1⁄4 in.). Private collection.

will be sufficient to afflict him, and enticing ones will be unable to bring him pleasure.[53]

Elsewhere, Su again wrote, "The problem is that people move about inside the realm of things, rather than outside it." And, to be a good collector, one must maintain a balance between attachment and detachment—"[to move] about outside the realm of things."[54] It evokes the proverbial warning: "Indulging in things destroys the will" (*wanwu sangzhi*).[55]

On the other hand, in the eye of the scholar-collector, ancient objects were historical material that documented and verified the classics and social institutions established by the sage kings. Compared to emperor-collectors, scholar-collectors were probably less interested in the political function of the ancient bronzes and more concerned with interpreting their meaning, especially their inscriptions. They used material evidence to reconstruct the history of the Three Dynasties; for example, the famous Song historian Ouyang Xiu was a keen collector of antiquities and inscriptions. In 1062 he catalogued his holdings in a book titled *Jigulu* (Record of Assembled Antiquities), writing in the preface:

> Knowing that a collection as large as this is bound eventually to be broken up, I have chosen the most important ones and entered them in a separate catalogue of colophons where I have also recorded the facts they contain that may be used to correct the textual historical record. It is my hope that this will be transmitted to future scholars as a contribution to learning. Some may belittle my efforts, saying that when things are accumulated in such quantity, it is difficult to keep the collection intact, and that sooner or later it will inevitably be broken up and scattered. So why am I making such a fuss over these things? I can only say, by way of reply, that doing so provides me joy. What harm is there if I grow old amusing myself with these things? Are not collections of ivory, rhinoceros horn, gold, and jade also bound to be scattered eventually? I simply cannot bring myself to exchange one for the other.[56]

Ouyang's motivation for collecting was not merely personal but also scholarly. To him, despite the inevitable fate of the things he acquired, they were to be cherished and recorded, so that they could be used as historical evidence and be transmitted to others for future learning.[57]

For scholar-collectors, collecting was a high-minded intellectual endeavor, and the idea of connoisseurship and authenticity played an important part. By collecting what they saw as "good" and "authentic" objects, they could then distinguish themselves. Art collections were seen not only as treasures with commercial value but also as social capital that elevated the owner's standing in society. In a special way, collecting was also a means of social bonding. Collectors who shared the same interests formed circles in which they often traded objects, sometimes for financial gain but mostly for friendship. Many famous collectors of the nineteenth century, such as Chen Jieqi, Pan Zuyin, Wang Yirong, and Wu Dacheng, interacted with each other on a regular basis, sharing their passion and knowledge; their friendship is often described as being as solid as "bronze and stone" (*jinshi zhijiao*).[58] This is exemplified in a painting by Qin Yuqi titled *Zhong Kui dedingtu* (Zhong Kui Obtaining a Cauldron), in which the historical figure Zhong Kui is depicted holding a bronze cauldron, implying auspiciousness and success (fig. 10). The painting was a present from Qin to his friend Wang Yirong who was on his way to the capital to take the metropolitan exam, which he passed that year, obtaining the *jinshi* (advanced scholar) degree. On the work both Pan Zuyin and Wu Dacheng wrote colophons to compliment this friendship, and Wu inscribed a name (*De ding*) onto the cauldron; the word *de* here means "to obtain"; Wu was making a pun of Wang's success in the exam.

Mirroring China's Past: Emperors, Scholars and Their Bronzes is devoted to an in-depth study of the tradition of collecting ancient bronzes in China. The focus of this project is not only how such works were produced and used in their original context, but also the different ways in which they were collected, classified, and understood throughout Chinese history. It aims to investigate how people have approached and appropriated bronzes; how a specialized culture developed around them that centered on the idea of antiquity; and how that culture made a significant impact on individuals and on society at large. Behind each object, there is always a story waiting to be told.

NOTES

1 | The Chinese word *li* has multiple meanings: it generally refers to rituals, ceremony, and social conventions and etiquette. But in philosophical contexts, it could also imply different things to different people. For a further discussion, see A. C. Graham, *Disputers of the Tao: Philosophical Argument in Ancient China* (La Salle, Illinois: Open Court, 1989), esp. 11–18, 22–25, 40, 57, 112, 158, 255–61, 270, and 301.

2 | See Dieter Kuhn and Helga Stahl, eds., *Perceptions of Antiquity in Chinese Civilization* (Heidelberg: Edition Forum, 2008), esp. Dieter Kuhn, "Reflections on the Concept of Antiquity in Chinese Civilization" (11–68), and Mu-Chou Poo, "The Formation of the Concept of Antiquity in Early China" (85–101).

3 | Evidence of the fifth millennium BC bronze alloy has recently been found in Serbia, but its dating and interpretation have been disputed. For this debate, see M. Radivojević, T. Rehren, J. Kuzmanović-Cvetković, M. Jovanović, and J. P. Northover, "Tainted Ores and the Rise of Tin Bronzes in Eurasia, c. 6500 Years Ago," *Antiquity* 87:338 (2013): 1030–45; Duško Sljivar and Dusan Boric, "Context Is Everything: Comments on Radivojević et al.," *Antiquity* 88:342 (2014): 1310–15; and M. Radivojević, T. Rehren, J. Kuzmanović-Cvetković, and M. Jovanović, "Context Is Everything Indeed: A Response to Sljivar and Boric," *Antiquity* 88:342 (2014): 1315–19.

4 | See Mou Yongkang and Wu Ruzuo, "A Discussion on the 'Jade Age,'" in Roderick Whitfield and Tao Wang, eds., *Exploration into China's Past* (London: Saffron Books, 1999), 41–44.

5 | See K. C. Chang, "China on the Eve of the Historical Period," in Michael Loewe and Edward L. Shaughnessy, eds., *The Cambridge History of Ancient China: From the Origins of Civilization to 221 B.C.* (Cambridge: Cambridge University Press, 1999), 37–73, where he summarized different views on the identification of the Xia dynasty. Chang himself believed that Erlitou belonged to the supposed Xia Dynasty.

6 | Sarah Allan, "The Myth of the Xia Dynasty," *Journal of the Royal Asiatic Society of Great Britain and Ireland* 116:2 (1984): 242–56. For discussions on the relationships between Erlitou and the Xia, see also Robert L. Thorp, "Erlitou and the Search for the Xia," Early China 16 (1991): 1–38; Sarah Allan, "Erlitou and the Formation of Chinese Civilization: Toward a New Paradigm," *Journal of Asian Studies* 66:2 (2007): 461–96; Liu Li and Xu Hong, "Rethinking Erlitou: Legend, History and Chinese Archaeology," *Antiquity* 81:314 (2007): 886–901; and Liu Li "Academic Freedom, Political Correctness, and Early Civilisation in Chinese Archaeology: The Debate on Xia-Erlitou Relations," *Antiquity* 83:321 (2009): 832–43.

7 | See Robert Bagley, "Shang Archaeology," in Loewe and Shaughnessy, *Cambridge History of Ancient China: From the Origins of Civilization to 221 B.C.*, 124–231.

8 | For the history and institutional involveents of Yinxu archaeology, see Robert L. Thorp, *China in the Early Bronze Age: Shang Civilization* (Philadelphia: University of Pennsylvania Press, 2006), esp. 117–71.

9 | See David Keightley, "The 'Science' of Ancestors: Divination, Curing, and Bronze-Casting in Late Shang China," *Asia Major* 14:2 (2001): 143–87.

10 | See Virginia C. Kane, "The Independent Bronze Industries in the South of China Contemporary with the Shang and Western Chou Dynasties," *Archives of Asian Art* 28 (1974/75): 77–107; and Robert W. Bagley, "Changjiang Bronzes and Shang Archaeology," in *Proceedings, International Colloquium on Chinese Art History, 1991, Antiquities, Part 1* (Taipei: National Palace Museum, 1992), 209–55.

11 | For this topic, see Charles D. Weber, *Chinese Pictorial Bronze Vessels of the Late Chou Period* (Ascona: Artibus Asiae, 1968); Esther Jacobson, "The Structure of Narrative in Early Chinese Pictorial Vessels," *Representations* 8 (1984): 61–83; and Alain Thote, "Intercultural Relations as Seen from Chinese Pictorial Bronzes of the Fifth Century B.C.E.," *RES: Anthropology and Aesthetics* 35 (1999): 10–41.

12 | See Donald B. Wagner, *Iron and Steel in Ancient China* (Leiden: Brill, 1993), esp. chaps. 2–4.

13 | See Su Rongyu's essay, "Bronze Casting Technology in the Late Shang Dynasty," in this catalogue, 32–37. See also Robert Bagley, "Shang Ritual Bronzes: Casting Technique and Vessel Design," *Archives of Asian Art* 43 (1990): 6–20.

14 | See Tao Wang, "Pottery to Bronze: A Cultural and Technological Transition in Early China," *Transactions of the Oriental Ceramics Society* 72 (2007/8): 34.

15 | See Anne P. Underhill, "Changing Patterns of Pottery Production during the Longshan Period of Northern China, c. 2500–2000 B.C." (PhD diss., University of British Columbia, 1990), and *Craft Production and Social Change in Northern China* (New York: Kluwer Academic/Plenum Publishers, 2002); and Li Liu, "'The Products of Minds as Well as of Hands': Production of Prestige Goods in the Neolithic and Early State Periods of China," *Asian Perspectives* 42:1 (2003): 1–40.

16 | See Rong Geng and Zhang Weichi, *Yin Zhou qingtongqi tonglun* [A General Survey of Bronzes of the Shang and Zhou Periods] (Beijing: Kexue chubanshe, 1958), esp. chaps. 4 and 5.

17 | Scholars have tried to use oracle bone inscriptions to study bronze vessels; for example, we can find the character *jue* (as a pictograph depicting the vessel) in oracle bone inscriptions where it is used as a verb, referring to some kind of wine offering. See, e.g., Elizabeth Child-Johnson, "The *Jue* and Its Ceremonial Use in the Ancestor Cult of China," *Artibus Asiae* 48:3/4 (1987): 171–96.

18 | To use these textual records, the reader must be aware of the question of the authenticity of the texts and the context in which they were compiled. For the three ritual books *Zhouli*, *Yili*, and *Liji*, see Michael Loewe, ed., *Early Chinese Texts: A Bibliographical Guide*, Early China Special Monographs 2 (Berkeley: Society for the Study of Early China and Institute of Asian Studies, 1993), esp. William Boltz, "Chou li" and "I li" (24–32 and 234–43), respectively, and Jeffery Riegel, "Li chi" (293–97).

19 | See, e.g., Tang Jigen, "The Burial Ritual of the Shang Dynasty: A Reconstruction," in Whitfield and Wang, *Exploration into China's Past*, 173–81.

20 | Institute of Archaeology, Chinese Academy of Social Sciences, *Yinxu Fu Hao mu* [Tomb of Lady Hao at Yinxu] (Beijing: Wenwu chubanshe, 1980).

21 | See Yu Weichao and Gao Ming, "Zhoudai yong ding zhidu yanjiu" [A Study of the Use of *Ding* Cauldrons during the Zhou Dynasty], *Beijing daxue xuebao* (*Shehui kexue ban*) [Bulletin of the Peking University (Social Sciences)] (1978/1): 84–98, (1978/2): 83–96, and (1979/1): 83–96.

22 | David Keightley, "The Religious Commitment: Shang Theology and the Genesis of Chinese Political Culture," *History of Religion* 17:3/4 (1978): 211–25.

23 | Yan Yun (pseud. Lin Yun), "Shangdai buci zhong de yezhu shiliao" [Metallurgical Evidence in Shang Oracle Bone Inscriptions], *Kaogu* (1973/5): 299.

24 | Jessica Rawson, "Ancient Chinese Ritual Bronzes: The Evidence from Tombs and Hoards of the Shang (c. 1500–1050 BCE) and Western Zhou (c. 1050–771 BCE)," *Antiquity* 67:257 (1993): 76.

25 | Jessica Rawson, "Late Shang Bronze Design: Meaning and Purpose," in Roderick Whitfield, ed., *The Problem of Meaning in Early Chinese Ritual Bronzes*, no. 15 (London: Percival David Foundation Colloquies on Art and Archaeology in Asia, 1993), 67–95.

26 | See Robert Bagley, "Ornament, Representation, and Imaginary Animals in Bronze Age China," *Arts Asiatiques* 61 (2006): 17–29.

27 | See Xu Lianggao, "Cong Shang Zhou renxiang yishu kan Zhongguo gudai wu ou-xiang chongbai chuantong" [There Is No Idol Worship in Ancient China as Reflected in the Figurative Art of the Shang and Zhou Periods], in Institute of Archaeology, Chinese Academy of Social Sciences, ed., *Kaogu qiuzhiji* [Seeking Knowledge in Archeology] (Beijing: Zhongguo shehuikexue chubanshe, 1997), 334–52.

28 | See Sarah Allan's essay, "Interpreting the Decoration on Early Chinese Bronzes," in this catalogue, 38–43. Other discussions include Jordan Paper, "The Meaning of the 'T'ao-T'ieh,'" *History of Religions* 18:1 (1978): 18–41; Ladislav Kesner, "The *Taotie* Reconsidered: Meanings and Functions of the Shang Theriomorphic Imagery," *Artibus Asiae* 51:1/2 (1991): 29–53; Tao Wang, "A Textual Investigation of the *Taotie*," in Whitfield, *The Problem of Meaning in Early Chinese Ritual Bronzes*, 102–18; and Wu Hung, *Monumentality in Early Chinese Art and Architecture* (Stanford: Stanford University Press, 1995), esp. 47–53.

29 | Max Loehr, *Ritual Vessels of Bronze Age China* (New York: Asia Society, 1968), 11.

30 | Ibid., esp. 12–14. For a further elaboration of Loehr's theory, see also Robert Bagley, "Meaning and Explanation," in Whitfield, *The Problem of Meaning in Early Chinese Ritual Bronzes*, 34–55, and a more recent publication, *Max Loehr and the Study of Chinese Bronzes: Style and Classification in the History of Art*, Cornell East Asia Series 141 (Ithaca: Cornell East Asia Program, 2008).

31 | Berhard Karlgren, "Notes on the Grammar of Early Bronze Décor," *Bulletin of the Museum of Far Eastern Antiquities* 23 (1951): 1080, "Marginalia on Some Bronze Albums," *Bulletin of the Museum of Far Eastern Antiquities* 31 (1959): 289–331, and "Marginalia on Some Bronze Albums II," *Bulletin of the Museum of Far Eastern Antiquities* 32 (1960): 1–24.

32 | Harrie A. Vanderstappen, "Shang Ceremonial Bronzes and Their Décor," in Harrie A. Vanderstappen, Richard A. Born, and Sue Taylor, eds., *Ritual and Reverence: Chinese Art at the University of Chicago* (Chicago: University of Chicago, 1989), 35.

33 | Martin J. Powers, "The Figure in the Carpet: Reflections on the Discourse of Ornament in Zhou China," *Monumenta Serica* 43 (1995): 211–33.

34 | Hong Liangji, *Chunqiu Zuozhuan gu* [Annotated *Zuo Commentary*] (Beijing: Zhonghua shuju, 1987), 401.

35 | See, e.g., Arjun Appadurai, ed., *The Social Life of Things: Commodities in Cultural Perspective* (Cambridge: Cambridge University Press, 1988); and Bill Brown, ed., *Things* (Chicago: University of Chicago Press, 2004).

36 | Bill Brown, "Thing Theory," *Critical Inquiry* 28:1 (2001): 1–22, esp. 4.

37 | Wu, *Monumentality in Early Chinese Art and Architecture*, 50.

38 | Ibid.

39 | See Tao Wang, "'Hu gui' mingwen zhong de 'chijin' jiqi xiangguan wenti [The Term "Red Metal" in the Inscription of the *Hu gui* Vessel, and Other Related Questions], in Tao Wang, *Yanse yu jisi: zhongguo gudai wenhua zhong yanse hanyi tanyou* [Color and Ritual: An Exploration of Meanings of Color in Early Chinese Culture] (Shanghai: Shanghai guji chubanshe, 2013), 280–96.

40 | Wu, *Monumentality in Early Chinese Art and Architecture*, 4–11.

41 | Eugene Y. Wang, "Afterlife Entertainment? The Cauldron and Bare-Torso Figures at the First Emperor's Tomb," in *Beyond the First Emperor's Mausoleum: New Perspectives on Qin Culture*, ed. Liu Yang (Minneapolis: Minneapolis Institute of Arts, 2015), 51-87.

42 | For a detailed study, see Xin Deyong, *Jianyuan yu gaiyuan: Xi Han Xinmang nianhao yanjiu* [Using and Changing the Reign Names: A Study of the Reign Names of the Western Han and the Xinmang Period] (Beijing: Zhonghua shuju, 2013), 2–102.

43 | Sima Qian, *Records of the Grand Historian: Han Dynasty II*, translated by Burton Watson, rev. ed. (New York: Columbia University Press, 1993), 33–35.

44 | See, e.g., John Elsner and Roger Cardinal, eds., *The Cultures of Collecting* (London: Reaktion Books, 1994).

45 | See Susan M. Pearce, *Museum, Objects, and Collections: A Cultural Study* (Leicester: Leicester University Press, 1992), esp. 69–88, where Pearce lists sixteen possible motivations for collecting. See also James Clifford, "On Collecting Art and Culture," in *The Predicament of Culture: Twentieth-Century Ethnography, Literature and Art* (Cambridge: Harvard University Press, 1988), 215–51.

46 | Krzysztof Pomian, *Collectors and Curiosities: Paris and Venice, 1500–1800*, trans. Elizabeth Wiles-Portier (Cambridge: Polity Press, 1990), 5–6, 9.

47 | See Joseph Alsop, *The Rare Art Traditions: The History of Art Collecting and Its Linked Phenomena Wherever These Have Appeared*, Bollingen Series 35.27 (New York: Harper and Row Publishers; Princeton: Princeton University Press, 1982), esp. 1–32, 243–51.

48| For a brief historic survey of the topic, see Scarlett Jang, "The Culture of Art Collecting in Imperial China," in *A Companion to Chinese Art*, ed. Martin Powers and Katherine Tsiang (Chichester: Wiley-Blackwell, 2015), 47–72.

49 | See Peter N. Miller and François Louis, eds., *Antiquarianism and Intellectual Life in Europe and China, 1500–1800* (Ann Arbor: University of Michigan Press, 2012), esp. Peter N. Miller and François Louis, "Introduction" (1–24). For a comparative study of antiquar-ianism, see Alain Schnapp, with Lothar von Falkenhausen, Peter N. Miller, and Tim Murray, eds., *World Antiquarianism: Comparative Perspectives* (Los Angeles: Getty Research Institute, 2013).

50 | Alain Schnapp, "The Many Dimensions of the Antiquary's Practice," in Miller and Louis, *Antiquarianism and Intellectual Life in Europe and China*, 58–79, 72.

51 | See Paola Dematte, "Emperors and Scholars: Collecting Culture and Late Imperial Antiquarianism," in Vimalin Rujivacharakul, ed., *Collecting China: The World, China, and a History of Collecting* (Newark: University of Delaware Press, 2011), 165–75.

52 | Lothar Ledderose, "Some Observations on the Imperial Art Collection in China," *Transactions of the Oriental Ceramic Society* 43 (1978–79): 33–46, 36, 34. See also Shih Shou-Chien, "Qingshi shoucang de xiandai zhuanhua—Jianlun qi yu Zhongguo meishushi yanjiu fanzhan zhi guanxi" [The Modern Transformation of the Qing Imperial Collections, with a Discussion on Its Relationship to the Study of the History of Chinese Art], *Gugong xueshu jikan* 23:1 (2005): 1–33.

53 | Kong Fanli, ed., *Su Shi wenji* [Collected Writings of Su Shi] (Beijing: Zhonghuashuju, 1986), vol. 2, *juan* 11, 356–57. See also Ronald Egan, *The Problem of Beauty: Aesthetic Thought and Pursuits in Northern Song Dynasty China*, Harvard East Asian Monographs 271 (Cambridge: Harvard University Asia Center, 2006), esp. 165–69.

54 | *Su Shi wenji*, vol. 2, *juan* 11, 351.

55 | This common saying was first used in the *Shangshu* (Book of Documents; 772–476 BC).

56 | Li Yian, ed. *Ouyang Xiu quanji* [Complete Works of Ouyang Xiu] (Beijing: Zhonghua shuju, 2001), *juan* 42, 599–600.

57 | For a detailed discussion of Ouyang Xiu's preface to *Jigulu*, see Egan, *Problem of Beauty*, 7–59.

58 | See Shana J. Brown, *Pastimes: From Art and Antiquarianism to Modern Chinese Historiography* (Honolulu: University of Hawai'i Press, 2001), esp. 35–72.

BRONZE-CASTING TECHNOLOGY IN THE LATE SHANG DYNASTY

SU RONGYU

Field archaeological studies have revealed that the continuous production of bronze vessels in China began with the Erlitou culture (c. 1900–1600 BC), named after a site discovered at Yanshi in Henan, which many scholars regard as the capital of the Xia dynasty (c. 2100–1600 BC), which preceded the Shang dynasty (c. 1600–1046 BC). The Erlitou site at Yanshi in Henan, in addition to yielding a wealth of bronze artifacts, has revealed bronze-casting workshops as well. These findings demonstrate clearly that since the beginning of the Bronze Age in China, just as distinctive typologies of bronze vessels and weapons had developed, so had particular methods of manufacturing bronzes. The site had no forged implements, suggesting that everything must have been made by casting—and yet the casting was done without stone molds or lost-wax techniques. Even the simplest of knives was cast by the ceramic piece-mold method. This technique is not appropriate for small-scale family or lineage workshops but rather is suited to large-scale factory production under the authority of the king or state. Thus it is evident that, by this time, Chinese bronze typologies and technical traditions were well established—and far more advanced than those of other civilizations.[1] Given the distinctive features of Chinese bronze casting, the claim that these technologies were transmitted from the Near East or central Asia is unconvincing, even though continuous production of bronzes began in China some two thousand years later than in those regions.

Chinese bronze making developed rapidly during the Erligang culture (c. 1600–1400 BC), which witnessed the rise of the Shang dynasty. A large number of bronzes has been excavated from graves in the areas surrounding the city of Zhengzhou, one of the major Erligang sites, and the ruins of two foundries also were unearthed. These discoveries demonstrate that during this period all bronze vessels continued to be made by piece-mold casting; they also show that the zoomorphic and other patterns cast in the vessels grew ever more abundant, diverse, and refined. The invention of casting and joining techniques enabled the production of large rectangular cauldrons (*fangding*) of up to a meter high. In addition, during this period the Shang culture began to spread to the Yangzi River valley region, perhaps owing to the copper resources in that area and the availability of tin to the south. The excavated bronze vessels from the important sites Panlongcheng in Huangpi (Hubei) and Wucheng in Zhangshu (Jiangxi) exhibit a number of technological innovations, including the use of riveting, binding, and lug techniques for casting and joining, especially employed in tandem with animal-form decorations. The use of spacers and the combination of high-relief patterning with corresponding concavities on the inner vessel walls makes the thickness of the walls as even as possible, which is consistent with the casting solidification process. Moreover, the use of these techniques gave rise to a distinctive southern style visible, for example, in vessels excavated in the Sichuan Basin of the Yangzi River valley, the Zhouyuan site in the Guanzhong Plain, the northern Loess Plateau, and even as far away as Beijing.

After the Erligang period, the Shang kings often moved their capitals. In the late fourteenth century BC, King Pangeng moved the capital to the Anyang area, and in the time of King Wuding (r. c. 1250–1192 BC) the capital was established in the modern-day village of Xiaotun, near Anyang, where it remained for over two hundred years. During this time, the production of

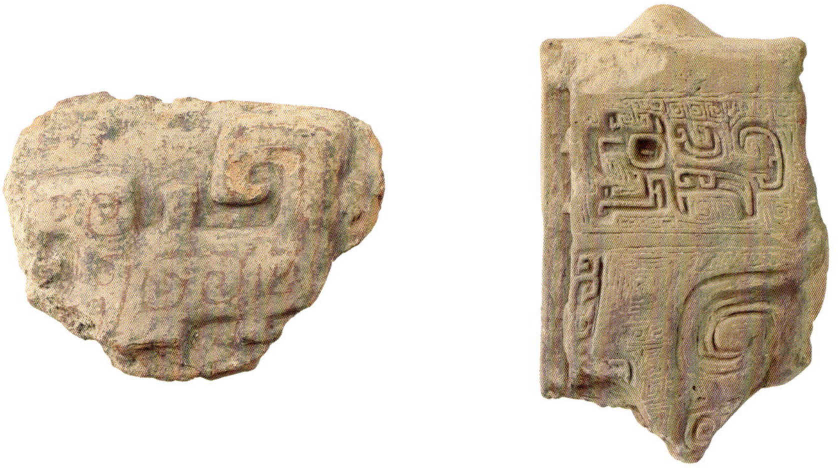

1 | Model and mold fragments with dragon motifs, late Shang dynasty (c. 1600–1046 BC). Terracotta; 8.3 × 5.8 × 1.4 cm (3¼ × 2¼ × 9/16 in.). From trench B128, Xiaotun, Anyang, Henan province. Collection of Institute of History and Philology, Academia Sinica, R016666.

bronze vessels reached its apogee. Bronze vessels from Anyang are generally highly ornate and often covered with dragons, phoenixes, birds, and the zoomorphic face motif known as the *taotie*. Many of the vessels have sophisticated decoration, although later pieces show a trend toward simpler patterns. Based on technological history, as well as comparison with Near Eastern and central Asian metalwork, the scholar Stephen Bushell and some subsequent scholars hypothesized that Chinese bronze casting used lost-wax techniques.[2] However, soon after the discovery of Anyang in 1928, wastes and implements from bronze production, including ceramic molds, were excavated there, showing definitively that the bronzes were not made by forging.[3] By matching the bronzes with the mold implements, scholars finally realized that bronze casting at Anyang was accomplished by the piece-mold method. The discoveries at Anyang have also provided more concrete reference points for establishing the dates and origins of bronzes that were unearthed long ago and are now found in Chinese and international private and public collections.

Over the past sixty years, more than ten thousand graves, several thousand bronze vessels, and seven foundry ruins have been unearthed at Anyang. These have presented a wealth of new data regarding production techniques, greatly expanding our knowledge of procedures at Anyang. Although these discoveries have raised a number of new questions about the details of bronze production, they also conclusively demonstrate that the Chinese compound word *taozhu* (to shape, cast, train, or nurture) reflects a profound connection between its component characters: *tao* (pottery) and *zhu* (metal casting). The model, mold, and core, as well as the craftwork employed in bronze casting, all originated in clay techniques; in other words, bronze casting began with the preparation of clay. Because bronze melting temperatures reach 2,012 degrees Fahrenheit, sifted yellow earth (loess) was washed to remove heat-intolerant clay particles, and fine sand was added. As the designs contain very fine details, the ceramic particles used to make the molds had to be fine as well. And, because the mold material also needed to be highly stable and malleable, vegetable ash was added to the mixture. Perhaps to maximize resources, the material in the inside of the mold is finer than that in the exterior of the mold. Petrographic analyses have shown that there was little or no plasticine material in the ceramic mixture, which raises the question of how it was bound together.[4] This matter is currently under investigation.

Archaeological excavations conducted at Anyang have taught us a great deal about the process of making the clay models and molds. The model is the primary step in piece-mold casting and once again, the Chinese language attests to this fact: the compound *mofan* (literally, model-mold) means exemplar or ideal.[5] In fact, a model for a square-shaped vessel (*fangyi*) found in the 1930s has red brush marks on its surface, some of which had already been cut and engraved into the surface, and parts of the zoomorphic pattern were applied by building onto the model (see fig. 1).[6] Subsequently, seven model fragments were also excavated from Miaopu Beidi, and yet more evidence of casting techniques comes from other bronze-casting ruins in Anyang, the largest of which is at the village of Xiaomintun, with an area of approximately thirty-one square miles.[7] Despite severe erosion to the site over the years, two excavations (conducted in

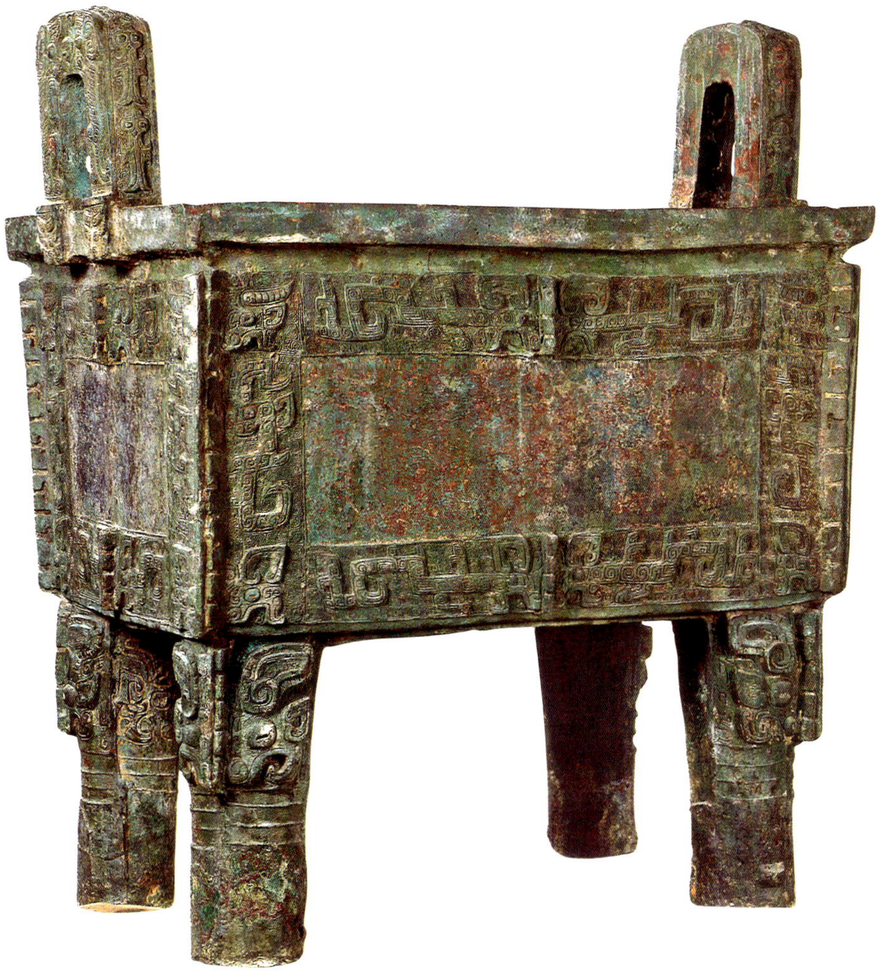

2 | *Square Cauldron of Simuwu* (*Simuwu Fangding*), late Shang dynasty (c. 1250–1046 BC). Bronze; 133 × 110 × 79 cm (52 3/8 × 43 5/16 × 31 1/8 in.). National Museum of China.

2000–2001 and 2003–4) yielded tens of thousands of artifacts related to bronze casting. The first excavation discovered over one hundred ceramic fragments of models, including ones for *gui* bodies, as well as vessel handles, chariot fittings, staff caps, ox-head ornaments, and other bronze implements. Over thirty thousand mold pieces were found for a number of bronze types, including cauldrons (*ding*), steamers (*yan*), food containers (*gui*), wine containers (*bu*, *yi*, and *lei*), buckets (*you*), beakers and goblets (*zun*, *gu*, *jue*, *jia*, *zhi*, and *gong*), water jars and basins (*he* and *pan*), and stemmed bowls (*dou*). Not only do these encompass almost all the varieties of vessels found in Anyang, but there are even ceramic molds for vessel types that so far have not been found.

It is now evident from the excavated models and molds that the decoration was first carved on the model. In some cases, the model was marked with a brush before carving; in a small minority of cases, a layer of ceramic material was applied to a rough model prior to carving. As for molds, some were impressed directly from the model; others initially took their rough shape from models prior to being inscribed with additional patterns.[8] In one of the architectural enclosures at Xiaomintun, archaeologists found a large casting platform constructed of tamped earth, approximately five feet in diameter, with a folded edge nearly three inches wide. Around it was a trough of fine sand, beyond which were scorch marks. This earth platform was specially made for casting a large bronze basin whose dimensions were even greater than the *Simuwu Fangding*, the largest vessel ever excavated in Anyang (fig. 2).[9] This discovery supports the studies of scholars, such as Wan Jiabao and Hu Jueming, regarding piece-mold structure.[10] Moreover, moveable pieces of models and molds were also found there. From the tomb of Lady Hao, a consort of King Wuding, archaeologists excavated 469 bronze vessels and weapons totaling approximately 3,500 pounds in weight (plus 109 small chariot fittings, known as *pao*).[11] The bronzes demonstrate the grand scale and magnificent quality of bronze production in the late Shang dynasty.

Bronzes occupied a special place in Shang society, and starting in the Erlitou period, the royal capitals all had bronze-casting workshops. Such workshops have seldom been found elsewhere, and those few that have been discovered were devoted to the production of weapons and tools rather than to the refined vessels necessary for ritual usage. This suggests that royal authority sponsored and controlled only the production of ritual bronze vessels. Nonetheless, the large quantity and unique style

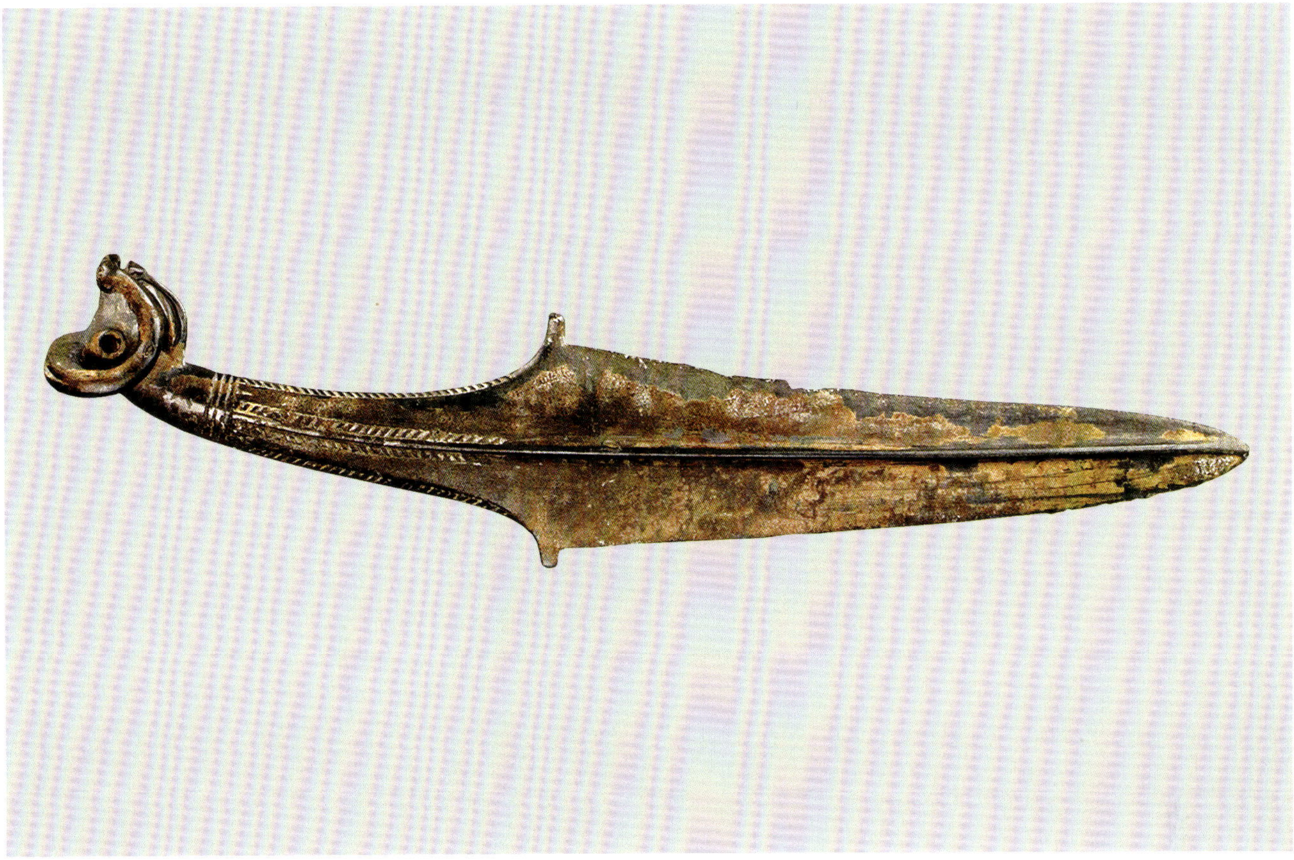

3 | Short sword with ram-shaped handle (*yang shou qu bing duan jian*), Shang dynasty (c. 13th–11th century BC). Bronze; l. of blade: 30.2 cm (11 7/8 in.); l. of handle: 22.6 cm (8 7/8 in.). From Qinglong, Hebei province. Cultural Relics Institute, Hubei province.

of the southern bronze vessels imply that a bronze industry developed out of the natural resources in the Jiangnan region; technological innovations here gave the vessels their unique style. When King Wuding conquered the Jiangnan regions, destroying the southern bronze factories and transferring their artisans to Anyang, this injected new blood into the royal foundries, immediately bringing about an efflorescence of bronze production that encompassed a range of diverse techniques and styles. This is evident in vessels from Fu Hao's tomb in Xiaotun (a larger city near Xiaomintun), such as the *ou fangyi* (a large rectangular wine container), an owl-shaped *zun* (wine vessel), a *yan* (segmented steamer), a *you* (handled bucket-like vessel), and an openwork *gu* (goblet), as well as the square cauldrons with ox and deer motifs excavated at the tomb designated HPKM1004 at Xibeigang, and other fine vessels such as the twin-handled *yu* water vessel from the tomb designated M54 at Huayuanzhuang. However, as the artisans from the south died out and the Shang kings monopolized bronze production, the bronzes made in Anyang gradually lost their vitality and became ever more rigid and monotonous. Certainly, the destruction of the southern bronze factories brought about the rapid demise of Shang-era southern-style bronzes.[12]

The culture in the southern Yangzi River valley was a subtype of Shang culture, whereas the northern part of the valley was open to the Eurasian steppe and in continuous interaction with central Asian cultures. Perforated axes were transmitted from this domain to Anyang, where they hybridized with the *ge* (local dagger-axe), resulting in perforated bronze weapons. In fact, lost-wax casting technology might also have arrived via this same channel: implements decorated with animals or animal heads in the round, and knife handles similar to those found in Eurasia, had already been transmitted to Great Wall regions by the late Shang dynasty (see fig. 3). Such implements constitute the distant source of lost-wax casting that developed in China after the sixth century BC.[13]

In lost-wax casting, wax envelops an earthen core and constitutes the model, and the mold is composed of ceramic material packed around the model. The casting is a single, integral process, and there is no need for division and reassembly of the sections of a complex piece-mold. For this reason, it became the standard means of casting complex bronze ornaments and other forms in Near Eastern and Eurasian cultures. The patterns and lines produced by the lost-wax method are relatively

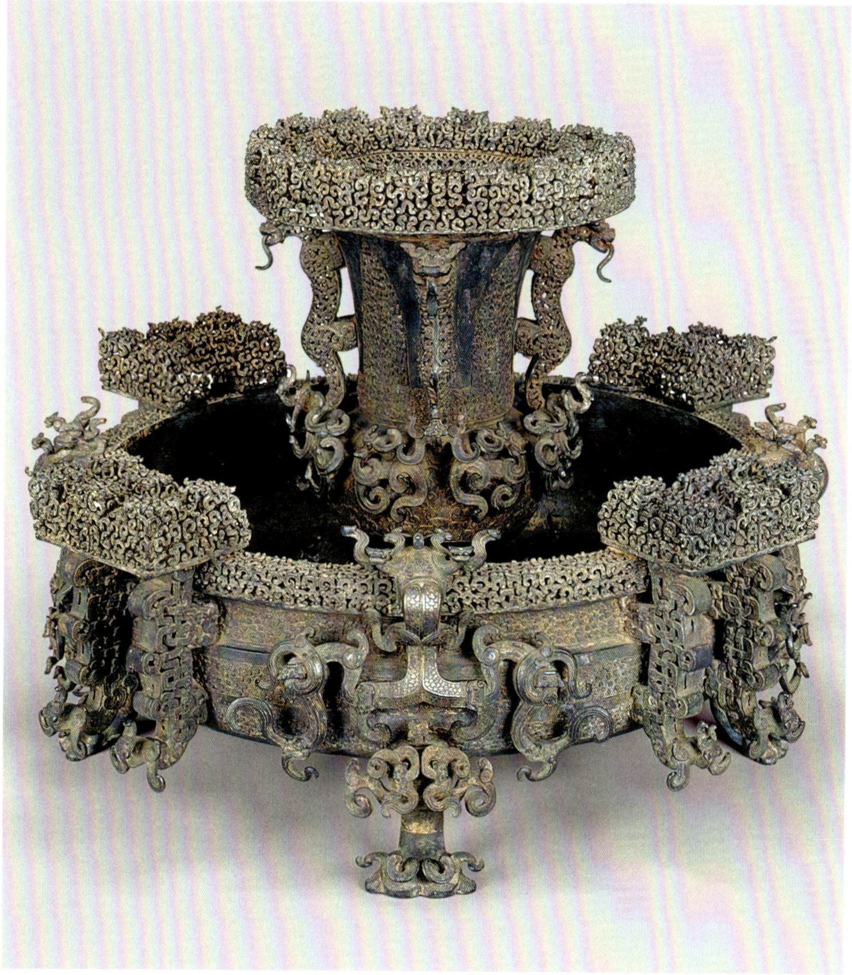

4 | *Wine Service Set from the Tomb of Zeng Hou Yi (Zeng Hou Yi Zun Pan)*, Warring States period (475–221 BC). From Suixian, Hubei province. Bronze; h. 41.6 cm (16 3/8 in.). Hubei Provincial Museum.

soft, unlike the sharp, bold designs achievable with piece-mold casting. We cannot confirm the use of lost-wax casting in Central Plains bronze work from the Erlitou to the Western Zhou (1046–771 BC) periods, nor, however, can we definitively conclude that the technique was not employed. Because lost-wax techniques can be used to make complex vessels or implements, naturally they can also be used to make simple objects.[14] The bulk of the evidence currently available indicates that lost-wax casting was not used in the Central Plains until the sixth century BC, when it was employed to produce complex ornamental vessel appendages that could not be made by piece-mold techniques; these ornamental appendages were subsequently welded or joined to vessel bodies made—as before—by piece-mold casting. We may label this unique use of lost-wax casting the Central Plains lost-wax technique.

In the revolutionary years of the Spring and Autumn period (770–476 BC), the feudal lords and nouveau riche challenged the limits of ostentation, and bronze craft did its best to oblige. It was only in these most extravagant of pieces that lost-wax techniques—transmitted to the north of China from Eurasia—were employed; for example, the bronze *jin* (altar table) from Xichuan Xiasi (Henan) and the *zun pan* (wine service set; see fig. 4) from the tomb of Zeng Hou Yi in Suixian Leigudun (Hubei) all show the combination of the piece-mold method with the lost-wax technique. Pieces such as these, however, are quite rare.

NOTES

1 | See Su Rongyu, "Erlitou wenhua yu Zhongguo zaoqi qingtongqi guojiaxing chutan: jianlun nifan kuaifan fa zhuzao qingtongqi de youguan wenti" [The Erlitou Culture and the Development of the State in Early China: A Discussion on Related Questions of the Piece-Mold Casting of Bronzes], in Xu Hong, ed., *Xia Shang duyi yu wenhua* [Urban Cultures of the Xia and Shang Periods], vol. 1 (Beijing: Zhongguo shehui kexue chubanshe, 2014), 342–72.

2 | Stephan W. Bushell, *Chinese Art*, vol. 1 (London: Wyman and Sons Limited, 1904), 61; W. Perceval Yetts, *The George Eumorfopoulos Collection: Catalogue of the Chinese and Corean Bronzes, Sculpture, Jades, Jewellery and Miscellaneous Objects*, vol. 1 (London: E. Benn, 1929), 35–38; and Herbert Maryon and Harold J. Plenderleith, "Fine Metal Work," in Charles Singer and Trevor Illtyd Williams, *A History of Technology*, vol. 1 (Oxford: Clarendon Press, 1954), 628.

3 | See Liu Yuxia, "Anyang ye tong shu yanjiu," [A Study of Methodology at Anyang] in *Anyang fajuebaogao* [Excavation Reports of Anyang], ed. Zhongyang yanjiuyuan lishi yuyan yanjiusuo [Institute of History and Philology, Academia Sinica], no. 4 (Nanjing: Zhongyang yanjiuyuan lishi yuyan yanjiusuo, 1933), 681–96.

4 | Yue Zhanwei, Jing Zhichun, Liu Yu, James B. Stoltman, and Jonathan Mark Kenoyer, "Yinxu qingtongqi zhuzao jishu xiangguan wenti" [Relevant Questions on the Casting Techinique of Shang Dynasty Bronzes from Yinxu], *Gugong wenwu yuekan* [National Palace Museum Monthly of Chinese Art] (2012/10): 47–54.

5 | In his article "Imperfect Symmetry: Re-Thinking Bronze Casting Technology in Ancient China," *Artibus Asiae* 66:1 (2006): 5–39, Lukas Nickel notes that some of the decorations on bronzes from Anyang seemed less than "ideal" (in that they lacked perfect symmetry), and he suggested that the casting therefore must have been done without models. This suggestion, however, neglects evidence from the Anyang foundries, revealing an inadequate understanding of piece-mold casting. Robert Bagley has provided a detailed and intelligent analysis and rebuttal of these claims; see Robert Bagley, "Anyang Mold-Making and the Decorated Model," *Artibus Asiae* 69:1 (2009): 39–90.

6 | Shi Zhangru, "Yinxu zuijinde zhongyao faxian, fulun Xiaotun diceng" [Recent Important Discoveries in Yinxu and the Question of the Stratification at the Xiaotun Site], *Zhongguo kaogu xuebao* [Reports of Chinese Archaeology] 2 (1947), 39–40.

7 | Institute of Archaeology, Chinese Academy of Social Sciences, "1958–1959 nian Anyang fajue jianbao" [Excavation Reports at Anyang from 1958–59], *Kaogu* [Archaeology] (1961/2): 68.

8 | Institute of Archaeology, Chinese Academy of Social Sciences, "2000–2001 nian Anyang Xiaomintun dongnan di Yindai zhutong yizhi fajue baogao" [Report of the Excavation Carried Out in 2000–2001 on Bronze Foundries at Areas Southeast of Xiaomintun], *Kaogu xuebao* [Acta Archaeological Sinica] (2006/3): 351–81.

9 | Yue Hongbin and Yue Zhanwei, "Shilun Yinxu Xiaomintun daxing zhufan de zhuzao gongyi he qixing; Jianlun Shangdai guanxi liyi" [Preliminary Discussion on Casting Techniques and Forms of the Large Mold Found at Xiaomintun in Yinxu, and the Related Question of Ritual Bath in the Shang Dynasty], *Kaogu* [Archaeology] (2009/6): 72–76.

10 | Wan Jiabao, "Anyang chutu qingtong sanzuqi de yanbian—Xianqin jishushi de gean kaocha zhiyi" [The Development of Bronze Tripods Unearthed at Anyang: A Case Study of History of Technology in Early China], *Dalu zazhi* [Journal of Mainland] 45:4 (1972): 201–12; and Hua Jueming, Feng Fugen, Wang Zhenjiang, and Bai Rongjin, "Fu Hao mu qingtongqi qun zhuzao jishu de yanjiu" [Study of the Casting Technology of Bronzes from the Lady Hao Tomb], in Institute of Archaeology, Chinese Academy of Social Sciences, ed., *Kaoguxue jikan* [Collection of Archaeological Papers] 1 (Beijing: Kexue chubanshe, 1981), 244–72.

11 | Institute of Archaeology, Chinese Academy of Social Sciences, *Yinxu Fu Hao mu* [The Tomb of Lady Hao at Yinxu] (Beijing: Wenwu chubanshe, 1980), 15.

12 | Su Rongyu, "Anyang Yinxu qingtong jishu yuanyuan de shangdai nanfang yinsu: Yi zhumao jiegou wei anlie de chubu tantao jianji Quanwu bowuguan suocang fengzhujia de niandai he shuxing" [The Southern Elements in the Origin of Late Shang Bronze Technology: A Discussion of the *Jia* Goblet with Phoenix Poles in the Sen-oku Hakuko Kan, Based on Riveting Techniques], in Sen-oku Hakuko Kan and Kyushu National Museum, eds., *Quanwu toushang: Quanwu bowuguan qingtongqi toushe saomiao jiexi* [Analysis of X-Rays and Scans of Bronzes in the Sen-oku Hakuko Kan] (Beijing: Kexue chubanshe, 2015), 352–86.

13 | See, e.g., William Watson, *Cultural Frontiers in Ancient East Asia* (Edinburgh: Edinburgh University Press, 1971), 44–61, 77–78; and Robert Bagley, *Shang Ritual Bronzes in the Arthur M. Sackler Collections* (Cambridge: Harvard University Press, 1987), 44–45.

14 | See Hua Jueming, "Shilafa de qiyuan he fazhan" [The Origin and Development of the Lost-Wax Techniques], in Institute for the History of Natural Sciences, Chinese Academy of Sciences, ed., *Kejishi wenji* [Essays on History of Sciences and Technology] 13 (Shanghai: Shanghai kexue jishu chubanshe, 1985), 63–81.

INTERPRETING THE DECORATION ON EARLY CHINESE BRONZE VESSELS

SARAH ALLAN

In order to understand the decoration on early Chinese bronzes, we must place them within their original context. As with most other ancient art, this context was religious. A core belief of traditional Chinese religion, commonly known as ancestor worship, was that, after people died, they continued to need food. Thus, their children and their descendants were obliged to provide them with offerings. In return, the ancestors would bring them good fortune or at least refrain from harming them. This belief in the needs of the dead was the origin of the Confucian ethical ideal of *xiao* (filial piety). Moreover, burial rites and offerings to the ancestors were an essential aspect of another Confucian ideal, *li* (ritual etiquette or propriety). It is impossible to ascertain when these beliefs originated, but pottery vessels containing food offerings were buried with the dead early in the Neolithic era (c. 6000–2000 BC).

By the late Shang period (c. 1250–1046 BC), the cult of ancestral offerings had become the driving force in the organization of a complex and far-reaching state centered at Yinxu, near Anyang, in Henan. Kings divined continuously by applying heated rods to previously prepared ox scapula and turtle plastrons and reading the resultant cracks. They often engraved the contents of these divinations on the cracked bones. The engraved divinations, now called *jiaguwen* (oracle bone inscriptions), convey a visceral fear of the potential harm of their ancestors' curses. Humans, as well as animals, wine, and grain were offered, and the sacrifices had to be appropriate in type, number, color, and combination. The Shang also developed an elaborate and sophisticated bronze-casting industry that was primarily devoted to the production of bronze vessels for making these ancestral offerings. The vessels had particular shapes, depending on their use, and included water basins for ritual ablutions; vessels for steeping, storing, pouring and drinking wine; and vessels for cooking, preparing, and serving grain and meat.

These bronze vessels, which were used to make offerings in ancestral temples as well as buried with the dead, were the supreme aesthetic and technological achievement of ancient China. Although the oracle bone inscriptions provide considerable information about the Shang spirit world, there is no direct correspondence between the imagery that decorates the vessels and the names found in oracle bone inscriptions. The primary motif on most Shang bronzes is a two-eyed zoomorph, traditionally called a *taotie*. In the late Shang period, this motif is characterized by mutability. It may be one animal with a split body or two creatures facing one another. Individual body parts, such as horns or wings, may become separate creatures. The parts of different animals (such as tigers, sheep, deer, goats, and humans) that make up the face combine and recombine. The suggested creature may be part-bird or part-dragon or have aspects of both. Because of this mutability, it is difficult to imagine that the motif depicts something specific—real or imagined. Nevertheless, if we interpret the imagery on the vessels in light of their function (to feed the ancestral spirits) and take this lack of realism as an essential aspect of their aesthetic form, we can understand the logic of the decoration, at least in a general sense.[1]

The term *taotie* was first applied to the motif on bronze vessels in the Song dynasty (960–1279) by the antiquarian Lü Dalin, who was the first Chinese scholar to make a catalogue of ancient vessels and jades found in later times. The historical context of the vessels

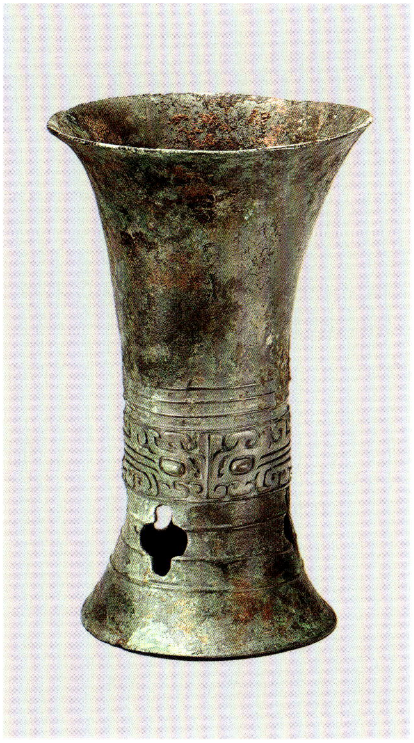

1 | Beaker (*gu*), early Shang dynasty, Erligang culture (c. 1600–1400 BC). Bronze; h. 15.5 (6 ⅛ in.); diam. 11 cm (4 5⁄16 in.). The Art Institute of Chicago, gift of Katherine and George Fan, 2011.51.

and the meaning of their motifs had long been lost, so he combed ancient literature for clues and concluded that the primary bronze vessel motif was a gluttonous creature described in the *Lüshi chunqiu* (Spring and Autumn Annals of Mr. Lü), compiled by Lü Buwei, which states: "The *ding* [vessels] of the Zhou display the *taotie*. It has a head and no body. It ate a person, but, before it could swallow it, it was destroyed itself."[2] There is, however, no reason to relate this statement to Shang or early Zhou dynasty (1046–771 BC) vessels. As Tao Wang has observed, other Song antiquarians identified this motif with other names found in the ancient texts, but none of their arguments are historically convincing.[3] For example, Luo Bi suggested that the motif represented another mythical figure, Chiyou, a rebel in the time of Huangdi (the Yellow Emperor). Luo's son, Luo Ping, glossed his father's identification with the observation that "[Chiyou's] nature and shape were never consistent. Bronzes from the three dynasties were often cast with Chiyou's portrait to warn those who are greedy."[4] There is no early evidence that any of the names suggested by these scholars were known during the Shang period, much less applied to the motif with which they decorated their vessels. Nevertheless, that the Song antiquarians understood the motif as an eating or devouring entity supports the idea that the open mouth of the *taotie* is critical to understanding its meaning.

In the early Shang period (c. 1600–1400 BC), the *taotie* is characterized by two eyes and the suggestion of a face. The eyes are either round or, like human eyes, have canthi with whites. The eyes are normally placed within a band of decoration and flanked on both sides by designs in which the image and the ground are not clearly differentiated (see fig. 1). Neolithic imagery throughout the world commonly emphasizes eyes. David Pearce and David Lewis-Williams have argued that hypnagogic experiences—vivid mental imagery, visions, or hallucinations experienced in states ranging from semiwakefulness to altered states of consciousness induced by such means as alcohol, rhythmic music and dancing, or psychotropic drugs—are neurologically engendered and common across all cultures. Brain experiments show that these hypnagogic experiences have common characteristics, including seeing bright geometric patterns, passages through tunnels, floating or flying images, and transformations of animals and humans into one another. The strangeness and vivid detail of these visions provide a rich source of imagery for ancient peoples, and the similarity of the visions around the world explains the occurrence of similar motifs in unrelated Neolithic cultures.[5]

In this light, it is significant that the earliest vessels cast in bronze (in the early second millennium BC) were a type of wine vessel, called a *jue*. These vessels have been found in burial assemblages that include two-eyed turquoise plaques found in the chest position of the decayed skeleton, small bronze clapper bells near the waist, and baton-like objects made of jade. The vessels had thin walls and were not decorated, but the two-eyed motif found on the turquoise plaques is the precursor of the early Shang *taotie*. The unusual accoutrements found in these tombs imply that the people buried in them were religious interlocutors or shamans, who used wine in ritual performances.[6]

By the late Shang period, the suggestion of a face in a band of decoration had been elaborated in an aesthetic language of mutating forms, split images, conjoined creatures, and other breaches of reality. The decoration was no longer confined to narrow bands of ornament, often filling the entire external space on the vessel. Although Pearce and Lewis-Williams attributed the

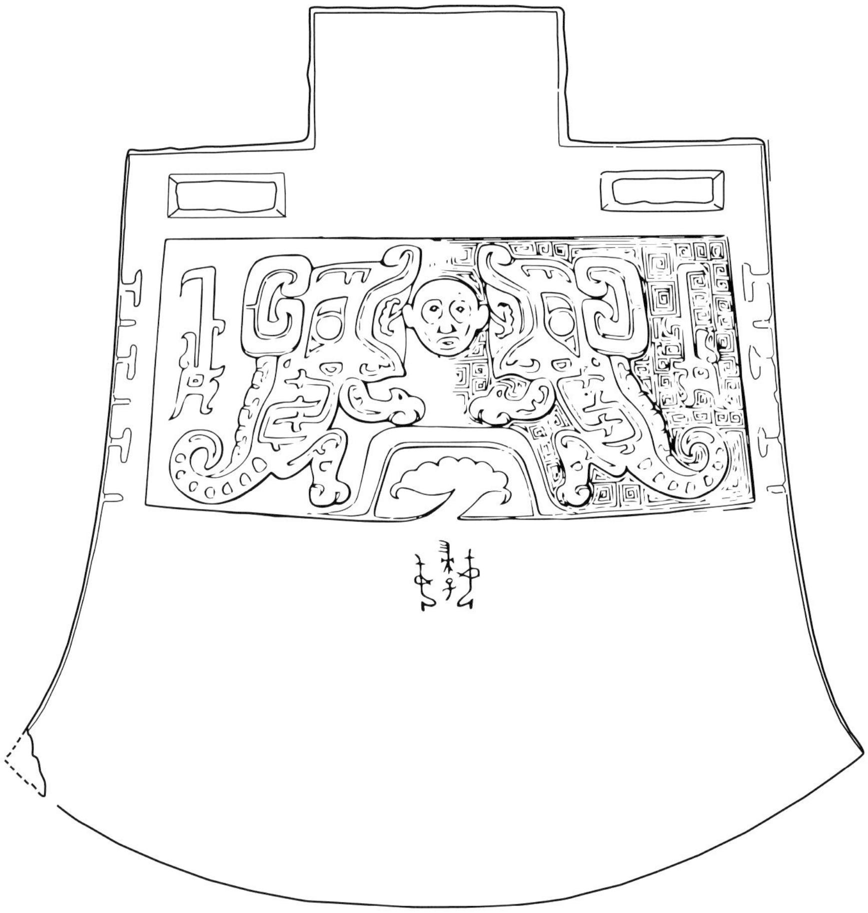

2 | A drawing of the axe (*yue*) from the tomb of Lady Hao. From Institute of Archaeology, Chinese Academy of Social Sciences, ed., *Yinxu Fu Hao mu* [The Tomb of Lady Hao at Yinxu] (Beijing: Wenwu chubanshe, 1980), 106, pl. 67.

importance of eyes in primitive art to the significance of neurologically engendered visions, it is worth noting that the feeling of being seen or watched also has a neurological effect, producing a sensation of unease, or even fear. Placing eyes on a vessel endows it with the power of sight. Thus, the supplicant—and his audience—are not seeing but being seen. That is, the eyes suggest another world, the world of the spirits who will consume the offerings.

Sacrifice is posited on a notion of transition between cosmological realms: the offering is sent from one part of the cosmos to another. In ancient China, the vessels served as the conduit between the people making the offerings and the ancestral spirits. We know from the oracle bones of the late Shang period that the ancestral spirits were still "living," in the sense that they needed food and were able to interfere with the lives of the living. This suggests that they could also still "see." This does not mean that the eyes on the vessels were those of particular ancestors but that, in a more general sense, the eyes of the *taotie* alluded to the spirits of the dead. Accordingly, the unreadability of the aesthetic form alludes to the ineffable nature of the world in which they dwell.

Besides eyes, the late Shang *taotie* usually has an open mouth, often with an abbreviated or absent lower jaw. Presumably, this open mouth was the reason that the Song dynasty antiquarians thought the motif represented a creature that was gluttonous. The mouth commonly has long catlike fangs, a convention associated with tigers, as on the ritual axe (see fig. 2) from the tomb of Lady Hao, a consort of King Wuding (r. c. 1250–1192 BC).[7] These two tigers, whose mouths enclose a human head, are probably a split image (see fig. 3a). The same mouth is found at the bottom of the image so that the blade of the axe appears to extend from a fanged mouth; that is, the tiger mouth and the blade are equated. These tigers also have the round C-shaped ears conventionally associated with tigers in Shang writing and art.

Large cats such as lions, tigers, and jaguars are night hunters and meat eaters, and they prey on humans as well as animals. Such animals are common in sacrificial rituals throughout the world, and their mouths commonly allude to the passage to another cosmological realm, or death, in myth and art. Tigers played a special role in hunting and sacrifice for the Shang kings. Divinations about their possible capture were made before royal hunts and their capture was sometimes recorded. An unusual carved and inlaid tiger humerus, now in the Royal Ontario Museum,

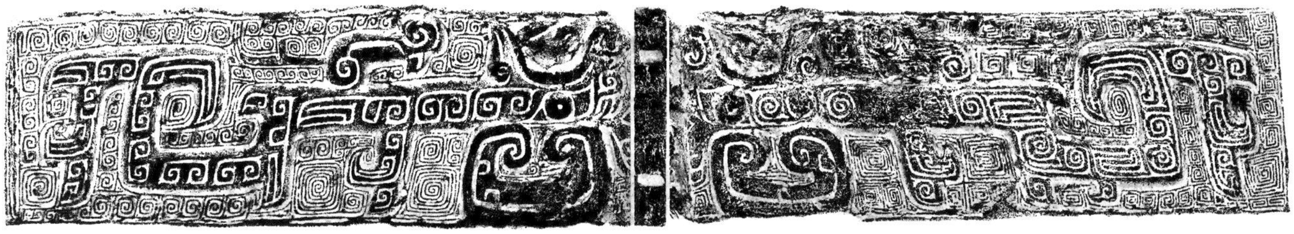

a

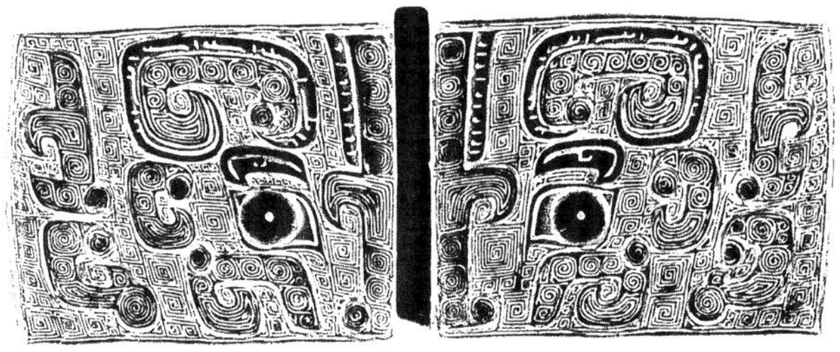

b

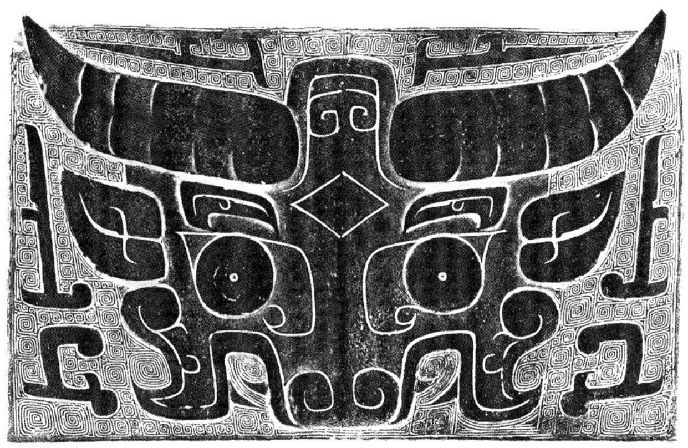

c

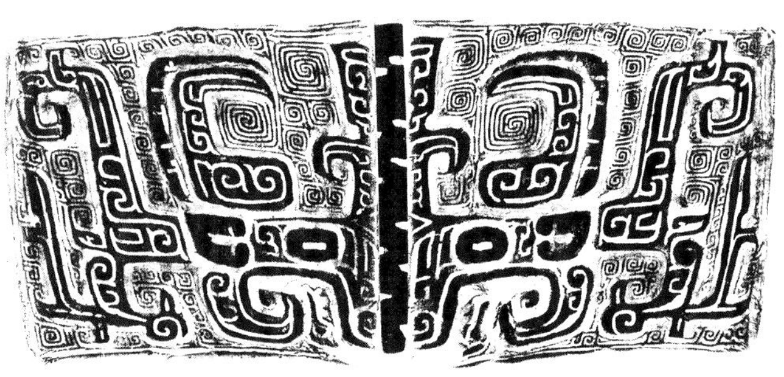

d

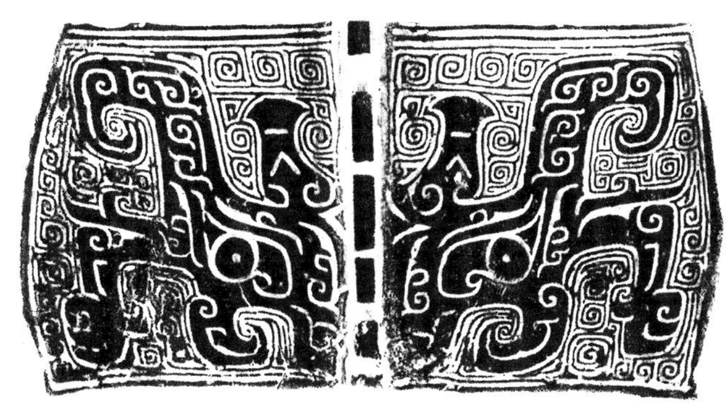

e

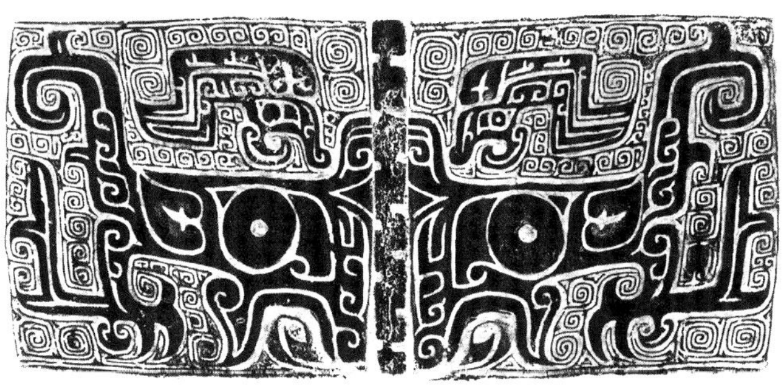

f

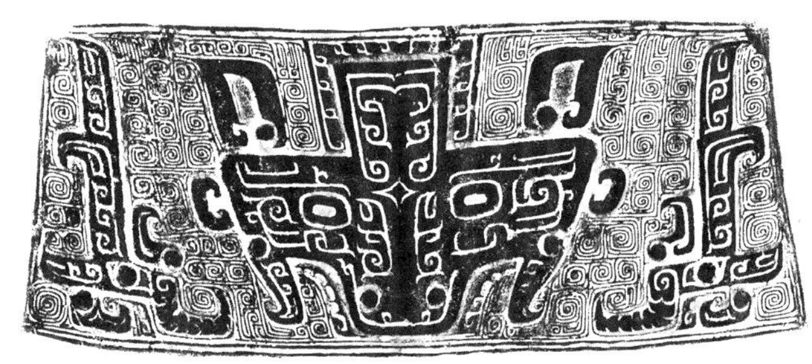

g

3a–3g | Rubbings of *taotie* motifs on bronze vessels from the late Shang dynasty (c. 1250–1046 BC). From Shanghai Museum Bronze Research Group, *Shang Zhou Qingtongqi Wenshi* [Motifs of Shang and Zhou Bronzes] (Beijing: Wenwu chubanshe, 1984), nos. 59, 35, 205, 81, 139, 145, and 203, respectively.

records the successful capture of a particularly large and ferocious tiger and a subsequent ritual offering, probably of the same animal.[8] The placement of a human head within the open mouth of a tiger is an unusual motif in Shang art, but we may deduce from it that the open tiger mouth in the *taotie* has a similar meaning and serves to transmit the vessel's contents to the ancestral spirits.

Horns, as well as tiger ears, are commonly found above the eyes in the *taotie*. The face may also have eyebrows, horns, or ears. Occasionally, the eyebrows are enlarged and fill the space (see pl. 156). Human ears sometimes appear at the sides of the head (see figs. 3b and 3g). The horn types allude to animals that were sacrificed by the Shang, for example, sheep (see figs. 3a and 3b), oxen (see fig. 3c), and goats (see fig. 3d). The so-called bottle horns (fig. 3e) probably reference the stalks of a young deer. The Jin Yin *gong* (pl. 37) shows an antler sprouting from the stalk by a deer-like ear. The twisted horn in another variant (see fig. 3f) is possibly also an antler.[9] The Qi Fu *li* (pl. 1) is unusual in having both tiger ears and ox horns above the eyes.

The mutability of the *taotie* imagery is evident in the changing relationship of the body or bodies and body parts to the face. Most commonly, two bodies with a single leg (or single pair of legs, since the image is in profile) and a tail are attached to each side of the *taotie* face (see fig. 3a). The *taotie* might be a two-bodied creature, but it also might be a single-bodied one seen from both sides. In other examples, the bodies are detached and may even dissolve into their individual parts, as on the Qi Fu *li*. Or, they may become whole creatures with their own heads. These may resemble another type of creature with a single leg, or single pair of legs since it is seen in profile, that frequently occurs independently of the *taotie* in its own register. These creatures are conventionally called *kui* dragons. They may be replaced by birds, or take on birdlike features, and both dragons and birds may both occur in registers. This pairing suggests the tiered cosmos, familiar from later texts, of a watery underworld and a celestial heaven. Cicadas and snakes are also commonly intermingled with the *taotie*. Thus, not only are the motifs of Shang bronze art continually transformed, their primary allusions are to transformations of states of being: eating and sacrifice; the watery underworld of the dead; and dragons that are also birds, snakes that slough their skins, deer that shed their antlers, and cicadas that emerge winged from the earth.

The legitimacy of the Shang king was based on a religious claim to the favor of the Lord on High, Shangdi. When the Zhou overthrew the Shang, they claimed that the Mandate of Heaven had devolved on them. Drawing on the Shang system of governance, the Zhou created a more organized governmental structure, establishing members of their family and allies as lords over states under their control. Although vessels were still used for making offerings to the ancestors, the sense of religious awe that inspired Shang sacrifices was replaced by a more this-worldly focus on the descendants who cast the vessels in honor of their ancestors and the relationship between the royal house and the aristocratic families. The inscriptions, once short ancestral dedications, now recorded glorious deeds, official appointments, and gratitude for gifts received. Cauldrons (*ding*), already an important marker of status, were paired with food containers (*gui*) in different numbers to reflect official or royal rank. After a transitional period, the ritual practices in which bronze vessels were used were altered, as reflected in the types of vessels that were cast. Moreover, the Zhou did not practice human sacrifice, and the wine vessels that were central to Shang ritual lost their importance. The decoration of bronze vessels changed in tandem with these religious and ideological shifts. In the transitional period, Zhou bronzes sometimes took a more flamboyant form than those of the Shang, but they continued to be decorated with the same motifs. However, interest in mutating forms eventually gave way to a preference for repeating ones. The *taotie* also lost its central role. The secondary motifs, such as birds and dragons, were retained and often became the basis of new forms. Novel types of birds and dragons with their heads turned backward toward their tails sometimes replaced the *taotie* in the central register of vessels (see pl. 19). However, the aesthetic focus of the vessels increasingly became the overall form of the vessels, with the decoration playing a supportive role. To this end, the birds and dragons were increasingly abstracted, sometimes reduced to undulating lines or patterning (see pl. 51). The *taotie*, to the extent that it was retained at all, now played a minor role in the overall design. In the Warring States period (475–221 BC), as the states gained more autonomy, bronze decoration became more varied, as regional styles emerged. Moreover, bronzes inlaid with gold and silver became popular, reflecting the influence of a new mercantile class (see pl. 50). Yet the social role of bronzes had changed with the development of early Chinese culture, and their decoration never regained the religious intensity of the Shang vessels.

NOTES

1 | The arguments presented in this essay are discussed in more detail and with fuller documentation in Sarah Allan, "The *Taotie* Motif on Early Chinese Ritual Bronzes," in Jerome Silbergeld and Eugene Wang, eds., *The Zoomorphic Imagination in Chinese Art and Culture* (Honolulu: Hawai'i University Press, 2016), 21–66. See also Sarah Allan, *The Shape of the Turtle: Myth, Art and Cosmos in Early China* (Albany: State University of New York Press, 1991), 138–49.

2 | Chen Qiyou, ed., *Lüshi chunqiu jiaoshi* [Concordance and Annotation of the Annals of Lü Buwei] (Shanghai: Xuelin chubanshe, 1984), *juan* 16.1, 947. Unless otherwise indicated, all translations are the author's own.

3 | Tao Wang, "A Textual Investigation of the *Taotie*," in Roderick Whitfield, ed., *The Problem of Meaning in Early Chinese Ritual Bronzes*, Colloquies on Art and Archaeology in Asia (London: Percival David Foundation of Chinese Art, School of Oriental and African Studies, 1992), 102–18.

4 | *Lushi* (Wayside History], *Sibu Beiyao* edition (Shanghai: Zonghua shuju, 1936), vol. 3, 2a, quoted in Wang, "A Textual Investigation of the *Taotie*," 115.

5 | David Pearce and David Lewis Williams, *Inside the Neolithic Mind* (London: Thames and Hudson, 2005).

6 | Sarah Allan, "Erlitou and the Formation of Chinese Civilization: Toward a New Paradigm." *Journal of Asian Studies* 66:2 (March 2007), 461–96. The "wine" was grain-based.

7 | For a more detailed discussion of the role of the tiger in Shang imagery and oracle bone inscriptions, see Sarah Allan, "He Flies Like a Bird, He Dives Like a Dragon, Who Is That Man in the Animal Mouth?: Shamanic Images in Shang and Western Zhou Art," *Orientations* 41:3 (April 2010), 45–51; and Allan, "*Taotie* Motif," 51–54.

8 | Chin-hsiung Hsu, *Oracle Bones from the White and Other Collections*, exh. cat. (Toronto: Royal Ontario Museum, 1979), cat. 1915; William Charles White, *Bone Culture of Ancient China* (Toronto: University of Toronto Press, 1945), 96–98.

9 | This identification was made by Elizabeth Childs-Johnson; see "The Metamorphic Image: A Predominant Theme in the Ritual Art of Shang China," *Bulletin of the Museum of Far Eastern Antiquities* 70 (1998): 20–31.

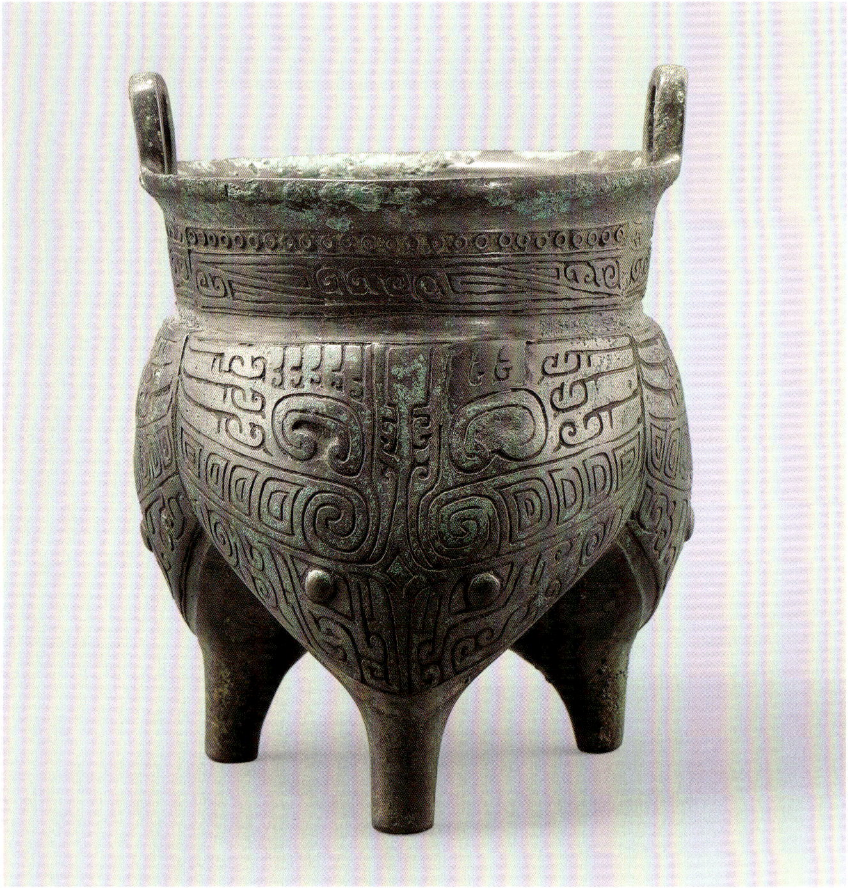

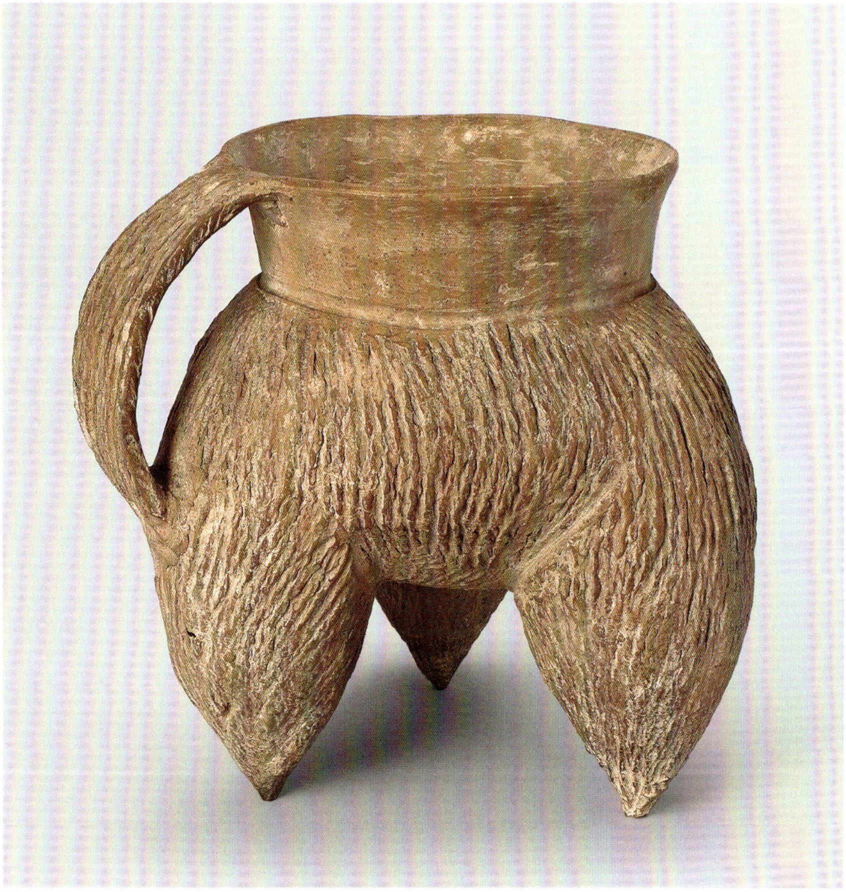

1 | LOBED TRIPOD CAULDRON OF LADY QI (*QI FU LI*), late Shang dynasty (c. 1250–1046 BC)

2 | LOBED TRIPOD CAULDRON (*LI*), Longshan culture (c. 2500–2000 BC)

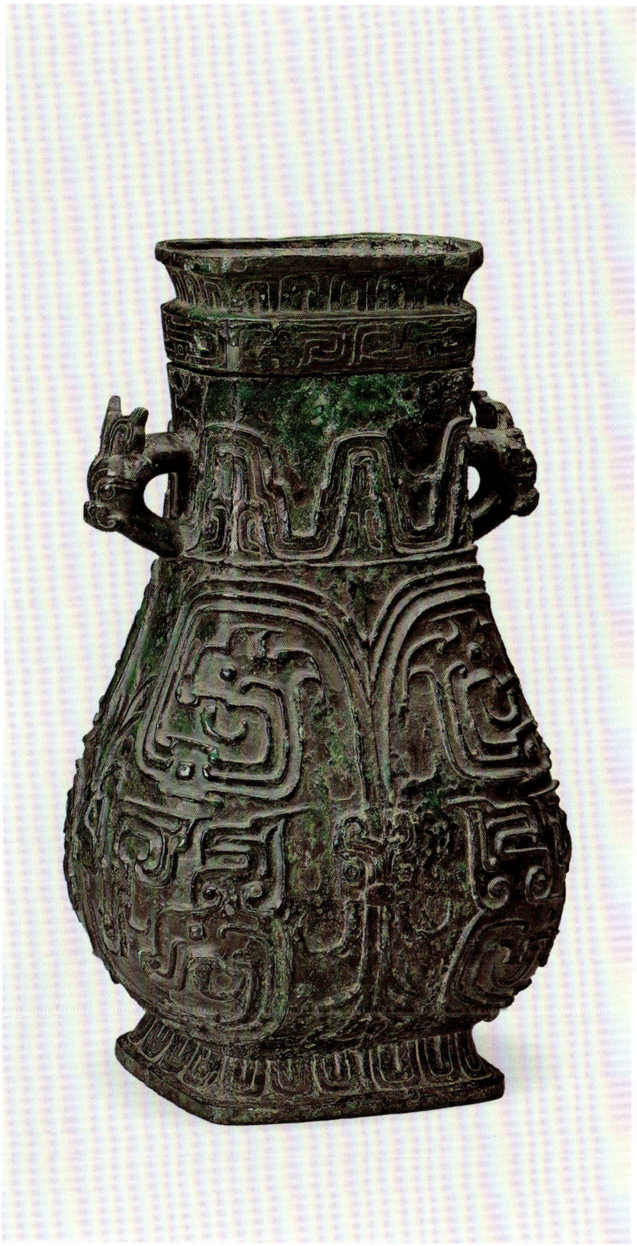

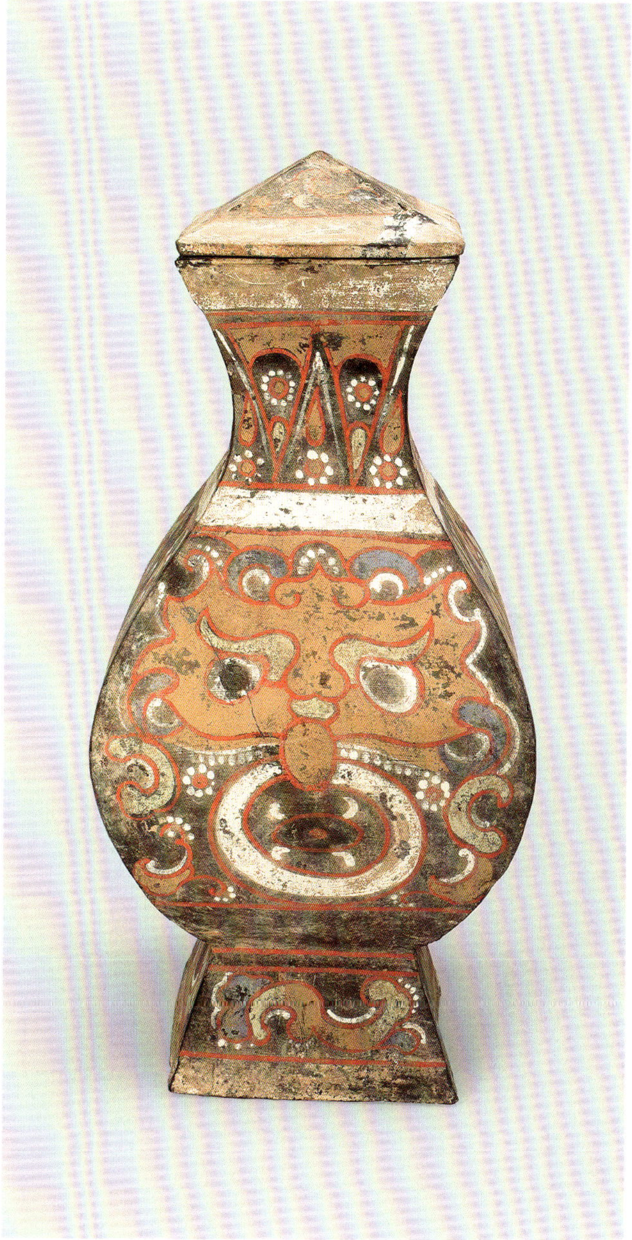

3 | JAR OF LORD RUI (*RUI GONG HU*), Western Zhou dynasty (1046–771 BC)

4 | CONTAINER IN THE FORM OF AN ANCIENT BRONZE JAR (*HU*), Western Han dynasty (206 BC–AD 9)

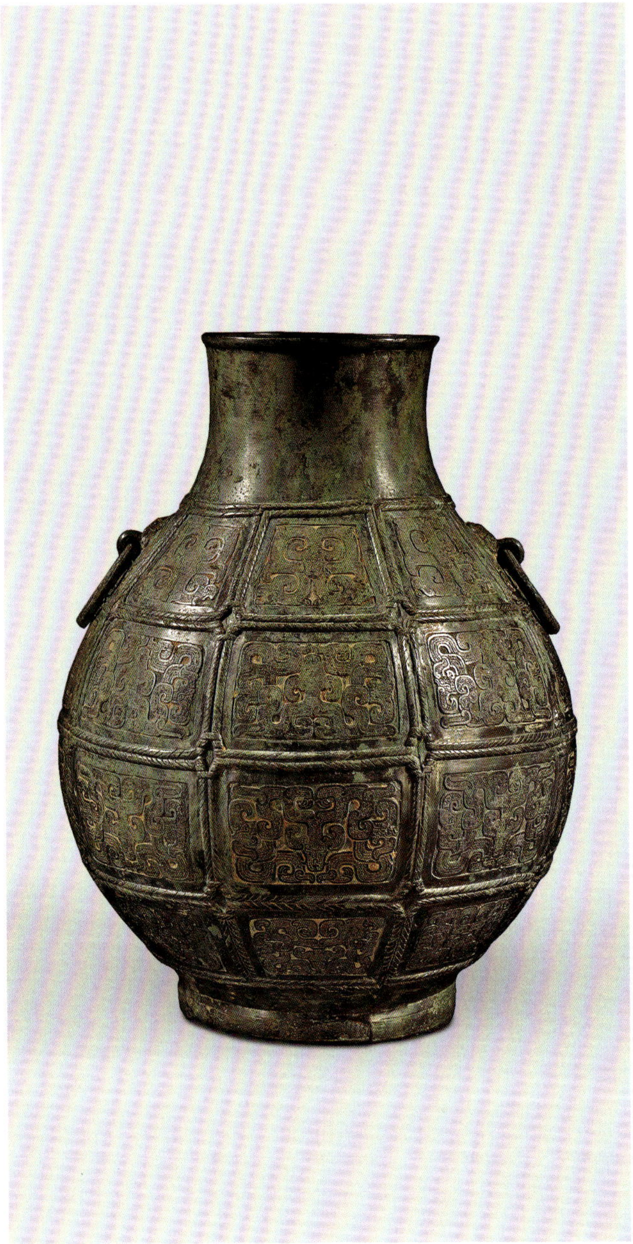

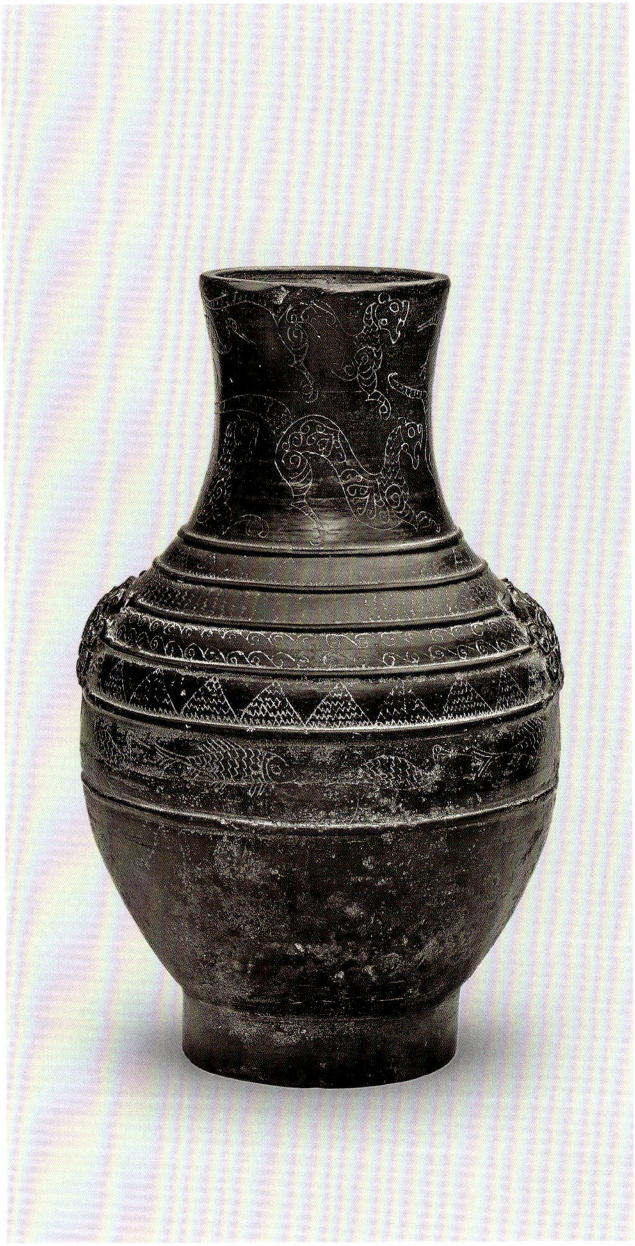

5 | JAR (*HU*), Warring States period (475–221 BC)

6 | CONTAINER IN THE FORM OF AN ANCIENT BRONZE JAR (*HU*), Warring States period (475–221 BC)

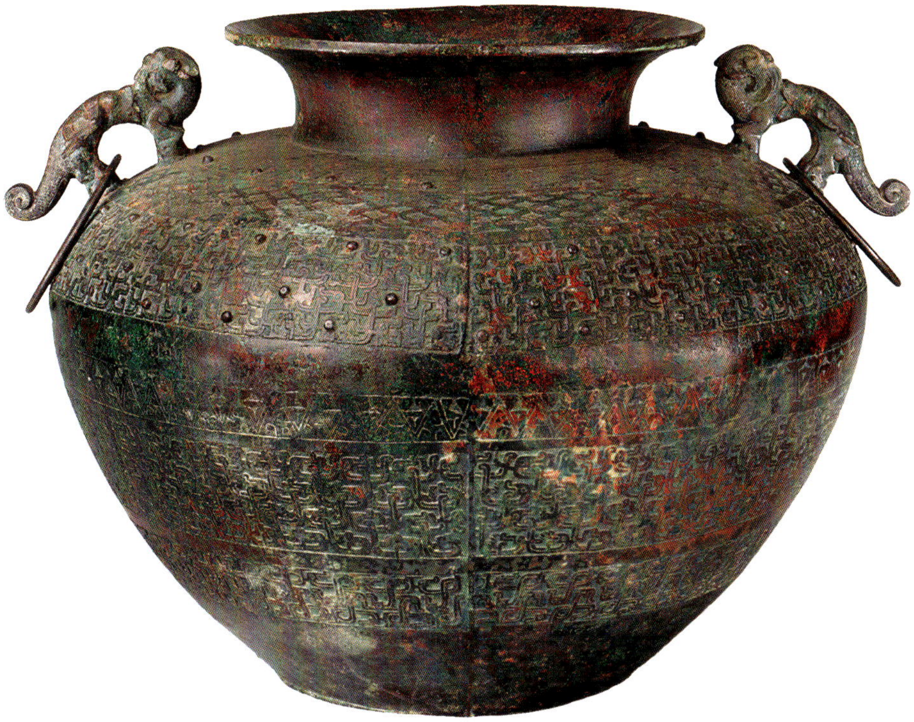

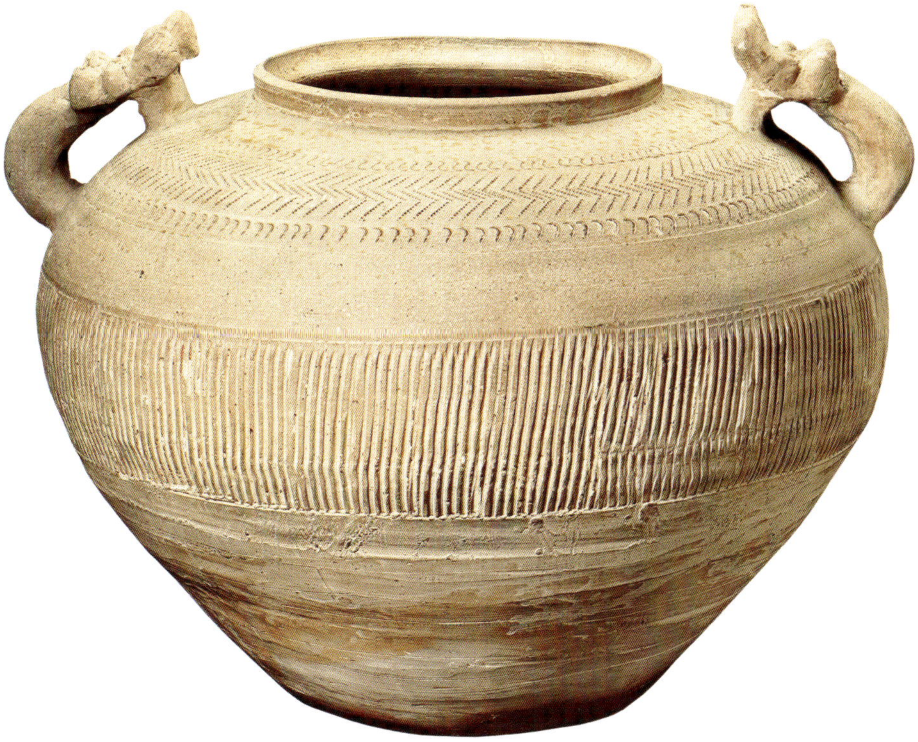

7 | CONTAINER (*LEI*), Spring and Autumn period (770–476 BC)

8 | JAR IN THE FORM OF AN ANCIENT BRONZE CONTAINER (*LEI*), Eastern Zhou dynasty, Warring States Period (475–221 BC)

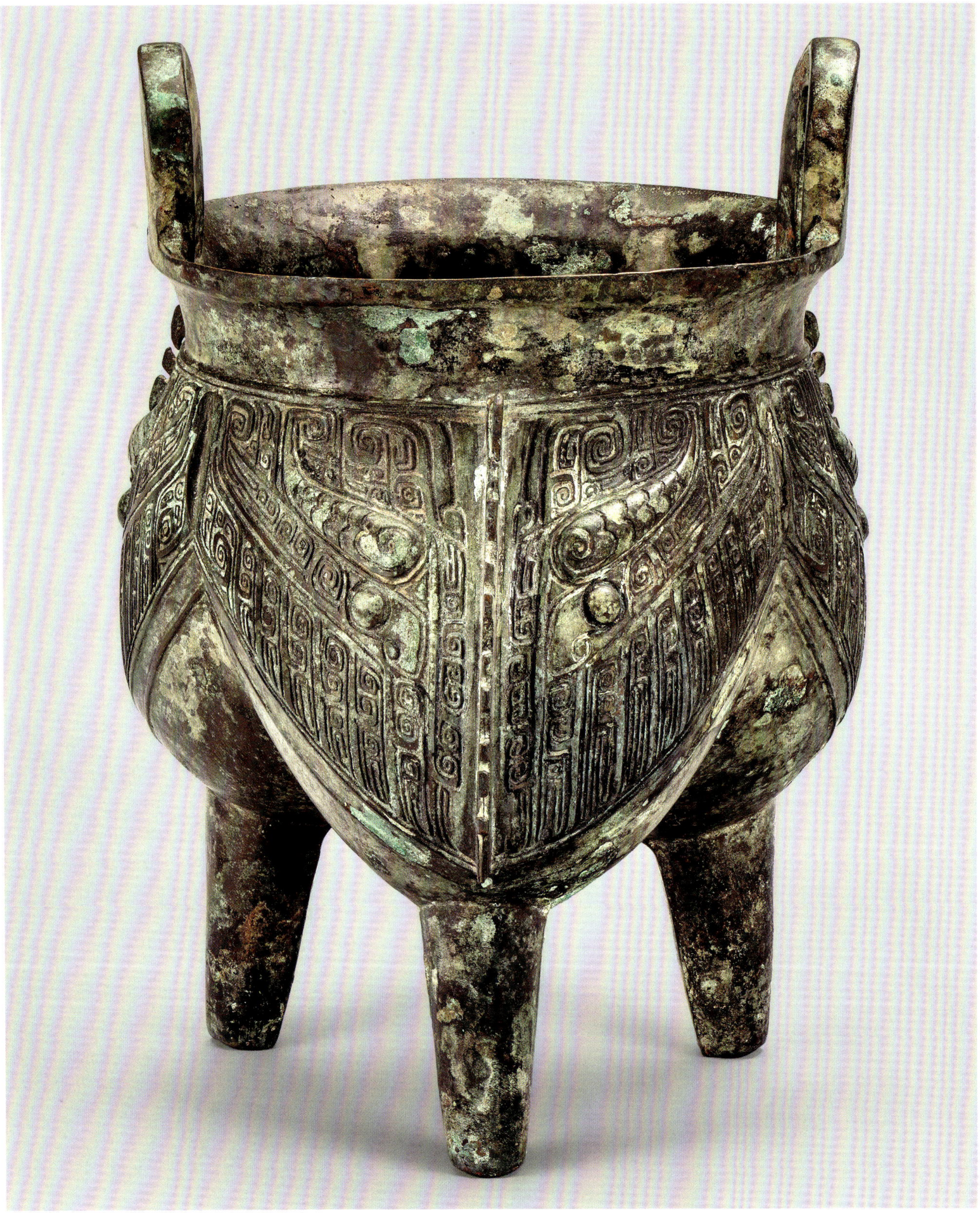

9 | LOBED TRIPOD CAULDRON (*LI*), late Shang dynasty (c. 1250–1046 BC)

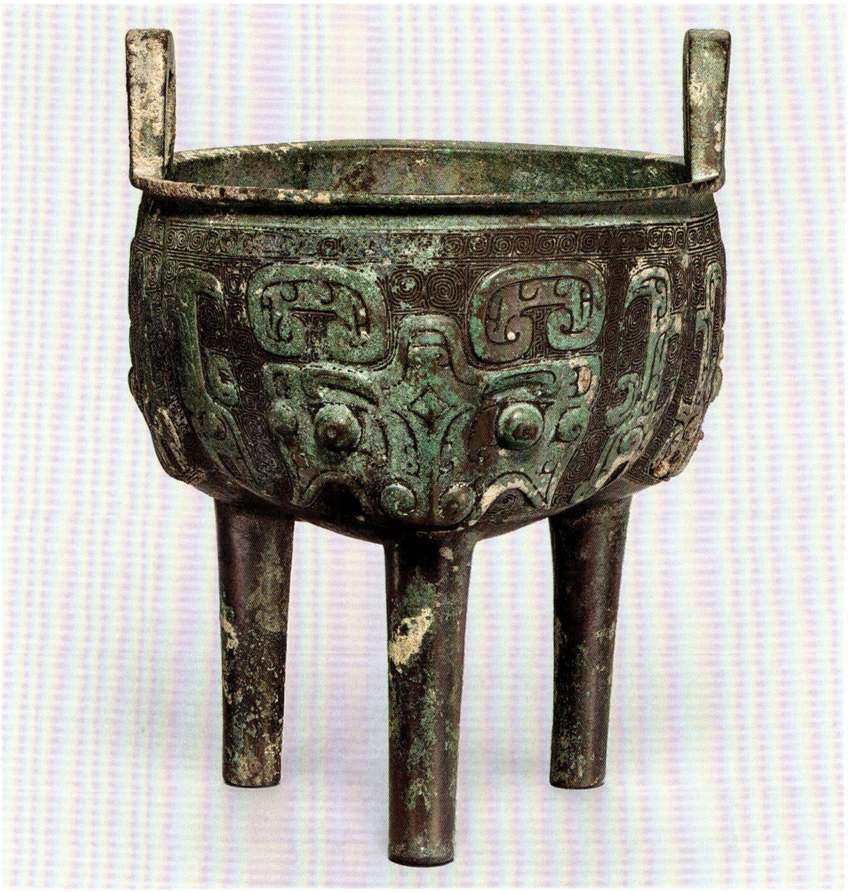

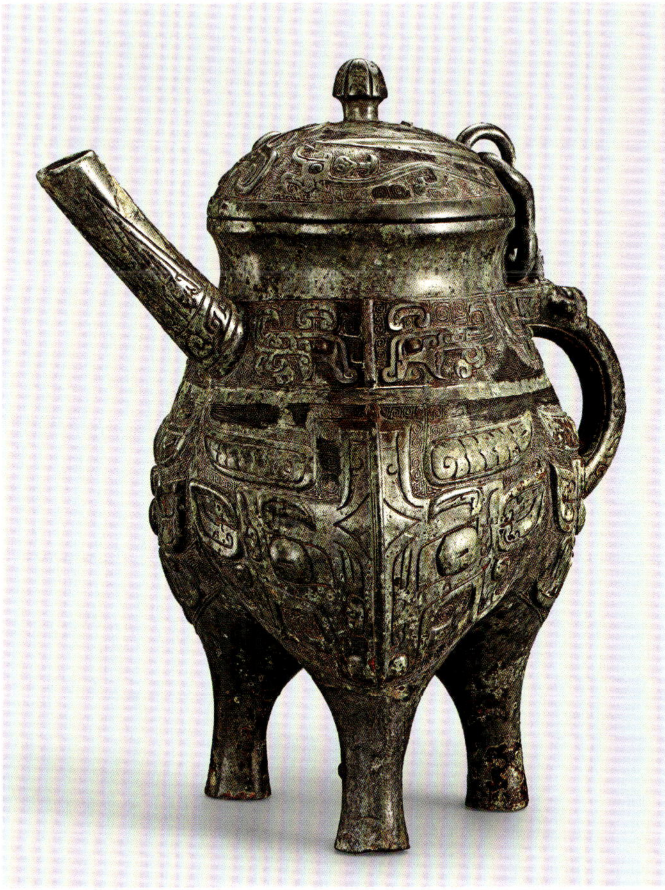

10 | TRIPOD CAULDRON (*DING*), late Shang dynasty (c. 1250–1046 BC)

11 | EWER OF FATHER YI (*FU YI HE*), late Shang dynasty (c. 1250–1046 BC)

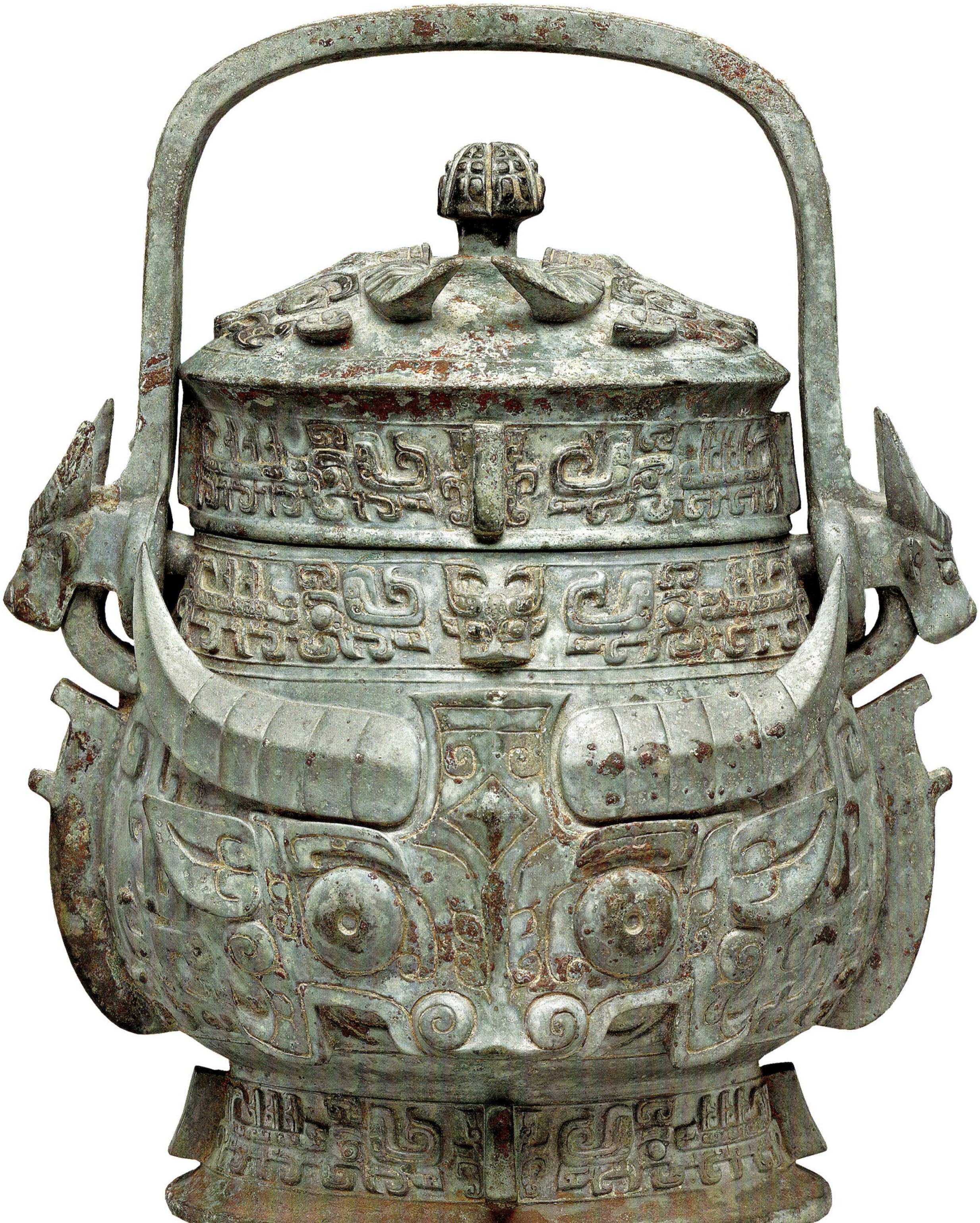

12 | BUCKET OF FU CHENG (*FU CHENG YOU*), late Shang dynasty (c. 1250–1046 BC)

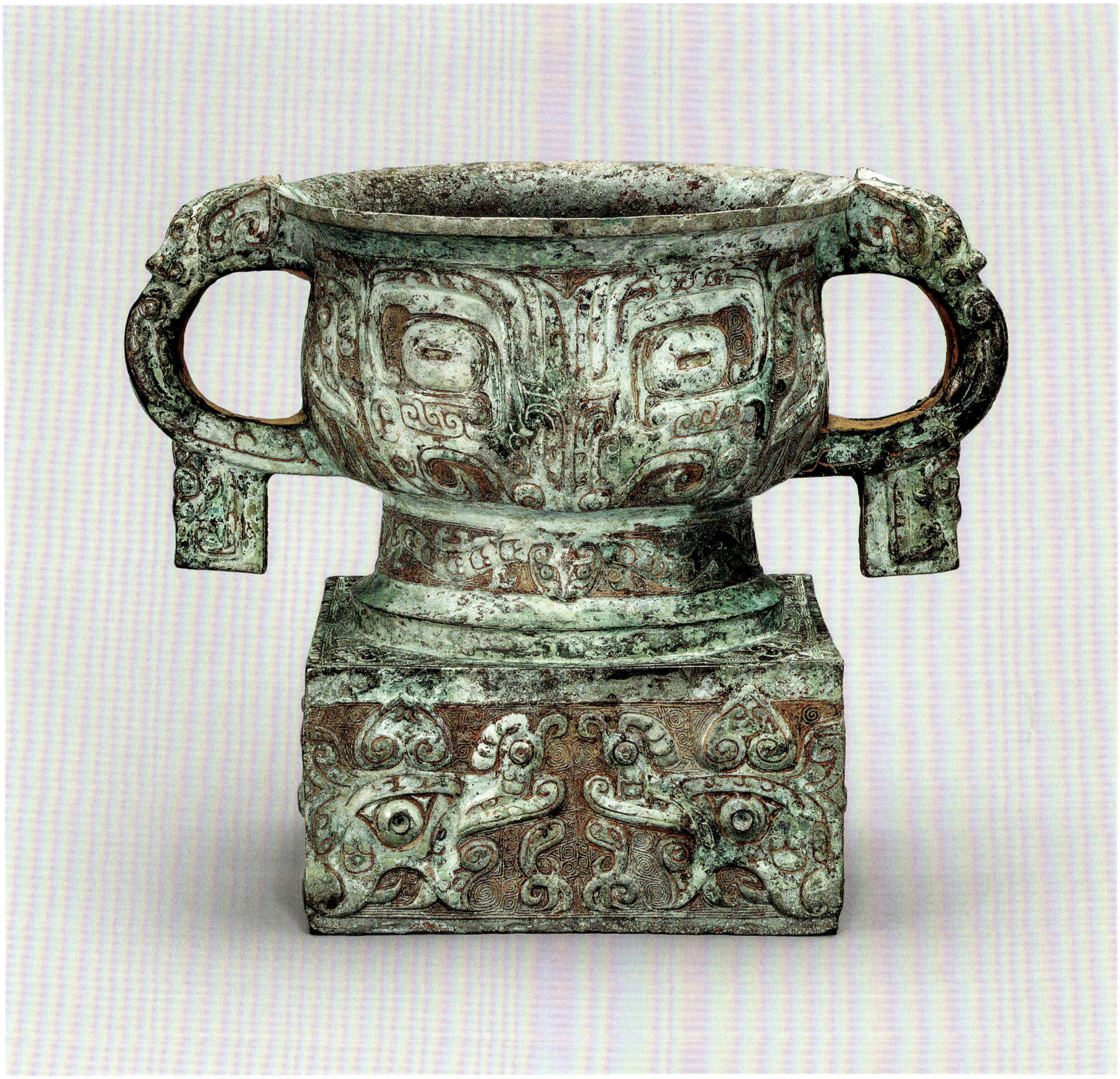

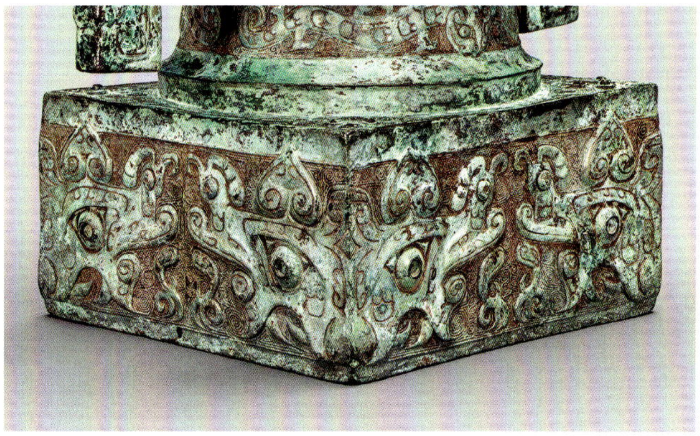

13 | PEDESTALED TUREEN OF DUKE JU (*BO JU GUI*), Western Zhou dynasty (1046–771 BC)

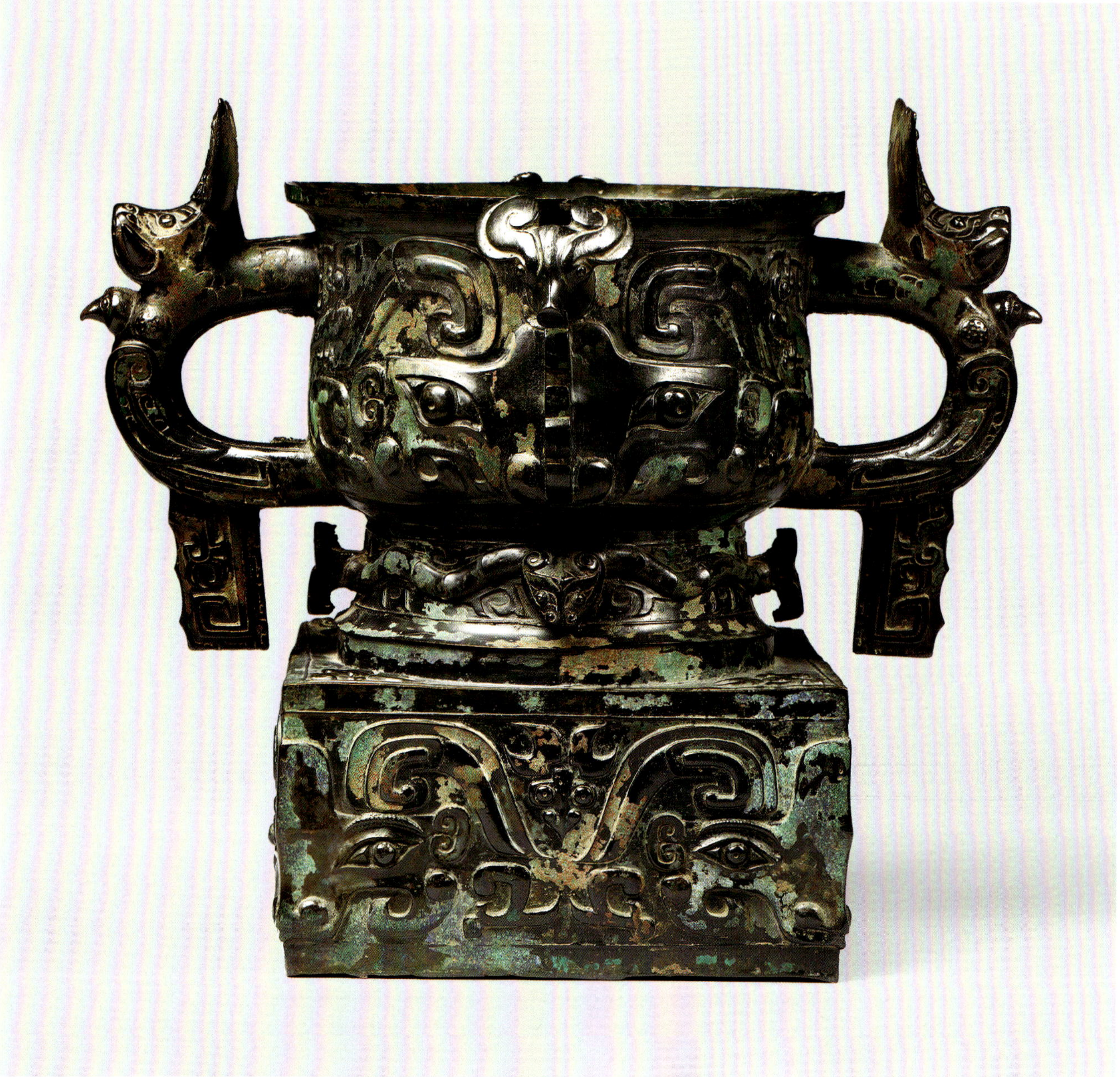

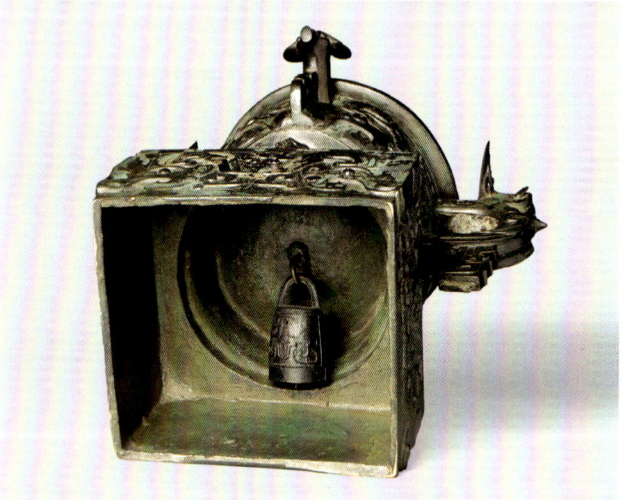

14 | PEDESTALED TUREEN OF DUKE HUAN (*JU BO HUAN GUI*), Western Zhou dynasty (1046–771 BC)

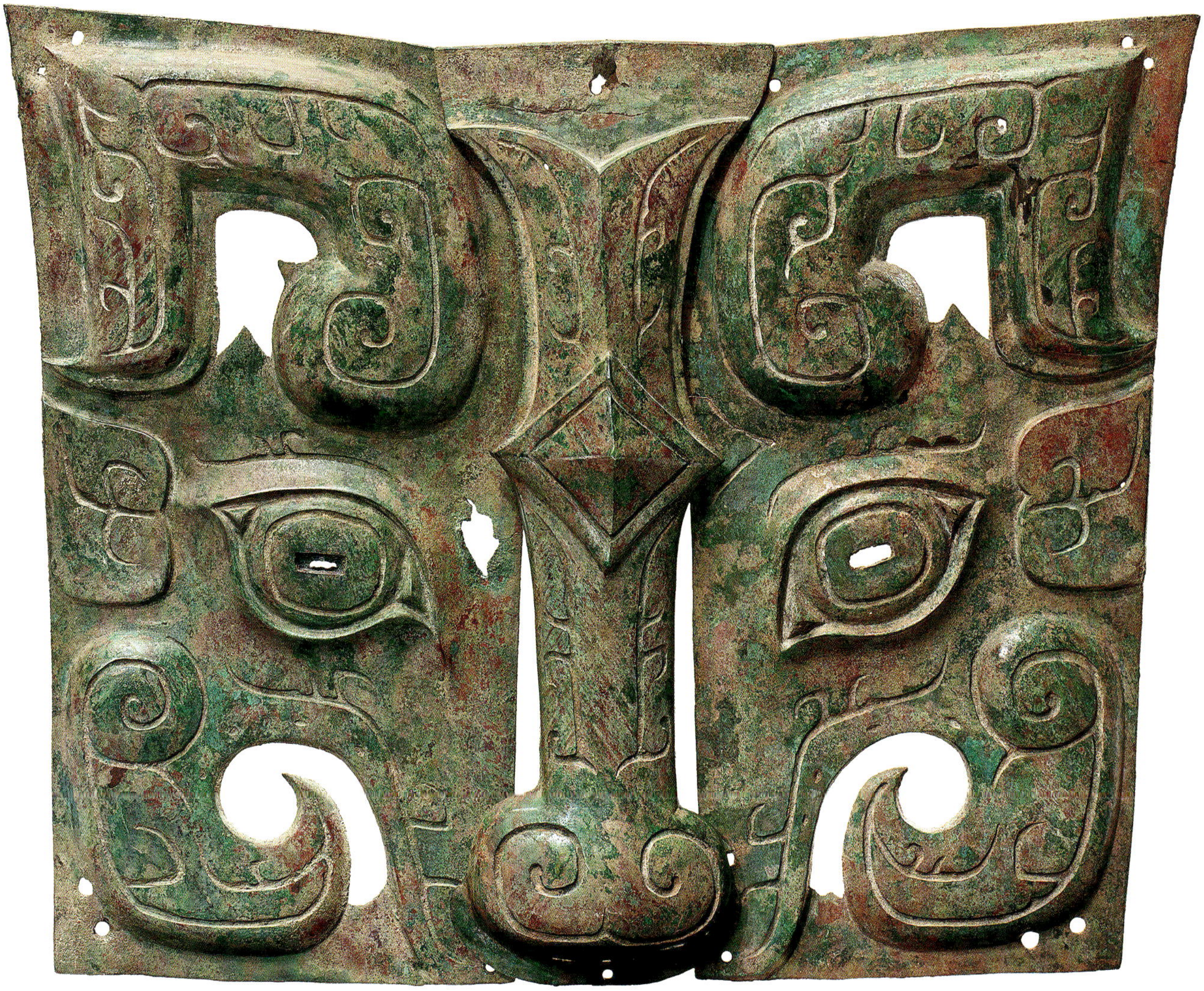

15 | MASK, Western Zhou dynasty (1046–771 BC)

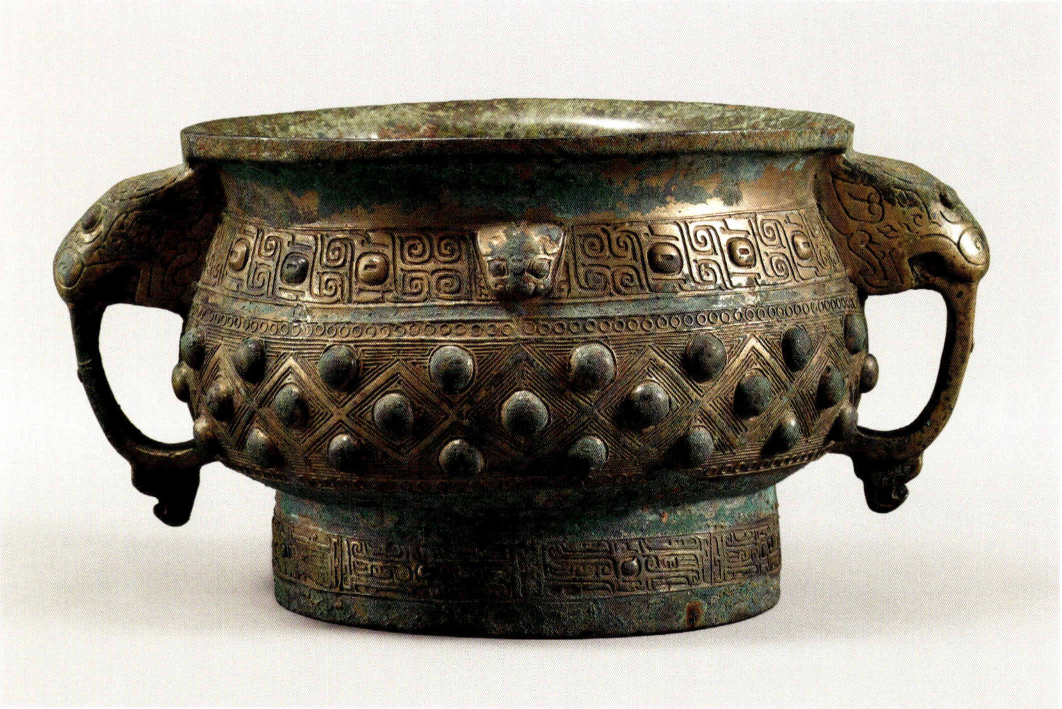

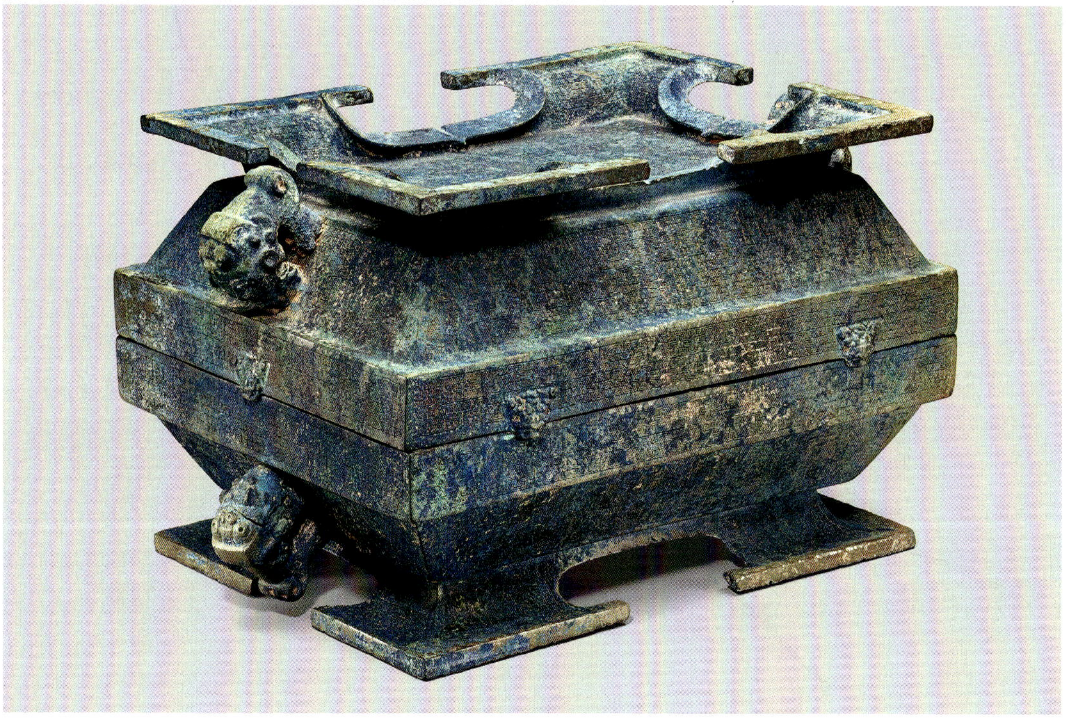

16 | TUREEN OF OFFICER SHI (*YA SHI GUI*), late Shang dynasty (c. 1250–1046 BC)

17 | RECTANGULAR TUREEN (*FU*), Spring and Autumn period (770–476 BC)

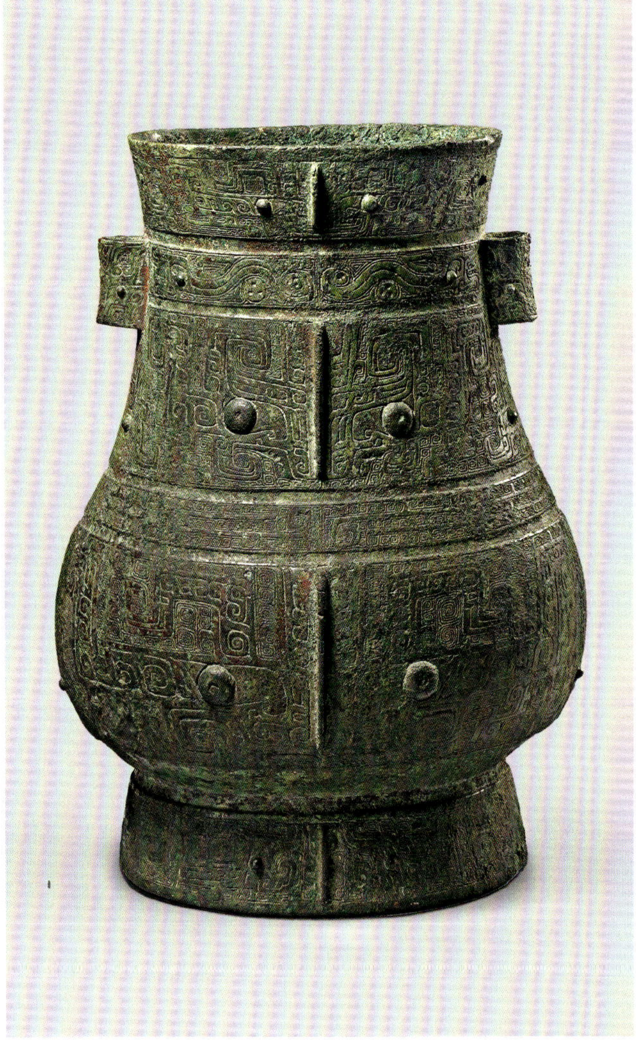

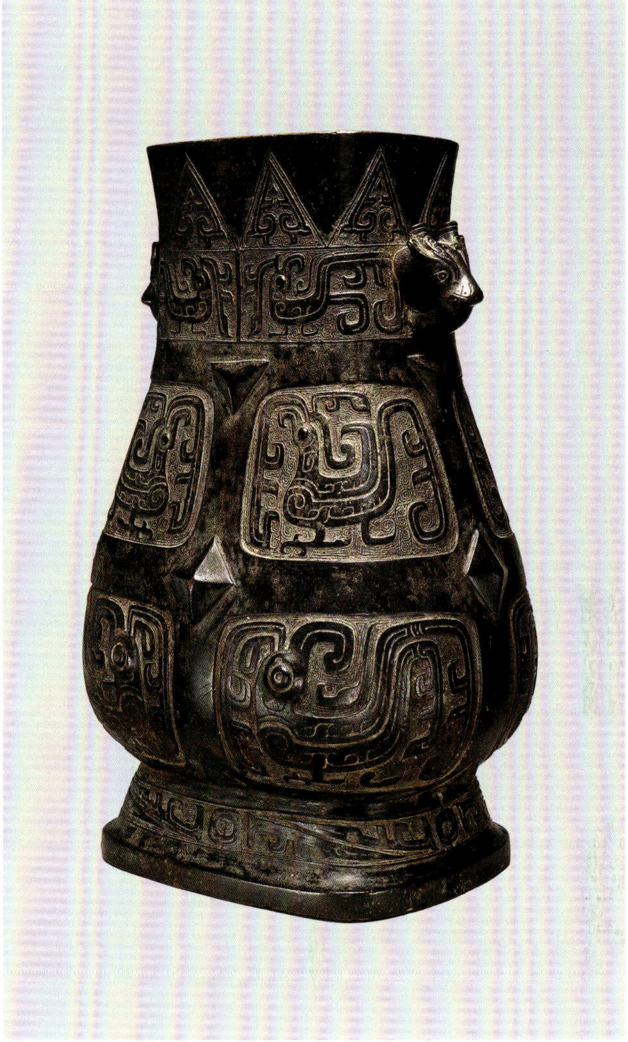

18 | JAR (*HU*), late Shang dynasty (c. 1250–1046 BC)

19 | JAR (*HU*), Western Zhou dynasty (1046–771 BC)

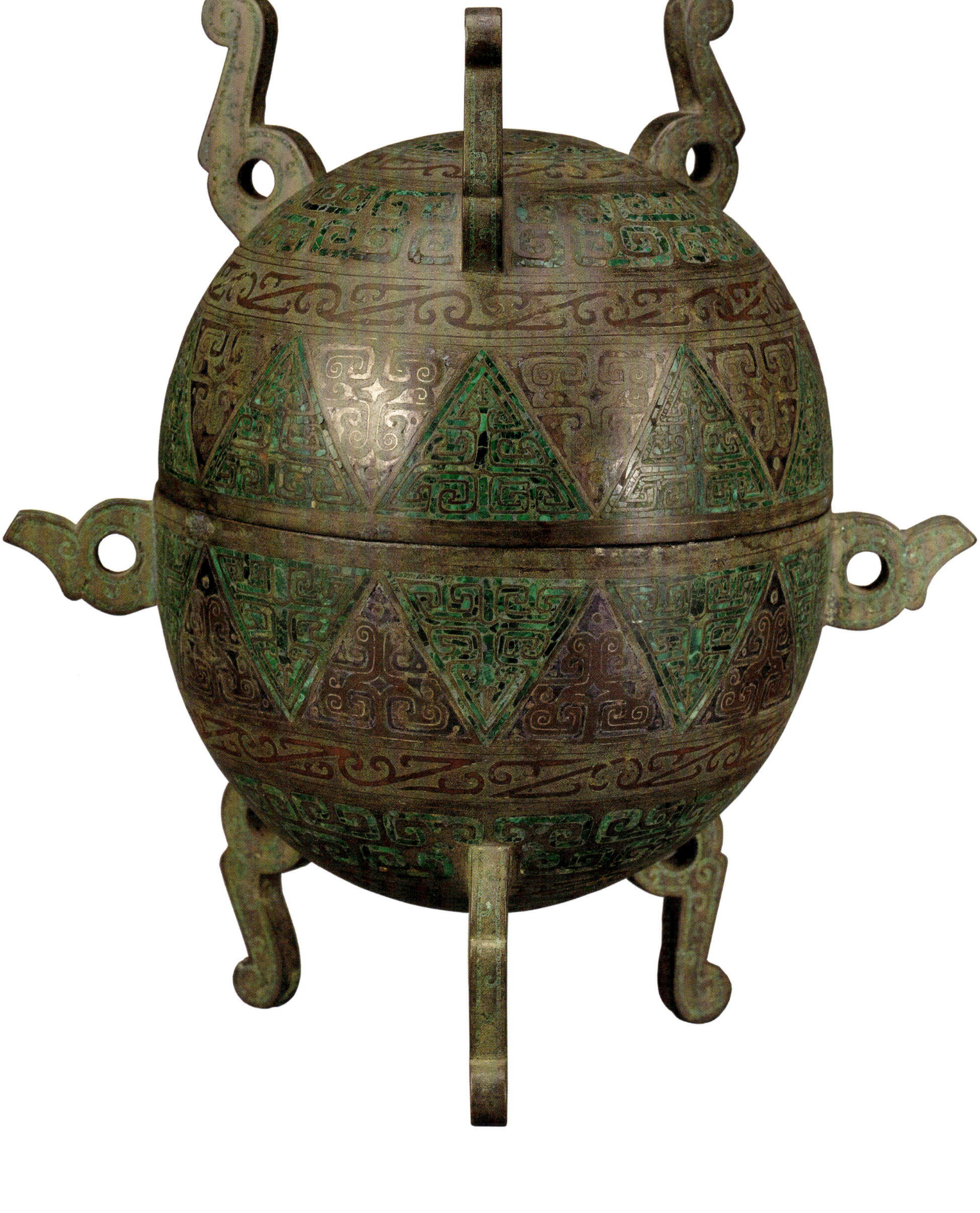

20 | BIPARTITE HEMISPHERICAL BOWL (*DUI*), Warring States period (475–221 BC)

21 | JAR (*HU* OR *ZHONG*), Western Han dynasty (206 BC–AD 9)

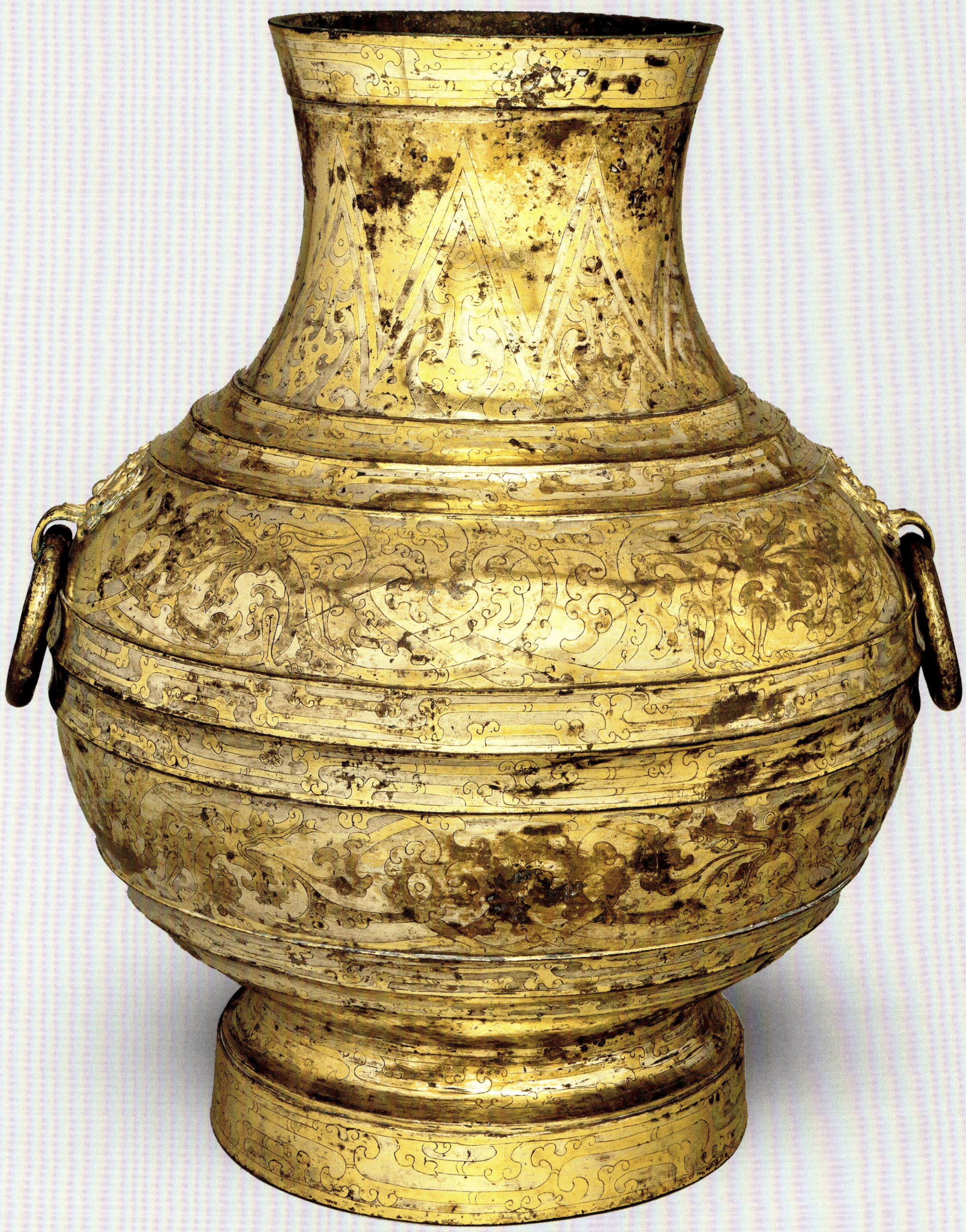

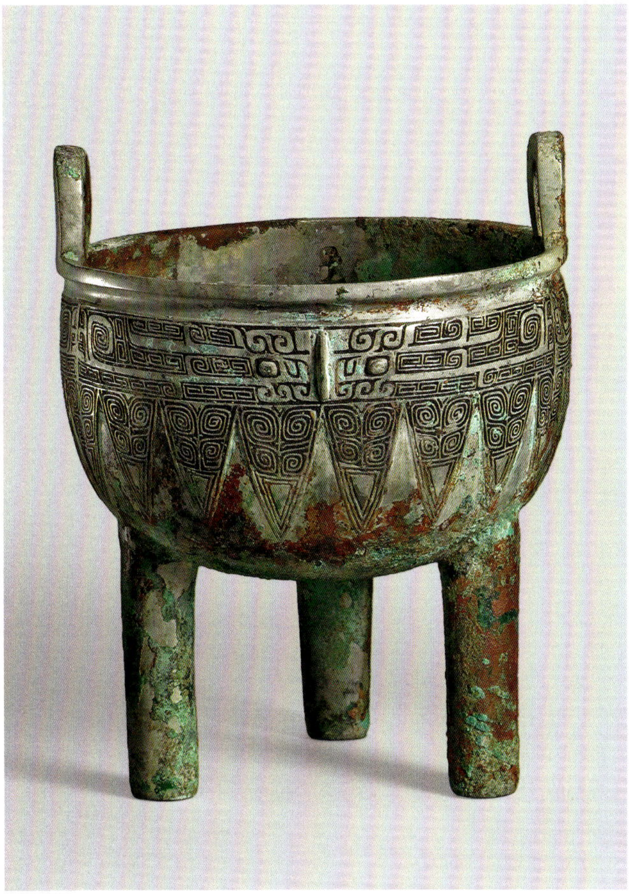

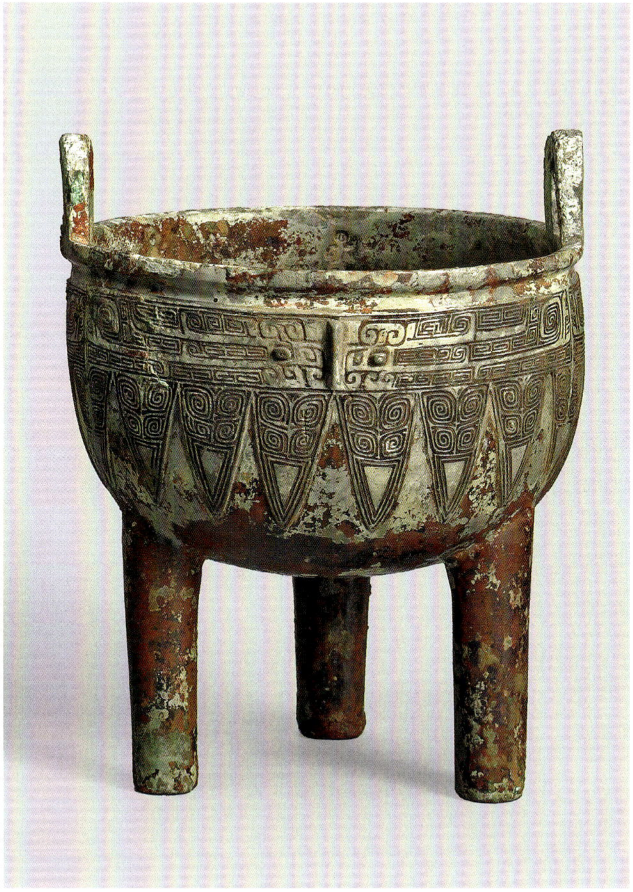

22–23 | PAIR OF TRIPOD CAULDRONS OF PRINCE GONG (*ZI GONG DING*), late Shang dynasty (c. 1250–1046 BC)

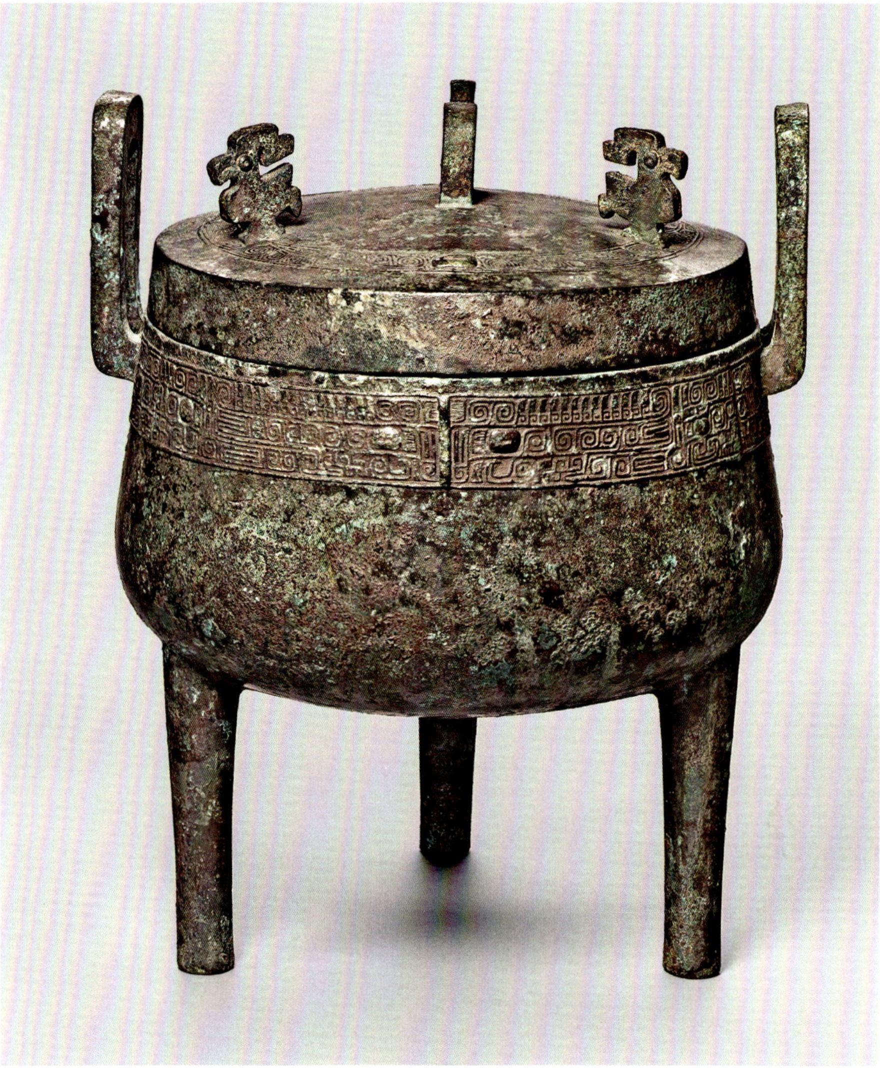

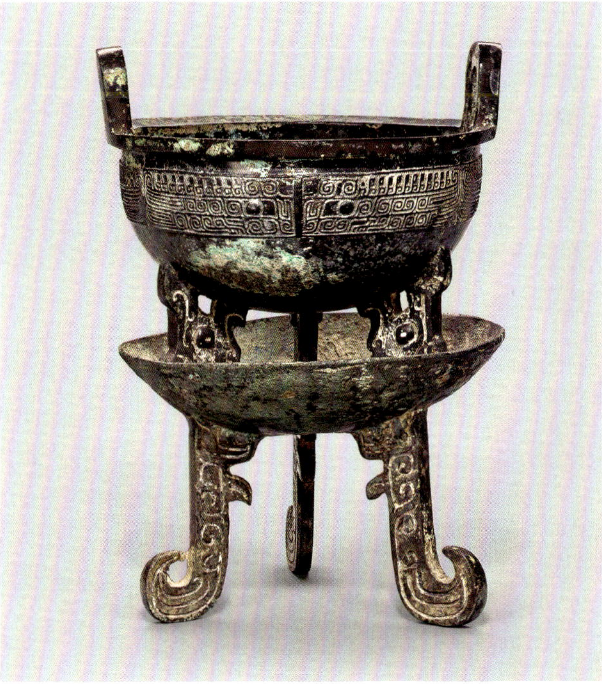

24 | TRIPOD CAULDRON (*DING*), Western Zhou dynasty (1046–771 BC)

25 | SMALL TRIPOD CAULDRON OF CHANG ZI (*CHANG ZI DING*), Western Zhou dynasty (1046–771 BC)

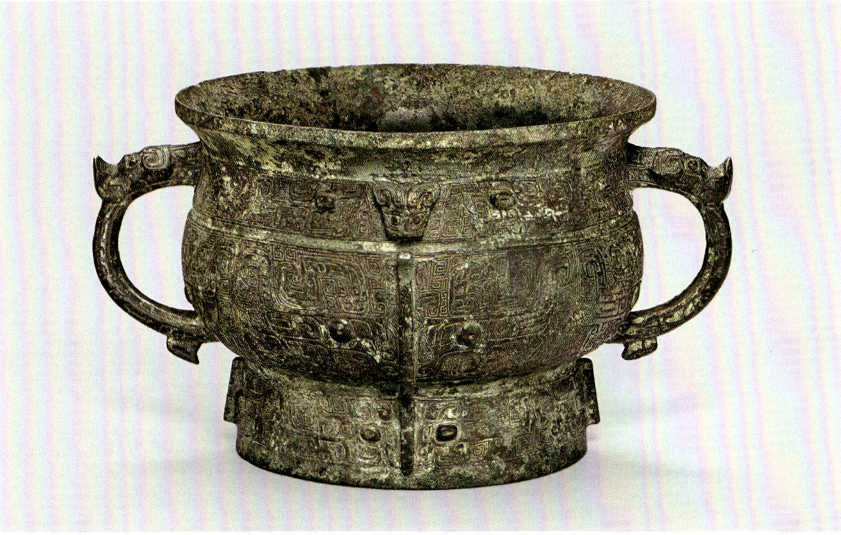

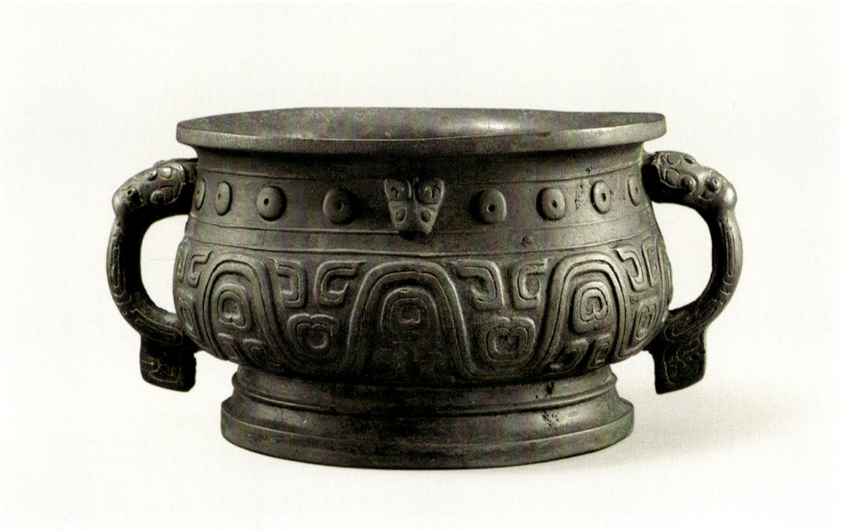

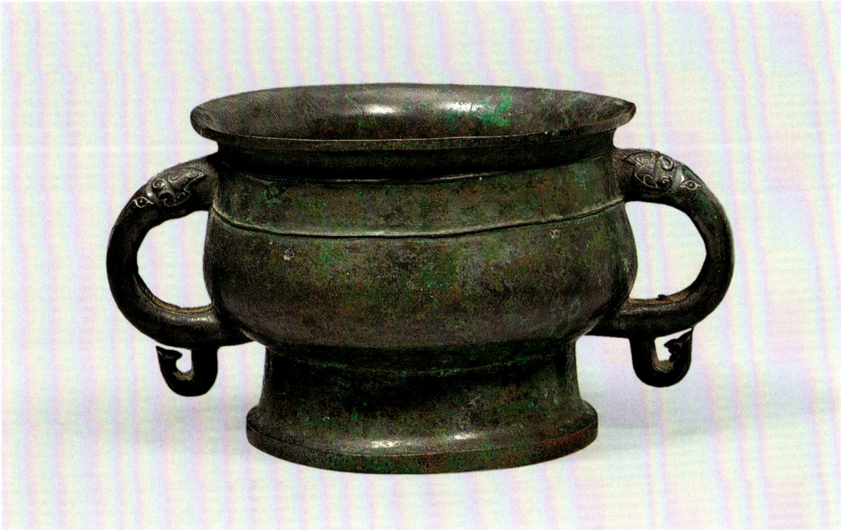

26 | TUREEN (*GUI*), late Shang dynasty (c. 1250–1046 BC)

27 | TUREEN OF MARQUIS CHEN (*CHEN HOU GUI*), Western Zhou dynasty (1046–771 BC)

28 | TUREEN OF LORD YING (*YING GONG GUI*), Western Zhou dynasty (1046–771 BC)

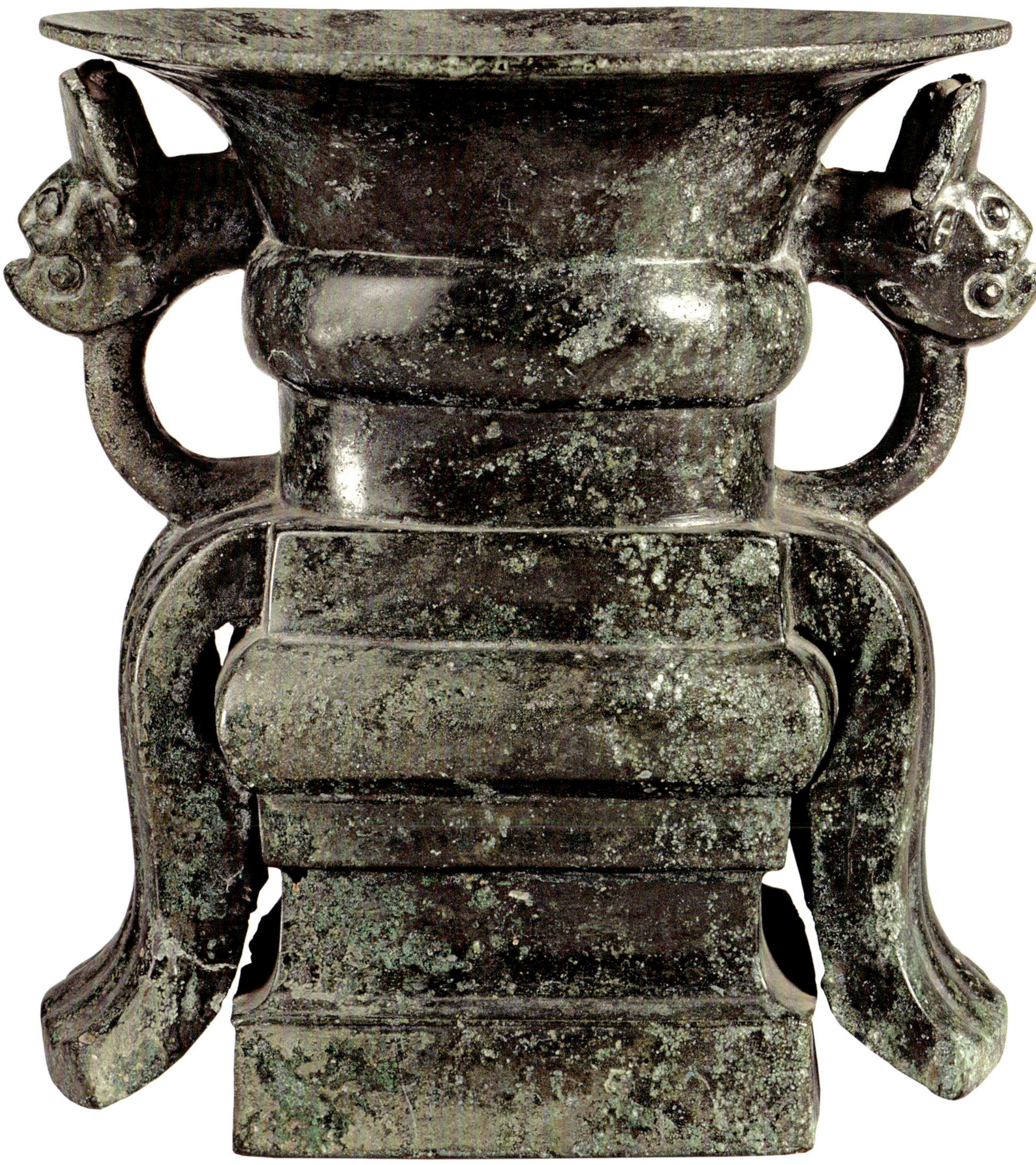

29 | PEDESTALED CONTAINER OF MARQUIS LU (*LU HOU ZUN*), Western Zhou dynasty (1046–771 BC)

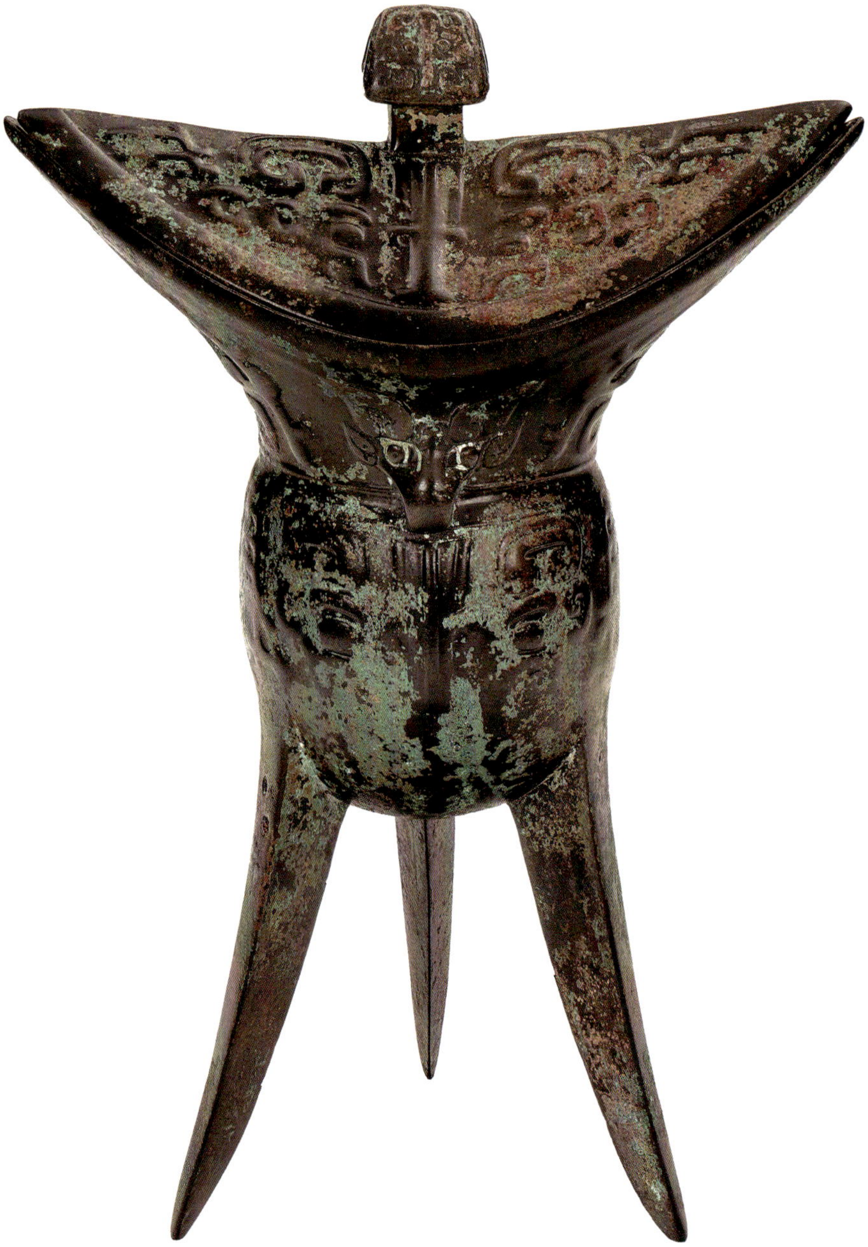

30 | GOBLET OF FATHER DING (*FU DING JUE* [OR *JIAO*]), Western Zhou dynasty (1046–771 BC)

31 | GOBLET (*JIA*), late Shang dynasty (c. 1250–1046 BC)

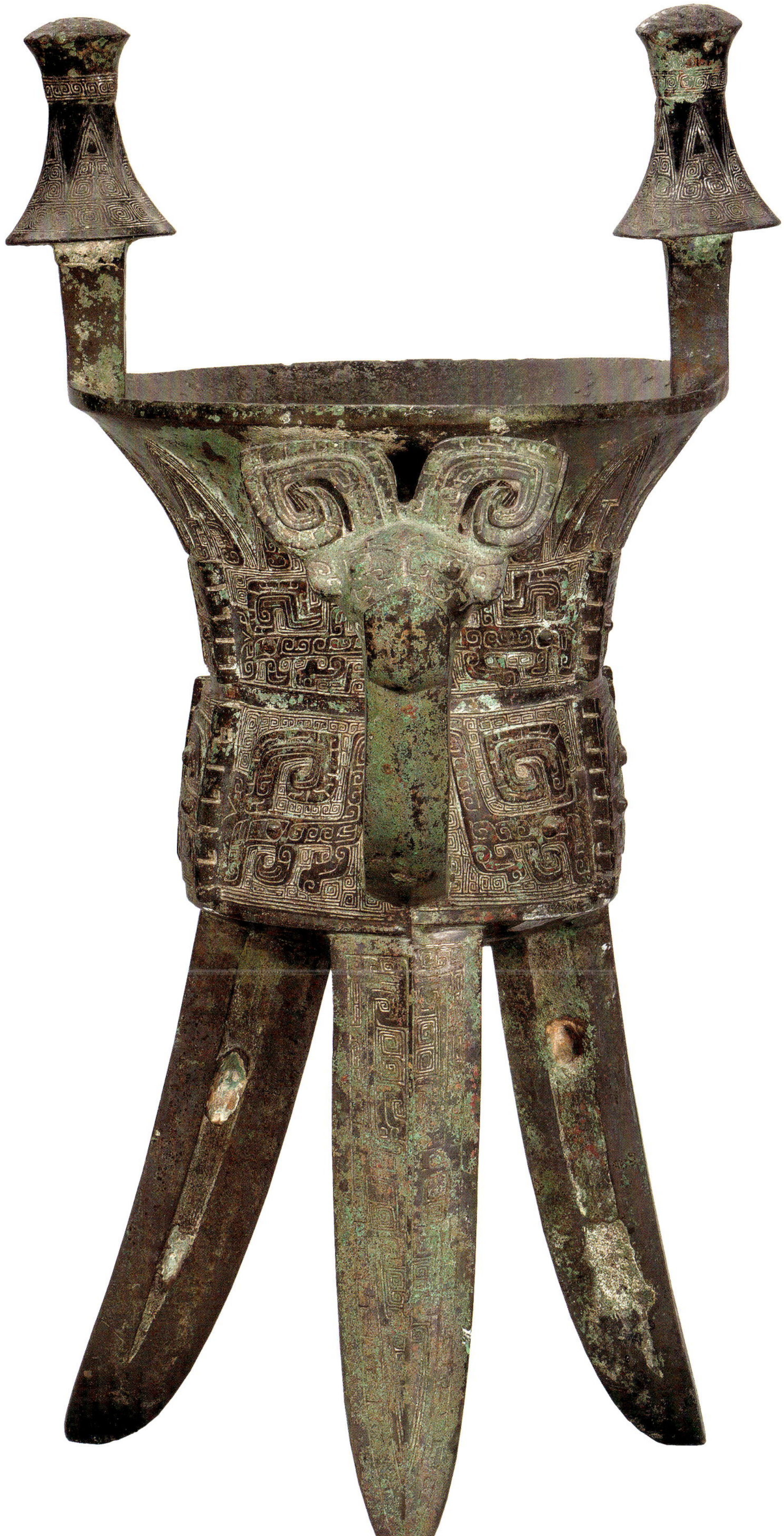

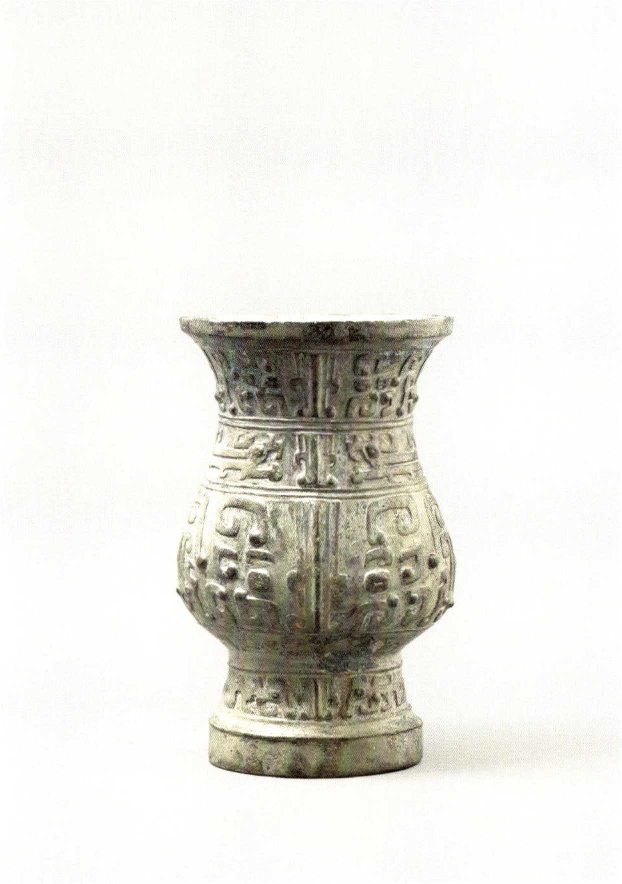

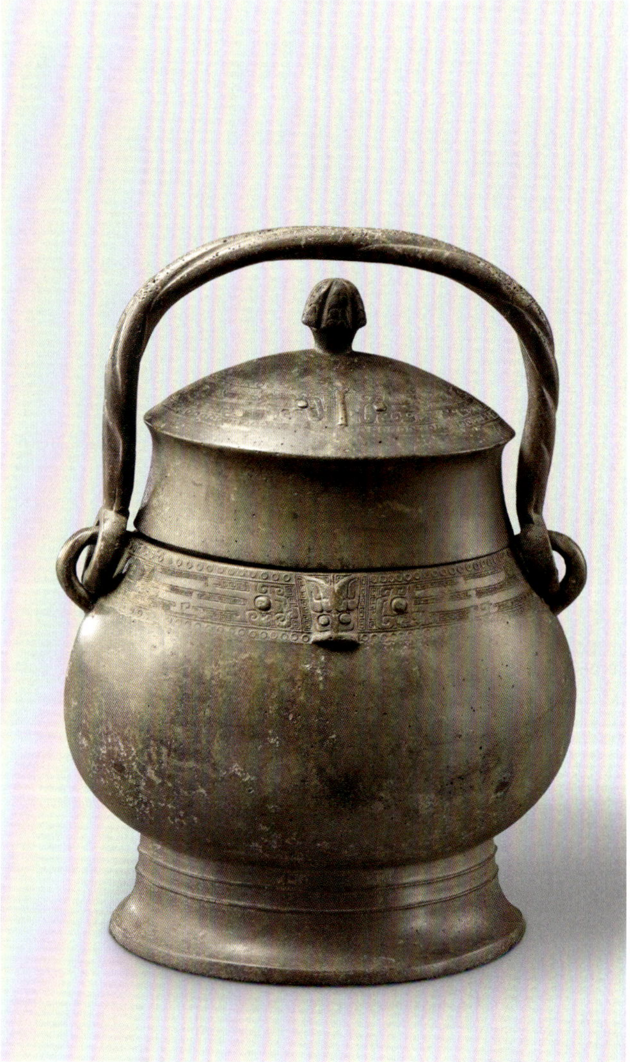

32 | CUP OF SHI (*SHI ZHI*), late Shang dynasty (c. 1250–1046 BC)

33 | BUCKET OF FATHER DING (*FU DING YOU*), late Shang dynasty (c. 1250–1046 BC)

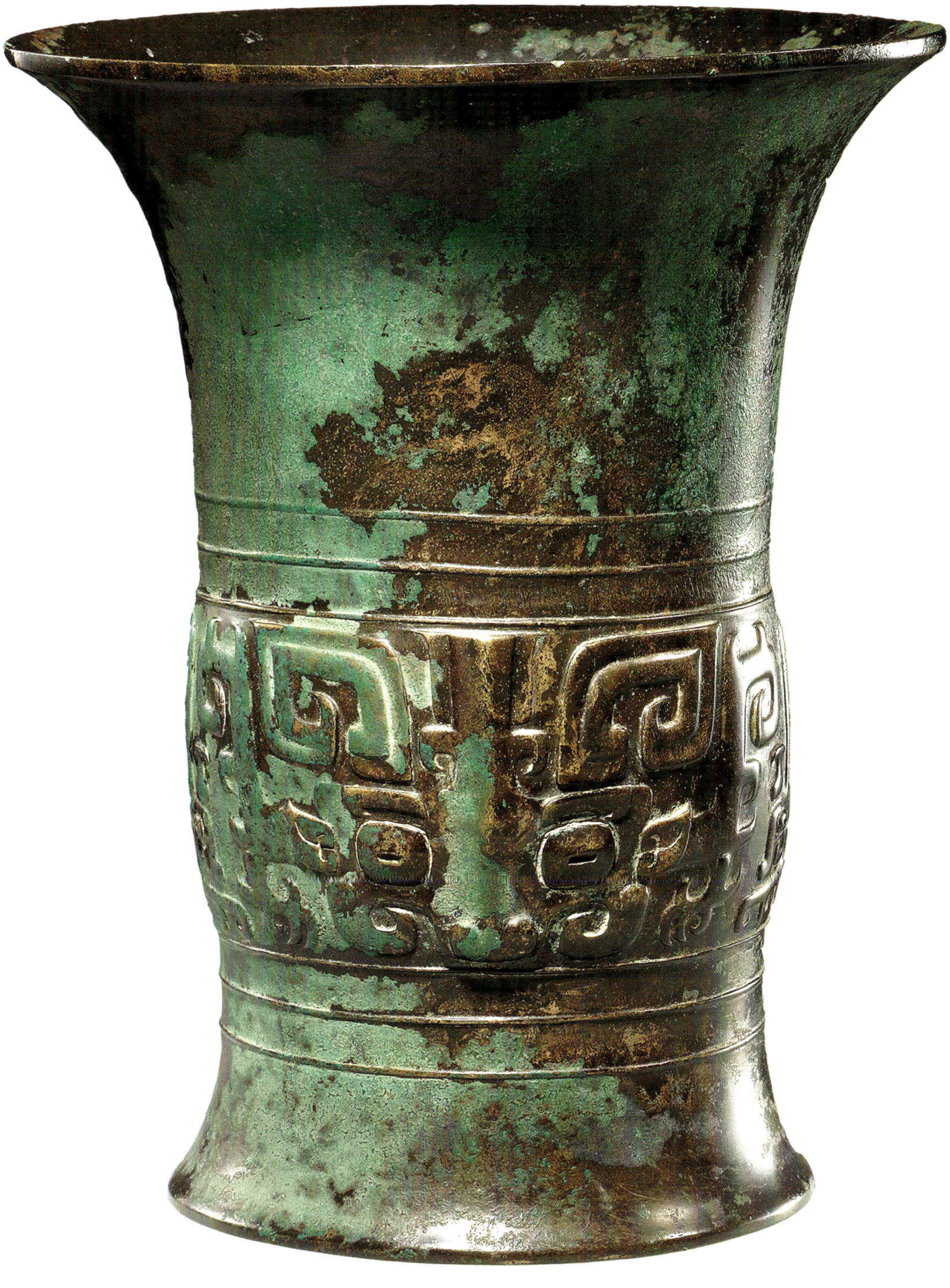

34 | BEAKER OF ER (*ER ZUN*), late Shang dynasty (c. 1250–1046 BC)

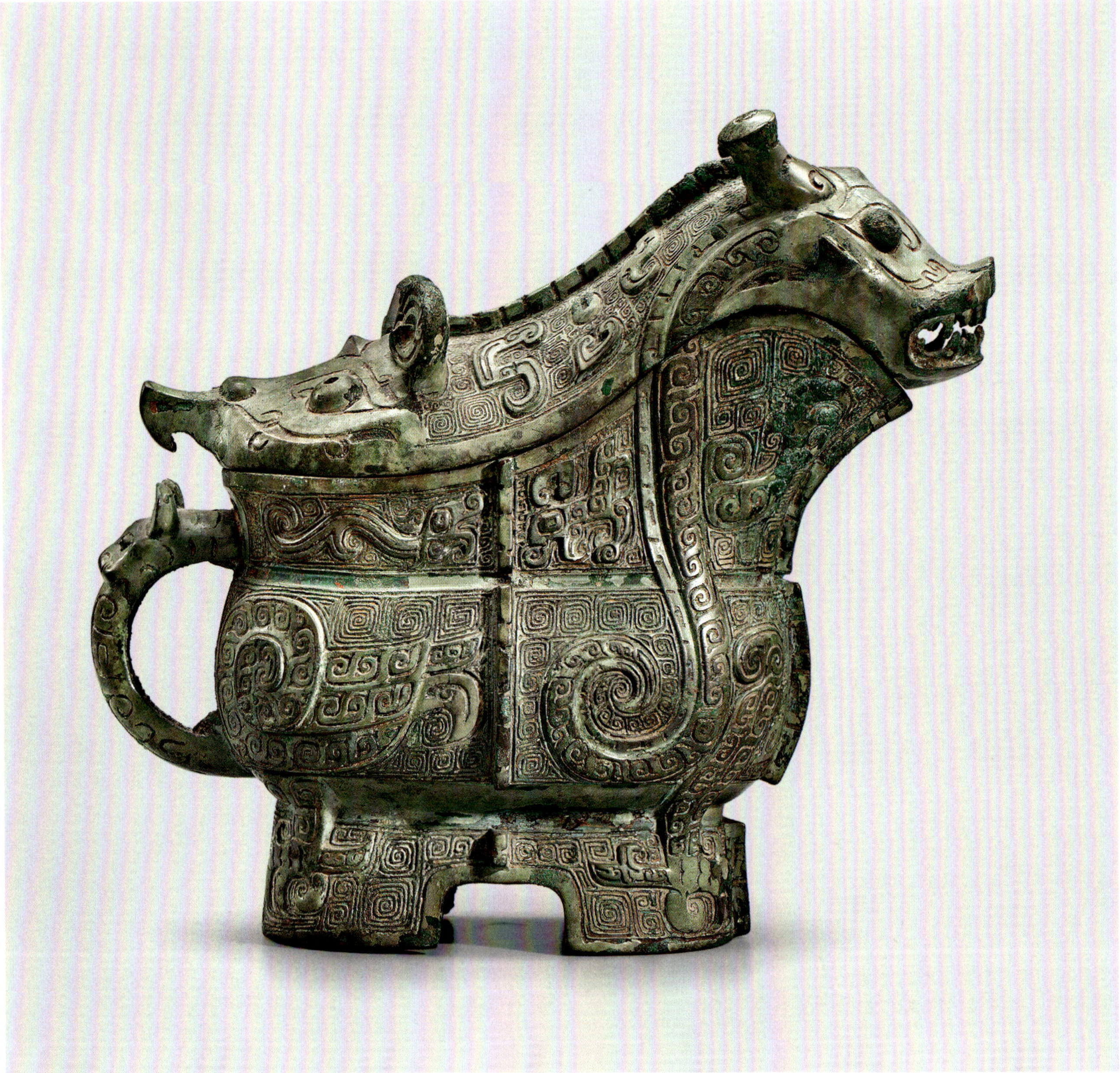

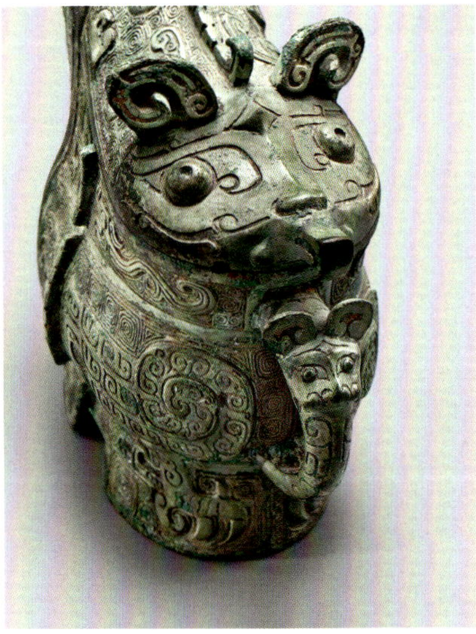

35 | PITCHER (*GONG*), late Shang dynasty (c. 1250–1046 BC)

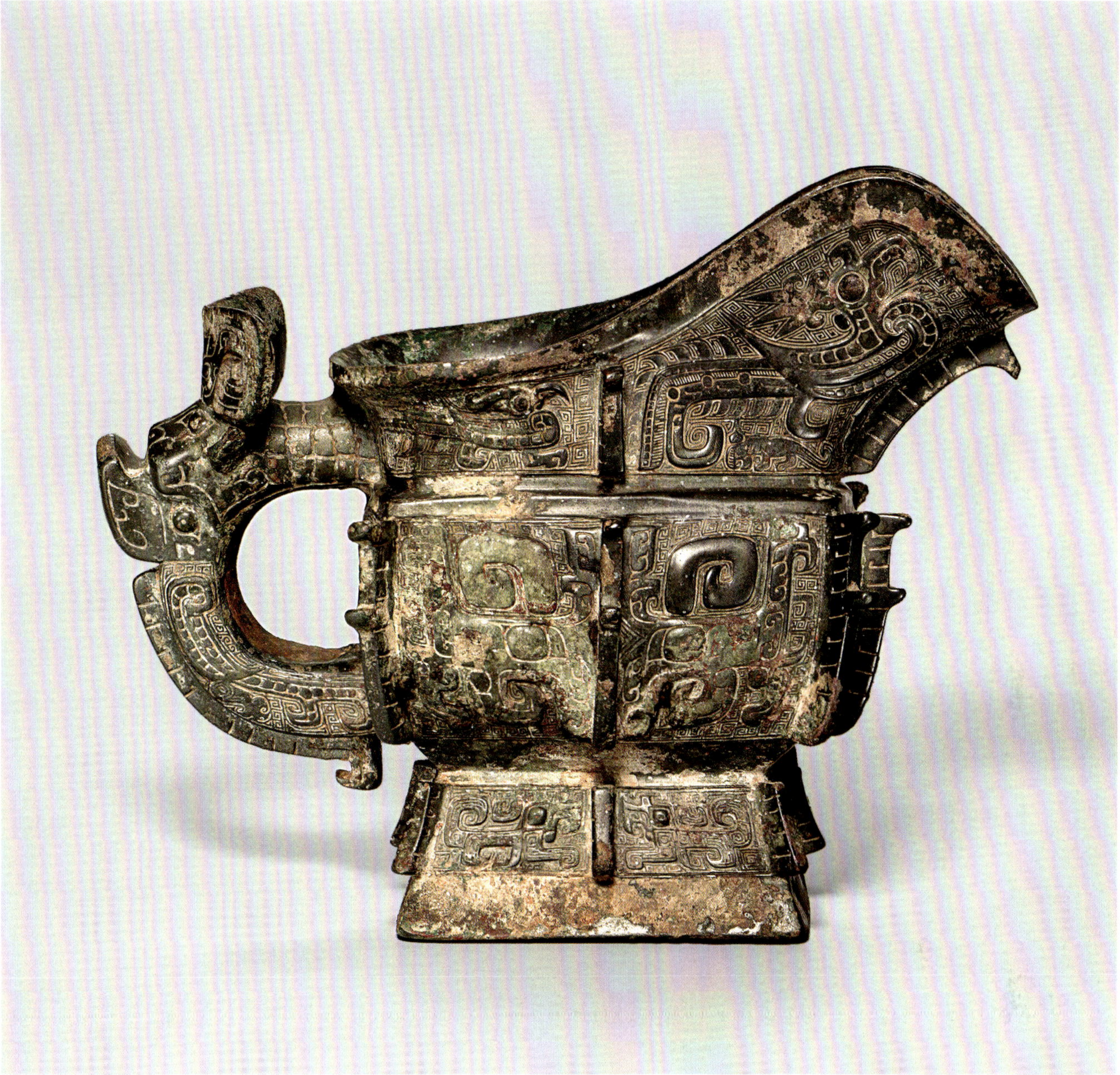

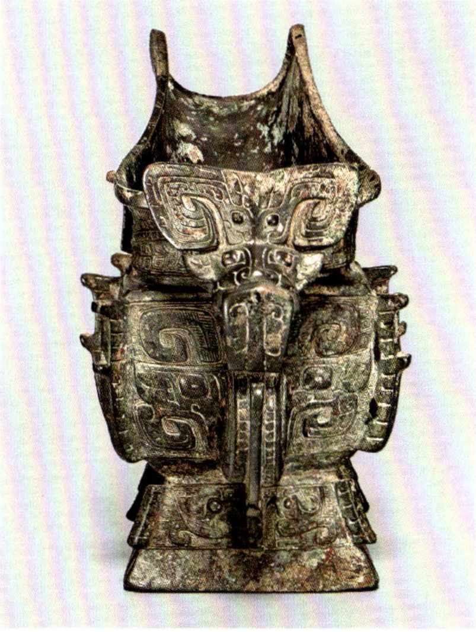

36 | PITCHER OF FATHER DING (*FU DING GONG*), late Shang dynasty (c. 1250–1046 BC)

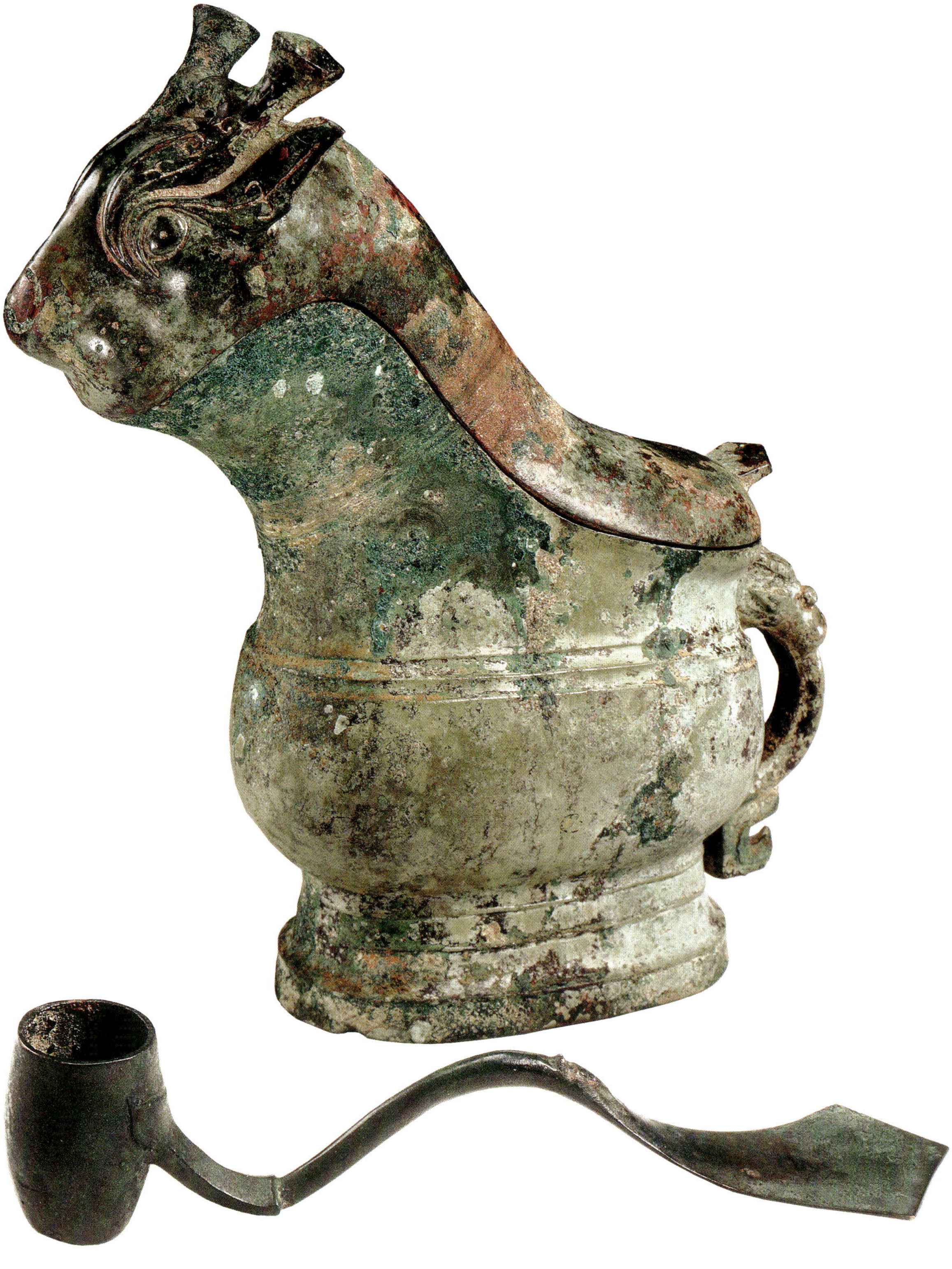

37 | PITCHER OF JIN YIN (*JIN YIN GONG*) AND LADLE, Western Zhou dynasty (1046–771 BC)

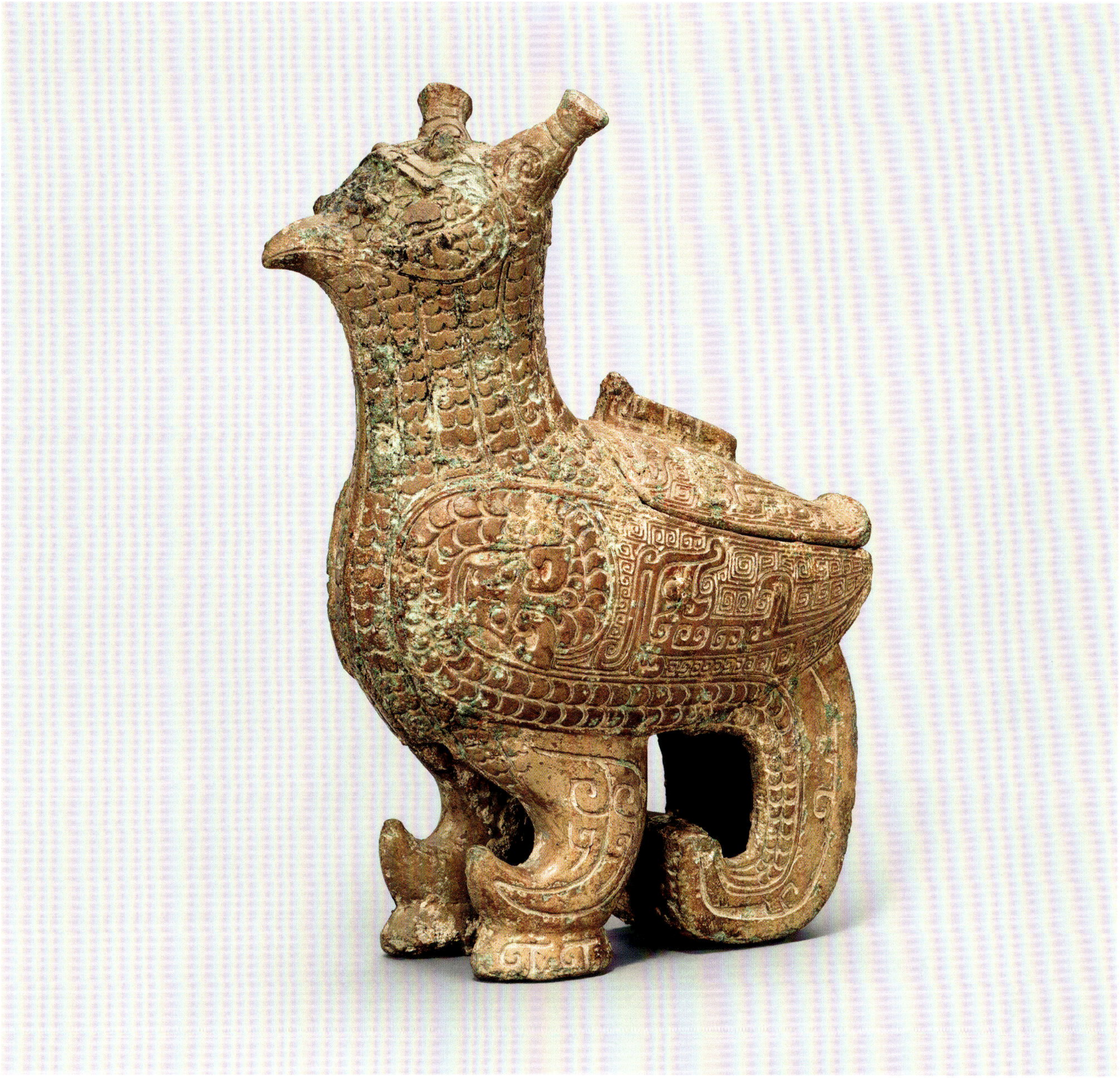

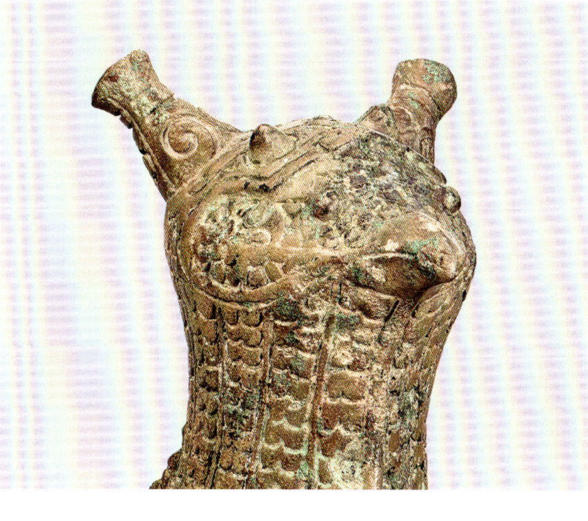

38 | BIRD-SHAPED CONTAINER (*ZUN*), late Shang dynasty (c. 1250–1046 BC)

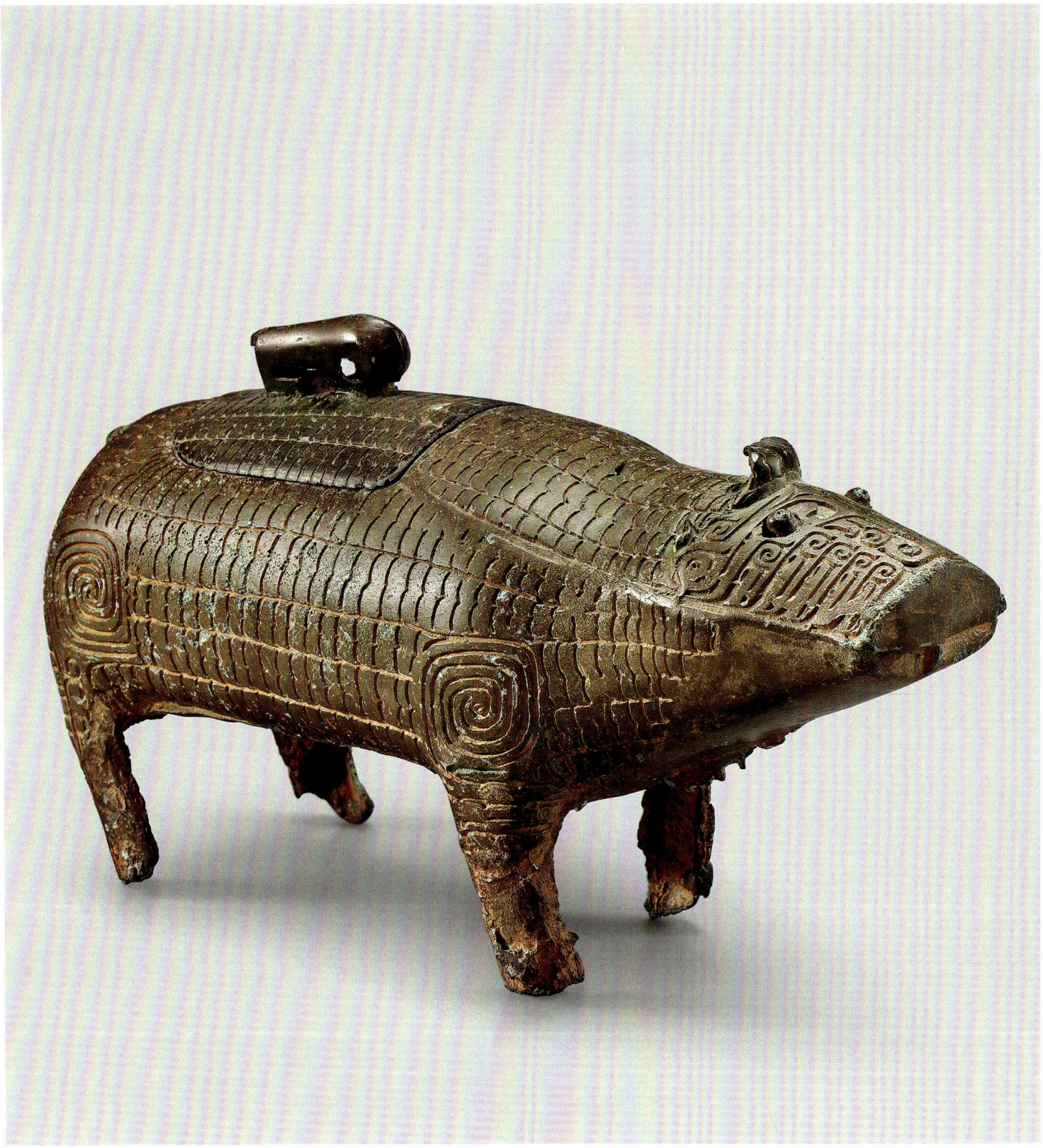

39 | OX-SHAPED CONTAINER (*ZUN*), Shang dynasty (c. 1600–1046 BC)

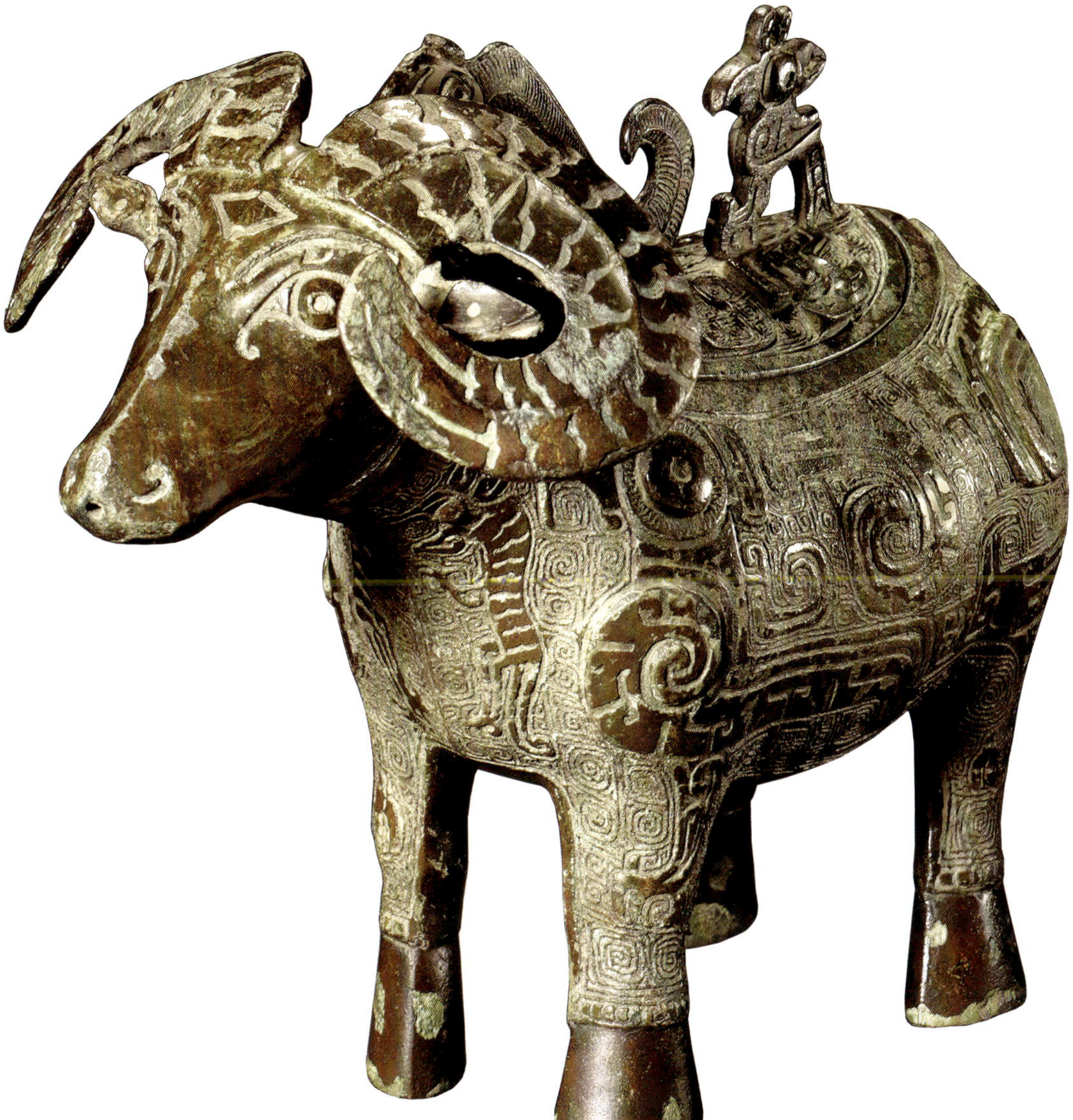

40 | RAM-SHAPED CONTAINER (*ZUN*), late Shang dynasty (c. 1250–1046 BC)

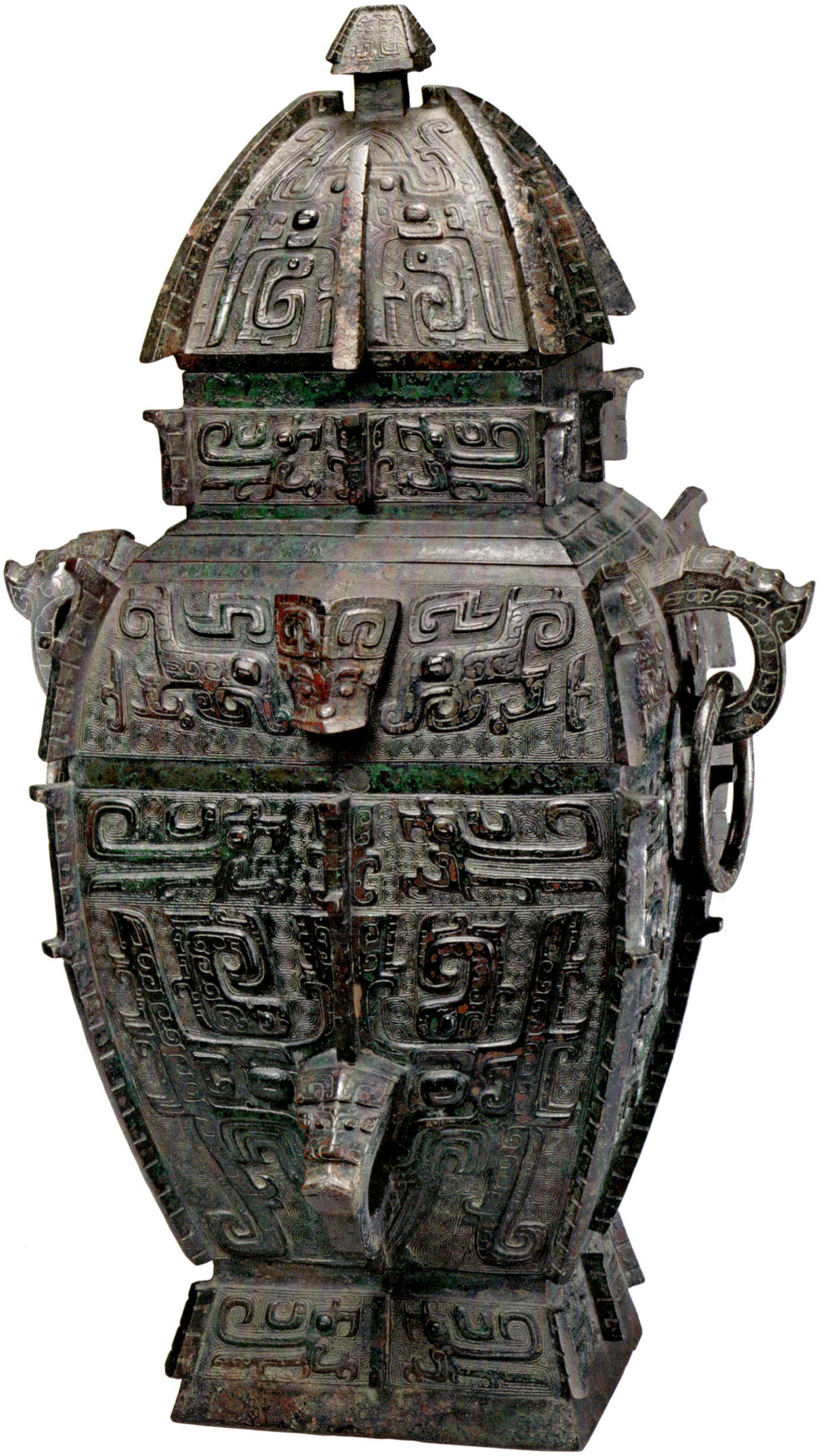

41 | SQUARE CONTAINER OF OFFICER CHOU (*YA CHOU FANGLEI*), late Shang dynasty (c. 1250–1046 BC)

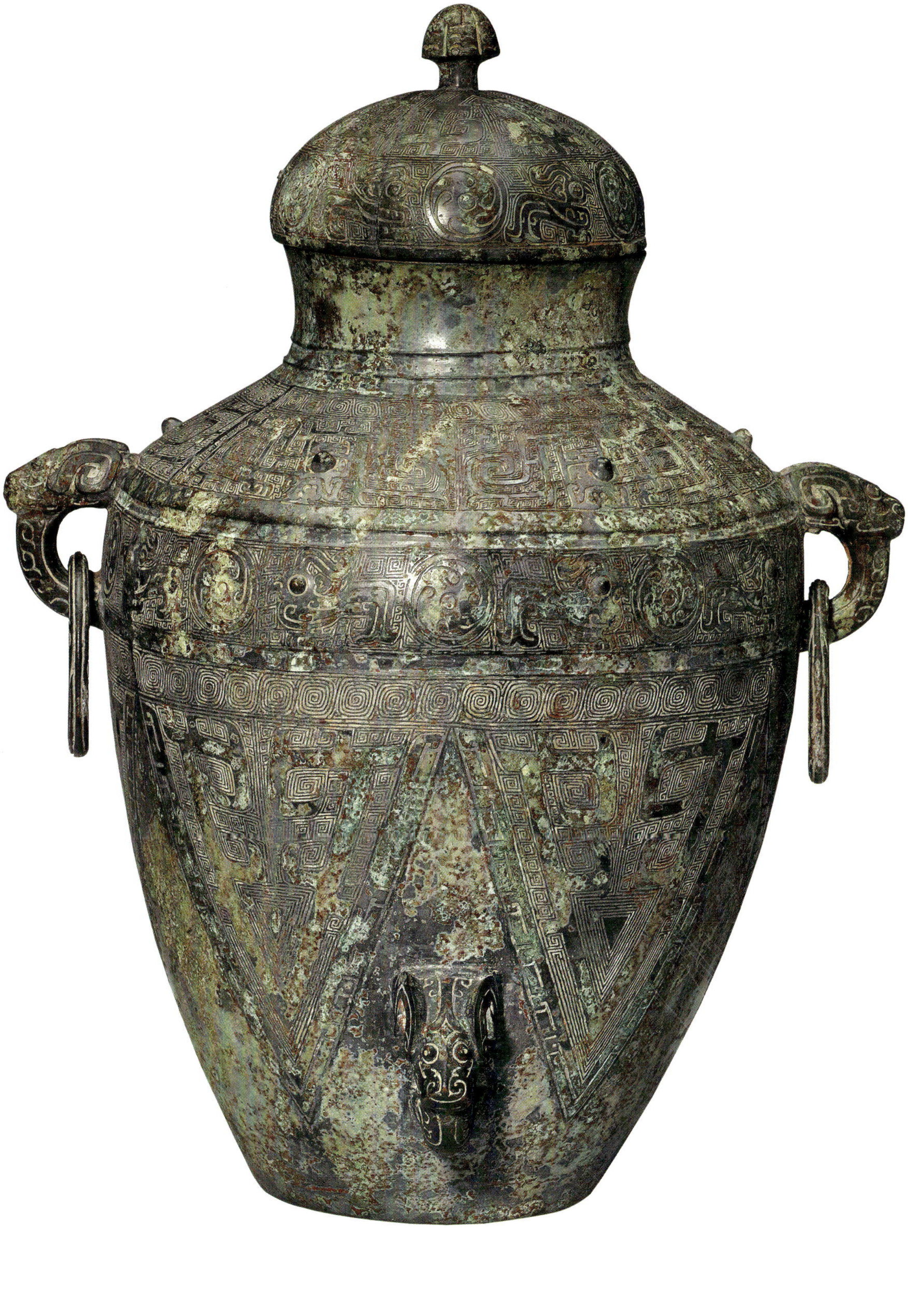

42 | CONTAINER OF OFFICER CHOU (*YA CHOU LEI*), late Shang dynasty (c. 1250–1046 BC)

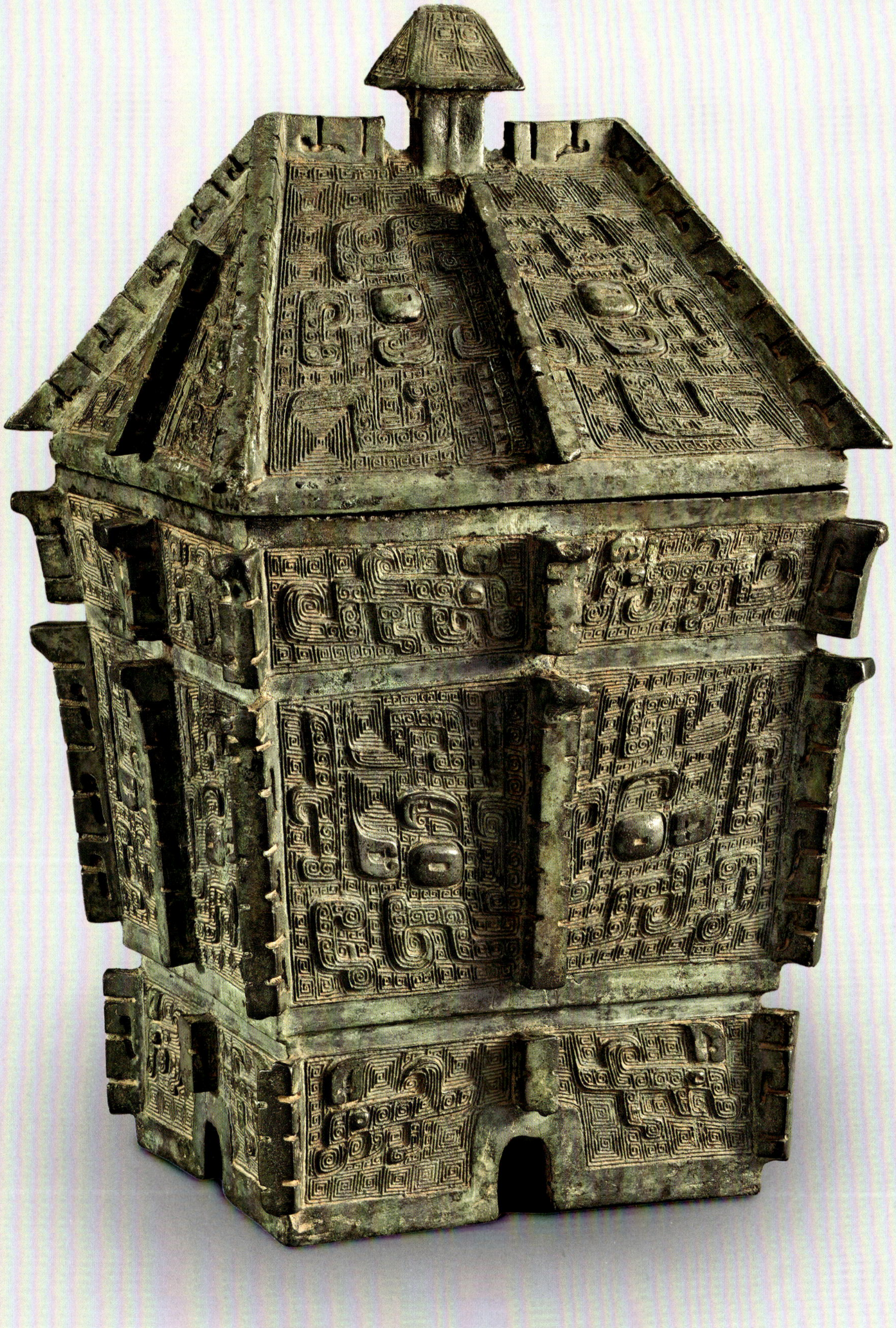

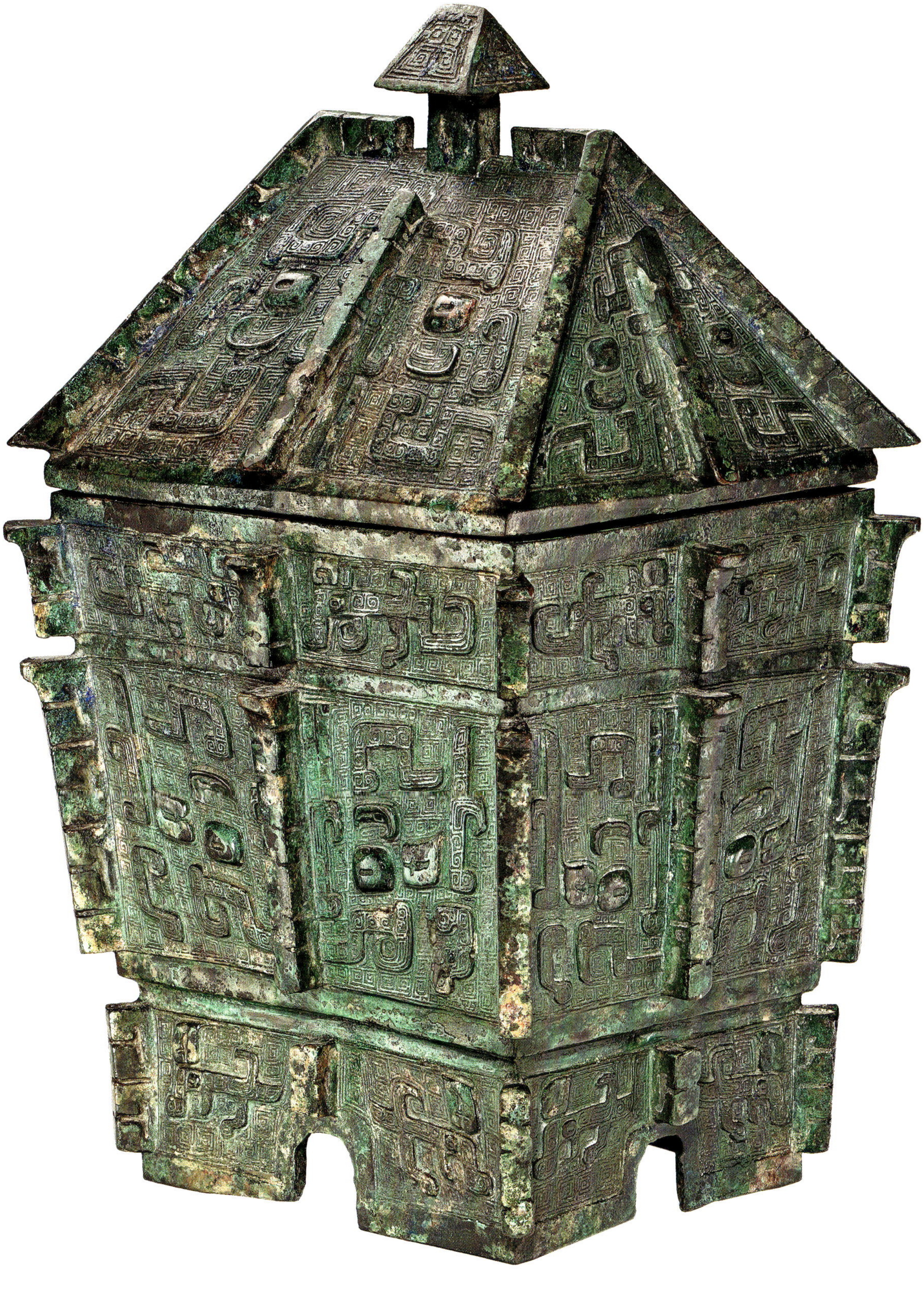

43–44 | TWO SQUARE CONTAINERS OF OFFICER RUO GUI (*YA RUO GUI FANGYI*), late Shang dynasty (c. 1250–1046 BC)

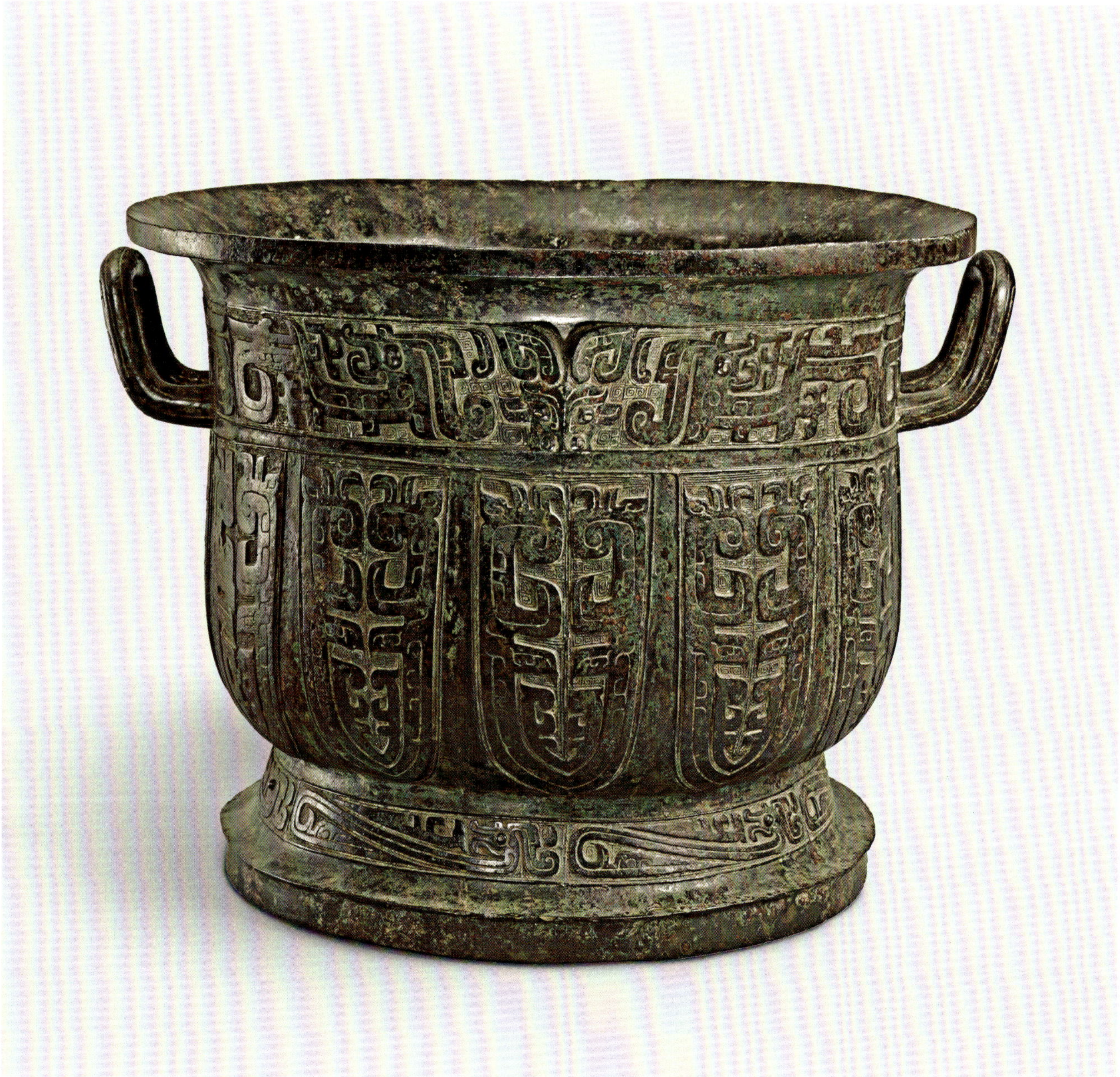

45 | CONTAINER OF BO (*BO YU*), Western Zhou dynasty (1046–771 BC)

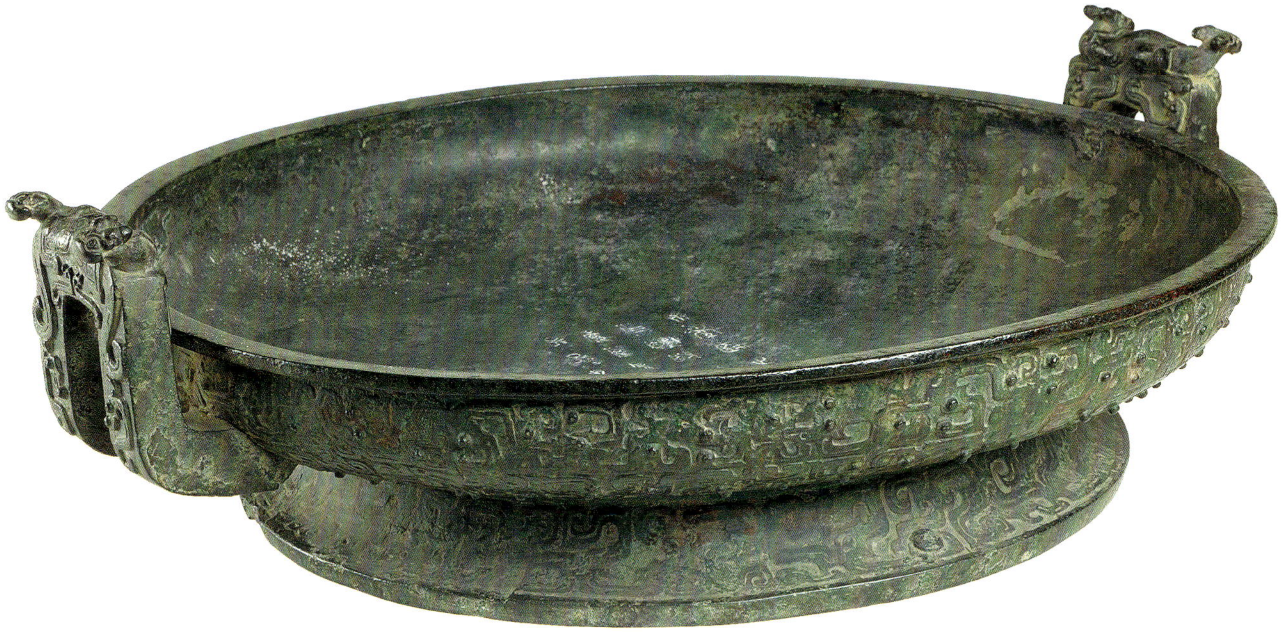

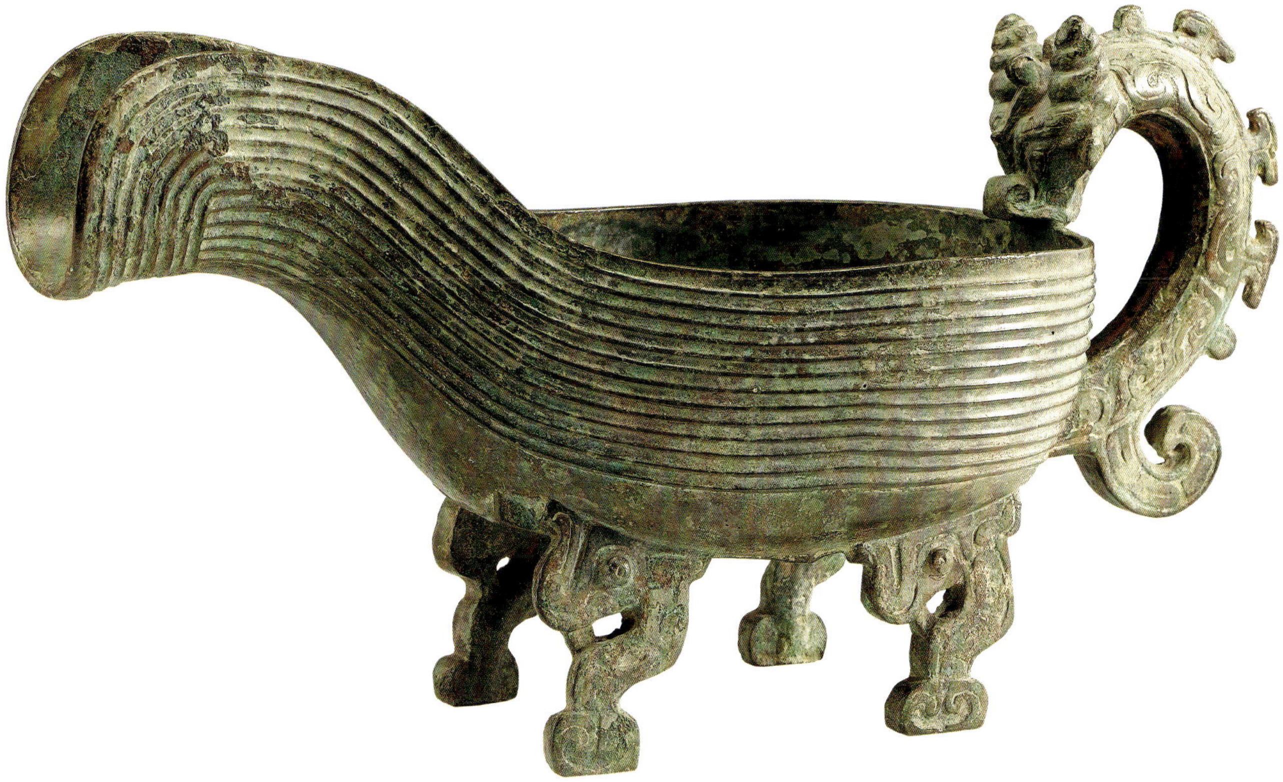

46 | BASIN OF CONSORT YING OF QI (*QI YING JI PAN*), Spring and Autumn period (770–476 BC)

47 | EWER OF MARQUIS QI (*QI HOU YI*), Western Zhou dynasty (1046–771 BC)

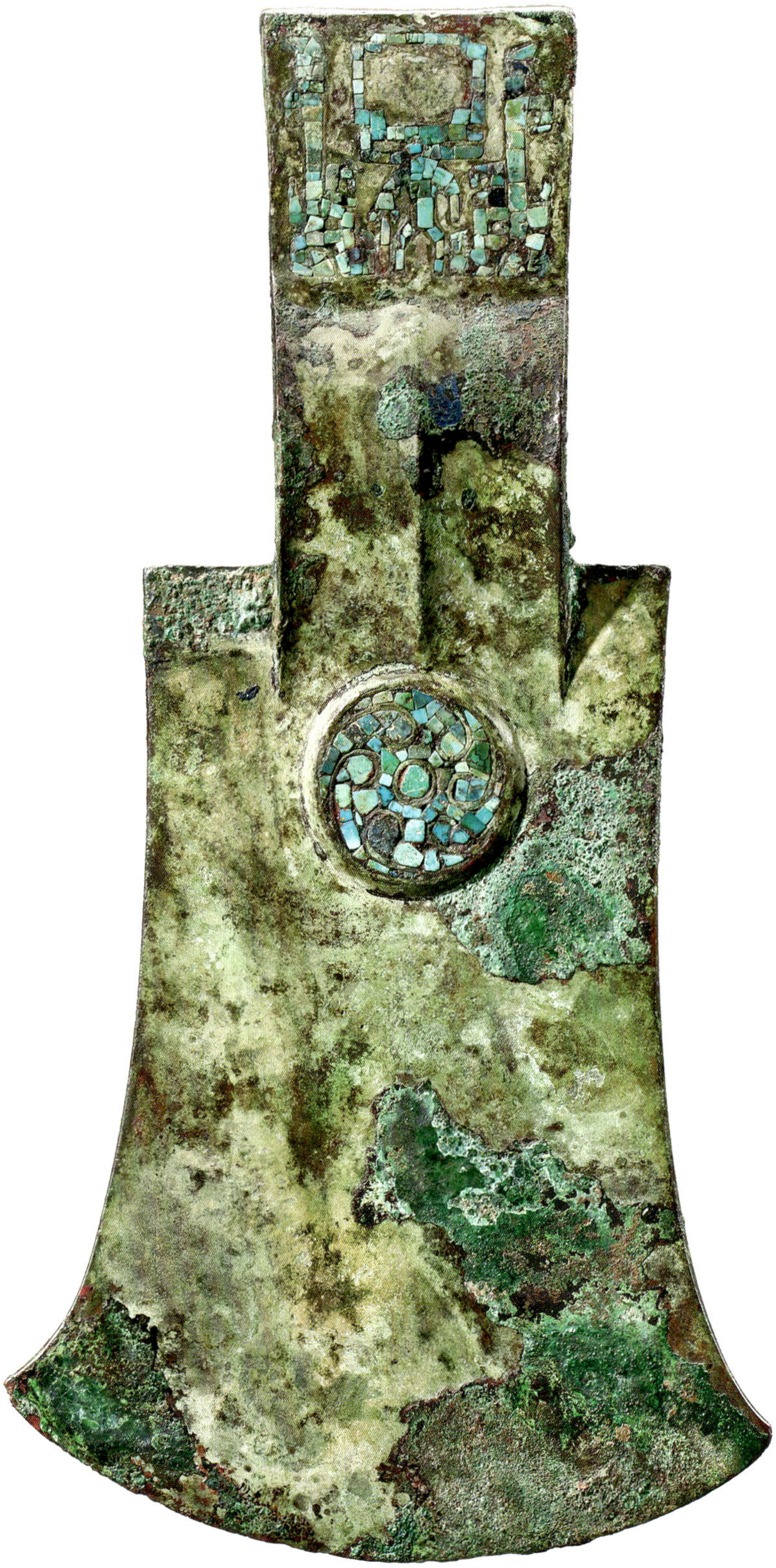

48 | AXE (*YUE*), late Shang dynasty (c. 1250–1046 BC)

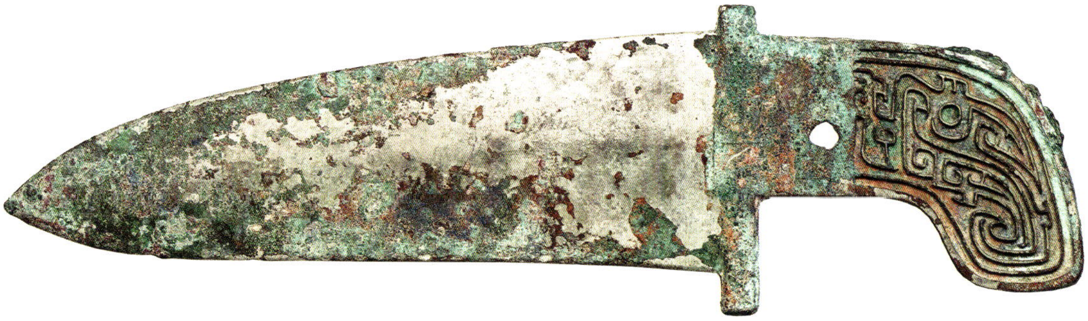

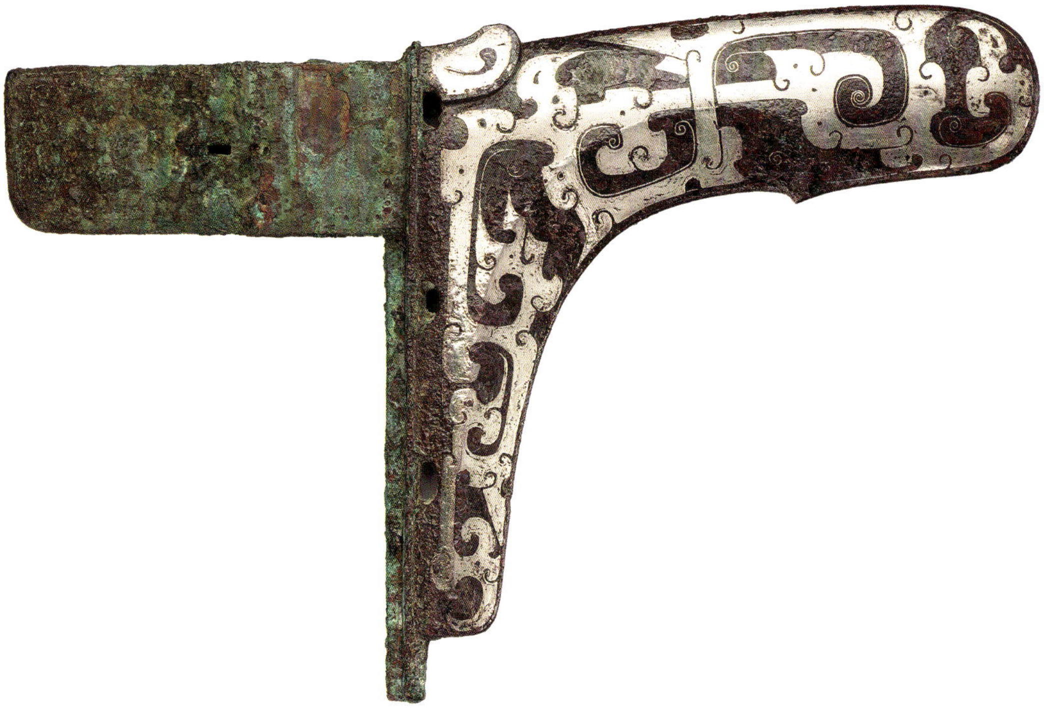

49 | DAGGER-AXE (*GE*), late Shang dynasty (c. 1250–1046 BC)

50 | DAGGER-AXE (*GE*), Warring States period (475–221 BC)

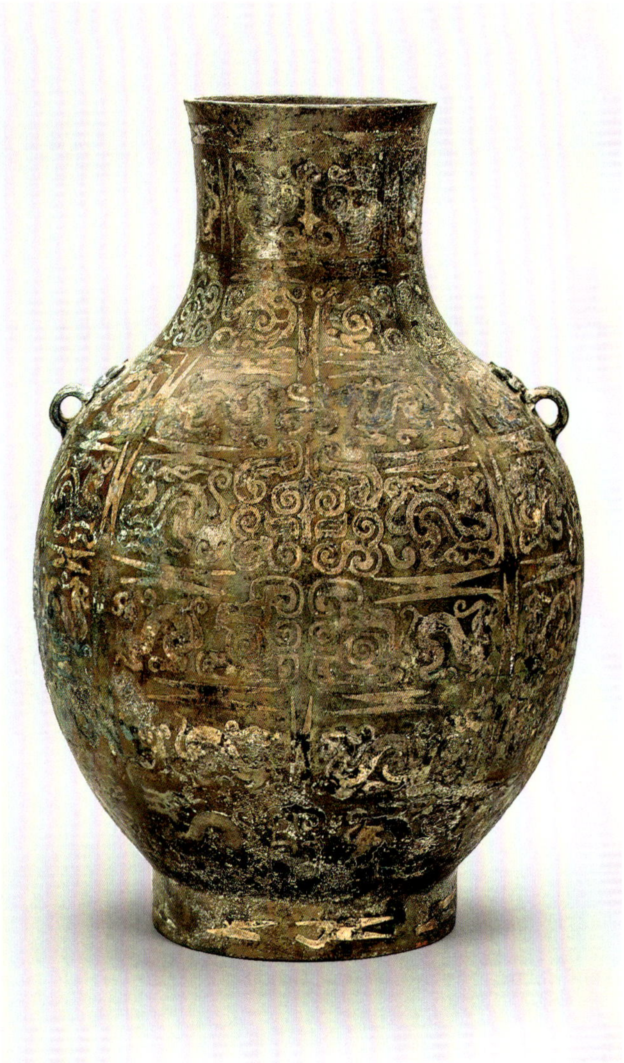

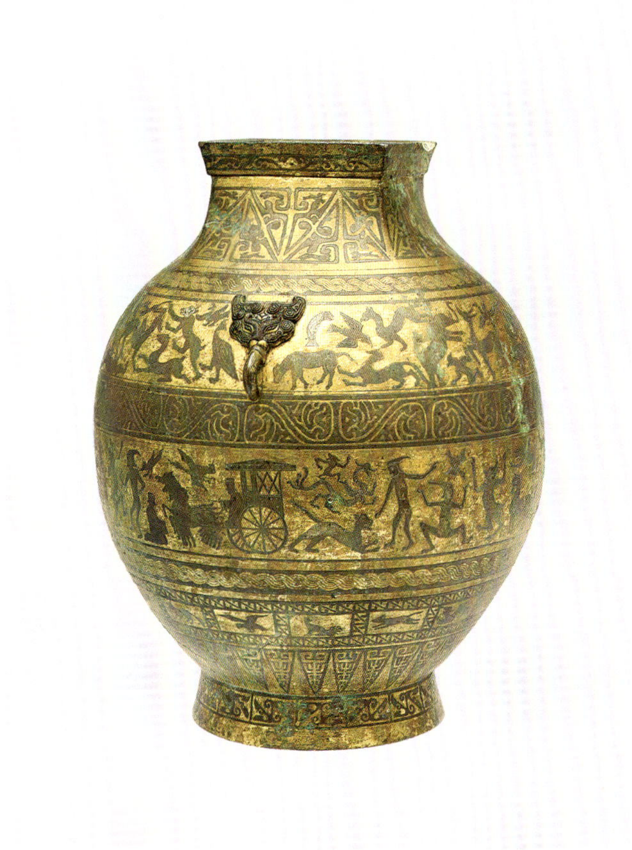

51 | JAR (*HU*), Warring States period (475–221 BC)

52 | JAR (*HU*), jar: Han dynasty (206 BC–AD 220), decoration: 20th century

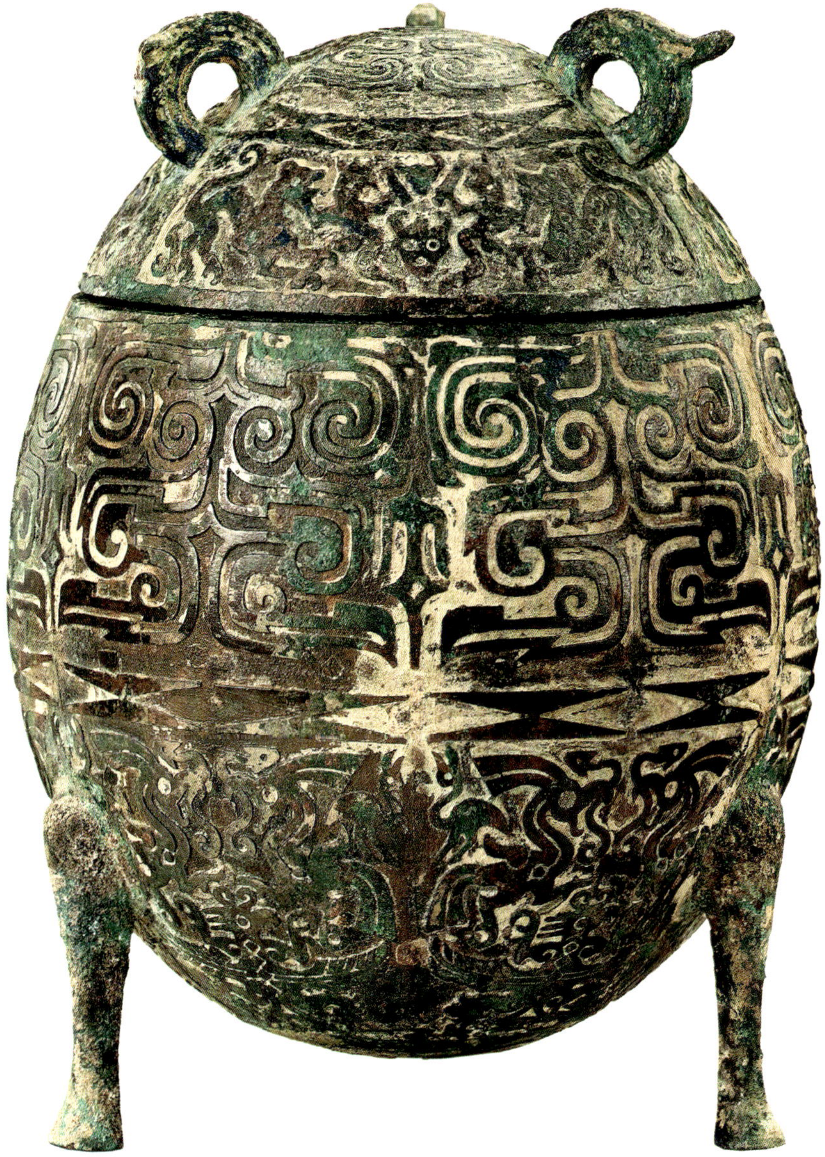

53 | BIPARTITE HEMISPHERICAL BOWL (*DUI*), Spring and Autumn period (770–476 BC)

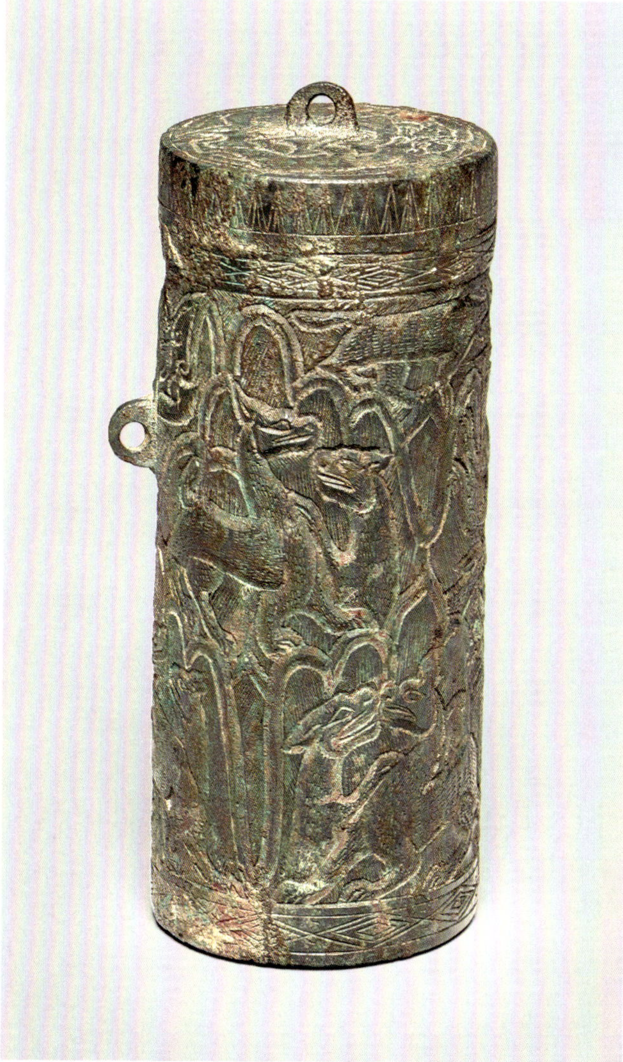

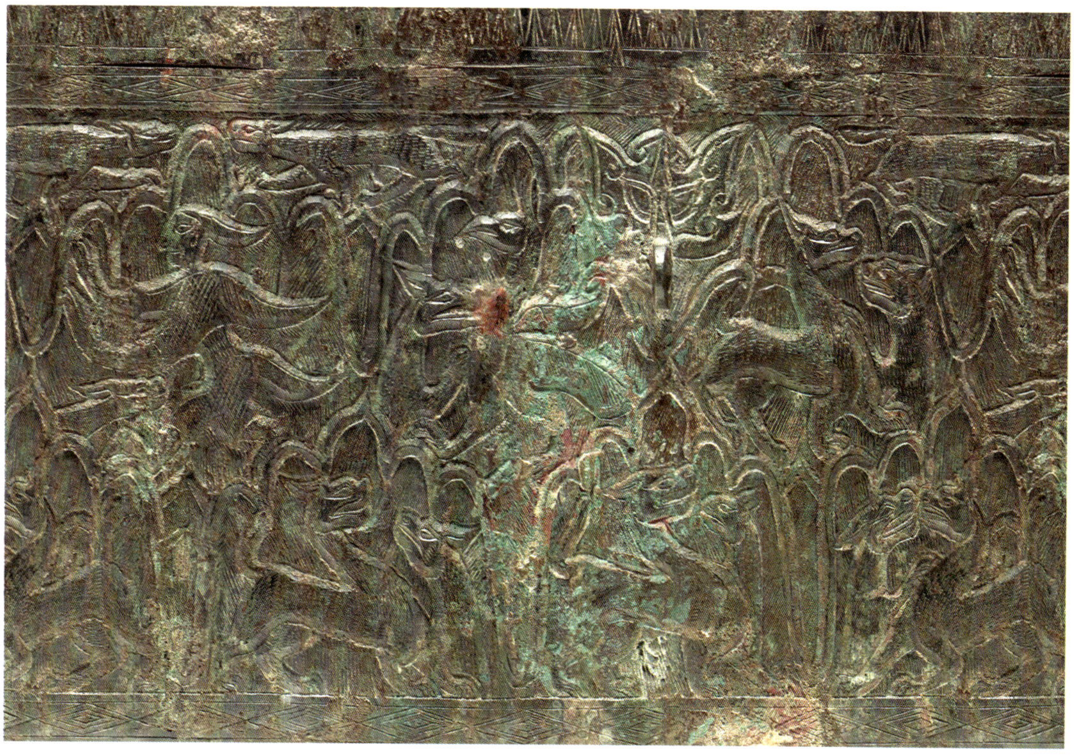

54 | CYLINDRICAL CONTAINER, Western Han dynasty (206 BC–AD 9), and a composite image showing the full circumference

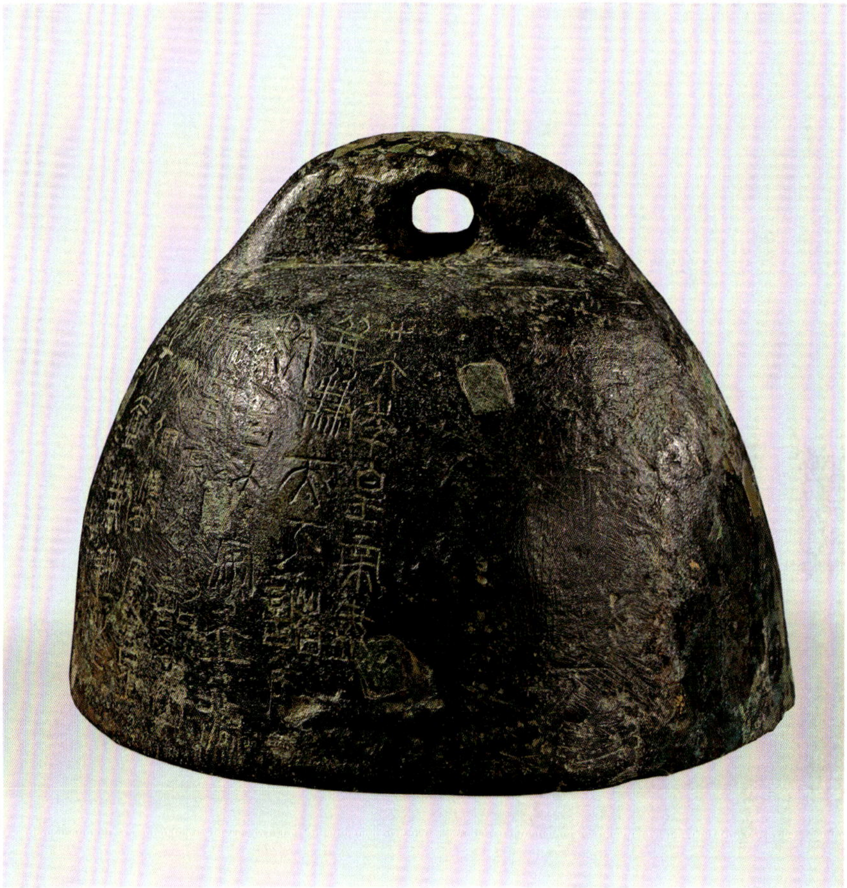

55 | WEIGHT (*QUAN*), Qin dynasty (221–206 BC)

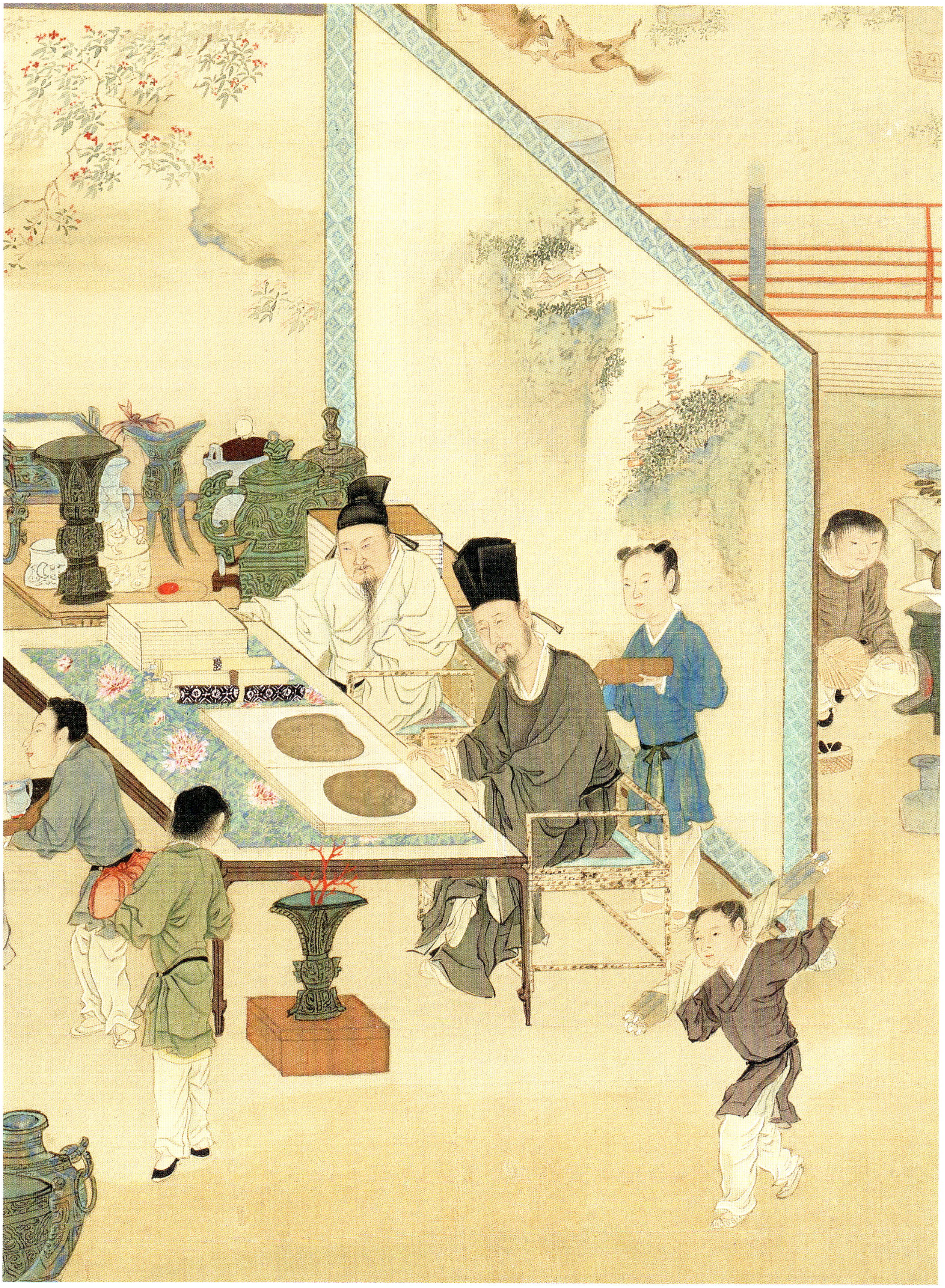

考古

LOST ARCHAEOLOGY

FROM ANTIQUITY TO PLAYTHING

TAO WANG

Antiquarianism in the Song Dynasty

The Song dynasty (960–1279) was a period of prosperity, when the population increased, the economy thrived, technologies advanced, and culture and arts flourished (see fig. 1). However, the dynasty was under constant threat of invasion along its northern borders, and there was considerable internal political upheaval. The crucial date is 1127. Until then, the Song emperors ruled from the capital at Bianjing (modern Kaifeng in Henan)—a northern city in the heartland of the Chinese empire, hence the name *Northern Song*. When the capital was lost in 1127 to the Jin dynasty of the nomadic Jurchens (from the steppe in the region now known as Manchuria), the Song dynasty was forced to move to the south of the Yangzi River, hence the term *Southern Song*.

One of the characteristics that distinguished the Song dynasty from preceding dynasties was its civil service examination system through which all government officials were selected. Differing from the Tang dynasty system, which focused on the candidates' skill in writing poems and essays, the Song examinations evaluated their knowledge of, and familiarity with, the Confucian classics, such as *Shijing* (Book of Poetry), *Shangshu* (Book of Documents), *Yijing* (Book of Changes), *Zhouli* (Rites of Zhou), and *Liji* (Notes on Rituals)—in other words, historical texts and literature handed down from the pre-Han periods (before the second century BC). This led to the formation of a powerful social class, the scholar-officials (*shidafu*). They came mostly from gentry families and were well educated in history, literature, philosophy, and the arts. Within this intellectual environment developed the discipline of *jinshixue*, which translates directly as "the study of bronze and stone," and was the Chinese equivalent of Western antiquarianism.[1]

The crucial element of any enlightened antiquarian study is a developed appreciation of history. In the Western tradition, the rise of antiquarianism coincided with the Renaissance in the fifteenth century but can be traced back to art collecting in late fourteenth-century Italy. The full emergence and diffusion of the European art-collecting tradition occurred in the seventeenth through nineteenth centuries.[2] In China, prior to the Song dynasty, there were many instances in which ancient bronzes were unexpectedly discovered, and scholars tried their hand at deciphering their inscriptions and interpreting their contexts. Yet Song dynasty scholars, together with the imperial court, were the first to approach the study of antiquities systematically, putting together collections and cataloguing them. They examined the objects closely and compared their observations against descriptions in the textual records, with which they were very well versed. The methodology they employed—their classification, dating, etymology, and interpretation—was advanced and far ahead of Western antiquaries at that time.[3]

Song antiquarianism not only influenced the fields of historiography, philology, philosophy, and literature, but also extended to scientific experiments and innovations. For example, Su Song, who was in charge of the making the world's first astronomical clock tower (see fig. 2), was a collector of antiquities.[4] His ingenious invention

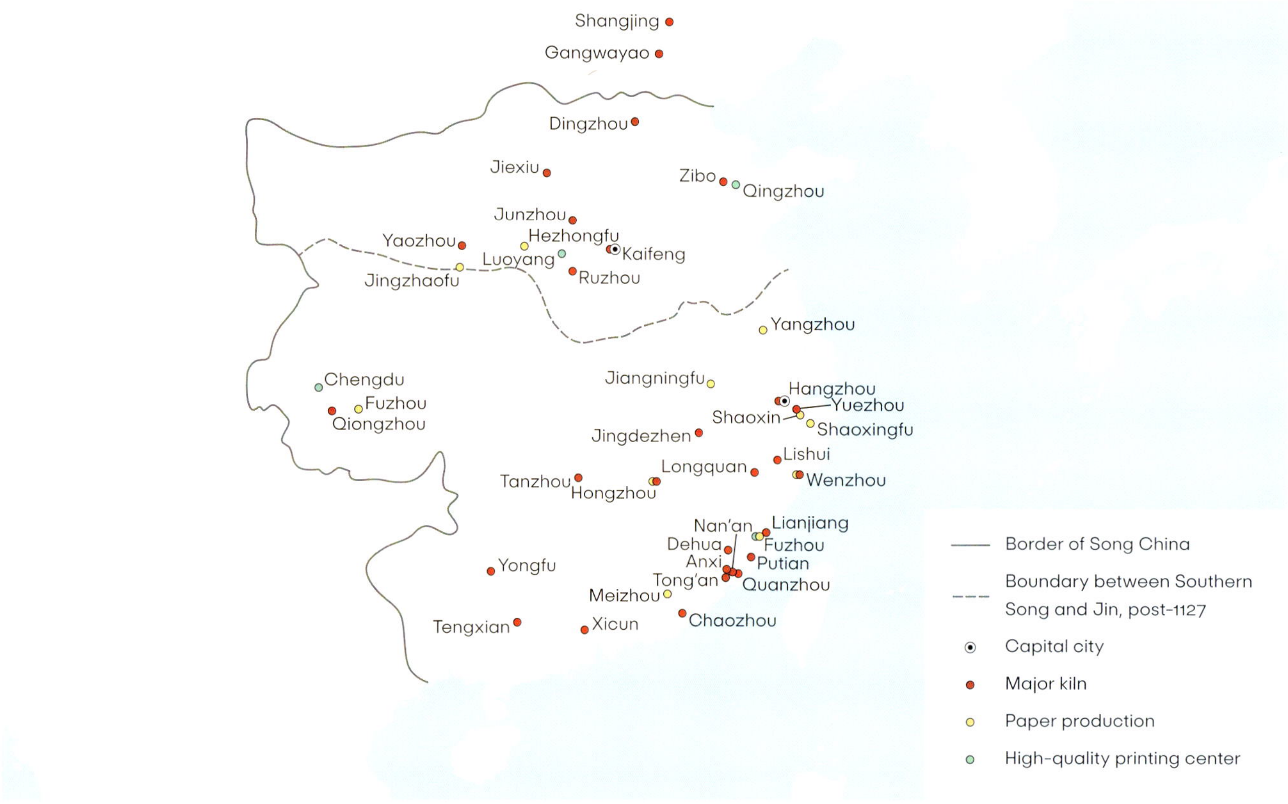

1 | Map of China during the Song dynasty (960–1279), showing important sites of ceramic production and printing.

was likely inspired by ancient bronzes, especially a Han dynasty (206 BC–AD 220) time-keeping device (*lou*). Another important scholar is Shen Kuo, who wrote the groundbreaking book *Mengxi bitang* (Dream Pool Essays; 1086–93), in which he discussed the metallurgy and manufacture of ancient weaponry, employing iconographical evidence to date Han dynasty reliefs and experimenting with optics to explain ancient mirrors. A musician, Shen even tried to explore the correct way to suspend bronze bells. His methodology was empirical. In addition, he was also an avid collector of ancient bronzes and made use of his knowledge of natural sciences when trying to understand the function and decoration of ritual vessels. Shen was probably the first person in history to advocate an interdisciplinary approach to archaeology and practice, even extending his interests to ancient geometry and meteorology.[5]

The Song dynasty emperors and scholars' investigation of antiquity on historical and philological grounds during the eleventh and twelfth centuries was antiquarian archaeology—an attempt to retrieve objects, preserve and study them, and publish books and catalogues of their findings. Some scholars have regarded such investigation as the foundation of Chinese indigenous archaeology, but the investigation did not extend as far as developing a methodology of field excavations. Such a methodology was introduced from the West in the early twentieth century, and this marks the real birth of modern archaeology in China.[6]

Ouyang Xiu, Liu Chang, and Li Gonglin

At the heart of Song antiquarianism were a few major personalities. One of the best ways to understand the principles of their new field of inquiry is to analyze their writings and the catalogues they compiled. The most significant and influential figure was Ouyang Xiu. Born into a modest official family in Jiangxi, he was mostly self-taught and began his civil service career after passing the imperial examination; he was awarded the *jinshi* (advanced scholar) degree in 1030, when he was twenty-four-years old. Ouyang's public career was not entirely smooth: he rose from being a fellow of the Imperial Hanlin Academy to local magistrate, vice commissioner of military affairs, vice minister of revenues, and assistant chief councilor, but he was also twice demoted and sent to the provinces—the first time in 1037, for supporting his friend the famous writer and politician Fan Zhongyan, and the second time in 1044, again because of his close connection to Fan's failed reforms of the government. He finally took early retirement and died in 1072 at age sixty-six.

Ouyang's literary talent made him famous.[7] He was the leading figure in the archaic-style prose writing movement (*guwen yundong*) and was renowned as a poet and calligrapher; he was also the historian in charge of the official compilation of the *Xin Tangshu* (New Tang History; 1054–60) and the private compilation of the *Xin Wudaishi* (New Historical Records of the Five Dynasties; 1053).

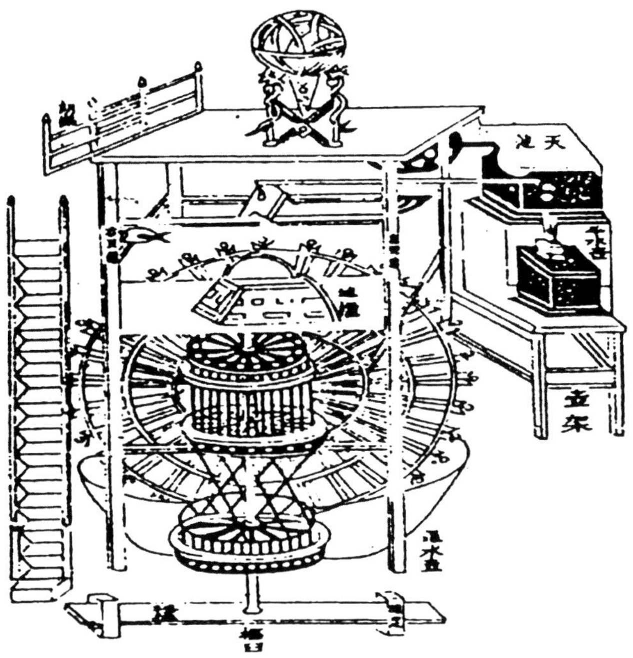

2 | A drawing of Su Song's water-powered astronomical clock from *Xin yixiang fayao* [New Design of the Astronomical Clock Tower, 1089], *Siku quanshu* edition, vol. 786, p. 4.

Ouyang's achievement in historical research is remarkable, and his approach differed from those of many of his contemporaries, including Sima Guang, who wrote the landmark chronicle *Zizhi tongjian* (A Comprehensive Mirror for Aid in Government; 1065–84), and the Daoist philosopher and historian Shao Yong, whose representative work was *Huangji jingshishu* (The August Ultimate Book for Ordering the World; c. 1072). Ouyang argued that in order to reconstruct the "true history," a historian must be factually reliable, using common sense; corroborate information from various sources when considering the picture of antiquity found in the classics; and be perfect in literary exposition to enable a historical narrative to accomplish its moral lessons. This methodology shaped his understanding of and approach to antiquity.[8]

Compared with his immense reputation as a historian and literary talent, Ouyang's contribution to *jinshixue* is perhaps less well known but of equal importance.[9] His interest in collecting started when he was a child, with rubbings of inscriptions on steles, which he perhaps used as an aid for calligraphy practices. Later on, in his spare time from official duties, Ouyang was an active collector of antiquities, in particular, inscriptions on ancient bronzes and steles in the form of ink rubbings. Rubbing is a particular way of making accurate impressions of carved surfaces using ink and paper; it was the most advanced technology available for duplicating inscriptions and patterns.[10] Clearly, Ouyang was interested in rubbings and antiquities not merely for their age and beauty but also for their historical value. Over a period of eighteen years, his collection increased to more than one thousand scrolls, and finally, he compiled a book of his collection, titled *Jigulu* (Record of Assembled Antiquities). In his preface, written in 1062, Ouyang explained his reason for collecting antiquities and his theory of antiquity and history. We should read this key document closely, since it begins with a definition of the "collector," who should be, in his eyes, someone who has a keen sense of history and art, not merely the means to collect: "As a rule, material things (*wu*) accumulate where they are enjoyed and are likewise processed where the resources to obtain them are greatest. If there are resources but no enjoyment, or enjoyment without resources, then even if the things in question are close at hand and easy to acquire, they will not be brought to you."[11]

In the following passage, Ouyang noted that there were fewer collectors of antiquities than of natural specimens such as the horns, tusks, and skins of elephants; leopards; rhinoceroses; tigers; and gold, jade, and pearls. However, for him, a "thing" (*wu*) was not limited to a natural object but included antiquities such as bronzes and steles, as well as works of calligraphy and writings. We read:

> King Tang's wash basin, Confucius's cauldron, the stone drums from Jiyang, the inscribed stones at Mt. Dai, Zhouyi, and Kuaiji; the great stele, sacrificial vessels, bronze inscriptions, poems, prefaces, and dedicatory essays written by sage rulers and worthy officials from the Han and Wei dynasties down to today; and calligraphy by various masters done in archaic, greater seal, lesser seal, *bafen*, and clerical scripts—all these are priceless treasures from the Three Dynasties and later times, and they are the most bizarre and extraordinary, majestic and striking, skillfully crafted, and delightful of material things [*wu*]. They are not found in remote places and acquiring them does not involve danger or risk. Why is it, then, that exposed to the elements and ravaged by war, they are abandoned and damaged, and lie strewn about on hillsides and in ruins where no one gathers them up? It is because those who enjoy such things are so few. Even if someone does know how to enjoy them, if his resources are inadequate, he will be lucky to obtain one or two of them and will be unable to make them truly accumulate before him.[12]

It is significant that Ouyang did not try to separate the bronze vessels, stones, and steles from their inscriptions. To him, writing was of primary importance, and in addition, he included various literary genres, such as essays, poems, and prefaces, as well as calligraphic styles, in a particular category of things that could be collected. They were, as he said in the excerpt quoted above, "the most bizarre and extraordinary, majestic and striking, skillfully crafted, and delightful of material things" (*guai qi wei li gongmiao kexi zhi wu*). By grouping together objects with writing, he created a new category of collectible.

As a collector of antiquities, Ouyang also described his personal fascination with the things he acquired:

> In general, resources are less important than finding enjoyment in the thing (*wu*), and normal enjoyment is not as good as focused concentration. By nature I am eccentric and am inordinately fond of antiquity. That which men of the world generally desire holds no interest for me. Consequently, I have been able to focus my enjoyment on these things. My enjoyment being extreme, I have been able to bring them into my possession despite having inadequate resources. Beginning with King Mu of the Zhou, down through the Qin and Han, the Sui and Tang, and the Five Dynasties, gathered from throughout the lands within the four seas and nine provinces, famous mountains and great marshes, sheer cliffs and precipitous valleys, overgrown forests and ruined graveyards, including even those that tell of gods, demons, and the anomalies, I have them all and have collected them together in what I call the *Record of Assembled Antiquities*.[13]

As mentioned earlier, Ouyang's personal collection consisted mainly of rubbings of bronze and stele inscriptions, and before his death he wrote more than four hundred colophons on the inscriptions in his possession. These are complex and informative, giving the provenance, transcription, and textual and historical commentary on each text. Among them there are eighteen on bronzes dating from the Shang to Han periods.[14]

Ouyang was known to have had only a few bronzes in his possession, two of which came as gifts from his close friend Liu Chang, a renowned collector of ancient bronzes. Like Ouyang, Liu also came from Jiangxi. He passed the metropolitan examination in 1046 and was appointed to a number of official positions. Ouyang described how Liu assisted him with his project of collecting and studying ancient inscriptions:

> During the Jiayou era [1056–64], the Hanlin scholar Liu Chang was appointed as prefect of Yongxing, and positioned in Chang'an (modern Xi'an in Shaanxi). Liu is very learned and loves antiquity, and has collected many ancient objects. He can read ancient scripts and inscriptions, as well as being able to investigate and understand the history of objects and makers. Chang'an was the ancient capital of Qin and Han dynasties, and frequently objects were unearthed there. Liu Chang purchased as many as possible for his collection. Knowing I've been compiling a book of assembled antiquities, each time when he acquired something new, he would always make a copy of the inscription and send to me.[15]

If Ouyang was the historian and literary talent, Liu was more the classicist and epigrapher. He was well versed in history and literature and able to decipher difficult ancient scripts. Liu had a sizable collection of ancient bronzes and also catalogued it in the *Xian Qin guqi ji* (Record of Ancient Vessels of the Pre-Qin Era; c. 1060), which contained eleven bronzes with long inscriptions. In the preface, he expressed an even broader view of antiquarianism than Ouyang: for him, ancient bronzes could "enlighten ritual experts with the codes of ceremonies, correct the characters studied by philologists, and fix the genealogical order of the deceased."[16] Although this publication is no longer extant, Liu's identifications and analyses of his bronzes were quoted in Ouyang's *Jigulu*. There, his friend also recorded antiquities that belonged to the imperial court and other collectors, including a bronze tureen (*dui*) found at the foot of Mount Zhongnan in Shaanxi, from the collection of the famous writer and calligrapher Su Shi.

Among all the Song antiquaries, one of the most significant was probably the celebrated artist Li Gonglin. Like the majority of his contemporaries, Li took the civil service examination and obtained his *jinshi* degree in 1070. He was appointed to a number of minor positions in the provinces and at the capital before finally retiring in 1100 to his hometown Shuzhou (modern Tongcheng in Anhui), where his residence was located on Sleeping Dragon Hill (*Longmianshan*). Li excelled at landscape and figurative painting, and was widely admired as a leading artist; a landscape painting in the Art Institute of Chicago is attributed to him (see fig. 3).[17] But, in the eye of his contemporaries, Li was viewed as an accomplished and skillful collector and connoisseur.[18] His paintings not only brought him fame and friendship with such notable figures as Su Shi, Huang Tingjian, Mi Fu, and Wang Shen, but also earned him enough money to acquire high quality works of art, in particular early bronzes, jades, paintings, and pieces of calligraphy. A contemporary writer described him as one who "always searched widely for ancient objects such as bells and cauldrons, and jade tablets and discs, which filled his house like a forest."[19]

Unlike Ouyang, Liu, and other Song antiquaries, Li also collected unusual objects that had little epigraphic significance, such as belt hooks, weapons, and weights. He did not treat these ancient artifacts as playthings for his own amusement but as physical evidence of the past, that is, as a way to connect with history. There is a difference between Li and the others in that he paid much greater

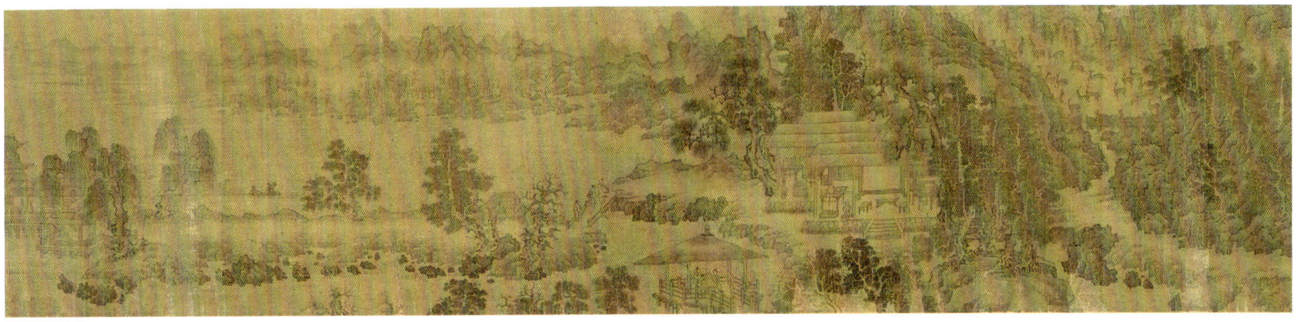

3 | Li Gonglin (Chinese, c. 1049–1106). *The Wangchuan Villa*, Jin dynasty (1115–1234), early 13th century. Handscroll, ink on silk; 26.3 × 554 cm (216 × 10 ¼ in). The Art Institute of Chicago, Kate S. Buckingham Fund, 1950.1369.

attention to the objects' form and decoration. According to *Zhoushi* (History of Ancient Scripts), a book written in the mid-twelfth century, Li compiled a catalogue of his own collection, *Kaogutu* (Illustrated Investigations of Antiquity; 1092), in which he made drawings of all his objects and wrote commentaries about their shape, decoration, and inscriptions, as well as their functions. The book was widely circulated, and from this, scholar-officials began to pay attention to the study of ancient bronzes. The book also quoted what Li said about their meaning:

> The sages made vessels and adorned them with forms, upholding the Way and giving warnings. In their functions there are some subtleties that cannot be easily expressed but must be passed on to later generations. Those who are learned will be able to seek forms through vessels, and seek intentions through forms. Their hearts could be enlightened and their eye could see the meaning of the name of the thing (*wu*); and they could then understand the principles of rituals and music whose secrets cannot be spoken about.[20]

Unfortunately, Li's own catalogue has not survived, but its contents and presentation had a lasting influence. He laid the foundation for the study of ancient bronzes, which was far beyond the traditional scope of epigraphy, and focused on the objects themselves; even today, the term *kaogu* (to investigate antiquity) is used to translate *archaeology*. Lü Dalin's 1092 *Kaogutu*—which is one of the most important Song antiquarian catalogues—shared the same title.

Lü Dalin and His *Kaogutu*

Lü Dalin's *Kaogutu* has been regarded as one of the most significant antiquarian studies in Chinese history, exemplifying the methodology and highest standards of Song scholarship. It has been admired and followed by later scholars, and remains significant in today's archaeological practices. Comprising ten volumes, it records a total of 214 bronzes, thirteen jades, and one stone chime. Each work is given a name, provenance, a line drawing, and an ink rubbing of the inscription, if the object bears one, as well as its transliteration, followed by a colophon about its place of discovery (if known), and its dimensions and weight; in many cases, an explanatory note about its function and textual references is included (for the structure of this and other Song catalogues, see Jeffery Moser, "Figuring Things," in this catalogue, 104–7). Clearly, the catalogue was a selection of the pieces to which Lü had access. It drew from both imperial and private collections: among the bronzes, there were nine from the Imperial Repository (*Mige*), six from the Court of Sacrifices (*Taichang*), and sixteen from the Palace Storehouse (*Neicang*), with the remaining from private collectors. The largest group and the highest-quality pieces—forty-nine bronzes and thirteen jades—came from the private collection of Li Gonglin. Li's notes on the objects were directly incorporated into Lü's commentaries, suggesting that Lü must have seen Li's original manuscript or his book. For instance, it was Li who first made the connection between the distinct mask motif found on Shang and Zhou bronzes and the *taotie* motif described in historical literature.

In *Kaogutu*, the author often drew references from classical literature such as the *Zuozhuan* (Zuo Commentaries) and *Erya* (Erya Dictionary) in which the ritual function and meaning of the types of bronzes, or the motifs on them, were mentioned. This leads us to some important questions: Why did Lü always try to find textual references in his interpretation of antiquities, and what were the motivations and criteria for his selection? To answer these questions, we must examine Lü's personal life, as well as his social and political background.

Lü was born into a prominent family in Guanzhong (Shaanxi). His father, Lü Fen, once held the position of director of the Department of Justice, and three of his brothers (Lü Dafang, Lü Dazhong, and Lü Dajun) all had high-ranking official appointments. Lü himself did not have any significant official positions, except in later life, when he was given the honorary titles of erudite of the Grand Academy and proofreader in the Palace Library. Lü gained his reputation through his scholarship. He was a pupil of the eminent scholar Zhang Zai and then studied under the famous Cheng brothers: Cheng Hao and Cheng Yi, the two most influential philosophers of *Daoxue* (Learning of the Way), who argued that human morality was immanent and part of the natural process of the cosmos, which could remain unchanged over time.[21] Lü wrote many books on metaphysics of the classics. By nature and training, he was more of a philosopher than an antiquarian, but he recognized that antiquity could be extremely effective in teaching the ritual system and its associated moral principles that were passed down from the sage kings (the semilegendary wise rulers of the Three Dynasties), and that collecting and studying ancient ritual bronzes and jades were important in achieving that goal.[22] In the preface to his *Kaogutu*, dated the second month of the seventh year (1092) of the Yuanyou era (1086–94), Lü wrote:

> The words of Yao, Shun, Yu and Gao Yao are all of investigation of antiquity. Confucius said that he himself was fond of antiquity and sought it diligently. Although what is called antiquity may be simply the old traces of the former kings, for those who investigate it and those who adore it must find out why it is a trace (*ji*), which is the embodiment of institutions, laws and models, remnants of the essential principles of the sages; those are the same things of the past and present, never changed for a hundred generations—how can we call them straw dogs or wheelwrights?[23]

Here, the sentiment and tone are very similar to that of Ouyang in his preface of *Jigulu*. But Lü was more interested in the use of antiquities to apprehend timeless moral principles rather than to reconstruct historical narrative; he continued:

> I have seen many bronzes in the homes of scholar-officials, and every time I obtained a tracing and rubbing; these have now formed a large collection. It is painful that my knowledge falls short and I am unable to research them more deeply. I must wait till I have more spare time, when I can write in great detail on each in turn. I dare not treat these vessels as playthings. By looking closely at the vessels, reciting the inscriptions on them, and describing their shape, we pursue the custom and influence of the Three Dynasties, as though we are face to face with the people [of those times]. In doing so, we seek out the original intentions and explore the sources of their creation. We can emend lost parts of the classics and commentaries and correct the mistakes of Confucian scholars. In the future, all people under Heaven should be able to examine these vessels—if ever they have any interest in antiquity.[24]

The expression "face to face with the people" (*ru jian qi ren*) is very significant. To comprehend the teaching and morality of the ancient sages, Lü emphasized the necessity of looking closely at the bronze vessels and reading their inscriptions. The bronzes were no longer a literary source of knowledge, but a direct visualization of the past. Like Li Gonglin, Lü seems to have shared the common belief that antiquities should be treated with respect, and their shared approach was to give priority to the bronzes over the textual records.

Lü's *Kaogutu* was also, to a degree, the product of a social act in a particular historical moment. It was obviously connected to the political milieu in which its author operated.[25] The latter half of the eleventh century was marked by fierce fighting among different political factions in the Song government. In 1069, spearheaded by the ambitious statesman Wang Anshi, who was also a talented scholar and writer, Emperor Shenzong (r. 1068–85) began wholesale reforms, changing every aspect of government policy: agriculture, civil service examinations, the military, state labor, and taxation. These efforts achieved some results but also met with resistance from farmers and more conservative-minded scholar-officials, including the eminent statesman and historian Sima Guang. Faced with such powerful lobbying, Wang eventually lost his position, and after the death of Shenzong, the new Emperor Zhezong (r. 1086–1100) and Empress Dowager Gao abandoned the reforms and reversed the policies. Under the more conservative Emperor Zhezong, and especially during the Yuanyou reign, many antireform scholars were appointed to important government positions. Known as the Yuanyou faction, they included Lü Dafang, the elder brother of Lü Dalin, who become chancellor. Lü Dalin supported the conservative policies, since they fit well with his philosophy and ideology.

In *Kaogutu*, the inclusion and presentation of the objects were influenced by Lü's own political connections. Many of the collectors who contributed substantially to the catalogue were either members of the Yuanyou faction or sympathetic to them, including Li Gonglin, Liu Fengshi (son of Liu Chang), Lü Dafang, Su Shi, Su Song, Wang Qinchen, Wen Yanbo, Xue Shaopeng, and Zhang Shunmin. It is probably because of these social connections that the cataloguing of antiquities was somehow seen as more than a scholarly activity. Thus, once court politics turned against the Yuanyou factions, *Kaogutu* also fell out of favor. In *Bogutu*, another important catalogue compiled under the imperial order of Emperor Huizong (r. 1101–1126), there is not a single mention of Lü and his work, even though *Bogutu* was largely based on *Kaogutu*.

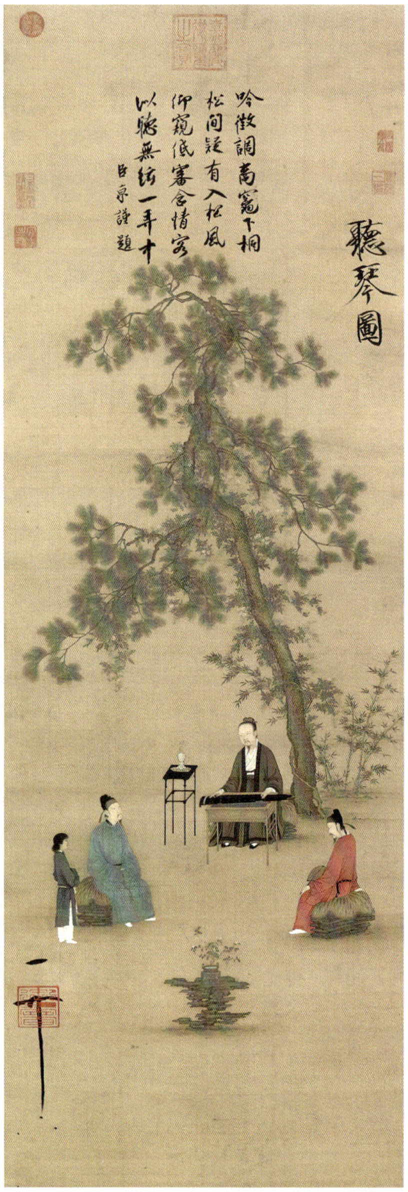

4 | Attributed to Emperor Huizong (Chinese, 1082–1135, r. 1101–26). *Listening to the Zither*, first half of the 12th century. Hanging scroll, ink and color on silk; 184.4 × 123.9 cm (72 5/8 × 48 3/4 in.). Palace Museum, Beijing.

Emperor Huizong and *Bogutu*

In the first month of 1101, Emperor Huizong ascended the throne and became the eighth emperor of the Song dynasty. His reign lasted for twenty-six years, and in 1126, he finally abdicated to his son, Emperor Qinzong, who ruled for only fourteen months (r. 1126–27). In 1127 the dynasty fell to the Jurchen invaders. In Chinese history, Huizong has often been portrayed as a disastrous political leader, yet an accomplished practitioner of fine arts, excelling in painting and calligraphy (see fig. 4).[26] However, a number of recent studies have thrown new light on this important historical figure, particularly regarding his double role as "emperor-artist," and some have questioned to what extent the paintings and works of calligraphy attributed to Huizong are actually from his own hand.[27]

As a sensitive and talented artist, the emperor had a strong personal interest in antiquities and classical art. For Huizong, antiquity played a unique role, and it is highly revealing to see the names he gave to the different compartments of his palace: Pursuing Antiquity (*Jigu*), Broadening Antiquity (*Bogu*), Honoring Antiquity (*Shanggu*), Deepening Antiquity (*Suigu*), Appreciating Antiquity (*Jiangu*), Creating Antiquity (*Zuogu*), Transmitting Antiquity (*Chuangu*), and Inner Secrets of Antiquity (*Migu*).[28] In those spaces, Huizong tried to live as an individual, as well as an emperor, negotiating between the public and private. In a piece of writing attributed to him, he described the palace as follows:

> The left side is filled with state papers and the classics and histories, which allow one to draw on antiquity in composing decrees and regulations. On the right are stored vessels of the Xia, Shang, and Zhou dynasties: cauldrons, libation cups, stands, raised dishes, tureens, pans, beakers, and tall jars. From observing the images on these vessels one can make vessels that reach the spirits during offerings at the altars and temples.
>
> On the eastern aisle are arranged the ancient and modern calligraphy and paintings, which have been classified according to quality. They allow one to amuse oneself and give free rein to thought. On the western aisle are [such scholar's objects as] zithers, brushes, and inkstones. With these one can flourish the brush and scatter ink, thus releasing sorrows and expressing emotions.[29]

However, once he had assumed his role as emperor, Huizong's relationship with antiquity became complicated. Antiquity was no longer a matter of personal aesthetic pursuit, but provided a model for state affairs, as well as the public demonstration of his rule.

Huizong was not a weak ruler. Soon after he was enthroned, he decided to reverse state policy and elevate the reformers who had lost favor at Zhezong's court. Many of the anti-reform scholar-officials were exiled and their works banned. Cai Jing, a crafty politician but a learned scholar and accomplished calligrapher, was appointed as the grand councillor. With Cai's assistance, Huizong then embarked on an ambitious project to implement a new political and ritual system that he believed could transform the country and make him equal to the sage kings of the past. It is significant that his political reforms revolved around the idea of the past as coded in classics such as *Zhouli* (Rites of Zhou).

Thus, collecting, and replicating, ancient ritual bronzes became an important part of Huizong's political initiatives, closely related to the reconstruction of the ritual system and political institution of the Three Dynasties. Between 1104 and 1107, on the advice of Cai Jing, the emperor decided to make a complete set of nine cauldrons. The inspiration might have come from the legend of the nine cauldrons documented in early classics such as *Zuozhuan* (Zuo Commentaries), in which the vessels were regarded as Heaven's blessing and the representation of political legitimacy. But Huizong's cauldrons were based on Daoist philosophy, and after their completion were placed in the Palace of Nine Accomplishments (*Jiuchenggong*). At the same time, he also cast a set of bronze bells, named *Dasheng* (Great Splendor), which were said to have been designed following the advice of the Daoist musician Wei Hanji, who was over ninety years old, and to have pitch pipes tuned according to the length of the emperor's fingers.[30] We can neither prove nor contest this story, but we know that Huizong believed in and promoted Daoism, and that there are extant Dacheng bells that were closely modeled on some Eastern Zhou (770–221 BC) examples unearthed in the Song dynasty.[31] After the fall of the Northern Song dynasty, the nine bronze cauldrons were never seen again and were perhaps destroyed. However, the bells survived and were reused by the Jurchens, who added new inscriptions to them.[32] Several are now in different collections, including the palace museums in Beijing and Taipei, Shanghai Museum, Tianjin Museum, Liaoning Provincial Museum, and Royal Ontario Museum in Toronto.[33] By looking closely at the surviving examples, we can see they were made in imitation of those illustrated in the catalogue of ancient bronzes in the Song imperial court.

In order to secure ancient ritual vessels that could be used for court ceremonies and simultaneously replicate them as closely as possible, Huizong established two new agencies, one for Deliberating on Ritual and the other for Instituting Rituals, as well as special workshops. Xue Ang, an official at the Song court, who presented the emperor with a report in 1108, said:

> I saw that ritual vessels used in the government offices, such as *zun* beakers, *jue* goblets, *fu* and *gui* grain containers, are of different forms from those ancient vessels in scholar-officials' collections. Those antiquities were mostly recovered from ruins and graves dating back more than a thousand years, and were surely derived from certain ritual systems. Thus, they cannot be forgeries. It is said that when rituals are lost, one can seek them in remote territories. As the court now intends to rectify the ritual system, if any of the vessels are worth investigation, the court should broaden the search and obtain evidence. I request that offices of all counties and prefectures be ordered to seek out scholar-officials or commoners who have ancient ritual vessels, dispatching someone to their homes to make drawings of the vessels and, after careful inspection and elimination of errors, send the drawings to the Agency for Deliberating on Ritual. The government should provide the pigments and supplies for drawing, which should not be loaned out or bring any inconvenience, and anyone who violates this will be treated as breaking the law and must be punished.[34]

Huizong approved this proposal. In the following decades, the court made a large number of bronze vessels for use at state and religious ceremonies, and as rewards to be given to loyal ministers.[35] The effectiveness of government rituals seemed to rely partially on the quality of the vessels employed. At the same time, the imperial collection of ancient bronzes grew ever larger, reaching into several thousands of pieces. Many of them came from uncontrolled excavations and the marketplace, but some were bought or confiscated from private collectors; for instance, a number of bronzes that belonged to Liu, Li Gonglin, and others were later incorporated into Huizong's collection.

Perhaps with the earlier private scholarly catalogues in mind, Huizong launched his own projects to catalogue the imperial collection, which included bronzes, paintings, and works of calligraphy. These are known as the Xuanhe catalogues, and refer to one of Huizong's palace halls and one of his reign names. The *Xuanhe huapu* (Xuanhe Catalogue of Paintings) was finished first, in 1120. The *Xuanhe shupu* (Xuanhe Catalogue of Calligraphy) was completed in 1122 or later. The catalogue of ancient bronzes took longer to finish, and its current version, probably concluded after 1123, is titled the *Chongxiu Xuanhe bogutu* (Illustrated Antiquities from the Xuanhe Hall, Revised), often shortened to *Bogutu*.[36]

Huizong's *Bogutu* comprises thirty volumes and records 839 bronzes. The presentation format is not so different from Lü's

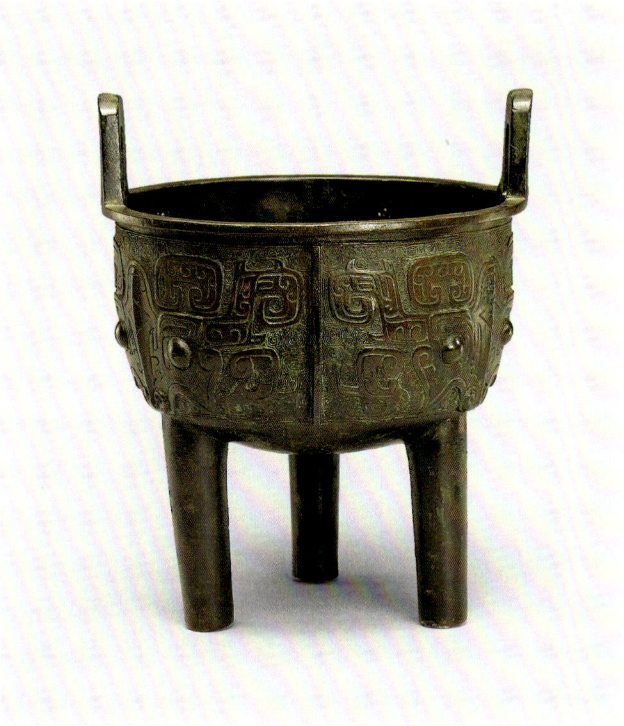

5 | Tripod vessel of the Zhenghe period (Zhenghe *ding*), Northern Song dynasty (960–1127), 1116. Bronze; h. 23 cm (9 1/16 in.); d. 10.7 cm (4 3/16 in.); diam. of rim 19.1 cm (7 1/2 in.). National Palace Museum, Taipei.

Kaogutu, and like that catalogue, there is also a selection from the thousands of bronzes in the imperial collection. Although there are different theories about the authorship of *Bogutu*—it may have been based on an earlier manuscript by the palace librarian Huang Bosi or compiled by one of Huizong's favorite ministers, Wang Fu—there is no doubt that the project was commissioned by the emperor himself and was under his close supervision.[37] A note found in *Bogutu* suggests that Huizong was, in fact, directly involved in its compilation: "Among all the vessels, this *lei* container is especially fine and of antiquity, which can serve as a model for later generations. I therefore issue an edict decreeing that the ritual officials should produce vessels based on it, for use at the temples of Heaven, Earth, or the ancestors. Thus, the system of the Three Dynasties can be splendidly revealed to people today. This is also a benefit of investigating antiquity."[38]

Obviously, the aim of the catalogue was not simply to make a record of the bronzes that were in the imperial collection, but to provide models that could be copied to make new replicas for government rituals and to serve as a political tool to control and deny oppositions. For instance, a bronze *ding* (see fig. 5) cast in the Zhenghe period (1110–18) was modeled on a Shang prototype. Like Lü's *Kaogutu*, *Bogutu* was also heavily colored by factionist divisions, as we read in the catalogue that the collectors of the Yuanyou era were accused of having presented the imperial court with forgeries and were condemned as "the wicked faction."[39] *Bogutu* conveyed a negative attitude toward *Kaogutu*, probably because Lü was associated with the Yuanyou faction. Also, while the emperor himself was busy acquiring ancient bronzes, private collecting was discouraged, perhaps to avoid situations in which the emperor and private collectors might compete over the same pieces. Moreover, Song society under Huizong was more autocratic than under previous dynasties, and private collections of ancient ritual objects could be a potential threat to the monopoly of the emperor and his government.[40] As Patricia Ebrey has argued, "In Song times, collecting and writing about books, art, and antiquities became an arena in which the educated elite and the throne subtly competed for cultural leadership."[41] The emperor was concerned not only with the age and authenticity of ancient ritual bronzes but also with the interpretations given to them.

Here, a comparison between *Bogutu* and *Kaogutu* is necessary. Compared to the latter, the former has some noticeable shortcomings. First, it pays little attention to each object's locality and provenance. Thus, from a modern perspective, *Bogutu* has an insufficiently archaeological approach. Second, in terms of interpretation, the author(s) of *Bogutu* relied heavily on moral and political explications, sometimes without solid philological grounding. This has led some scholars, such as Hong Mai of the Southern Song period, to describe its mistakes as "absurd and laughable."[42]

However, we can also see that there are certain strengths and advanced features in *Bogutu*. For example, it presents, for the first time, a systematic treatment of the typology of ancient bronzes. Whereas *Kaogutu* still suffers a number of faults and inconsistencies, *Bogutu* takes a much more coherent approach to the classification and nomenclature of ancient bronzes. It arranges all objects into twenty categories, according to their forms and functions, and gives a general introduction to each. Though the introductory essays are usually full of moral teachings and political overtones, the classification system is well developed and reasonable. It has been passed down through the dynasties and is still being used today by contemporary scholars. Also, unlike Lü Dalin's ambivalent approach toward dating the object, *Bogutu* assigns a period to each object: the Shang, the Zhou, or later periods, such as the Han (206 BC–AD 220), the Six Dynasties (220–589), and the Tang (618–907). This method was based on inscriptions, historical texts, forms, and decorations. Since Huizong needed the bronzes to serve as models of antiquity, establishing their dates was crucial.

Modern scholars have noted that there are theoretical as well as technical differences between Huizong's catalogue of bronzes and other scholars' works. Even when they include the same objects or share a similar presentational format, the underlying philosophy and motivation vary. For Huizong, ancient bronzes were important to help to reconstruct court ritual, which made them tools for political and social

reforms. But for scholars such as Ouyang, Su Shi, Li, and Lü, history, philology, and art were important, because antiquity provided them with a means to distinguish themselves as a distinct social group. As Yun-Chiahn Sena argues, these different stances reflected the multiple views of antiquity appearing in Song antiquarian scholarship.[43]

Southern Song Antiquarianism

The stories of antiquities often tell the fates of history. In 1127 the Jin dynasty of the Jurchens ransacked the Song capital at Bianjing. Huizong and his son Emperor Qinzong were taken as captives, together with thousands of men and women, gold and silver, valuables, libraries, and imperial art collections of bronzes, calligraphy, and paintings, which were all sent back to the Jin capital at Yanjing (today's Beijing). Huizong himself later died in humiliation. The Song imperial collection met with an uneven fate. While painting and calligraphy continued to be treasured by the Jurchen rulers, ancient ritual bronzes were singled out as being bad omens, and many were destroyed.

After losing territory and political control north of the Yangzi River to the Jurchens, Emperor Gaozong (r. 1127–62), the ninth son of Huizong, escaped to the south and finally settled at Lin'an (modern Hangzhou in Zhejiang)—the old capital of the Wuyue state (907–968) and one of the richest and most fertile cities in southern China. Struggling to rebuild a new government, he remembered what his father had done and knew that in order to carry out stable and effective policies, he must restore the ritual system to legitimize his rule. For this purpose, Gaozong needed to cast new bronze vessels that could be used for state rituals and ceremonies. But because he no longer had the collection of ancient bronzes and the imperial catalogues such as *Bogutu*, which were temporarily taken by the Jurchens, Gaozong's reproduction of ritual vessels, mostly in ceramics, could rely only on old printed books such as *Sanlitu* (Illustrations of the Three Ritual Classics) for reference. *Sanlitu* was compiled and presented by the Five Dynasties official Nie Chongyi to the newly established Song court in 962; it is full of explications of rituals accompanied by fanciful illustrations of ancient ritual vessels. Later, when a copy of *Bogutu* was discovered in 1143 and brought back to Lin'an by a Southern Song ambassador who had traveled to Jin territory, the Ministry of Ritual requested that multiple copies of the book be made, and that reproductions of ritual vessels should follow the correct "ancient system" recorded by *Bogutu*.[44] The Southern Song court was also actively collecting antique bronzes they found in the marketplace. Two years later, in 1145, the court again issued a new ritual handbook, *Shaoxing zhizao liqi tu* (Shaoxing Illustrations for the Production of Ritual Objects).

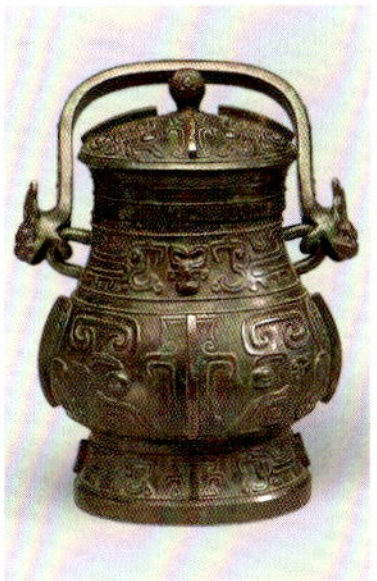

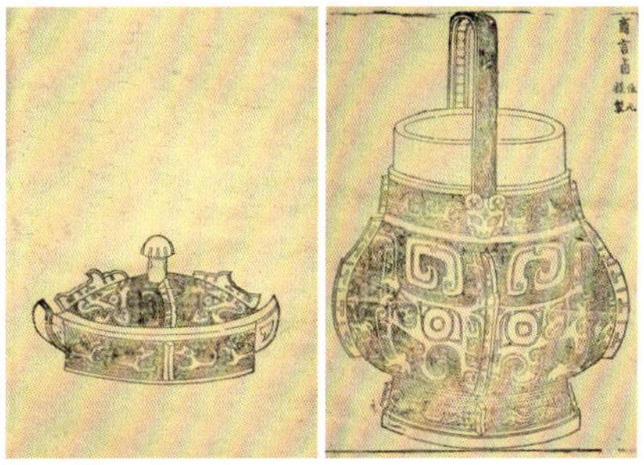

6a | Bucket (*you*), Southern Song dynasty (1127–1279) or Ming dynasty (1368–1644). Bronze; 35.3 × 33 × 21.5 cm (13 7/8 × 13 × 8 7/16 in.). National Palace Museum, Taipei.

6b | Illustration of a bucket (*you*) in Wang Fu et al., *Bogutu* [Illustrated Broad Manifestation of Antiquity], *Yizhengtang* edition (compiled 1107–10, 1752), 9.10.

The original pictures are now lost, but we can see examples from a shortened version, *Shaoxi zhouxian shidianyitu* (Shaoxi Illustrated Compendium for Sacrificing to Confucius in the Provinces; 1155–94), which is said to have been compiled by the famous southern Song philosopher Zhu Xi. This attribution is uncertain, but we know that one of Zhu's achievements was indeed to combine ancient objects and ancient texts with his Neo-Confucian (*lixue*) philosophy, and that this book was widely circulated and followed.[45]

In recent years, many bronzes of the Southern Song period have been unearthed around the country, from the capital at Hangzhou to Sichuan (a peripheral region of the empire).[46] These works are of varied quality, but all are related to the illustrated catalogues and guides to state rituals. Moreover, they are mostly altar sets comprising candleholders, flower vases, and incense burners. Bronze production was localized, and vessels were made in an archaistic style and widely circulated in both public and private spaces, apparently forming new sets and performing new roles. Ancient bronzes, many from the Three Dynasties, were no longer being used for offering food and drink to ancestors, but were employed in local Buddhist, Daoist, and Confucian temples and family shrines. In a new social environment, the manufacture and use of bronze vessels had to change, as did their meanings. A perfect example of this can be seen in a poem by the famous writer Fan Chengda, who lamented the repurposing of an ancient cauldron as an incense burner:

> Clouds, thunder, and circling bands formed
> the ancient decoration;
>
> Sons and grandsons treasured it for eternity
> with offerings;
>
> Inscriptions were painstakingly cast on to it,
> but for what?
>
> It is now destitute and used for burning incense.
>
> Sadly, the antiques that had once been much
> revered and carefully studied by emperors

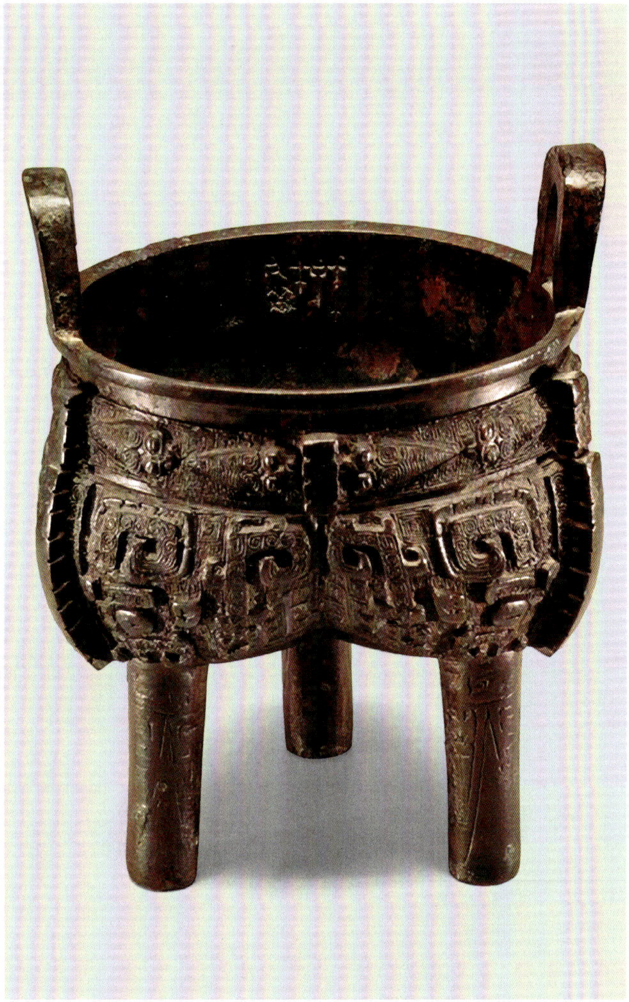

7a | *Tripod Vessel of Fu Gui* (*Fu Gui Ding*), late Shang dynasty (c. 1250–1046 BC). Bronze; h. 22.5 cm (8 7/8 in); diam. of mouth: 16.5 cm (6 1/2 in.). National Palace Museum, Taipei.

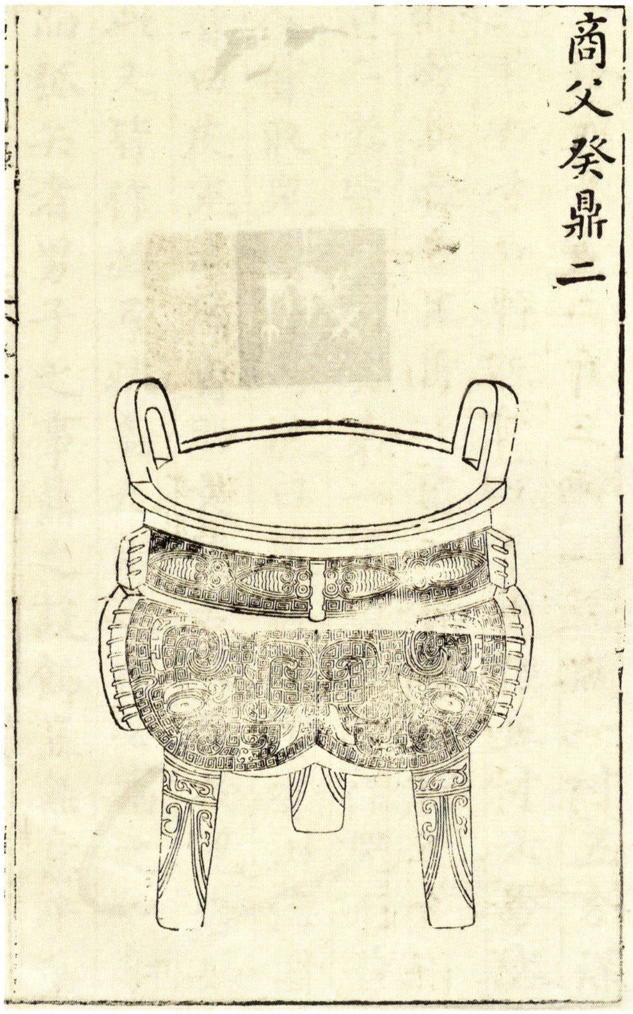

7b | Illustration of a tripod vessel in Wang Fu et al., *Bogutu* [Illustrated Broad Manifestation of Antiquity], *Yizhengtang* edition (compiled 1107–10, 1752), 1.26. This illustration is most likely of the same vessel shown in fig. 7a.

> and scholars have become little more than playthings and incense burners![47]

The tradition of art collecting was also transformed in the Southern Song dynasty. Those who had lost their holdings during those turbulent years still remembered them with regret. An example of this is recorded by the noted poet Li Qingzhao, wife of collector Zhao Mingcheng. To escape the invading Jurchen troops, Zhao told his wife: "Follow the crowds. If you can't do otherwise, abandon the household goods first, then the clothes, then the books and scrolls, then the old bronzes, but carry the sacrificial vessels for the ancestral temple yourself; live or die with them; don't give them up." After her husband died, Li wrote about the joy of acquiring antiquities, but also the anguish of parting with them, lamenting: "Why are they are so hard to obtain, but so easy to lose?!"[48] Lingering resentment and the desire to regain their culture drove Southern Song collectors to find as many antiquities as they possibly could.

Although Southern Song collectors were still interested in ancient bronzes, it became very hard for them to find genuine pieces. To meet the increasing demand, craftsmen used printed images to make a very large number of reproductions in bronze and ceramics, although there seemed no need to model them very closely on the originals. For example, a bronze bucket in the National Palace Museum's collection was copied from an illustration in *Bogutu* (see figs. 6a and 6b). The inclination to use antiquities as decorative objects for personal enjoyment, combined with the decrease in scholarly appreciation of bronzes, eventually led to the decline of *jinshixue* in the following five hundred years—until the revival of rigorous evidence-based scholarship in the eighteenth century during the Qing dynasty.

Some Surviving Bronzes from Song Collections

Very few of the bronzes that were recorded in the Song dynasty catalogues have survived today. A well-known exception is the Shang tripod *Fu Gui ding* now in the collection of the National Palace Museum in Taipei (fig. 7a).[49] Judging by its similar form and inscription, this work must be the same

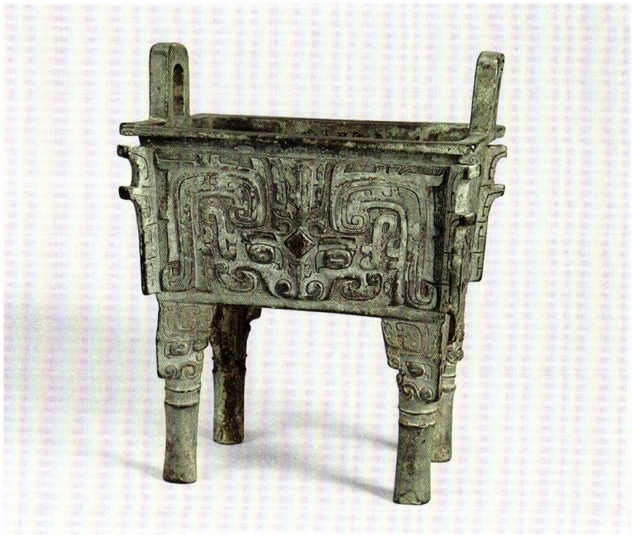

8a | *Square Cauldron of Hou Chuo* (*Hou Chuo Fangding*), mid-Western Zhou Dynasty, 927–850 BC. Bronze; h. 21.3 cm (8 3/8 in.); diam. of rim: 17.4 cm (6 7/8 in.). Shanghai Museum, 41544.

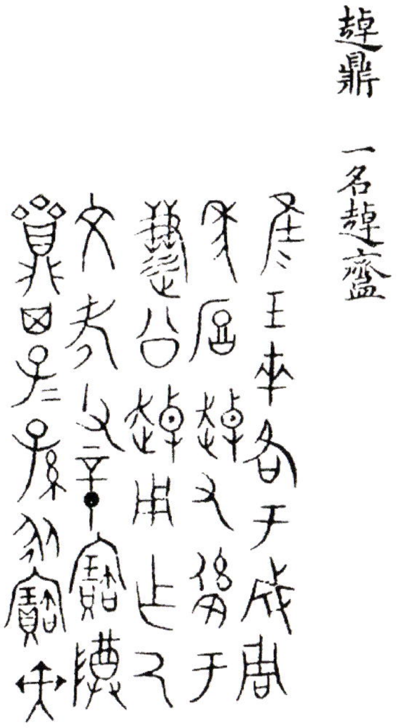

8c | The same inscription as on fig. 8a, recorded in Xue Shanggong, *Lidai zhongding yiqi kuanzhi fatie* [Model Inscriptions from Ritual Bronzes from Successive Dynasties] (1144), 9.87.

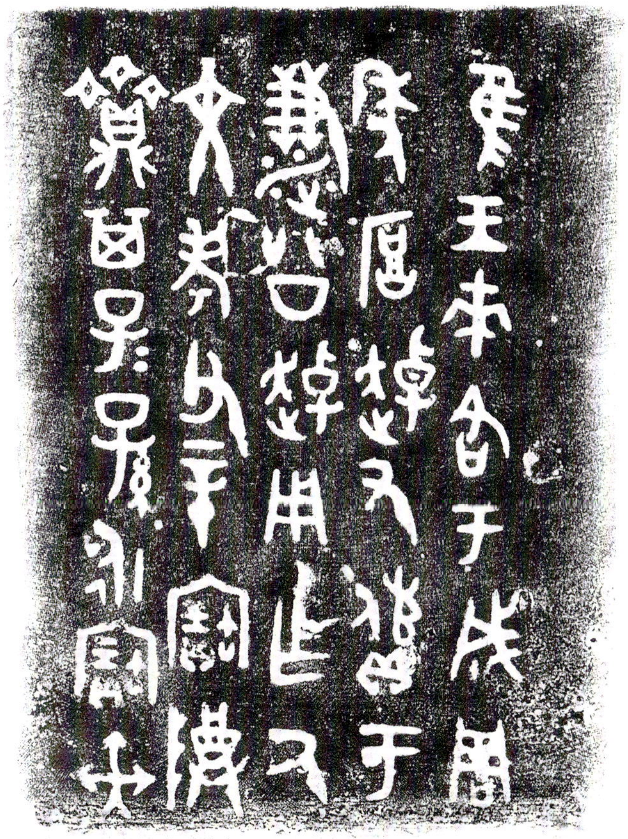

8b | Rubbing of the inscription on fig. 8a.

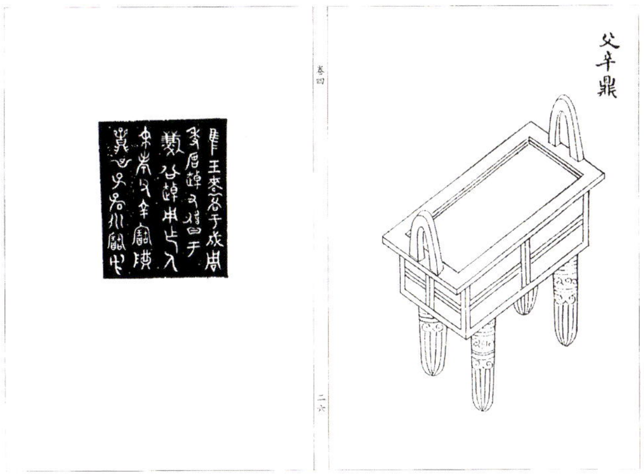

8d | The same inscription as on fig. 8a, recorded in Lü Dalin (attributed), *Xu Kaogutu* (Supplement to "Illustrated Catalogue for the Study of Antiquity"), probably Southern Song (1127–1279), 4.26.

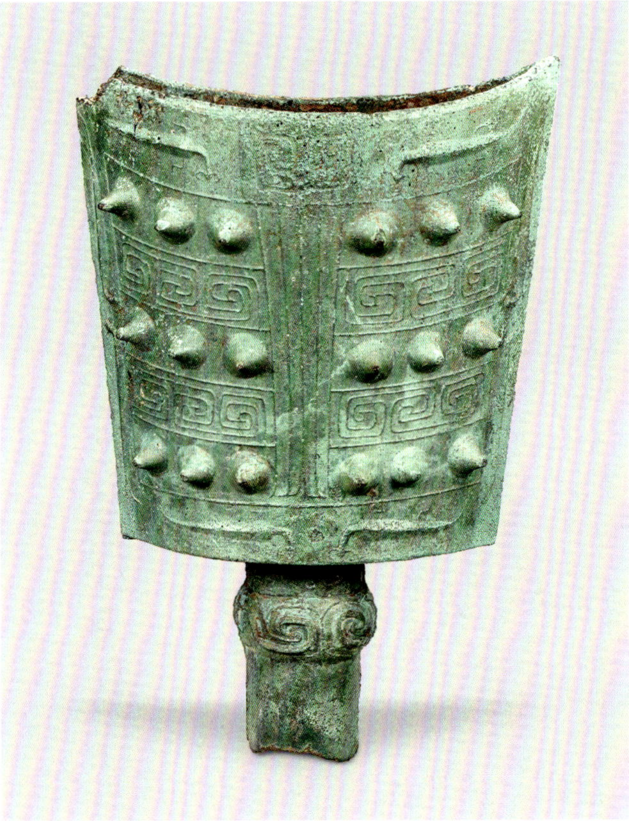

9a | Bell (*nao*), Western Zhou dynasty (1046–771 BC). Bronze; h. 41.7 cm (16 ½ in); diam. 28 cm (11 ⅜ in). The Art Institute of Chicago, Lucy Maud Buckingham Collection, 1924.243. See pl. 57.

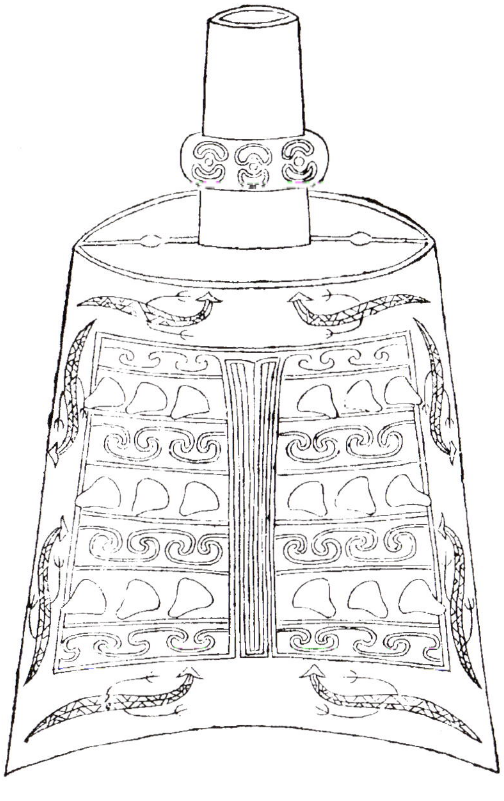

9b | Illustration in *Bogutu*, no. 23.14, of a *nao* bell very similar to fig. 9a.

one recorded in *Bogutu* (fig. 7b).[50] Another example, included in this exhibition, is the *Hou Chou fangding* in the Shanghai Museum (figs. 8a and 8b), which originally came from the collection of the famous nineteenth-century scholar Chen Jieqi. An identical inscription (fig. 8c) is found in the *Lidai zhongding yiqi kuanzhi fatie* (Model Inscriptions from Ritual Bronzes from Succesive Dynasties; 1144), by the Southern Song scholar Xue Shanggong. This object was included in another catalogue, *Xu Kaogutu* (Supplement to the Illustrated Investigation of Antiquity; fig. 8d), attributed to Lü Dalin, but of a late date. This time, the inscription was published together with an illustration of a square-shaped cauldron. Considering the rarity of the inscription, we have reason to believe that the square cauldron in the Shanghai Museum is likely the same one published in Xue's book. The illustration in the *Xu Kaogutu* does not quite match the real piece, but as the book is known to contain errors, it could be a mismatch, or a case of the author drawing an imagined illustration without actually having seen the vessel. In these two instances, the inscriptions play a crucial role in the identification and in making the connection between the illustration and the objects. However, it is much more difficult to identify pieces without inscriptions. The Art Institute has a bronze *nao* bell that has a distinctive shape and unique decoration (fig. 9a), and we can find a very close illustration in *Bogutu* (see fig. 9b). Are they the same piece? The answer is uncertain since there are less than half a dozen similar bells, including those excavated recently in Hunan, of which the Art Institute's piece and the illustration in *Bogutu* are the closest match. But because there is a huge gap of over one thousand years and about which we have little information, and the pictorial evidence is not always accurate, the identification has to be speculative.

NOTES

1 | For a general introduction of Song dynasty *jinshixue*, see Wang Guowei, "Songdai zhi jinshixue," *Guoxue lunheng* 1:3/4 (1927): 45–49 [English translation by Liu Chongxiong, "Archaeology in the Sung Dynasty," *China Journal* 6:5 (1927): 222–31]; Rong Geng, "Songdai jijin shuji shuping" [Review of Song Dynasty Publications on Bronzes and Stones], in *Rong Geng xuanji* [Selected Writings of Rong Geng] (Tianjin: Tianjin renmin chubanshe, 1994), 3–73; and Ye Guoliang, *Songdai jinshixue yanjiu* [Study of Song Antiquarianism] (Taipei: Taiwan shuju chubanshe, 2011).

2 | See Joseph Alsop, *The Rare Art Traditions: The History of Art Collecting and Its Linked Phenomena Wherever These Have Appeared*, Bollingen Series 35.27 (Princeton: Princeton University Press/New York: Harper and Row, 1982), esp. 298–336.

3 | R. C. Rudolph, "Preliminary Notes on Sung Archaeology," *Journal of Asian Studies* 22:2 (1963): 169–77.

4 | See Joseph Needham, Wang Ling, and Derek J. de Solla Price, *Heavenly Clockwork: The Great Astronomical Clocks of Medieval China*, 2nd ed. (Cambridge: Cambridge University Press, 1986).

5 | See Xia Nai, "Shen Kuo yu kaoguxue" [Shen Kuo and Archaeology], in Institute of Archaeology, Chinese Academy of Social Sciences, *Xia Nai wenji* [Collected Writings of Xia Nai] (Beijing: Shehui kexue wenxian chubanshe, 2000), 465–80.

6 | For discussion on the relationship between the traditional antiquarian learning and modern archaeology, see K. C. Chang, "Archaeology and Chinese Historiography," *World Archaeology* 13:2 (1981): 156–69; Su Rongyu, "The Reception of 'Archaeology' and 'Prehistory' and the Founding of Archaeology in Late Imperial China," in Michael Lackner and Natascha Vittinghof, eds., *Mapping Meanings: The Field of New Learning in Late Qing China* (Leiden: Brill, 2004), 423–49; and Denis Thouard and Tao Wang, "Making New Classics: The Archaeology of Luo Zhenyu and Victor Segalen," in Sarah C. Humphrey and Rudolf G. Wagner, eds., *Modernity's Classics* (Verlag Berlin Heidelberg: Springer, 2013), 231–60.

7 | See James T. C. Liu, *Ou-yang Hsiu: An Eleventh-Century Neo-Confucianist* (Stanford: Stanford University Press, 1967).

8 | See Thomas H. Lee, "Skepticist Reconstruction and Sagely Truth in Tension: Song Attempts to Draw the Boundaries of Historical Antiquity," in Dieter Kuhn and Helga Stahl, eds., *Perceptions of Antiquity in Chinese Civilization* (Heidelberg: Edition Forum, 2008), 253–89.

9 | For a brief discussion on Ouyang Xiu's collecting activities, see Yun Chiahn C. Sena, "Ouyang Xiu's Conceptual Collection of Antiquity," in Alain Schnapp, with Lothar von Falkenhausen, Peter N. Miller, and Tim Murray, eds., *World Antiquarianism: Comparative Perspectives* (Los Angeles: Getty Research Institute, 2013), 212–29.

10 | In ink-squeezed rubbing, the most common method of the period, damp paper is placed over the inscription, then tamped with a brush. Ink is applied to the paper with an ink pad, and the raised parts catch the ink, whereas the depressed parts remain white. For a brief discussion on the techniques and its cultural significance, see Tseng Yu-ho Ecke, "The Importance of Ink-Imprints" (24–27), and Lothar Ledderose, "Rubbings in Art History" (28–36), in Hartmut Walravens, ed., *Catalogue of Chinese Rubbings from the Field Museum*, Fieldiana Anthropology, New Series 3 (Chicago: Field Museum of Natural History, 1981).

11 | Li Yian, ed., *Ouyang Xiu quanji* [Complete Works of Ouyang Xiu] (Beijing: Zhonghua shuju, 2001), *juan* 42, 599–600. The translation is from Ronald Egan, *The Problem of Beauty: Aesthetic Thought and Pursuits in Northern Song Dynasty China*, Harvard East Asian Monographs 271 (Cambridge: Harvard University Asia Center, 2006), 11–12.

12 | Ibid.

13 | Ibid.

14 | Li, *Ouyang Xiu quanji*, *juan* 134, 2061–*juan* 143, 2327.

15 | Ibid., 2063.

16 | Liu Chang, *Gongshiji* [Collected Writings of Gongshi], in *Baibu congshu jicheng* edition (Taipei: Yiwen yinshuguan, 1965), 27, 58–59, 36, 13b–14a.

17 | For an exhibition devoted to Li Gonglin's art, see Richard Barnhart, Robert E. Harrist Jr., and Hui-liang J. Chu, *Li Kung-Lin's "Classic of Filial Piety,"* exh. cat. (New York: Metropolitan Museum of Art, 1993).

18 | See Robert Harrist, "The Artist as Antiquarian: Li Gonglin and His Study of Early Chinese Art," *Artibus Asiae* 55 (1995): 237–80; Zhang Linsheng, "Li Gonglin yu Bei Song guqiwuxue de farren" [Li Gonglin and the Beginning of the Study of Ancient Objects in the Northern Song Dynasty], in National Palace Museum, *Qianxi nian Songdai wenwu dazhan* [China at the Inception of the Second Millennium: Art and Culture of the Sung Dynasty, 960–1279], exh. cat. (Taipei: National Palace Museum, 2000), 19–46.

19 | Deng Chun, *Huaji* [Continuation of Paintings], in *Huashi congshu* edition (Shanghai: Renmin meishu chubanshe, 1963), *juan* 3, 12.

20 | Zhai Qinian, *Zhoushi* [History of Scripts], *Congshu jicheng chubian* edition (Shanghai: Shangwu yinshuguan, 1935/40), 11–12.

21 | See A. C. Graham, *Two Chinese Philosophers: The Metaphysics of the Brothers Ch'eng*, 2nd ed. (La Salle: Open Court, 1992).

22 | See Jeffery Moser, "Recasting Antiquity: Ancient Bronzes and Ritual Hermeneutics in the Song Dynasty" (PhD diss., Harvard University, 2010), 124–59, and "The Ethics of Immutable Things: Interpreting Lü Dalin's Illustrated Investigations of Antiquity," *Harvard Journal of Asiatic Studies* 72:2 (2012): 259–93.

23 | Lü Dalin and Zhao Jiucheng, *Kaogutu, Xu Kaogutu, Kaogutu shiwen* [Illustrated Catalogue for the Study of Antiquity, Supplement to the "Illustrated Catalogue for the Study of Antiquity," Explanation of the "Illustrated Catalogue for the Study of Antiquity"], *Siku quanshu edition* (Beijing: Zhonghua shuju, 1987), 2.

24 | Moser, "Recasting Antiquity," 131f7.

25 | See Ya-Hwei Hsu, "Reshaping Chinese Material Culture: The Revival of Antiquity in the Era of Print, 960–1729" (PhD diss., Yale University, 2010), esp. 47–61, and "Antiquaries and Politics: Antiquarian Culture of the Northern Song, 9960–1127," in Schnapp, with von Falkenhausen, Miller, and Murray, *World Antiquarianism*, 230–48.

26 | See Tseng Yu-ho Ecke, "Emperor Hui Tsung, The Artist: 1082–1136" (PhD diss., New York University, 1972). For a recent and comprehensive study, see Patricia B. Ebery, *Accumulating Culture: The Collections of Emperor Huizong* (Seattle: University of Washington Press, 2008).

27 | See Maggie Bickford, "Huizong's Paintings: Art and the Art of Emperorship," in Patricia B. Ebery and Maggie Bickford, eds., *Emperor Huizong and Late Northern Song China: The Politics of Culture and the Culture of Politics* (Cambridge: Harvard University Asia Center, 2006), 453–513.

28 | Recorded in Huang Yizhou et al., *Xu zizhi tongjian changbian shibu* [Additions to the Supplement to the Extended Version of the Comprehensive Mirror for Aid in Government] (Beijing: Zhonghua shuju, 2004), *juan* 40, 1251.

29 | Ibid., *juan* 32, 1061. The translation is from Ebery, *Accumulating Culture*, 113.

30 | See Patricia Ebery, "Replicating Zhou Bells at the Northern Song Court," in Wu Hung, ed., *Reinventing the Past: Archaism and Antiquarianism in Chinese Art and Visual Culture* (Chicago: Center for the Art of East Asia, University of Chicago/Art Media Resources, 2009), 179–99, and *Accumulating Culture*, 159–66.

31 | Ibid.

32 | See Richard C. Rudolph, "Dynastic Booty: An Altered Chinese Bronze," *Harvard Journal of Asiatic Studies* 11 (1948): 174–80.

33 | Chen Mengjia, "Song Dacheng bianzhong kaoshu" [Investigation of the Dacheng Bells], in *Cheng Mengjia xueshu lunwenji* [Academic Essays by Chen Mengjia] (Beijing: Zhonghua shuju, 2016), 528–33.

34 | Huang et al., *Xu zizhi tongjian changbian shibu*, *juan* 28, 950. See also Ebery, *Accumulating Culture*, 167; and Hsu, "Reshaping Chinese Material Culture," 79. My translation differs slightly from Ebery's.

35 | See Chen Fangmei, "Zaixian sandai: Cong Gugong Songdai fanggu tongqi shuoqi" [Representing the Three Dynasties: On the Song Archaistic Bronzes in the Palace Museum], in National Palace Museum, *Qianxi nian Songdai wenwu dazhan*, 293–320.

36 | There are various editions of *Bogutu*. Among them, the *Yizhengtang* edition of 1752, which is based on the fine editions of 1603 and 1588, is the best, and I have used it for this catalogue: Liu Qingzhu, Duan Zhihong, and Feng Shi, eds., *Jinwen wenxian jicheng* [Compendium of Publications on Bronze Inscriptions] (Beijing: Xian zhuang shuju, 2005), vol. 2. For a discussion on its production and editions, see Robert Poor, "Notes on the Sung Dynasty Archaeological Catalogs," *Archives of the Chinese Art Society of America* 19 (1965): 33–44; and Ebery, *Accumulating Culture*, 355–70.

37 | For discussions on the authorship, see Ebery, *Accumulating Culture*, 355–72; Hsu, "Reshaping Chinese Material Culture," 74–76; and Wang Hongsheng, "*Xuehe Bogutu* zuozhe yu chengshu kao" [Investigation on the Authorship of *Xuehe Bogutu* and the Time of Its Completion], *Zhongguo dianji yu wenhua* [Chinese Books and Culture] (2007/3).

38 | *Bogutu*, 7, 39.

39 | Hsu, "Reshaping Chinese Material Culture," 58–60.

40 | See Peter K. Bol, "Emperors Can Claim Antiquity Too: Emperorship and Autocracy Under the New Policies," in Ebery and Bickford, *Emperor Huizong and Late Northern Song China*, 173–205.

41 | Ebery, *Accumulating Culture*, 17.

42 | Hong Mai, *Rongzhai suibi* [Essays from the Rongzhai Studio] (Shanghai: Shanghai guji chubanshe, 1978), 14, 181.

43 | Yun-Chiahn C. Sena, "Cataloguing Antiquity: A Comparative Study of the *Kaogu tu* and *Bogu tu*," in Wu, *Reinventing the Past*, 200–28.

44 | See Hsu, "Reshaping Chinese Material Culture," 169–71.

45 | See Chen Fangmei, "'Yu Sandai tongfeng': Zhu Xi dui 'shidianyishi' dexingcheng ji ying-xiang" [Fashioned as the Three Dynasties: Zhu Xi's Influence to the Formation of the "Compendium for Sacrificing"], in Chen Fangmei, *Qingtongqi yu Songdai wenhuashi* [Bronzes and the Cultural History of the Song Dynasty] (Taipei: Taiwan University Publication Center, 2016), 191–255.

46 | See Hsu, "Reshaping Chinese Material Culture," 197–233; and Moser, "Recasting Antiquity," 246–67.

47 | *Quan Songshi* [Complete Collection of Song Dynasty Poems] (Beijing: Beijing daxue chubanshe, 1998), *juan* 41, 2269, 26018.

48 | Wang Zhongwen, *Li Qingzhao ji jiao zhu* [Collation and Annotations of Li Qingzhao's Writings] (Beijing: Renmin wenxue chubanshe, 1979), 179–80. The translation is from Stephen Owen, *Remembrance: The Experience of the Past in Classical Chinese Literature* (Cambridge: Harvard University Press, 1986), 90.

49 | Wen Fong and James Watt, eds., *Possessing the Past: Treasures from the National Palace Museum*, Taipei (New York: Metropolitan Museum of Art/Taipei: National Palace Museum, 1996), 221.

50 | *Bogutu*, 1, 26.

CHEN MENGJIA AND THE READING OF BRONZE INSCRIPTIONS AS HISTORICAL SOURCES

EDWARD L. SHAUGHNESSY

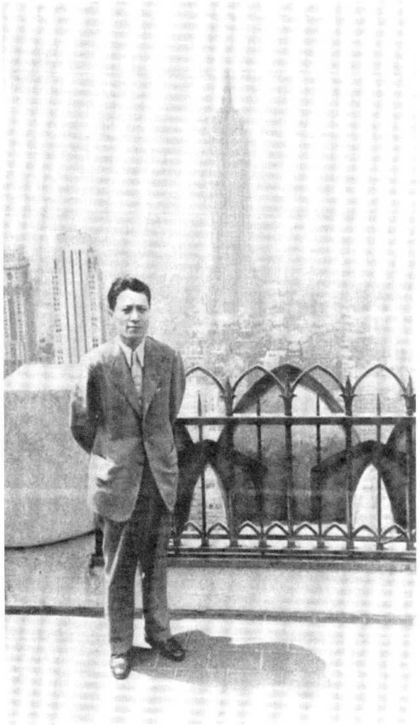

1 | Chen Mengjia, c. 1946.

The "study of bronze and stone" (*jinshixue*), the traditional name in China for paleography or the study of inscriptions, is conventionally traced back almost one thousand years to Ouyang Xiu, the great scholar-statesman of the Song dynasty (960–1279). A noted historian and the author of both the *Xin Wudaishi* (New Historical Records of the Five Dynasties; 1053) and also the *Xin Tangshu* (New Tang History; 1054–60), Ouyang was also an avid collector of inscriptions on ancient bronze vessels and more recent stone steles. In the preface to his publication of these inscriptions, *Jigulu bawei* (Notes on a Record of Collecting Antiquity; 1062), he noted two reasons why historians in particular should value such inscriptions. First, they often mention people and events not found in the traditional historical record. Second, being cast in bronze or carved into stone, the inscriptions are available to be read as they were first written, and were not subject to mistakes created through copying and recopying, as is the case with texts written on such perishable materials as bamboo and silk, or later on paper.[1] To this day, these two reasons remain the fundamental premises with which historians approach paleographic sources. However, it would be almost a thousand years after Ouyang's time before historians began to exploit these sources systematically to reconstruct ancient history.

The modern study of bronze inscriptions has developed in tandem with the study of ancient Chinese history. In China, this study is associated with some of the greatest historians of the modern era, including especially Wang Guowei, Guo Moruo, and Chen Mengjia (also known as Ch'en Meng-chia; see fig. 1). Although the first two of these scholars were more celebrated in their lifetimes, it was Chen Mengjia who doubtless made the more significant contribution to the study of paleography, or at least of bronze vessels and their inscriptions. That he also had a special connection with the Art Institute of Chicago merits celebration in the context of the present catalogue.

Chen was a visiting scholar at the University of Chicago from late 1944 until August 1947, collecting sources for a book to be called *Chinese Bronzes in American Collections: A Catalogue and Comprehensive Study of Chinese Bronzes*. In June 1947, shortly before he returned to China, Chen submitted to the Harvard-Yenching Institute of Harvard University a nearly six-hundred-page draft supplemented by a catalogue with photographs of eight hundred fifty bronze vessels in American collections. This work pioneered a multifaceted approach to the study of bronze vessels, combining historical, archaeological, art historical, and anthropological perspectives, demonstrating relationships among different bronze vessels and showing how these relationships could be used for historical purposes. Unfortunately, this book was never published, at least in the form Chen envisioned.[2] Although the Harvard-Yenching Institute had promised to publish the book, after Chen's return to China—and especially after the Communist Revolution there two years later—publication apparently became inconvenient, and Chen's original typescript was lost.

Fortunately, several of Chen's other writings during his time in Chicago did appear in print. The most important of these was a major contribution to *Chinese Bronzes from the Buckingham Collection*, the catalogue of the bronze vessels in the collection of the Art Institute of Chicago. Indeed, so important was Chen's contribution that Charles Fabens Kelley, then the museum's curator of Oriental Art, listed Chen as coauthor of the book.[3] It is still the definitive publication of the Art Institute's permanent collection of Chinese bronzes. Chen contributed a commentary that spelled out his understanding of the periodization of bronze vessels, as well as a notes section that provided translations of all the inscriptions on vessels in the collection.

After he returned to China, Chen published—in Chinese—a multipart article that expanded the scope of *Chinese Bronzes in American Collections* to encompass all bronze vessels that were known at that time: "Xi Zhou tongqi duandai" (Periodization of Western Zhou Bronzes). This was by no means just a journal article or technical study of periodization. Rather, in six parts, Chen produced a draft history of the first seven or eight reigns of the Western Zhou dynasty (1046–771 BC). His discussions of bronze inscriptions from these reigns include considerations of the Zhou conquest of Shang and its immediate aftermath, the Zhou colonization of eastern China and regional variation in bronze vessels, the performance of ritual and its significance at the Zhou court, military affairs and relations with peoples living on the periphery of the Zhou realm, and the staffing of the royal government, among other topics. Taken together, they constitute a synoptic history of the Western Zhou period, largely based on the inscriptions cast into bronze vessels. Unfortunately, Chen's fate in his homeland was not much better than it had been in the United States, and publication of his work was stopped before he could complete the sections on the final reigns of the dynasty.[4]

While at the University of Chicago, Chen was at least nominally a colleague of Herrlee Glessner Creel, already then one of the West's preeminent historians of ancient China.[5] Before joining the faculty at the university, Creel had spent nearly four years (1932–36) living in Beijing, studying paleography with Liu Jie, the director of the National Central Library's Department of Bronze and Stone Inscriptions. One of Creel's first published articles was "Bronze Inscriptions of the Western Chou Dynasty as Historical Documents," in which he suggested "a few of the occasions for which these bronze vessels were cast," and thus some of the ways in which bronze inscriptions can be used to study the history of the period:

> Let us consider a few of the occasions for which these bronze vessels were cast. A vassal is enfeoffed by the king, in a court ceremony which may include a moral and religious lecture written for the king in advance by his ministers, and presented with certain ritual gifts; he makes a bronze vessel to record the fact, giving details of the ceremony in the inscription. A vassal, having performed some service for the king, is rewarded with ceremony, and in commemoration of the fact makes a vessel dedicated to his ancestors and designed to be used for sacrifice, to secure for himself blessings and long life without end, and to be used by his descendants forever. On a military raid to "punish" certain barbarians, a rich spoil of shell money is obtained; the maker of the vessel records that he used his share of the loot to make this vessel. The transfer of lands is recorded, with details of the areas involved. A treaty, cast on bronze, defines the boundaries between states. Two feudal lords dispute over a piece of land; the king settles the quarrel, but he has to send an army to subdue the loser. Complicated commercial transactions involving horses, slaves, silk, and metal used as money are recorded. An instance of acceptance of a fine, in lieu of punishment, is recorded as a case of unusual clemency.[6]

The first of these "occasions"—a court ceremony recorded in the inscription—was actually the most common occasion for the casting of a bronze vessel. Creel went on to describe the ceremony and noted also its significance for the existence of written records at the Zhou court:

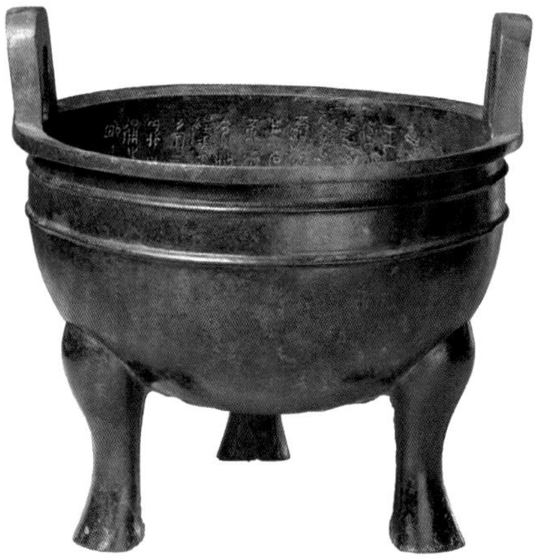

2a | *Song Tripod Cauldron* (*Song Ding*), Western Zhou dynasty (1046–771 BC). Bronze; h. 38.4 cm (15 1/8 in.); diam. of rim: 30.3 cm (11 15/16 in.). The Palace Museum, Beijing, GU77390.

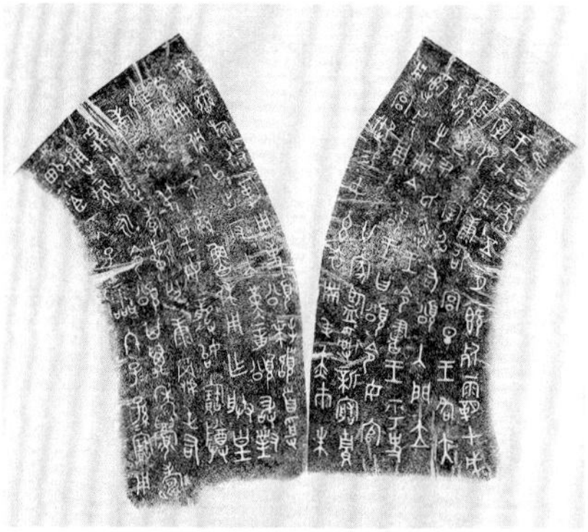

2b | Rubbing of the inscription on fig. 2a.

> It was the custom, when the king or, in some cases, other rulers gave land or other gifts to their vassals, to accompany the gift with a speech of presentation. Although this might be spoken, it was usually (in the case of presentations important enough to be commemorated by the casting of a vessel) written in advance by an official, and read aloud at the order of the ruler. At the conclusion of the ceremony this written document was handed to the recipient of the gift, who thrust it in his girdle and withdrew. The same ceremony is described in the *I Li* [*Yili*]. When the recipient cast a bronze he copied this document, verbatim, into its inscription, in a number of cases.[7]

As evidence of this practice, Creel cited the inscription on a vessel that just happens to be included in the present catalogue: the *Song Ding*, in the collection of the Palace Museum in Beijing (fig. 2a and pl. 59).[8] He did not provide a translation, but it is worth examining the vessel and its inscription in more detail.

The *Song Ding* is a typical late Western Zhou cauldron, with a hemispherical belly; three cabriole legs, known in the Chinese tradition as *mati* (horse-hoof legs); two inverted U-shaped handles (also known as ears) rising from a slightly everted rim; and two simple bowstrings running across the otherwise unadorned surface of the vessel. The inscription (see fig. 2b) contains 149 characters, which—as Creel noted earlier in his article—is longer than some of the shorter chapters of the *Shangshu* (Book of Documents), putatively the oldest of the Chinese classics.[9] It reads:

> It was the third year, fifth month, after the dying brightness, day 11 [*jiaxu*]; the king was at the Kang-Zhao Palace in Zhou. At dawn, the king entered the Grand Chamber and assumed position. Intendant Yin entered the gate to the right of Song and stood in the middle of the court. Master Yin received the king's command document. The king called out to Scribe Guo Sheng to record the command to Song.
>
> The king said: "Song, I command you to officiate over and supervise twenty warehouses in Chengzhou, and to oversee and supervise the newly constructed warehouses, and to use these for the palace supply. I award you a black jacket with embroidered hem, red kneepads, a scarlet jade-pendant, a pennant with jingle bells, and a bridle with bit and cheek pieces; use them to serve."
>
> Song bowed and touched his head to the ground, received the command, put the strips in his sash, and exited. He returned with a jade tablet. The text on the tablet read, "Song dares in response to extol the Son of Heaven's illustriously fine beneficence, herewith making for my august deceased-father Gong Shu and august mother Gong Si this treasured offertory cauldron with which to pursue filial piety, and to entreat and beseech vigorous joy, pure blessings, penetrating wealth, and an eternal mandate. May Song for ten thousand years be long lived, truly ministering to the Son of Heaven until a numinous end, and have descendants eternally to treasure and use this vessel.[10]

We can learn much from this inscription about the history of the period in which it was created. The date "third year, fifth month, after the dying brightness, *jiaxu*" corresponds to May 9, 825 BC. The Kang-Zhao Palace was located in the Zhou capital, at modern-day Xi'an, and was dedicated to a deceased Zhou king, King Zhao (r. 977–957 BC). Court ceremonies regularly featured an extensive cast of characters: here, the king and Song, the person receiving the king's command; Intendant Yin, Song's sponsor who is said to have entered at Song's right; a Master Yin, the head of the secretarial corps, who here serves as the master of ceremonies; and Guo Sheng, a *shi* (scribe or secretary), who wrote the command document in advance of the ceremony and read it out loud during the ceremony. We also learn some details about Song in particular: that he was put in charge of tax receipts in Chengzhou, the capital of the Zhou regions in the east; that his father and mother were both dead; and that the mother was descended from a family, Si, different from that of the Zhou royal family. However, perhaps the most important thing to learn from this inscription concerns the administration of the Zhou court. A court scribe prepared the *ming shu* (command document), copying it on bamboo strips, prior to the court ceremony, and presented it to Song at the conclusion of the ceremony. When Song subsequently cast this bronze vessel (and it is important to note that at the same time he cast at least three [and probably several more] *ding* cauldrons, six *gui* tureens, two *hu* vases, and at least one *pan* basin), he had them cast with the text of the command document, apparently "verbatim," as Creel put it.[11] This demonstrates that the bronze inscriptions that we now read were but copies of copies of documents that other evidence suggests were stored in an archive or archives at the Zhou court. Nevertheless, as Ouyang Xiu noted almost one thousand years ago, these tertiary copies have not been copied yet again and so appear to us very much as they did to Song when he first had these bronze vessels cast almost three thousand years ago. And even though Song left no other trace in the traditional historical record, we can use his inscriptions to learn at least a little about him and quite a bit about the time in which he lived.

NOTES

1 | See Ouyang Xiu, *Jigulu bawei* [Notes on a Record of Collecting Antiquity] in *Jinshi congshu* edition, 1.10a, concerning bronze inscriptions. He makes similar observations throughout his comments on stone stele inscriptions.

2 | For a fascinating account of Chen's time in Chicago, see Elinor Pearlstein, "Chen Mengjia: Chinese Bronzes, Western Collections, International Perspectives" (unpublished manuscript).

3 | Charles Fabens Kelley and Ch'en Meng-chia, *Chinese Bronzes from the Buckingham Collection* (Chicago: Art Institute of Chicago, 1946).

4 | Chen Mengjia, "Xi Zhou tongqi duandai [Periodization of Western Zhou Bronzes]," *Kaogu xuebao* [Journal of Archaeology] part 1 (1955/9): 137–75; part 2 (1955/10): 69–142; part 3, (1956/1): 65–114; part 4 (1956/2): 85–94; part 5 (1956/3): 105–27; and part 6 (1956/4): 85–122. In 1956, while these installments were being published, Chen was branded as a rightist in the first of the Communist purges;thereafter he was prohibited from publishing. It was not until the late 1970s, more thana decade after he committed suicide at the beginning of the Cultural Revolution, that his status was "rehabilitated." Finally, in 2004, these studies were republished in a sumptuous two-volume edition, together with thereto-fore unpublished notes for the succeeding sections. Not only does this edition contain studies of more than twice as many bronzes than the earlier *Kaogu xuebao* version, but it also includes sections on "History," "Geography," "Ritual," and "Vessel Shape and Ornamentation"; see Chen Mengjia, *Cheng Mengjia zhuzuoji: Xi Zhou tongqi duandai* [Collected Works of Chen Mengjia: Periodization of Western Zhou Bronzes] (Beijing: Zhonghua shuju, 2004). Other planned sections on "Paleography and Linguistics," "Land System and Social Economy," and "Chronology" were never written.

5 | It is not clear whether Chen and Creel ever met in Chicago. For the first two years of Chen's tenure in the city, Creel was in the United States Army, stationed in Washington, DC. After his release from the army, Creel remained in Washington, DC, during the 1946–47 academic year, doing research at the Library of Congress. He seems not to have returned to Chicago until September 1947, after Chen had already left for China. Chen and Creel certainly did meet at the Bicentennial Conference on Far Eastern Culture and Society held at Princeton University on April 1–3, 1947, and they also corresponded at least once.

6 | Herrlee G. Creel, "Bronze Inscriptions of the Western Chou Dynasty as Historical Documents," *Journal of the American Oriental Society* 56 (1936): 339.

7 | Ibid., 342.

8 | Actually, Creel's citation, to "*Chün Ku Lu Chin Wên*, 3 *hsia*. 4b" (i.e., *Jun gu lu jinwen*) seems to be to another version of the Song *ding* currently in the collection of the Shanghai Museum: Wu Shifen, *Jun gu lu jinwen* (N.p.: Wu Zhongxi, 1895), *juan* 3. The Palace Museum version is given on the following page of the catalogue to which Creel referred.

9 | Creel, "Bronze Inscriptions of the Western Chou Dynasty as Historical Documents," 342.

10 | Translation is author's own.

11 | Creel, "Bronze Inscriptions of the Western Chou Dynasty as Historical Documents," 342.

FIGURING THINGS: EARLY SCHOLARSHIP ON CHINESE BRONZES

JEFFREY MOSER

This exhibition catalogue is heir to one of the longest uninterrupted traditions of scholarship in world history. The techniques used to represent ancient bronzes in these pages—their nomenclature and typology, the visualization of the inscriptions on their surfaces, even the angles from which they are photographed—derive in large measure from methods of antiquarian scholarship and representation that date back to the eleventh-century heyday of the Northern Song dynasty (960–1127). Chinese literati of the eleventh century produced the first systematic treatises on ancient ritual bronzes, and they articulated their scholarship in the form of illustrated catalogues that are not, at least structurally speaking, radically dissimilar from the art catalogues of modern museums.

Most of these early catalogues are lost. *Kaogutu* (Illustrated Investigations of Antiquity), by the famous literatus, collector, and painter Li Gonglin, is known only from excerpts preserved in the antiquarian writings of Li's contemporaries;[1] all that survives of Liu Chang's once-influential *Xian Qin guqi ji* (Record of Ancient Vessels of the Pre-Qin Era, c. 1060) is its preface.[2] The earliest work on early bronzes to survive in its entirety is Lü Dalin's *Kaogutu* (1092), which shares the same name and frequently cites Li Gonglin's aforementioned catalogue, while simultaneously articulating Lü Dalin's distinctive understanding of ancient bronzes as catalysts for contemporary moral self-cultivation (see Tao Wang's essay "Lost Archaeology" in this catalogue, 85–99).[3] It features illustrated entries on more than two hundred bronzes that Lü examined and selected from the collections of over forty individuals and institutions.

The other major Northern Song catalogue of bronzes to survive is the *Chongxiu Xuanhe bogutu* (Illustrated Antiquities from the Xuanhe Hall, Revised; after 1123), often shortened to *Bogutu*. Unlike *Kaogutu*, which was compiled by a single individual as a private scholarly endeavor, this latter catalogue was an imperial project conducted at court under the auspices of Emperor Huizong (r. 1101–1126), one of the most famous patrons of the arts in all of Chinese history. Written by a team of scholars, *Bogutu* was the culmination of years of research on Huizong's enormous collection of ancient bronzes, which at its height is estimated to have included more than six thousand discrete objects.[4] *Bogutu* features just over eight hundred of them.[5]

Both catalogues were first printed in the Song dynasty, reprinted multiple times over the course of the Yuan (1271–1368) and Ming (1368–1644) dynasties, and ultimately transmitted down to the scholars of the Qing (1644–1911) court, whose research is examined in the next section in the present publication. The earliest surviving editions of the two catalogues date to 1299 and 1308–11, respectively.[6] The layout, treatment of text, and quality and detail of illustrations varies in small but significant ways from one edition to the next (see figs. 1 and 2). Bibliographic evidence suggests that the recension preserved in the eighteenth-century *Siku quanshu* (Complete Library of Four Treasures) edition of *Kaogutu* most closely approximates the essential conventions of Northern Song antiquarian representation.[7]

The page illustrated here (fig. 3) represents a typical entry, on a vessel similar to the ewer (*yi*) of Marquis Qi (see pl. 47). The first page features an illustration of the object. The elevated perspective, just left of center, reveals the complete contour of the vessel's rim and conveys the broad spacing

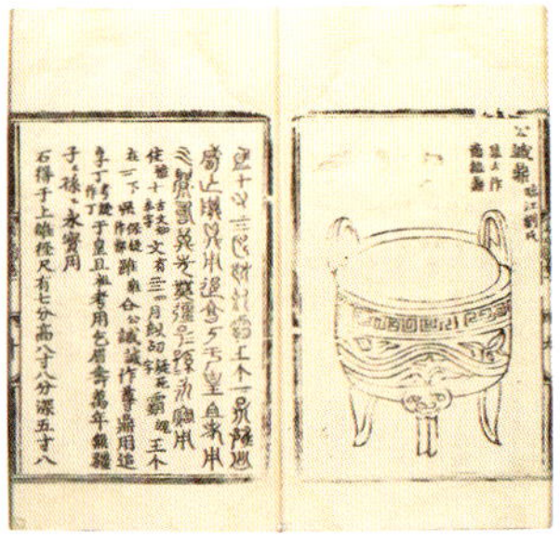

1 | Illustration of the *Gong Cheng Ding* (Ding of Duke Cheng) in the 1299 edition of Lü Dalin's *Kaogutu*, collated by Luo Gengweng. Harvard-Yenching Library, Cambridge, Massachusetts.

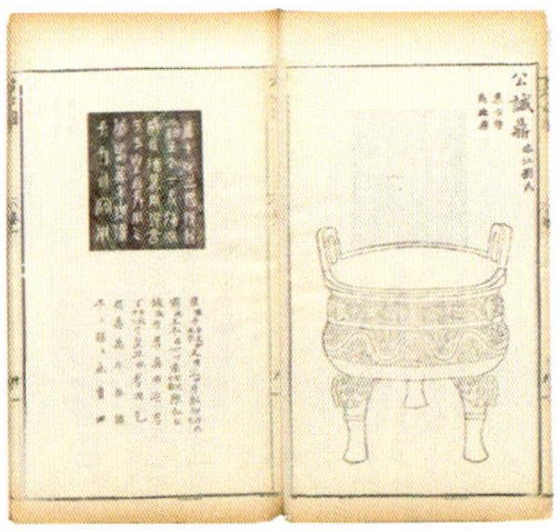

2 | Illustration of the *Gong Cheng Ding* (Ding of Duke Cheng) in the 1752 Yizhengtang Printing House edition of Lü Dalin's *Kaogutu*. Harvard-Yenching Library, Cambridge, Massachusetts.

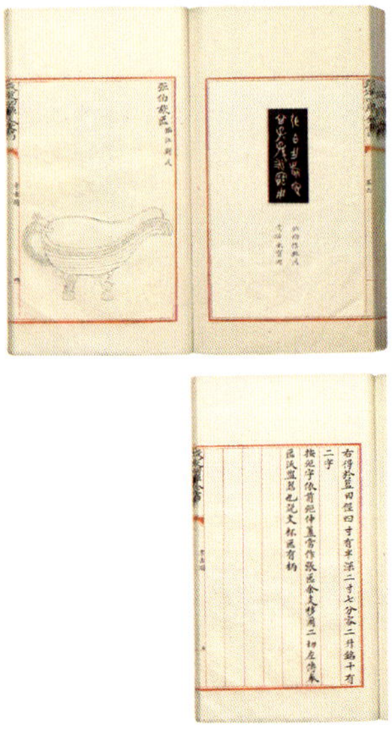

3 | Entry for the *Ju Bo Luyi* (Ranked *yi* vessel of Count Ju, collection of Liu Chang of Linjiang) in Lü Dalin's *Kaogutu*. National Palace Museum, Taipei.

of its four legs. The desire for legibility clearly trumped the commitment to unified perspective, as the head of the creature at the junction between the handle and the rim is shown from an alternate angle, right of center, presumably to distinguish the creature's two horns from one another. The fine lines of the monochrome illustration clearly delineate the decoration while eliding all traces of the vessel's age: there is no suggestion of color, patina, or corrosion. The inscription in the upper-right corner of the page identifies the vessel as the *Ranked Yi of Count Ju*. The smaller four characters below identify the vessel as belonging to the aforementioned Northern Song scholar Liu Chang.

The second page features a hand-drawn copy of the vessel's inscription, the white-on-black lettering evoking the rubbing on which it was presumably based. Immediately below is a transcription of the archaic logographs of the inscription into standard script. The contents of the inscription are highly conventional: *Count Ju made this* yi *for placement* [on his altar]. *May his descendants use it reverently for all time.*

The text on the final page provides the artifact's dimensions and place of discovery, and identifies the number of characters in its inscription. It then uses the orthography and semantics of the inscription to decipher a problematic character in one of the previous inscriptions in the catalogue. Next it proceeds to identify the pronunciation of the fourth character in the vessel's inscription—*yi*—which identifies the typological category to which the vessel belongs. It closes with citations from two classical sources that confirm the identification of the vessel as an *yi* and suggest its original function. A passage from the *Zuozhuan* (Zuo Commentaries) indicates that "the *yi* is a vessel for pouring water for washing," while a reference from *Shuowen jiezi* (Explanation of Graphs and Explication of Characters; hereafter *Shuowen*) explains that "*yi* vessels are cups with handles."

The entry on the *yi* highlights the primary methods and concerns of Northern Song bronze scholarship. Illustrations were more diagrammatic than representational, more focused on conveying the vessel's structural features, proportions, and decorative patterning than expressing how they appeared to the eye. Dimensions mattered, but they were conveyed by text rather than by picture. Considerable attention was dedicated to epigraphy and paleography—both the semantic content of the inscription and the forms of the logographs used to write it.

Although some entries on bronzes with particularly lengthy inscriptions associated with known historical figures offer extensive disquisitions on the history of the vessel, in most cases the particular story of the vessel as a unique historical artifact was less important than the identification of the type to which the vessel belongs. Song cataloguing was, first and foremost, a matter of grouping vessels into generic categories that could be correlated with individual, known logographs in the classical canons of Confucian ritual. It was a matter of determining which vessels were *ding*, which were *zun*, which were *yi*, and so on. The diagrammatic quality of the illustrations, their tendency to reduce the experiential totality of the bronze to a series of nameable forms and features, reinforced this "categorical imperative." The notion of the ancient bronze as a unique, irreproducible, and coherent thing-in-itself, colored and worn by the ravages of time, did not, by and large, absorb the imagination of Song antiquarian cataloguers to the extent that it fascinates modern collectors.

Because later scholars not only used Northern Song bronze catalogues as resources for information on specific bronzes, but also adopted the

catalogues' broader taxonomies and representational methods, there has been a tendency for historians of Chinese archaeology, art history, epigraphy, and other modern disciplines to interpret these catalogues through reference to the influence that they exerted on later scholarship. The desire of modern disciplines to trace their intellectual genealogy encourages readings of earlier texts on the basis of what they came to mean later. Over the course of the past two decades, the burgeoning literature on Song antiquarianism has increasingly come to recognize such retrospective interpretations as anachronistic and has endeavored to resituate Song bronze catalogues in the intellectual milieu of their own day. The balance of this essay aims to synthesize current understandings of how this wider world of Northern Song thought facilitated the emergence of the illustrated antiquities catalogue as a new genre of scholarship.[8]

From its inception in the mid-tenth century, the Northern Song dynasty witnessed intense and sustained debate over fundamental moral and aesthetic values. Over the course of the first half of the eleventh century, those who claimed allegiance to the so-called *guwen* (ancient style) tradition of Han Yu gradually came to dominate the intellectual landscape.[9] These scholars, who included among their ranks most of those who wrote about ancient bronzes, attempted to interpret the Confucian classics in ways that were fundamentally extratextual, in that they relied on sources external to the classic text and received commentaries to establish its meaning. In some cases, these external referents were a priori principles that Song scholars regarded as having preceded the classics and informed the sages who compiled them.[10] In other cases, they were physical entities manifest in the phenomenal world, such as geographic features, plants and animals, and historical artifacts. This interest in external verification extended to the reception of other, noncanonical texts, traditions, legends, and stories of all sorts.[11] On the whole, Song scholars endeavored to substantiate what they read in the ground of their lived experience.

Interest in extratextual verification brought two previously distinct domains of scholarship—lexicography and ritual studies—into dialogue with one another. Since the compilation of China's oldest comprehensive dictionary, *Shuowen*, in the second century AD, one of the primary aims of Chinese lexicography was the correlation of contemporary with archaic scripts. In his postface to *Shuowen*, the compiler Xu Shen explains his attempt to recover the *guwen* (here, Old Script) and *dazhuan* (Greater Formal Script) of the ancient Zhou by tracing its transmission through the diverse scripts of the *zhuhou* (feudal lords), the eight scripts of the Qin, and the orthographic corruptions of the Wang Mang interregnum. He notes that in addition to the various transmitted collections of these scripts, he also consulted the inscriptions of "ritual vessels found in the wilderness."[12] The editing and republication of *Shuowen* by the brothers Xu Kai and Xu Xuan in the early Song sparked renewed interest in the variant orthographies of bronze inscriptions.[13] Scholars like Liu Chang attempted to correlate the characters found in newly discovered inscriptions with those known from *Shuowen*.

Since the canonization of the *Sanli* (Three Ritual Classics)—*Liji* (Notes on Rites), *Yili* (Book of Rites), and the *Zhouli* (Rites of Zhou)—in the commentaries of the late Han scholar Zheng Xuan, scholars had endeavored to identify the myriad vestments, offertory vessels, and other ceremonial implements named in the texts. Although the *Sanli* were understood as a blueprint for the practice of ritual at the ancient Zhou court, they offered little concrete description. They made it clear that vessels with names like *ding*, *zun*, and *yi* were important for the effective performance of ritual, but failed to explain what these vessels were supposed to look like or how they were to be made. This paucity of description sparked centuries of elaborate exegetical attempts to give shape to these names with illustrations and dimensions. Song literati understood this commentarial tradition principally through the scholarship of Nie Chongyi, who submitted an authoritative digest of earlier exegeses known as *Sanlitu* (Illustrations of the Three Ritual Classics) to the newly established Song court in 961.[14]

As scholars deciphered the inscriptions of ancient bronzes, they discovered that these inscriptions included typological names. An antiquarian like Liu Chang could recognize the four-footed bronze pitcher in his collection as an *yi* because it called itself an *yi*. But more importantly, the presence of these names on the surface of a material object established a direct, verifiable connection between a classical name and a manifest, apprehensible thing. As soon as scholars began comparing the bronzes with inscribed names to pictures with the same names in *Sanlitu*, they realized Nie Chongyi's reconstructions were based on assumptions that had very little to do with the actual material practices of ritual in antiquity.[15] This realization sparked wide-ranging efforts to rethink the way names in the classics were related to forms in the phenomenal world. It endorsed the extratextual logic of Song classicism, and facilitated the recalibration of Confucian hermeneutics more generally.[16]

Under Emperor Huizong, efforts were made to mobilize the results of Northern Song bronze scholarship to develop new templates for the manufacture and use of ritual implements that were, at least superficially, more consistent

with ancient forms than those promulgated by earlier Song emperors.[17] The Dasheng bell illustrated in this catalogue (pl. 56) is one example of the physically-verified archaism that dominated the material culture of Confucian ritual in the wake of Huizong's ritual reforms.

In sum, the introduction of new graphs into the lexicography of known scripts facilitated the introduction of new objects into the taxonomy of legible things. Deciphering made the physical traces of antiquity nameable, and thus knowable. It expanded the repertoire of sources that scholars could call upon to make sense of the ancient past and inspired new approaches to the persistent challenge of emulating the normative order of antiquity in the novel circumstances of the present.

The compilation, printing, and dissemination of antiquarian catalogues in the Song also preserved a tremendous amount of information that is unlikely to have survived otherwise. Because bronze is a liquid asset that is easily melted down and transformed into coin, statuary, tools, and weapons, bronze objects are more vulnerable than things made from less readily reusable materials like pottery and stone. The fact that East Asian currency regimes before the twentieth century were predominantly copper-based made bronze vessels especially prone to predation. Ultimately, excavation of bronzes from their earthen graves dramatically shortened their lifespans. With but one or two possible exceptions, none of the nearly one thousand bronzes recorded in the catalogues of the Northern Song survives to this day.[18] Thus the Song passion for collecting bronzes simultaneously preserved and imperiled the material record of China's ancient past.

NOTES

1 | Robert Harrist, "The Artist as Antiquarian: Li Gonglin and His Study of Early Chinese Art," *Artibus Asiae* 55:3/4 (1995): 237–80.

2 | Liu Chang, "Xian Qin guqi ji" [Record of Ancient Vessels of the Pre-Qin Era] in Zeng Zaozhuang and Liu Lin, eds., *Quan Song wen* [Complete Writings of the Song Dynasty], vol. 59 (Shanghai: Shanghai cishu chubanshe, 2006), 363.

3 | Jeffrey Moser, "The Ethics of Immutable Things: Interpreting Lü Dalin's *Illustrated Investigations of Antiquity*," *Harvard Journal of Asiatic Studies* 72:2 (2012): 259–93.

4 | Ya-hwei Hsu (Xu Yahui), "Antiquities, Ritual Reform, and the Shaping of New Taste at Huizong's Court," *Artibus Asiae* 73:1 (2013): 144.

5 | For a thorough discussion of bronze collecting and cataloguing under Emperor Huizong, see Patricia Ebrey, *Accumulating Culture: The Collections of Emperor Huizong* (Seattle: University of Washington Press, 2008), 150–203.

6 | On the publication history of the two catalogues, see Hsu Ya-hwei (Xu Yahui), "Zhida chongxiu Xuanhe bogu tulu de banyin tedian yu liuchuan" [The Characteristics and Transmission of Recension of the Zhida-Era Edition of Illustrated Antiquities from Xuanhe Hall, Revised], *Gujin lunheng* [Inquisitions on the Past and Present] 18 (October 2008): 76–96; and "Reshaping Chinese Material Culture: The Revival of Antiquity in the Era of Print, 960–1279" (PhD diss., Yale University, 2010), 275–84.

7 | Moser, "Ethics of Immutable Things," 261n4.

8 | In addition to the aforementioned studies, some of the most important recent work on Song antiquarianism includes Chen Fangmei, "Song guqiwuxue de xingqi yu Song fanggu tongqi" [The Rise of Song Antiquarianism and the Imitation of Archaic Bronzes], *Meishushi yanjiu jikan* [Taida Journal of Art History] 10 (2001): 37–160; "Zhui sandai yu dingyi zhi jian—Songren de cong 'kaogu' dao 'wangu' de zhuanbian" [Seeking the Three Dynasties Among the Ritual Vessels of Old: The Song Dynasty Move from "Investigating Antiquity" to "Appreciating Antiquity"], *Gugong xueshu jikan* [National Palace Museum Research Quarterly] 23:1 (2005), 267–332; Christian de Pee, *The Writing of Weddings in Middle-Period China* (Albany: State University of New York Press, 2007), 21–87; and Yun-chiahn Sena, "Pursuing Antiquity: Chinese Antiquarianism from the Tenth to the Thirteenth Century" (PhD diss., University of Chicago, 2007). For an overview of the history of scholarship on Song antiquarianism, see Xu Yahui, "Guanyu Songdai guwuxue zhi yanjiu yu taolun" [Review of Studies on Song Antiquarianism], *Zhongguo shixue* [Studies in Chinese History] 21 (2011): 67–77.

9 | See Peter K. Bol, *This Culture of Ours: Intellectual Transitions in T'ang and Sung China* (Stanford: Stanford University Press, 1992), 148–211.

10 | Ibid.

11 | One of the best known exemplars of this empirical tendency is the polymath Shen Gua. See Ya Zuo, "Capricious Destiny: Shen Gua (1031–1085) and His Age" (PhD diss., Princeton University, 2011), 287–91.

12 | For a translation of Xu Shen's postface and an up-to-date summary of scholarship on the *Shuowen jiezi*, see Timothy O'Neill, "Xu Shen's Scholarly Agenda: A New Interpretation of the Postface of the *Shuowen jiezi*," *Journal of the American Oriental Society* 133: 3 (Summer 2013): 413–40.

13 | William G. Boltz, "Shuo wen chieh tzu," in Michael Loewe, ed., *Early Chinese Texts: A Bibliographical Guide* (Berkeley: Society for the Study of Early China, 1993): 435–36.

14 | François Louis, *Design by the Book: Chinese Ritual Objects and the "Sanli tu"* (New York: Bard Graduate Center, 2016).

15 | Chen, "Song guqiwuxue de xingqi," 48.

16 | De Pee, *Writing of Weddings*, 21–87.

17 | The literature on Huizong's ritual reforms is legion. A recent discussion, with thorough references to earlier scholarship on the subject, is Hsu, "Antiquities, Ritual Reform, and the Shaping of New Taste at Huizong's Court," 137–80.

18 | Ebrey, *Accumulating Culture*, 152.

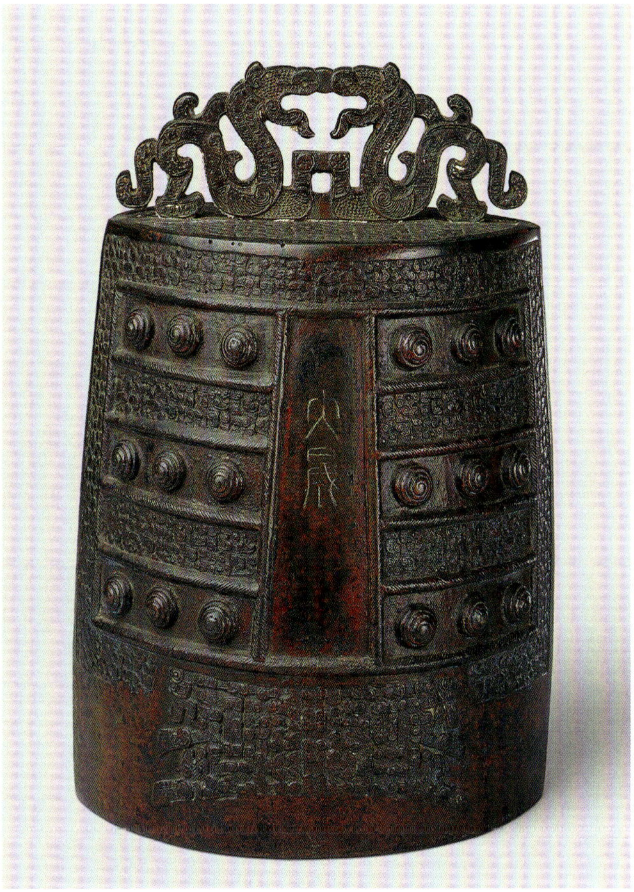

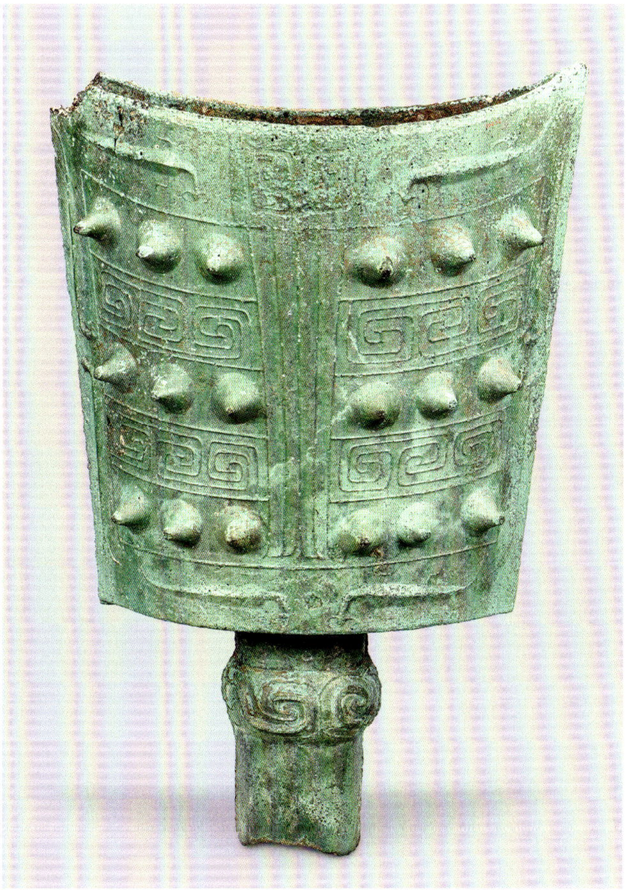

56 | *BO* BELL OF GREAT SPLENDOR (*DASHENG BOZHONG*), Northern Song dynasty (960–1127)

57 | BELL (*NAO*), Zhou period (c. 10th–7th century BC)

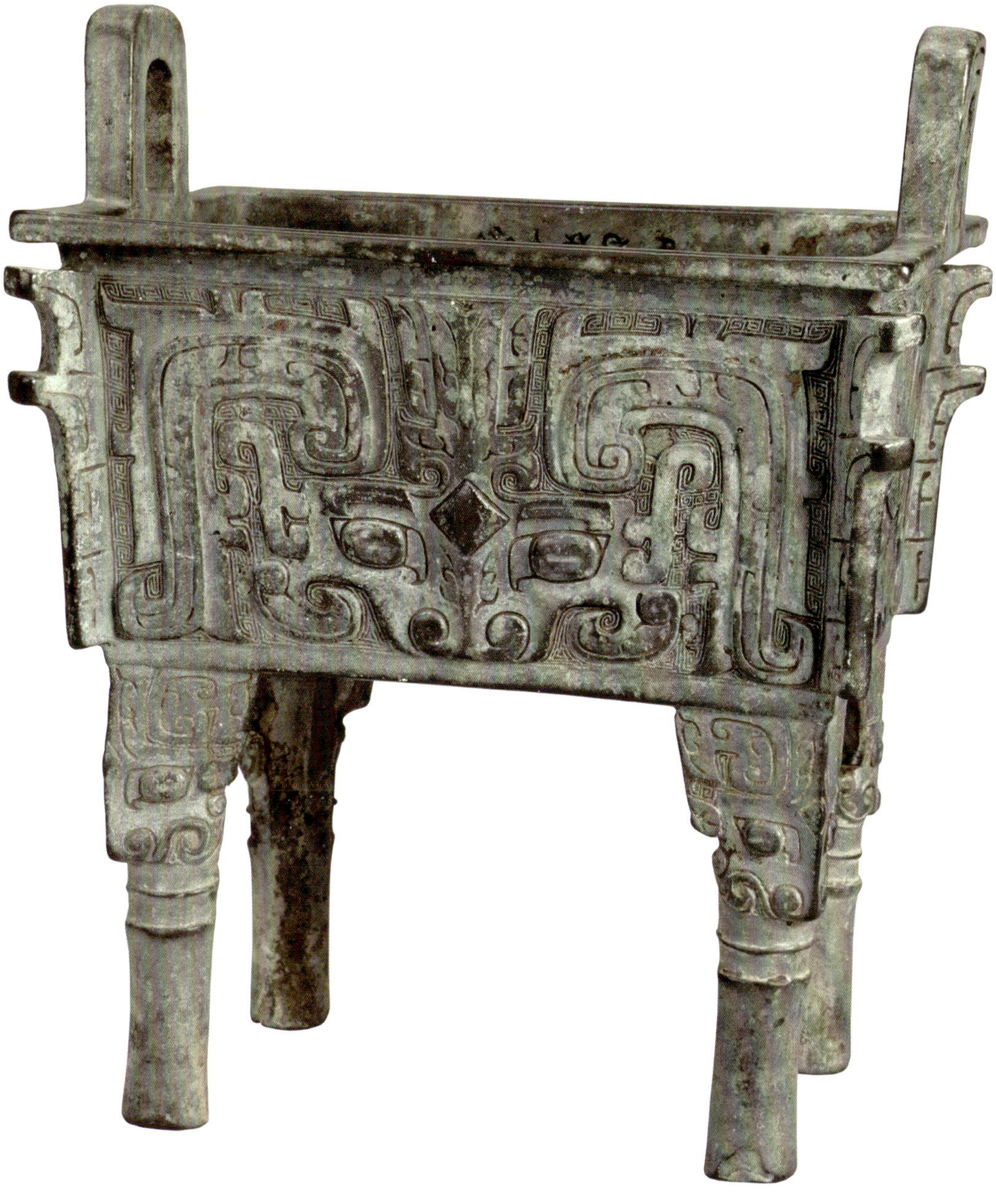

58 | RECTANGULAR CAULDRON OF HOU CHUO (*HOU CHUO FANGDING*), Western Zhou dynasty (1046–771 BC)

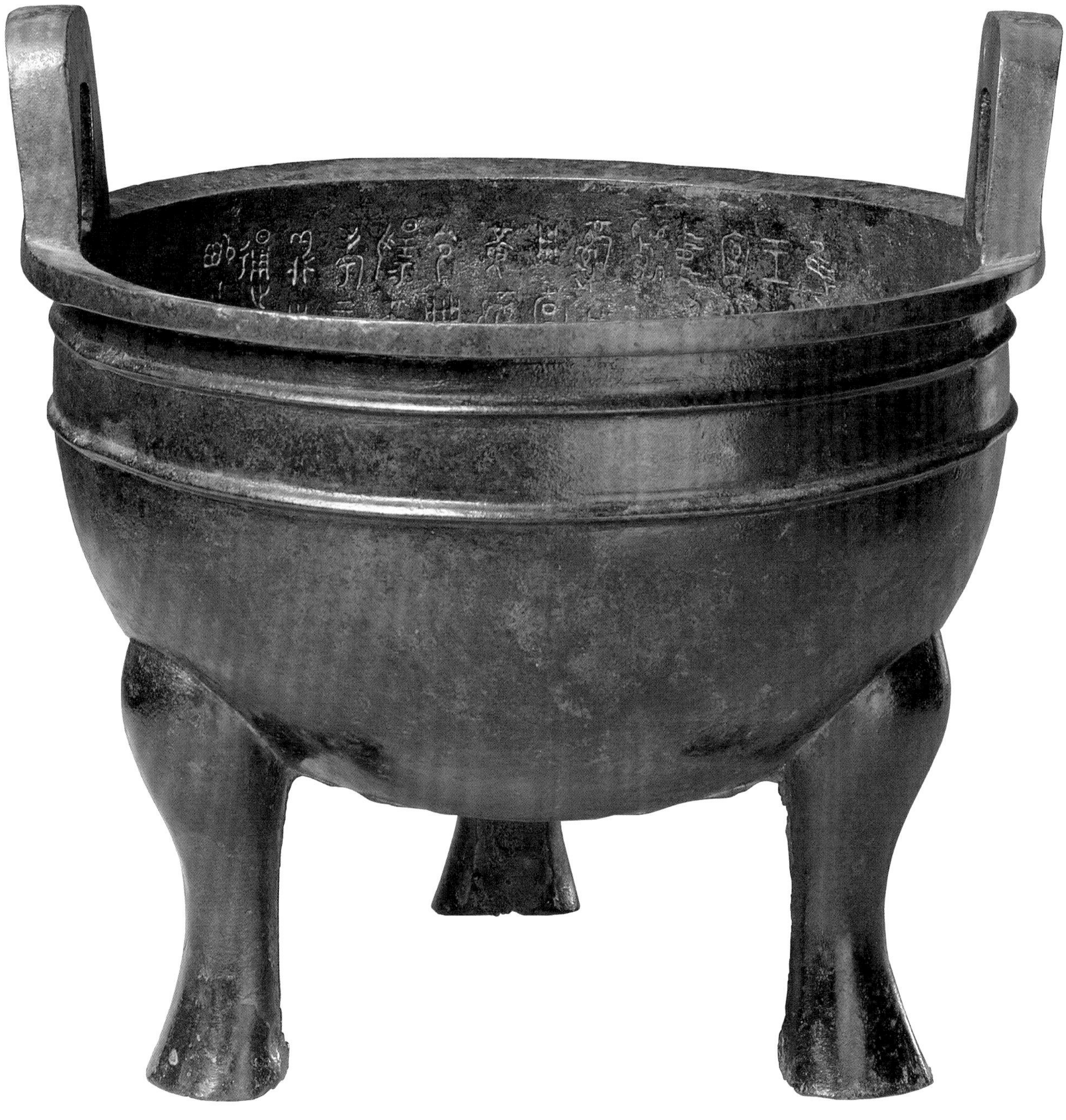

59 | TRIPOD CAULDRON OF SONG (*SONG DING*), Western Zhou dynasty (1046–771 BC)

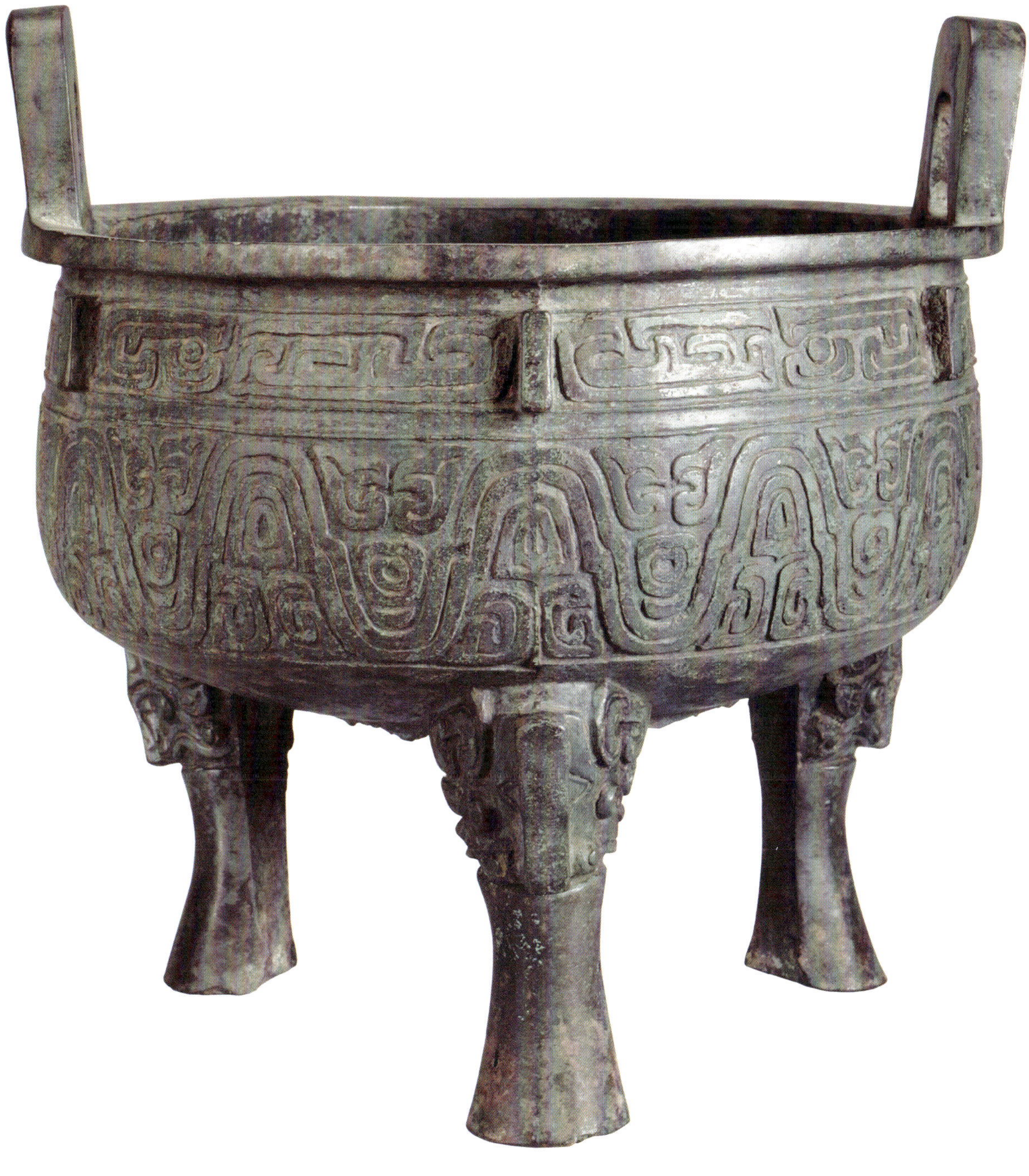

60 | TRIPOD CAULDRON OF SCRIBE SONG (*SHI SONG DING*), Western Zhou dynasty (1046–771 BC)

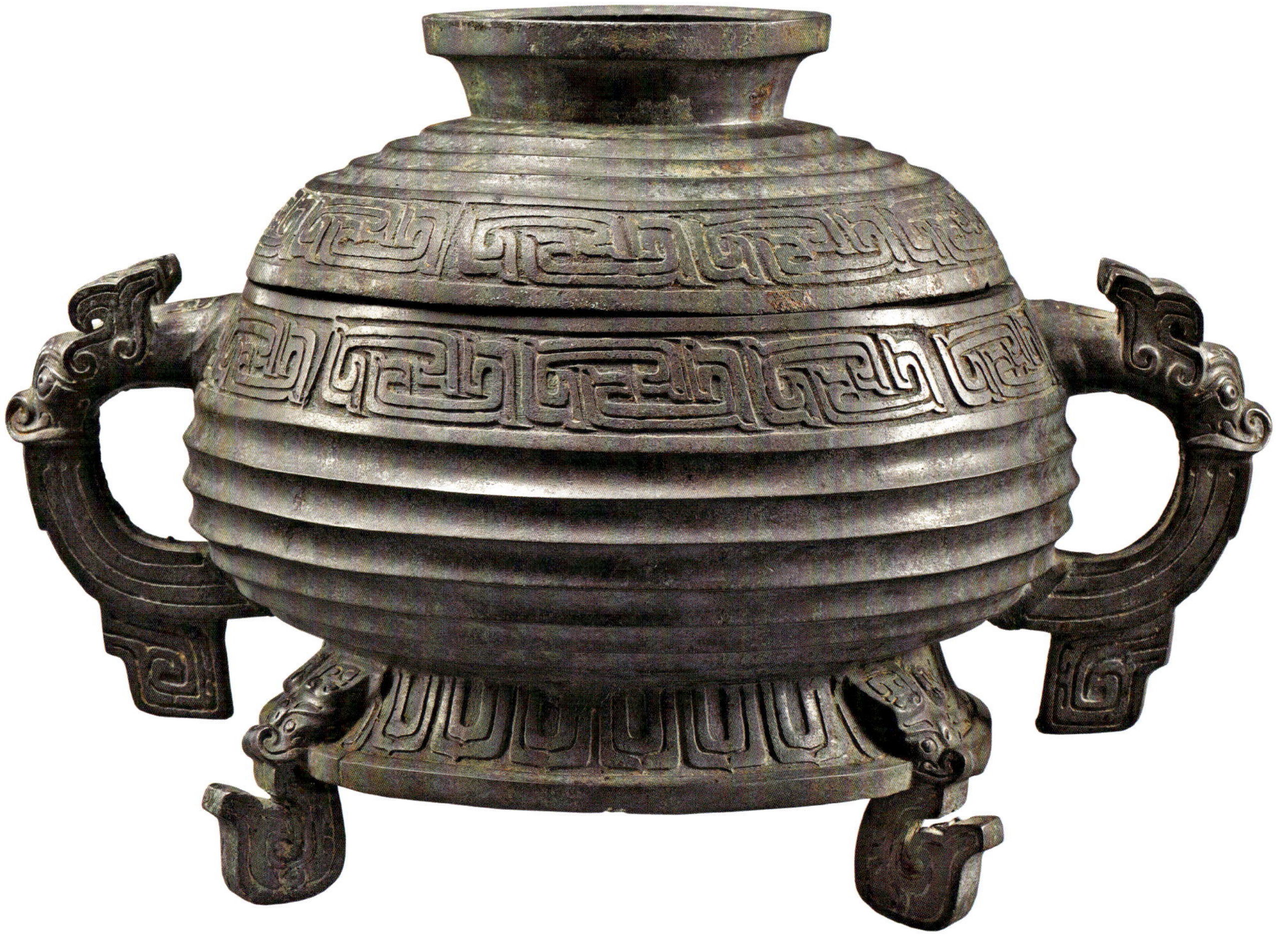

61 | TUREEN OF SCRIBE SONG (*SHI SONG GUI*), Western Zhou dynasty (1046–771 BC)

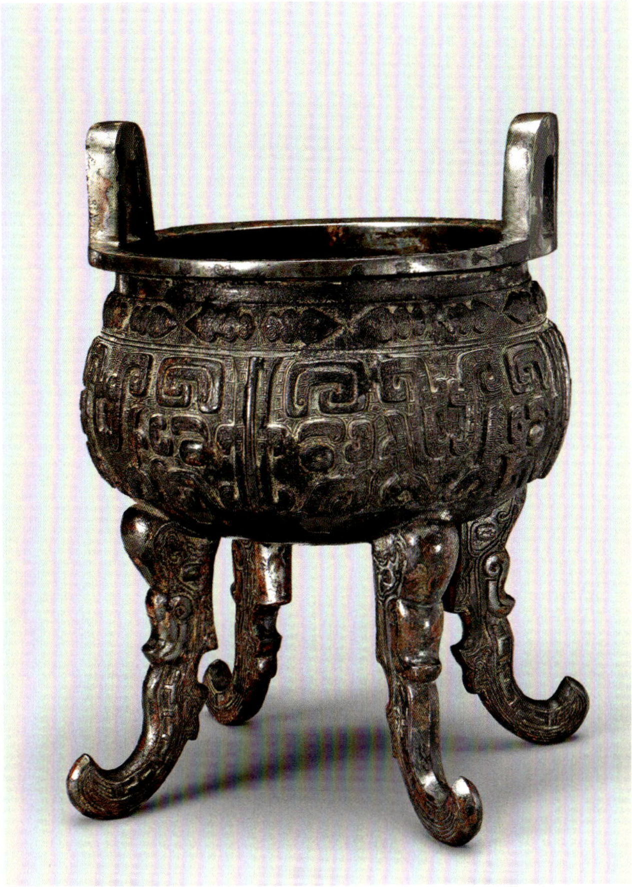 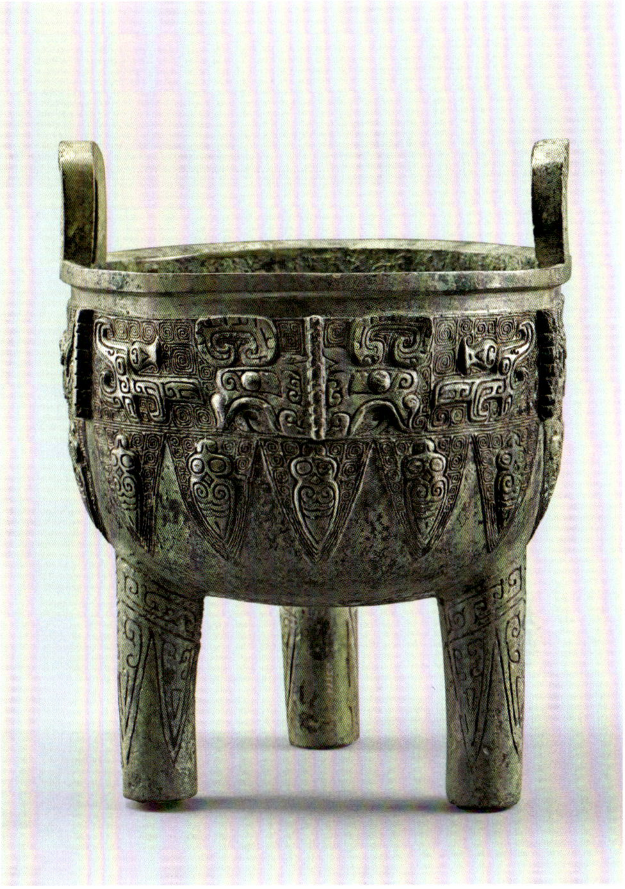

62 | CAULDRON MADE IN THE NINTH YEAR OF EMPEROR CHONGZHEN'S REIGN IN THE STATE OF LU (*CHONGZHEN JIUNIAN DING*), Ming dynasty (1368–1644), Chongzhen reign (1628–44), 1636

63 | TRIPOD CAULDRON OF SHE NÜ (*SHE NÜ DING*), late Shang dynasty (c. 1250–1046 BC)

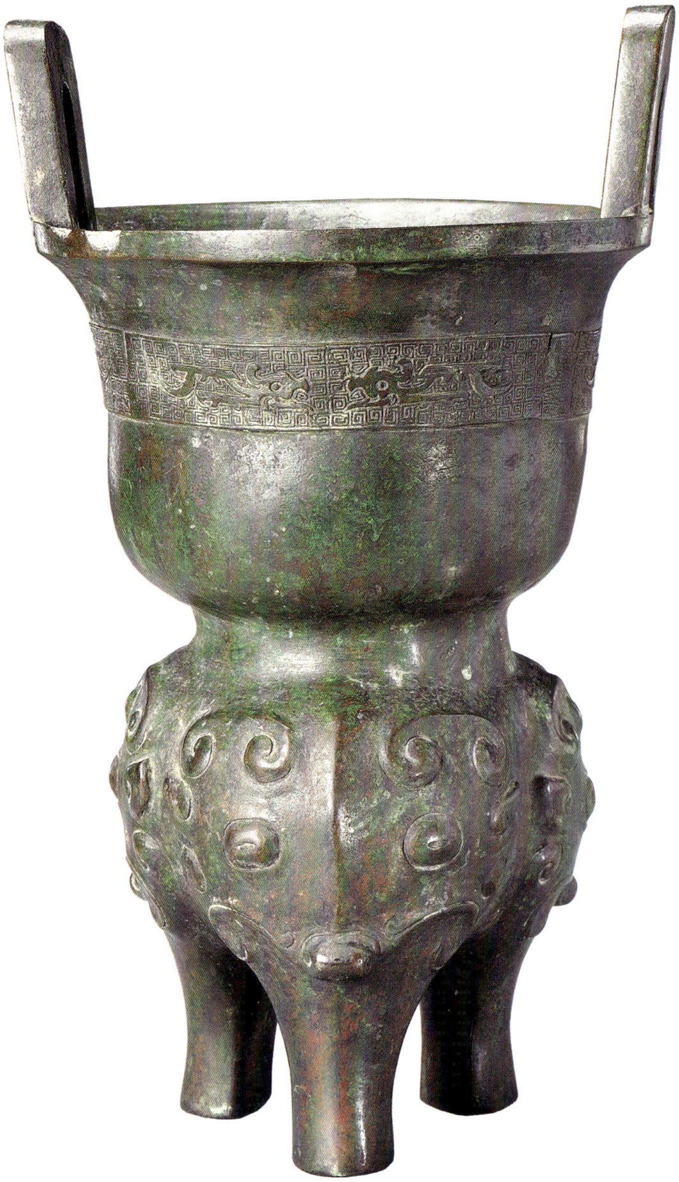

64 | STEAMER (*YAN*), Ming dynasty (1368–1644)

65 | STEAMER (*YAN*), late Shang dynasty (c. 1250–1046 BC)

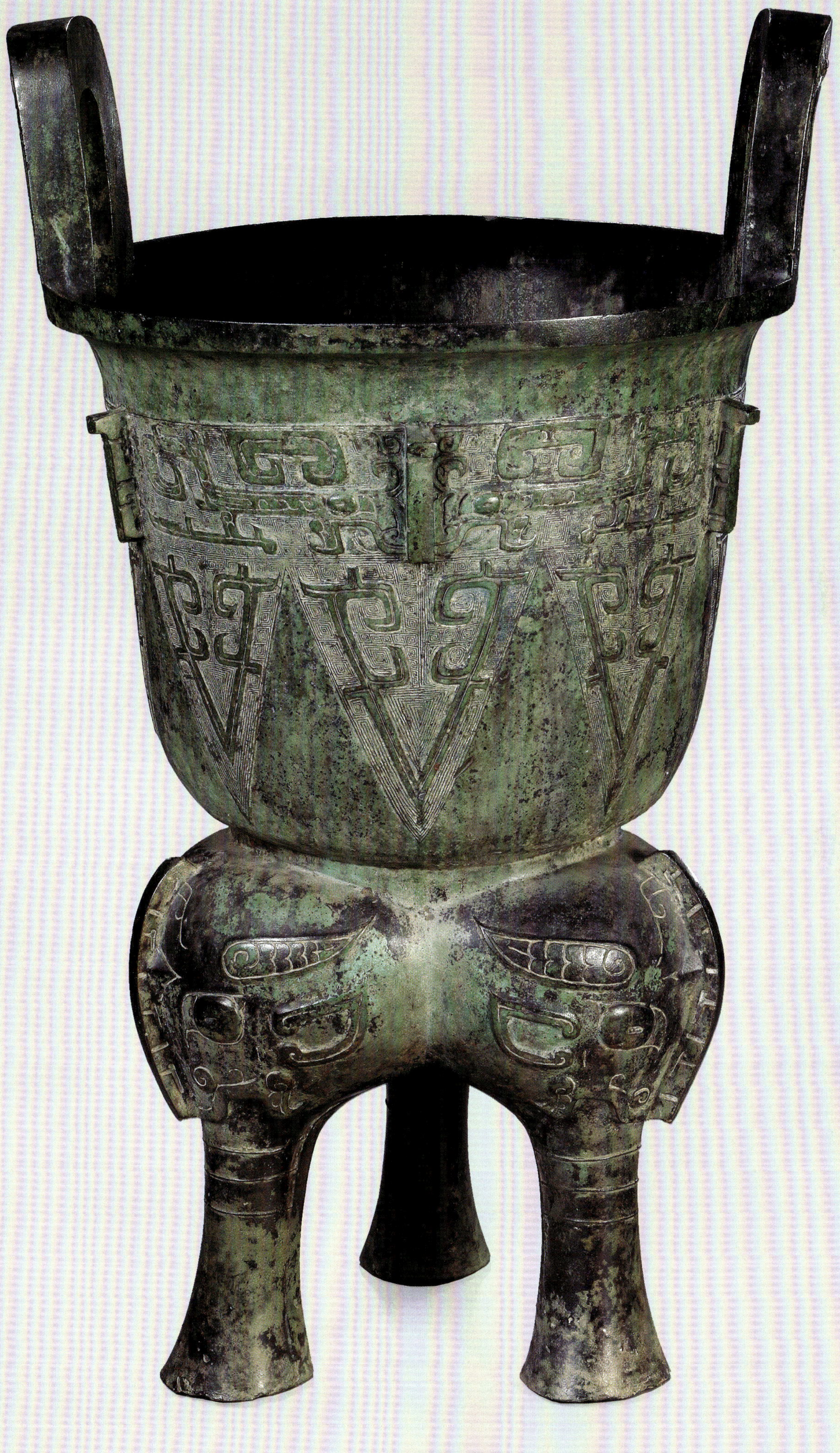

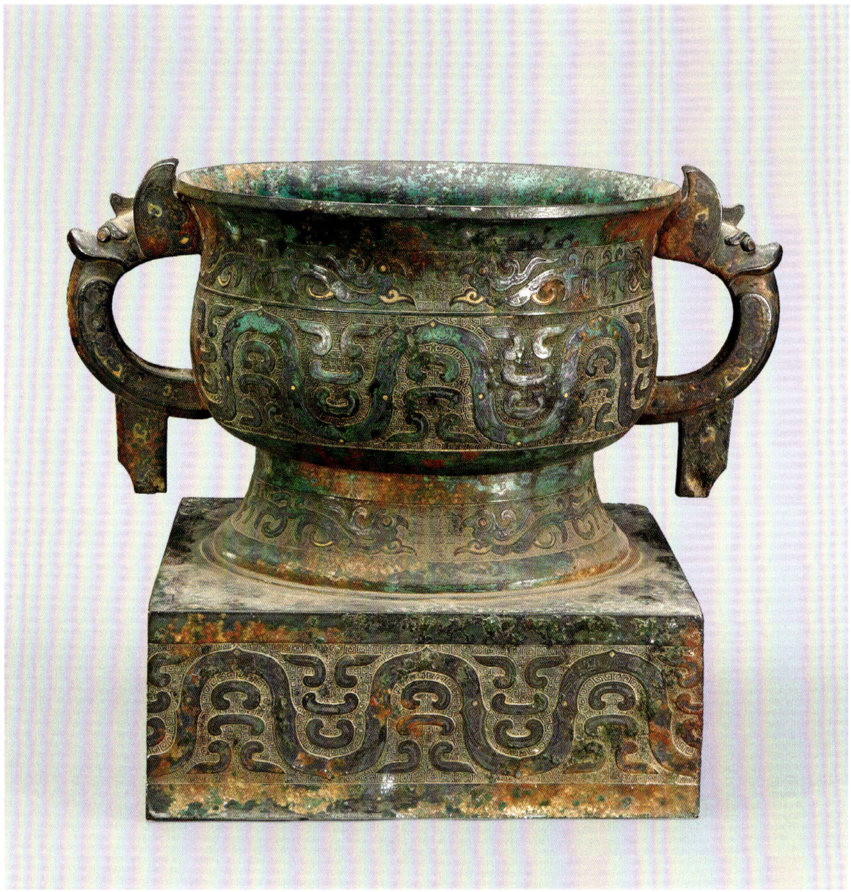

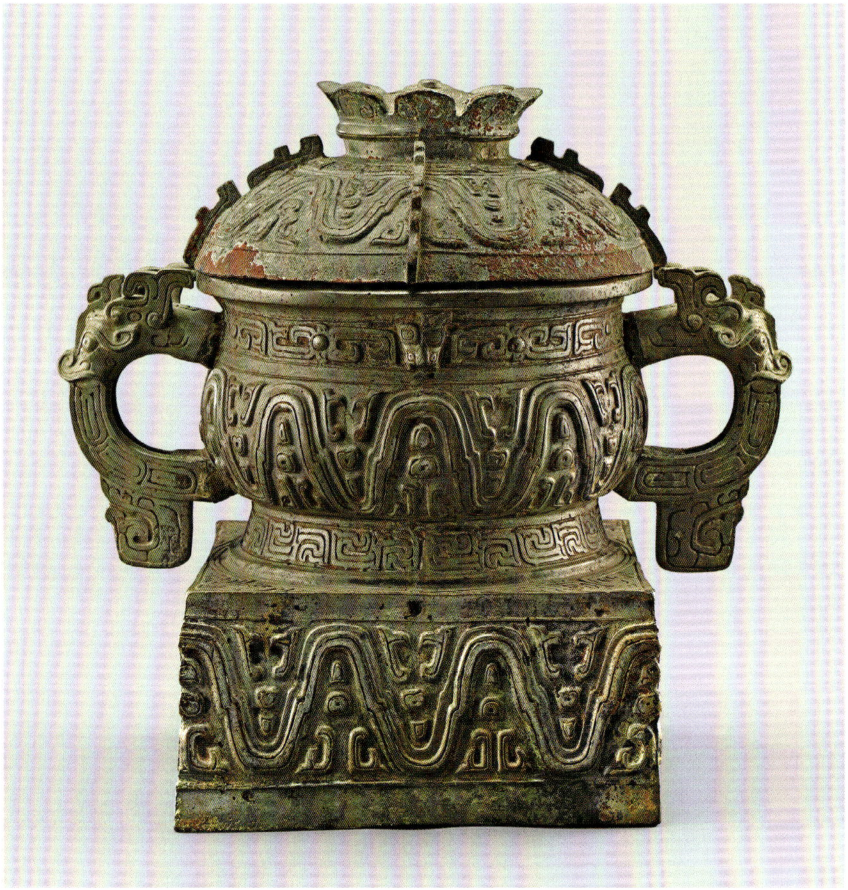

66 | TUREEN WITH SQUARE PEDESTAL (*GUI*), Song dynasty (960–1279)

67 | PEDESTALED TUREEN OF HU (*HU GUI*), Western Zhou dynasty (1046–771 BC)

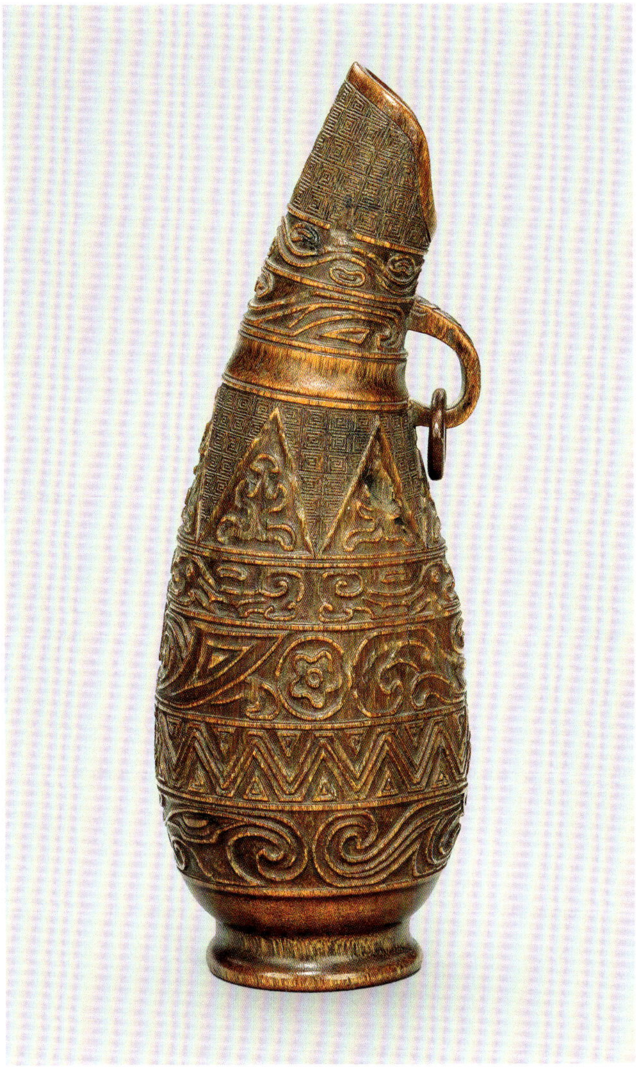

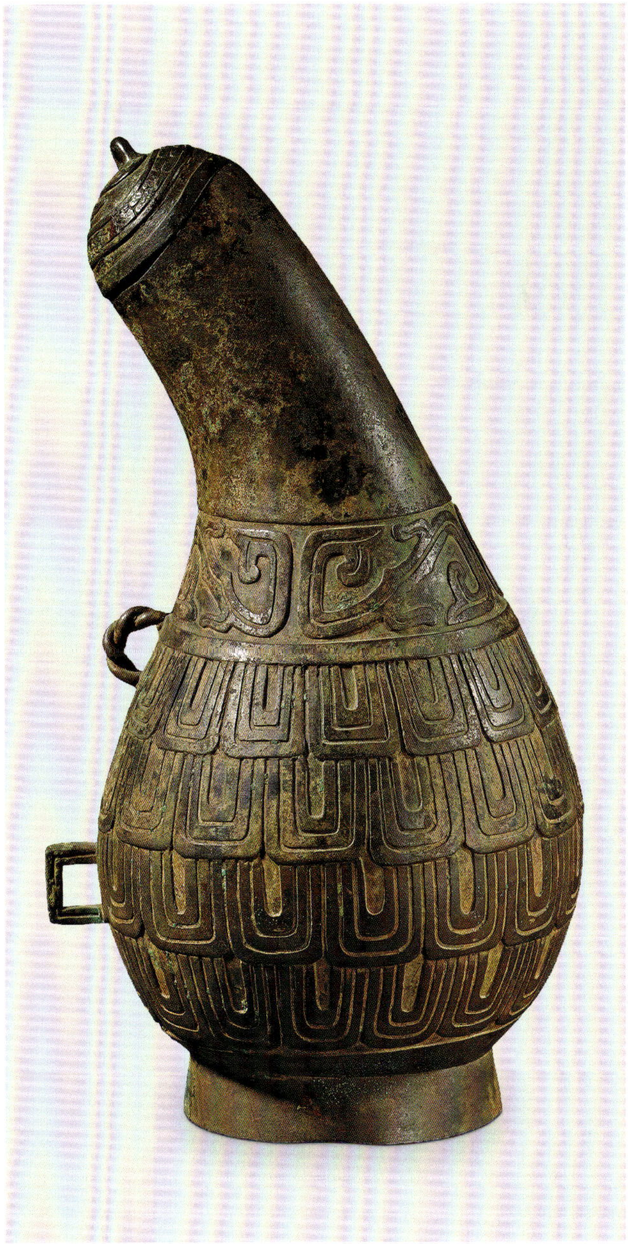

68 | MINIATURE BOTTLE IN THE FORM OF AN ANCIENT BRONZE JAR (*HU*), Ming dynasty (1368–1644)

69 | GOURD-SHAPED JAR (*HU*), Spring and Autumn period (770–476 BC)

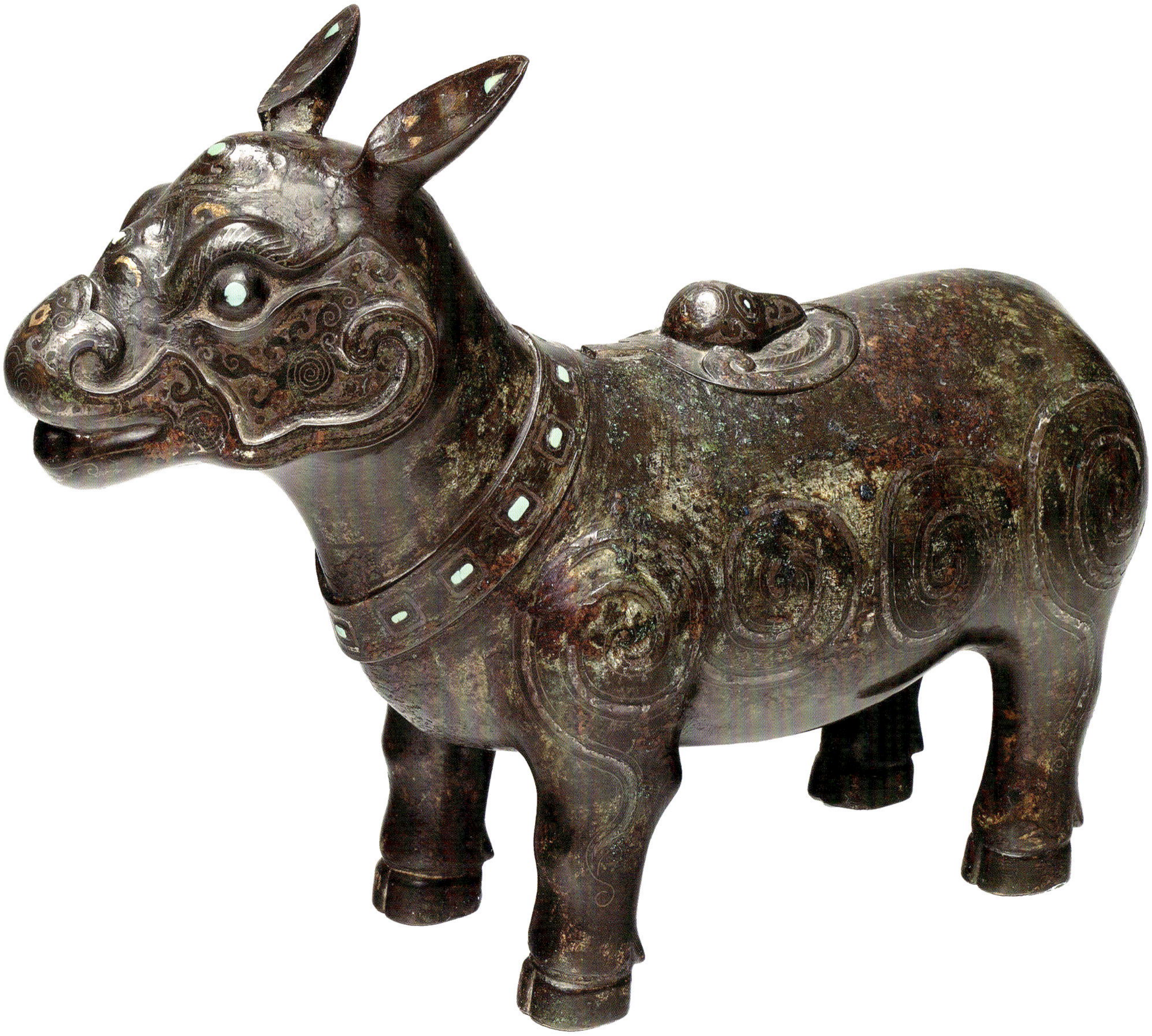

70 | TAPIR-SHAPED CONTAINER (*XI ZUN*), Song dynasty (960–1279) or Ming dynasty (1368–1644)

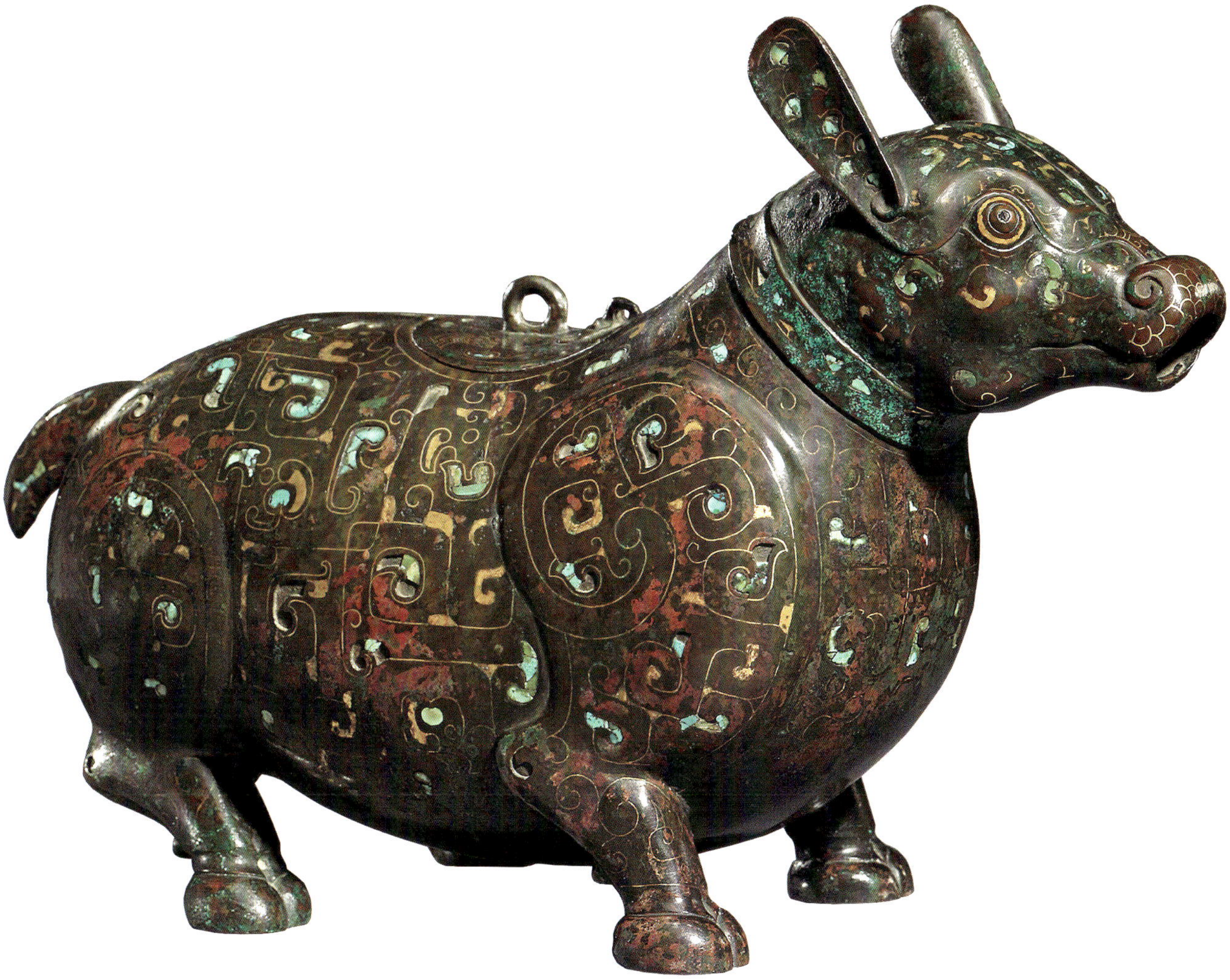

71 | TAPIR-SHAPED CONTAINER (*XI ZUN*), Warring States period (475–221 BC)

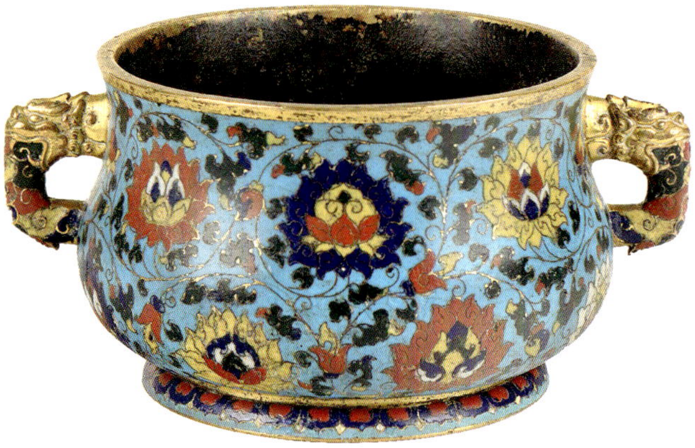

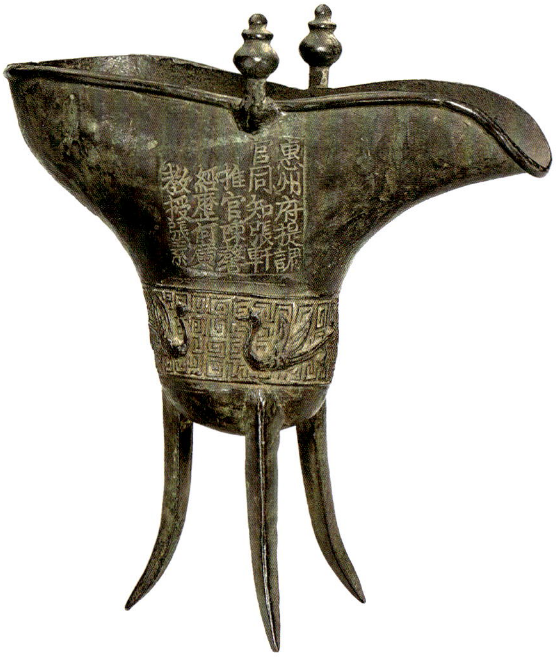

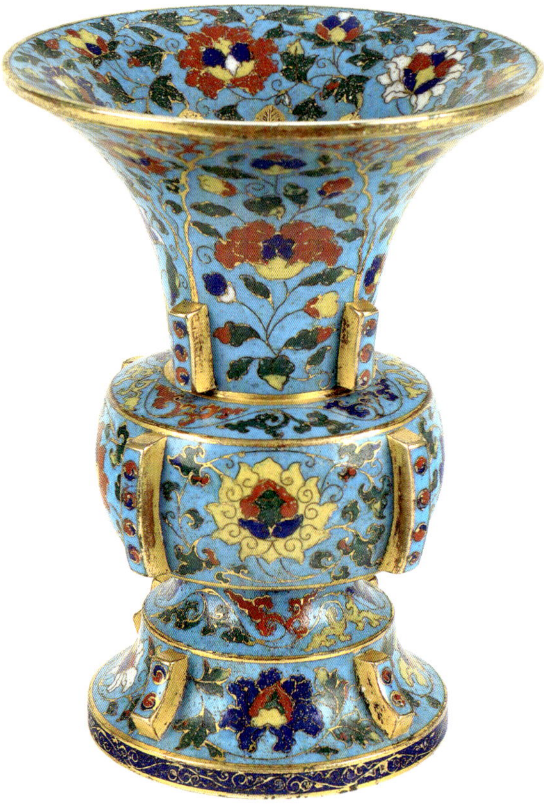

clockwise from top left

72 | GOBLET (*JUE*), Ming dynasty (1368–1644), Tianshun reign (1457–64), 1464

73 | CENSER IN THE FORM OF AN ANCIENT BRONZE TUREEN (*GUI*), Ming dynasty (1368–1644)

74 | BEAKER IN THE FORM OF AN ANCIENT BRONZE CONTAINER (*ZUN*), Ming dynasty (1368–1644)

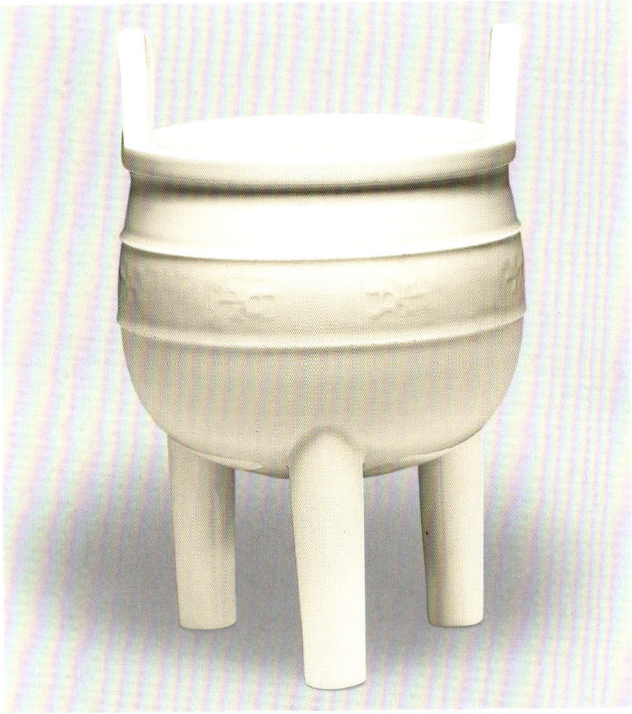

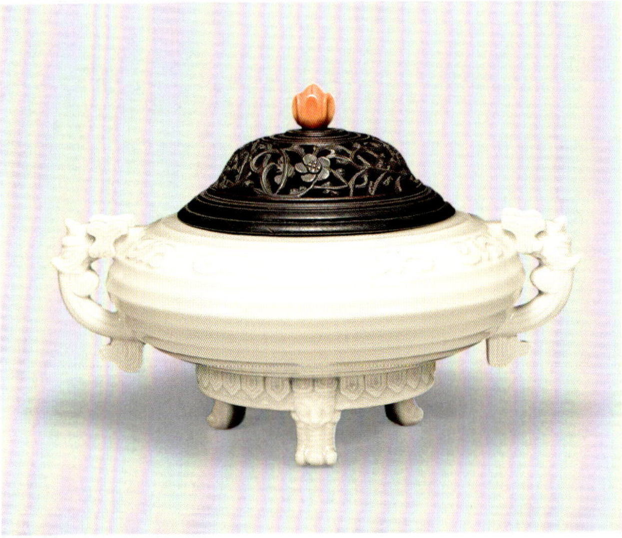

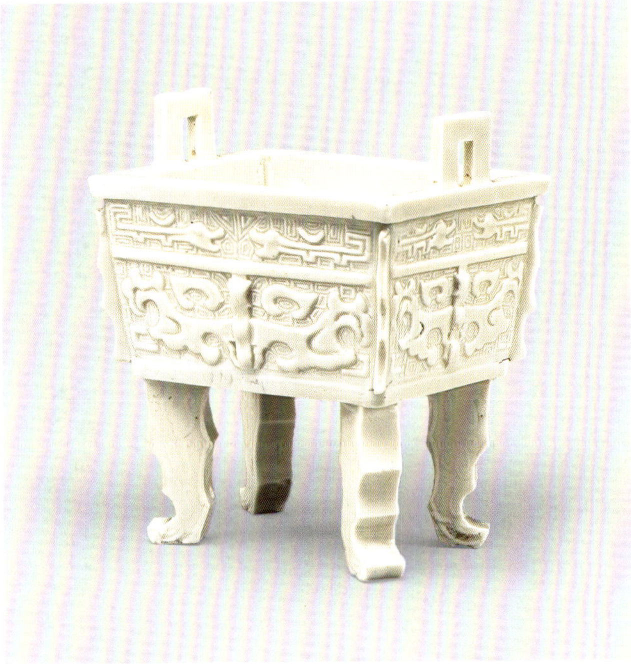

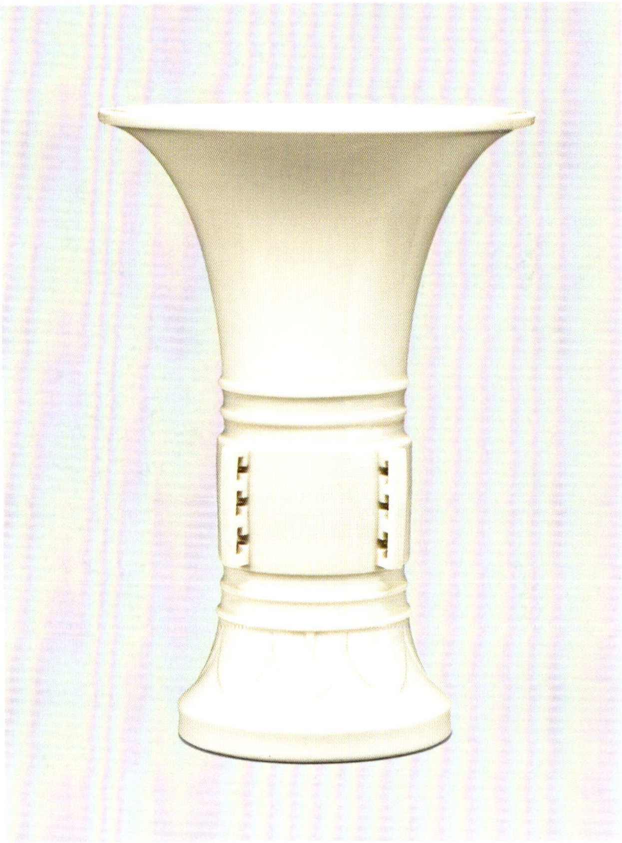

clockwise from top left

75 | CENSER IN THE FORM OF AN ANCIENT BRONZE TRIPOD CAULDRON (*DING*), Qing dynasty (1644–1911)

76 | CENSER IN THE FORM OF AN ANCIENT BRONZE TUREEN (*GUI*), Qing dynasty (1644–1911)

77 | BEAKER IN THE FORM OF AN ANCIENT BRONZE CONTAINER (*ZUN*), Qing dynasty (1644–1911)

78 | CENSER IN THE FORM OF AN ANCIENT BRONZE RECTANGULAR CAULDRON (*FANGDING*), Qing dynasty (1644–1911)

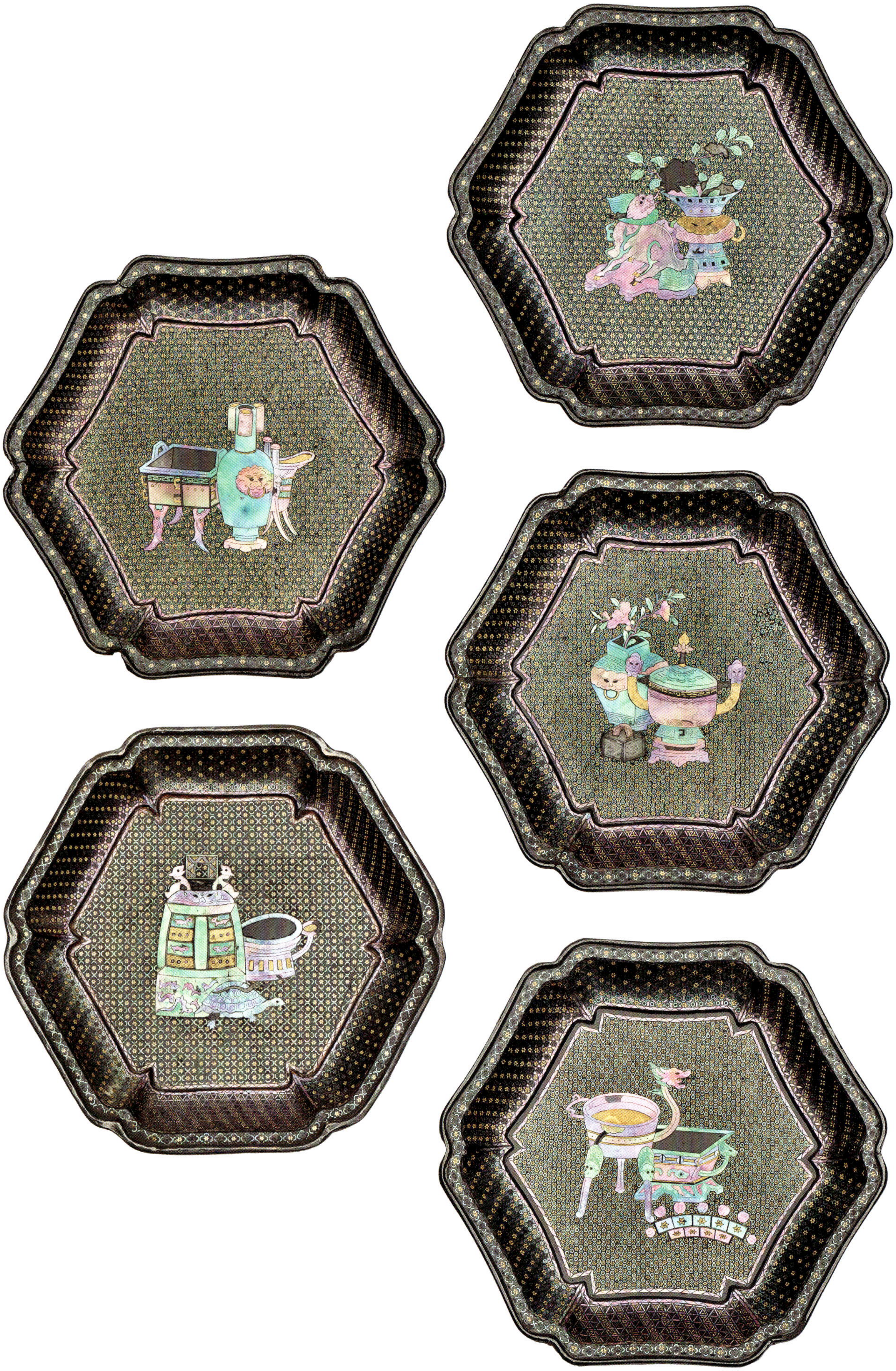

79–83 | DISHES INLAID WITH IMAGES OF ANCIENT BRONZES, Qing dynasty (1644–1911)

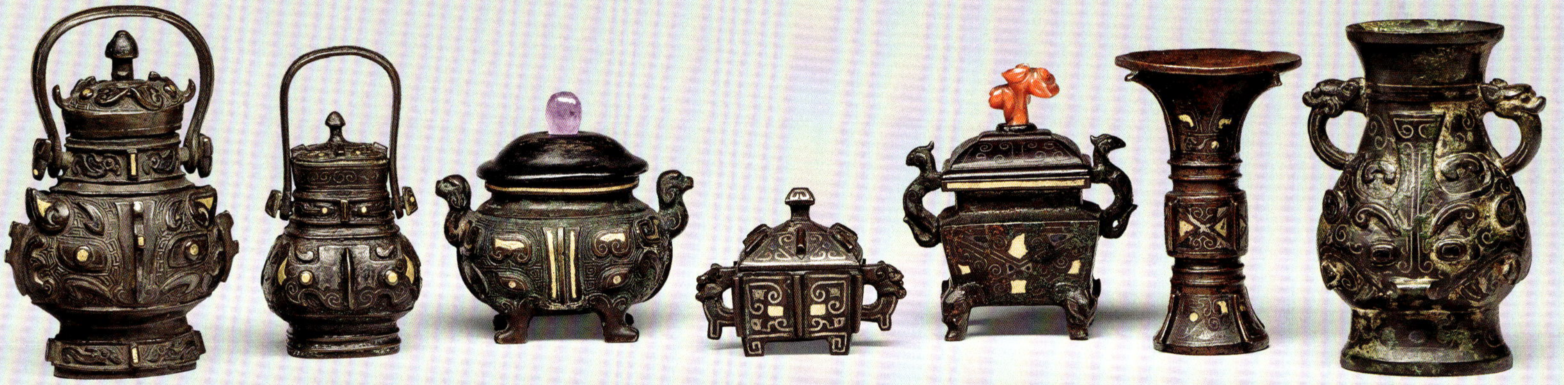

84–90 | MINIATURE VESSELS, Ming dynasty (1368–1644) or Qing dynasty (1644–1911)

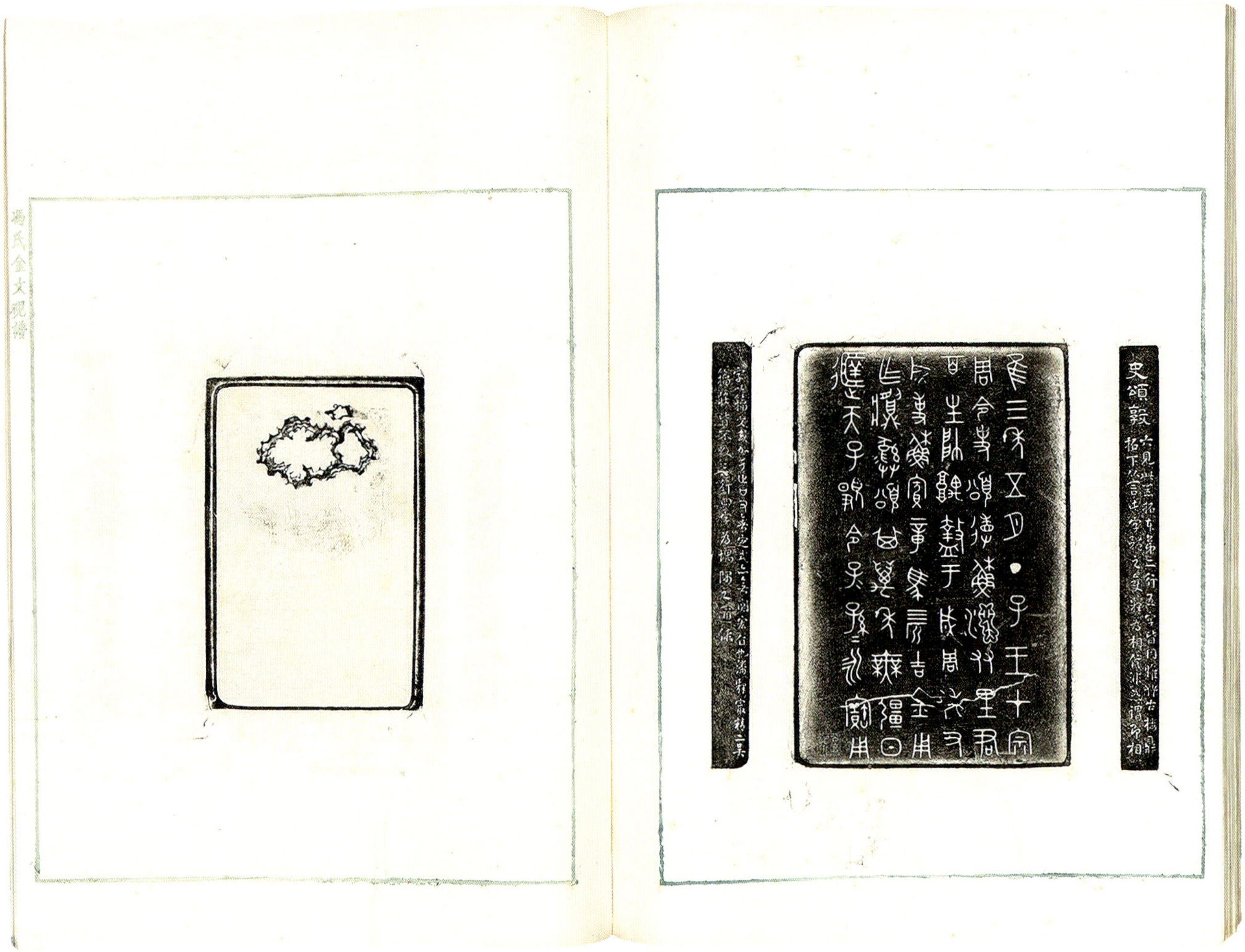

91 | Feng Shu (Chinese, 1867–1948). BOOK OF RUBBINGS OF BRONZE INSCRIPTIONS ON INK STONES, 1930

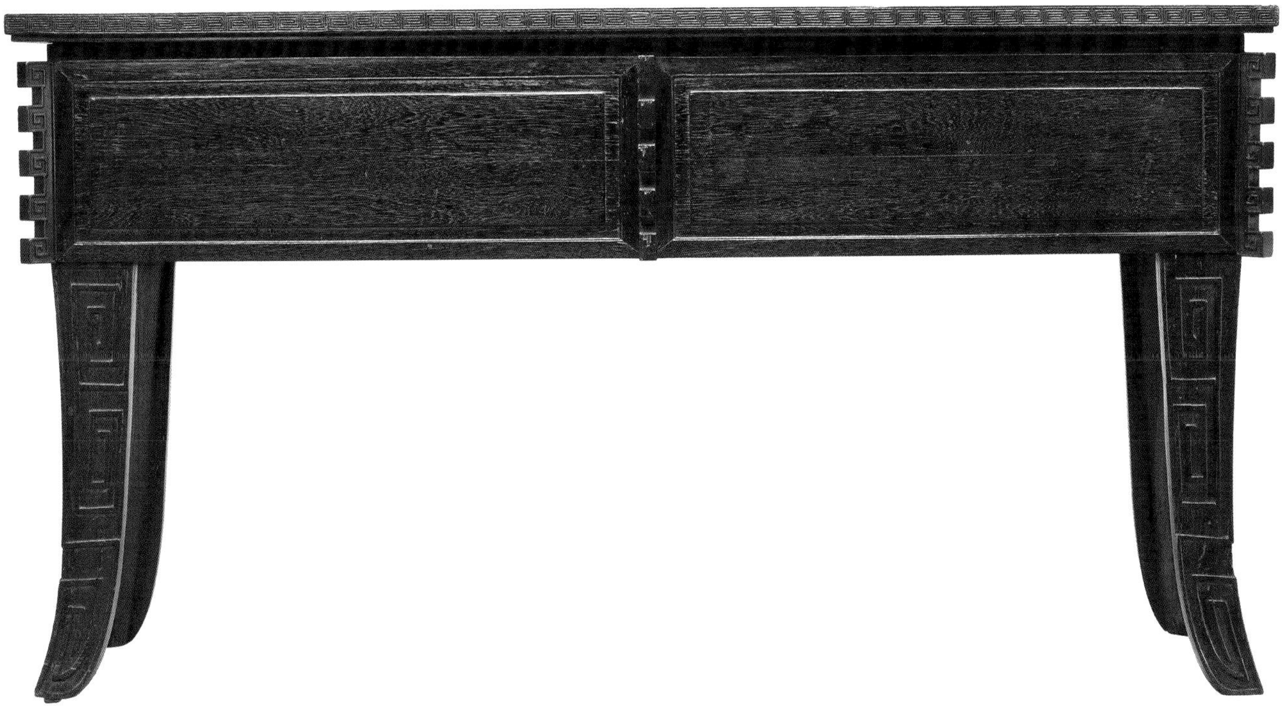

92 | TABLE IN THE FORM OF AN ANCIENT BRONZE VESSEL, Qing dynasty (1644–1911)

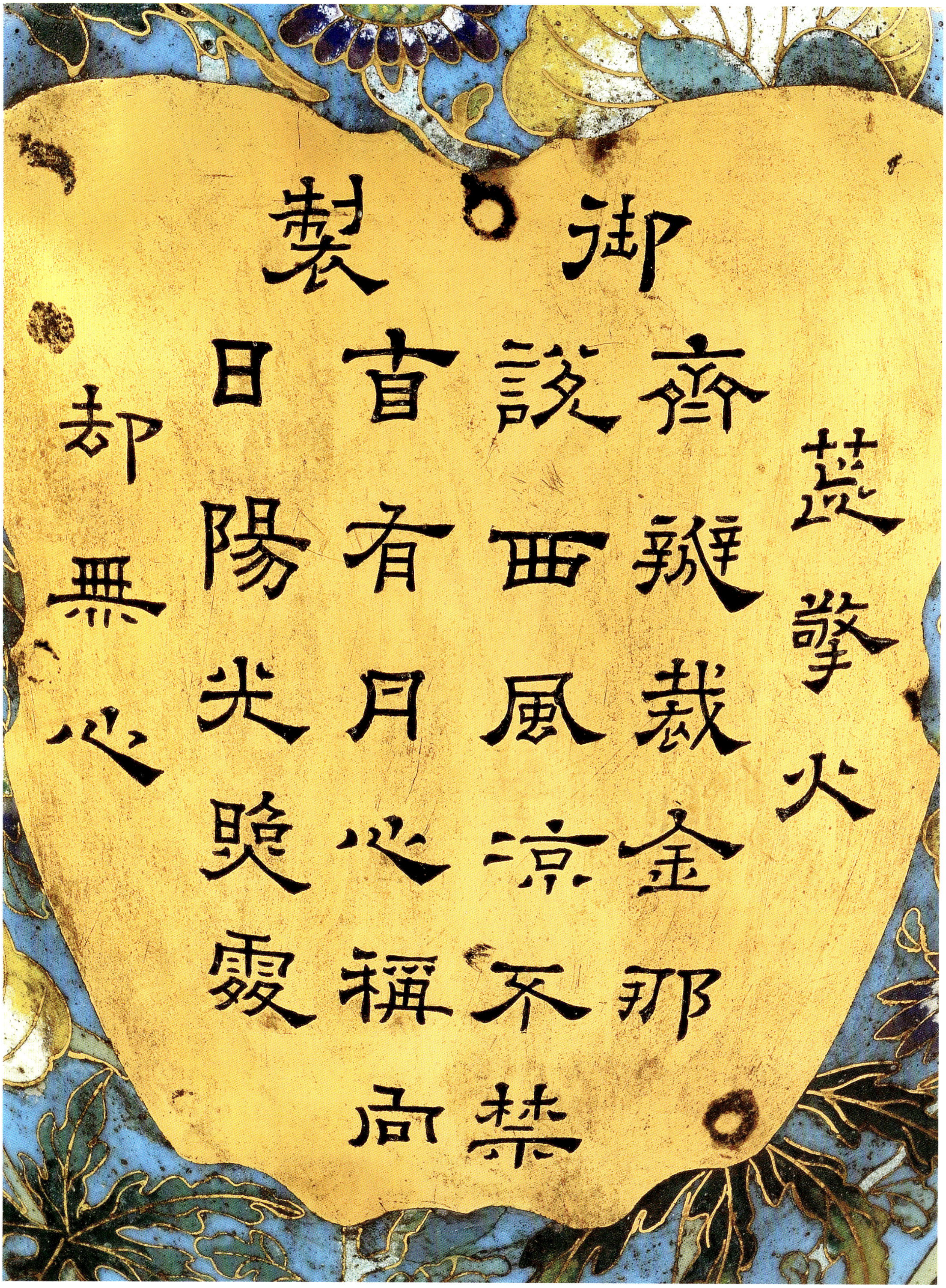
御製
芝擎火
齊紈裁金那
設西風涼不禁
直有月心稱向
日陽光晚霞
却無心

鑑古

MIRRORING THE PAST

EMPEROR QIANLONG AND HIS BRONZES

TAO WANG

Qianlong's Heritage

Historians have long called Emperor Qianlong (r. 1735–96) a "Renaissance man."[1] He was highly regarded for his diligence, ambition, and political skills, as well as for his extraordinary passion for art and ability as a writer. He was prolific, with nearly forty thousand poems and thirteen thousand essays attributed to him. Having great authority and abundant resources at his disposal, Qianlong amassed an unparalleled collection of art treasures—probably the largest in history—that included thousands of classical paintings, works of calligraphy, ancient jades, ceramics, and bronzes, as well as works by contemporary artists and craftsmen.[2] Although not considered the equal of Emperor Huizong (r. 1100–26) of the Song dynasty (960–1279), Qianlong was nonetheless an able painter and competent calligrapher; he loved to imitate early masters and add inscriptions to ancient artworks.[3]

We should perhaps look first at Qianlong's imperial and artistic heritage, as well as the historical background of his rule. The Qing dynasty was established by the Manchus in 1644 after the fall of the Ming dynasty (1368–1644). Before that, the Manchus, descendants of the Jurchens who destroyed the Northern Song dynasty in the twelfth century, already had developed a political system and administrative organization in the style of a Chinese dynasty, and the rulers of the early Qing dynasty managed to unite different ethnic groups, laying the foundation of a multicultural society.[4] By the time of Qianlong, after the reigns of Shunzhi (r. 1644–61), Kangxi (r. 1662–1722), and Yongzheng (r. 1722–35), anti-Manchu resistance from the Han Chinese population had to a large degree dissipated, and the country was brought entirely under Manchu rule (see fig. 1).

All Manchu emperors recognized that in order to rule a multiethnic empire effectively, they needed not only a strong military to manage the populace but also the power of culture to mold and keep them in check. To achieve their goals, nothing proved more useful than controlling, and gaining support of, the Chinese intelligentsia. Kangxi launched and Yongzheng continued the project of compiling a great imperial encyclopedia *Gujin tushu jicheng* (Complete Collection of Illustrations and Writings from the Earliest to Current Times; 1726), which consisted of ten thousand volumes and was divided into six categories: cosmology, economy, geography, nature, philosophy, and society.

Qianlong was in many ways the ideal successor to his father and grandfather. Under his rule, China became the largest and most powerful empire in East Asia. Unprecedented success in both domestic and foreign affairs allowed Qianlong to regard himself as a universal ruler who could achieve whatever he chose and control and possess anything he wanted. His most remarkable cultural achievement was the compilation of the *Siku quanshu* (Complete Library of Four Treasures; see fig. 2), which exemplifies his cultural ambition and managerial skill. The compilation began in 1773 and took fifteen years to complete. Directed by a number of high-ranking officials, and with the famous scholar Ji Yun as chief compiler,

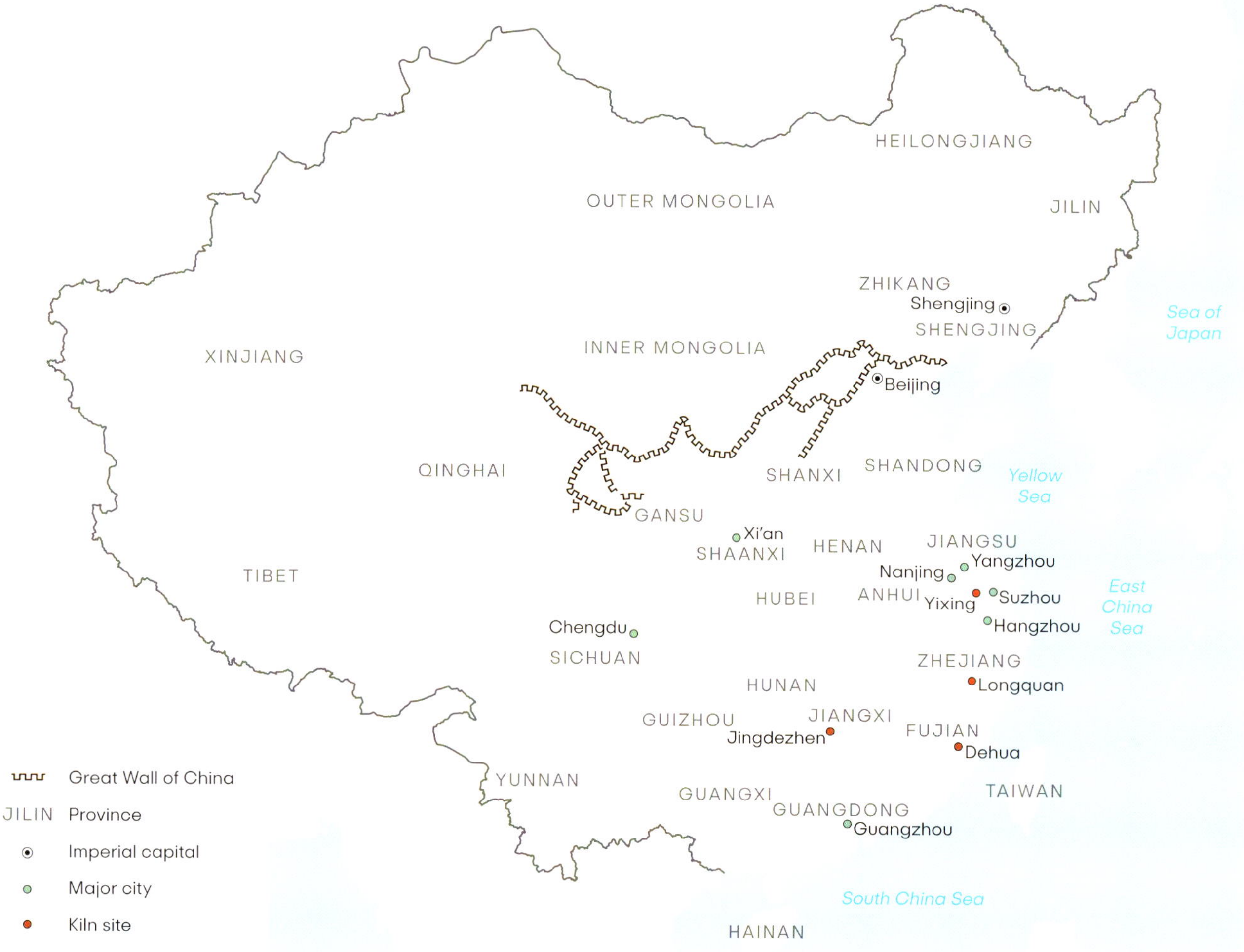

1 | Map of China during the Qing dynasty (1644–1911), showing imperial capitals, major cities, and kiln sites.

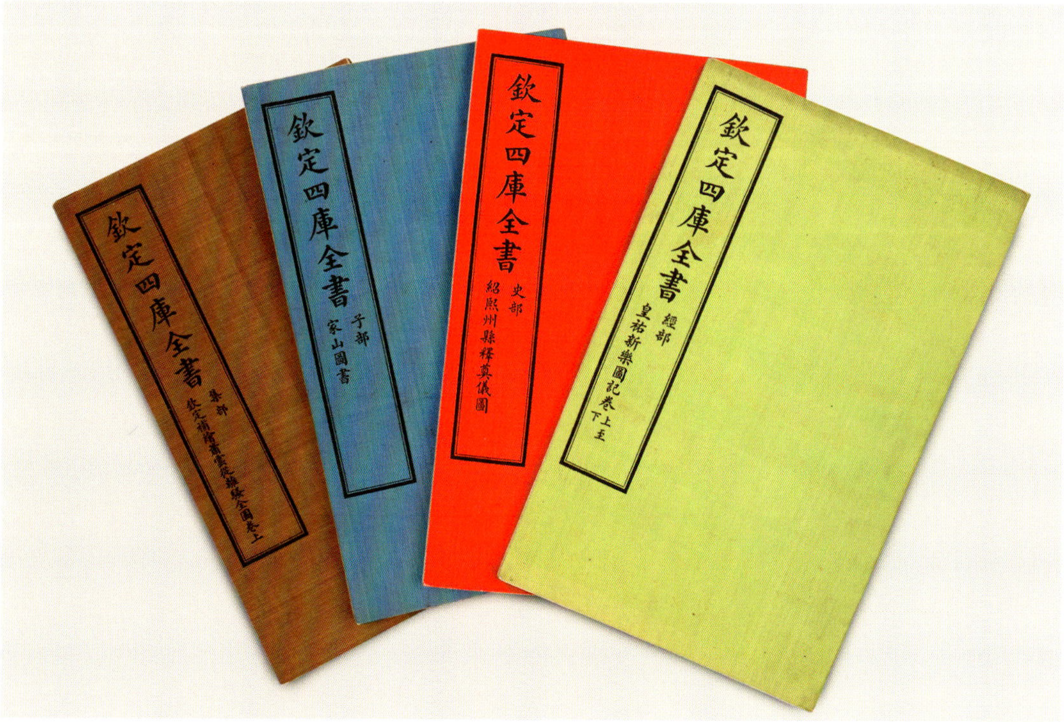

2 | Volumes from the *Siku quanshu* (Complete Library of Four Treasures) (Beijing: Imperial Court, 1773–82). Palace Museum, Beijing, Xian 49192–49197.

the project involved more than 3,600 scholars, as well as 3,800 copyists. The book was arranged in four categories—classics, history, masters of philosophy, and collections of belles lettres—and there were 44 sections, encompassing 3,503 individual titles and 79,337 volumes. It overtook the *Gujin tushu jicheng* to become the grandest collection of texts in Chinese history.

In addition to compiling the book, Qianlong also ordered the construction of seven strategically located imperial libraries. The Pavilion of Literary Profundity (*Wenyuange*) in the Forbidden City, the Pavilion of the Origins of Literature (*Wenyuange*) in the Garden of Perfect Brightness (*Yuanmingyuan*), the Pavilion of the Source of Literature (*Wensuoge*) in the Old Palace in Mukden (today's Shenyang), and the Pavilion of Literary Delights (*Wenjinge*) in the Summer Palace in Rehe (now Chengde) were collectively known as the Four Pavilions of the Inner Court (*Neiting sige*). The Pavilion of the Purpose of Literature (*Wenzongge*) in Jinshan Monastery in Zhenjiang, the Pavilion of Literary Confluence (*Wenhuige*) in the Great Observation Hall in Yangzhou, and the Pavilion of Literary Magnificence (*Wenlange*) near the West Lake in Hangzhou were collectively known as the Three Southern Pavilions (*Jiang Zhe sange*). When the *Siku quanshu* was completed, multiple copies were made, and each of the libraries received one.[5]

This huge project exemplifies Qianlong's ambition and cultural strategy: to standardize the classical texts geared toward learning and promoting Confucian orthodoxy and to project his own image as a sage king (on the model of the semilegendary wise rulers of the Three Dynasties) and man of letters. The comprehensiveness of the *Siku quanshu* is astonishing, and it was intended to showcase the unity and prosperity of the country, the emperor's combination of morality and authority, and the intellectual link between the past and present. As Qianlong stated in his edict: "By such means, the unity of scholarship past and present can be made manifest. Let the provincial governors be ordered to collect all books . . . that clarify the essential methods of government or concern human nature."[6] There can be no doubt that Qianlong understood the power of texts and printing. While bringing about this phenomenal project, he also sought to control the production and circulation of other books. Although the *Siku quanshu* included nearly eight hundred thousand volumes, Qianlong also banned and destroyed almost the same number.

Thus, we should recognize the emperor's cultural interests and achievements as an integrated part of his political agenda, as well as an element of his worldview. As Mark Elliott points out:

> In its proper context, we should see it, together with his love of travel and hunting, as part of his overall dedication to a model of imperial rulership according to which the sovereign should be master of everything. It reflected his desire to impose order—and, by extension, ownership—upon his world. Qianlong's wish to "inspect," as it were, artistic and literary endeavors was like his wish to inspect the different corners of his realm to comprehend within his ken the entire range of creative activity known to his subjects and to put his stamp on it. In short, it mirrored the tendency toward universalism we have seen in other aspects of Qianlong's rule.[7]

Qianlong and His Collections

In his study of the formation of the Qing imperial collections, Gerald Holzwarth divided them into four categories.[8] The first group is composed of classical calligraphy, paintings, ancient jades, ceramics, and bronzes, which were usually kept from public view. The second included pieces commissioned with the intention of display, functioning as political statements and works of art. The third contained ritual objects used for various religious occasions. The fourth consisted of things for daily use, such as clothing and accessories, as well as decorative objects from the palace interiors. Although this taxonomy is useful for analytical purposes, a further investigation reveals a much more complicated picture.

The Qing inherited a large number of artworks from previous dynasties.[9] Kangxi and Yongzheng, Qianlong's father and grandfather, were lovers of Chinese literature and art. They reestablished the palace workshop inside the Forbidden City and reopened the imperial porcelain factory at Jingdezhen (Jiangxi). Although Kangxi was rather frugal, he loved porcelain and European-style arts and crafts; during his reign, he hired Italian Jesuit painter Giuseppe Castiglione as a court painter. Yongzheng, in particular, was a man of refined taste and a patron of art, and he was personally involved with the design and production of porcelain ware. He increased substantially the size of the imperial collection and had illustrations and paintings made of his beloved antiquities. Two scrolls, commissioned by Yongzheng, both titled *Guwantu* (Illustrations of Ancient Playthings), are now in the collections of the Percival David Foundation (British Museum) and the Victoria and Albert Museum in London. One of the scrolls (fig. 3) dates to the sixth year of Yongzheng's reign (1728). On this 20-meter-long work, 223 antiquities are portrayed, including 106 ceramics, 83 jades, and 20 bronzes.[10] Also, a set of twelve paintings (fig. 4) commissioned by Yongzheng when he was still a crown prince depicts antiquities together with his favorite palace consorts known as *meiren* (court

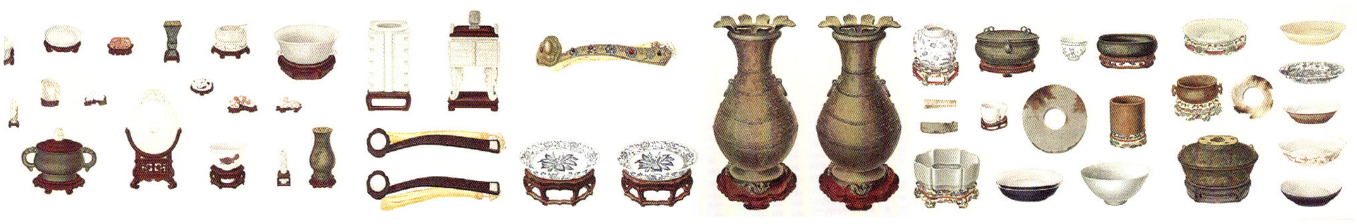

3 | Artists unknown. Section of *Illustrations of Ancient Playthings* (*Guwantu*), 1728. Handscroll, ink and color on paper; 502 × 62.5 cm (591 5/16 × 24 5/8 in.). Percival David Foundation of Chinese Art, London, PDF X01.

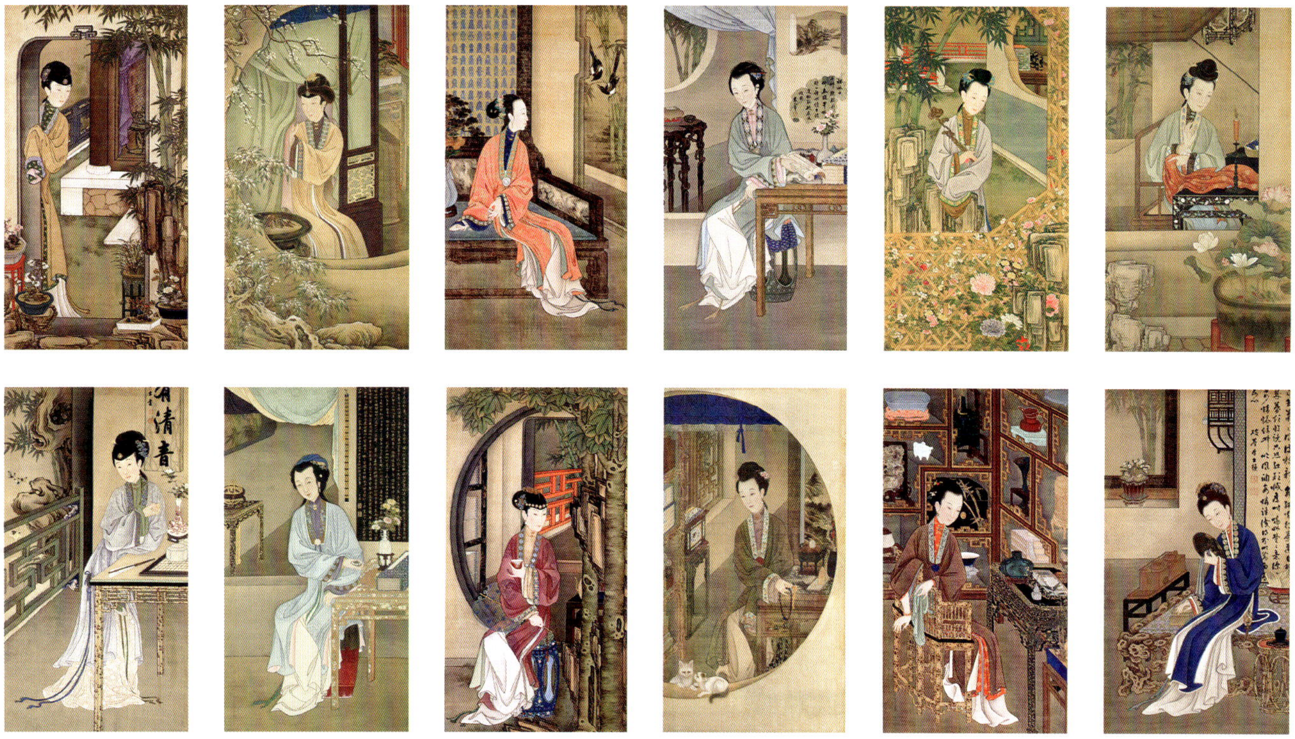

4 | Artists unknown. *Twelve Beauties at Leisure Painted for Prince Yinzhen, the Future Yongzheng Emperor,* late Kangxi reign (1709–1723). Set of twelve screen paintings, ink and color on silk; 184 × 98 cm (72 7/16 × 38 9/16 in.). Palace Museum, Beijing, GU6458, 1–12.

beauties). Two paintings are included in the exhibition (see pls. 97 and 136). One painting (pl. 136) portrays a young woman wearing a Han-style robe who is sitting at a lacquer table on which rests a Han dynasty bronze *hu* (jar); she is surrounded by cabinets full of antiquities, including a Shang dynasty *gu* (goblet) and a Zhou dynasty *bo* bell. The other painting (pl. 97) shows a woman (possibly the same person) sitting on a couch fashioned from tree roots and looking into a bronze mirror, and on the screen behind her is a poem written in the *caoshu* (grass script) style of calligraphy, signed by "Buddhist Layman beyond Worldly Affairs" (Pochenjushi, Yongzheng's nickname when he was still prince), which laments being lonely and lovelorn, but also suggests a special meaning for the bronze mirror as an emblem of solitude.[11]

Qianlong's passion for antiquities and art surpassed that of both his father and grandfather. Moreover, he began to document the imperial collections. As early as 1743, he ordered a team of officials and scholars of the Imperial Hanlin Academy to classify and catalogue his art treasures. Two years later, in 1745, two separate catalogues were published: *Midian zhulin* (Pearl Forest of the Secret Hall; see fig. 5) and *Shiqu baoji* (Precious Collection of the Stone Moat; see fig. 6), which listed religious and secular works, respectively, totaling approximately four thousand paintings and pieces of calligraphy. The names *Secret Hall* and *Stone Moat* are derived from the imperial library and archive of the Han dynasty (206 BC–AD 220), indicating Qianlong's desire to associate his art collecting with China's revered imperial past. As the collection grew, a second supplement (*Xubian*) was compiled in 1793, including an additional 3,600 works. A third supplement (*Sanbian*) was completed in 1815/16 by his son Emperor Jiaqing (r. 1796–1820) after Qianlong's death.

In 1749, four years after the completion of the first painting and calligraphy catalogues, Qianlong launched a new project to survey the bronzes in the palace collection. The undertaking was supervised by two princes, Yunlu and Hongyan,

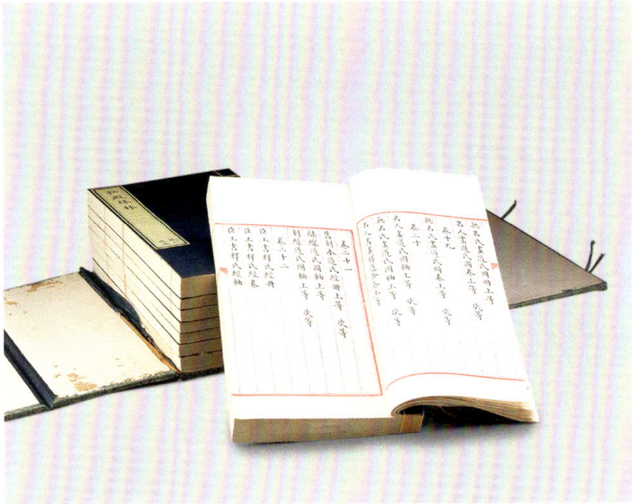

5 | *Midian zhulin* (Pearl Forest of the Secret Hall) (Beijing: Imperial Court, 1745). Palace Museum, Beijing.

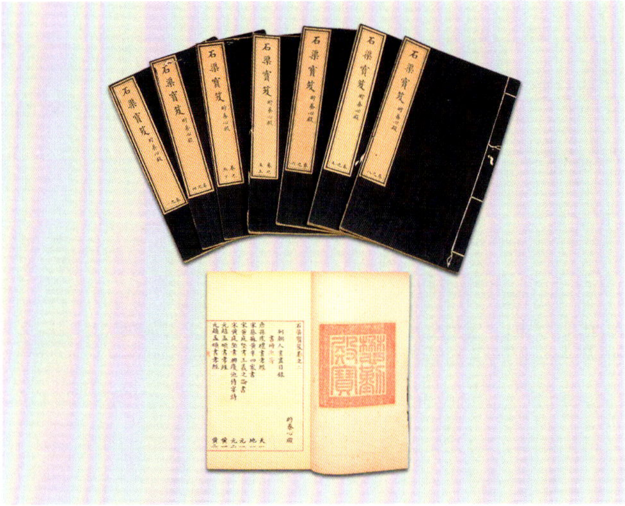

6 | *Shiqu baoji* (Precious Collection of the Stone Moat) (Beijing: Imperial Court, 1745). Palace Museum, Beijing, 000009–000047.

and carried out by a number of high-ranking ministers, including Liang Shizheng and Yu Minzhong, who also had been previously involved with the cataloguing of the paintings and calligraphy. A team of scholars, court artists, copyists, and proofreaders assisted them. A total of four catalogues of bronzes were produced. The first, printed in 1755, was *Xiqing gujian* (Ancient Mirror of Western Clarity), documenting 1,529 pieces. *Xiqing* (western clarity) is a literary term meaning purity or tranquility, but here it refers to the palace library (*Nanshufang*) where many of the bronzes were originally stored and catalogued. But, the term *gujian* (ancient mirror) is used in a more abstract and metaphysical way; only a small portion of the catalogue (two of forty volumes) is devoted to mirrors, whereas most of it is devoted to vessels. Thus, its title is probably better understood as "mirroring antiquity" or a "reflection of the past"; as Eugene Wang argues, "the mirror metaphor thus evolved into a pattern of moralizing historiography or historicizing homily."[12]

The second catalogue, *Ningshou jiangu* (Reflections on Antiquity from the Palace of Tranquil Longevity), compiled more than twenty years later, listed 600 ritual bronzes and 102 bronze mirrors that were housed in the Ningshou Palace, which was Qianlong's retirement quarter. *Jiangu* (a play on words with *gujian* in the title of the previous catalogue) can be translated as "mirroring the past" or "appreciating antiquity," which accurately reflects the intention of the emperor. Two sequels appeared between 1781 and 1793, *Xiqing xujian jiabian* (Supplement A) and *Xiqing xujian yibian* (Supplement B), comprising 1,850 bronzes that had not yet been catalogued, including those kept in the palace repository and the old palace at Mukden.[13]

Qianlong himself explained the motivation for, and purpose of, the bronze catalogue, in a decree printed at the beginning of the first volume:

Of all the model things [*fawu*], transmitted from the remote past, only bronzes such as the *zun* and yi wine vessels, *ding* and *nai* cauldrons have lasted for generations. This is because they are solid in substance and heavy in construction, undamaged by either dry climate or dampness, and resistant to corrosion. Their mysterious brightness is profound, revealing the greatness and aura of the Three Dynasties of the distant past. Thus, many antiquaries are eager to acquire ancient bronzes. The *Xuanhe bogutu* has been widely circulated among scholars and artists, as well as Lü Dalin's *Kaogutu*. But, besides these two catalogues, few records about the ancient bronzes still exist, not for the lack of resources of collectors but because it is indeed very difficult to assemble a collection. It is not worth recording if one only sees a small number of examples.

In our dynasty, the discipline is not to indulge oneself in entertainment and superfluous things. But we do not forbid people to take part in the activities of collecting and appreciating antiquities; after all, my palaces are full of such displays and the imperial collection is rich. In my spare time between official duties, I enjoy appreciating and putting inscriptions onto these antiquities. Considering that many of them have never been recorded before, and that many ancient objects may fall into obscurity, if we don't record them and publish them, how can investigators in the future obtain their evidence? I hereby order the ministers Liang Shizheng, Jiang Pu, and Wang Youdun, leading Hanlin scholars of the inner court, to follow the example of *Bogutu* and compile the catalogue *Xiqing gujian*, providing

> accurate illustrations and tracings of inscriptions. This would enable us to use the reserve of energy accumulated from working with the arts and to embody the thoughts we have gained from reflection on the past; all these activities surely can be considered as prosperity and elegance.[14]

Here, Qianlong used the term *fawu* when referring to the ancient bronze vessels—a combination of *fa*, which means "model," "law," "method," and "pattern," as well as "to imitate," and *wu*, which means "thing(s)." To treat ancient ritual bronzes as models was not new to Qianlong, and the overtone of his decree sounds very similar to that of Song dynasty antiquarianism, as discussed in previous essays in this publication. However, it is clear that the emperor was not against private collecting and, as he put it so vividly, the catalogue was to be used as "the reserve of energy accumulated from working with the arts and embody the thoughts we have gained from reflection on the past" (*yi youyi zhi yigong, ji jiangu zhi yuansi*).

Qianlong's publications followed the conventional format of earlier Song dynasty catalogues, such as *Kaogutu* and *Bogutu*, offering an entry for each bronze that contains a name and a line-drawing illustration; the item's measurements and weight; a tracing of the inscription, if there was one; the literary transcription; and, occasionally, an explanatory note. These books represent the revival of *jinshixue* scholarship in eighteenth-century China. However, they lack the systematic classification of *Bogutu*, which was compiled under Emperor Huizong, and fall short of the rigorous epigraphic scholarship that was demonstrated by the Song antiquarian scholar Lü Dalin.[15] Although a highly knowledgeable connoisseur of ancient jades and ceramics, Qianlong was clearly less competent with ancient bronzes. Indeed, a high proportion of the imperial collection recorded in his catalogues has been proven to be fake, and mistakes have been found in the classification and dating of the ancient bronzes.[16] For example, a bronze *yan* steamer that is included in this exhibition (fig. 7a) is an obvious reproduction of the Ming period, but is presented in the *Xiqing gujian* as from the Zhou dynasty (fig. 7b), and a Shang-dynasty *yan* (fig. 8a) is wrongly dated to the Han dynasty (see fig. 8b).

Indeed, the emperor had an ambivalent attitude toward ancient bronzes. On the one hand, they were still revered and employed for state rituals. Between 1768 and 1779, Qianlong presented as many as thirty pieces to the Confucian temples at the Imperial Academy (*Guozijian*) in the capital, at Queli—Confucius's birth place in Qufu—and at the imperial summer resort in Jehol (Rehe). Confucius had long been regarded as the uncrowned sage king (*suwang*) in China, but Qianlong was the only emperor who employed genuine Shang and Zhou bronzes to perform sacrifices to him.[17]

On the other hand, during the Qing period, porcelain was used more commonly than bronze for making ritual vessels. According to the *Da Qing huidian zeli* (Regulations and Statues of the Great Qing; 1764), at the beginning of the Qing dynasty, following the Ming dynasty tradition, the majority of ritual vessels were ceramics. But during Yongzheng's reign, the emphasis shifted toward bronzes. This trend continued, and under Qianlong, many bronze vessels were made to replace the ceramic ones. In the twelfth year of his reign (1747), he ordered that for ancestral worship, the ritual vessels should be given the ancient nomenclature and follow the ancient system. Thus, objects made of ceramic and bronze—based on their shapes and colors—were offered at different altars and temples.[18] This trend was followed through uniformly, since many Qianlong-period examples were made of ceramic but took the forms of ancient bronzes. In fact, both Yongzheng and Qianlong used ancient bronzes as models, and a great number of reproductions were produced using various materials—bamboo, enamel, jade, lacquer, and porcelain.[19] These reproductions were not direct copies of ancient works, but rather were inspired by them, and featured variations and new elements. Thus, it is useful to distinguish the different kinds of "archaism" at work here; as Jessica Rawson suggests, Qing archaism was not much concerned with reviving ancient rituals, but rather with creating collections, catalogues, and encyclopedias, in which the past could be used as a decorative style.[20] These archaic objects were popular at the Qing court. They were often stored and displayed together with the genuine ancient pieces, not in any ritual context but as a part of palace interiors (see fig. 9).[21]

In addition, Qianlong does not appear to have had the same kind of familiarity and intimacy with bronzes that we see in his relationship with other antiquities. Thomas Lawton has argued that, while there are plenty of examples of paintings and pieces of calligraphy that bear numerous, even tiresome, colophons and seal impressions stamped by Qianlong, it was not common practice to add inscriptions onto bronzes. But why? According to Lawton, it is quite easy to scratch and cut into bronze, and the emperor did have inscriptions carved onto much harder and more fragile materials, such as jade and ceramics. If he had wanted to inscribe bronzes, he could certainly have done so. It seems, rather, that he did not wish to.[22]

Yet it was certainly not the case that Qianlong was uninterested in ancient bronzes. In fact, he had a particular fascination with certain types of bronzes, such as mirrors. There is a rare example, recorded in the *Xiqing gujian*, of a bronze mirror inscribed with one of his poems (see figs. 10a and 10b):[23]

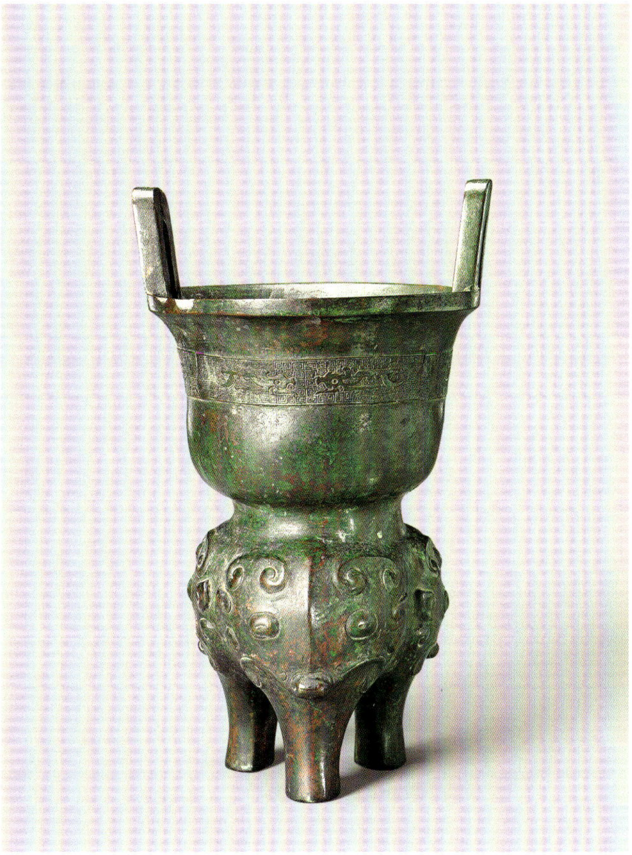

7a | Food steamer (*yan*), Ming dynasty (1368–1644). Bronze; 37.8 × 22.9 cm (14 7/8 × 9 in); diam. 21.6 cm (8 1/2 in.). Palace Museum, Beijing, GU77911. See pl. 64.

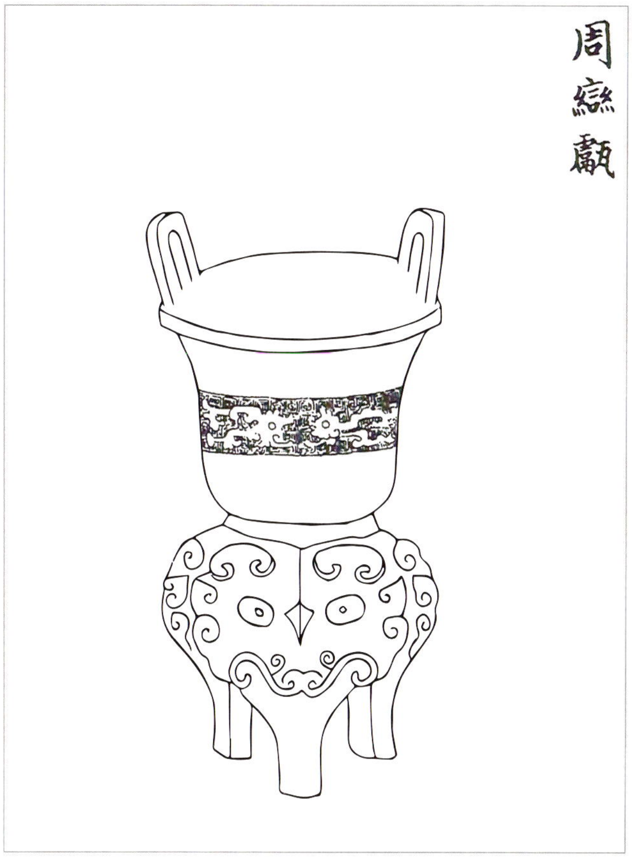

7b | Illustration of fig. 9a in *Xiqing xujian jiabian* (Ancient Mirror of Western Clarity) [Supplement A] (Beijing: Imperial Court, 1871–93), 13.21.

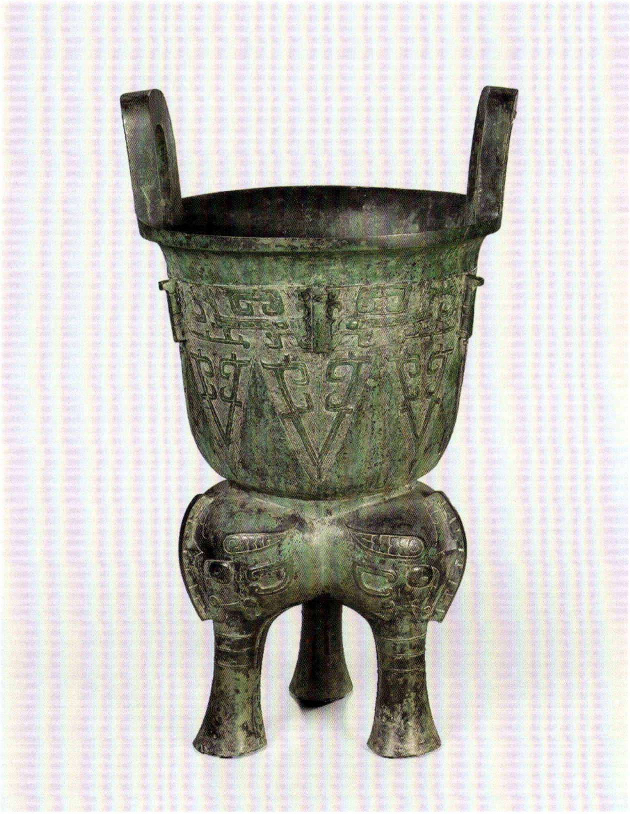

8a | Food steamer (*yan*). Late Shang dynasty (c. 1250–1046 century BC). Bronze; 80.9 × 44.9 cm (31 7/8 × 17 11/16 in.). Palace Museum, Beijing, GU76893. See pl. 65.

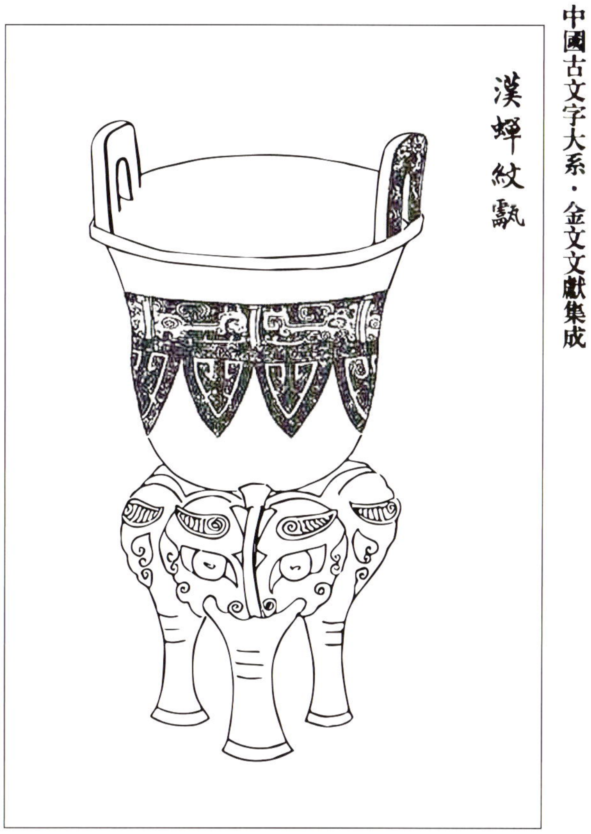

8b | Illustration of fig. 10a in *Xiqing xujian jiabian* (Ancient Mirror of Western Clarity) [Supplement A] (Beijing: Imperial Court, 11871–93), 13.21.

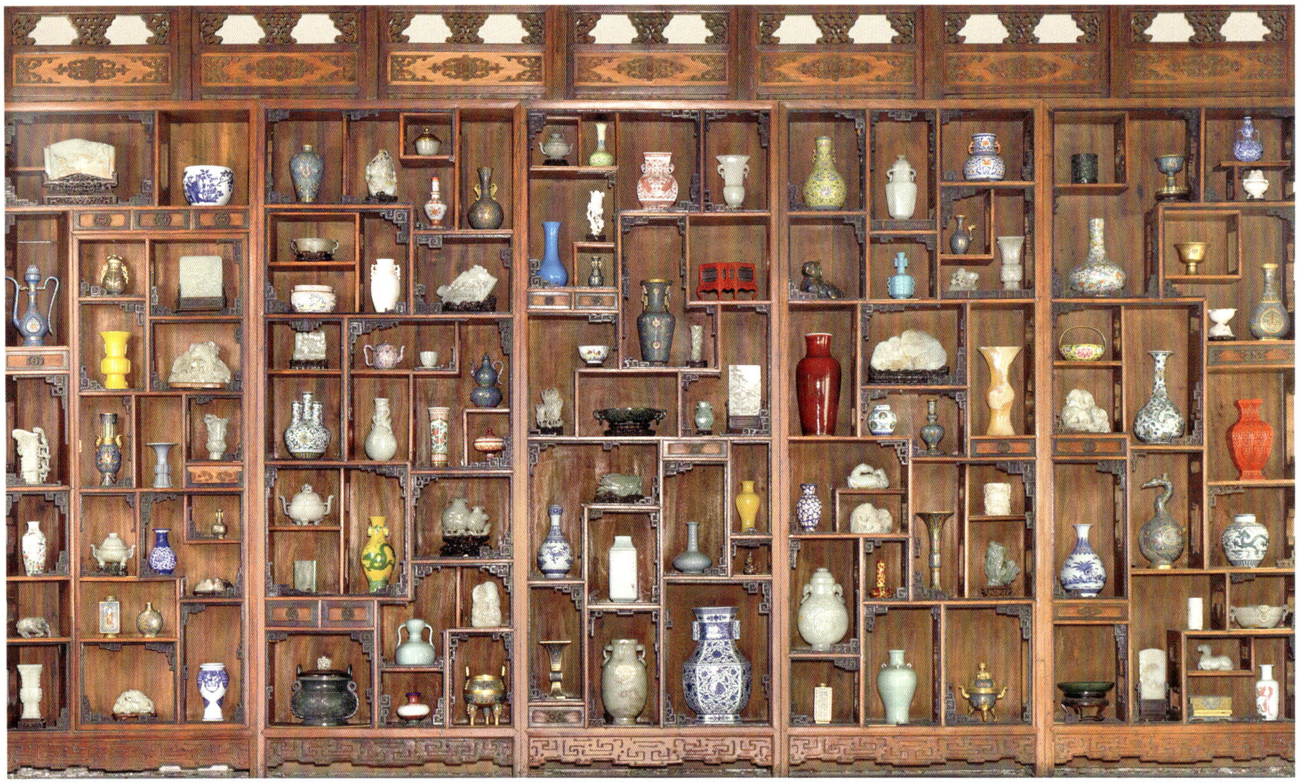

9 | Display of treasures preserved in shelves in the Forbidden City Palace Museum, Beijing, 2017.

Xuanyuan [the Yellow Emperor] melted metal
to cast this divine thing [*shenwu*];

Its virtue conjunctures Heaven and Earth
and is bright as the sun and the moon.

Containing the essence and energy of yin
and yang;

It could not be diminished even after eighteen
thousand years.

Protected by heavenly solders from demons;

Its light radiates from the central circle
as green clouds.

Like stars turning repeatedly at the celestial gate;

The four spirits of cardinal directions and five
holy mountains cannot ratify its existence.

Vulgar productions of the Han and Tang dynasties
cannot compete with its energy;

The auspiciousness will not allow Qu Yuan to
suffer injustice.

Mirrors illuminate the good from the treacherous,
revealing their hearts and bones.[24]

Qianlong called the mirror *shenwu*, or "divine thing." This poem paraphrased the "general discussion of mirrors" of *Bogutu*, which recorded 113 such objects. Emperor Huizong from the Song dynasty also seems to have had a special interest in mirrors, perhaps because of their association with Daoism.[25]

Included in the exhibition is a very large bronze mirror (pl. 96) that has been mounted as a table screen and also bears another Qianlong inscription, dated to spring 1776. It reads:

> Pure, and with a big knob, it has the form of a mirror of the Han dynasty: a round disc with a diameter exceeding one foot. On the reverse of the precious bronze are carved several motifs, an elegant adornment of dispersed seahorses and grapes. Brought out of the earth after a thousand years, it is of a bright green color. Which lady used it in her fragrant dressing case we cannot know. Was she a singer at the theater, accompanied by fans of silk, declining the splendid and virtuous regulations of the Inner Palace? Or was she a woman of peace and harmony, attached to a prince, striving for beauty with rouge and powder and jealously adhering to virtue? In the end their beautiful eyebrows were all reflected, virtuous or not, as far apart as the sky and sea; she had to decide by herself. Alas, mirror! Alas, mirror! What was entrusted to you, you don't know! How can you wait for the beautiful and ugly alike to turn their face to you!

Qianlong's appreciation for mirrors can also be gleaned from the special packaging and presentation he gave them: each was carefully stored in a designated box, which also included paintings and calligraphy by ministers and renowned artists.

Like paintings and works of calligraphy, mirrors were ranked as top grade (*toudeng*) or second grade (*cideng*).[26]

The emperor also had a penchant for converting small ancient bronzes into scholarly objects or *wenwan* (things for cultural enjoyment). For instance, among the old imperial collections are several treasure boxes that contain small bronzes of different dates, from the Shang to the Qing periods; these were given names such as *Fanjin zuoze* (Model Bronzes Establish the Pattern; see fig. 11) or *Jijin yaocai* (Auspicious Bronzes Shine with Brightness). Matching stands or covers were specially made for these works. Sometimes they were converted into water droppers or brush rests and accompanied with albums of color illustrations.[27] Turning ancient objects into playthings was not uncommon, especially in the Ming and Qing periods, and Qianlong had a vested interest in this practice. This seems very much against the principle of not treating antiquities as *wanwu* (playthings), which was established by Song antiquarianism.

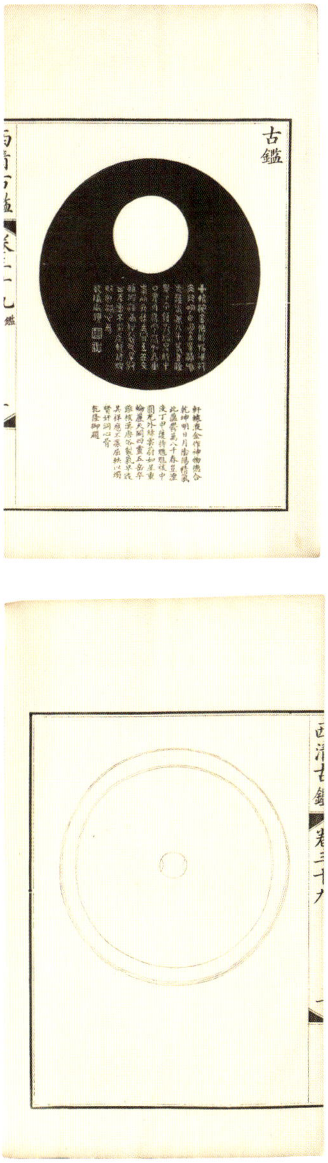

10a–b | Illustrations of a bronze mirror inscribed with one of Qianlong's poems in *Xiqing xujian jiabian* [Ancient Mirror of Western Clarity], Supplement A (1781–93), 39, 1. Palace Museum, Beijing.

Here, we see a contradiction in Qianlong's approach to antiquity. His collecting and connoisseurship is inevitably intertwined with his rulership. An exquisite example of this can be seen in a set of bronze bells, known as *Zhejian zhong*, whose discovery, restoration, exhibition, and reproduction show that the emperor fully recognized that ancient bronzes could perform a social and political role.[28] The bells were discovered in the twenty-sixth year of his reign (1761) in Linjiang (Jiangxi) when some farmers were digging a field. The local governor sent these finds to the capital as gifts to the emperor. Although Qianlong had previously acquired other bells, this was the first time he had received a set of eleven. Among them, six bear a long inscription of eighty-three characters, and four have an inscription of twenty-eight characters, noting that they were commissioned in the fifth century BC by a prince named Zhejian of the ancient Wu state. The emperor and his scholars correctly identified them as Zhou dynasty *bozhong* bells. The date of the bells is indeed probably around the fifth century BC, during the late Spring and Autumn period (770–476 BC).

To commemorate his significant archaeological discovery, Qianlong wrote an essay, "Yungutang ji" (An Account of the Hall of Rhyming with the Past), and nine poems.[29] He also believed that the complete set should have twelve bells, representing the twelve standard pitches, so he ordered a replica to be made. The eleven bells, plus the new one, were all recorded in the imperial catalogue *Xiqing xujian*,which provided illustrations, descriptions, and inscriptions, along with a substantial introduction, which reads, in part:

> In the past, music was made according to the scales and measurements of the twelve pitches and twelve notes, because the twelve sounds

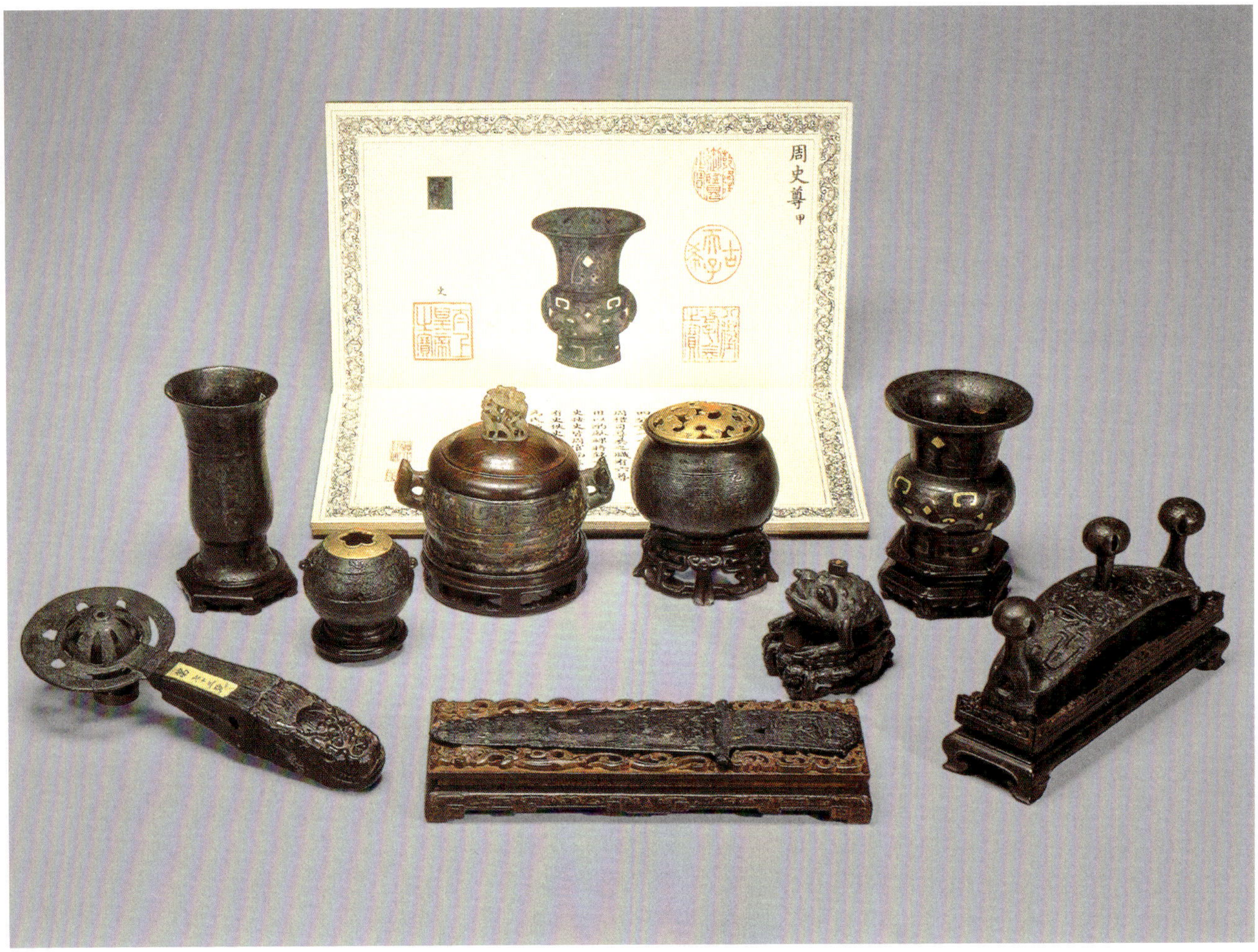

11 | *Fanjin zuoze* curio box, Qing dynasty (1644–1911), Qianlong reign (1735–96). Bronze, wood, and paper; 40 × 44 cm (15 3/4 × 17 6/16 in.). National Palace Museum, Taipei.

> are most even, following the way of heaven. Having preserved auspiciousness for a long time, our empire is increasingly prosperous. To celebrate the moment of victory of our troops in the west, heaven and earth have responded and the precious objects that have been hidden for over two thousand years all suddenly appear, and now suspended from the frames, manifest our mighty military achievements. They play an elegant melody with harmony, accompanied by ecstasy and happiness from the ancient music. Such grandness the history and books have not yet managed to record.[30]

The completed set was then put on view at the Hall of Rhyming with the Past (*Yungutang*) in the Western Park at the Forbidden City. These bells were perhaps the most publicly displayed bronzes from the imperial collection. During his reign, Qianlong had the Board of Music (*Yuebu*) cast no less than sixty-four replicas of the Linjiang bells, and he placed them at important palaces including the Hall of Grand Harmony (*Taihedian*), the Palace of Heavenly Clarity (*Qianqinggong*), and the Palace of Tranquil Longevity (*Ningshougong*). They were played at state banquets and court audiences. One example is included in this exhibition (see fig. 12 and pl. 106).

Hui-chun Yu argues that this story illustrates how Qianlong considered the bronze bells magical treasures and charged his bureaucracy with authenticating them for the imperial collection and displaying them in public. In this way, according to Yu, "collectorship and connoisseurship were completely institutionalized into his emperorship."[31] Yu has also used another example to show how Qianlong manipulated the imperial collection for political gain.[32] The collection appears at the end of *Xiqing xujian jiabian* as a supplement that includes thirty-eight objects. They are bronze buckets, coins, seals, and weapons related to the victories of Qianlong's military campaigns, as well as some that came as tributes from Middle Eastern countries, such as thirteenth-century Islamic metalwork. Qianlong personally wrote commentaries for some of these pieces, and also displayed them in the Pavilion of Purple Light (*Ziguangge*), where the emperors received foreign envoys. As Yu points out, he seemed to be more attached to these more modern bronzes than to his collection of ancient ones; for the emperor, the latter merely evoked a longing for the legendary golden

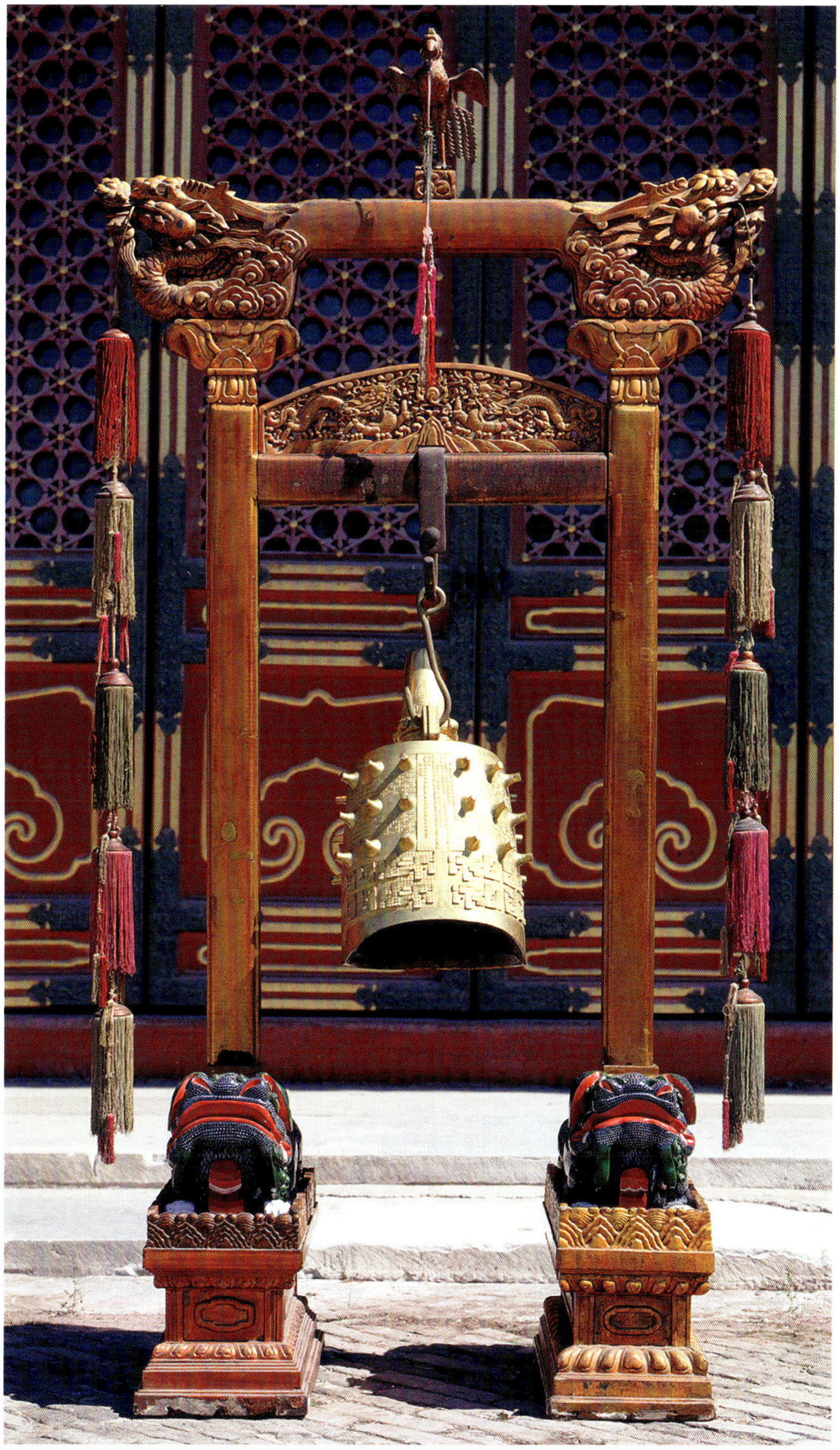

12 | *Bo* bell, Qing dynasty, Qianlong reign (1735–96), 1761. Gilt bronze and wood; 340 × 180 cm (133 7/8 × 70 7/8 in.). Palace Museum, Beijing. See pl. 106.

age, but the former brought him the recognition that he was in fact creating the history of his own empire.[33]

Western art historians have observed that from the Renaissance onward, and in the seventeenth century in particular, many European rulers were consumed with collecting art competitively; they wanted the magnificence of their holdings to fill their rivals with awe.[34] Qianlong's comprehensive collection of every kind of art was surely impressive enough to qualify as magnificent. But, beyond the grandeur, was his collecting behavior different from that of other emperors? And to what degree was his collection of ancient bronzes defined by his worldview and his own image making?

Comparing the habits of Huizong and Qianlong, Patricia Ebery has noted that both were mega-collectors, and imperial resources and institutional structures allowed them to acquire in a similar fashion. However, their intellectual frameworks were different, and they faced different audiences.[35] During his reign, Qianlong commissioned a number of portraits of the same composition, one of them is included in this exhibition (pl. 138). The subject is perhaps related to the tradition of *jiangutu* (enjoyment of antiquities), but the emperor added an inscription to suggest his multiple identities. At the same time, the painting depicts Qianlong's complex relationship to his art collection.[36] Indeed, it is very hard to separate his political agenda from his personal interests. Scholars agree that the emperor was a passionate connoisseur, obsessive about pursuing all kinds of antiquities. His personality and authority were intertwined with his objects, which he used to craft not only his own special relationship with history but also the image he wanted to project. Harold Kahn points out that Qianlong's collecting activities were connected with what he calls "the politics of monumentalism"—a public art demonstrating hegemonic sovereignty and cosmological harmony.[37] By performing multiple roles (artist, militant, politician, priest, and scholar), the emperor embraced universal kingship and the cosmos. It was through such modes that he created what Kahn described as a "legacy of taste for unshakable imperial pomp, massive projects, and occasional displays of what can only be called elephantine delicacy."[38] It is perhaps more than reasonable to treat imperial collecting (and perhaps collecting in general) as the product of an individual personality operating within unique circumstances. As a case study, Qianlong's collecting and collating delivered a strong message: antiquity is at once private and public; of the past but also of the present.

NOTES

1 | Mark C. Elliott, *Emperor Qianlong: Son of Heaven, Man of the World* (New Jersey: Pearson Education, 2009), 107.

2 | For more on Qianlong's achievements, see Elliott, *Emperor Qianlong*, esp. chap. 7, 107–24; see also National Palace Museum, *Qianlong huangdi de wenhua daye* [Emperor Qianlong's Grand Cultural Enterprise], exh. cat. (Taipei: National Palace Museum, 2002), and *Shiquan Qianlong: Qing Gaozong de yishu pinwei* [The All Complete Qianlong: The Aesthetic Tastes of the Qing Emperor Gaozong], exh. cat. (Taipei: National Palace Museum, 2002).

3 | For examples, see National Palace Museum, *Qianlong huangdi de wenhua daye*, pl. I-10, 30, pl. I-12, and *Shiquan Qianlong: Qing Gaozong de yishu pinwei*, pls. III-2.14, III-2.16, III-2.18, and III-2.20–24.

4 | See Evelyn S. Rawski, "Presidential Address: Reenvisoning the Qing: The Significance of the Qing Period in Chinese History," *Journal of Asian Studies* 55:4 (1996): 829–50.

5 | For a study of the project, see R. Kent Guy, *The Emperor's Four Treasuries: Scholars and the State in the Late Ch'ien-lung Era* (Cambridge: Harvard University Asia Center, 1987).

6 | Qianlong's edict of 1722, reprinted in *Siku quanshu* [Complete Library of Four Treasures], *Wenyuange* edition (repr., Taipei: Shangwu yinshuguan, 1983), quoted in Elliott, *Emperor Qianlong*, 119.

7 | Ibid., 124.

8 | Gerald Holzwarth, "The Qianlong Emperor as Art Patron and the Formation of the Collections of the Palace Museum, Beijing," in Evelyn S. Rawski and Jessica Rawson, eds., *China: The Three Emperors 1662–1795* (London: Royal Academy of Arts, 2005), 41–53.

9 | See Chang Lin-Sheng, "The National Palace Museum: A History of the Collection," in Wen Fong and James Watt, eds., *Possessing the Past: Treasures from the National Palace Museum, Taipei*, exh. cat. (New York: Metropolitan Museum of Art and Taipei: National Palace Museum, 1996), 3–25.

10 | See Shane McCausland, "The Emperor's Old Toys: Rethinking the Yongzheng (1723–35) *Scroll of Antiquities* in the Percival David Foundation," *Transactions of the Oriental Ceramic Society* 66 (2001–2): 65–75.

11 | See Yang Xin, "*Yinzhen weiping meiren tu tanmi*" [Research on the Set of Paintings *Yinzhen Weiping meiren tu*], *Gugong bowuyuan yuankan* [Bulletin of the Palace Museum] 154 (2011/2): 6–23.

12 | Eugene Yuejin Wang, "Mirror, Death, and Rhetoric: Reading Later Han Chinese Bronze Artifacts," *Art Bulletin* 76:3 (1994): 511–34.

13 | See Liu Yu, "Emperor Qianlong's Four Catalogues on Bronzes," in this catalogue, 140–43. See also Yu Hui-chun, "The Intersection of Past and Present: The Qianlong Emperor and His Ancient Bronzes" (PhD diss., Princeton University, 2007), esp. chap. 1, 21–71; Zhu Shuai, "*Xiqing gujian* yanjiu" [Study of *Xiqing gujian*] (MA thesis, Zhongguo meishu xueyuan, 2013); and Wei Xinying, "Qinggong cang qingtongqi pulu: 'Qianlong sijian' xiangguan wenti tanxi" [The Bronze Records of the Qing Palace: Analysis of Relevant Issues on "Qianlong sijian"], *Gugong xuekan* [Journal of Gugong Studies] (2015/1): 340–54.

14 | *Xiqing gujian* [Imperial Preface]. I use the facsimile edition that was based on the copy printed by the court in 1755, reprinted in Liu Qingzhu, Duan Zhihong, and Feng Shi, eds., *Jinwen wenxian jicheng* [Compendium of Publications on Bronze Inscriptions], 47 vols. (Beijing: Xianzhuang shuju, 2005), vol. 3, 92–93.

15 | See Rong Geng, "Qingdai jijin shuji shu-ping" [Reviews of Publications of Studies on Bronzes and Steles of the Qing Dynasty], in *Rong Geng xueshu zhuzuo quanji* [Complete Collection of Rong Geng's Academic Writings] (Beijing: Zhonghua shuju, 2011), vol. 22, 68–78.

16 | See Liu Yu, *Qianlong sijian zonglibiao* [Collation Table of Qianlong's Four Bronze Catalogues] (Beijing: Zhonghua shuju, 1989).

17 | See Yu, "Intersection of Past and Present," chap. 2, 112–39.

18 | *Da Qing huidian zeli, juan* 75, in *Siku quanshu, Wenyuange* edition. This is also found in Zhao Erxu et al., *Qingshigao* [Draft History of Qing Dynasty] (Beijing: Zhonghua shuju, 1977), 2494.

19 | See Liu Yue, "Wangu reng cun shigu qing: Qianlong shiqi gongting gongyi fanggu fengge de chengyin yu tedian [The Reasons and Characteristics of Archaism in Court Craft Production during the Qianlong Period], *Zijingcheng* [Forbidden City] (2006/2): 42–47, (2006/3): 59–61, and (2006/4): 36–45.

20 | See Jessica Rawson, "Novelties in Antiquarian Revivals: The Case of the Chinese Bronzes," *National Palace Museum Research Quarterly* 22:1 (2004): 1–34.

21 | See Wang Zilin, *Ming Qing huanggong cheshe* [Interior of the Imperial Palaces in the Ming and Qing Dynasties] (Beijing: Gugong chubanshe, 2011), 44, 57–68, 145–6, 208–11, 256, 258, for examples of how ancient bronzes were installed and displayed at various palaces.

22 | Thomas Lawton, "An Imperial Legacy Revisited: Bronze Vessels from the Qing Palace Collection," *Asian Art* 1:1 (1987/88): 53, and "Jin Futing: A 19th Century Chinese Collector-Connoisseur," *Transactions of the Oriental Ceramic Society* 1989–1990 (1991): 35–61, in which Lawton has cited a few examples in which collectors' seals and inscriptions were added to ancient bronzes.

23 | See Yu, "Intersection of Past and Present," 47–49.

24 | *Xiqing gujian, juan* 39, 1–2. Qu Yuan was a patriotic poet who lived in the Chu State during the Warring States period.

25 | For more on mirrors in Daoism, see Ebrey, *Accumulating Culture*, 184–203.

26 | See Wu Hsiao-yun, ed., *Qianlong huangdi de jingzi: Qinggong jingjian wenhua yu diancang* [Reflections of the Emperor: The Collection and Culture of Mirrors at the Qing Court], exh. cat. (Taipei: National Palace Museum, 2015), esp. 290–303.

27 | See Chang Lin-Sheng, "Jifan liu hui" [Auspicious Molds Shine], *Gugong wenwu yuekan* [National Palace Museum Monthly of Chinese Art] 3:6 (1985): 4–12; *De Jiaqu: Qianlong huangdi de taoci pinwei* [Obtaining Refined Enjoyment: The Qianlong Emperor's Taste in Ceramics], ed. Yu Pei-chin, exh. cat. (Taipei: National Palace Museum, 2012), 26–32, 263–78.

28 | See Yu, "Intersection of Past and Present," chap. 4, 140–71, and "Qianlong's Divine Treasures: The Bells in Rhyming-the-Old Hall," *Asia Major*, Third Series, 22:2 (2009): 121–44.

29 | *Qinding rixia jiuwen kao, juan* 22 [Investigation of the Old Stories of the Capital], in *Siku quanshu, Wenyuange* edition.

30 | *Xiqing xujian jiabian, juan* 17, 1–3, in Liu, Duan, and Feng, *Jinwen wenxian jicheng*, vol. 5, 432–41.

31 | Yu, "Qianlong's Divine Treasures," 143.

32 | Yu, "Intersection of Past and Present," chap. 5, 172–225, and "Bronzes from Afar: Ch'ien-lung's 'Hsi-ch'ing Hsü-chien Chia-pien Fu-lu,'" *Meishushi yanjiu jikan* [Essays on Art History] 31 (2011): 151–96.

33 | Yu, "Bronzes from Afar," 189.

34 | See Jonathan Brown, *Kings and Connoisseurs: Collecting Art in Seventeenth-Century Europe* (Princeton: Princeton University Press, 1995).

35 | Ebrey, *Accumulating Culture*, 341–47.

36 | For a more detailed discussion of these portraits, see Lu Zhang's essay, "*One or Two?*," in this catalogue, 144–47. See also, among others, Wu Hung, *The Double Screen: Medium and Representation in Chinese Painting* (Chicago: University of Chicago Press, 1996), 231–36; and Kristina Kleutghen, "One or Two, Repictured," *Archives of Asian Art* 62 (2012): 25–46.

37 | Harold L. Kahn, "A Master of Taste: The Monumental and Exotic in the Qianlong Reign," in Ju-hsi Chou and Claudia Brown, eds., *The Elegant Brush: Chinese Painting under the Qianlong Emperor 1735–1795*, exh. cat. (Phoenix: Phoenix Art Museum, 1985), 288–302.

38 | Ibid., 291.

EMPEROR QIANLONG'S FOUR CATALOGUES ON BRONZES

LIU YU

During a forty-year period of his reign, which lasted from 1735 to 1796, Qianlong, one of the most powerful emperors in the history of China, oversaw the documentation of his bronze collection, which totaled 4,105 pieces and included, among other items, vessels and mirrors.[1] Under his patronage, four catalogues were published, which greatly promoted antiquarian study during the Qing and continue to serve scholars today. The resulting books were named *Xiqing gujian* (Ancient Mirror of Western Clarity; hereafter referred to as *Xiqing*; 1755; see fig. 1), *Ningshou jiangu* (Reflections on Antiquity from the Palace of Tranquil Longevity, hereafter referred to as *Ningshou*), *Xiqing xujian jiabian* (Supplement A to *Xiqing*; hereafter referred to as *Xijia*; 1781–93), and *Xiqing xujian yibian* (Supplement B to *Xiqing*, hereafter referred to as *Xiyi*; 1781–93; see pl. 98). Because each of the four catalogues all contain the character *jian* (reflection) in their titles, together they are called "Qianlong's four *jian*."

The names Qianlong gave these compilations indicate either the place where the catalogues were prepared or the palace where the bronzes documented in the catalogues were kept. Three use the term *xiqing*, which literally translates as "western clarity." The word is first seen in Sima Qian's *Shiji* (Records of the Grand Historian; 94 BC). It first appears in the chapter titled "Biography of Sima Xiangru": "Green dragons slither from the eastern pavilion; elephant-carved carriages prance from the hall of Western Clarity (*xiqing*)."[2] In an annotation to *Shiji*, the Eastern Jin dynasty scholar Guo Pu wrote, "*xiqing* means a quiet place in the west wing."[3] Later, *xiqing* is used to indicate a peaceful and relaxing place in the imperial palace. Probably inspired by *Shiji*, Qing emperors used the same word to describe the *Nanshufang*, the Southern Library in the Forbidden City, where scholars from the Imperial Hanlin Academy prepared the bronze catalogues and many other important catalogues of the imperial art collections. *Ningshou*, which literally translates as "tranquil longevity," is the name of the palace in the Forbidden City that Qianlong built for his retirement, but which he never moved into, having abdicated in 1796. *Ningshou* includes bronzes kept in the Palace of Tranquil Longevity.

Qianlong regarded ancient bronze vessels as embodiments of ritual, power, and venerability. In the edict that served as a preface to *Xiqing*, the emperor explained, "the *zun* and *yi* wine vessels, *ding* and *nai* cauldrons have lasted for generations" and he believed that "collecting and studying ancient bronzes would enable us to use the reserve of energy accumulated from working with the arts and to embody the ideas we have gained from reflection on the past; which surely can also be called in the name of prosperity and elegance."

The study of ancient bronzes and inscriptions had flourished during the Song dynasty (960–1279), with the publication of numerous antiquarian studies, such as *Kaogutu* (Illustrated Investigations of Antiquity; 1092), *Chongxiu Xuanhe bogutu* [Illustrated Broad Manifestation of Antiquity], and *Lidai zhongding yiqi kuanzhi fatie* (Model Inscriptions from Ritual Bronzes from Successive Dynasties; 1144). Famous antiquarian scholar-elites such as Lü Dalin, Xue Shanggong, and Zhao Mingcheng collected and wrote during this time. However, the following two dynasties, the Yuan (1271–1368) and Ming (1368–1644), witnessed little progress in the field. Research was reignited under Qianlong with *Xiqing*. Qianlong's four *jian* follow the Song dynasty bronze cataloguing tradition, which not only enumerated the distinctive features of each bronze, such as the dimension, weight, and capacity, but also included a beautiful line drawing of the object done by a professional painter. The inscriptions were hand copied from the actual objects, which makes them potentially less accurate than ink-squeezed rubbings but still a reliable resource for research purposes. The four *jian* have fewer printing errors than the Song dynasty catalogues such as *Kaogutu*, since the latter has been reprinted many times.

Xiqing was the first catalogue and was initiated in 1749. Qianlong authorized the project in an imperial edict issued on the seventh day of the eleventh lunar month of the fourteenth year of his reign. It was finished on the fifth month of 1751, and was printed four years later, in 1755, by the imperial printing house. However, the emperor's bronze collection kept growing. According to the catalogue's postscript, in the forty-sixth year of his reign, thirty years after *Xiqing* was written, Qianlong commissioned a supplemental catalogue, *Xijia*, to record his bronzes that were housed in the Forbidden City. The catalogue took thirteen years to compile and was completed in 1793, the fifty-eighth year of his reign. The postscript to *Xijia* mentions that Qianlong also ordered a second supplemental catalogue, the *Xiyi*, to catalogue the bronzes that he kept in his palace in Mukden (now Shenyang in Liaoning), the old capital of the Manchu empire before it conquered the Ming dynasty in 1644. These two supplemental catalogues were written at around the same time (1781–93), but addressed bronzes in different locations; comparison of the contents of the two catalogues shows that they do not overlap. Unlike *Xiqing* and its two supplemental catalogues, *Ningshou* has neither a preface nor a postscript to indicate the compilation date or authorship. Since the Ningshou Palace was completed in 1776, the forty-first year of Qianlong's reign, we can assume that this catalogue was started some time after 1776. Because the description and examination sections in both *Xijia* and *Xiyi* cite *Ningshou* as a reference for several entries, *Ningshou* must have been compiled before the two supplemental catalogues. Therefore, we may assume that *Ningshou* was compiled at some point between 1776 and 1781.

Xiqing, composed of forty volumes, is the first bronze catalogue that comprehensively documents the Qing dynasty's imperial collection of ancient bronzes. Both the format and cataloguing principles of the book imitate *Bogutu*, which was compiled during the Daguan reign of Emperor Huizong (r. 1101–26) of the Northern Song dynasty (960–1127). *Xiqing* recorded in total 1,529 bronze objects, ranging from the Shang and Zhou periods (c. 1600–256 BC) to the Tang dynasty (618–907). The objects include different types of bronze vessels, such as *ding* (cauldrons with three or four legs), *zun* (a type of wine container), *lei* (tall wine jars), *yi* (a type of bowl), *you* (lidded wine buckets), *ping* (a type of bottle), *hu* (pear-shaped jars), *fu* and *gui* (food containers), and a number of bronze mirrors; 586 of the objects bear inscriptions. *Xiqing* lists the dimensions, weight, and inscriptions for each bronze, and every object is illustrated by one of the court painters: Liang Guan, Li Huilin, or Ding Guanpeng.[4] *Ningshou*, which also includes the dimensions, weight, and inscriptions, as well as an illustration for each bronze, has 16 volumes recording 701 ancient bronzes selected from the collection at Ningshou Palace, including 144 objects with inscriptions. *Xijia* consists of 20 volumes, listing 941 newly added bronzes, of which 257 have inscriptions; in addition, it also includes 31 seals and weapons. The *Xiyi*, which also consists of 20 volumes, documented 900 bronzes kept in the Shengjing imperial palace, including 192 inscribed objects. In total, the emperor's four catalogues list 4,105 bronze objects, and among these, 1,179 are inscribed (not including the 114 bronze mirrors).

Qianlong directly authorized and oversaw the compilation and editing of all four bronze catalogues. According to an edict issued in 1749, the purpose, cataloguing principles, editorial boards, and illustration teams were all determined by the emperor himself. Moreover, after each volume was completed, he reviewed and edited the manuscript. Therefore, for all four catalogues, the editors reported to the emperor, fully following his orders on all matters, from the writing and editing to the publishing. Indeed, Qianlong appointed two imperial princes as associate supervisors for the editorial work: Prince Yunlu, the sixteenth son of the Emperor Kangxi (r. 1662–1722), who had mastered mathematics and music theory; and Prince Hongyan, the sixth son of the Emperor Yongzheng (r. 1723–35), who was famous for his accomplishments in poetry and book collecting. These appointments further demonstrated that the bronze cataloguing project strictly followed imperial orders. A massive project, the cataloguing took several decades and documented thousands of bronzes; the editorial team comprised over thirty-five people, including major literary officials and skilled painters who were responsible for drawing illustrations, transcribing inscriptions, explaining the objects, and researching the annotations.

Xiqing has gone through seven editions. The first edition, which is considered the best, was woodblock printed by the imperial printing house at Wuying Palace in the twentieth year of Qianlong's reign (1755); it is known variously as the *Wuyingdianben* (Wuying Palace edition), *dianben* (the Palace edition), or the *neifuben* (the imperial household edition). The print block of this edition measures 11 5⁄8 × 8 7⁄8 inches, and the paper is a fine quality southern paper known as *kaihuazhi*, renowned

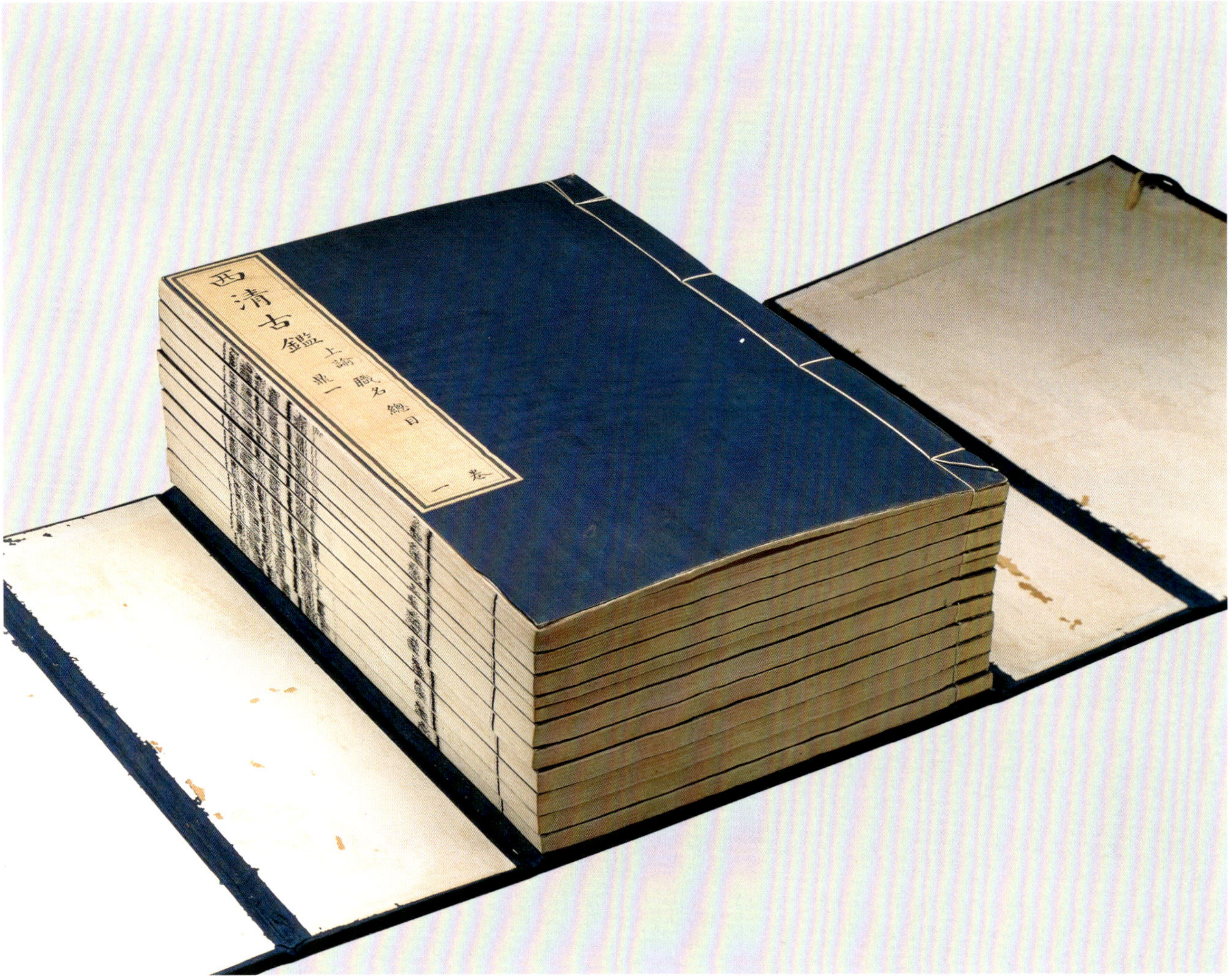

1 | Liang Shizheng (Chinese, 1697–1763) and others. *Xiang gujian* [Ancient Mirror of Western Clarity], *Wuyingdian* edition, Qing dynasty (1644–1911), Qianlong reign (1735–96). The Palace Museum, Beijing. See pl. 98.

for being white, smooth, thin, and long lasting. In the fourteenth year of Emperor Guangxu's reign (1888; r. 1875–1908), a Japanese publishing house, Maisong Book Houses, printed a high-quality edition of *Xiqing* using copperplate printing technology; it is thus called "the Japanese copperplate edition." Its plates were close in size to those of the Wuying Palace edition and its images are even sharper, but the images and inscriptions are slightly smaller, and there are some transcription errors. During the late Qing and the Republican periods (late 19th century to 1949), three more lithographic editions were published, using the above two editions as models. Qianlong also ordered that the *Xiqing* be included in the *Siku quanshu* (Complete Library of Four Treasures). Based on the Wuying Palace edition, this edition was completed in November 1784 and is known as the *Siku quanshu* edition. However, it contains many errors and is probably the worst of the printed editions.

In addition to the printed versions, Qianlong also commissioned a hand-painted copy of *Xiqing*. The Institute of Archaeology of the Chinese Academy of Social Sciences (then the Chinese Academy of Sciences) purchased four volumes of this rare edition in 1956. It is seven inches tall and the volumes are in *jingzhe zhuang* (folding sutra) format, but without block binding or page numbers. The contents are identical to volume thirty-two of the Wuying Palace edition, but the sequence of the bronzes and the calligraphy and inscription tracings are not the same. The illustrations are in the meticulous, delicate, fine-line style of Chinese *gongbi* painting but were clearly influenced by European naturalism, as they look as though they were drawn directly from the vessels themselves, with a three-dimensional appearance and realistic representation of color, patina, and texture.

The earliest edition of the *Ningshou* known today is the manuscript produced by the imperial household of the Ningshou Palace, which totals sixteen volumes and is currently in the ancient books collection of the National Library in Beijing. The printing block of this edition is 11 5/8 inches tall. The first edition of *Xijia* was also produced by the Ningshou Palace, and copies are now in both the Palace Museum, Beijing, and the National Palace Museum, Taipei. Its printing block is 11 5/8 inches tall as well.[5] Shangwu Yinshuguan (Commercial Press) of Shanghai published excellent-quality lithographic editions of *Ningshou* and *Xijia* in 1910 and 1913, respectively. These editions were based on the first editions, but their print block was reduced in size to 6 13/16 inches tall. The manuscript of the first edition of *Xiyi* was also produced by the Ningshou Palace and should have the same dimensions as the other three catalogues, but its current location is unknown. In 1931 the Peking Antiquities Exhibition Institute, the first national museum established in China, founded during the Republican period within the old imperial place, published a reduced-size lithographic version of *Xiyi*, based on the first edition. Its print block is 6 13/16 inches tall, the same as the other two prints published by Shangwu Yinshuguan, and is also of high quality.

A major criticism of Qianlong's four catalogues is that the authors were unable to distinguish reproductions from authentic pieces, so the books include many fakes. Rong Geng, a leading scholar on ancient Chinese bronzes, studied all the 1,179 inscribed bronzes recorded in the compilations and found 189 likely fakes and 336 definite fakes. My own study, based on Geng's research, shows 81 questionable pieces and 317 inauthentic pieces. This clearly shows that almost a third of the inscribed bronzes recorded in the four Qianlong catalogues are problematic. Because none of the original compilers were epigraphic specialists, their analyses of the inscriptions and their dating were flawed. For instance, for the date of each object, the authors gave only a dynastic term, such as Shang, or Zhou, or Han, and many were incorrect. Thus these aspects of the catalogues cannot be used as reliable scholarship for contemporary research.

Despite such shortcomings, the historical catalogues offer an invaluable resource for contemporary study of ancient bronze inscriptions. Since many bronzes documented in the catalogues do not survive, these records are the only source of information on those objects—as the four *jian* compiled under Qianlong's patronage attest. For example, the eighth volume of *Xiqing* records a bronze wine vessel, now lost, that was commissioned by someone named Mai and is thus known as the *Mai zun*. It was inscribed with a 163 character-long essay documenting how the Zhou king rode in a boat and performed the Dafeng rite, an archery ritual, at Biyong Lake. Similarly, the *Geng hu* recorded in the sixteenth volume of *Xijia* bears a long inscription of over 200 characters; this inscription was published in the *Shang Zhou jinwen luyi* (Collected Records of Shang and Zhou Bronze Inscriptions; 1957) by Yu Xingwu, but its line-drawing image is only recorded in *Xijia*. There are many similar examples. Of the 1,179 inscribed objects documented in the four catalogues, only 203 pieces are extant; the rest are missing. Nonetheless, we can study the description, drawing, and inscription of each of the missing objects in the four catalogues. In this way, the catalogues contribute significantly to preserving ancient bronzes, one of the most important legacies of ancient Chinese culture.

NOTES

1 | The term *bronze* is used here in a loose sense to include all metal works.

2 | For an English translation, see Sima Qian, "Biography of Sima Xiangru," in *Records of the Grand Historian, Han Dynasty II*, trans. Burton Watson, rev. ed. (New York: Columbia University Press, 1993), 276.

3 | Unless otherwise noted, all translations are by the translators of this essay.

4 | In the fifteenth year of his reign (1750), Qianlong called Liang Shizheng, the chief editor of *Xiqing*, to compile a catalogue of the 567 ancient coins kept in the imperial household. The resulting *Qian lu* (Catalogue of Money) consists of sixteen volumes, finished in 1751, the same year as *Xiqing*. It was attached to *Xiqing* as an appendix.

5 | The measurements given by two museums vary slightly. The Palace Museum, Beijing, records it as 29.5 × 22.6 cm, whereas the National Palace Museum, Taipei, gives 29.4 × 21.5 cm. The discrepancy is probably due to the manner in which the printing blocks were measured at the two institutions.

ONE OR TWO?: SELF-REPRESENTATION IN EMPEROR QIANLONG'S PORTRAITURE

LU ZHANG

One or two?

Neither come together; nor separate.

Can be a Confucian scholar;
can be a Mohist.

Why should I worry, or even
contemplate?

—Emperor Qianlong[1]

One or Two?, a dual portrait of Emperor Qianlong (r. 1736–1795) of the Qing dynasty (1644–1911), is a famous painting that exists in five versions, four of which are frequently exhibited. In all versions, the emperor sits on a couch-bed surrounded by his collection of ancient bronzes, ceramics, jades, and books. The painting presents a carefully crafted image of Qianlong. It not only highlights his connoisseurship and enthusiasm for art collecting but also his philosophical perspective. Above all, it depicts him as inhabiting multiple identities: Manchu ruler, traditional Chinese literatus, a practitioner of the Buddhist faith, and a proponent of both Confucianism and Mohism.[2] All five surviving versions of *One or Two?* are preserved in the Palace Museum in Beijing. One is in poor condition and very little is known about it because it cannot be safely unrolled.[3] The other four versions have been extensively studied and widely exhibited. Each was inscribed by Qianlong himself with the short poem cited at the beginning of this essay, which the emperor personally composed. The painting's title, *One or Two?*, comes from the first line of this poem. The inscription on each version differs only in the place name that follows the poem. All but one of the versions derive their name from this place name: *Eternal Spring Studio* (Changchun Shuwu; fig. 1a), *Mental Cultivation Hall* (Yangxin Dian; fig. 1b and pl. 138), and *The Cave of Narayana* (Naluoyan ku; fig. 1c). Another version, also inscribed *Eternal Spring Studio*, is called *Plum Screen* after the motif in the screen at center (fig. 1d). In both their similarities and differences, they show how the image was, for Qianlong, a highly self-conscious means of symbolically legitimizing his rule. As sovereign of a foreign (Manchu) regime, the emperor aimed to position himself as an educated connoisseur in the tradition of the literati, the most respected members of the ethnic Chinese (Han) society under his control.

The four studied versions of *One or Two?* share a composition. In all, Qianlong wears the black horsehair hat and flowing robe of Han Chinese scholars. He sits on a wide wood couchbed in the center of the painting, holding a scroll in his left hand and a brush in his right. Behind the couch bed is a large standing screen. In one version (fig. 1d), this screen simply displays a blossoming plum. In each of the other three versions, however, the screen bears a landscape that enhances the room's atmosphere and affords a sense of depth that contrasts with the relatively shallow space of the interior. A bust-length portrait of the emperor hangs over the left side of the screen, facing the "real" emperor; both Qianlongs wear the black hat and robe. The double portrait dramatizes the first two lines of the inscribed poem: "Is there one person in the painting? Or are there two? Am I the same person in reality as I am depicted in the portrait?"

The portrait-within-a-portrait composition predates Qianlong's era. An album leaf (fig. 2) that Qianlong acquired when he was a prince is likely a primary inspiration for *One or Two?*.[4] Although the paintings differ in size, their major elements are the same. Both have a double-portrait design and depict the same individual items, including the screen, the books, the rolled paintings and antiquities sitting on the tables or couch-bed, and especially the dress and position of the scholar and his attendant.

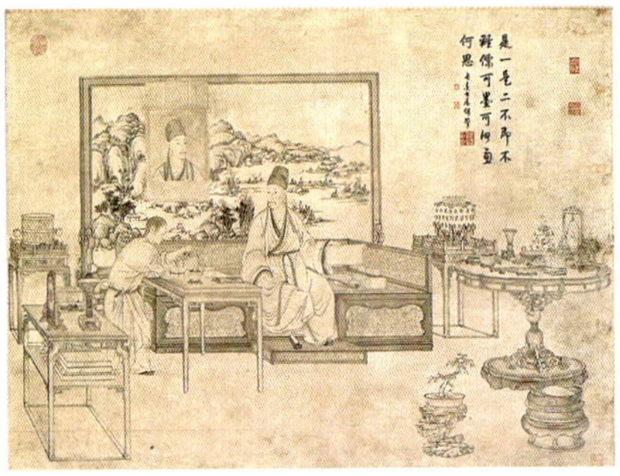

1a. *Eternal Spring Studio* version. 75 × 150 cm (29 ½ × 59 in.). Acc. no. GU005313.

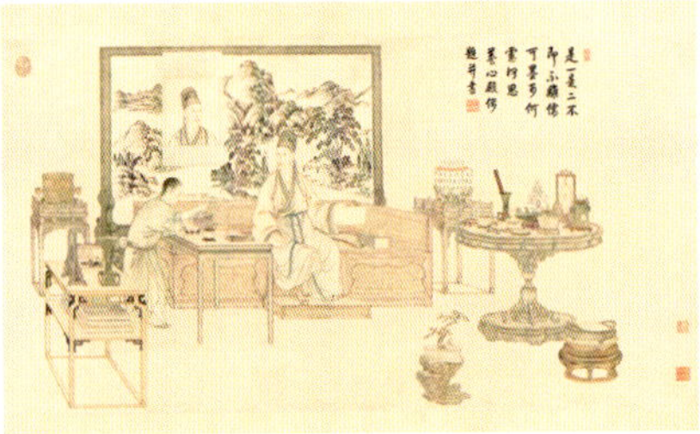

1b. *Mental Cultivation* version. 230 × 168 cm (90 9/16 × 66 1/8 in.).

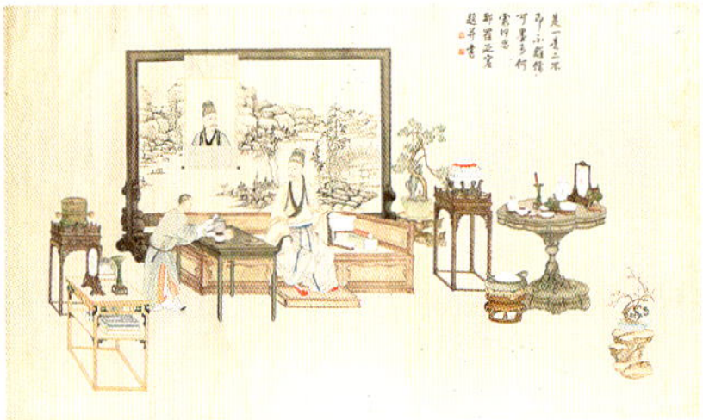

1c. *The Cave of Narayana* version. 75 × 150 cm (29 ½ × 59 in.). Acc. no. GU006491.

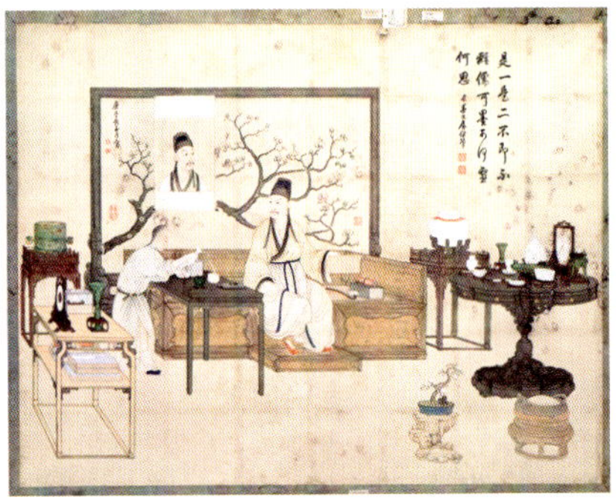

1d. *Plum Screen* version, 1780. 75 × 150 cm (29 ½ × 59 in.). Acc. no. GU006492.

1 | The four studied versions of *One or Two?*, Qing dynasty, Qianlong reign (1736–1795). Affixed hanging for standing screen, remounted as a hanging scroll. a: ink on paper, b–d: ink and color on paper. Palace Museum, Beijing.

The references to the earlier painting are not accidental; it was long linked to Emperor Huizong (r. 1101–1126), with whom Qianlong likely sought to associate himself. Although some scholars now date the work to the Ming dynasty (1368–1644), *Scholar* was previously thought to be a Song work, mainly based on the seals that appear on it.[5] Indeed, Qianlong may have believed that this painting was collected by Huizong, or even a depiction of Huizong himself. Of all Qianlong's predecessors, Huizong was the most renowned for his art collection. He was also known for his talents in painting, calligraphy, poetry, and music—the so called "Four Accomplishments" of the scholar-gentleman. The composition of *One or Two?* suggests that Qianlong may have intended to emulate Huizong, portraying himself as a collector and connoisseur of equal distinction to the earlier, Han Chinese emperor, thereby asserting the legitimacy of his rule.

During the Qing dynasty, the educated elite—both Manchu and Han Chinese—commissioned portraits of themselves appreciating antiquities as a testament to their erudition, connoisseurship, and antiquarian interests. By contrast, Qianlong skillfully used his relationship to the arts to express his political identity. In all four studied versions of *One or Two?*, his clothing is that of a traditional Chinese literatus, not the Manchu ruler that he was, and the scroll and brush he holds attest to his allegiance to the values of Han Chinese intellectuals and connoisseurs.[6] But it is perhaps the works of art surrounding him that do the most symbolic work. These imperial possessions, including ancient bronze vessels, jades, ceramics, books, and scrolls of painting and calligraphy, span about four thousand years, from the Three Dynasties period (c. 2100–206 BC) to Qianlong's own day. The bronze standard measure (*jialiang*; fig. 3) to the left of the screen is particularly meaningful. Commissioned by Wang Mang during the first year of the Xin dynasty (AD 9–23), it was also recorded in Qianlong's catalogue of his imperial bronze collection, *Xiqing gujian* (Ancient Mirror of Western Clarity).[7] Wang Mang usurped the Han dynasty throne for a mere fourteen years but was a visionary and social and economic reformer who aimed to devise laws in accord with classical texts. Each section of the *jialiang* represents a standard unit of volume—*yue*, *ge*, *sheng*, *dou*, and *hu*.[8] As the power to issue standards for weights and measures was strictly reserved for the emperor, the *jialiang* in *One or Two?* attests less to Qianlong's antiquarianism than to his supreme authority. In all four versions of the painting, the *jialiang* is elaborately depicted, with traces of its long inscription visible.

Five bronze ritual vessels are also depicted in each of the paintings. These include two beakers (*gu*), one on the wood table to the left of the couch bed and one on the round Baroque-style lacquer table to the right. The latter table also features a second beaker, as well as a large water vessel (*pan*) and a wine goblet (*jia*). Bronze vessels had been used by royal and noble families of the Three Dynasties in the worship of ancestors and heaven, and the vessels later came to be valued as symbols of power and political status. The accidental discovery of a bronze vessel was considered an auspicious omen—heavenly approval of rulership—starting in at least the Han dynasty (206 BC–AD 220). The belief in bronzes as moral symbols of a virtuous state naturally encouraged emperors to collect these vessels. The ancient bronze vessels in *One or Two?* thus symbolize Qianlong's heavenly mandate to rule.

A blue-and-white porcelain jar on a tall wood table to the right of the screen presents a very different symbol of Qianlong's authority. Scholars have dated this vessel (fig. 4) to the reign of the Emperor Xuande (r. 1426–35) of the Ming dynasty, who was well known

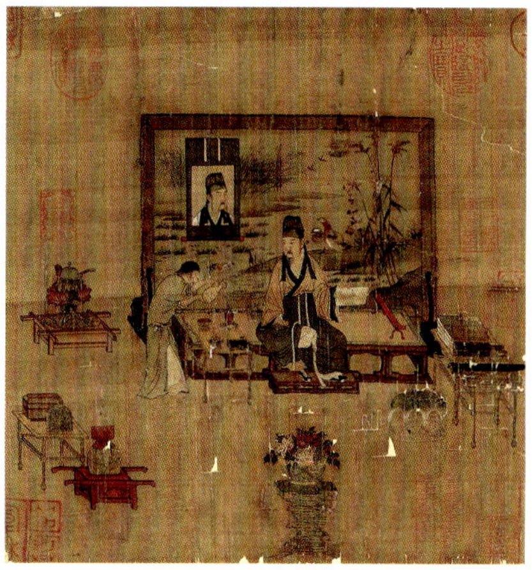

2 | Artist unknown. *Scholar*, Song dynasty (960–1279). Album leaf, ink and color on silk; 29 × 27.8 cm (11 3/8 × 11 in.). National Palace Museum, Taipei, acc. no. Guhua 001261-1.

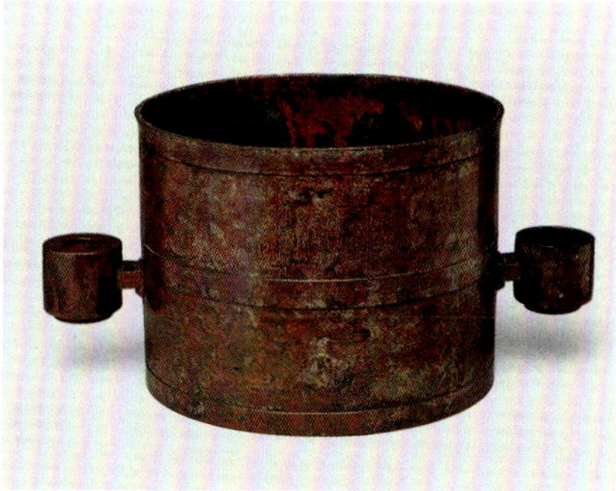

3 | Standard measure (*jialiang*), Wang Mang Interregnum (AD 9–23), AD 9. Bronze; h. 10 1/16 (25.6 cm); diam. of mouth 13 3/8 in. (34 cm). National Palace Museum, Taipei, acc. no. Gutong 2384.

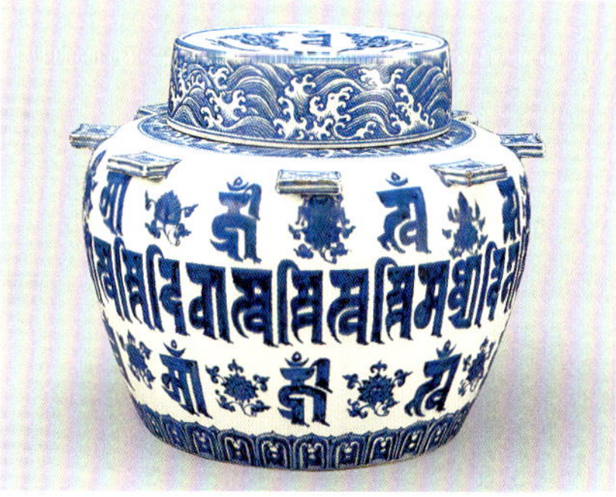

4 | Blue-and-white porcelain jar painted with lanca script, Ming dynasty, Xuande period (1426–1435). Porcelain; h. 28.7 cm (11 5/16 in.), diam. 19.7 cm (7 3/4 in.). Palace Museum, Beijing, acc. no. GU145578.

for his patronage of Tibetan Buddhism. With its mandala-shaped cover and Sanskrit inscription in underglaze blue on the body, it was probably used in Tantric rituals at court. The vessel was depicted in the *Guwantu* (Scroll of Antiquities; see fig. 3 on p. 130)—a set of long handscrolls commissioned by Qianlong's father, Emperor Yongzheng (r. 1723–1735) to record selected artwoks in the Qing imperial collection.[9] Like his father and grandfather, Qianlong was an important patron of Tibetan Buddhism. This religion was not only his personal faith but also a tool for maintaining peace with the Mongols and Tibetans he ruled. The blue-and-white jar therefore constitutes a visual metaphor for the vast expanse of Qianlong's regime—a political concept not seen in paintings with traditional literati themes such as scholarly gatherings and the appreciation of antiquities.

There are, however, differences among the four studied versions, and these differences reveal their relative age. *Eternal Spring Studio* and *Mental Cultivation Hall* were probably painted at about the same time and perhaps by the same artist or workshop. Their distinctly Western features—detailed and nuanced execution of the emperor's double portraits and three-dimensional rendering of the interior space and furnishings—suggest the Italian Jesuit court painter Giuseppe Castiglione was involved in the conception and execution of each[10] The upper left corner of *Plum Screen* bears Qianlong's signature—"imperial signature written in the month of the summer solstice of the *gengzi* year (1780)." If this signature is accepted, this version of *One or Two?* can be precisely dated. *The Cave of Narayana* was probably made at roughly the same time as *Plum Screen*, if not earlier, because its composition, especially the landscape motif of the standing screen, closely resembles the design of the first two versions. Both *Plum Screen* and *The Cave of Narayana* depict the emperor's face as wrinkled and his eyes as slightly puffy, underlined with bags. These features strongly suggest that the ruler portrayed in these two paintings is considerably older than the man in *Eternal Spring Studio* and *Mental Cultivation Hall*.

One or Two? may be the only painting that Qianlong commissioned in multiple versions, which attests to his affinity for the composition. The absence of any inscriptions besides the emperor's own poem render him the central focus of the work. The poem serves a critical function, operating separately from the image to tell viewers about the monarch's diverse identities—as a Confucian and/or Mohist scholar, and as a Buddhist layperson. The decor in each painting—the self-portrait that presides directly over the emperor, as well as the antiquities that surround him—allows the future Qianlong to view his own past. The juxtaposition of the ruler's two portraits, together with the poem of his own composition, written in his own hand, identify the emperor as both subject and observer, and suggest he played an active role in conceiving this composition as a symbol of his self-image as the moral and historically conscious Chinese sovereign.

For example, it is likely that the decoration on the screen in one of the studied versions was a highly deliberate choice. *Plum Screen* alone bears a blossoming plum branch on its screen. Recent scholarship has convincingly demonstrated that this motif was probably painted by the emperor himself.[11] As the first tree to bloom in late winter, the plum has traditionally been regarded by Chinese literati as a symbol of inner beauty, humility, and fortitude. Thus, that Qianlong chose the blossoming plum to enhance this screen was undoubtedly not arbitrary.

Emperor Qianlong clearly used *One or Two?* to present a carefully crafted, multidimensional image of himself

as a cultivated Chinese gentleman. Like the most important antiquities in his vast collection, these paintings were far more than objects to be enjoyed and admired in leisure or connoisseurship. Rather, they were a means of asserting his political legitimacy in the present and of idealizing his character in the future.

NOTES

1 | The translation is from Wu Hung, *The Double Screen: Medium and Representation in Chinese Painting* (Chicago: University of Chicago Press, 1996), 235.

2 | For a discussion of Mohism, see Frederic W. Mote, "Mo Tzu: His Philosophical Ideas," *Intellectual Foundations of China*, 2nd ed. (New York: McGraw Hill, 1989), 77–83.

3 | This version is acc. no. GU006490. Zhang Zhen, curator of Chinese painting at the Palace Museum, to Lu Zhang, August 7, 2017.

4 | Two seals, *Zhenghe* and *Xuanhe*, are era names of Huizong, and two seals, *Shaoxing* and *Qiangua*, belong to Emperor Gaozong (r. 1127–1162). For Qianlong's acquisition of the painting, see Craig Clunas, *Chinese Painting and Its Audiences* (Princeton: Princeton University Press, 2017), 103. For *Scholar* as an inspiration for *One or Two?*, see Hung, *The Double Screen*, 235.

5 | The National Palace Museum, Taipei, dates this painting to the Song dynasty. See *Shiquan Qianlong: Qing Gaozong de yishu pinwei* [The All Complete Qianlong: The Aesthetic Tastes of the Qing Emperor Gaozong], ed. National Palace Museum (Taipei: National Palace Museum, 2013), 331. But recently some major Western scholars have concluded that the seals were likely added later and that the composition most closely approximates that of the paintings depicting Ming literati gatherings in which members are shown appreciating and evaluating antiquities. See James Cahill, *An Index of Early Chinese Paintings and Paintings: T'ang, Sung, and Yuan* (Berkeley: University of California Press, 1980), 221; Hung, *The Double Screen*, 232; and Kristina Kleutghen, "*One or Two*, Repictured," *Archives of Asian Art* 62 (2012), 31.

6 | Wu Hung, "Emperor's Masquerade: 'Costume Portraits" of Yongzheng and Qianlong," *Orientations* 26, no. 7 (July/August 1995): 25–41.

7 | Liang Shizheng (1697–1763), Jiang Pu (1708–1761), eds., *Qinding Xiqing Gujian* [Ancient Mirror of Western Clarity], Qing dynasty, 1749–55. vol. 34, 5, in the collection of the Palace Museum, Beijing.

8 | A 249-character edict encircling the exterior of the vessel not only records its casting process, but also identifies the five measures and asserts that these standard units would last forever. See Wen C. Fong and James C. Y. Watt, *Processing the Past: Treasures from the National Palace Museum*, Taipei (New York: Metropolitan Museum of Art/Taipei: National Palace Museum, 1996), 94–95.

9 | Shane McCausland, "The Emperor's Old Toys: Rethinking the Yongzheng (1723–35) Scroll of Antiquities in the Percival David Foundation," *Transactions of the Oriental Ceramic Society* 66 (2001–2), 71.

10 | Gerald Holzwarth, "*One or Two?*," in *China: The Three Emperors* 1662–1795, ed. Evelyn S. Rawski and Jessica Rawson (London: Royal Academy of Arts, 2005), 439–440; Jason Steuber, "Qing Dynasty Emperors Kangxi and Qianlong: Rule through Replication in Architecture and the Arts," in *Original Intentions: Essays on Production, Reproduction, and Interpretation in the Arts of China*, ed. Nick Pearce and Jason Steuber (Gainesville: University of Florida Press, 2012), 161; Kleutghen, "*One or Two*, Repictured," 28; and Clunas, *Chinese Paintings and Its Audiences*, 105. Castiglione served the Qing court for half a century. Qianlong in particular favored Castiglione's extraordinary blend of the color, perspective, and light found in Italian Renaissance art with the conventions of traditional Chinese brushwork.

11 | Kristina Kleutghen, "The Qianlong Emperor's Perspective: Illusionistic Painting in Eighteenth-Century China" (PhD diss., Harvard University, 2010), 115; Kleutghen, "*One or Two*, Repictured," 38–39.

THE *HEZI YOU* VESSELS: A CASE STUDY IN AUTHENTICITY AND FORGERY

ZHOU YA

The Qing imperial catalogue *Xiqing gujian* (Ancient Mirror of Western Clarity; 1755; hereafter *Xiqing*) records two bronze vessels that are known as the *Hezi You* (Wine Buckets Made for Chief He); they are labeled A (*Xiqing juan* 15, no. 9 [15.9]; fig. 1) and B (*Xiqing juan* 15, no. 11 [15.11]; fig. 2) in this essay. According to the illustrations and inscriptions recorded in the *Xiqing*, there are several noticeable differences between the two vessels. First, the lid of vessel A has a pair of hornlike protrusions on either side and a ring-shaped knob on top, whereas the lid of vessel B lacks horns and has a mushroom-shaped knob. Second, both vessels display a horizontally banded deer motif, but both the lid and body of B exhibit a zoomorphic face design absent on A. Third, the text of the inscription is parsed differently on each vessel: the last two vertical lines of A's inscription each have five characters, while the last two lines of B's have, respectively, six and four characters. There are now two *Hezi You*: one, without lid, is in the Shanghai Museum (see pl. 107), and the other, with both a lid and body, in the Minneapolis Institute of Art (see pl. 108). Their authenticity has long been debated among scholars, and I will offer my observations and assessment here.

It was probably during the reign of the Qing emperor Guangxu (r. 1875–1908) that the former Qing official and famous collector Pan Zuyin obtained a *Hezi You*. Fang Junyi wrote a note after the inscription of the *Hezi You*: "This vessel is recorded in *Xiqing gujian*, but at present it is held in the collection of Minister Pan Zuyin, with its lid missing."[1] Fang thought that Pan's vessel body was the same vessel described in *Xiqing* 15.9. Another famous collector and Qing official, Wu Dacheng, included in his *Kezhai jigulu* (Record of Antiquities Collected by Kezhai; 1918) a rubbing of the inscription on the body of vessel A. Next to the rubbing is a seal impression (see fig. 3) that reads "From Pan Zuyin's prized collection of ritual vessels of the Three Dynasties." These are the earliest clues about the location of the body of vessel A, which was eventually obtained by Li Yinxuan, and after he passed away, donated in 1979 by his wife Qiu Hui to the Shanghai Museum.

The lid of vessel A and the body of vessel B somehow left the Qing palace together and were purchased by Li Zongdai (date unknown), a famous collector who was the former Qing salt commissioner and provincial administrator of Shandong. Later, the vessel was sold by antique dealers to the American collector Alfred F. Pillsbury and is now in the collection of the Minneapolis Institute of Art. However, the whereabouts of the lid of vessel B remains unknown.

As mentioned above, in his publication, Fang Junyi identified the inscription on the body of vessel A as being "held in the collection of Minister Pan Zuyin." But in the same book he also recorded the inscription on the lid of A and noted, "This vessel is complete and now in the collection of Li Zongdai." It is evident that Fang Junyi never saw the *Hezi You* itself; his inscription entries were tracings based on rubbings made by Pan Zuyin and another late Qing collector, Wu Jiechen, and from a letter he received from Pan Zuyin, in which Pan stated that "one complete *Hezi You* vessel with lid was held by Li Zongdai; the one I got was somehow missing the lid." Clearly, Pan knew that there were two *Hezi You* vessels. Although Fang Junyi's record is not inaccurate, it is easily misunderstood as indicating that Pan Zuyin had the body of A, and that Li Zongdai had both the body and lid of B. The confusion is further exacerbated by the fact that Liu Chenggan put the rubbings of the inscriptions on the lids of both vessels A and B together, saying the bronze *you* was "in the collection of Mr. Li of Nanhai (Li Zongdai)."[2]

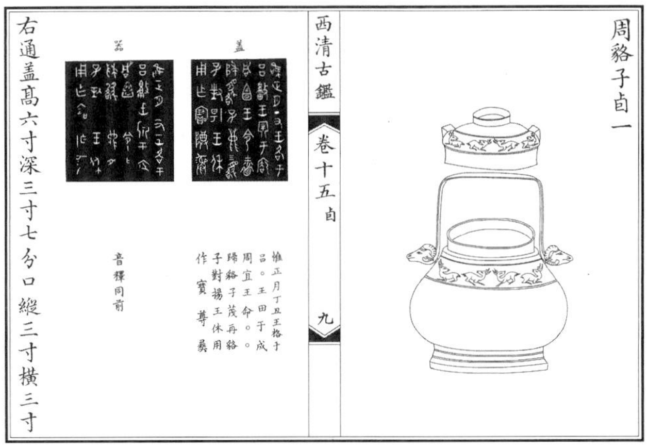

1 | *Hezi You* A in *Xiqing gujian* juan 15, no. 9.

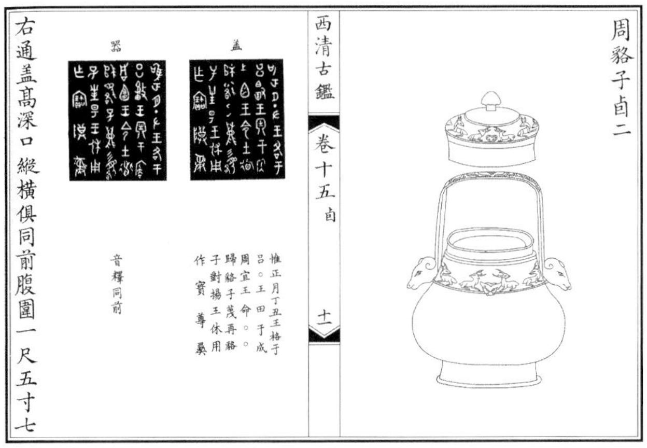

2 | *Hezi You* B in *Xiqing gujian* juan 15, no. 11.

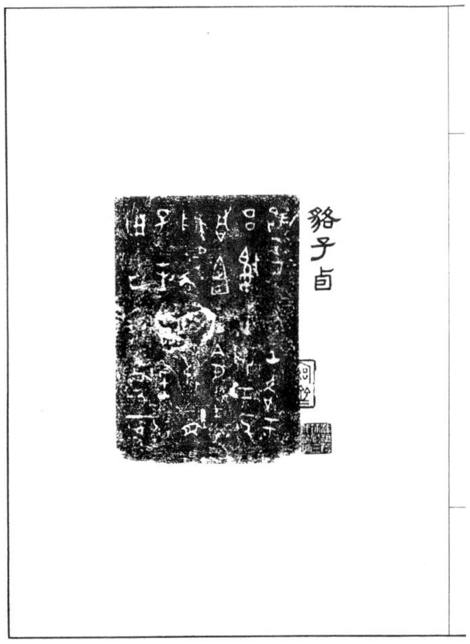

3 | Impression of the seal on *Hezi You* A in Wu Dacheng, *Kezhai jigulu* [Record of Antiquities Collected by Kezhai], 19.24.2.

The esteemed scholar Chen Mengjia managed to most clearly describe the origins and dispersal of the *Hezi You* vessels. In one publication he wrote: "The account in Fang Junyi's *Zhuiyizhai yiqi kuanzhi kaoshi* needs to be corrected. Of the two vessels originally in the Qing palace, for vessel A, Pan [Pan Zuyin] got the body and Li [Li Zongdai] got the lid. As to vessel B, Li got the body and the original lid got lost. The vessel once in Li Zongdai's collection has now been bought by A. F. Pillsbury of Minneapolis, but the lid is that of vessel A, and the body [that] of vessel B."[3] Furthermore, Chen elaborated that:

> The vessel body that Pan held and the lid that Li had are from vessel A in the *Xiqing*, as the inscriptions and layout of the lines are the same. This should be the original set; the knob on the lid of this vessel is ring shaped and is typical of early Western Zhou style. But, the layout of the inscription on B differs from that on A: examination of the inscription indicates that it must have been made in imitation of A, due to some errors. The lid of this vessel has a cap-shaped knob, which is an even earlier style than that of A. In the spring of 1945, I was able to examine the original vessel numerous times at Mr. Pillsbury's house, reaching the conclusion that the lid is that of vessel A, and is authentic, but the body is that of B and is a forgery.[4]

Chen's appraisal was soon almost universally accepted by scholars, such that many subsequent catalogues of bronze vessels included only one *Hezi You*: vessel A (*Xiqing* 15.9)—the body of which was at the Shanghai Museum and the lid of which was held by the Minneapolis Institute of Art. In these and a number of other publications, there is no longer any trace of vessel B.

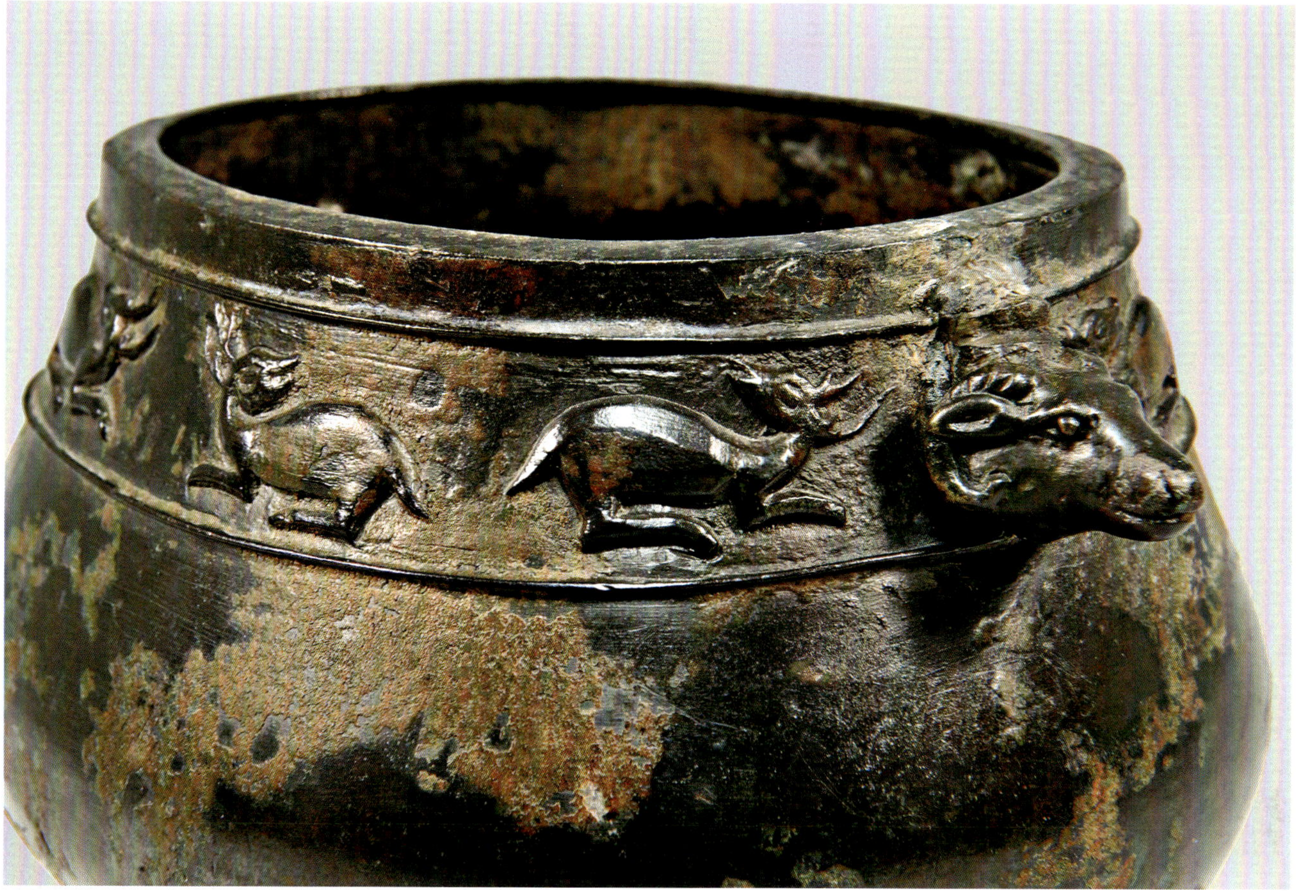

4 | Traces of cutting and knife marks around the deer motifs on the Shanghai Museum *Hezi You*.

My own conclusions about the authenticity of *Hezi You* vessels differ, however, from those of Chen Mengjia. A number of doubts remain about the *Hezi You* vessel body in the Shanghai Museum, alleged to be *Xiqing* 15.9, or what Chen called "Pan's vessel." First, although the form of this vessel is close to that of other *you* vessels dating from the early to mid-Western Zhou dynasty (ninth century BC), the comparison also presents a number of incongruities. In the Shang dynasty (c. 1600–1046 BC) and Western Zhou dynasty (1046–771 BC), lids for this type of oblong bronze bucket are usually bigger than the smaller mouth of the vessel, and the recessed rims have the same thickness as the lids, so that when the lid was on, it would be more or less even with the vessel wall. Examples of this type include the *Ya Guan you* excavated from Miaopubeidi T172 at Anyang (Henan), and the *Zuo Baozunyi you* excavated in 1978 from Qijiacun T19 in Fufeng (Shaanxi). The Shanghai Museum vessel, although superficially similar to these examples, has an inset rim that is only 0.8 millimeters high (by contrast, the inset rim on these other vessels stands several centimeters tall). Most importantly, however, the outer circumference of the rim is in fact on the same arc of the vessel's abdomen—the decorative band of deer that stands in relief on the vessel gives the false impression that the rim is inset. But it is clear that this type of rim design does not allow the lid to fit around the rim, which is not in keeping with the design principles of this type of vessel.

Second, the swing handles of *you* buckets are most commonly cast into two semicircular rings at the shoulders of the vessel body so that the handles can move freely. A minority of vessels employ two protruding stubs at the shoulders, around which are cast a zoomorphic head at each end of the swing handle, also allowing the handle to move. However, on the Shanghai Museum *you* vessel two ram heads appear on either side, a design not seen on other Shang or Zhou vessels. What is more dubious, however, is that the heads are not cast around protruding stubs nor into semicircular rings but are instead riveted onto the outer wall of the vessel. For this reason, the two ram heads are fixed rigidly to the vessel body, partly disrupting the two decorative bow lines. As a result, the swing handle cannot move and loses its customary functionality: the two ram heads merely indicate the presence of a handle. It is possible that the original handle was broken and lost, and that the ram heads were riveted during restoration. I have, however, examined the vessel closely, and no evidence suggests that there once were rings or stubs that had been broken off. Thus, the two ram heads must not have been an original feature of the vessel.

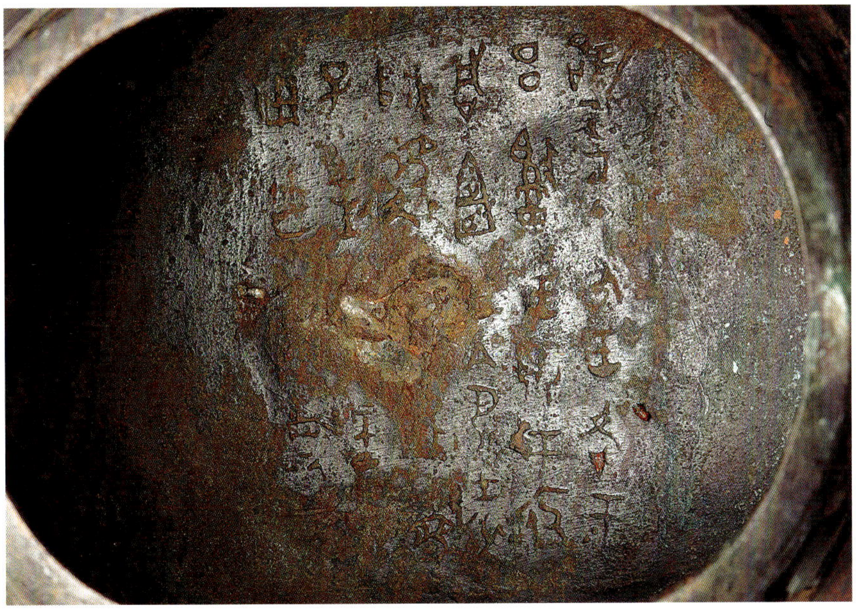

5 | The inscription on the Shanghai Museum *Hezi You*.

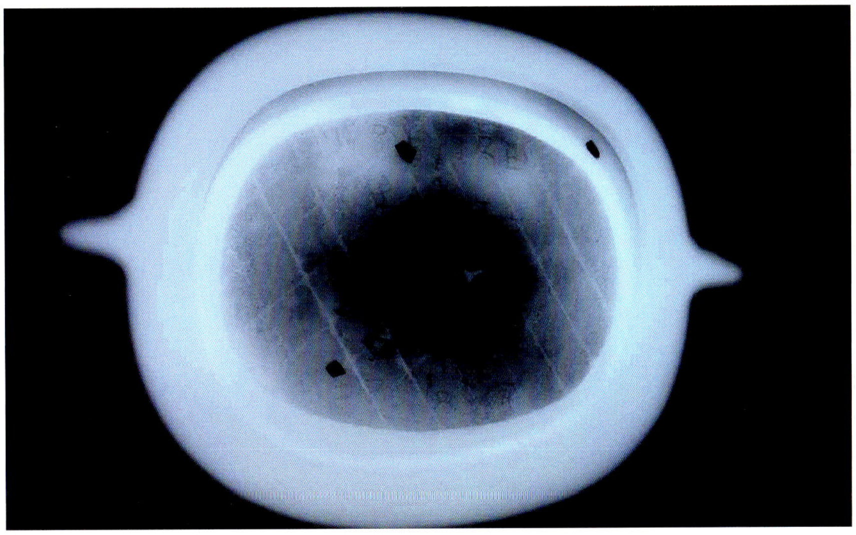

6 | An X-ray of the Shanghai Museum *Hezi You* showing that the repaired patch was previously the site of a large hole.

Additionally, in the *Xiqing*, vessel A is shown as having a handle, but in the Shanghai Museum piece, on top of the ram head there are no signs that a break occurred after the vessel was cast. On the contrary, the patina on the joining surface is completely indistinguishable from that on the rest of the body, which suggests that a surface treatment was applied to the vessel and ram heads at the same time. This is a common sign of forgery.

Third, there are various physical signs that the piece was cast and inscribed by means other than those used in Shang or Zhou bronze work. Comparison of the deer decoration on the Shanghai Museum *you* with that of the Minneapolis example reveals that the former is considerably less elegant. Not only are the fine details such as those in the eyes and mouth of the deer unclear, but the curves in the legs and feet seem stiff and unnatural, and the horns are relatively coarsely rendered. Especially noteworthy is that all around the deer motifs are traces of cutting and knife marks (see fig. 4), which are not seen in the Minneapolis *you* or in any other Shang or Zhou vessels. These are clearly markings that were cut into a wax slab, indicating that the piece was cast by a lost-wax process, a method not used in Shang or Zhou bronze work, which exclusively employed piece-mold casting. Moreover, many of the characters inscribed on the Shanghai Museum *you* are murky and indistinct, with some discontinuous lines that appear as if they are connected by dots (see fig. 5), and the middle of the inscription has a repaired patch, which an X-ray (fig. 6) has shown was previously the site of a large hole. These features suggest that the inscription was likely made using a chemical corrosion process. This process might cause discontinuities in the script but could also, if the wax seal leaked, cut too deeply and go all the way through the bronze, creating a hole. It is possible that the forgers did this on purpose to mimic a swath of the inscription that appears lost in the *Xiqing* catalogue drawing. Finally, careful inspection of the Shanghai Museum *you* reveals no trace of piece-mold casting: not only are there no seams from the piece-molds but also there is no sign of the use of spacers either (which was confirmed by an X-ray). In sum, the Shanghai Museum *Hezi You* is a late forgery made using the lost-wax process.

In May 2016, with the permission and aid of Dr. Liu Yang, curator of Chinese art at the Minneapolis Institute of Art, I examined the *Hezi You* vessel in the Minneapolis collection—the lid to vessel A and body of vessel B recorded in the *Xiqing*. In form, decoration, and casting process, the body and lid show no trace of forgery. This runs counter to Chen's claim, quoted above, that this *you* body is a forgery; the assertion rests on the fact that the spacing of the inscription on vessel B differs from that on vessel A, and that the former is a copy of the latter. Although the inscription on the Minneapolis *you* body indeed has a few strokes missing due to the casting process and the layout does differ from that on vessel A, such absences and discrepancies are commonly seen in authentic vessel inscriptions and do not prove that the vessel is a forgery. Furthermore, as it is already clear that the body of A in the Shanghai Museum is a forgery, Chen's assertion that B "must have been made in imitation of A" is implausible. By contrast, the position of the casting seams on B, as well as the use of spacers and their position (especially their distribution in and around the inscription on the lid and body), all accord with the conventions of the piece-mold casting process used in the Shang and Zhou periods. In addition, the traces of the inscription mold having been placed into the casting mold can be seen all around the inscription, conclusively demonstrating that the inscription on the vessel body was also made by piece-mold casting, rather than inscribed subsequently.

Based on the preceding analysis of the vessels' form, decoration, inscriptions, and casting processes, we can conclude that the Shanghai Museum *Hezi You* is counterfeit; it cannot be a genuine Western Zhou piece. Both the lid and body of the Minneapolis *Hezi You* are authentic, and Chen's appraisal to the contrary was wrong. Having established which of the *Hezi You* vessels are authentic, the question remains: is the Shanghai Museum piece *Xiqing* 15.9? Discrepancies between the two raise doubts that must be addressed. The illustration in *Xiqing* 15.9 shows the vessel body to have a relatively tall inset rim, which accords with conventions of *you* vessel form, but this is absent in the Shanghai Museum *you*. In addition, the *Xiqing* line drawings depict a swing handle and ram heads apparently made according to customary techniques, but the Shanghai Museum *you*'s ram heads are riveted on. Furthermore, the *Xiqing* drawing shows a handle that is missing in the Shanghai Museum vessel, and the latter's patina does not indicate that the handle was broken off (this could perhaps be explained by the fact that the forger decided it was more troublesome to cast a moveable handle than a passable semblance of a broken one). Finally, and perhaps most importantly, the rim on the neck of the Shanghai Museum bucket has an outer rim that is 11.3 × 13.9 cm (4 7/16 × 5 1/2 in.), whereas the inner rim of the Minneapolis vessel lid measures 9.8 × 12.8 cm (3 7/8 × 5 1/16 in.). There is no way this lid could cover the lip of the Shanghai Museum vessel, proving that the lid of the Minneapolis vessel does not belong to the vessel body in Shanghai. I doubt that the author of the *Xiqing* would have mistaken two vessels of different dimensions as a single vessel; in any case, though, the lid and vessels cannot all have come from the Qing imperial collection. The Shanghai Museum vessel does not match the dimensions recorded in the *Xiqing*, which state that the mouth of A "is 3.0 cun long by 3.9 *cun* wide." Ten *cun* is one *chi* and one *chi* corresponds to approximately thirty-two centimeters, making the mouth of vessel 9.6 × 12.5 cm (3 3/4 × 4 15/16 in.). The Shanghai Museum vessel obviously cannot be vessel A (*Xiqing* 15.9).[5]

The evidence shows clearly that the Shanghai Museum vessel is not the same one recorded in the *Xiqing*. Most likely it was made by a dealer or foundry in imitation of the *Xiqing* catalogue illustration before the vessel came into Pan's possession. Of course, we also cannot rule out the possibility that it is an imitation produced by artisans within the palace workshop.

Is one of the vessels in the *Xiqing* a forgery? This question arises because, except for a small difference in their abdominal measurements, the measurements of the two vessels recorded in the *Xiqing* are completely identical. In pairs of Western Zhou bronze *you* vessels, one vessel is always slightly larger than the other. This is the case, for example, in the pair of *Bo Ge you* vessels excavated from the Western Zhou tomb (M7) at the Zhuyuangou site in Baoji, and the pair of *Zuo Baozunyi you* from another tomb (M8) at the same site.[6] Having two *you* vessels of the same size would be inconsistent with Western Zhou practice.

Aside from the problem of the vessel size, the lid shapes of the *Xiqing* vessels are different: B has a mushroom-shaped knob, whereas A has a ring-shaped knob; A has horns protruding from the sides, whereas B does not; and B has a zoomorphic face amid the deer band, whereas A does not. These discrepancies also violate the design norms of Western Zhou vessels, which dictate that vessel pairs have identical form, decoration, and inscriptions.

These phenomena all suggest that one of the vessels in the *Xiqing* catalogue is likely a later replica. So how could it be that the Minneapolis *you* is composed of the lid of *Xiqing* 15.9 and the body of *Xiqing* 15.11, and yet neither lid nor body is fake? It is possible that the lids of A and B were reversed when they were illustrated in the *Xiqing*—that is, the lid of A belongs properly with the body of B, and thus the Minneapolis *you* is complete, authentic, and properly matched. Although this may seem to solve the problem, it is still the case that there are zoomorphic heads in relief amid the deer motifs on the vessel and lid of B, but not on A. It would also violate Western Zhou vessel design norms for the patterning on lid and body not to match. It seems, therefore, that a complete solution to the puzzle of the *Hezi You* still lies in the future—perhaps when the lid of *Xiqing* 15.11 reappears.

NOTES

1 | Fang Junyi, *Zhuiyizhai yiqi kuanzhi kaoshi* [Studies of Inscriptions on Ritual vessels from the Zhuiyizhai Studio], *juan* 2, p. 12. Fang's manuscript was first written in 1877 and finalized in 1894, but it was not published until 1935. It is reprinted in Liu Qingzhu, Duan Zhihong, and Feng Shi, eds., *Jinwen wenxian jicheng* [Compendium of Publications on Bronze Inscriptions], vol. 14 (Beijing: Xianzhuang shuju, 2005). All translations are by the translator of this essay, unless otherwise noted.

2 | Liu Zonggan, *Xigulou jinshi cuipian* [Compiled Collection of Bronzes and Stones of Xigulou] (Huizhou: Xigulou, 1915–33), *juan* 5, p. 14.

3 | Chen Mengjia, *Xizhou tongqi duandai* [Periodization of Western Zhou Bronzes] (Beijing: Zhonghua shuju, 2004), vol. 1, 122–23.

4 | Ibid.

5 | In the Qing dynasty measurement, one *chi* ("foot") was ten *cun* ("inches"), corresponding to today's thirty-two centimeters. I would like to thank Qiu Guangming for this information.

6 | For the *Bo Ge You* vessels, see Lu Liancheng and Hu Zhisheng, *Baoji yuguo mudi* [Yu State Cemetery in Baoji] (Beijing: Wenwu chubanshe, 1988), 103–4, color pl. 12.10. For the *Zuo Baozunyi You*, see Lu and Hu, *Baoji yuguo mudi*, 178, color pl. 8.2.

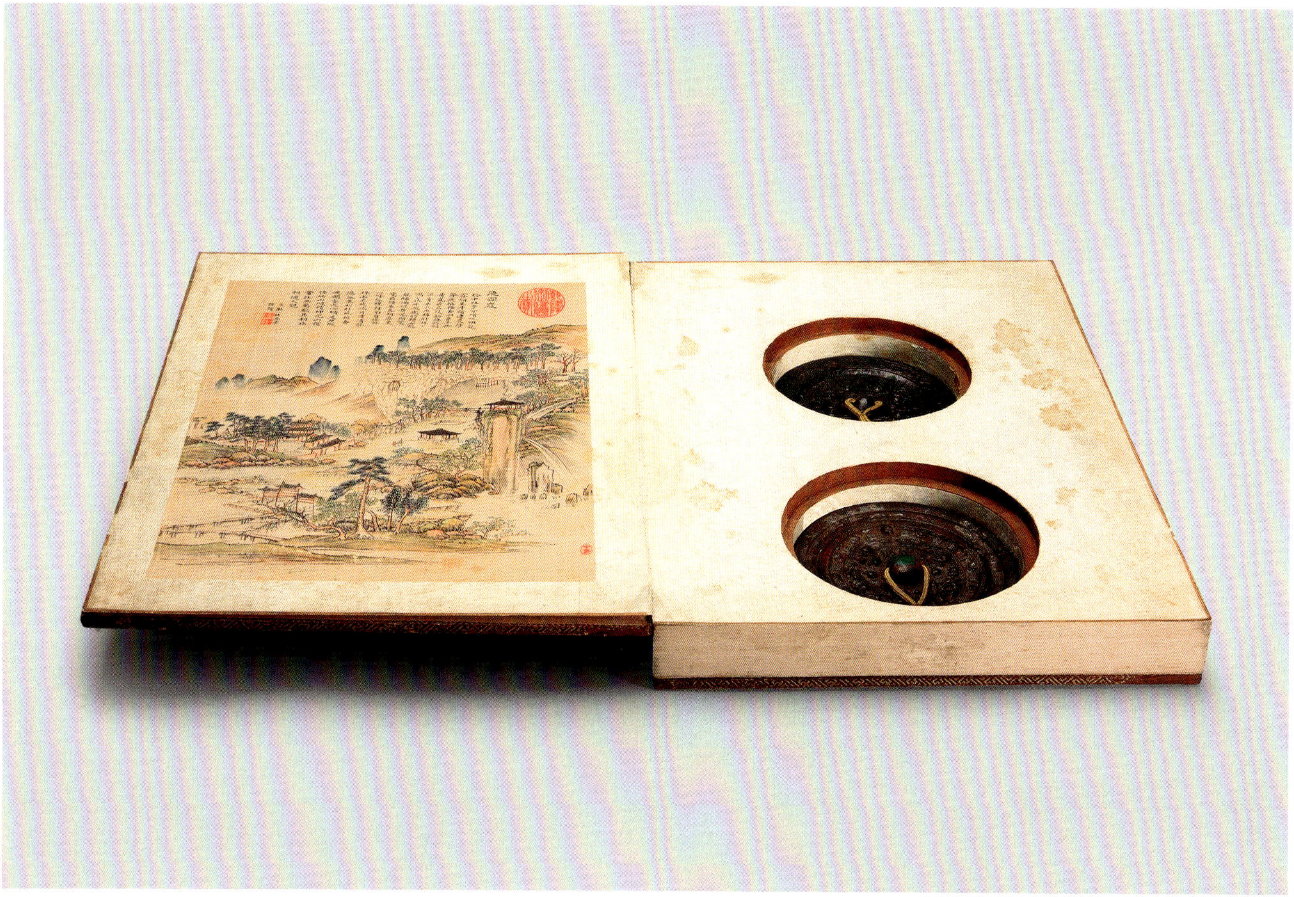

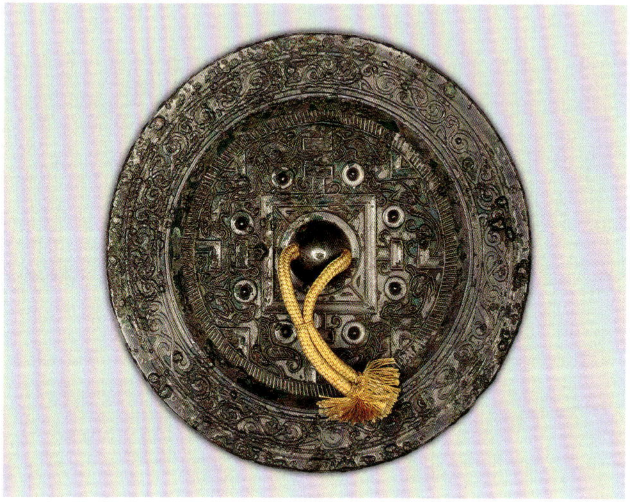

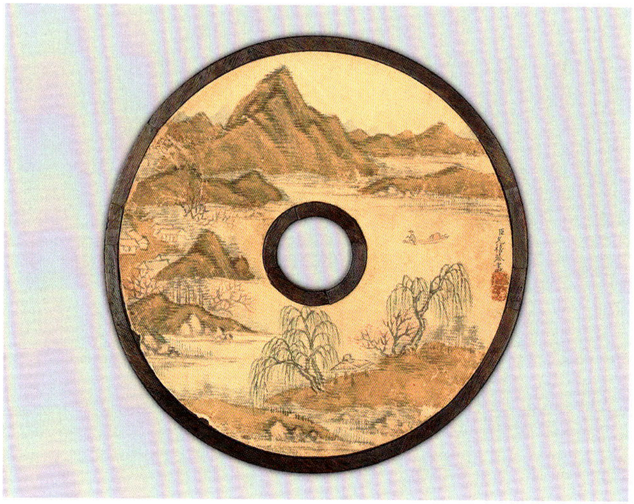

93 | BRONZE MIRRORS WITH BOX, VOLUME ONE OF *ANCIENT MIRROR OF WESTERN CLARITY* (*XIQING GUJIAN*), mirrors: Han dynasty (206 BC–AD 220); box and paintings: Qing dynasty (1644–1911), Qianlong reign (1735–96)

opposite page

94 | BRONZE MIRRORS WITH BOX, VOLUME EIGHT OF *ANCIENT MIRROR OF WESTERN CLARITY* (*XIQING GUJIAN*), mirror on top: Han dynasty (206 BC–AD 220); mirror on bottom: Tang dynasty (618–907); box and paintings: Qing dynasty (1644–1911), Qianlong reign (1735–96)

95 | BRONZE MIRRORS WITH BOX, VOLUME FORTY-TWO OF *ANCIENT MIRROR OF WESTERN CLARITY* (*XIQING GUJIAN*), mirror on top: Han dynasty (206 BC–AD 220); mirror on bottom: Tang dynasty (618–907); box and paintings: Qing dynasty, Qianlong reign (1735–96)

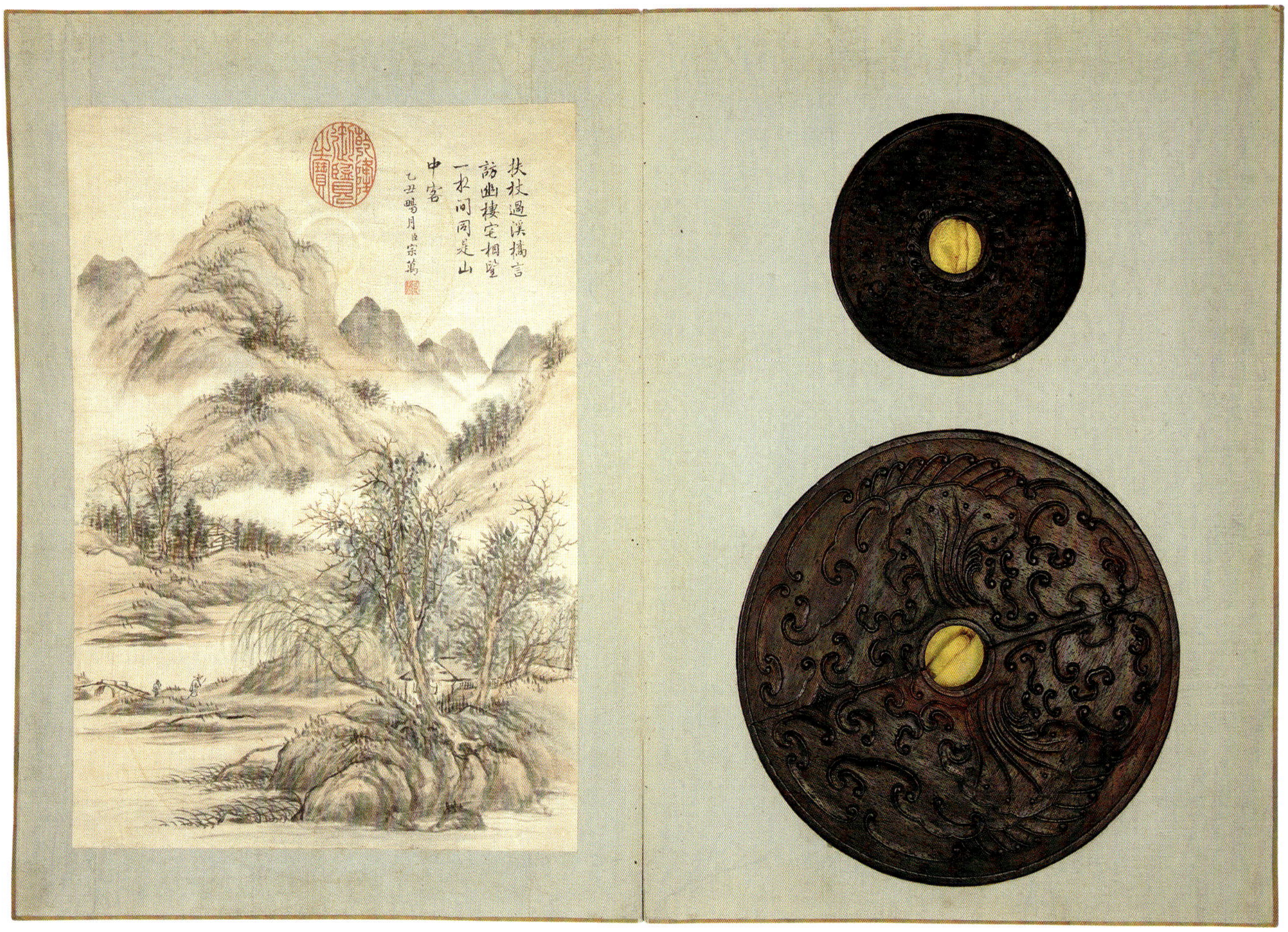
扶杖過溪橋言訪幽棲宅相望一水間同是山中客
乙丑暘月臣宗萬

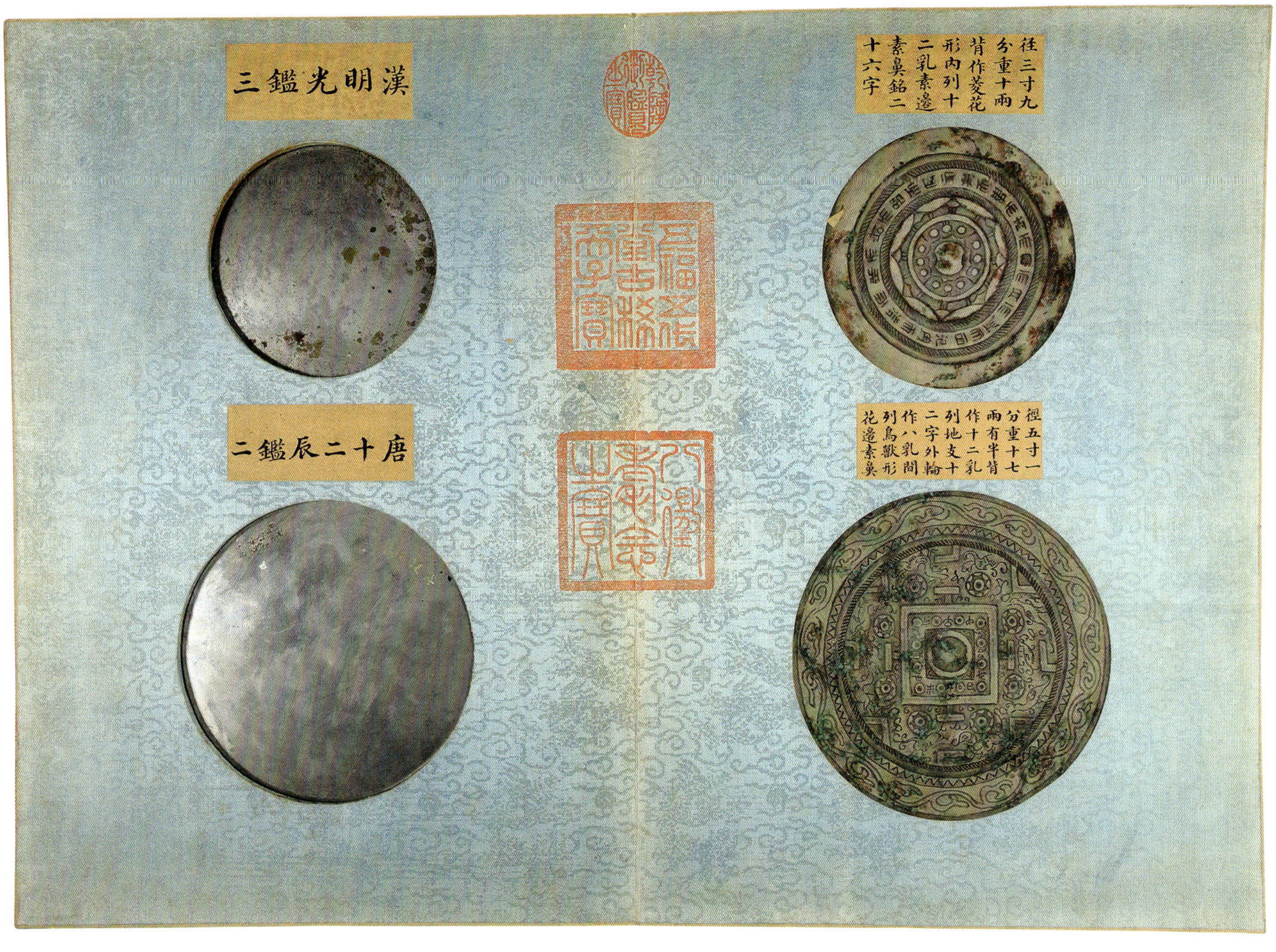
漢明光鑑三
唐十二辰鑑二
徑三寸九分重十兩背作菱花形內列十二乳素邊素奧銘二十六字
徑五寸一分重十七兩有半背作十二乳列地支十二字外輪作八乳間列鳥獸形花邊素奧

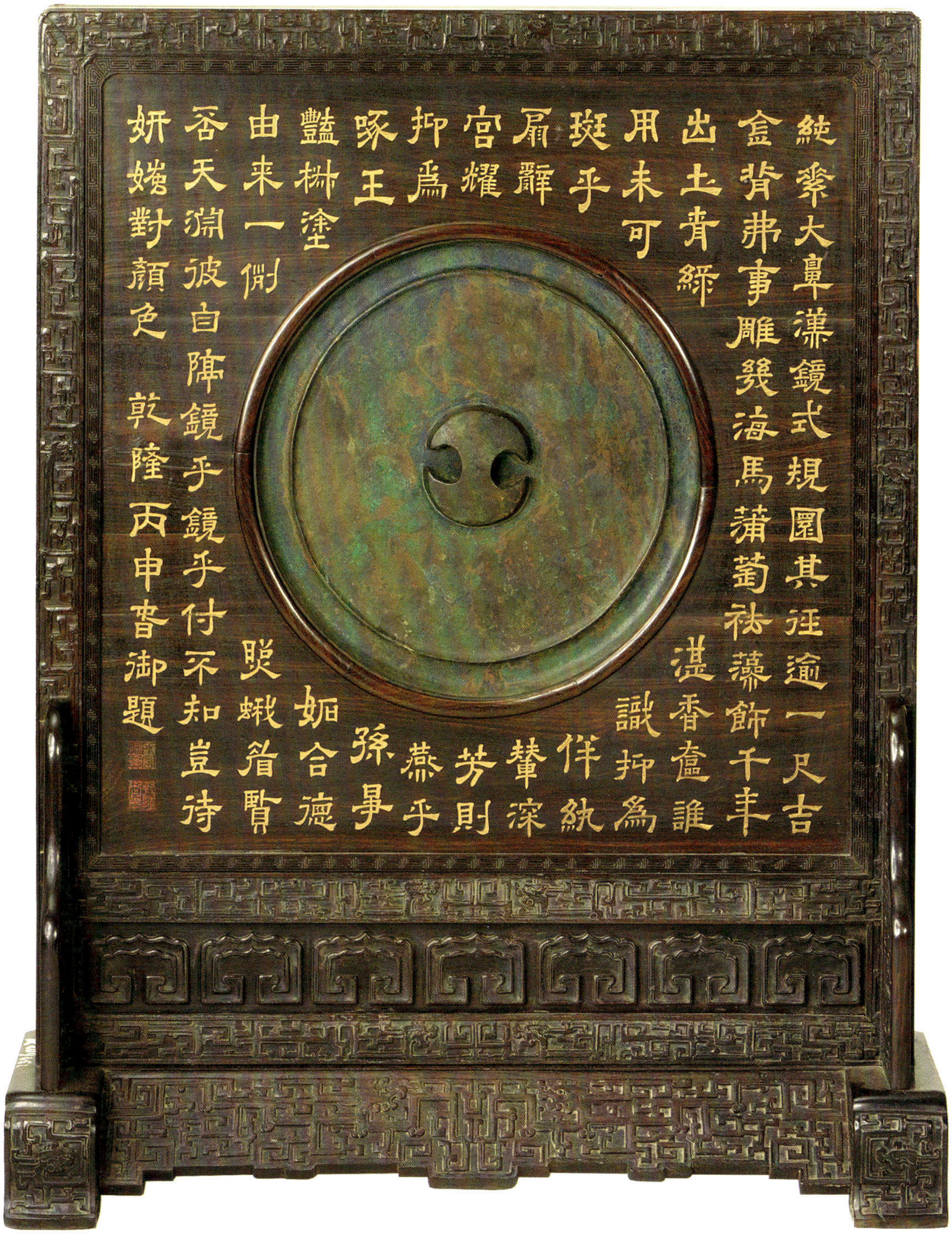

96 | SCREEN INLAID WITH BRONZE MIRROR, mirror: Han dynasty (206 BC–AD 220); screen: Qing dynasty, Qianlong reign (1735–96), 1776

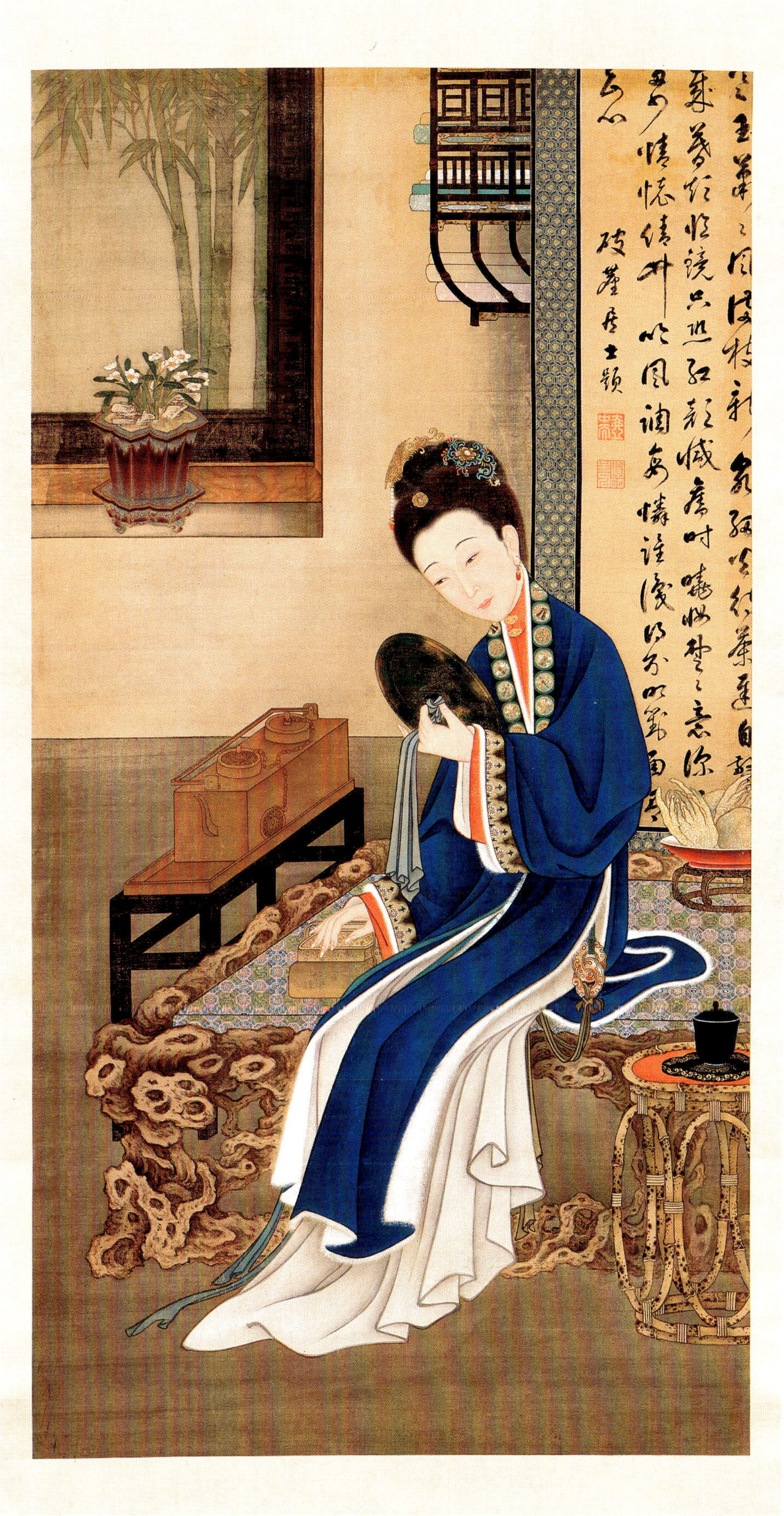

97 | Artist unknown. "COURT LADY LOOKING IN A MIRROR," FROM "TWELVE BEAUTIES," Qing dynasty (1644–1911), late Kangxi reign (1709–22)

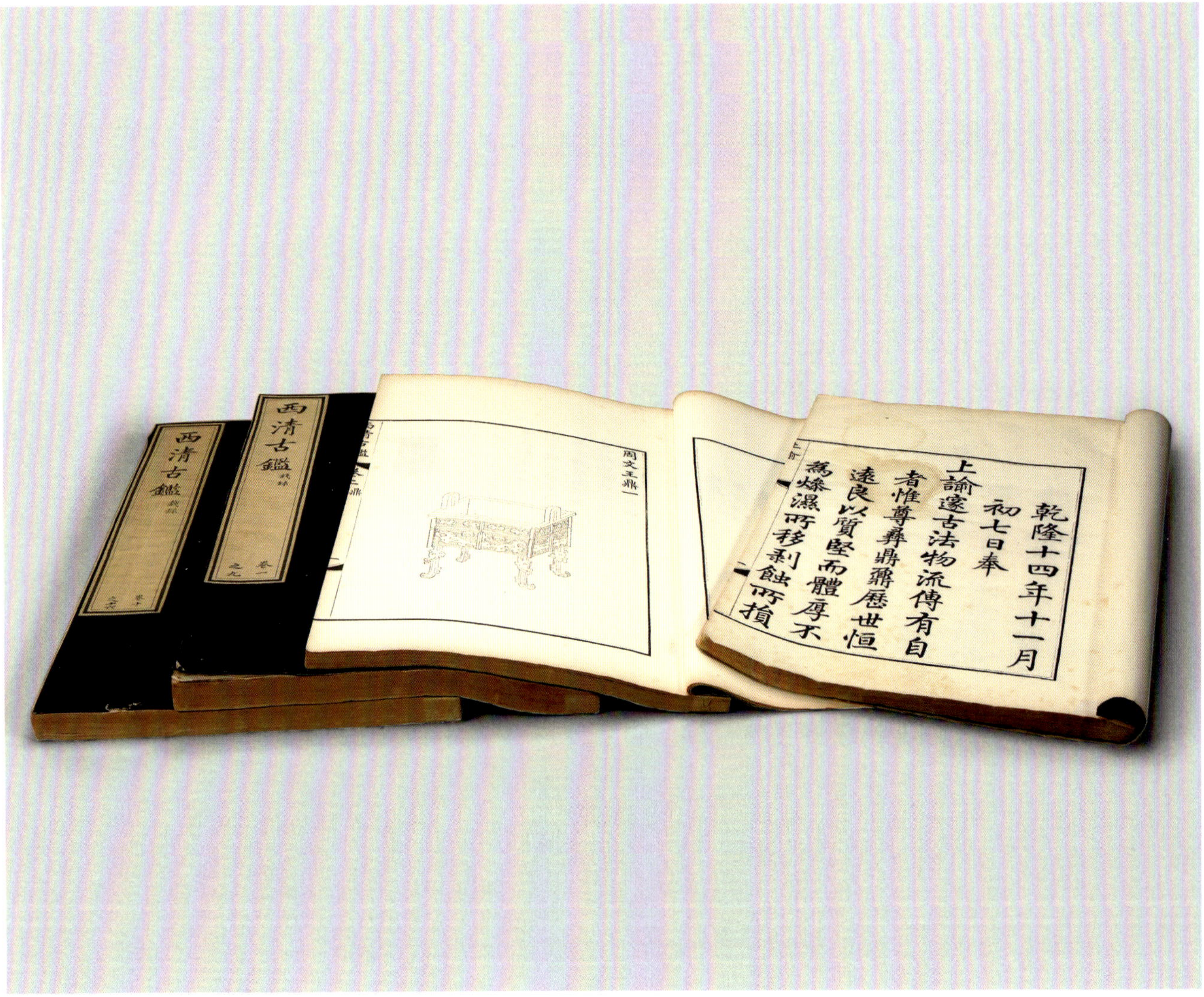

98 | Liang Shizheng (Chinese, 1697–1763) and others. ANCIENT MIRROR OF WESTERN CLARITY (*XIQING GUJIAN*), *Wuyingdian* edition, Qing dynasty (1644–1911), Qianlong reign (1735–96), and interior pages opposite

周螭梁盉六

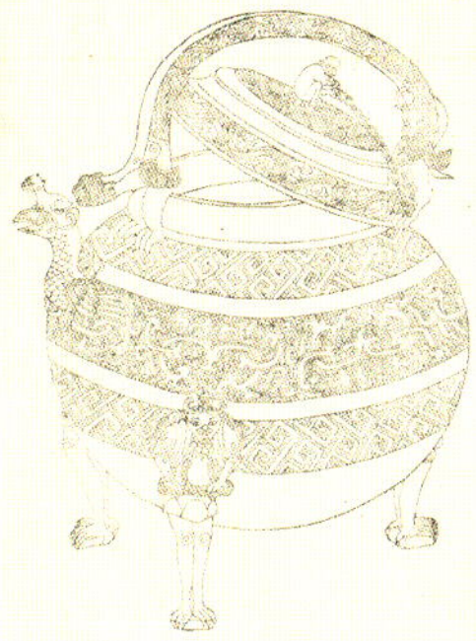

右通蓋高六寸五分深四寸五分口徑三寸一分腹圍一尺九寸重九十八兩有流有提梁三足

漢長區

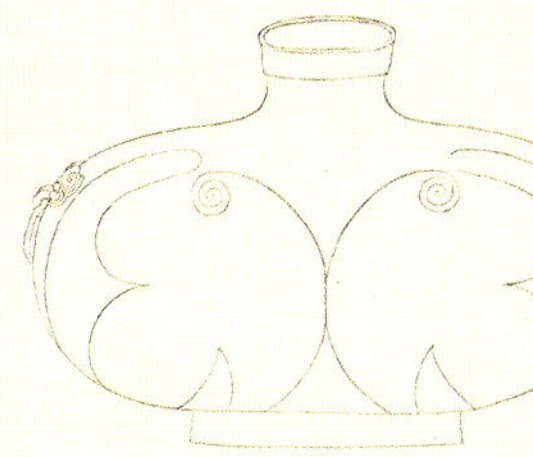

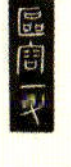

長區容一斗

右高六寸九分深五寸二分口徑二寸一分腹縱七寸二分橫三寸二分重五十兩兩耳有環左氏傳齊舊四量豆區釜鍾杜預注四豆為區區容十六升而此銘曰長區容一斗蓋自春秋至漢制之廣狹已不侔矣

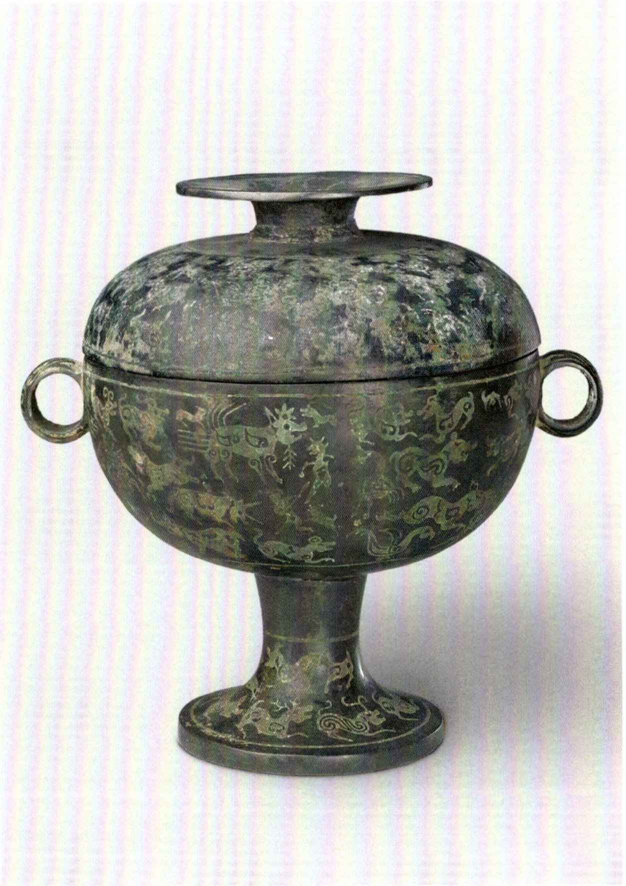 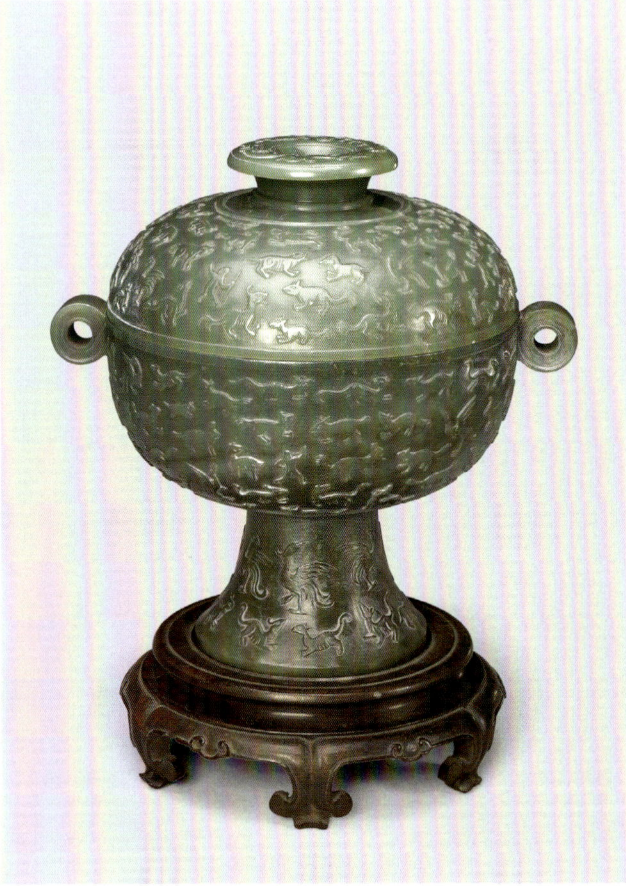

99 | STEMMED BOWL (*DOU*), Eastern Zhou period (770–221 BC)

100 | VESSEL IN THE FORM OF AN ANCIENT BRONZE STEMMED BOWL (*DOU*), Qing dynasty (1644–1911), Qianlong reign (1735–96)

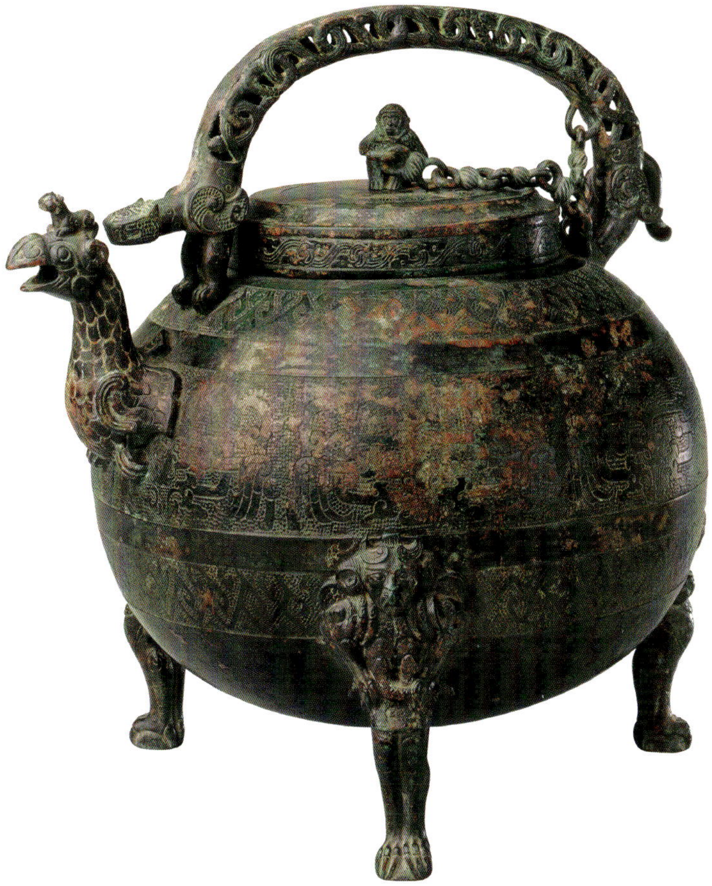

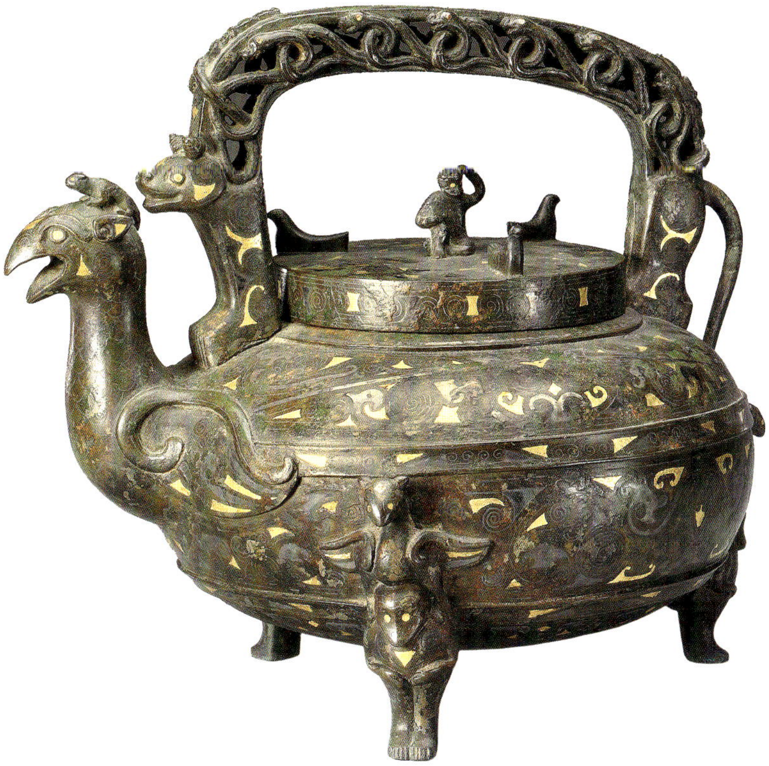

101 | EWER (*HE*), Warring States period (475–221 BC)

102 | VESSEL IN THE FORM OF AN ANCIENT BRONZE EWER (*HE*), Ming dynasty (1368–1644) or Qing dynasty (1644–1911), Qianlong reign (1735–96)

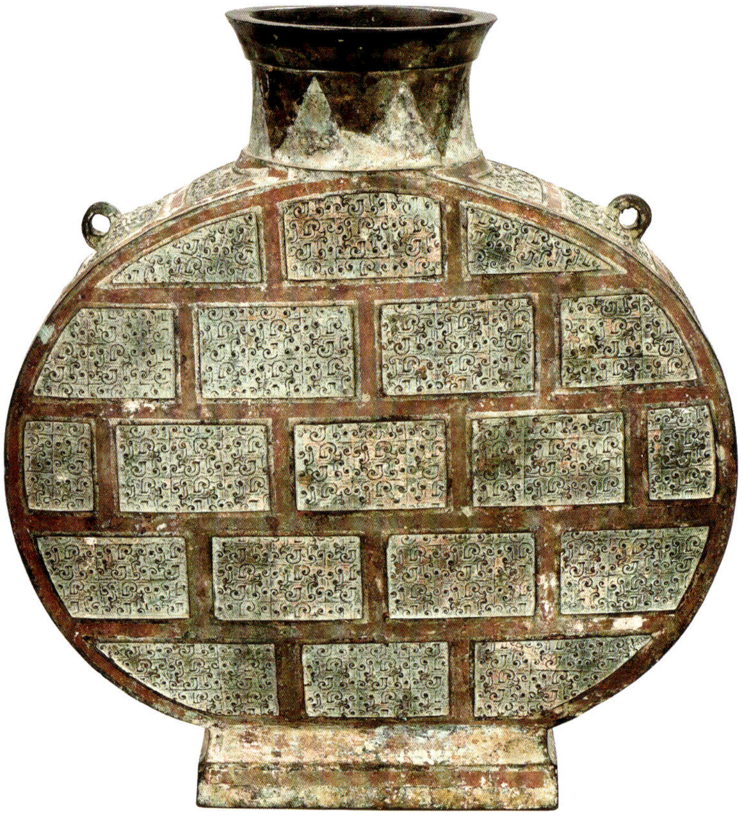

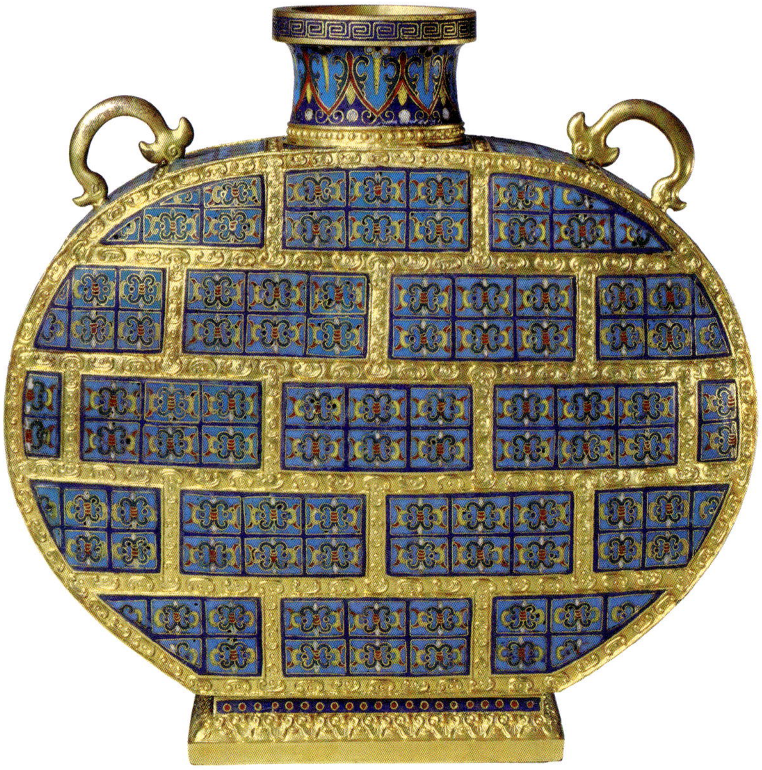

103 | FLASK (*BIANHU*), Warring States period (475–221 BC)

104 | VESSEL IN THE FORM OF AN ANCIENT BRONZE FLASK (*BIANHU*), Qing dynasty (1644–1911), Qianlong reign (1735–96)

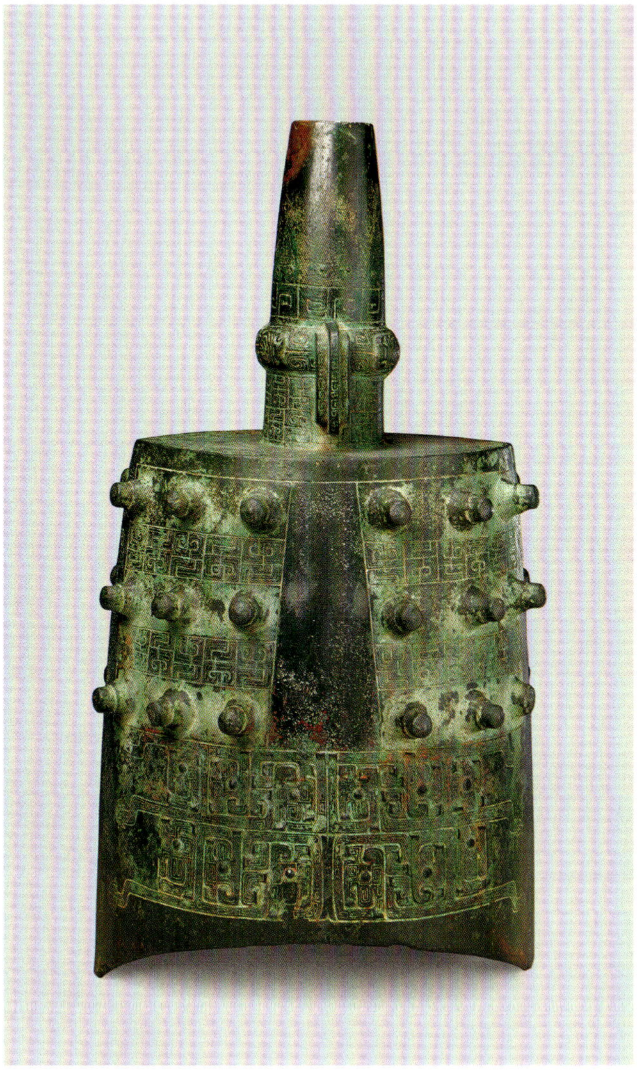

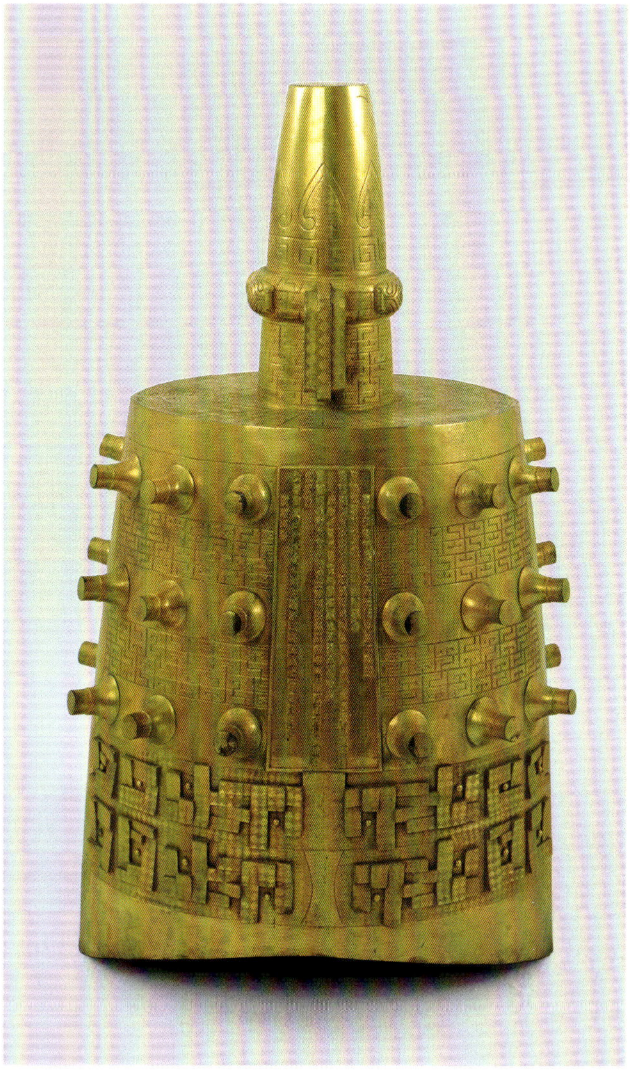

105 | *BO* BELL OF ZHE JIAN (*ZHE JIAN ZHONG*), Eastern Zhou dynasty, Spring and Autumn period (770–476 BC)

106 | BELL IN THE FORM OF AN ANCIENT BRONZE *BO* BELL, Qing dynasty (1644–1911), Qianlong reign (1735–96), 1761

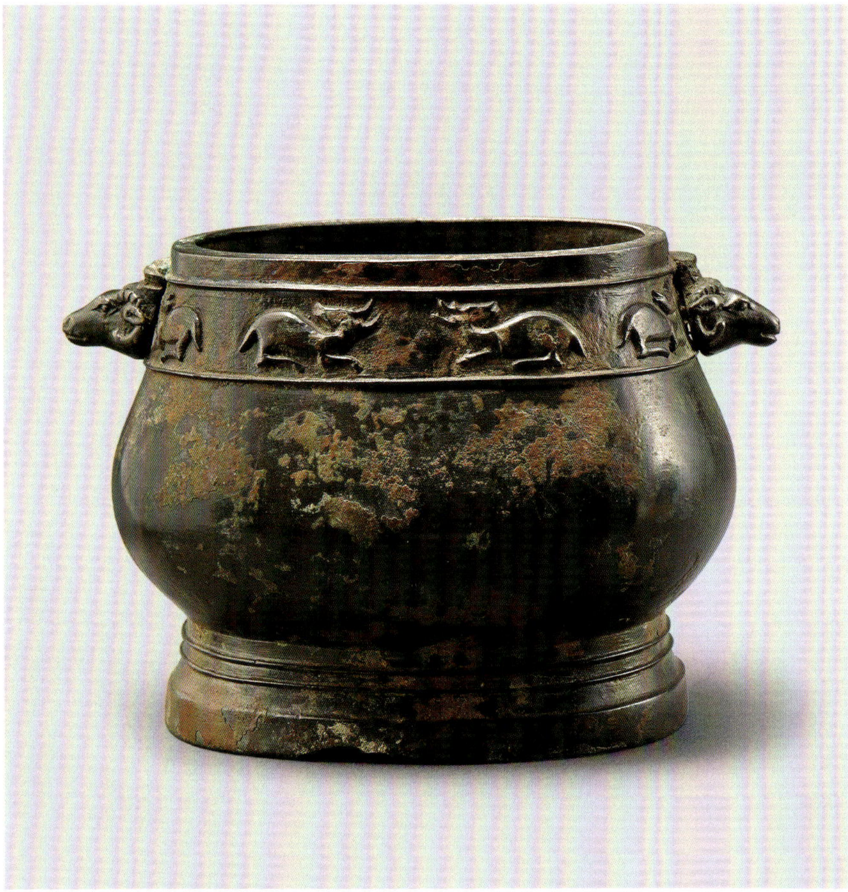

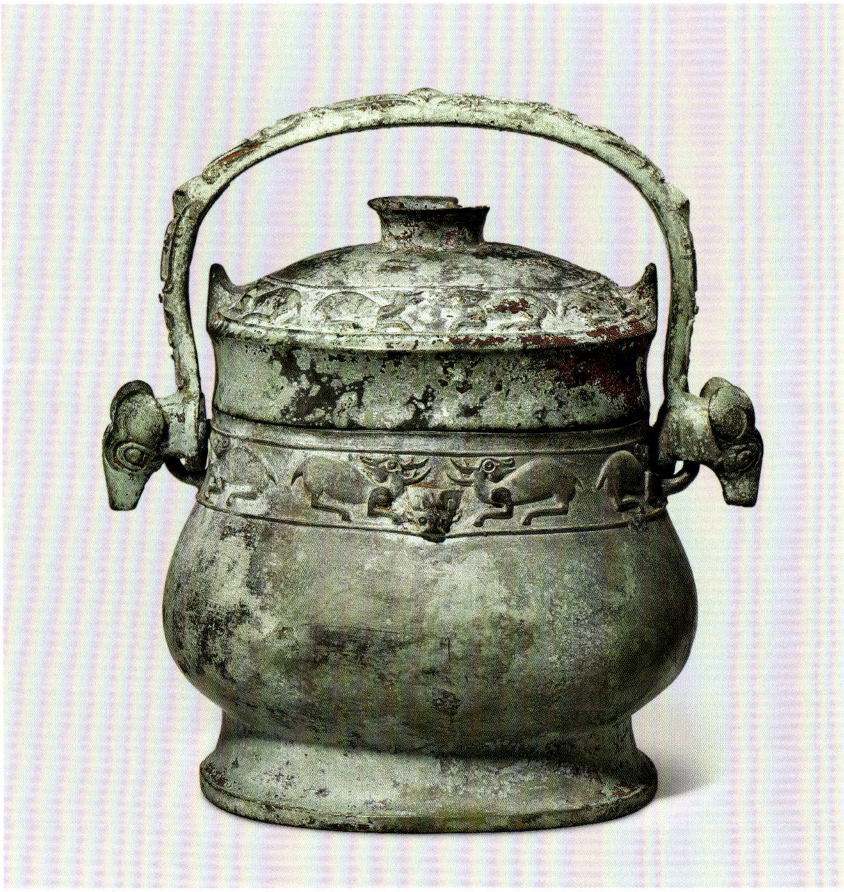

107 | LATE COPY OF THE BUCKET OF HEZI (*HEZI YOU*), Qing dynasty (1644–1911)

108 | BUCKET OF HEZI (*HEZI YOU*), Western Zhou dynasty (1046–771 BC)

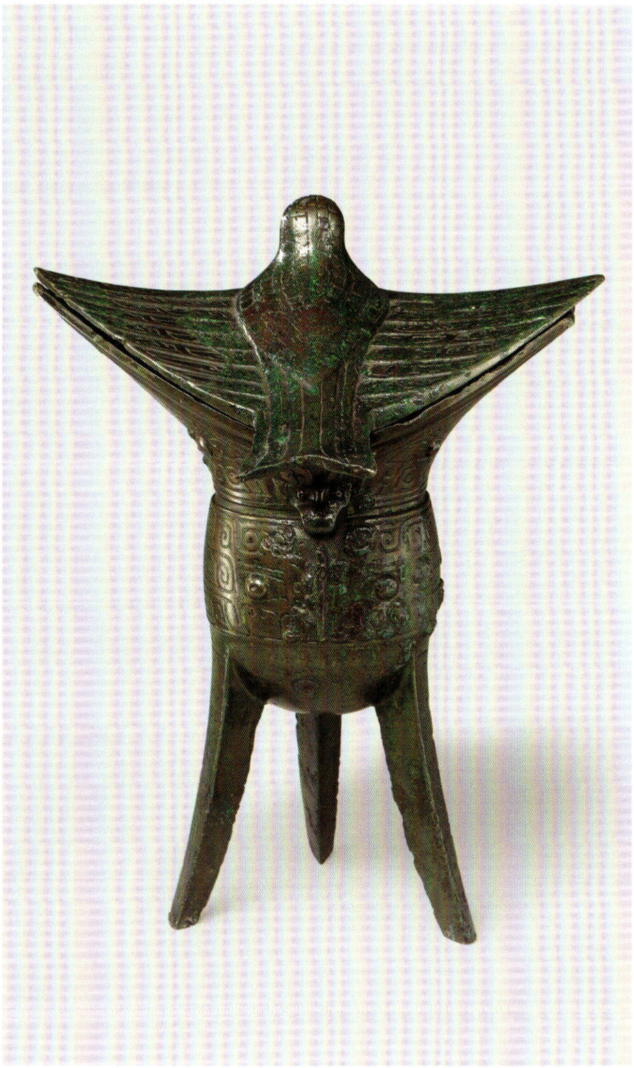

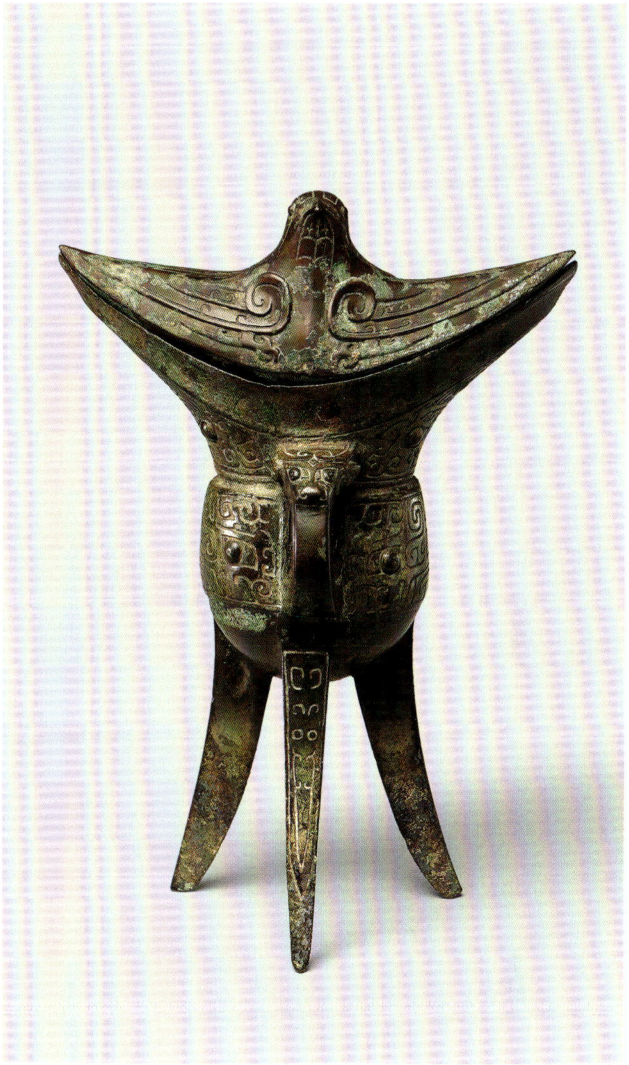

109 | GOBLET (*JUE*), Probably Ming dynasty (1368–1644)

110 | GOBLET (*JUE* OR *JIAO*), goblet: late Shang dynasty (c. 1250–1046 BC), lid: early 20th century

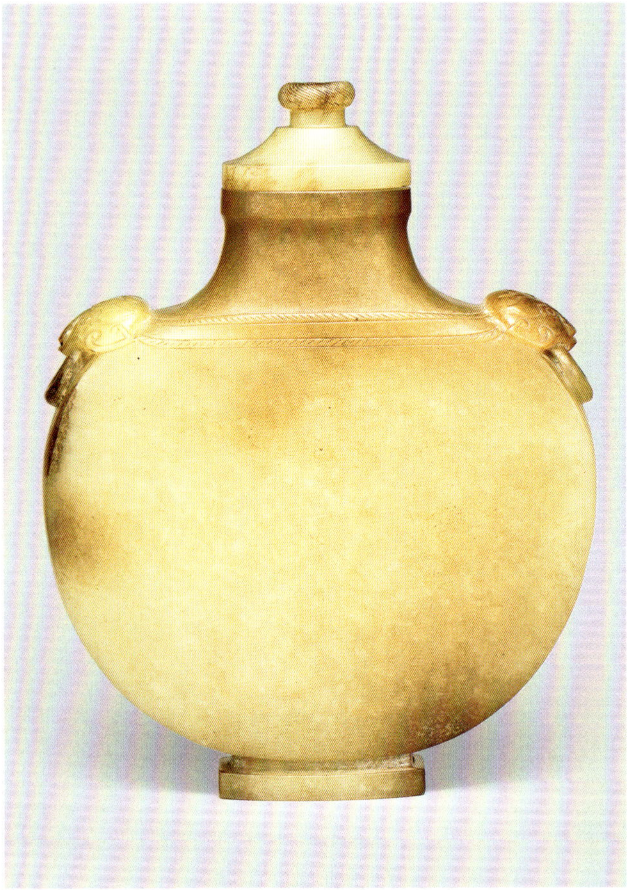

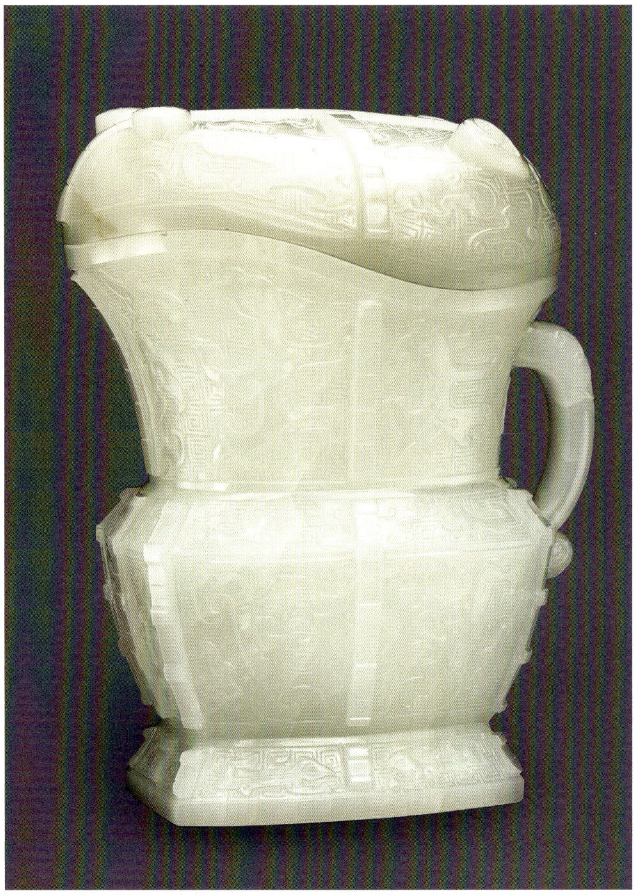

111 | VESSEL IN THE FORM OF AN ANCIENT BRONZE FLASK (*BIANHU*), Ming dynasty (1368–1644) or Qing dynasty (1644–1911)

112 | VESSEL IN THE FORM OF AN ANCIENT BRONZE PITCHER (*GONG*), Qing dynasty (1644–1911)

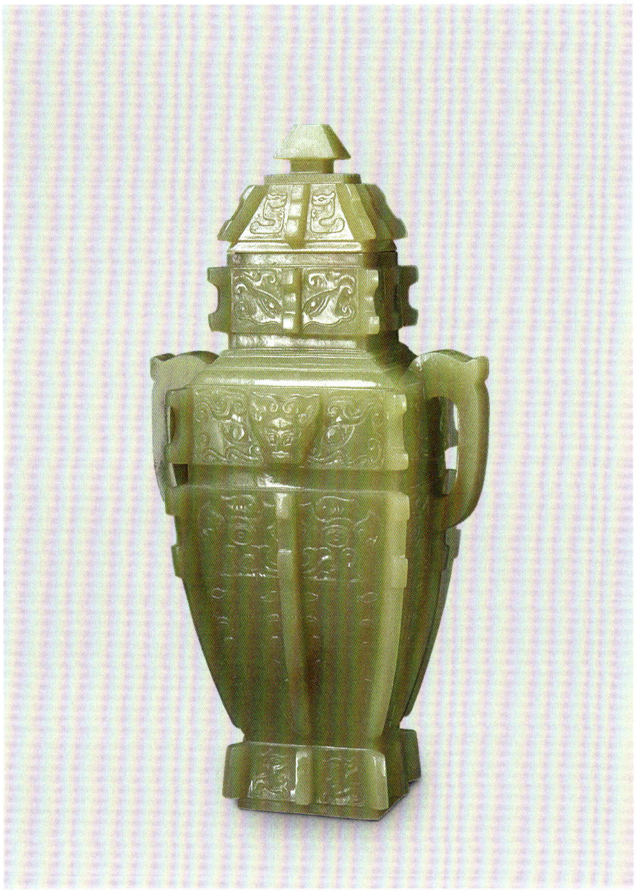

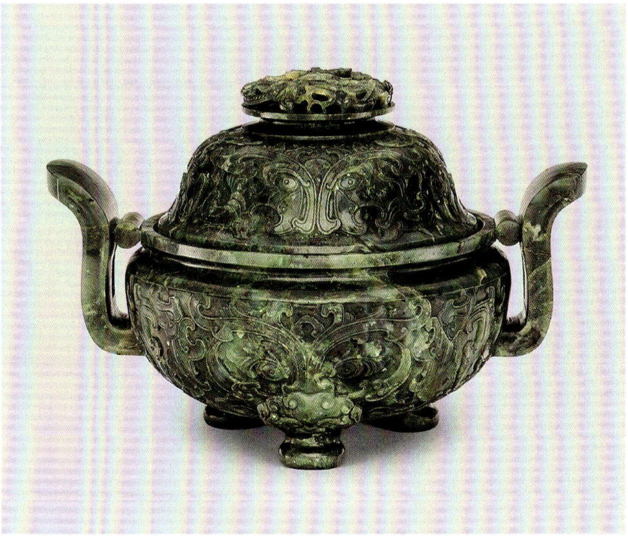

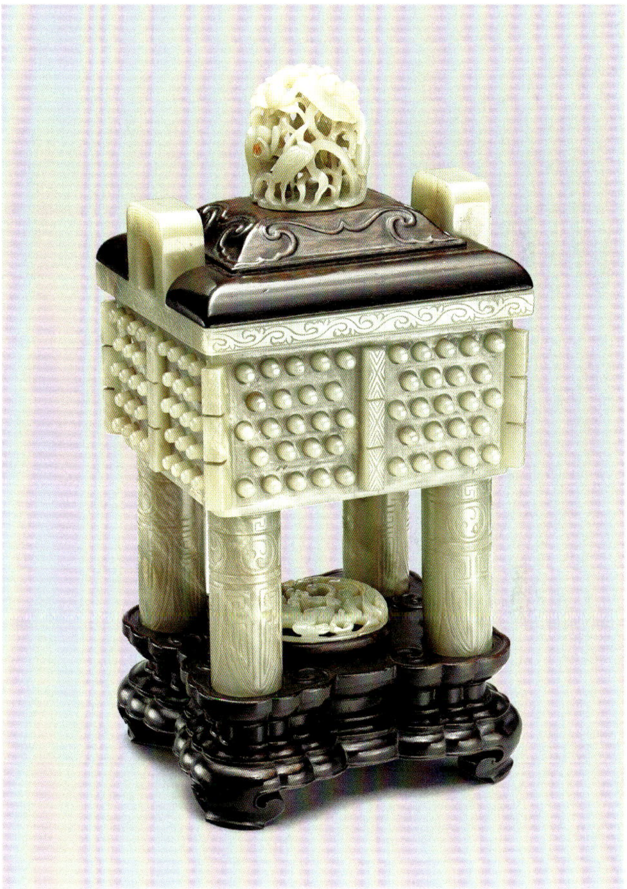

clockwise from top left

113 | LIDDED VESSEL IN THE FORM OF AN ANCIENT BRONZE CONTAINER (*LEI*), Qing dynasty (1644–1911), Qianlong reign (1735–96)

114 | CENSER IN THE FORM OF AN ANCIENT BRONZE TRIPOD CAULDRON (*DING*), Qing dynasty (1644–1911)

115 | CENSER IN THE FORM OF AN ANCIENT BRONZE RECTANGULAR CAULDRON (*FANGDING*), Qing dynasty (1644–1911)

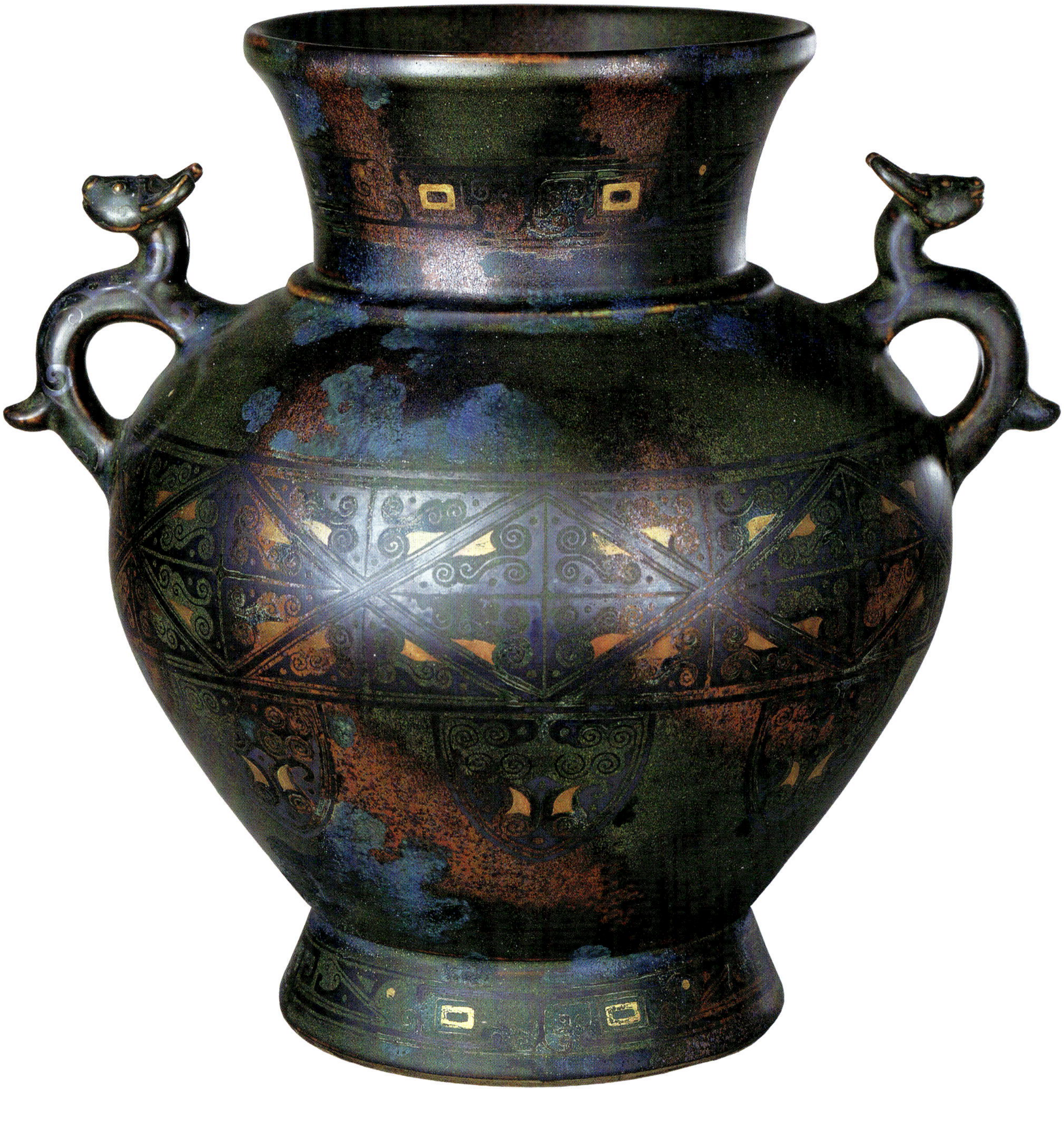

116 | VESSEL IN THE FORM OF AN ANCIENT BRONZE JAR (*HU*), Qing dynasty (1644–1911), Qianlong reign (1735–96)

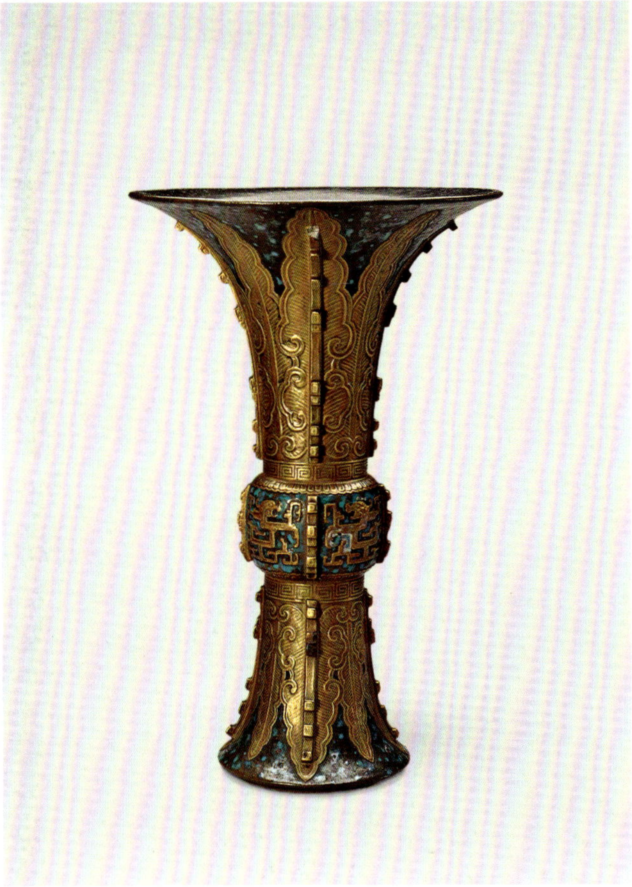

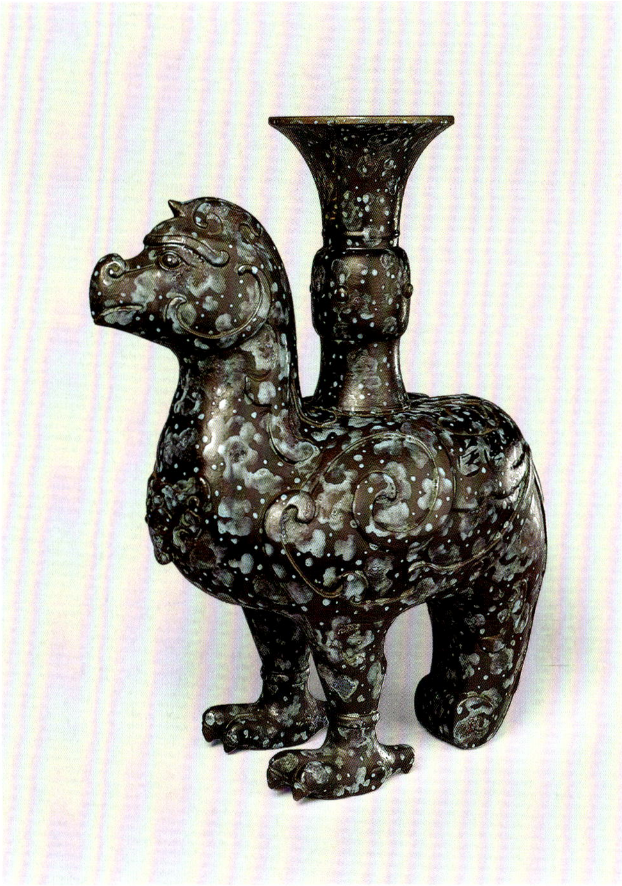

117 | VESSEL IN THE FORM OF AN ANCIENT BRONZE GOBLET (*GU*), Qing dynasty (1644–1911), Qianlong reign (1735–96)

118 | BIRD-SHAPED VESSEL IN THE FORM OF AN ANCIENT BRONZE CONTAINER (*ZUN*), Qing dynasty (1644–1911), Qianlong reign (1735–96)

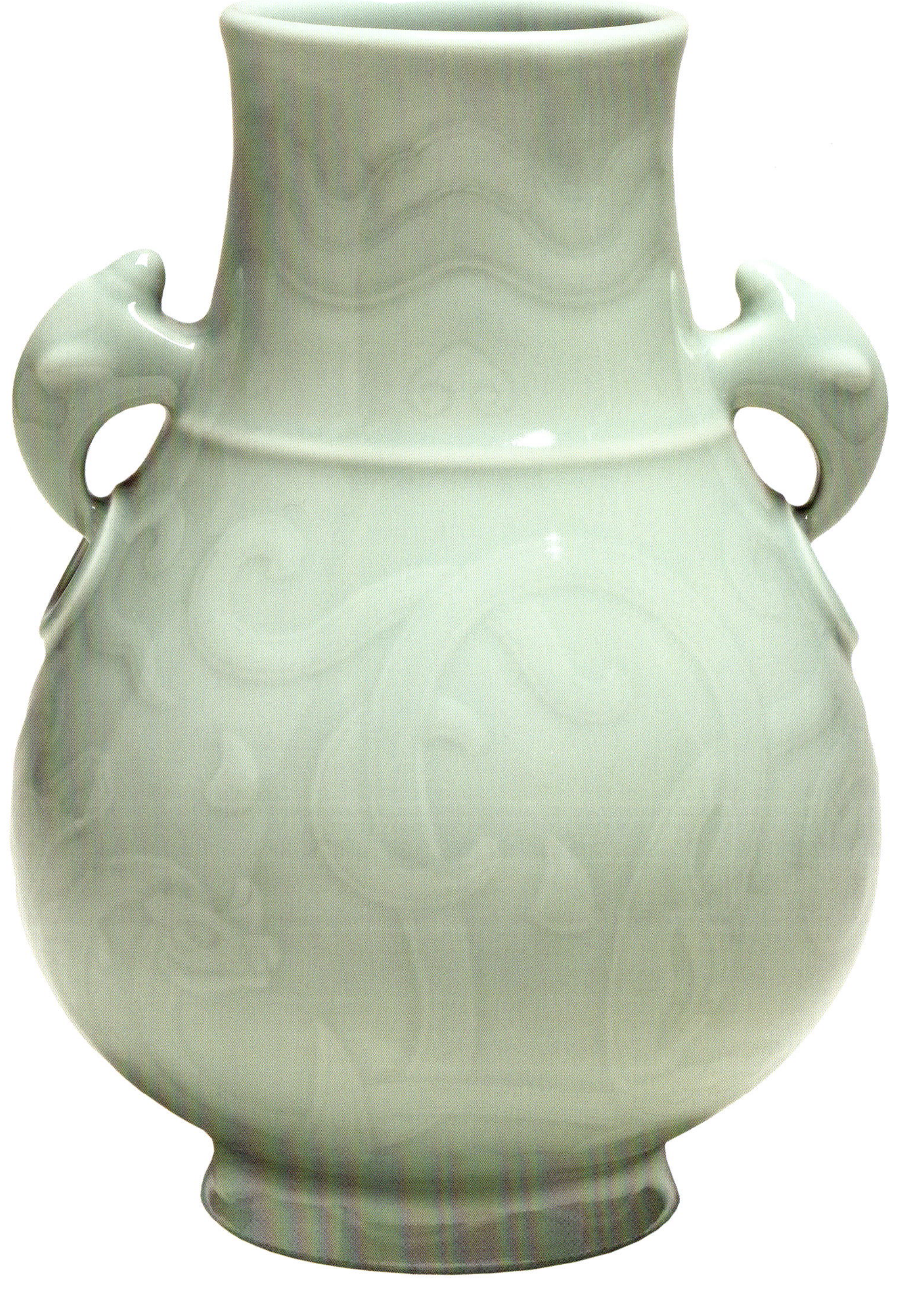

119–20 | VESSELS IN THE FORM OF AN ANCIENT BRONZE JAR (*HU*), Qing dynasty (1644–1911), Qianlong reign (1735–96)

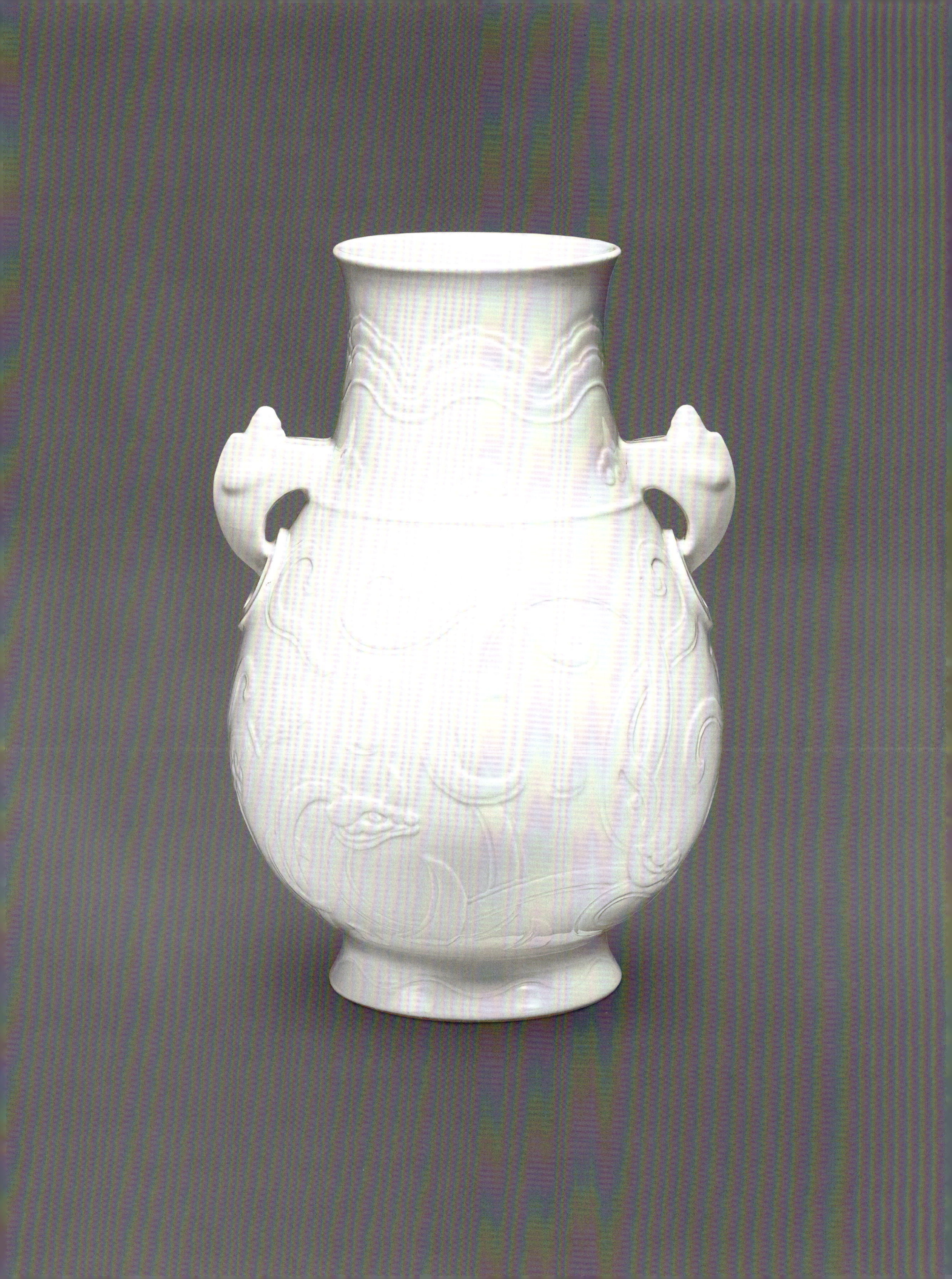

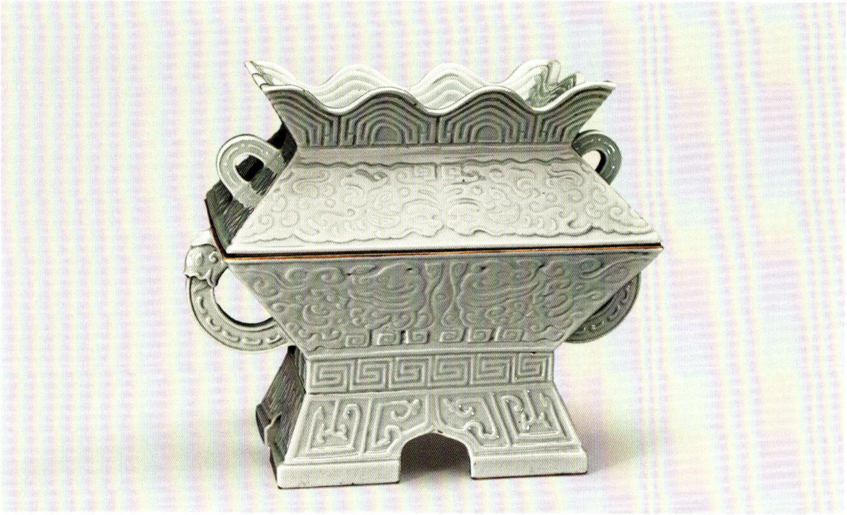

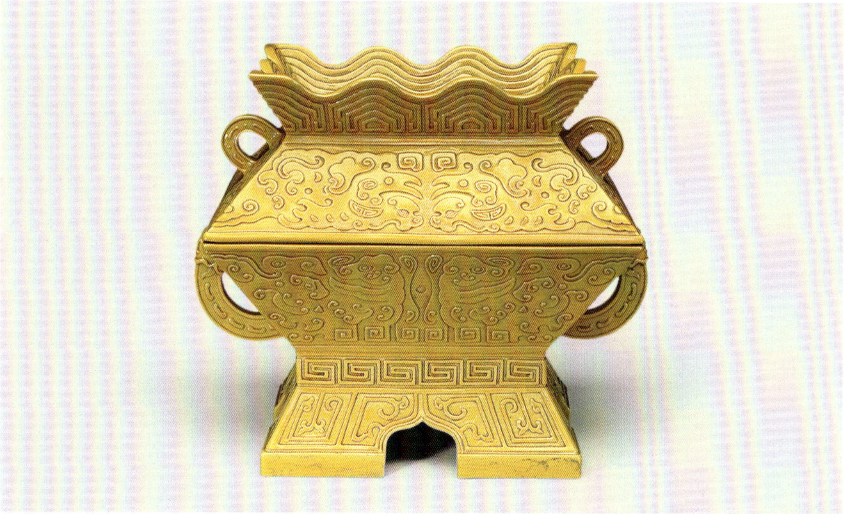

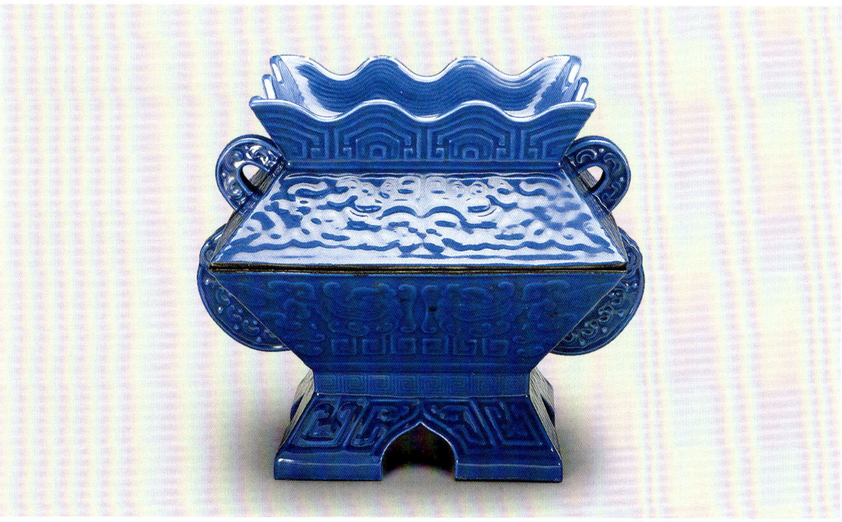

121–23 | BIPARTITE VESSELS IN THE FORM OF AN ANCIENT BRONZE RECTANGULAR TUREEN (*XU*), top and center: Qing dynasty (1644–1911), Qianlong reign (1735–96), bottom: Jiaqing reign (1796–1820)

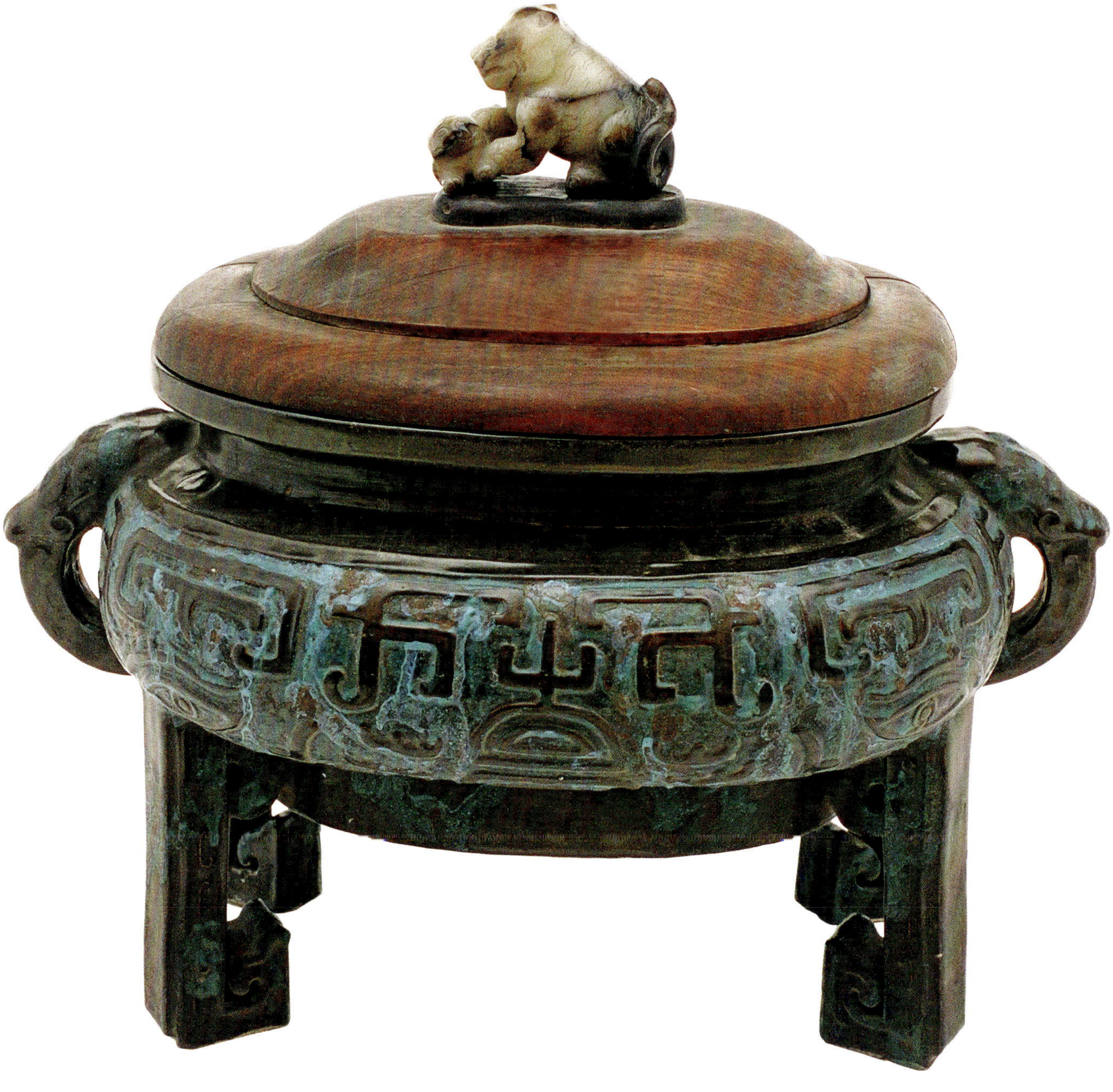

124 | VESSEL IN THE FORM OF THE WESTERN ZHOU BRONZE TUREEN OF BAN (*BAN GUI*), Qing dynasty (1644–1911), Qianlong reign (1735–96)

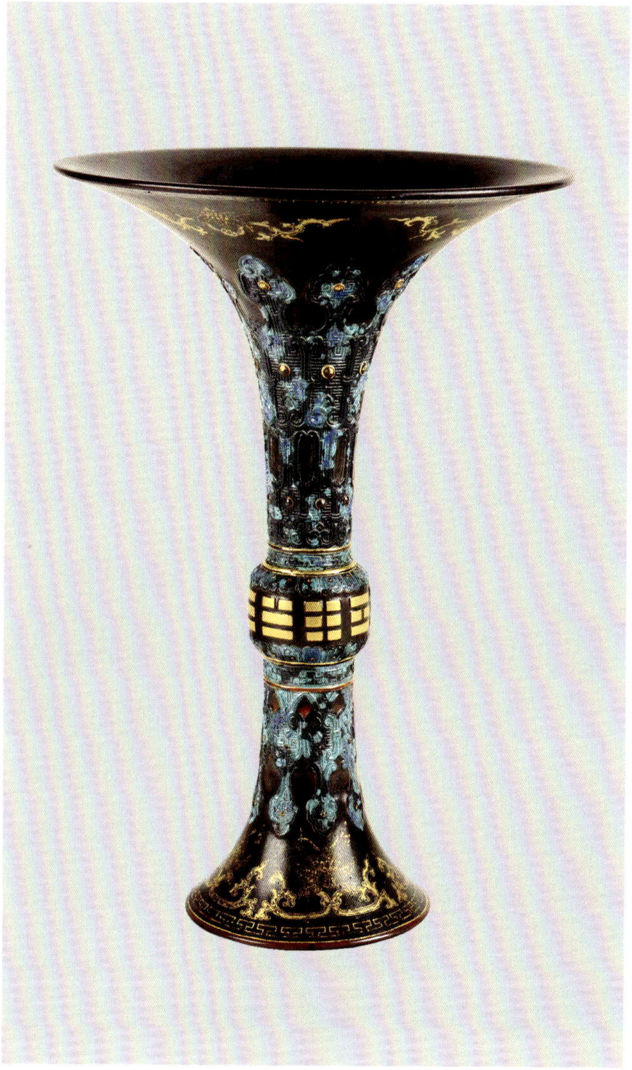

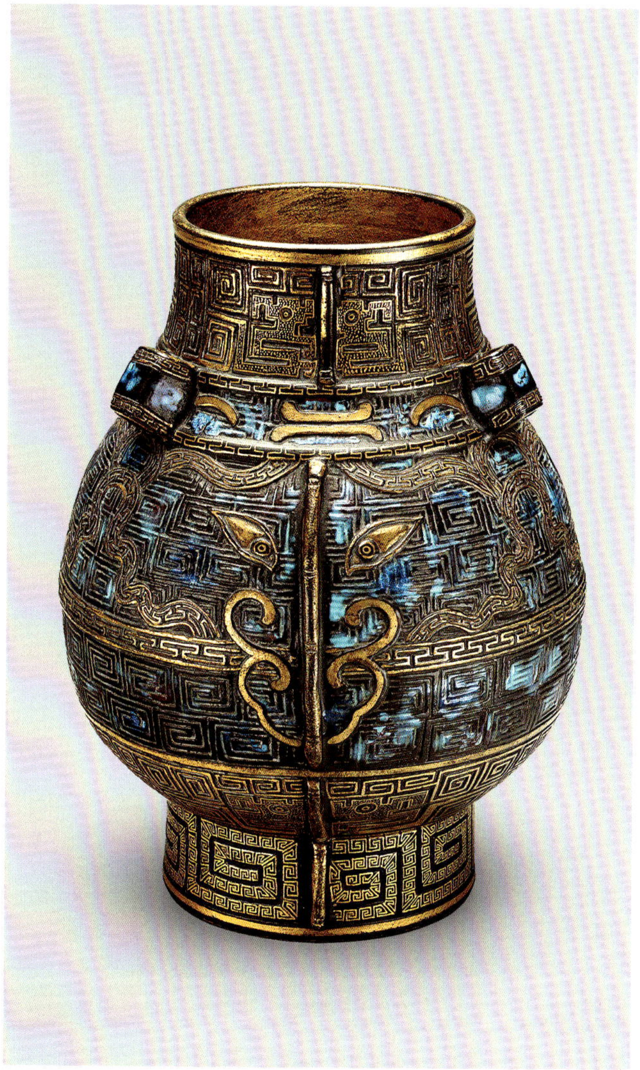

125 | VESSEL IN THE FORM OF AN ANCIENT BRONZE BEAKER (*GU*), Qing dynasty (1644–1911), Qianlong reign (1735–96)

126 | VESSEL IN THE FORM OF AN ANCIENT BRONZE JAR (*HU*), Qing dynasty (1644–1911), Qianlong reign (1735–96)

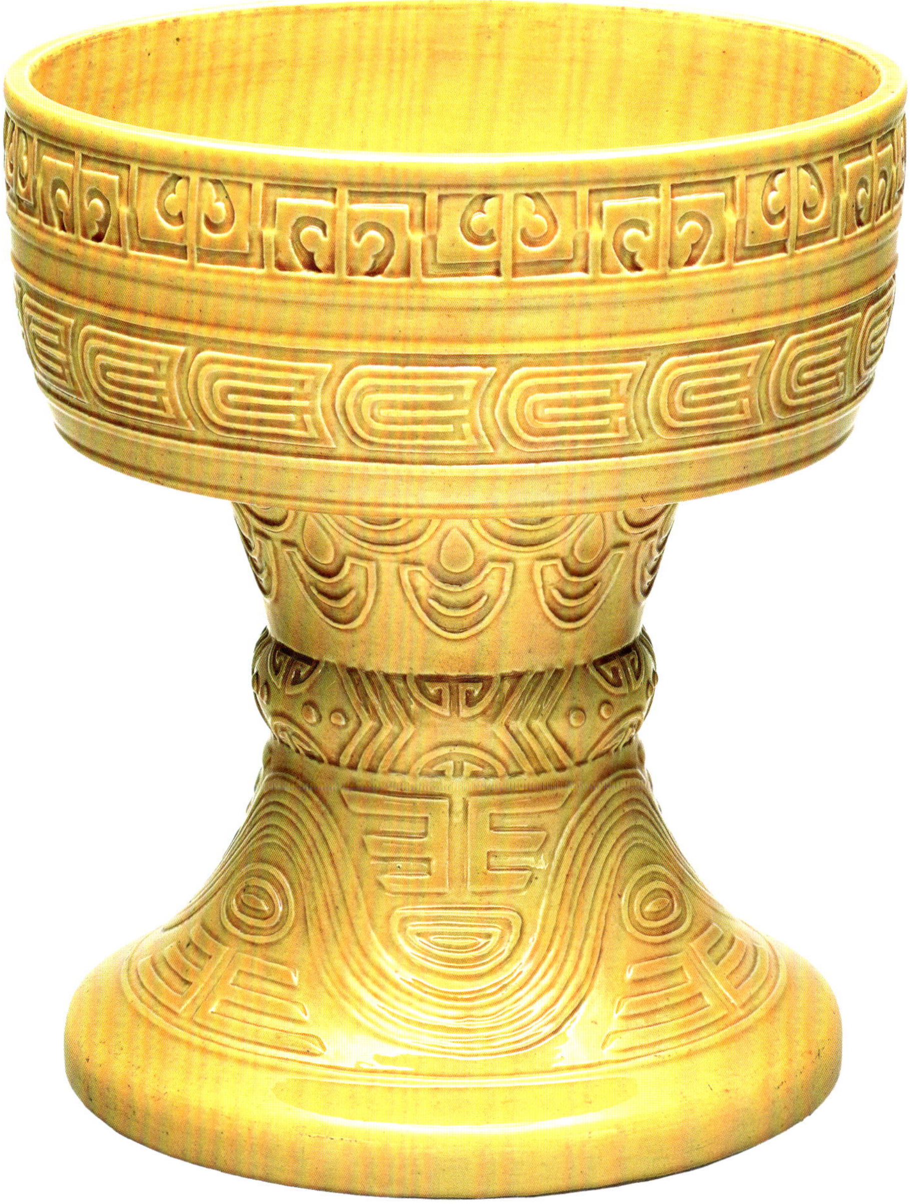

127 | VESSEL IN THE FORM OF AN ANCIENT BRONZE STEMMED BOWL (*DOU*), Qing dynasty (1644–1911)

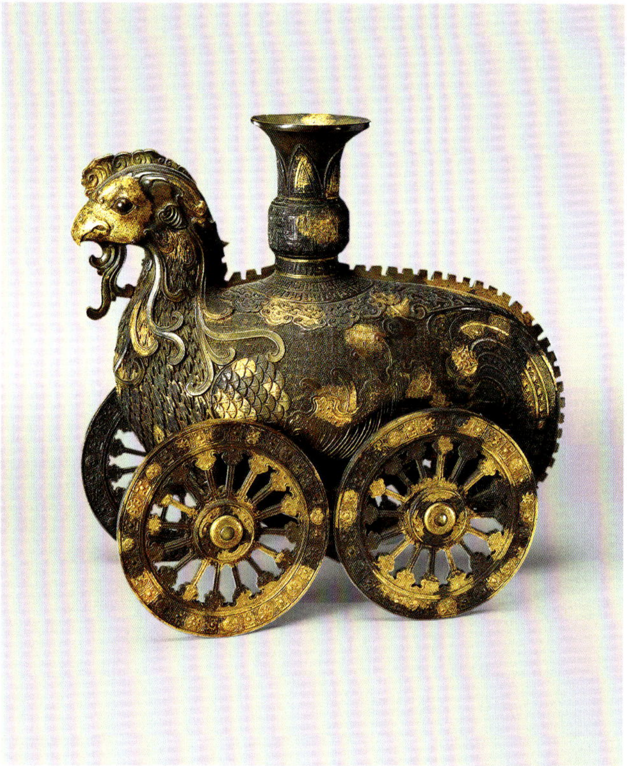

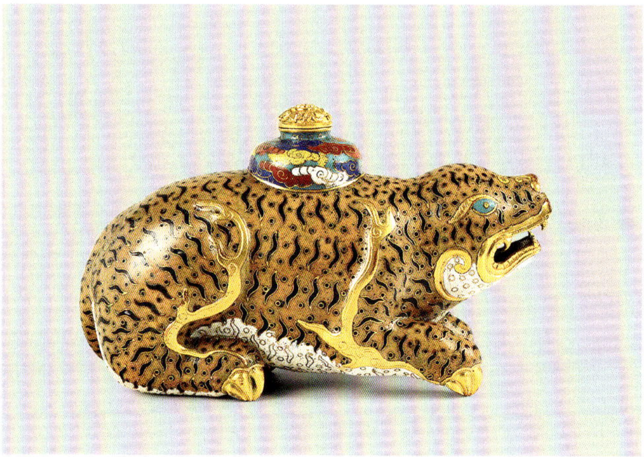

128 | WHEELED BIRD-SHAPED VESSEL (*ZUN*), Qing dynasty (1644–1911), Qianlong reign (1735–96)

129 | WATERPOT (*SHUICHENG*), Qing dynasty (1644–1911), Qianlong reign (1735–96)

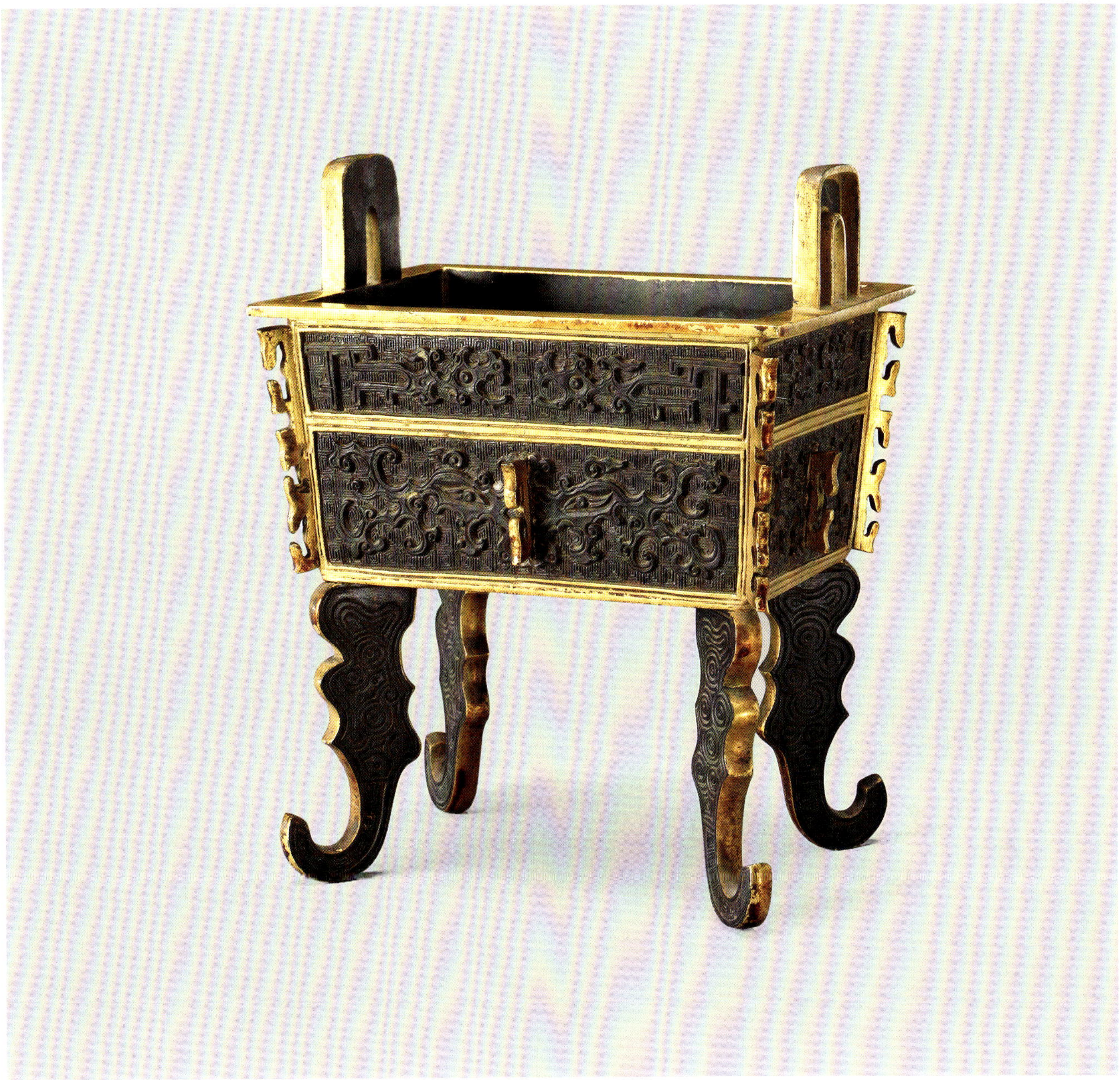

130 | RECTANGULAR CENSER IN THE FORM OF AN ANCIENT BRONZE CAULDRON (*FANGDING*), Qing dynasty (1644–1911), Qianlong reign (1735–96)

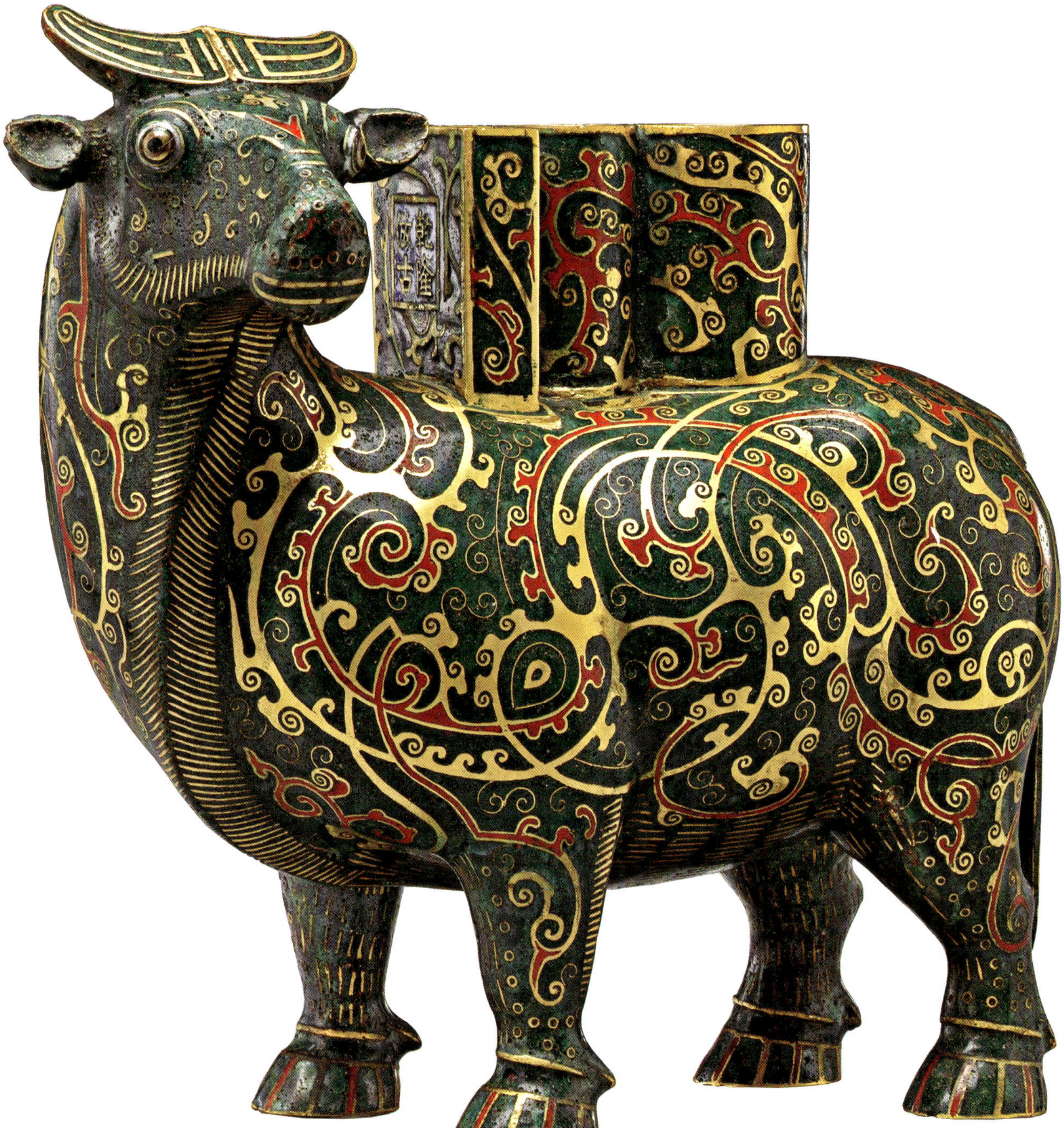

131 | OX-SHAPED CONTAINER (*ZUN*), Qing dynasty (1644–1911), Qianlong reign (1735–96)

132 | VESSEL IN THE FORM OF AN ANCIENT BRONZE JAR (*HU*), Qing dynasty (1644–1911), Qianlong reign (1735–96)

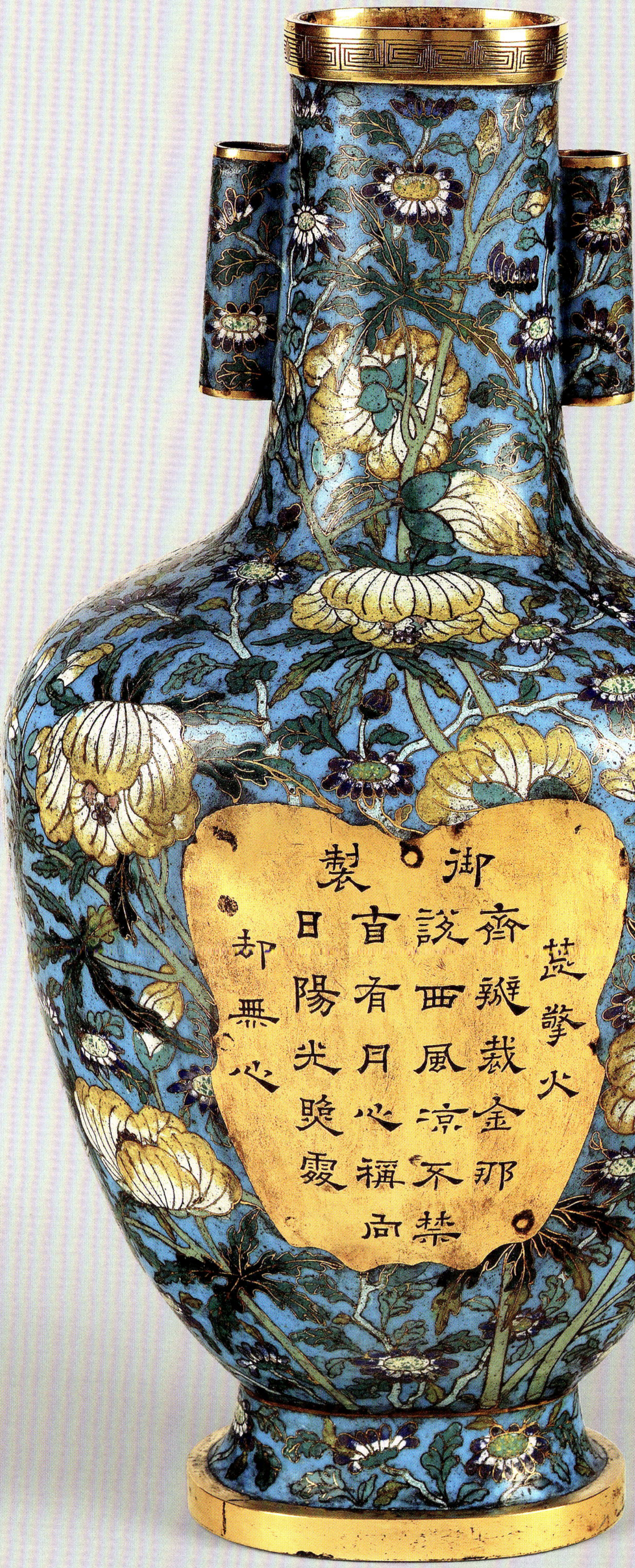

蓖擎火
御
齊瓣裁金那
說西風涼不禁
占有月心稱向
製
日陽光照霞
却無心

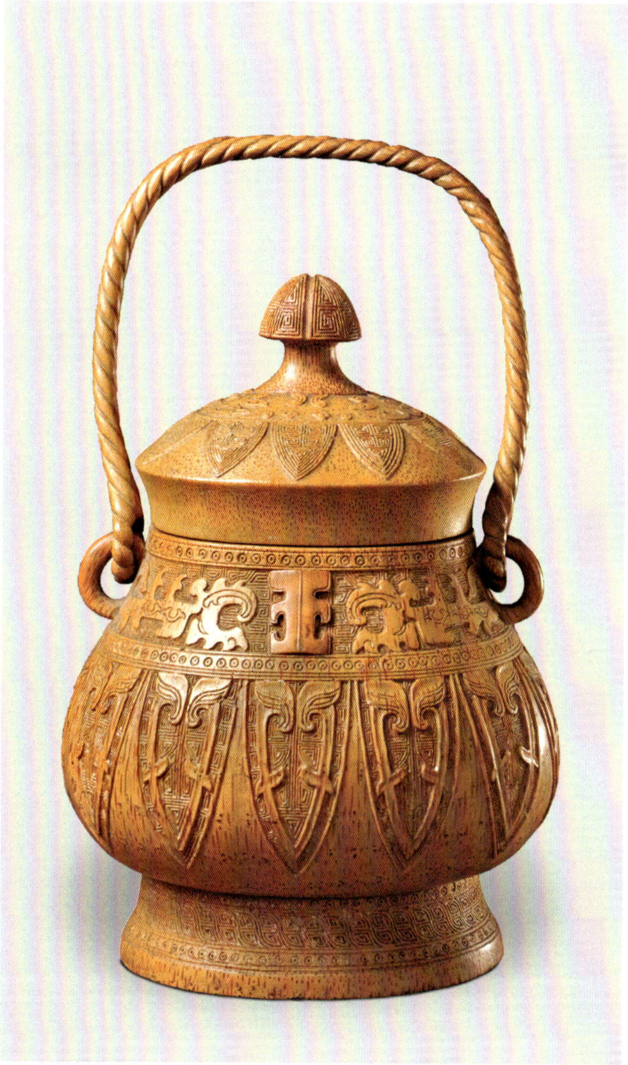

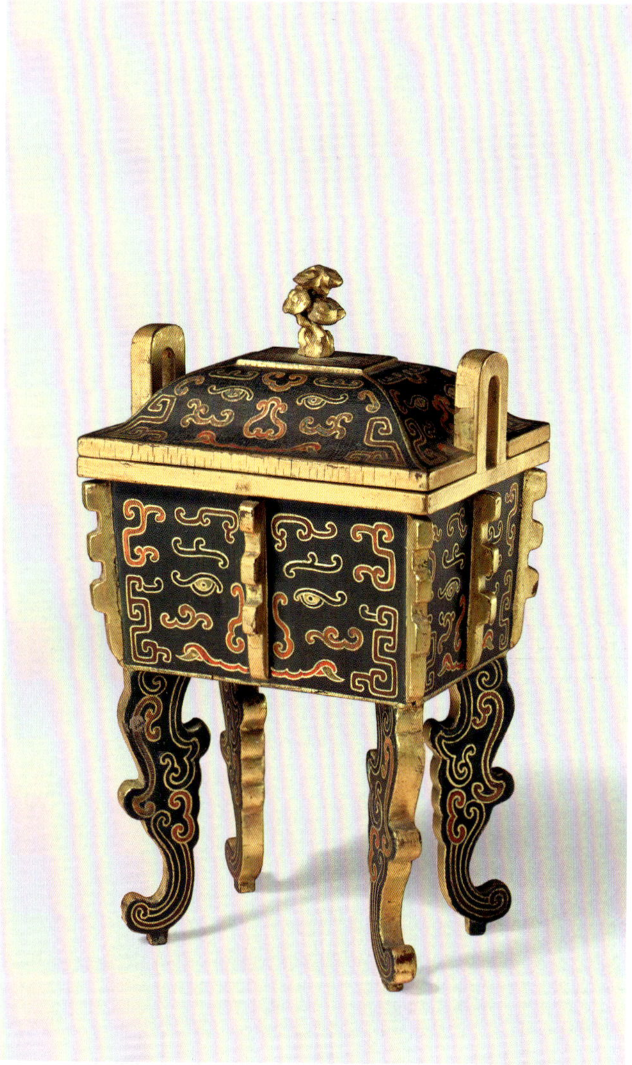

133 | VESSEL IN THE FORM OF AN ANCIENT BRONZE BUCKET (*YOU*), Qing dynasty (1644–1911)

134 | CENSER IN THE FORM OF AN ANCIENT BRONZE RECTANGULAR CAULDRON (*FANGDING*), Qing dynasty (1644–1911)

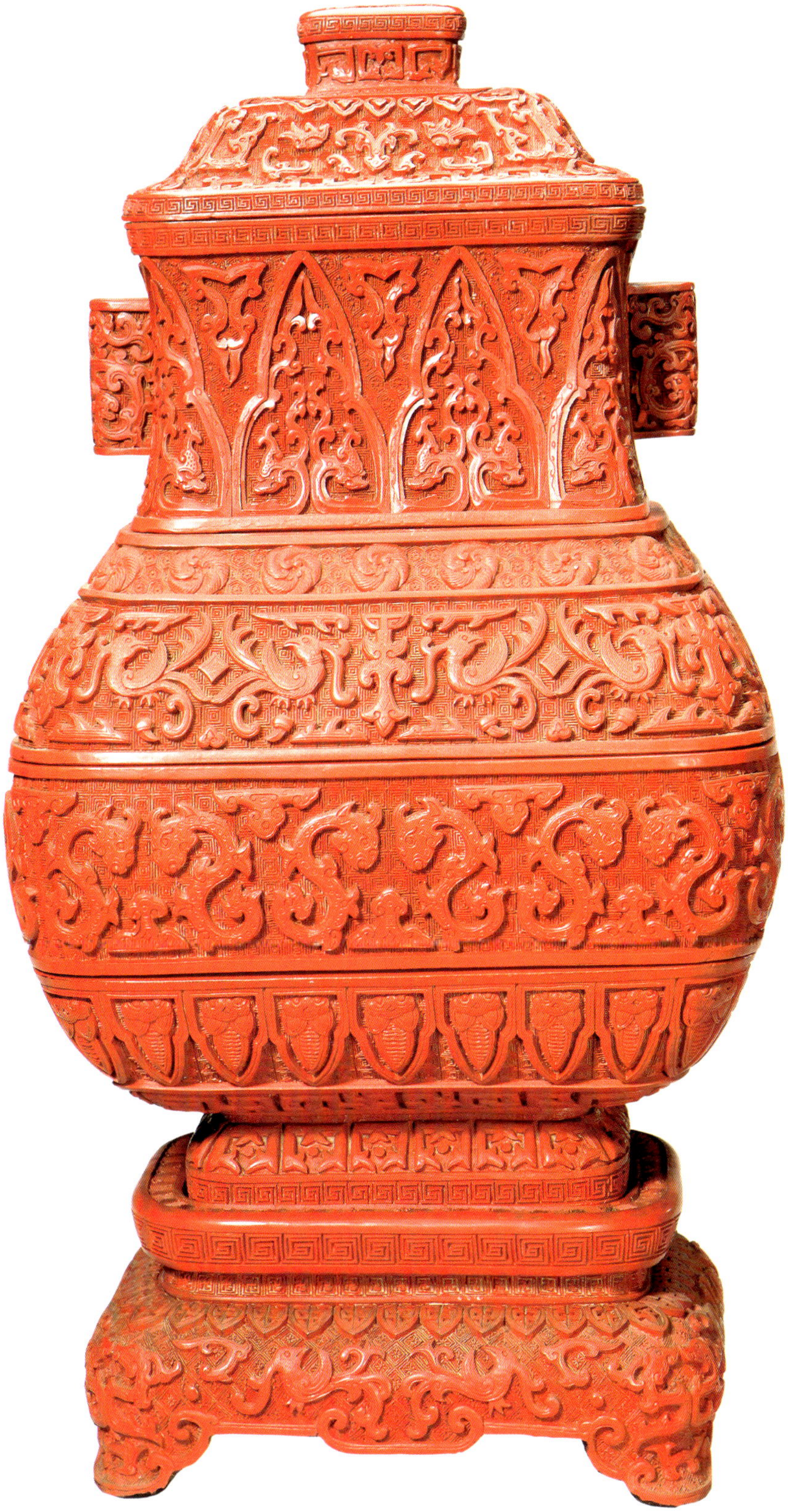

135 | BOX SET IN THE FORM OF AN ANCIENT BRONZE JAR (*HU*), Qing dynasty (1644–1911)

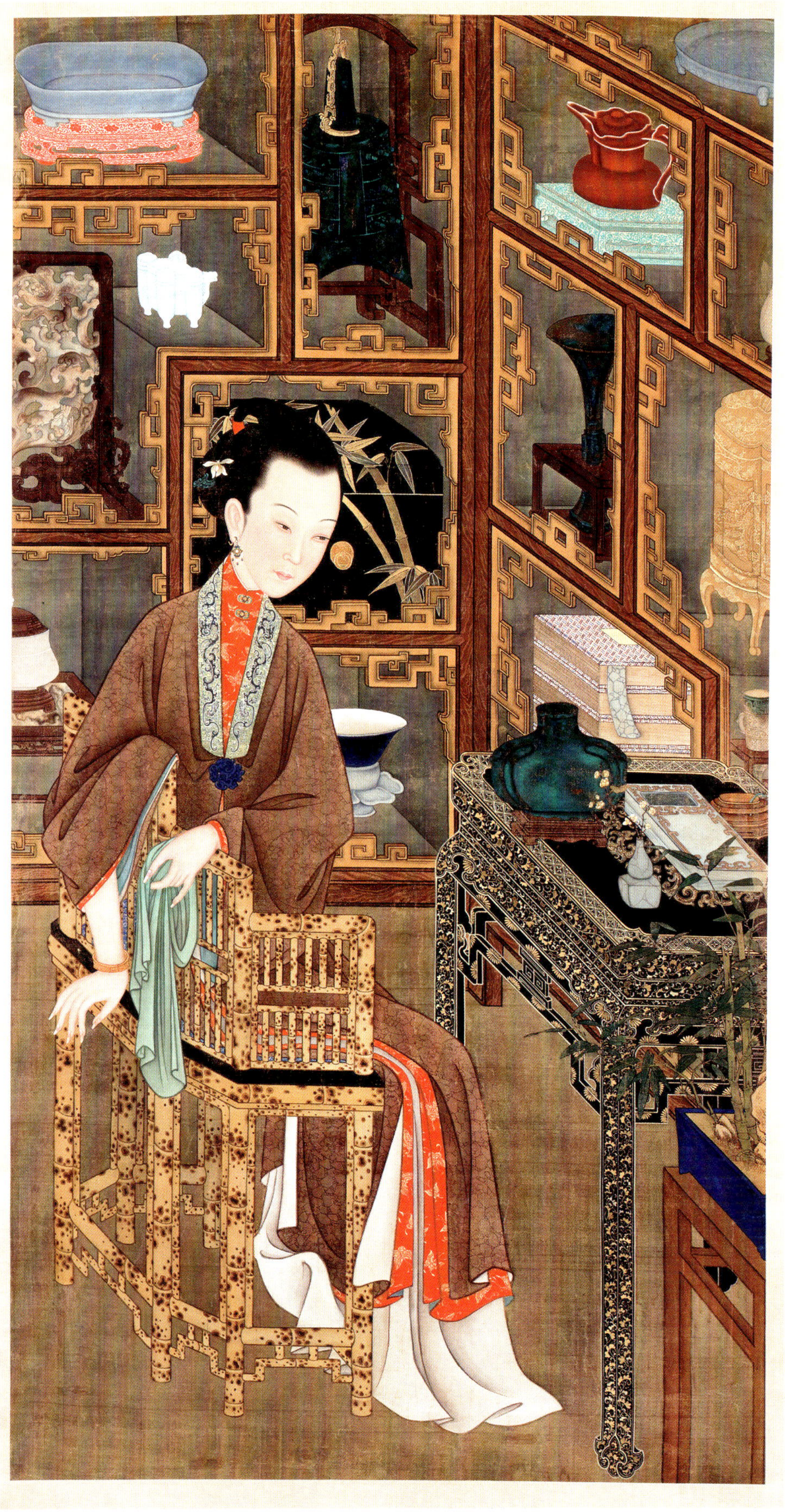

136 | Artist unknown. "COURT LADY APPRECIATING ANTIQUITIES," FROM "TWELVE BEAUTIES," Qing dynasty (1644–1911), late Kangxi reign (1709–22)

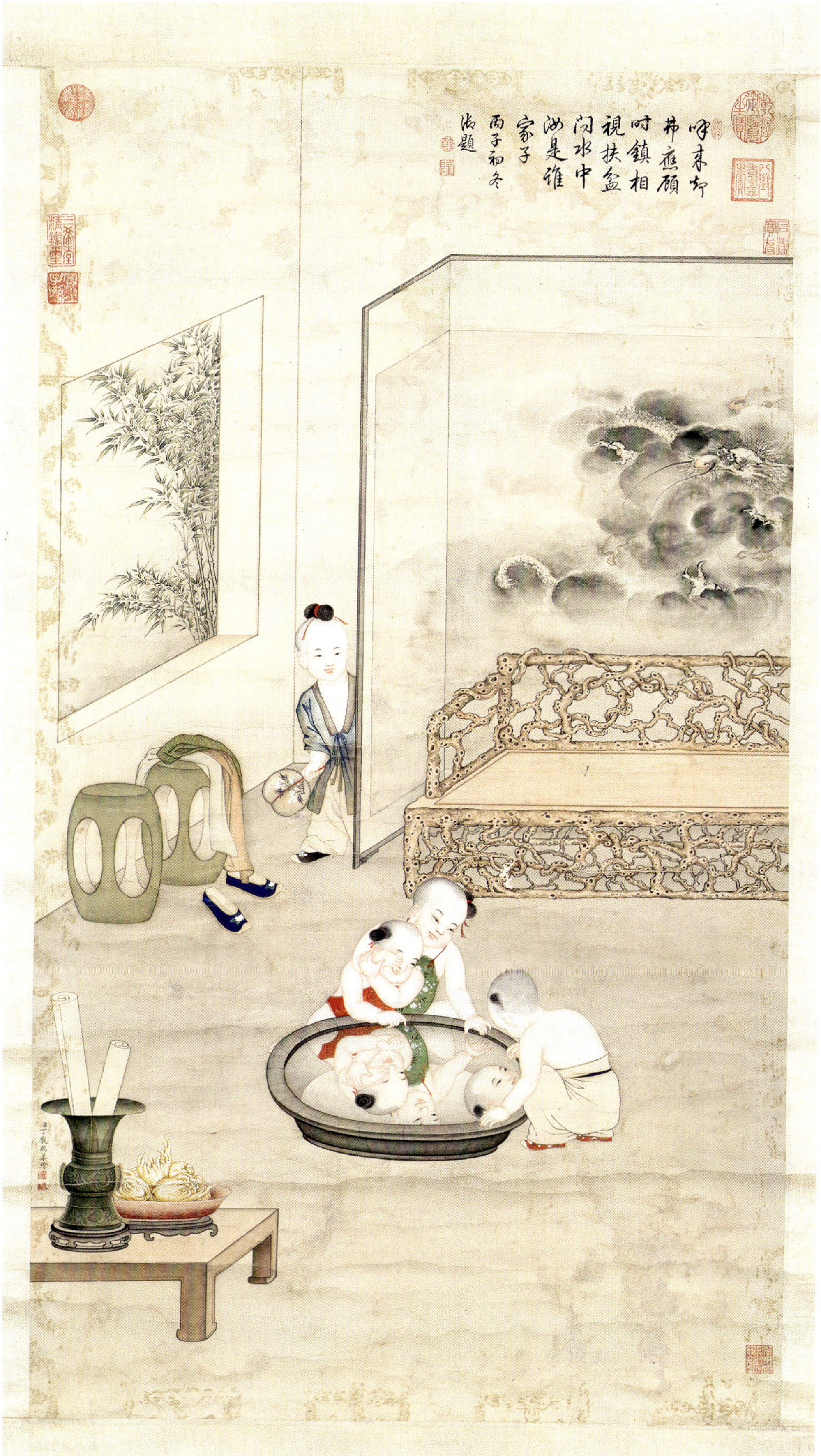

137 | Ding Guanpeng (Chinese, 1708–1771). CHILDREN PLAYING, Qing dynasty (1644–1911), Qianlong reign (1735–96)

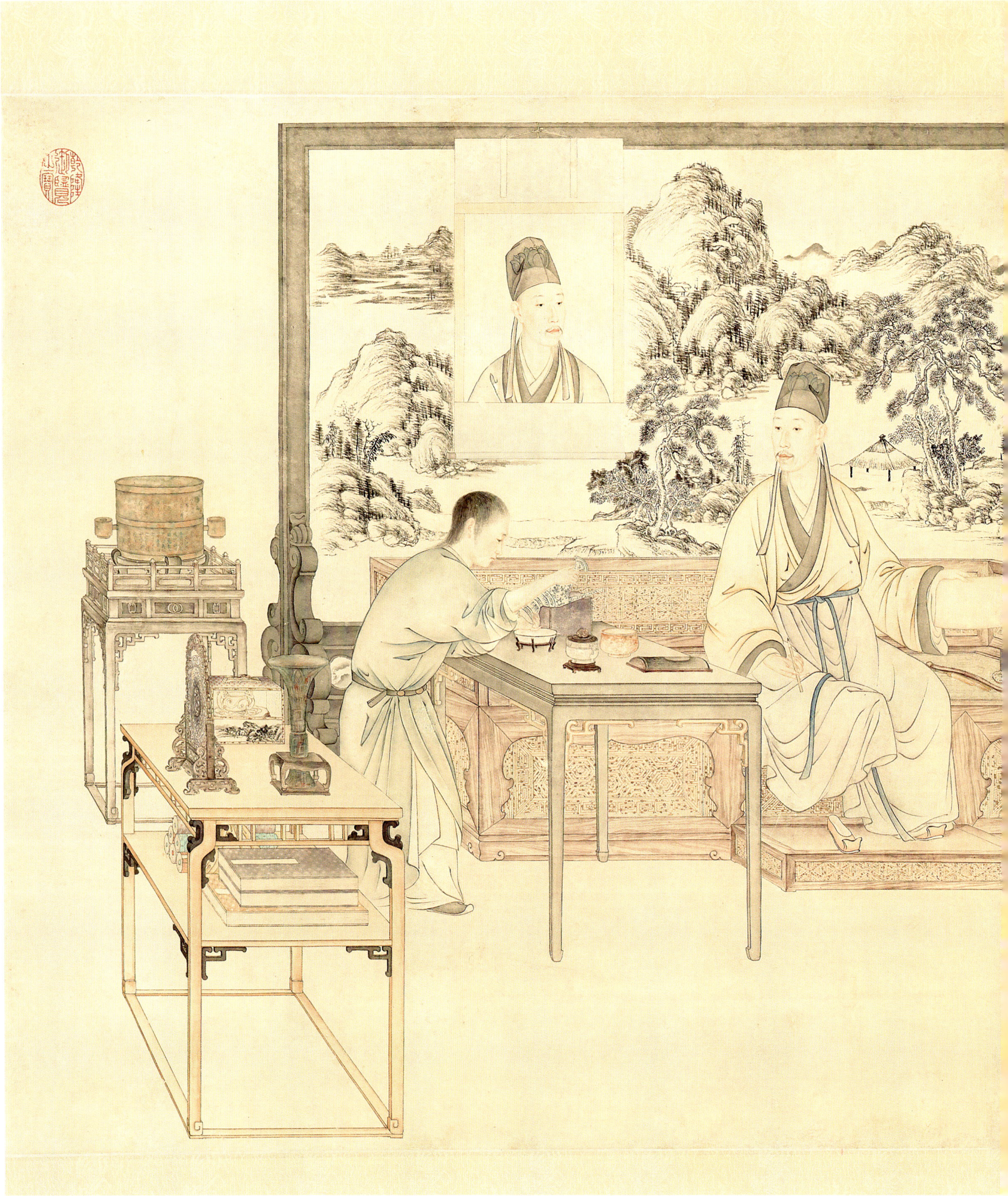

138 | Artists unknown. ONE OR TWO? (*SHIYI SHIER TU*), MENTAL CULTIVATION HALL (*YANGXINDIAN*) VERSION, Qing dynasty (1644–1911), Qianlong reign (1735–96)

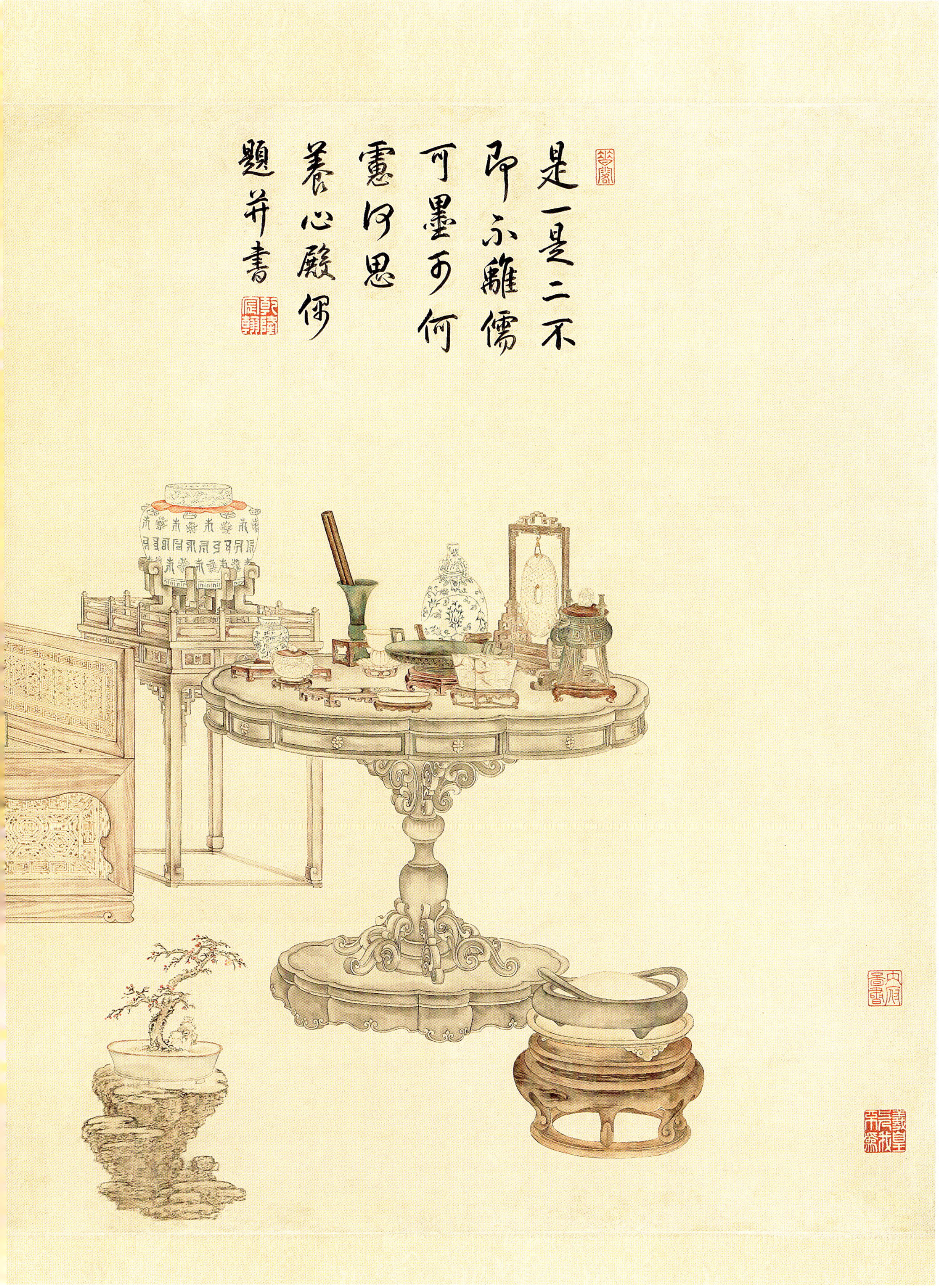
是一是二不
即不離儒
可墨可何
慮何思
養心殿御
題并書

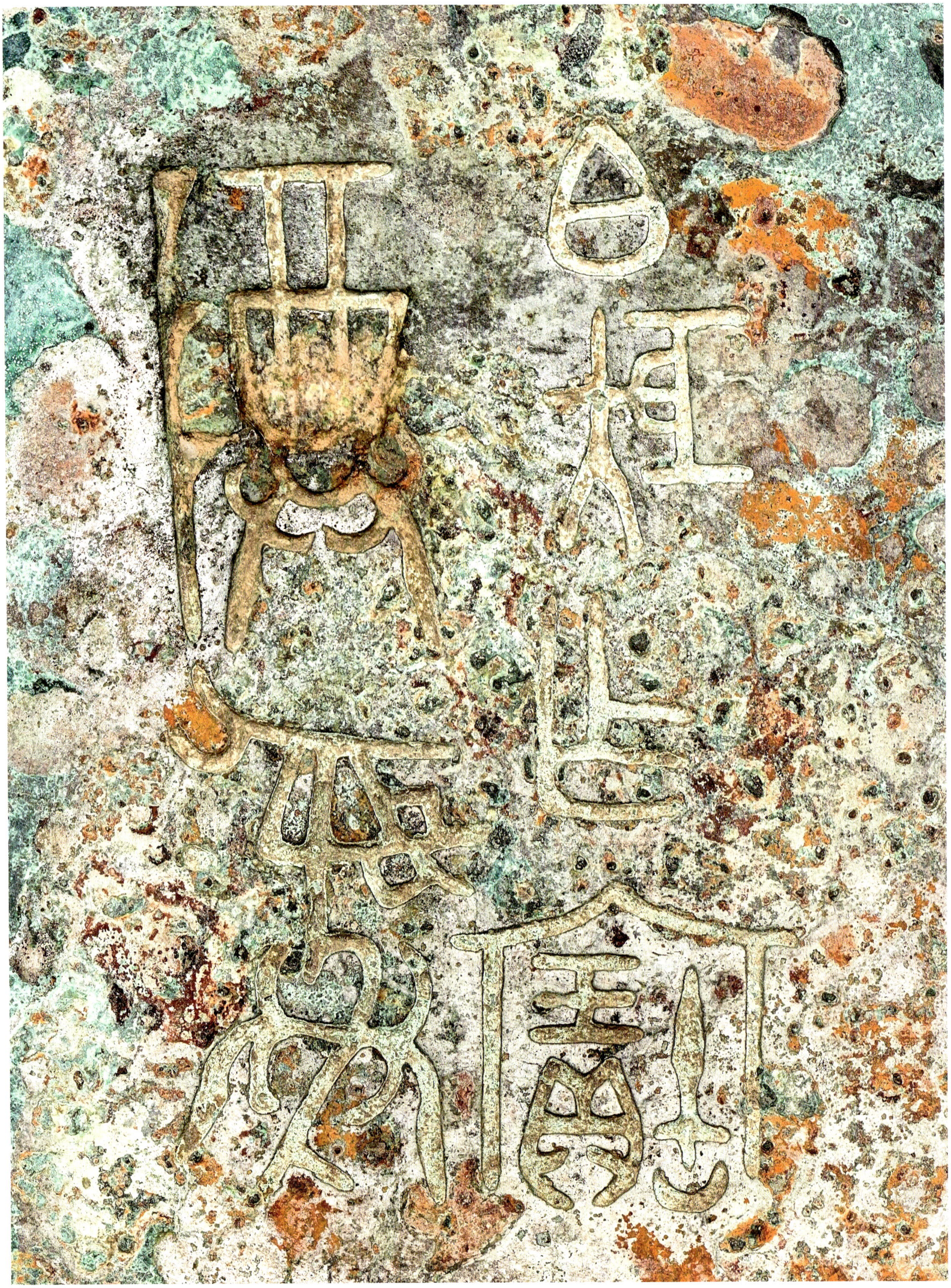

畏友

RIVALS AND FRIENDS

SCHOLAR-COLLECTORS AND THEIR CIRCLES

TAO WANG

Yaji: Elegant Gathering

Imagine a spring day in a rocky landscaped garden, with a stream flowing under a stone bridge and a gentle breeze blowing through bamboo and pine trees. A group of sixteen guests and their attendants, some sitting and some standing, are all busily reading, meditating, painting, doing calligraphy, making music, and appreciating antiquities. This scene is known as the Elegant Gathering in the Western Garden (*Xiyuan yaji*). According to legend, in the Northern Song dynasty in 1087, the powerful imperial son-in-law Wang Shen, who was also a renowned landscape painter and art collector, invited a group of celebrities to assemble and engage in activities that were widely regarded as the epitome of cultural refinement. His guests included famous writers, calligraphers, painters, a Japanese monk, and a Daoist. Wang Shen commissioned the famous antiquarian and artist Li Gonglin to immortalize this memorable occasion in a painting. "There is nothing that can be compared in human society with this most clear and profound joy!" sighed the painter, poet, and collector Mi Fu in his essay about the event.[1]

Li's painting is now lost, and although several contemporary art historians have questioned whether the Elegant Gathering ever actually happened, it became a popular subject for Chinese artists.[2] No fewer than forty existing paintings depict a similar scene. One of them (fig. 1), attributed to the Southern Song court artist Ma Yuan and now in the Nelson-Atkins Museum of Art in Kansas City, shows a group of ancient bronzes displayed on a flat garden rock. This painting is probably the earliest surviving visual record of collectors appreciating ancient bronzes.[3]

Qing Antiquarianism and Visuality

From the Southern Song (1127–1279) to the Qing (1644–1911) periods, many paintings depict scholars with their collections of antiquities. These are typically given titles ending in *gutu* (literally "picture of antiquity"): for example, *Shugutu* (Narrating Antiquity), *Bogutu* (Broad Manifestation of Antiquity), *Pingutu* (Appreciating Antiquity), *Jiangutu* (Authenticating Antiquity), and *Wangutu* (Playing with Antiquity). The famous Song poet and scholar Su Shi is often the main figure in these paintings.[4] For example, two works in this exhibition, one an album leaf by the famous Ming dynasty artist Qiu Ying (see pl. 162) and the other two fan paintings by the seventeenth- to eighteenth-century artists Zheng Zhong and Xiao Chen (see pls. 163 and 164), depict Su Shi sitting at a table with friends, appreciating antiquities. On the table are paintings and a group of bronze vessels. Although Su was a collector of antiquities, he eschewed ostentation and expressed reservation about attachment to things.[5] These representations of art collecting celebrate scholarly pursuits and simultaneously warn collectors of the danger of overindulging in material things and losing their purpose in life.

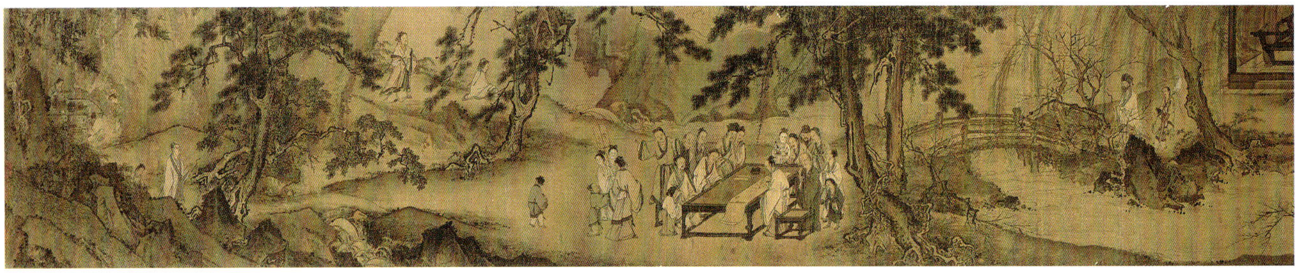

1 | Attributed to Ma Yuan (Chinese, 1190–1225). *Composing Poetry on a Spring Outing* [Chunyou fushi tu], 1127/1279. Ink and color on silk; 302.3 × 29.5 cm (119 × 11 5/8 in.). The Nelson-Atkins Museum of Art, Kansas City, Missouri, 63-19.

Despite scholar-officials' high-minded attitude, having a personal collection of art and antiques did serve to indicate high social status. Such holdings showcased the refined taste of the elite class and provided an effective way of social networking.[6] After the Song dynasty, ancient bronzes remained sought-after, but the imperial courts and private collectors of the Yuan, Ming, and early Qing periods appreciated them as curios and playthings; ancient bronze vessels were used for burning incense, displaying flowers, and studio decorations. Very little serious scholarship was produced on the subject; as a general survey states: "the Yuan dynasty found it difficult to succeed upon the flowering [of antiquarianism] during the Song dynasty, because their prevailing customs did not emphasize concrete learning, and therefore few bronzes and steles were discovered. . . . Being even more appreciative of non-empiricism, and unable to distinguish between real and counterfeit, but still flaunting their subjective talk with virtually no textual research, was the failing of Ming literati scholarship."[7]

However, the situation began to change in the late eighteenth century, when the Qianlong (r. 1735–96) and Jiaqing (r. 1796–1820) emperors engaged enthusiastically with collecting and cataloguing of collections. At the same time, many scholar-officials also became passionate collectors of antiquities and resourceful patrons of art. This attention was partially the result of the Manchu rulers' strict censorship policy, but it was also related to the rise of *kaojuxue* (evidential learning) in textual criticism and historical research.[8] With the completion of the imperial project, known as the *Siku quanshu* (Complete Library of Four Treasures; 1773–84), which is the largest collection of Chinese literature and scholarship, and the publication of the catalogues of imperial collections, private collectors now had the incentive, as well as the necessary references, to build their own holdings and publish their own catalogues.

Among these were many eminent scholar-officials, such as Chen Jieqi, Duanfang, Liu Xihai, Pan Zuyin, Ruan Yuan, Wu Dacheng, and Wu Shifen, all of whom contributed to the revival of the antiquarian discipline *jinshixue* (study of metal and stone), which was initiated by Song dynasty scholars. Ruan is regarded as the doyen of the Qing antiquarians. He was born in Yangzhou (Jiangsu) to a family of high-ranking officials.[9] Yangzhou was one of the most important southern cities in the Qing period and a regular stopping place for Qianlong's southern inspection tours.[10] Indeed, it is said that the young Ruan had his first audience with the emperor on a boat during one of these southern tours and that Qianlong was deeply impressed by his talent. Yangzhou was also the location of the Pavilion of Literary Confluence (*Wenhuige*), one of the six libraries holding the *Siku quanshu*.

Ruan passed the metropolitan examination, obtained the *jinshi* (advanced scholar) degree in 1789, and was appointed to the Imperial Hanlin Academy. He held a number of prominent official positions under the Jiaqing and Daoguang (r. 1821–50) emperors, including chancellor of Hunan; governorships of Yunnan-Guizhou, and Guangdong-Guangxi; and grand secretary. But Ruan is perhaps better known for his scholarship in textual criticism and for his achievements in education. In Hangzhou he founded an academic school, *Gujing jingshe* (Academy for Studying the Classics), to teach astronomy, geometry, literature, and mathematics. Later, in Guangzhou, he established the *Xuehaitang* (Hall of the Sea of Learning) to promote *kaojuxue*. Ruan also wrote and published many books on natural sciences and textual criticism, including *Chouren zhuang* (Biographies of Astronomers and Mathematicians; 1795–99) and *Shisanjing zhushu* (Commentaries and Notes to the Thirteen Classics; 1816).

Ruan collected antiquities and was a very accomplished epigrapher of bronze inscriptions. In his seminal 1804 work *Jiguzhai zhongdingyiqi kuanzhi* (Inscriptions on Ritual Vessels and Bells from the *Jiguzhai* [Studio of Accumulating Antiquity]), Ruan recorded, transcribed, and analyzed 560 bronze inscriptions. Like the Song antiquarians, he saw ancient bronzes not only as physical remains of the past but also as historical evidence and the embodiment of moral principles. He wrote: "Above the physical form is the Way [*dao*] and below is what we call objects [*qi*]. The Way of the Shang and Zhou dynasties remained in the nine classics, but very rarely do we find any objects of that age. Only bronzes such as bells and tripods could have survived . . . When we wish to comprehend the Way and objects of the Three Dynasties, outside of the nine classics, where can we find this other than with the bronze bells and tripods?"[11] For Ruan, recording the bronzes' inscriptions was more important than preserving their physical form. Once printed, the catalogue could outlast the bronzes themselves, as is the case with many of the ancient works recorded by the Song antiquarians—the printed images are still in circulation, although the objects have not survived. In the *Jiguzhai zhongdingyiqi kuanzhi*, Ruan recorded as many inscriptions as he could obtain and added to his own those collected by his friends and associates, whom he named: He Yuanxi, Jiang Deliang, Jiang Fan, Qin Enfu, Qian Dian, Song Baochun, Sun Xinyan, Weng Shupei, Zhang Tingji, Zhao Bingchong, Zhao Wei, and Zhu Weibi. Most of these individuals had obtained advanced-scholar degrees and held official positions, although a few were probably better known for their artistic talent and scholarly reputation, their rich collections of ancient bronzes and inscriptions, or their family connections. Weng Shupei was the son of Weng Fanggang, a famed calligrapher and high-ranking official. Qian Dian, a famous calligrapher, was the nephew of the great historian and linguist Qian Daxin, a leading figure of evidential learning. Zhang Tingji did not hold the *jinshi* degree but had one of the best collections of ancient bronzes. He was personally very close to Ruan, and their friendship has been described as "strong as metal and stone" (*jinshijiao*), another pleasing example of wordplay—*jinshixue* and *jinshijiao*—implying that their relationship was based on a shared antiquarian interest.[12] It is also worth noting that many of Ruan's associates originally came from the Jiangnan region (Jiangsu and Zhejiang); indeed, Qin Enfu and Jiang Fan shared the same hometown as Ruan.

Collectors from Shandong and Suzhou

Local traditions also played a significant part in the development of art collecting in the Qing period. Many important collectors came mainly from two regions: Shandong (the coastal province south of Beijing) and Jiangnan (in the south). The first Shandong collector who made his name is Liu Xihai. Liu came from a prominent family in Zhucheng. His great uncle was Liu Yong, the famed calligrapher and academician of the grand secretariat of Emperor Qianlong. Liu passed the provincial examination with the *juren* (provincial graduate) degree in 1816 and was subsequently appointed to various official posts in Fujian, Shaanxi, Sichuan, and Zhejiang. His early collecting interest was in coins, which then extended to bronzes, steles, and rare books. He lost his job while in Zhejiang, having been accused of spending too much time collecting antiquities.[13] He wrote and compiled

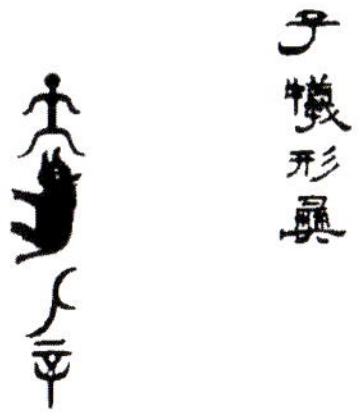

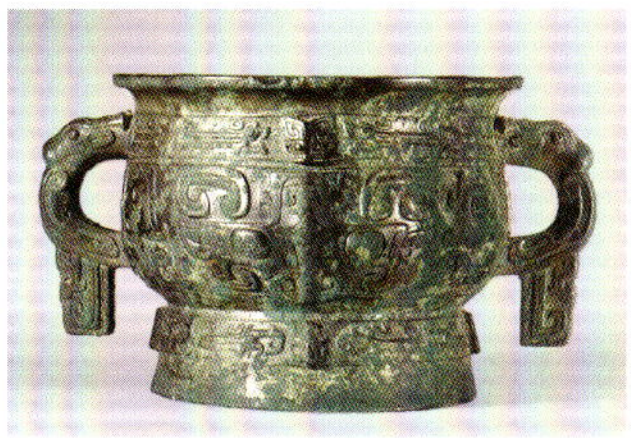

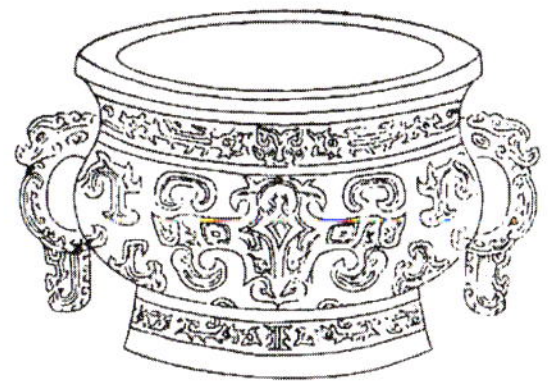

2a | *Tureen of Tian Shi* (*Tian Shi Gui*), early Western Zhou dynasty (1046–927 BC). Bronze; h. 16.5 cm (6 ½ in.). Private collection.

2b | Drawing of fig 2a published in Liu Xihai, *Chang'an huogubian* [Compilation of Antiquities Acquired in Chang'an] (1905).

a number of books covering a range of antiquarian subjects, such as *Guquan yuan* (Garden of Ancient Coins; unpublished), which contained more than four thousand coin rubbings, and two manuscripts, *Chang'an huogubian* (Compilation of Antiquities Acquired from Chang'an) and *Haidong jinshi yuan* (Garden of Metals and Stone at the East of the Sea), which appeared after his death.[14] While in Sichuan, Liu also investigated and recorded many local stele inscriptions and published a book in 1846, but the main part of his manuscript remained unpublished until recently.[15] He amassed a sizable collection of ancient bronzes, and one of them, known as *Tian Shi gui* (Tureen of Tian Shi; fig. 2a), appears in *Chang'an huogubian* (see fig. 2b). It was also recorded by Wu Shifen in his *Jungulu jinwen* (Bronze Inscriptions from the Record of Pursuing Antiquities; 1895) and later entered the collection of Wang Yirong.[16]

The second most important collector from Shandong is Wu Shifen, who was three years younger than Liu Xihai. Wu was born in Beijing, but his family was originally from a powerful gentry clan in Haifeng (Shandong). Over the years the family had nine "advanced-degree scholars," including Wu Shifen himself. Wu held many official posts and was promoted to high positions, such as academician of the grand secretariat and vice minister of the Department of Rites. But Wu is perhaps better known today for his historical scholarship and collection of antiquities. The famous *Zuo Ce Huan you* included in this catalogue once belonged to him (see pl. 140). His representative publications include the *Jungulu* (Record of Pursuing Antiquities), compiled with the assistance of his friend Xu Han, which lists over eighteen thousand bronze and stone inscriptions, and *Jungulu jinwen* (Record of Pursuing Antiquities—Bronze Inscriptions), issued by his sons in 1895 after his death, which contains his analysis of more than 1,300 bronze inscriptions.[17] Another book on seal impressions, *Fengni kaoluo* (A Brief Study of Clay Bullae), printed in 1904,

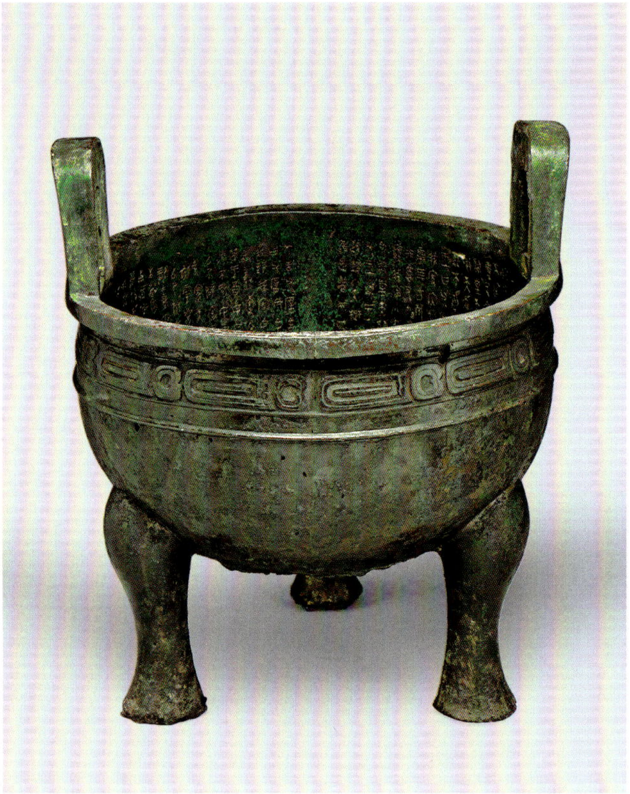

3a | *Ding of Maogong (Maogong Ding)*, late Western Zhou (850–771 BC). Bronze; 47.9 × 53.8 cm (18 7/8 × 21 3/16 in.). National Palace Museum, Taipei.

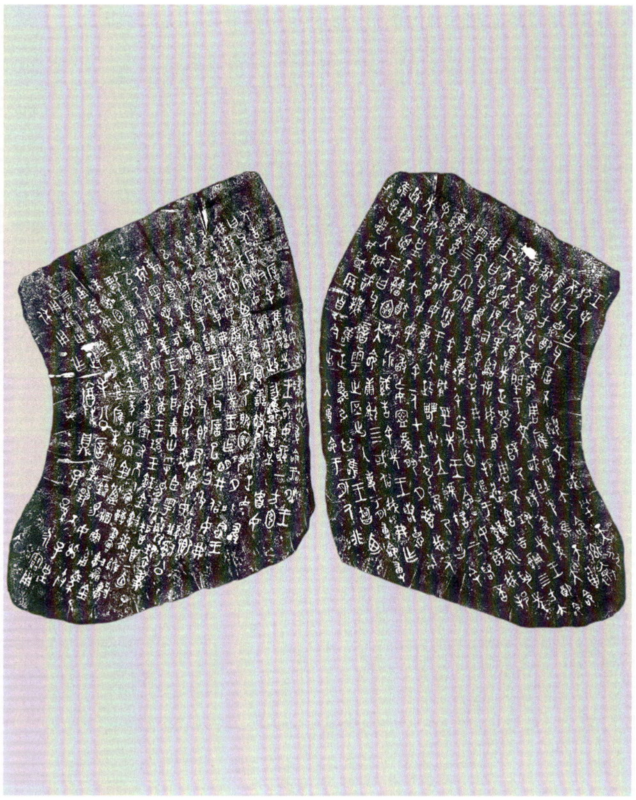

3b | Rubbing of the inscription on fig. 3a.

was prepared in collaboration with Chen Jieqi, a younger, acclaimed antiquarian scholar from Weixian (Shandong), who was related to him by marriage.

Chen was the most revered epigrapher and connoisseur of his generation. He obtained his advanced-scholar degree in 1845 and then served for about ten years as compiler of the Imperial Hanlin Academy in the capital. While in Beijing, he came to know Ruan Yuan personally and befriended many other like-minded scholar-officials such as He Shaoji and Wu. In 1854 he retired to his hometown and devoted all his time to collecting and studying antiquities. Chen had broad tastes, and his collection comprised more than seven thousand bronze seals and clay bullae (seal impressions); more than two hundred bronze mirrors; and 253 vessels, including the famous Western Zhou dynasty *Maogong Ding* tripod (fig. 3a) that bore an inscription of 499 characters (see fig. 3b); as well as many other types of objects, such as stone carvings and Buddhist statues. Chen emphasized inscriptions rather than the overall aesthetics of the objects; for example, his collection also contained a Han dynasty measuring vessel (see figs. 4a and 4b), which has a plain and rudimentary form but bears an inscription (see fig. 4b) and offers valuable information on Han economic history. Besides being an able epigrapher who deciphered difficult inscriptions, Chen was also very good at authenticating ancient bronzes and making rubbings, which he often exchanged with, and sometimes sold to, other collectors.

Among Chen's many friends was Pan Zuyin, who was probably the most celebrated collector of his time.[18] His ancestors originally came from Huizhou (Anhui), but migrated to Wuxian (modern Suzhou in Jiangsu) in the late Ming period, when the city was developing into a commercial and cultural center in the Jiangnan region. The Pan family made their money in the salt trade and began to invest heavily in the education of the their younger members. Pan's grandfather Pan Shi'en was awarded first place (*zhuangyuan*) in the metropolitan examination in 1793 and consequently held a number of senior government appointments. Pan was born and raised in Beijing, where his father, Pan Zengshan, and his grandfather were both working at the imperial court. In 1852, the second year of the Xianfeng reign, Pan passed the metropolitan examination and distinguished himself in the final imperial exam. He then was appointed as compiler of the Imperial Hanlin Academy and later as commissioner in charge of the civic examinations. In his official career, Pan held a number of high-level government appointments, including minister of justice, minister of war, minister of work, and grand minister of the state. These powerful positions enabled him to build one of the largest and best private collections of all times.

Although his family had a long tradition of art collecting, Pan managed to distinguish himself nonetheless. He collected a large number of antiquities, rare books, paintings, and calligraphic works, including more than five hundred ancient bronzes. A number of the latter in his collection came from the old imperial collection of Qianlong, including some that appear in this catalogue (see pls. 29, 107, and 143). According to Pan's own account, he was first introduced to the great antiquarian scholar Ruan when he was only eight years old. Ruan Yuan gave him a rubbing of an inscription taken from a work in his own collection, the *Qi Hou Lei*, a bronze wine jar of Lord Qi of the Zhou dynasty, which sparked his lifelong interest in ancient bronzes.[19] As a young man, Pan also studied epigraphy with the scholar Chen Songnan from Fujian. Later, while working at various imperial departments in the capital, he took the opportunity to expand his collection, particularly of rare books and ancient bronzes, and made friends with many fellow scholar-officials who shared the same interests. He wrote: "I spent all my salary purchasing ancient ritual bronzes and books. There were many people with whom I met frequently to discuss bronzes and books, including Qingqing [Wu Dacheng], Liansheng [Wang Yirong], Xiangtao [Zhang Zhidong], Zhou Mengbo [he passed the metropolitan exam in 1846 and was Wang Yirong's teacher], and Hu Shicha. Not a single day passed without us putting time into the study and investigation of such things. Each time a bronze was obtained, we would pass it around among us to study and appreciate. What an enjoyable time!"[20]

Mentioned here is Wu Dacheng, another distinguished collector who also came from Suzhou and was connected to Pan through marriage. Like Pan, he was born into a family of high-ranking scholar officials, and, after passing the metropolitan examination in 1868, was appointed compiler of the Imperial Hanlin Academy. Afterward, for about thirty years, Wu held various official positions in different provinces, including Fujian, Guangdong, Hebei, Henan, Jilin, and Shaanxi, eventually becoming governor of Hunan. His official career came to end in 1895, when the Japanese defeated the troops he led in the first Sino-Japanese War (1894–95). Dismissed immediately from his position as commander, Wu was subject to further investigations and, three years later, was barred permanently from government service. In the final years of his life, he was the headmaster at Dragon Gate Academy (*Longmen shuyuan*) in Shanghai, teaching private students.

Wu Dacheng was an accomplished epigrapher and connoisseur of all kinds of antiquities, as well as a competent calligrapher and painter. He was well known and highly respected, and communicated frequently with other collectors, including Chen Jieqi, Liu Xihai, Pan Zuyin, Wang Yirong, Wu Shifen, Wu Yun, and Shengyu, who discussed the antiquities they acquired and issues relating to their interpretation. He also enjoyed a close relationship with Pan, at times exchanging letters on a daily basis. Reading these, we see that Wu often acted as a go-between for his friend,

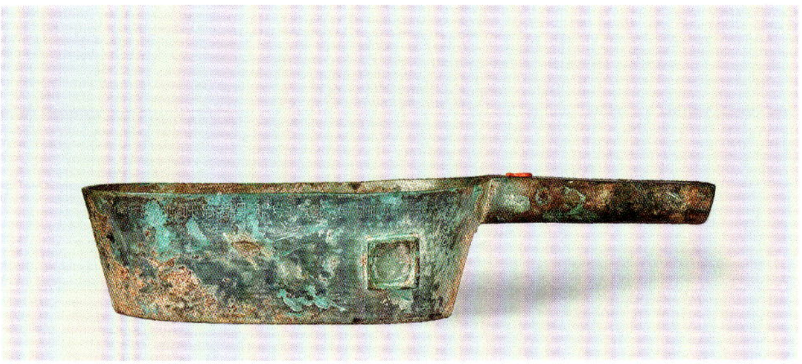

4a | Measuring vessel (*liang*), Wang-Mang Reign (9–13 AD). Bronze; without handle: 39 × 13 × 7.5 cm (15 3/8 × 5 1/8 × 2 15/16 in). Private collection.

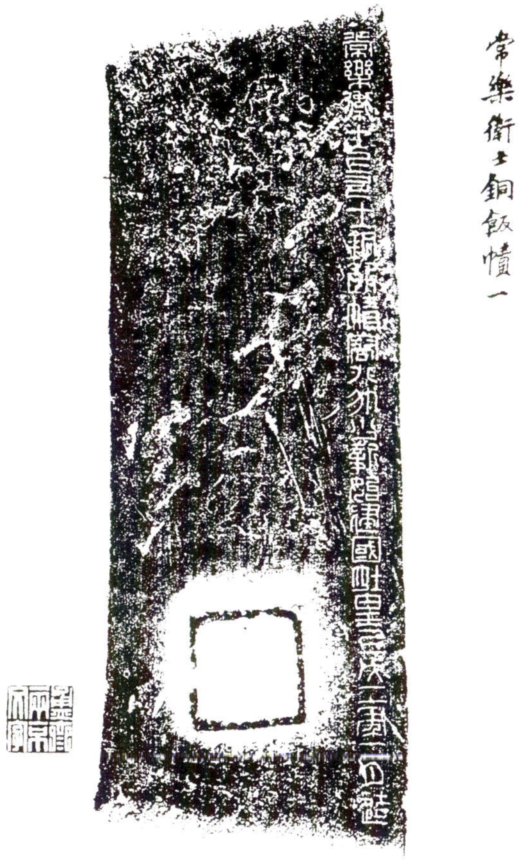

4b | Rubbing of the inscription on fig. 4a published in Chen Jiegi, *Fuzhai jijinlu* [Auspicious Metals Collected by Fuzhai], ed. Deng Shi (Shanghai: 1918), 5.31.

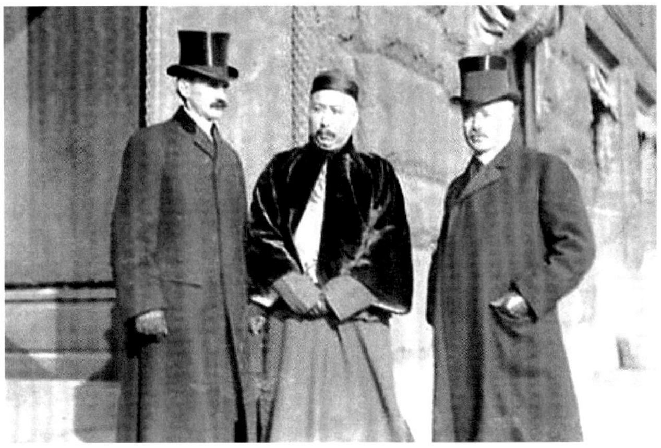

5 | Duanfang with his American hosts in front of the Congress Hotel, Chicago, 1906.

searching for and buying ancient bronzes, authenticating items, making drawings of objects, and tracing inscriptions on them. Wu's deep knowledge of antiquities, as well as his official duties that took him around the country, provided opportunities for him to locate good pieces. Yet, he was a keen collector himself, and inevitably some competition arose. There were times when Wu furtively bought bronzes that he knew were of interest to Pan, purchases he was too ashamed to mention to his mentor.[21]

East and West: Duanfang

The late nineteenth and early twentieth centuries witnessed dramatic changes in Chinese society, as well as intense interaction between China and the West. Duanfang toured the United States in 1906 as imperial envoy, visiting San Francisco, Chicago, and New York (see fig. 5). He was very impressed by what he saw in the United States—not only its political and economic institutions but also its museums. On his return to China, Duanfang promoted the reforms of the country's old political and educational systems, including the establishment of Western-style museums. He also became friends with foreign scholars, including American missionary and art collector John C. Ferguson.[22]

Duanfang's personal collection included ancient bronzes, clay bricks, jades, paintings, pieces of calligraphy, seals, and steles; assisted by his scholar friends such as Kuang Zhouyi, Li Baoxuan, Yang Shoujing, and Zhu Deyi, he published no less than six catalogues of his holdings. *Taozhai jijinlu* (Records of Auspicious Bronzes from Taozhai; 1908–9), for example, contained more than four hundred objects, including a bronze now in the collection of the Art Institute of Chicago (fig. 6a). The book was thoughtfully produced, with ink rubbings of all inscriptions and line drawings of the objects (see fig. 6b), and it was printed using the new lithographic technology. Duanfang is probably the first Chinese collector who was interested in foreign, in particular Native American and ancient Egyptian, artifacts; in this sense, he was truly exceptional for his time.[23] Both for him and for other scholars who shared his ideas and approach, collecting and connoisseurship were no longer merely private activities. As Jason Steuber points out, "The connoisseurship activities of late Qing imperial officials indicates attempts to resolve social and political turmoil by 'self-strengthening.'"[24]

Unfortunately, on November 27, 1911, on his way to suppress a riot in Sichuan during the chaos of the final moments of the Qing dynasty, Duanfang was assassinated by an officer in his own troop. His friends and colleagues mourned this tragic event and sent letters of condolence and memorial notes. Zhang Jian, who, in 1905, founded the first Chinese public museum, the Nantong Bowuyuan, wrote a pair of couplets summarizing Duanfang's cultural achievements and lamenting his untimely death:

> Things collected for enjoyment,
> you had the ability to assemble them,
> And they may bring world fame.
>
> Your collections were stored in the capital,
> but published in the southern city,
> Named as "Catalogue of Taozhai [Tao Studio]."
>
> Protecting them, but not your family;
> changes brought sadness.
>
> The soul may return halfway,
> and may gather gray clouds;
>
> May we all grieve forever and chant:
> "The Road to Sichuan is hard."[25]

With the collapse of the last imperial dynasty, traditional learning and art also suffered a final blow. The encounters between West and East changed relationships not only among countries but also between people and objects. The holdings of both the imperial palace and private individuals were scattered, mirroring the dramatic changes occurring in Chinese society more broadly; for instance, many bronzes recorded in Qianlong's catalogues are now found in various private and public collections throughout the world.[26] Following this dispersal, the ancient bronzes could no longer perform their role as embodiments of the heavenly mandate or as cultural symbols of orthodox ideology and institutions. One of the prizes of Duanfang's collection—a full set of Western Zhou bronze wine vessels and their original stand—was bought by the Metropolitan Museum of Art, New York, in 1924, becoming a permanent fixture in its galleries (see Zhixin Jaxon Sun, "A Legend Retold," in this catalogue, 198–203).

Art of Rubbings

Apart from pursuing antiquities, scholar-officials were eager to create catalogues that contained their own and other collections. No fewer than sixty books of bronzes

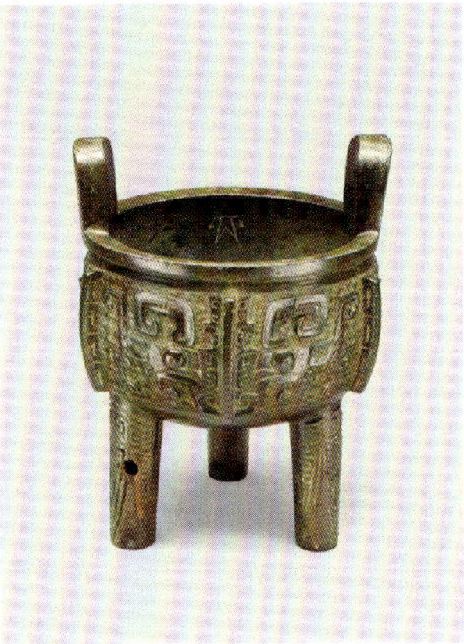

6a | Tripod cauldron (*ding*), late Shang dynasty (1250–1046 BC). Bronze; overall: h. 24.4 cm (9 5⁄8 in.); diam. 18.9 cm (7 1⁄6 in.); without handles: h. 19.1 cm (7 1⁄2 in.); diam. 18.9 cm (7 7⁄16 in.). The Art Institute of Chicago, Lucy Maud Buckingham Collection, 1928.167. See pl. 157.

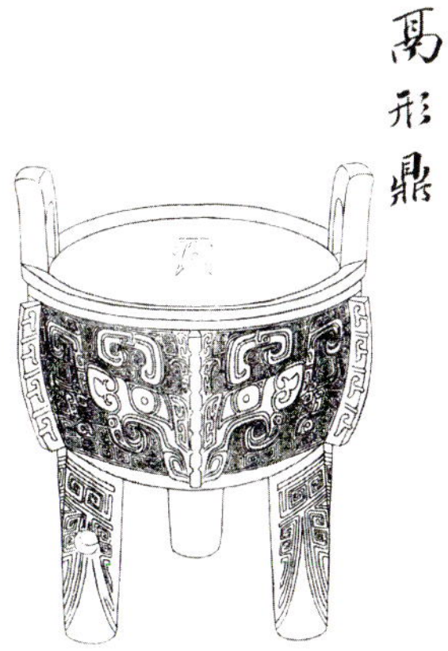

6b | Drawing of 8a published in Duanfang's *Taozhai jijinlu* (Records of Auspicious Bronzes from Taozhai) (1908), 18.

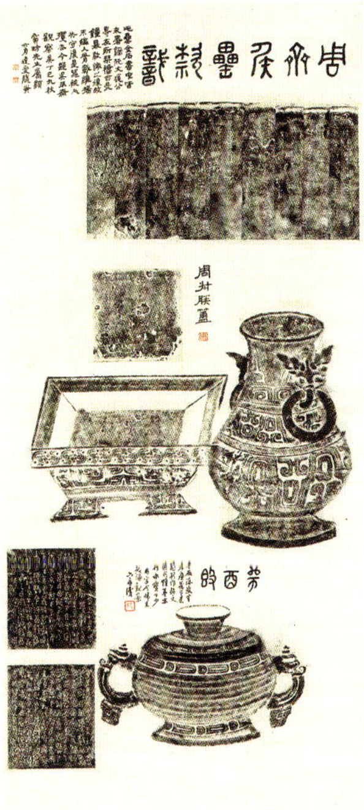

7 | Dashou (Chinese, 1791–1858). Composite rubbings made for Ruan Yuan, 19th century. Handscroll, ink rubbing on paper; 130 × 59 cm (51 3⁄16 × 23 1⁄4 in.). Zhejiang Provincial Museum.

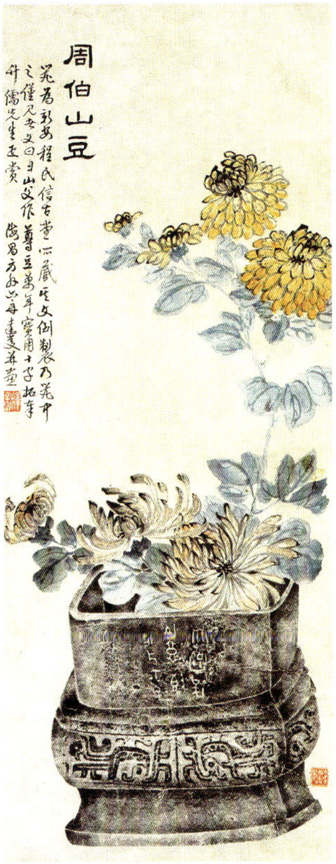

8 | Dashou (Chinese, 1791–1858). Painted chrysanthemum flowers with rubbing of a bronze lid, 19th century. Handscroll, ink rubbing on paper; 59 × 23.5 cm (23 1⁄4 × 9 1⁄4 in.). Xiling Seal Society.

and inscriptions were compiled between 1700 and 1910. These private projects contained new features that had not appeared in the earlier catalogues of the Song antiquarians or Qianlong's imperial publications. For example, in their presentation of inscriptions, they began to employ a tracing technique (*toumo*), as well as ink-squeezed rubbings (*taben*), first seen in Qian Dian's *Shiliu changletang guqi kuanzhi kao* (A Study of Inscriptions on Ancient Vessels from the Shiliuchangletang; 1796) and Chen Jing's *Qiugujingshe jinshilu* (Record of Bronzes and Stele at the Qiugujingshe; 1813). These methods were much more faithful to the original than was hand copying, as well as more beautiful and collectible. Although the use of ink rubbings to record bronze inscriptions began in the Northern Song dynasty, before the nineteenth century published works of inscriptions were usually hand copied and printed with carved woodblocks.

By the time of emperors Jiaqing and Daoguang (r. 1796–1820, r. 1821–50), the full-figured rubbing (*quanxingta*) had been invented, which allowed the recorder to capture the three-dimensional quality of bronze vessels. It was, in fact, a way of combining rubbing and painting techniques, of making hand-drawn outlines and taking rubbings of different parts of the object and then rejoining them to create composite images.[27] The new technique is attributed to the mysterious figure Ma Qifeng, from Jiaxing (Zhejiang), and the earliest example is an unadorned Han dynasty bronze basin, which was published in Bao Changxi's *Jinshixie* (Scraps of Bronzes and Stele; 1876) and dated by a *ganzhi* (the traditional system for reckoning time) on the rubbing to 1798, although this date is not confirmed.[28] However, we have more reliable evidence showing that the method of composite rubbings matured in the hands of Dashou (also known as Liuzhou, or Six Boats), a Buddhist monk who made a number of them for famous collectors, including Ruan Yuan and Cheng Hongpu from Anhui (see figs. 7 and 8).[29] Many scholar-collectors, such as Chen Jieqi and Wu Dacheng, also trained in this technique and were renowned for their skills.[30] But as the process was time consuming and labor intensive, most preferred to employ professionals to undertake them. For example, Wu had three people working for him on a regular basis: Chen Zizhen, Yin Bohuan, and Huang Mufu; on one occasion he commissioned Yin to make a number of composite rubbings, which then were mounted on several hanging scrolls and handscrolls (fig. 9).[31]

Two of the latter, now in the Shanghai Museum, are titled *Kezhai jigutu* (Illustrations of Antiquities Collected by Kezhai; see pl. 146).[32] The scroll is almost fifty feet long and presents forty-five bronze vessels in composite rubbings, each with a transcription of its inscription and its name, as well as a short annotation written by Wu. The handscrolls share the same title as his catalogue *Kezhai jigulu* (Record of Antiquities Collected by Kezhai), although that work records not the

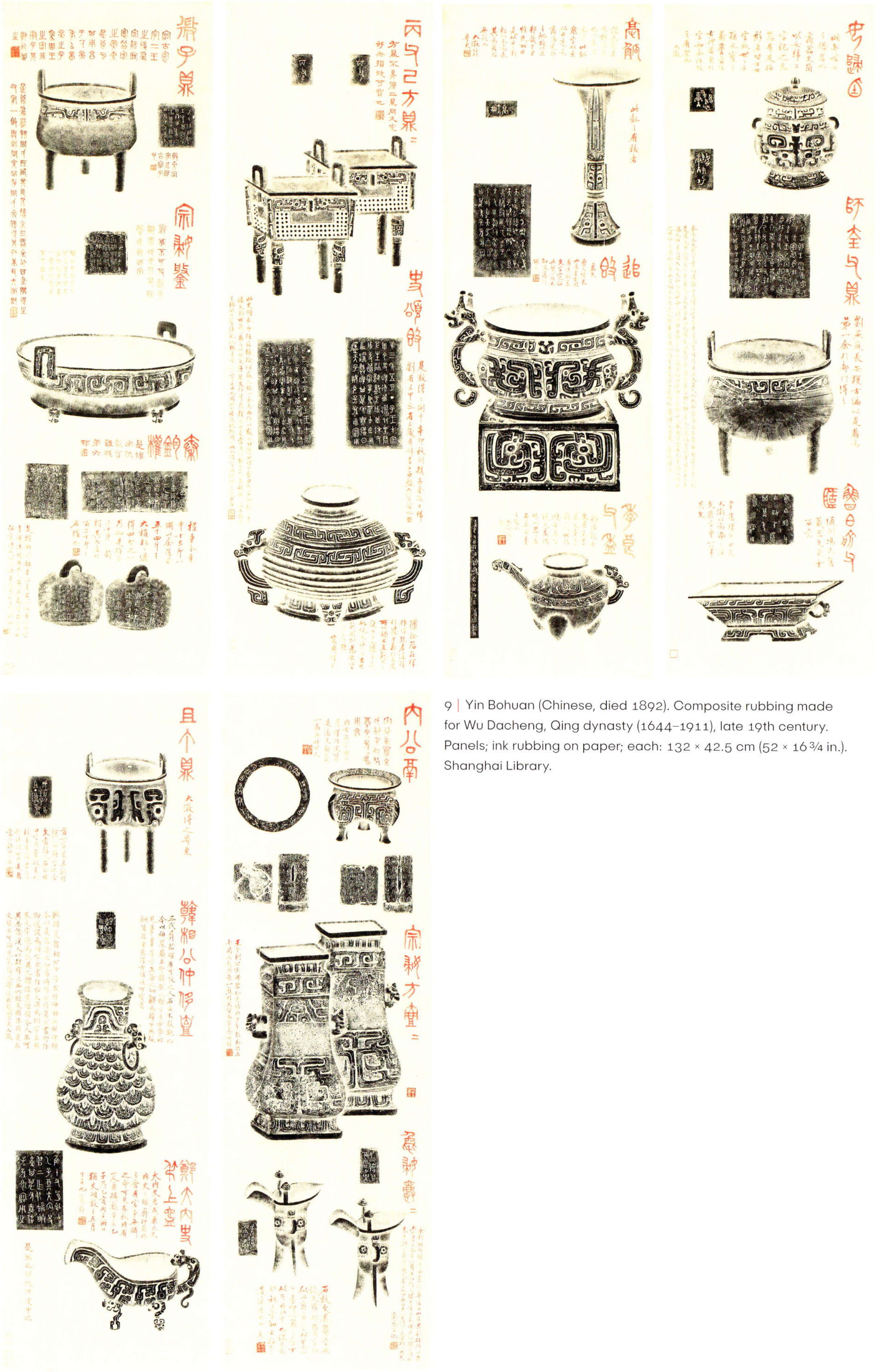

9 | Yin Bohuan (Chinese, died 1892). Composite rubbing made for Wu Dacheng, Qing dynasty (1644–1911), late 19th century. Panels; ink rubbing on paper; each: 132 × 42.5 cm (52 × 16 3/4 in.). Shanghai Library.

bronzes themselves but only the inscriptions, which were on objects that belonged to other collectors. By contrast, the handscrolls present both the inscriptions and the bronzes from which they were made; all of them from Wu's own collection. Moreover, the frontispiece of the scroll is a portrait of Wu, sitting on a wood bench in front of a landscape screen, surrounded by his bronzes (see pl. 146). The portrait is neither signed nor dated; according to Wu Dacheng's grandson, Wu Hufan, it was created jointly by a professional painter, Hu Xiang, and one of Wu's own students, Lu Hui, in 1892.

The composition of the painting reminds us of Qianlong's portrait *One or Two?* (see Tao Wang, "Mirroring the Past," 131–43, and Lu Zhang, *"One or Two?,"* in this catalogue, 144–47). The two images display comparable settings, in which the emperor and the private scholar are both depicted as owners of the material products of the past. Both paintings represent the a new identity that emerges from the relationship between person and object. The format itself can be traced back to earlier Ming and Song models that show scholars and artists sitting with their beloved books and antiquities against background paintings of unchanging landscape.[33]

The format of Wu's handscrolls seems to have followed another, slightly earlier example now in the National Library in Beijing (fig. 10). That handscroll is titled *Jigulu* (Illustration of Assembled Antiquities; 1802) and contains rubbings of 102 bronzes and seals and their inscriptions; the frontispiece is a painting, commissioned by Ruan Yuan and executed by Zhou Zan, showing Ruan appreciating bronzes together with his son Ruan Changsheng and friend Zhu Weibi.[34] During the late Qing period, rubbings of bronzes and steles were very sought after by scholar-officials, who regarded them as an important part of their lifestyle and social networks.[35]

If we consider this cultural significance, we appreciate the beauty of composite rubbings all the more. They are artworks in their own right, and their execution requires superior skills and a deep understanding of the materials and tools. Furthermore, a successful rubbing must catch every nuance and detail of surface decoration and of the inscription inside the vessel in order to make an accurate representation. The varied applications of ink and use of multiple perspectives add to the visual impact of the images, presenting something that the eyes alone cannot see. For these reasons, the composite rubbings demand recognition not only for their documentary value but also for their aesthetic quality. Even after the introduction of Western photography in the mid-nineteenth century, many Chinese scholars still preferred to have their bronzes published in this particular way. In the late nineteenth and early twentieth centuries, a popular trend emerged in which artists incorporated composite rubbings into figurative and flower paintings, thus creating a new genre known as *jinshihua* (painting of metal and stone).[36] For example, on the rubbings (see pls. 160 and 161) of the famous Qi Hou *lei* (Wine Jar of the Duke of Qi; pl. 159), there are colophons and annotations from many scholars, including Duanfang, He Weipu, Kuang Zhouyi, Luo Zhenyu, Zhu Deyi, and Zou An. The celebrated artist Wu Changshi (or Wu Changshuo) also painted onto the rubbings of chrysanthemums and plum blossoms. Sometimes such paintings employ mulitple colors, contrasting with the ink tone of the rubbings. The popularity of *jinshihua* during the late Qing period, as Chuang Shen points out, "not only resulted from a more realistic artistic technique but also reflects the larger historical trend of increasingly empirical approaches to classical and archaeological materials."[37] The incorporation of rubbings of real ancient bronzes into ink-and-color paintings of flowers brought the past into direct dialogue with the present.[38] The tension and contrast between the solidity and history of the vessels and the fleeting freshness of the delicate flowers also reflected artists' nostalgia and anxiety at a moment of historical change.

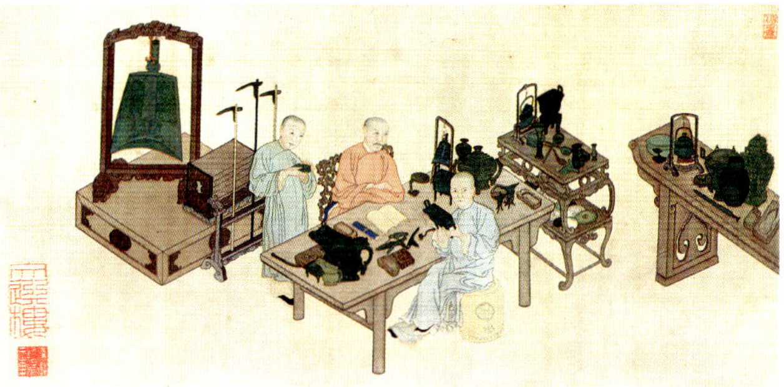

10 | Zhou Zan (Chinese, active 19th century). Frontispiece from *Jigulu* [Illustration of Assembled Antiquities], 1802. Ink and color on paper; 1640 × 38 cm (645 11/16 × 14 15/16 in.). National Library, Beijing.

NOTES

1 | Guests included Cai Xiang, Huang Tingjian, Li Gonglin, Mi Fu, Qin Guan, Su Shi, and Su Shi's brother Su Che. Mi Fu, *Baojin yingguanji (fu buyi)* [Brightness of Flowers from Baojin Studio—with Supplement], in *Congshujicheng chubian* edition (Shanghai: Shangwu yinshuguan, 1939), 76. For its English translation, see Osvald Siren, *A History of Early Chinese Painting* (London: Taylor and Francis, 1933), vol. 2, 53–54.

2 | See, e.g., Ellen Laing, "Real or Ideal: The Problem of the 'Elegant Gathering in the Western Garden' in Chinese Historical and Art Historical Records," *Journal of the American Oriental Society* 88:3 (1968): 419–35; and Liao Yaocheng, "The Epigraphy Studies of Li Gonglin and the Northern Song Literati," *Diancang* [Art and Collection] 14 (2015/5): 48–53.

3 | See Itakura Masaaki, "Ba en 'Seien gashu zu kan' (Nerusan-Atokinzu Bijutsukan) no shi teki ichi-kyoko to shite no 'Seien gashu' to so no kaigaka o megutte" [The Historical Position of Ma Yuan's 'Elegant Gathering in the Western Garden'" (The Nelson-Atkins Museum of Art): Concerning the Pictorialization of This Theme as Fiction], *Bijutsushi Ronso* [Studies in Art History] 16 (1999): 49–78.

4 | See, e.g., Yang Xin, "Quwei chunzhen, huaiyuan lishi: Qiu Ying kuan 'Xiyuan Yajitu' yanjin" [A Study on the "Xiyuan yajitu" attributed to Qiu Ying], *Zhongguo lishi wenwu* [Historical Relics of China] (2008/2): 2, 6–11, 58, 91; Sun Zhenzhen, "Mingdai zhonghouqi 'Xiyuan yaji' ticai liuxing yuanyin tanxi" [An Analysis on the Popularity of the Theme of "Xiyuan yaji" in the Middle and Late Ming Dynasty], *Wenxuejie* [Theory] (2012/5): 247–49; and Shi Jiong, "'Dongpo bogu': 'Xiyuan yajitu de yige bianti'" ["Dongpo bogu": A Variation of the "Xiyuan yaji tu"], *Xin Meishu* [New Fine Art] (2016/3): 19–31.

5 | See Ronald Egan, *The Problem of Beauty: Aesthetic Thought and Pursuits in Northern Song Dynasty China*, Harvard East Asian Monographs 271 (Cambridge: Harvard University Asia Center, 2006), esp. 170–93.

6 | See Craig Clunas, *Superfluous Things: Material Culture and Social Status in Early Modern China* (Urbana: University of Illinois Press, 1991); and Kathlyn Maureen Liscomb, "Social Status and Art Collecting: The Collections of Shen Zhou and Wang Zhen," *Art Bulletin* 78:1 (1996): 111–36.

7 | Zhu Jianxin, *Jinshixue* [Studies of Bronzes and Steles] (Hong Kong: Shangwu yinshuguan, 1964), 33, translated and quoted in Shana J. Brown, *Pastimes: From Art and Antiquarianism to Modern Chinese Historiography* (Honolulu: University of Hawai'i Press, 2001), 24.

8 | See Benjamin Elman, *From Philosophy to Philology: Intellectual and Social Aspects of Change in Late Imperial China* (Cambridge: Harvard University Press, 1984); and Q. Edward Wang, "Beyond East and West: Antiquarianism, Evidential Learning, and Global Trends in Historical Study, *Journal of World History* 19:4 (2008): 489–519. There is a pleasing parallel in terminology here: *kaoguxue* was the study of the past from objects, whereas *kaojuxue* was the study of the past from texts.

9 | See Betty Peh-T'i Wei, *Ruan Yuan, 1764–1849: The Life and Work of a Major Scholar-Official in Nineteenth-Century China before the Opium War* (Hong Kong: Hong Kong University Press, 2006).

10 | See Michael G. Chang, "Envisioning the Spectacles of Emperor Qianlong's Tours of Southern China: An Exercise in Historical Imagination," in James A. Cook, Joshua L. Goldstein, Matthew D. Johnson, and Sigrid Schmalzer, eds., *Visualizing Modern China: Image, History, and Memory, 1750–Present* (New York: Lexington Books, 2014), 25–46.

11 | Ruan Yuan, *Jiguzhai zhongdingyiqi kuanzhi*, 1804, as reprinted in Liu Qingzhu, Duan Zhihong, and Feng Shi, eds., *Jinwen wenxian jicheng* [Compendium of Publications on Bronze Inscriptions] (Beijing: Xianzhuang shuju, 2005), vol. 10, 54.

12 | See Shen Huixing, "Cong 'Qingyige suocang guqiwu wen' kan Zhang Tingji de jinshi shenghuo" [Zhang Tingji's Antiquarian Life Reflected in His "Qingyige suocang guqiwu wen"], *Sina*, May 20, 2014, blog.sina.com.cn/s/blog_4969983f0101gect.html.

13 | See Hu Cangjian, "Liu Xihai nianpu" [Chronicle of Liu Xihai], *Wenxian jikan* [Essays on Archival Documents] (2000/2): 133–51.

14 | All these works had been written before 1840 and were privately printed and circulated among Liu's friends. Bao Kang, Liu's friend and a well-known numismatist, reprinted two of them (*Guquanyuan* and *Haidong jinshiyuan*) between 1873 and 1876. The *Chang'an huogubian* was reprinted later by Liu Er in 1905. For a brief discussion on Liu Xihai and his books, see Lin Zihui, "Qingmo cangshujia Liu Xihai [The Late Qing Book Collector Liu Xihai]," *Shandong xingzheng xueyuan xuebao* [Bulletin of Shandong Administrative College] 8:135 (2014/8): 92–96; and Liu Zheng, "Lidai jinwen jingdian zhuzuo yingyin congkan jieti" [Brief Introduction to the Reprinted Series of Important Publications on *Jinshixue*] 29, http://blog.sciencenet.cn/u/kyotosizumoto.

15 | Liu Xihai, *Yanting jinshi conggao* [Yanting's Manuscript on Metals and Stones], *Shike shiliao xinbian* [New Compilation of Historical Sources from Stone Carvings], 3:32 (Taipei: Xinwenfeng, 1986), 467–668. This manuscript is now kept at the Institute of History and Philology, Academia Sinica.

16 | Wu Dacheng, *Hengxuan suojian suocang jijinlu* [Record of Auscpicious Metals Collected and Examined at Hengxuan], *juan* 1–2, 1885, 41.

17 | The book has twenty volumes, printed by his sons in the early twentieth century, but without an exact date. It is partially published in Qingzhu, Zhihong, and Shi, *Jinwen wenxian jicheng*, vol. 18, 185.

18 | For a full treatment of the Pan family collections, see Yi-Hsin Lin, "The Cultures and Collecting in Late Imperial China and Early Republican China: The Pan Family Collection in Suzhou" (PhD diss., University of London), 2012.

19 | Pan Zuyin, "Shuowen guzhou bu xu" [Preface to "Shuowen guzhou"; 1883], in Liu, Duan, and Feng, *Jinwen wenxian jicheng*, vol. 17, 203.

20 | Ibid.

21 | Lin, "Cultures and Collecting," 236–43.

22 | See Lara J. Netting, *A Perpetual Fire: John C. Ferguson and His Quest for Chinese Art and Culture* (Hong Kong: Hong Kong University Press, 2013), 30–36.

23 | See Thomas Lawton, *A Time of Transition: Two Collectors of Chinese Art* (Lawrence: University of Kansas Spencer Museum of Art, 1991).

24 | Jason Steuber, "Politics and Art in Qing China: The Duanfang Collection," *Apollo* (November 200): 67.

25 | Mei Yi, *Tiexue huanian: Xinhai geming nayiqiang* [Bloody and Glorious Time: The Gunshot of the Xinhai Revolution] (Beijing: Huayi chubanshe, 2008), 81.

26 | See, e.g., Thomas Lawton, "An Imperial Legacy Revisited: Bronze Vessels from the Qing Palace Collection," *Asian Art* (Fall/Winter 1987–88): 56–78; and Tao Wang, "'Zhou Zha hu' de liuchuan jiqi zhulu" [Transmission and Record of the *Zhou Zha* Jar], *Chutu wenxian yu guwenzi yanjiu* [Studies of Excavated Texts and Epigraphy] 6 (Shanghai: Shanghai guji chubanshe, 2015): 153–61.

27 | Thomas Lawton, "Rubbings of Chinese Bronzes," *Bulletin of the Museum of Far Eastern Antiquities* 67 (1995): 7–48; and Kenneth Starr, *Black Tiger: A Grammar of Chinese Rubbings* (Seattle: University of Washington Press, 2008), 128–44.

28 | Lawton, "Rubbings of Chinese Bronzes," fig. 1, p. 27. The date on the rubbing is *wuwu*, which could be either the third year of Jiaqing's reign (1798), which is what Lawton follows here, or the eighth year of the Xianfeng emperor (1858). There are two other known rubbings by Ma, dated 1833 and 1859. Thus, it is more likely that Ma lived around 1800–1860, which makes the early date of 1798 unlikely.

29 | Zhejiangsheng bowuguan [Zhejiangsheng Provincial Museum], ed., *Liuzhou: Yiwei jinshi seng de yishu shijie* [The Artistic World of Liuzhou: A Monk of Metal and Stone] , exh. cat. (Hangzhou: Xiling yinshe chubanshe, 2014), 22–23, 42. For a discussion on Liuzhou's rubbings, see Sang Shen, "Liuzhou yu zaoqi quanxingta" [Liuzhou and Early Full-Form Rubbings], in *Liuzhou: Yiwei jinshi seng de yishu shijie*, 9–19.

30 | Chen Jieqi, *Chuangu bielu* [Separate Record on Transmitting Antiquity], in *Pangxizhai congshu* edition (Suzhou: privately printed, 1862–1908), *juan* 28. See also Starr, *Black Tiger*, 68–70.

31 | See Bai Qianshen, *Wu Dacheng he tade duogong* [Wu Dacheng and the Men who Took Rubbings for him] (Beijing: Haitun chubanshe, 2013).

32 | *Kezhai* is a nickname of Wu Dacheng. The two rubbing scrolls are published in Zhou Ya, *Kezhai jigutu jianzhu* [Annotation and Explanation to *Kezhai jigutu*] (Shanghai: Shanghai guji chubanshe, 2012). In addition to the two scrolls in the Shanghai Museum, one titled *Jijintu* (Illustration of Auspicious Bronzes) was sold at Sotheby's New York on March 18, 2014, on which Wu Dacheng's grandson Wu Hufan wrote that there were five scrolls made. For more studies on the Shanghai Museum scrolls, see Qianshen Bai, "Composite Rubbings in Nineteenth-Century China: The Case of Wu Dacheng (1835–1902) and His Friends," in Wu Hung, ed. *Reinventing the Past: Archaism and Antiquarianism in Chinese Art and Visual Culture* (Chicago: Paragon Books, 2010), 291–319; Clarissa von Spee, "Wu Dacheng at 58: Two Handscrolls with Bronze Rubbings from the Shanghai Museum, *Orientations* 42:2 (2011): 124–30; and Jay Xu, "Art Collecting at the Dawn of Modern China: The Case of Wu Dacheng (1835–1902)," *Lotus Leaves: Society for Asian Art* 12:2 (2010): 1–7.

33 | See Wu Hung, *The Double Screen* (Chicago: University of Chicago Press, 1997), esp. 231–36.

34 | Eric Lefebvre, "'L'Image des antiquités accumulées' de Ruan Yuan: La représentation d'une collection privée en Chine a l'époque pré-moderne," *Arts Asiatiques* 63 (2008): 61–72.

35 | See Cheng Zhangcan, "Wanwu: Wan-Qing shifeng yu beita liutong" [Playthings: The Exchange of Rubbings as a Way of Living Among Late Qing Scholar-Officials], *Xueshu yanjiu* [Academic Researches] (2015/12): 141–50.

36 | See, e.g., Qianshen Bai, "From Composite Rubbing to Picture of Antiques and Flowers (*Bogu huahui*): The Case of Wu Yun," *Orientations* 38:3 (April 2007): 52–60. For a comprehensive study, see Tang Jianwei, *Jinshi ru hua: Qingdai Dao Xian shiqi jinshi shuhua yanjiu* [Painting Bronzes and Stones: Study on the Bronze-and-Stone Motif Painting and Calligraphy of Daoguang and Xianfeng Periods of the Qing Dynasty] (Shanghai: Shanghai guji chubanshe, 2013).

37 | Chuang Shen, "Archaeology in Late Qing Dynasty Painting," *Ars Orientalis* 24 (1994): 100.

38 | See, e.g., Wu Hung, "On Rubbings: Their Materiality and Historicity," in Judith T. Zeitlin and Lydia H. Liu, eds., *Writing and Materiality in China* (Cambridge: Harvard University Press, 2003), 29–72; and Wei-Cheng Lin, "Replicating the Past: Ink Rubbing and Its Related Ideas in Contemporary Chinese Art," in Wu, *Reinventing the Past*, 213–35.

A LEGEND RETOLD: THE DUANFANG BRONZES' JOURNEY TO THE METROPOLITAN MUSEUM OF ART

ZHIXIN JASON SUN

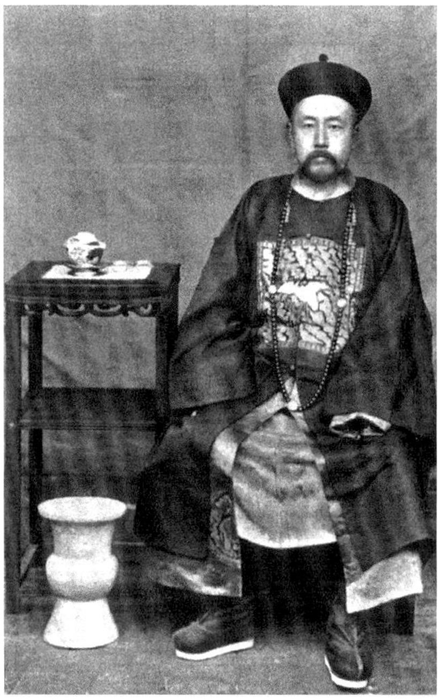

1 | Duanfang.

On the morning of February 4, 1906, Duanfang (see fig. 1), the official envoy from the Qing court to America, visited the Metropolitan Museum of Art, located on the east side of New York's Central Park. Dai Hongci, who had accompanied Duanfang on the diplomatic trip, recorded the event in his travel journal: "[The museum] has a rich collection of Western ceramics, bronzes, oil paintings, sculptures, clay vessels, antiquities, and arms and armor; however, it also houses a decent amount of decorative art and jade objects from China."[1] The Metropolitan, which aimed to educate the general public about history and culture, must have made a deep impression on Duanfang. It was after this visit that he founded the Nanyang Industrial Exposition in Nanjing (1910), the first Chinese exposition with a pronounced international outlook. And yet Duanfang, who died a mere five years after his visit to the museum, would never know that the most famous set of Western Zhou (1046–771 BC) ritual bronzes in his private collection, including an exceptionally rare altar table (*jin*), would enter the Metropolitan in 1926, becoming one of the most important object groups in the museum's renowned holdings (see pl. 145).

Duanfang was from a prominent family of the Manchu ethnic group, which conquered the Han Chinese Ming dynasty (1368–1644) and established the Qing dynasty (1644–1911). He was also known by his courtesy name Wuqiao, and literary name Taozhai among his friends and associates. In 1882, through family inheritance, he became a provincial graduate (*juren*), a qualified candidate for the final imperial examination in the Chinese civil service examination system. Because he helped protect the royal family during the Boxer Rebellion of 1899–1901, he was appointed provincial administration commissioner of Shaanxi and worked for the provincial governor. He later became provincial administration commissioner of Henan; governor of Hubei; acting viceroy of Hubei and Hunan; governor of Anhui, Jiangsu, and Jiangxi; and governor of Hunan province. He was one of the most open-minded and capable officials in the Manchu court during the late Qing dynasty. As a powerful bureaucrat who possessed courage and insight, he not only pushed forward government reforms but also supported the modernization of education and dispatched Chinese students to study in the West.

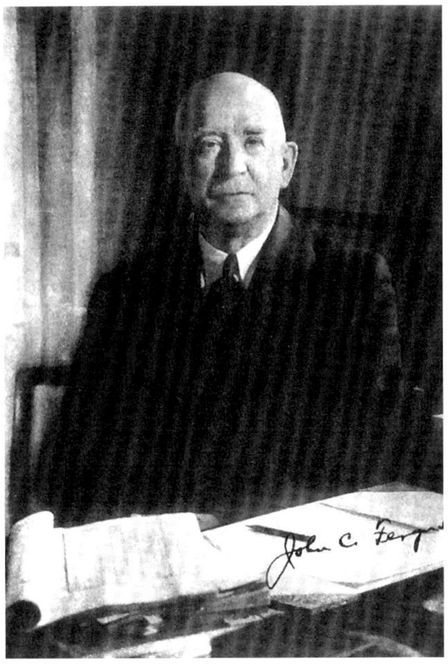

2 | John Calvin Ferguson.

An ardent student in his youth, Duanfang was well educated by his cultured family and had close ties to literary and cultural circles in the capital of Beijing. At an early age, he became fascinated by Chinese painting and calligraphy, rare books, and epigraphy, or the study of inscriptions. He conducted serious research on these subjects, publishing his findings widely. During his official expedition abroad, he passionately sought and acquired antiquities from other cultures, such as Greek carvings and Egyptian polychrome paintings, becoming one of the first Chinese individuals to take a formal interest in studying world civilization.

Duanfang's passion for Chinese art was contagious. He met Canadian missionary John C. Ferguson (see fig. 2) during his tenure as governor of Hubei and viceroy of Hubei and Hunan, sparking Ferguson's lifelong passion for the study of China's history and culture, in particular painting, calligraphy, and epigraphy. Ferguson, the son of a Methodist minister, grew up in Ontario and received his bachelor's degree from Boston University. He and his wife were initially posted to a Methodist mission in Zhenjiang, where he learned Chinese. Through various connections, he became an influential advisor for several modernizing industrialists and officials. In 1902 Ferguson was hired as an advisor to Duanfang, assisting him with foreign affairs during the so-called Self-Strengthening Movement of about 1861–95, when the Qing government instituted Westernizing economic and military reforms in response to defeats by foreign powers. The two men were in constant communication, with Ferguson periodically traveling between Shanghai and Wuchang, and then between Shanghai and Nanjing, to work in Duanfuang's official residences. During this period, Ferguson had direct access to the official's personal art collection and participated in the frequent salons at the official's private residence. Duanfang's circle of friends and acquaintances included several prominent scholars and connoisseurs, and they often gathered to discuss and appreciate works of art. This experience initiated Ferguson into connoisseurship and art appreciation. Many years later, Ferguson still remembered how Duanfang's eyes glittered with excitement and his body was taut in anticipation, as he handled an ancient artwork. Ferguson moved to Beijing some years later and became a renowned collector and scholar of Chinese art, as well as an agent who obtained Asian art for several American art museums.

In the early nineteenth century, Americans had limited understanding and experience of Chinese art. They were most familiar with Chinese export porcelain and souvenirs usually sold to foreign tourists; these mementos included glass paintings and folding fans that were brought back by sailors. Therefore, American scholars generally regarded Chinese art as mere ethnic specimens, and ordinary Americans considered Chinese artifacts as expensive luxury objects or kitschy daily utensils. In short, for Westerners, China did not have its own "fine art" equivalent to Western painting and sculpture. This perception began to change after the Opium Wars of 1839 to 1860, when political interactions and trade between China and the United States increased. No longer did only sailors on trade ships cross the oceans but so, too, did diplomatic envoys, commercial delegates, and art dealers. They started to bring back art objects acquired from the local market, and, for the first time, Americans witnessed high-quality, exquisite porcelain made for Chinese domestic consumption. This deeply changed how Americans understood the country's art.

Japan's late-nineteenth-century modernization and opening up to the West under the Meiji Restoration

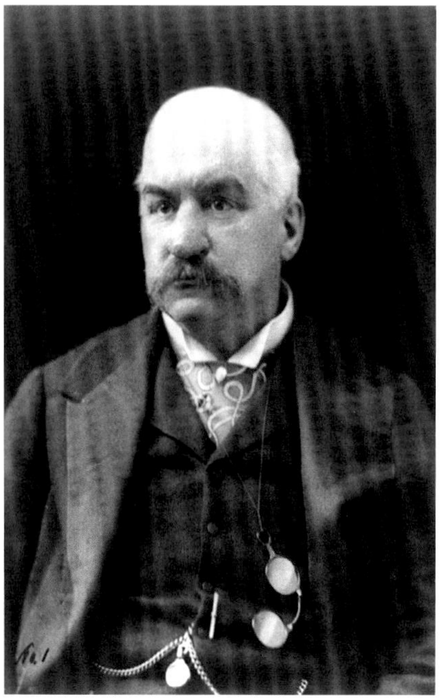

3 | John Pierpont Morgan, c. 1902. Library of Congress, Prints and Photographs Division.

also increased American appreciation of Chinese art. Even as Japan imported Western culture on a large scale, it actively introduced Japanese art and culture to the West. Americans and Europeans were fascinated by not only Japanese ceramics and ukiyo-e prints but also ink landscape paintings and Buddhist sculptures that were inspired by Chinese art. Westerners thus began to learn about and became increasingly interested in art from premodern China and came to realize that Chinese art was as worthy of appreciation and study as the work produced by other ancient civilizations.

The American industrialist J. Pierpont Morgan (see fig. 3), who was the president of the Metropolitan Museum of Art from 1904 to 1913, shared this interest in Chinese art. He was also aware of the importance of Chinese history and culture. He donated his private collection to the museum and decided to acquire bronzes, ceramics, paintings, pieces of calligraphy, and stone sculpture directly for the institution. When Ferguson met with Robert W. de Forest, vice president of the museum, in New York in 1912, it was a critical moment in his life and career. Following the political turmoil of the Chinese Revolution of 1911, Ferguson had lost his job and was trying his luck in America, serving as China's delegate to the Ninth International Red Cross Conference in 1912. Having known Morgan for more than a decade, he was hired as an agent for the museum, with the mission of acquiring Chinese art.

Even after this position expired in 1915, Ferguson continued to correspond with the Metropolitan. He hosted curator of Far Eastern art and Chinese ceramics specialist S. C. Bosch Reitz and de Forest at his private residence at No. 3 Xique Hutong in Beijing. He followed the art market closely, paying special attention to objects sold by prominent collectors and constantly watching for high-quality works that would meet the museum's standards. The opportunity finally came in 1924 when family members of Duanfang became willing to sell his set of Western Zhou ritual bronzes—the world's only known surviving set of this type.

Uncovered in 1901 from a tomb in Doujitai (approximately nine miles outside of Baoji County in Shaanxi), the set (see fig. 4) consists of fourteen separate items, including one *zun* ritual wine container; two *you* ritual wine containers; one *jia* ritual wine warmer; one *he* spouted ritual water vessel; one *jue* ritual wine warmer; one *jiao* ritual wine warmer; one *gu* ritual wine beaker; one *dou* ritual ladle; four *zhi* ritual wine cups; and, most remarkably, a ritual altar table called a *jin*, which was the only bronze altar table known in the world at the time of its discovery. In 1911 Duanfang was appointed the official supervisor of the Chuan-Han and Yue-Han railways, and he was on his way to Sichuan when he was killed in a military uprising in response to the Railway Protection Movement, a protest against the Qing government's attempt to nationalize local railway development projects. His fortunes fell into disarray after his death, and his family had to sell his personal art collection. As Ferguson and Duanfang had shared a long friendship and the former was familiar with domestic and international collectors, museums, and art dealers, the family agreed to have Ferguson oversee the liquidation of Duanfang's art collection. Over the next ten years, Ferguson recommended a few works to the Metropolitan, but the museum was not willing to acquire any of them. Nor was Duanfang's family inclined to sell the bronze set yet. Only in 1924, when the family became burdened by financial difficulties, did they agree to find a buyer for the bronzes. This rare set of items naturally caught the attention of many collectors, not only in the United States but also in Britain, France, Germany, and Japan. According to Ferguson, the family

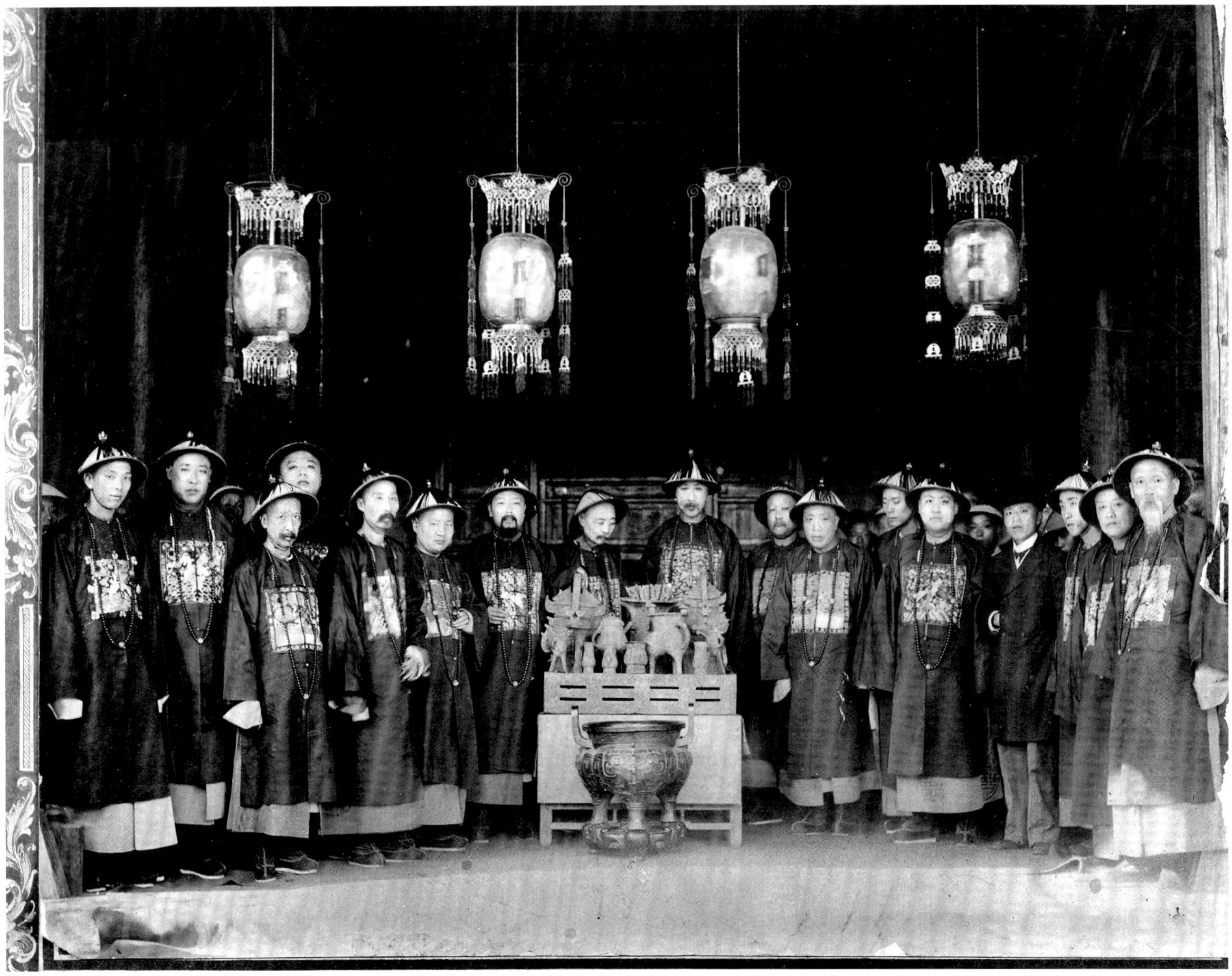

4 | Duanfang (fourth from left in the front row) and Manchu officials with the bronze altar set (pl. 145) that is now in the Metropolitan Museum of Art in New York, c. 1907. Freer Gallery of Art and Arthur M. Sackler Gallery Archives, Smithsonian Institution, Washington, DC, Gift of Thomas Lawton, FSA A2004.03.

was never able to conclude a deal with a potential buyer, however, because they had unrealistic expectations of the set's market value.[2] In spring 1923 Duanfang's widow and son decided to let Ferguson manage the sale.

This was an extraordinary opportunity for Ferguson, but he faced a strong competitor: Yamanaka & Co., one of Japan's oldest and wealthiest Asian art dealers, with a global network of branches in the United States, China, Europe, and Japan. The dealer offered Duanfang's family 200,000 Mexican silver trade dollars for the set—an astonishing amount of money in the early twentieth century. With this same amount, one could acquire tens to hundreds of properties in the booming New York real estate market, or multiple Impressionist paintings, even though their prices were already sky-rocketing.[3] The dealer also promised to waive the 10,000 trade-dollar debt that the family owed the company. Shortly after, Yamanaka added another 10,000 trade dollars to their offer, bringing it to a total of 220,000 trade dollars. Ferguson advised the Metropolitan that it must match or beat the Yamanaka bid if it was to have any hope of acquiring the set. In a letter to Bosch Reitz, he wrote, "The possession of this table and vessels would easily place the Museum in the front rank for all time in the department of ancient Chinese bronzes . . . . If an expedition were organized for the purpose of excavating in China there could be but little hope that it could result after many years in such a find as can now be purchased by obtaining the table and vessels."[4]

The museum called a board meeting to discuss this important acquisition, and after heated discussion it agreed to offer $100,000 (the equivalent of 200,000 Mexican silver trade dollars). However, Ferguson was still worried about the arrangement because the museum's offer merely matched Yamanaka's original amount and did not include any additional benefits. Fate intervened on the Metropolitan's behalf: a terrible earthquake hit Japan that year and hurt the country's economy, rendering Yamanaka unable to honor their offer and forcing them to withdraw it. But even this did not relieve Ferguson of his worries, as the conflicts within Duanfang's family continued to prove more troublesome than the art market competition. In letters written to the museum, he noted that this was the most difficult ordeal in his many years in the Chinese art market. The bronze set was in Duanfang's widow's possession, but by Chinese practice she could not claim sole ownership because she was not his first wife. Duanfang's son with his late first wife was the actual heir of the patriarch's art collection. The son did not get along with his stepmother and was also separated from his own wife. Although the individual family members bore deep animosity toward each other, they had to collectively sign off on matters related to the sale of Duanfang's collection, which meant that Duanfang's widow, his son, his son's wife, and his daughter and her husband all had to agree with one another.

Ferguson well understood Chinese ways of life and family affairs. He knew that the period shortly before Chinese New Year was when families usually settled their debts and were often in need of cash. Having been Duanfang's aide and confidant for many years and having acted as an agent overseeing the sale of the rest of Duanfang's collection, Ferguson was able to approach each family member separately at the end of the lunar year and was finally able to persuade them to reach a consensus. The bronze set was fully assembled in Tianjin on January 5, 1924, and the owners concluded the deal with the Metropolitan. In a letter to Bosch Reitz, Ferguson wrote, "I paid into their hands the order from the international Banking Corporation and they delivered to me the table and its accessories. I carefully examined each piece, replaced it in its box, and immediately transferred the whole lot to the home of the American Consul General, Mr. Jay C. Huston, who is my son-in-law. I called an insurance agent at once and placed upon the articles a policy covering their full value from Saturday, January 5th, at 4 o'clock."[5] Ferguson was extremely pleased to have acquired this rare set of fourteen bronze vessels for the museum. He wrote again, "I had not seen these pieces for seventeen years, but thought that my familiarity with them many years ago was such that I appreciated to the full these wonderful objects. However, as I opened box after box and placed these wonderful vessels upon the bronze table, I was carried away with enthusiasm at the wonderful acquisition made by the Museum."[6] Ferguson also found unexpected pleasure in the fact that through his tireless engagement and persuasion, Duanfang's family members had been able to set aside their differences and finally reach an agreement.

Two weeks later, after a short stop in Beijing, Ferguson returned to Tianjin with three weathered technicians from Liulichang, a Beijing street well known for antiques, and one Mr. Pei, the manager of Ruguxuan, an antique shop, who were to create rubbings of the bronze set and package it for transport. These were all experienced professionals in the antique art market; the sixty-five-year-old Pei had been working at Liulichang for more than four decades. Yet when they opened the boxes and took out the *jin* altar, then placed the *you* and *zun* ritual wine containers on top, they exclaimed in delight. According to Ferguson, "Their faces lighted up, eyes flashed; they wrung their hands, and often stood for a long space of time gazing steadily at some one feature which especially impressed them."[7] Pei even became tearful, started to clap his hands, and repeatedly remarked on the fine quality of the set: "I have not spent my long life in vain, for I have lived to see the most wonderful bronzes that were ever made!"[8] This was a surprise for Ferguson as well, for although he had lived in China for decades, he had never seen these art market veterans so thrilled.

It took the team ten days to create the rubbings and prepare the set for transport. Each vessel was wrapped with great care. On January 24, 1924, the bronzes set sail from Tianjin to Shanghai aboard the commercial carrier SS Shuntien. At Shanghai the bronzes went on the ocean liner SS President Harrison, which left the city on February 1 and arrived in New York on March 25. In June 1925, the Metropolitan announced the new acquisition and published the bronze set in its bulletin. The precious objects were lavishly displayed in the galleries.

Decades later, in the 1980s, the museum's remodeled galleries of ancient Chinese art were opened to the public, and this extraordinary set of bronzes was given pride of place. For millions of visitors from all around the world, the set embodies the long history and sophisticated culture of China. But it also tells the story of an important chapter in the museum's history of collecting Chinese art that is representative of Western attitudes toward Chinese art in general. Since the early twentieth century, the West has gradually come to recognize the complexity and importance of Chinese art. The bronze set's legendary journey from China to New York symbolizes this evolution, attesting to the moment when Chinese art first began to be recognized as an integral part of art history of the world and to emerge as an object for serious study and research.

NOTES

This essay is adapted from a more extensive Chinese version, "Duanfang, Mogen, Fukaisen: Xi Zhou Qingtong jin rucang daduhui bowuguan de yiduan chuanqi"] that was originally published in *Zhou ye lu min* [Noble Life of the Zhou: Bronzes Unearthed from the Cemetery of the Western Zhou Aristocrats at Shigushan of Baoji], exh. cat. (Shanghai: Shanghai shuhua chubanshe, 2014), 41–50. The author wishes to acknowledge Anne Feng and Thomas Kelly for their translation.

1 | Dai Hongci, *Chushi jiuguo riji* [Travelogue of Nine Countries] (Changsha: Hunanrenmin chubanshe, 1982), 89.

2 | John C. Ferguson to S. C. Bosch Reitz, July 28, 1923, "Ferguson to S. C. Bosch Reitz Correspondences," Metropolitan Museum of Art Archives.

3 | For more information on American real estate prices in the 1920s, see Tom Nicholas and Anna Scherbina, "Real Estate Prices During the Roaring Twenties and the Great Depression," *Real Estate Economics* 41:2 (2013): 278–309. For the price of Impressionist paintings in the 1920s, see Madeleine Korn, "Collecting Paintings by Van Gogh in Britain before the Second World War," *Van Gogh Journal* (2002): 120–37; and Nathalie Heinch, *The Glory of Van Gogh: An Anthropology of Admiration*, trans. Paul Leduc Browne (Princeton: Princeton University Press, 1996).

4 | John C. Ferguson to S. C. Bosch Reitz, July 28, 1923, "Ferguson to S. C. Bosch Reitz Correspondences," Metropolitan Museum of Art Archives.

5 | Ibid., January 10, 1924.

6 | Ibid.

7 | Ibid., January 24, 1924.

8 | Ibid.

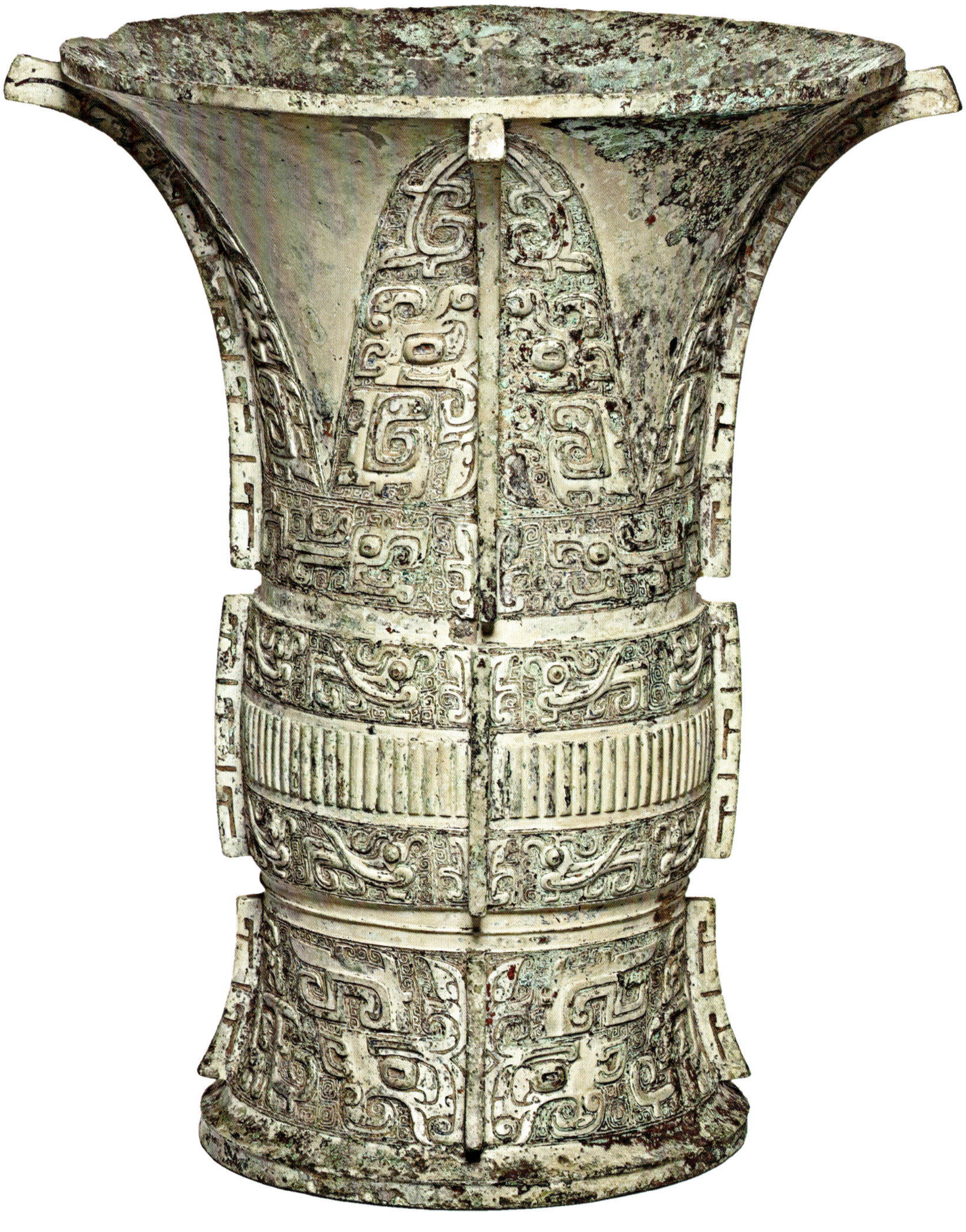

139 | BEAKER OF MOTHER XIN (*MU XIN ZUN*), Western Zhou dynasty (1046–771 BC)

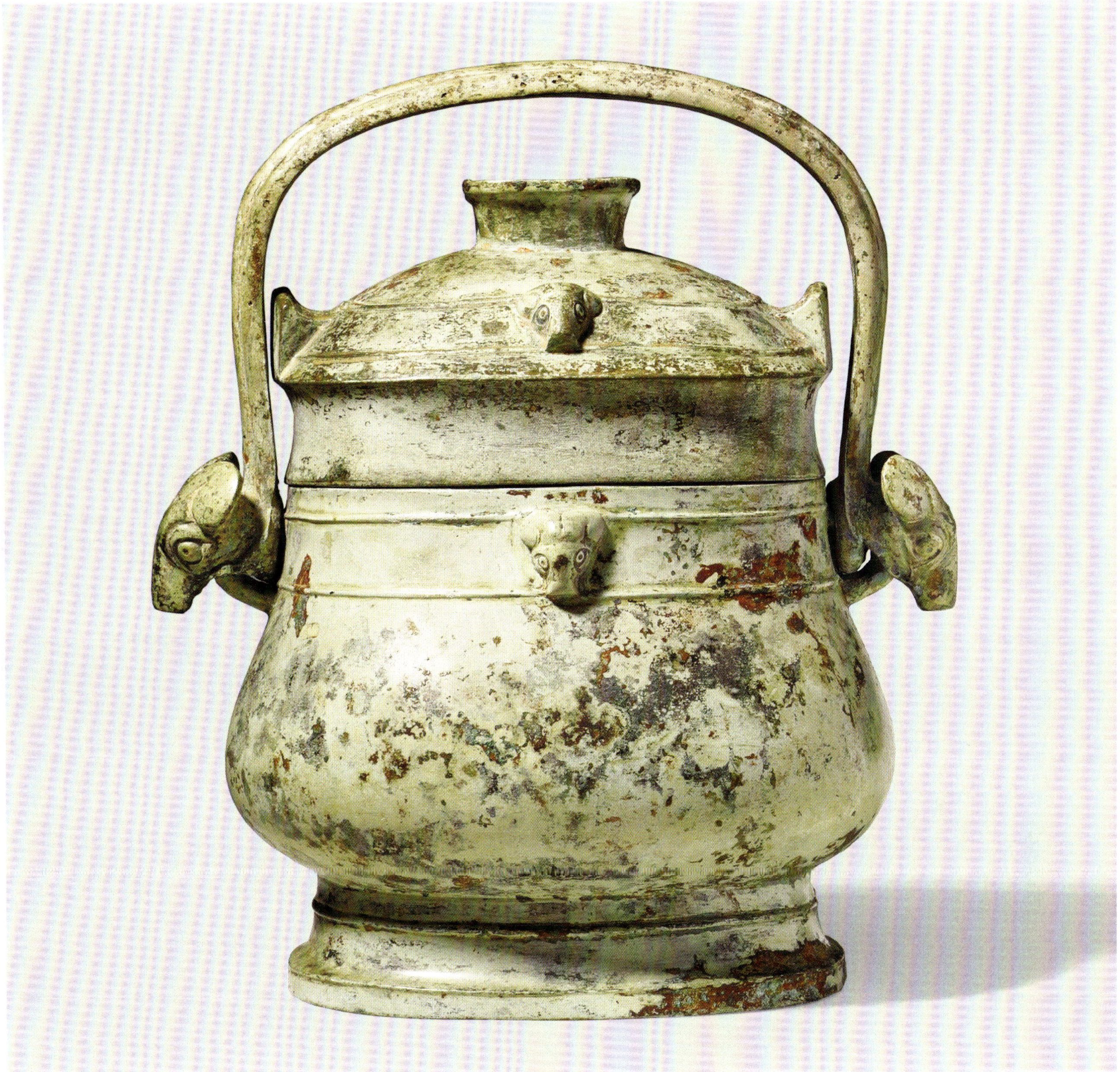

140 | BUCKET OF RECORDER HUAN (*ZUO CE HUAN YOU*), Western Zhou dynasty (1046–771 BC)

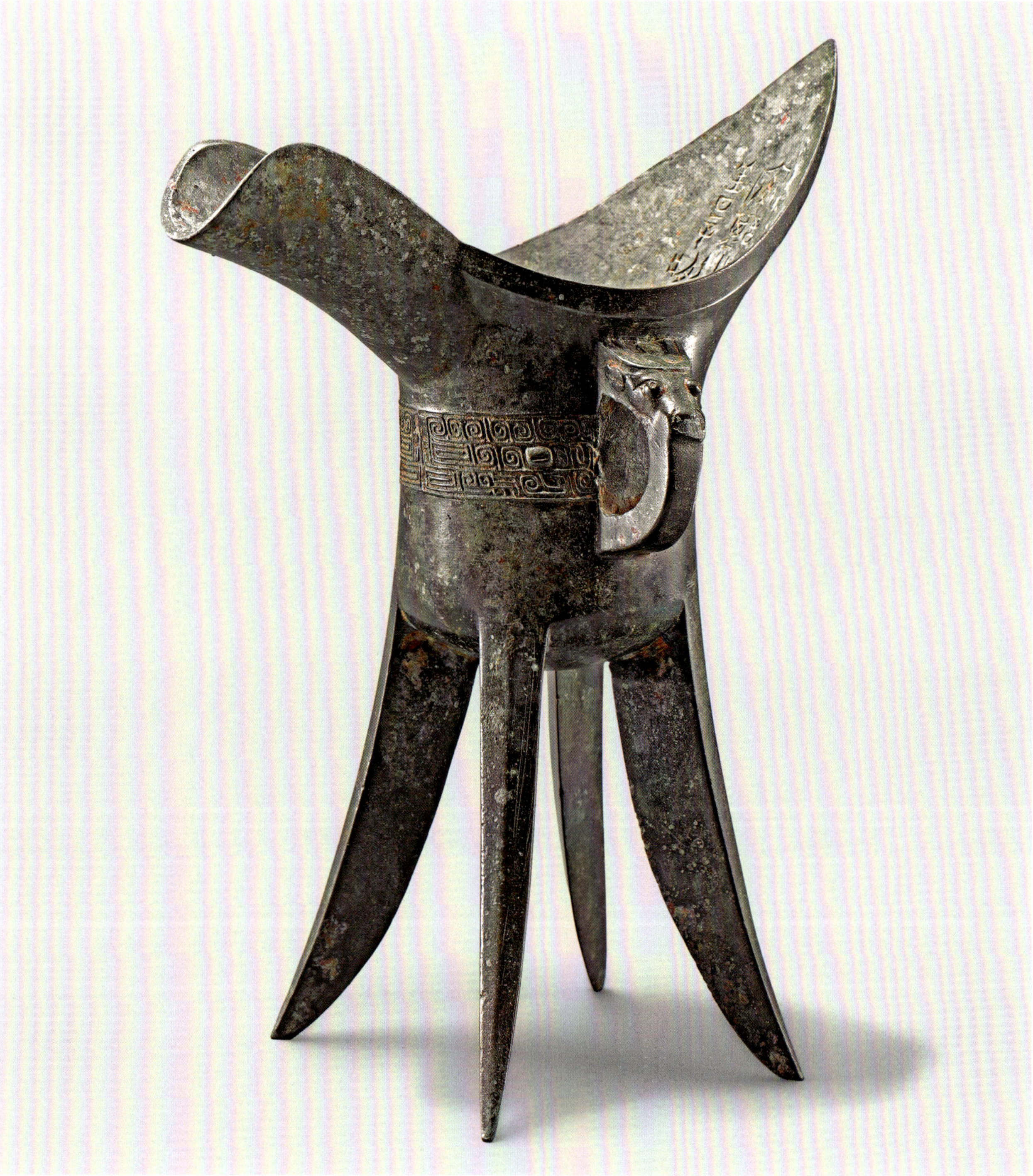

141 | GOBLET OF SUO QI (*SUO QI JUE*), Western Zhou dynasty (1046–771 BC)

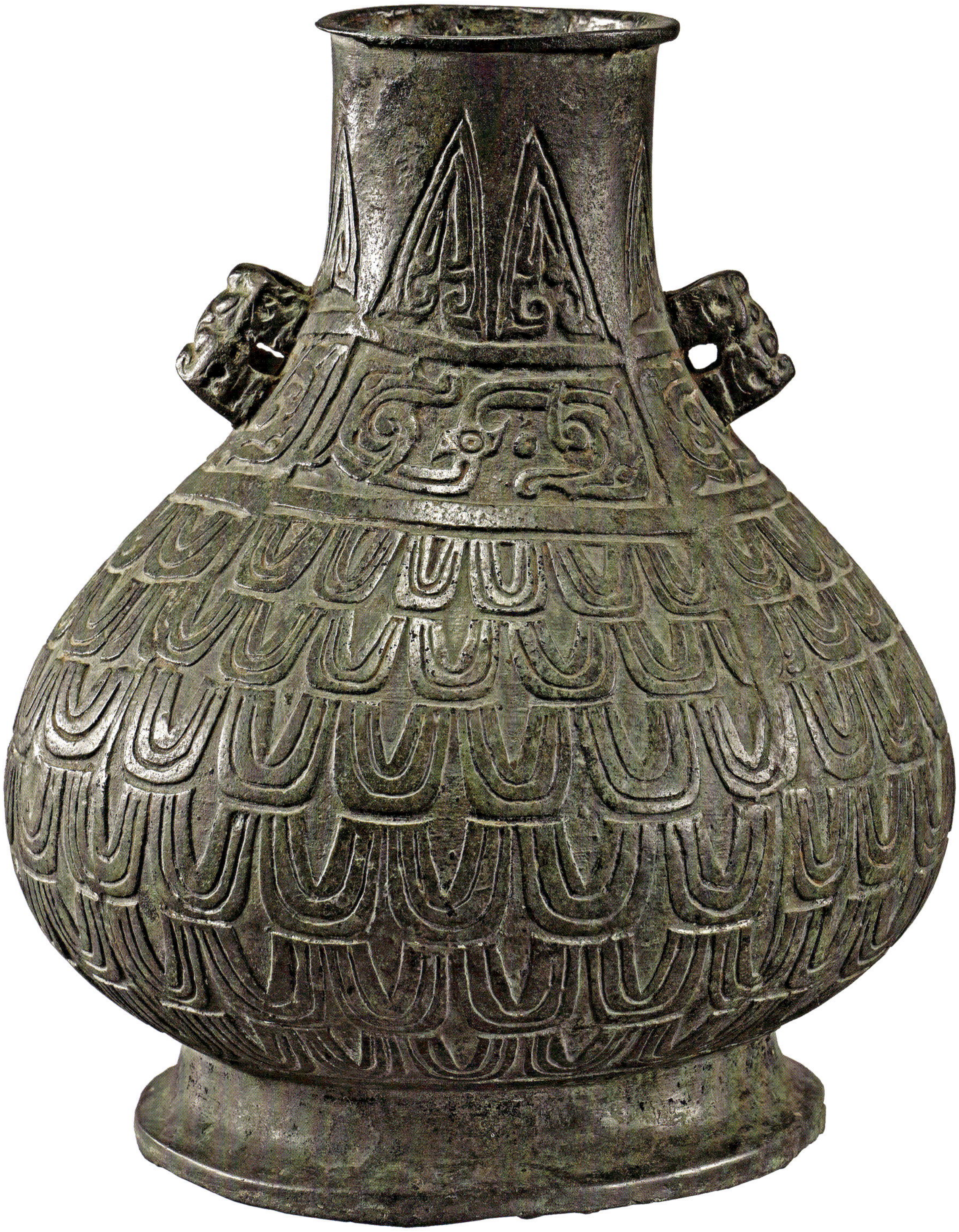

142 | JAR OF DUKE DUO FU (*BO DUO FU HU*), Western Zhou dynasty (1046–771 BC)

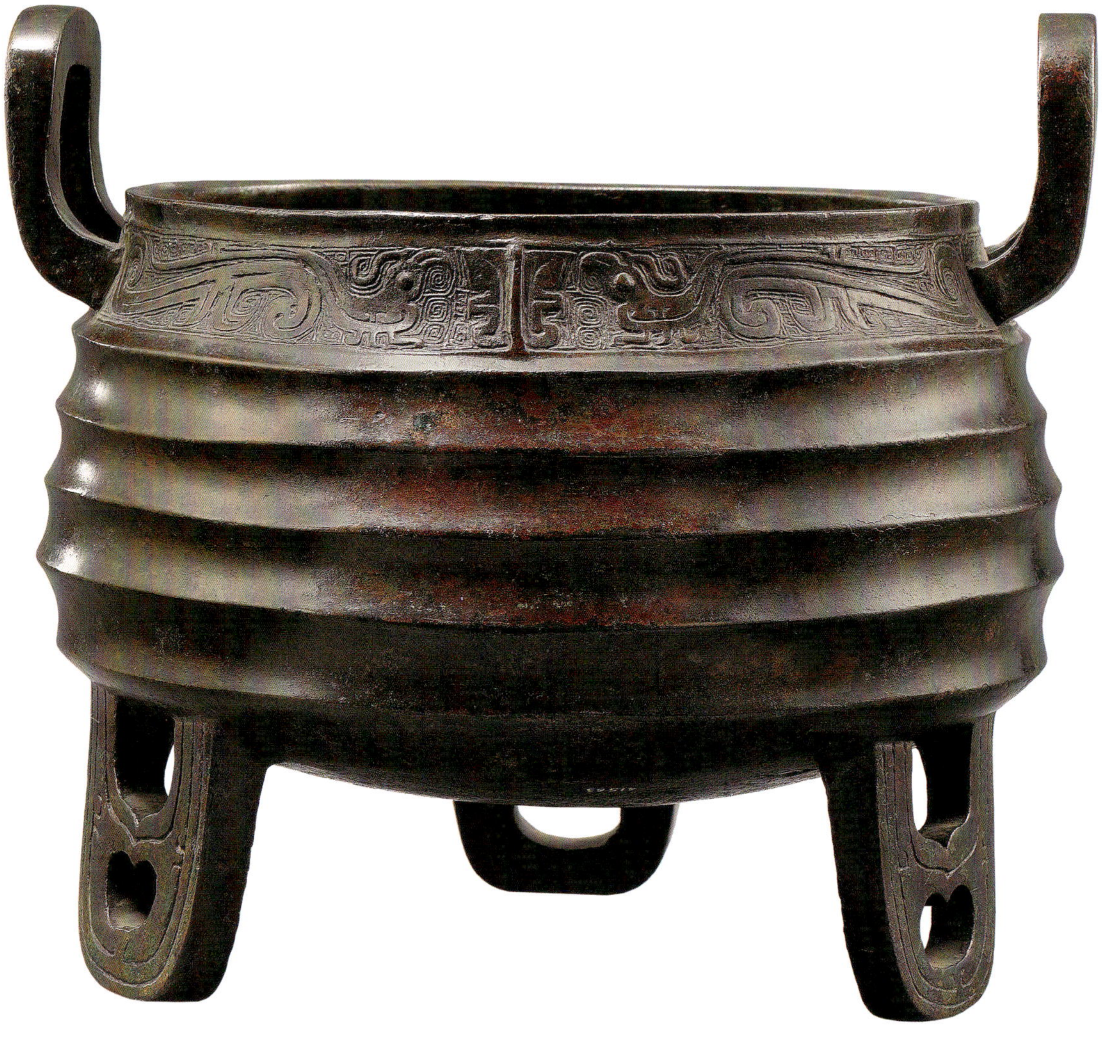

143 | TUREEN OF JI ZHI (*JI ZHI GUI*), Western Zhou dynasty (1046–771 BC)

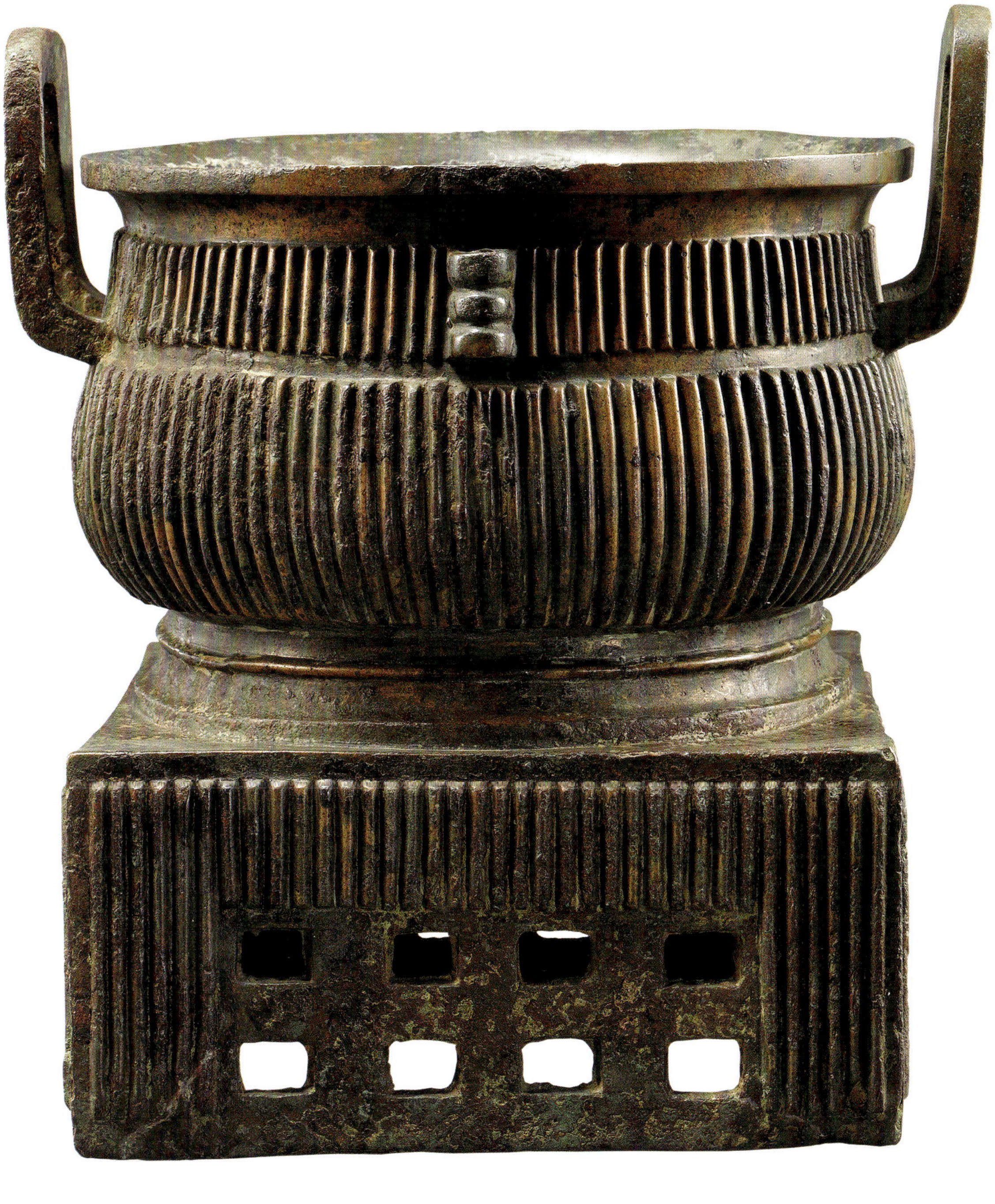

144 | PEDESTALED TUREEN OF SHI XIE (*SHI XIE GUI*), Western Zhou dynasty (1046–771 BC)

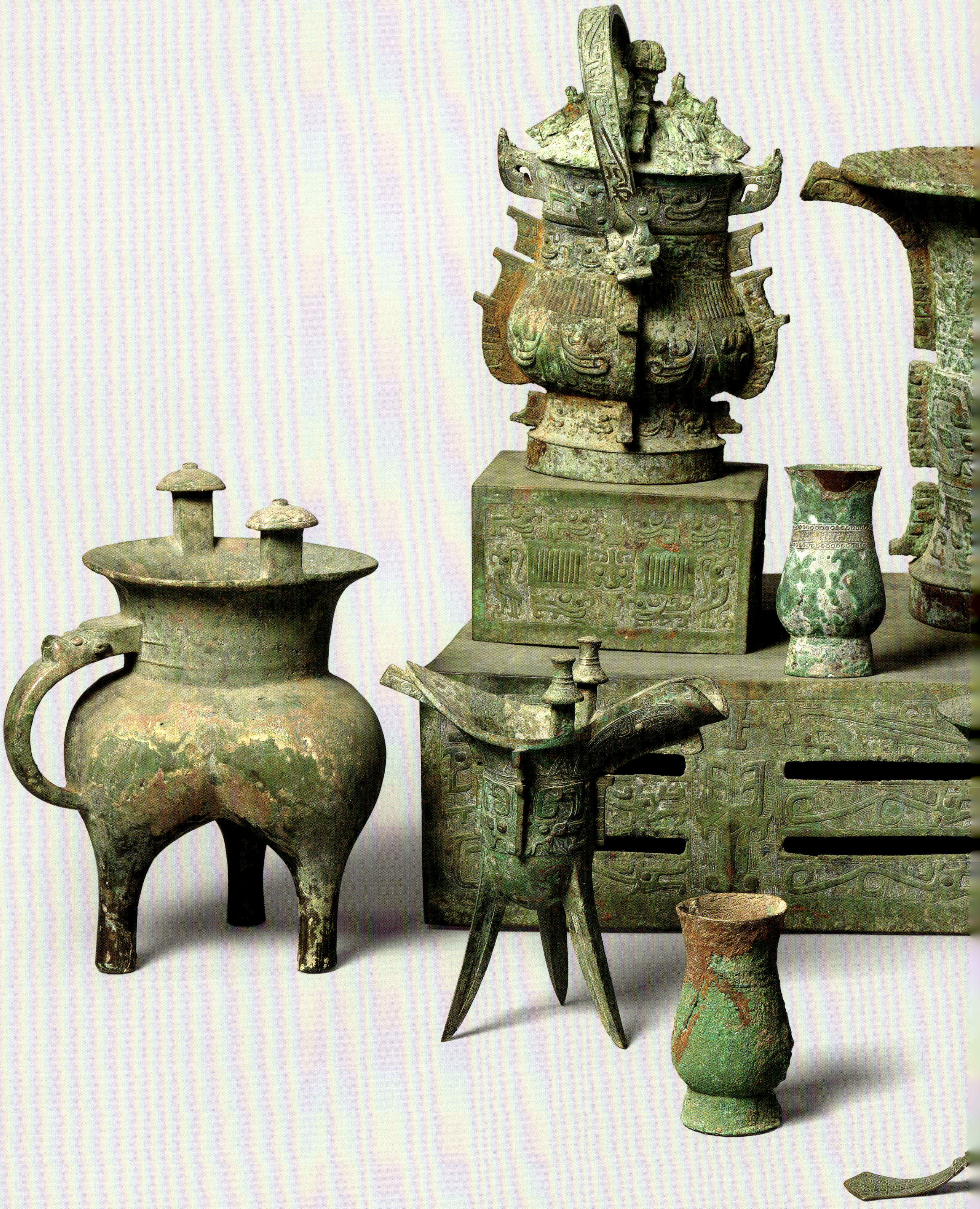

145 | ALTAR SET (*JIN*), Western Zhou dynasty (1046–771 BC)

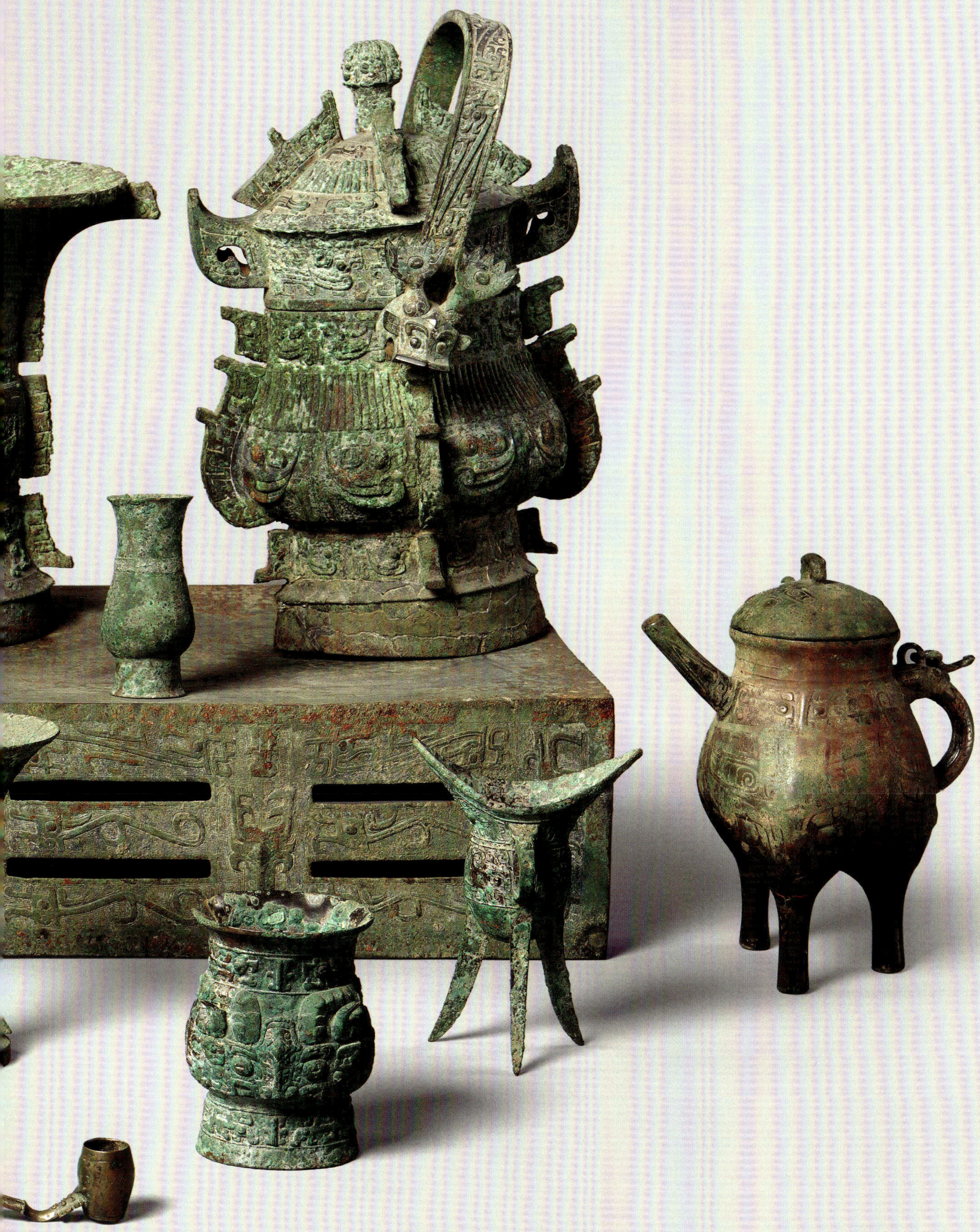

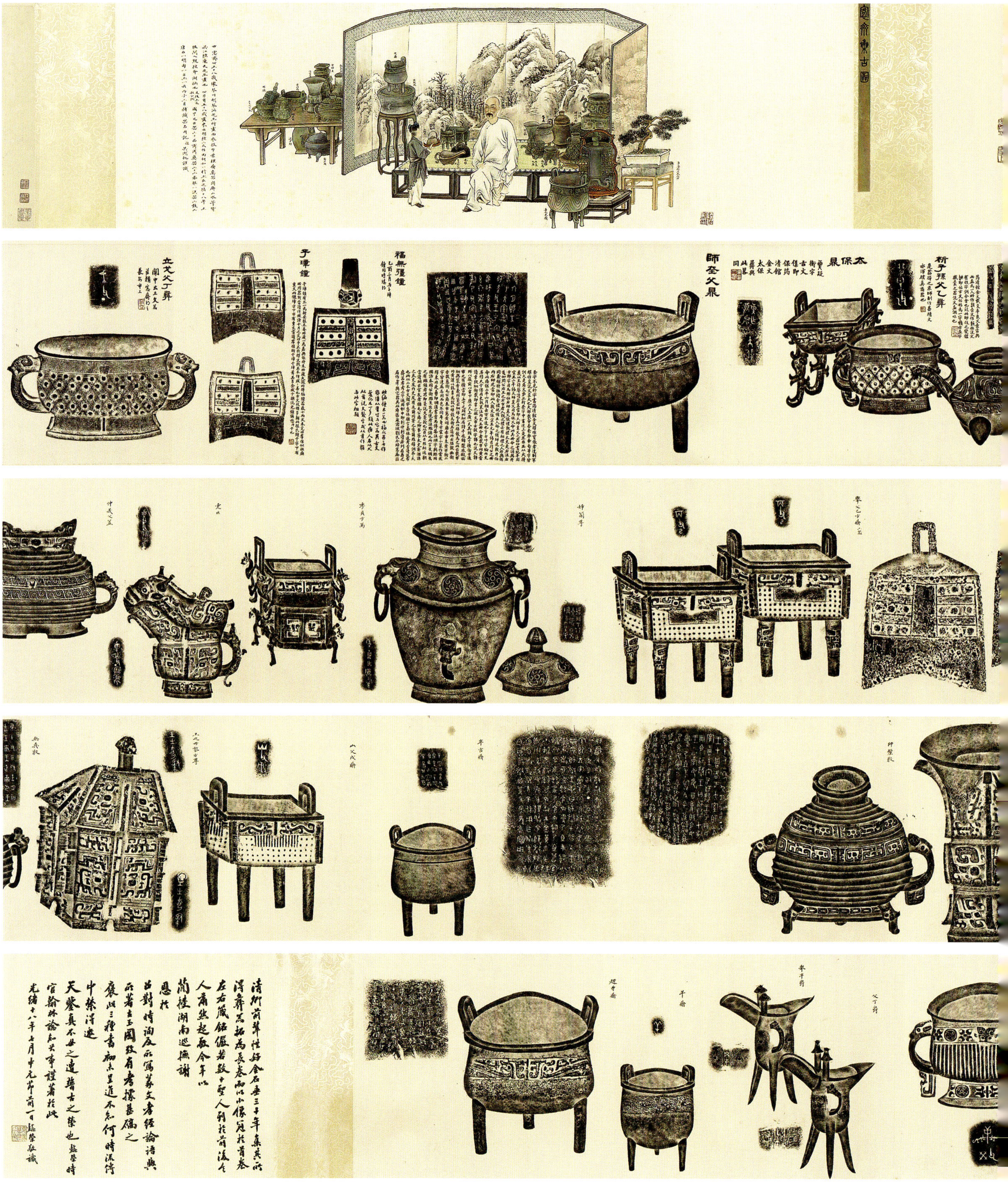

146 | Wu Dacheng (Chinese, 1835–1902) and others. COLLECTED ANTIQUITIES AT KEZHAI (*KEZHAI JIGUTU*), before 1892.

愙齋集古圖

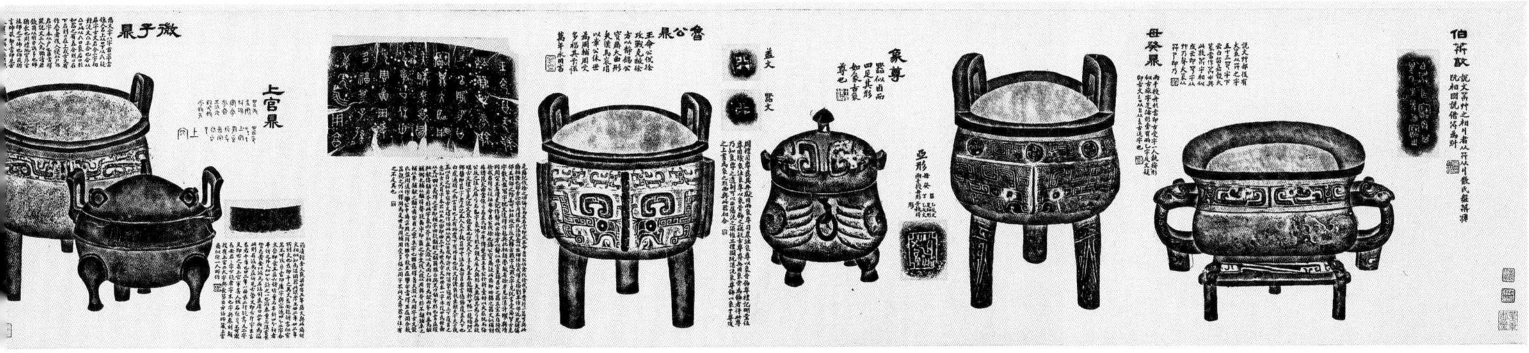

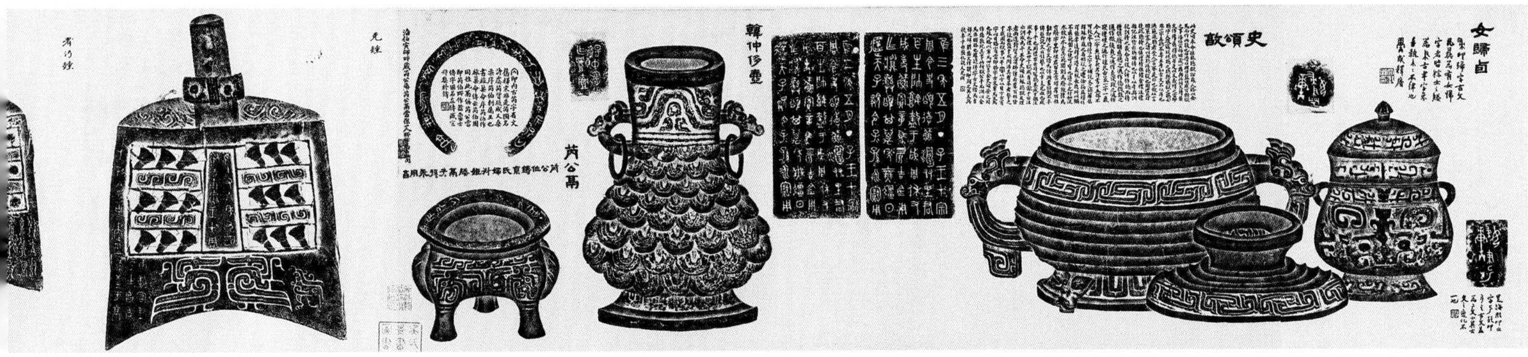

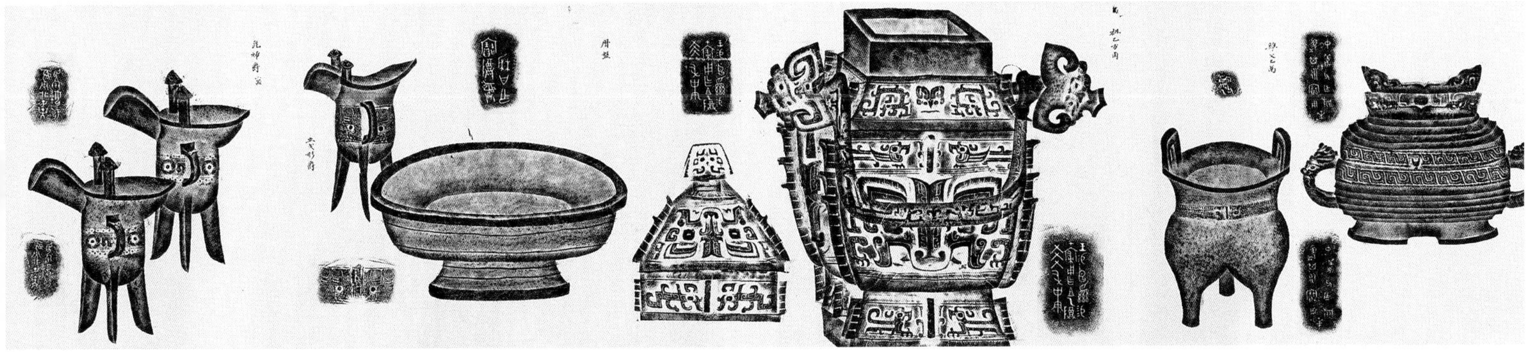

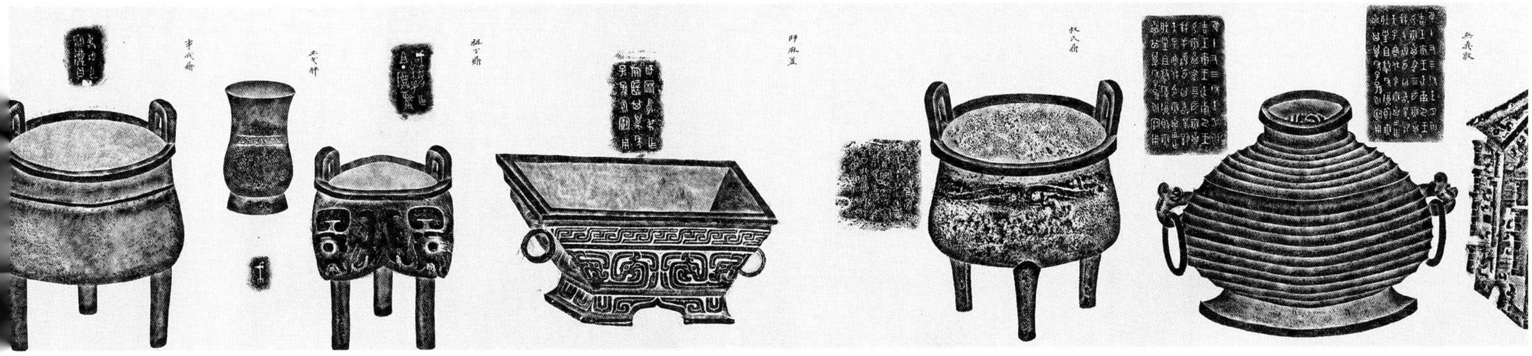

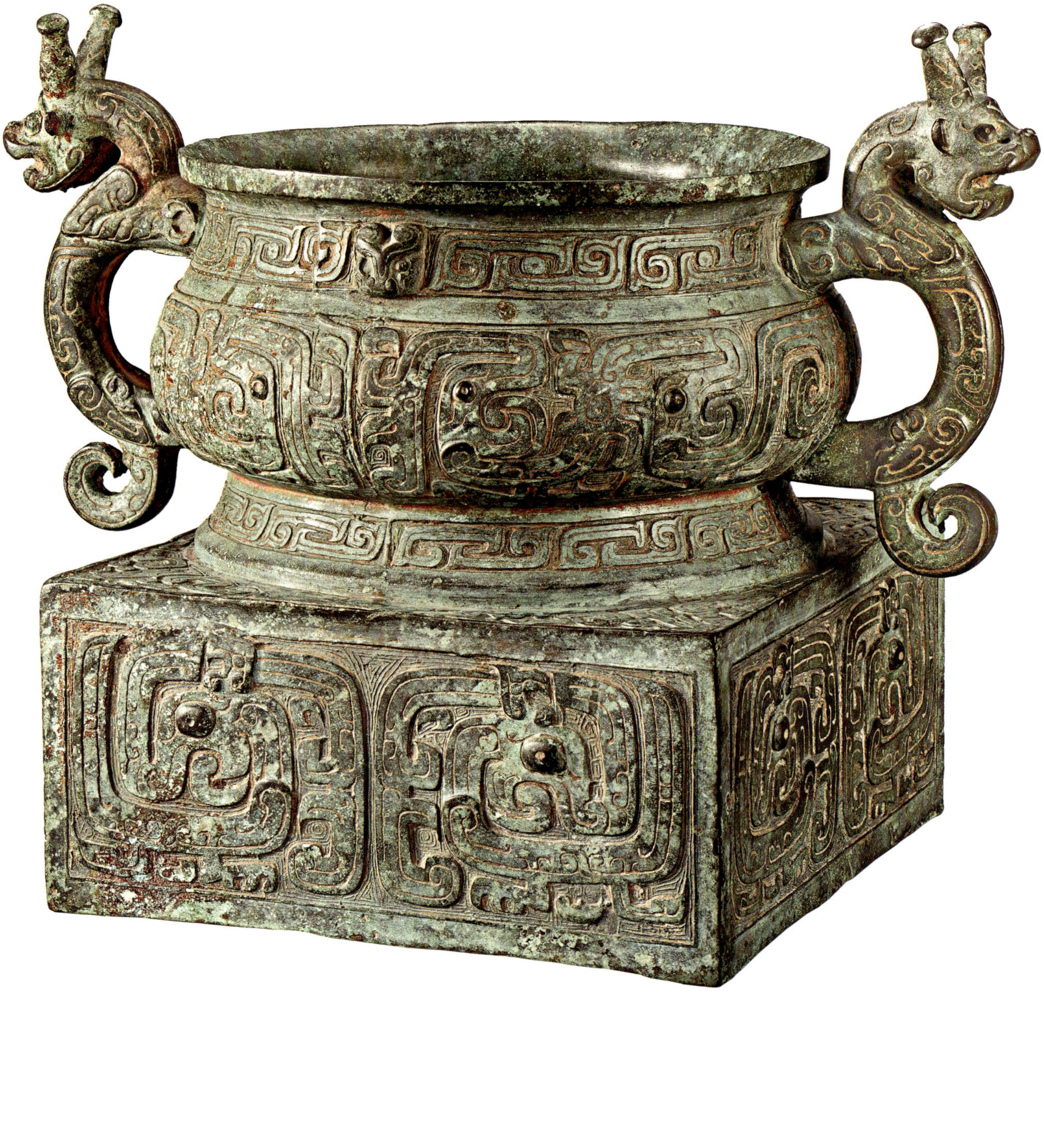

147 | PEDESTALED TUREEN OF ZHUI (*ZHUI GUI*), Western Zhou dynasty (1046–771 BC)

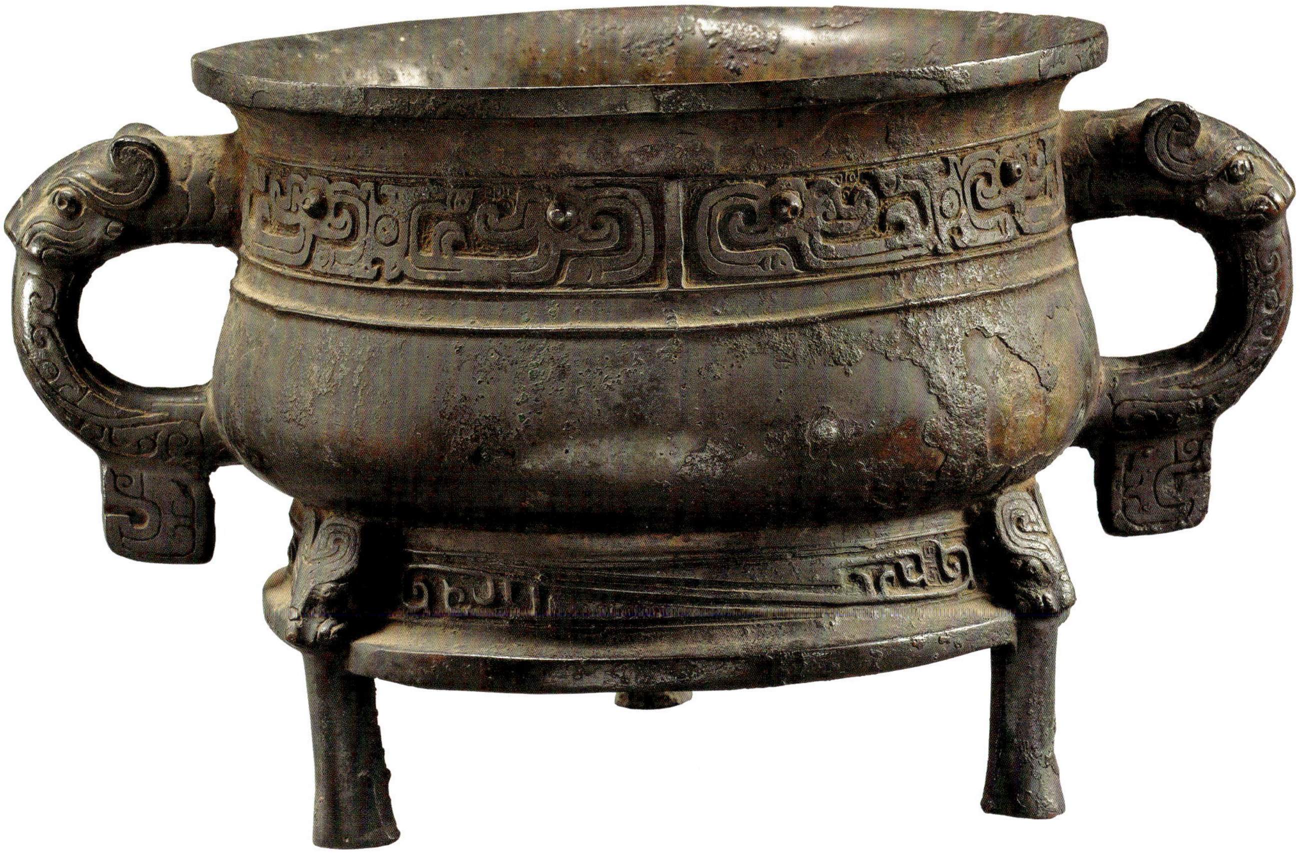

148 | TUREEN OF DUKE NAI (*BO NAI GUI*), Western Zhou dynasty (1046–771 BC)

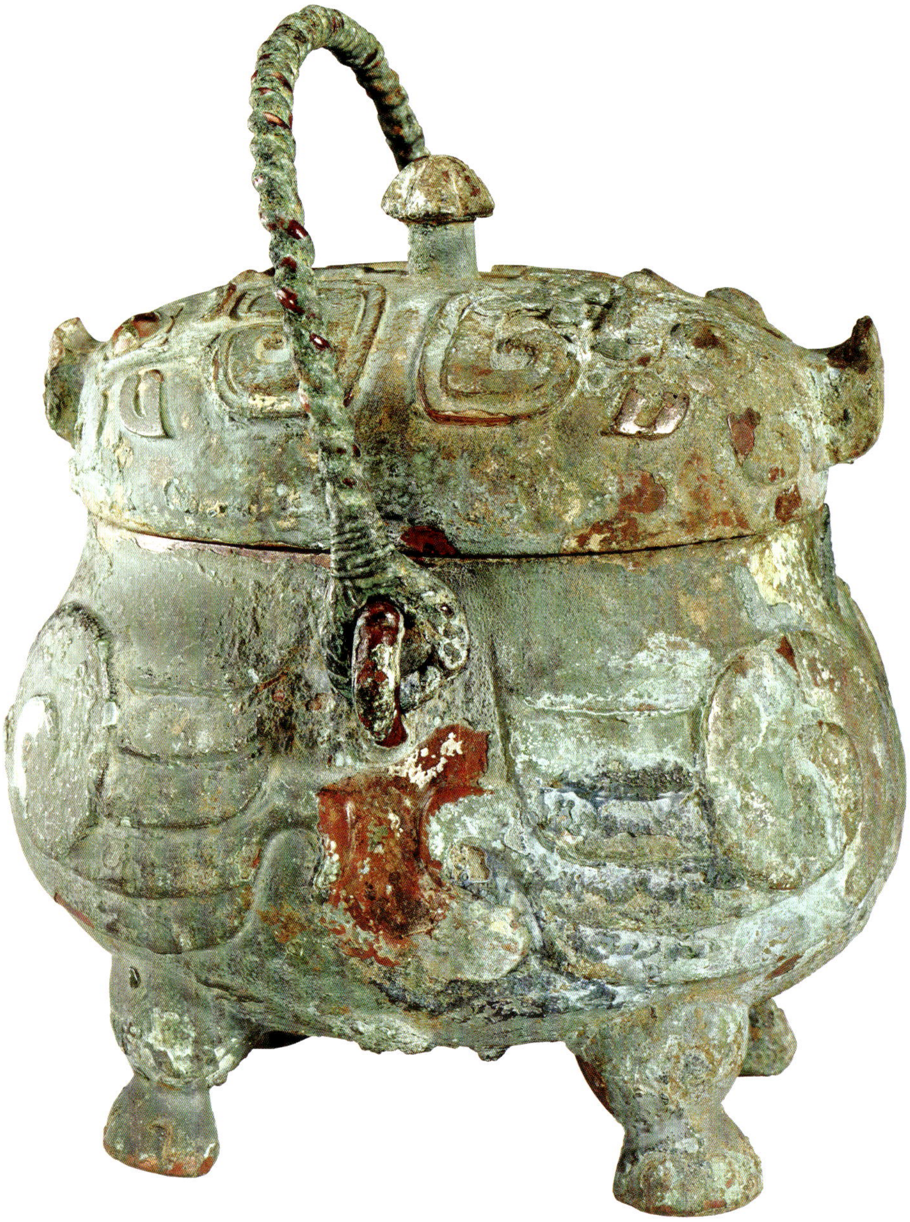

149 | OWL-SHAPED BUCKET OF XI (*XI YOU*), late Shang dynasty (c. 1250–1046 BC)

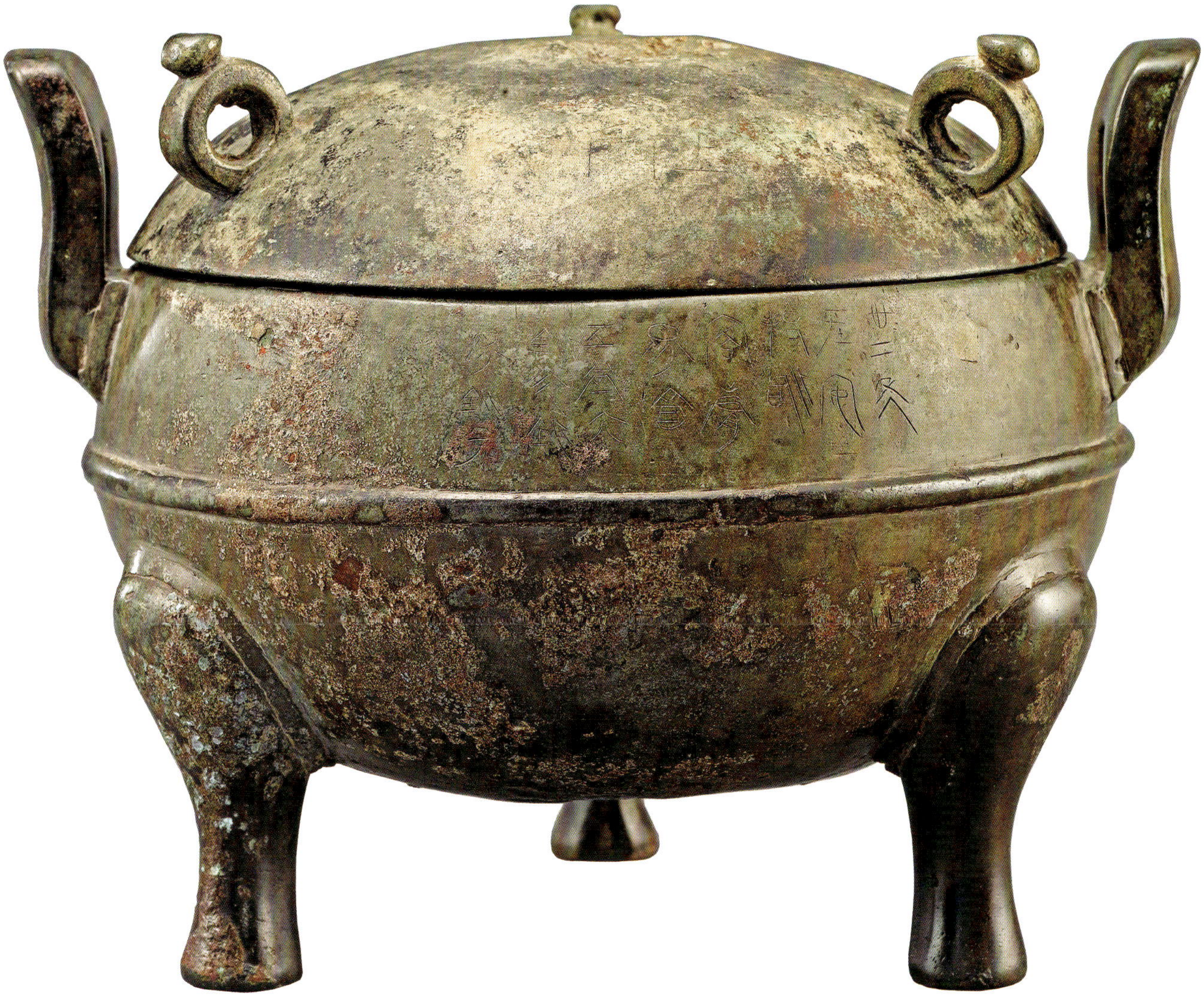

150 | TRIPOD CAULDRON OF PING AN (*PING AN JUN DING*), Warring States period (475–221 BC)

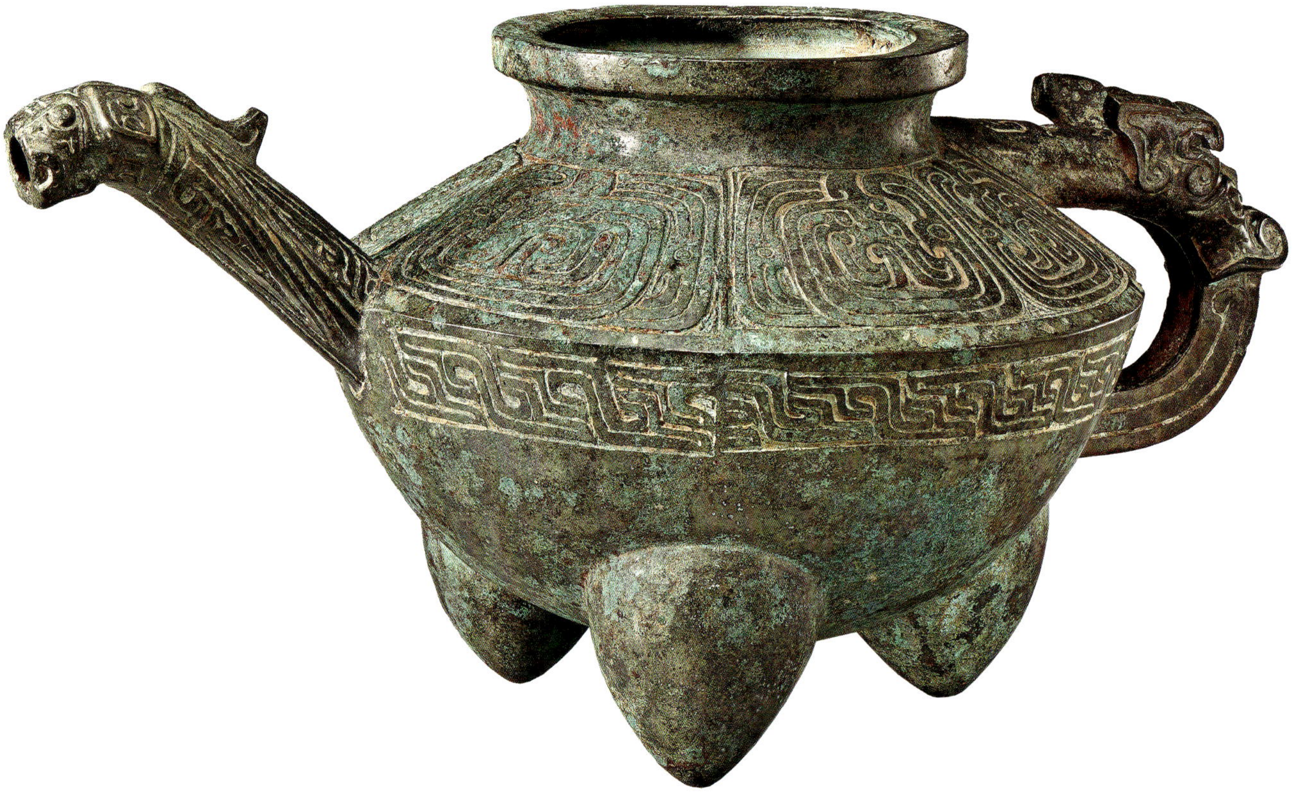

151 | EWER OF FATHER JI LIANG (*JI LIANG FU HE*), Western Zhou dynasty (1046–771 BC)

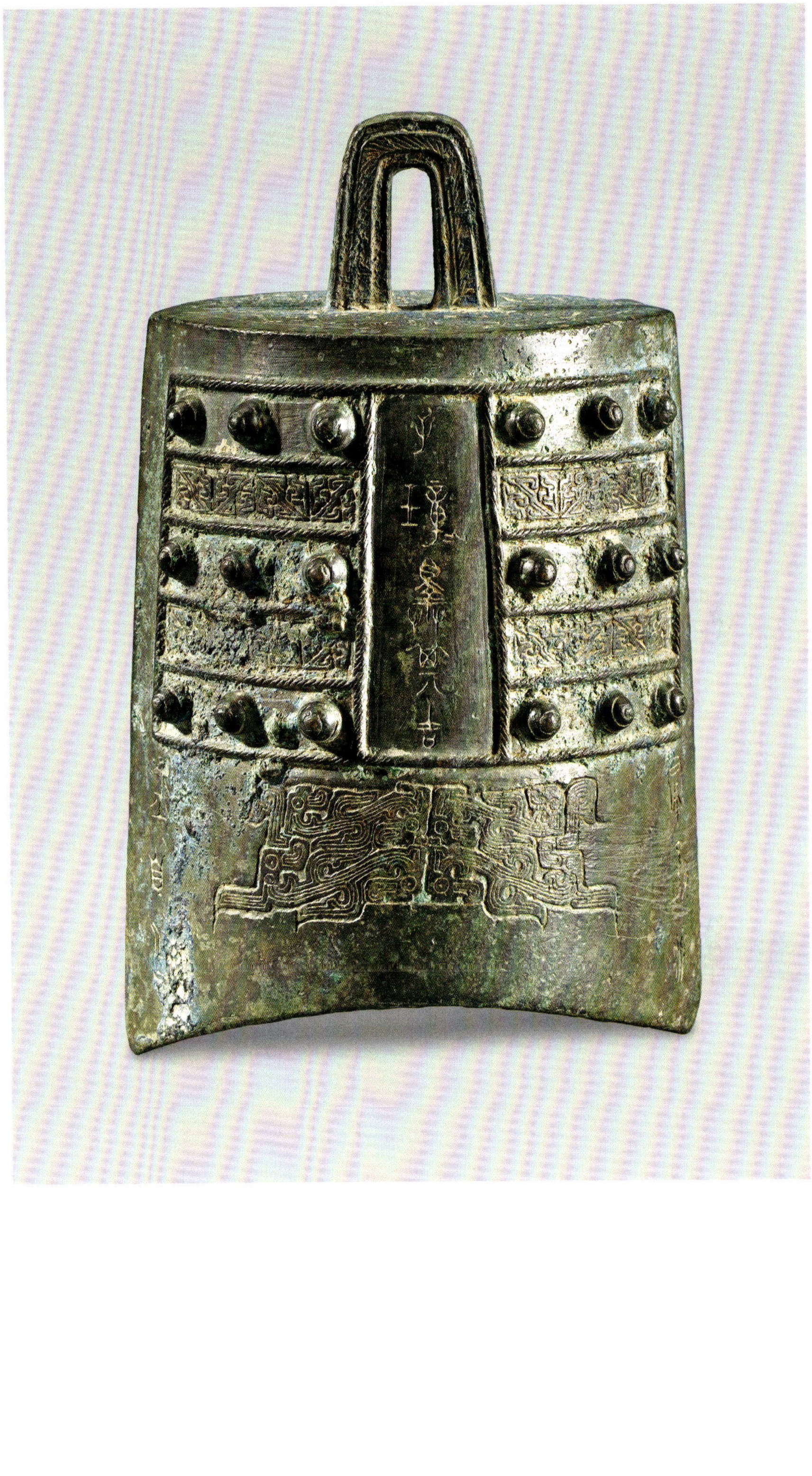

152 | BELL OF PRINCE ZHANG (*ZI ZHANG ZHONG*), Eastern Zhou dynasty, Spring and Autumn period (770–476 BC)

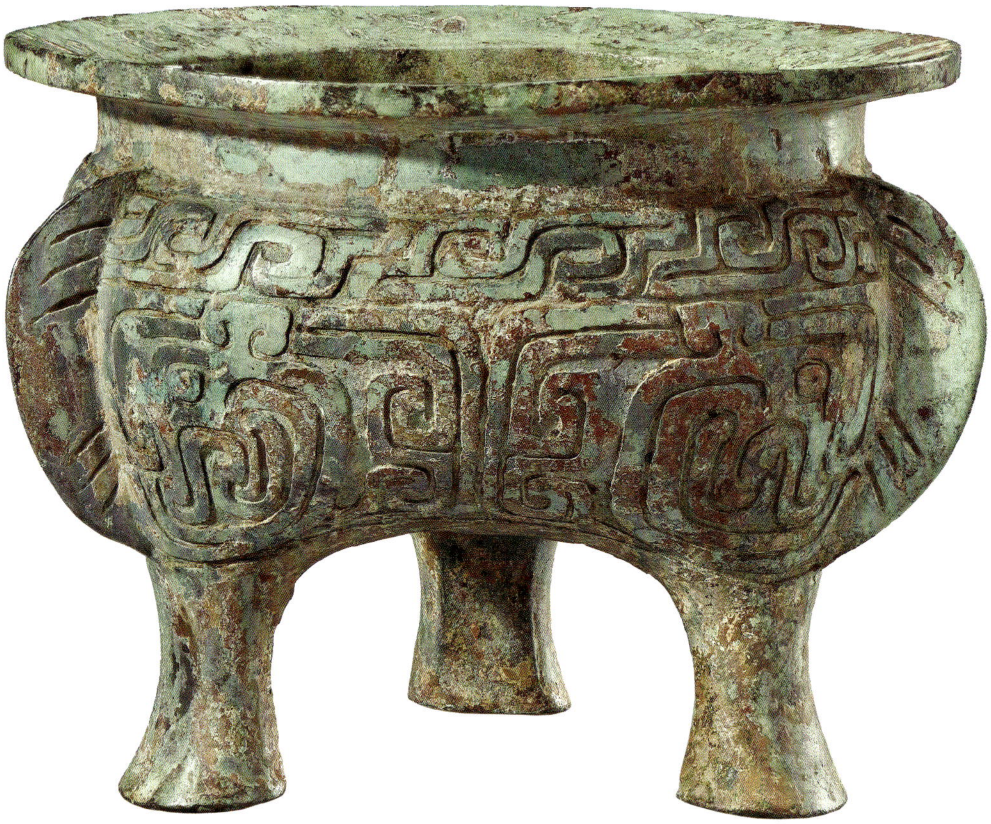

153 | TRIPOD CAULDRON OF LORD RUI (*RUI GONG LI*), Western Zhou dynasty (1046–771 BC)

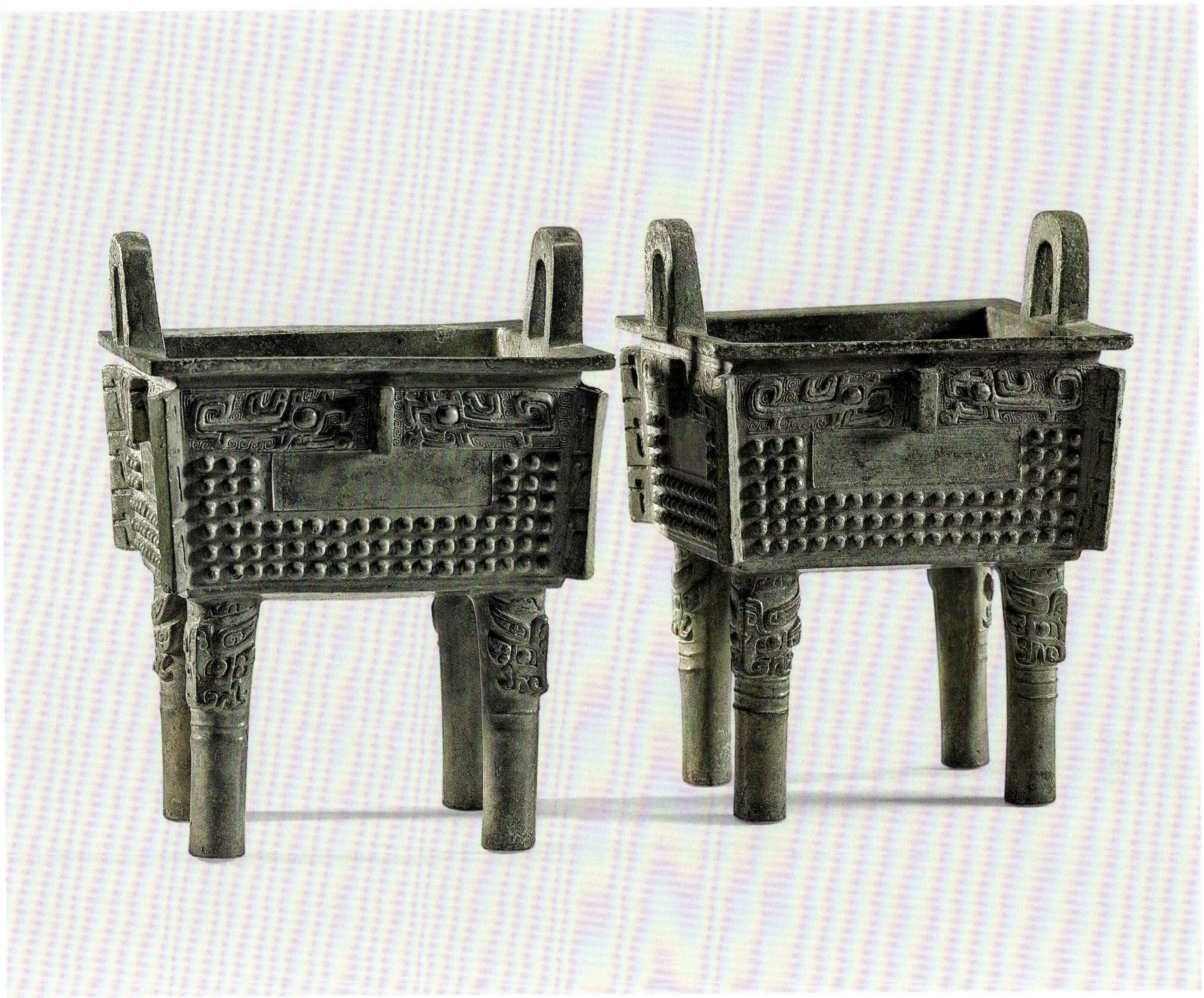

154 | TWO RECTANGULAR CAULDRONS OF JU FU JI (*JU FU JI FANGDING*), late Shang dynasty (c. 1250–1046 BC)

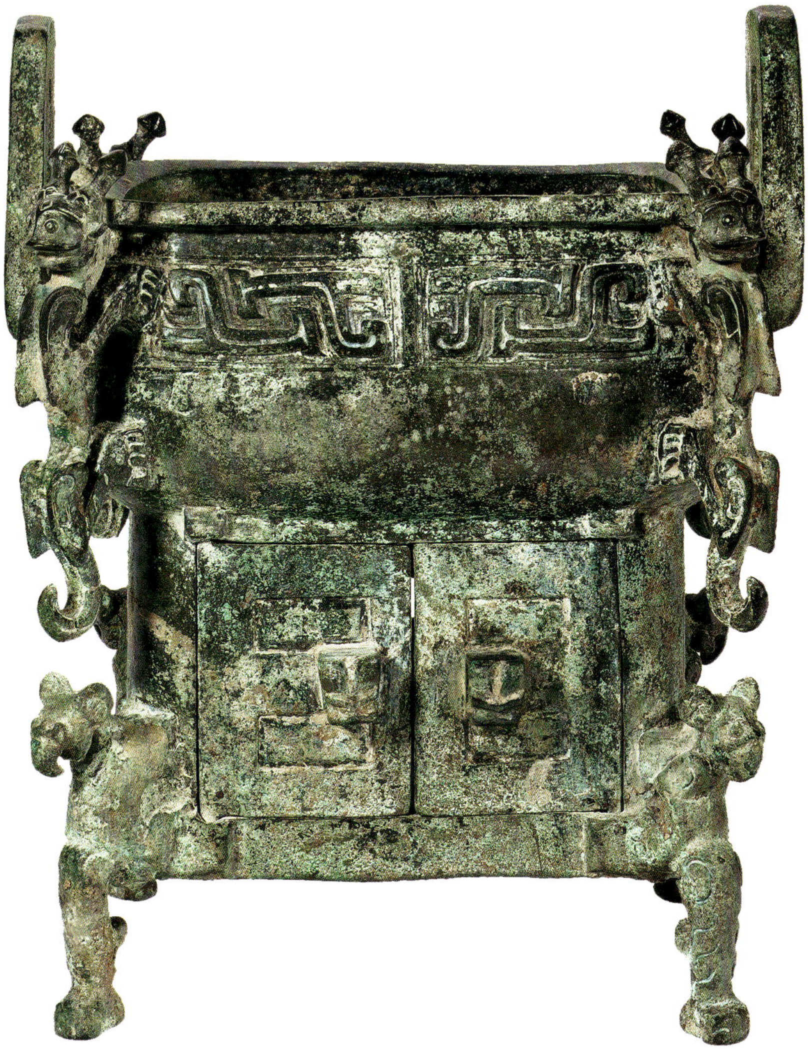

155 | SQUARE CAULDRON WITH STOVE OF JI ZHEN (*JI ZHEN FANGLI*), Western Zhou dynasty (1046–771 BC)

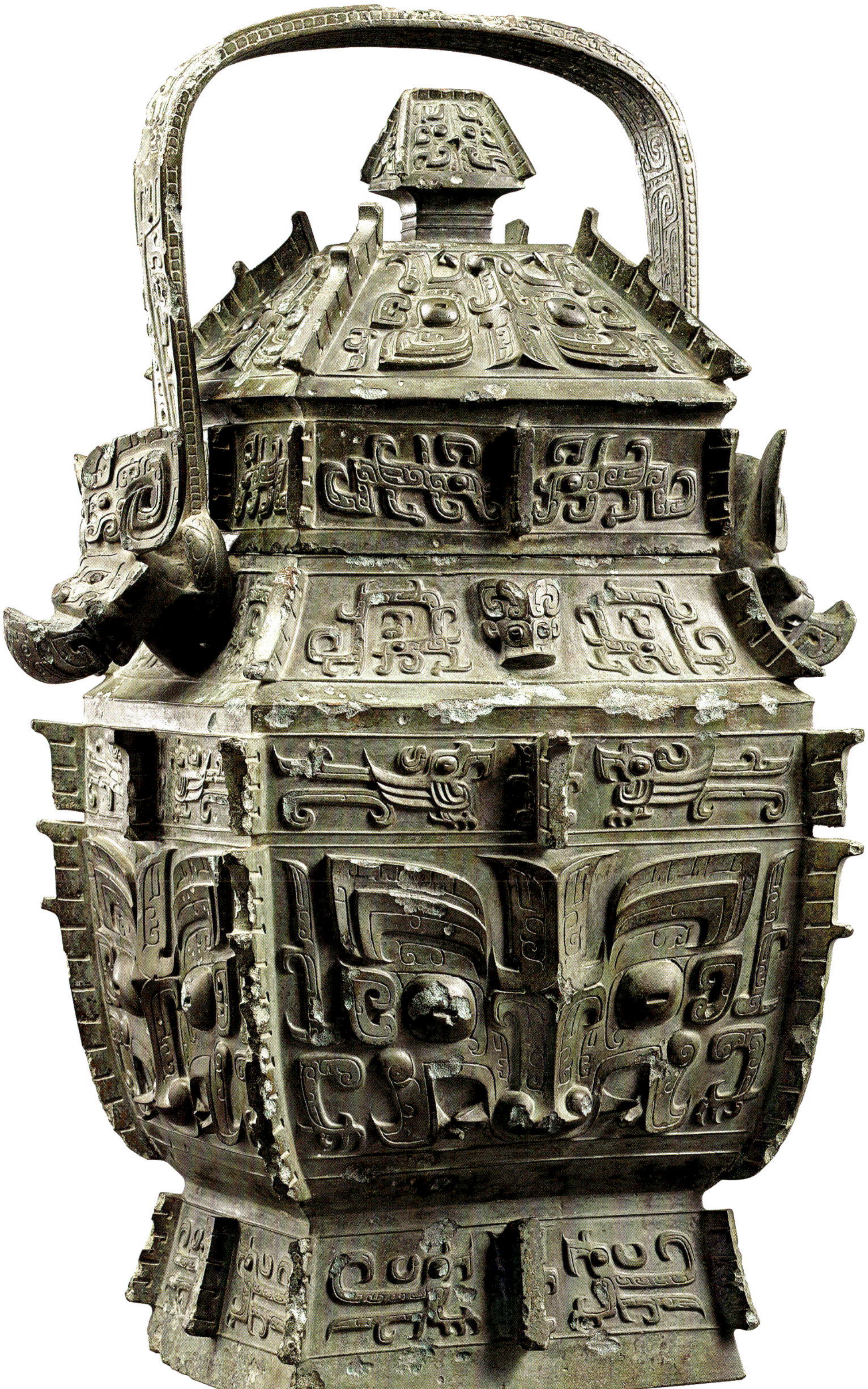

156 | BUCKET OF MINISTER XI (*XIAO CHEN XI YOU*), late Shang dynasty (c. 1250–1046 BC)

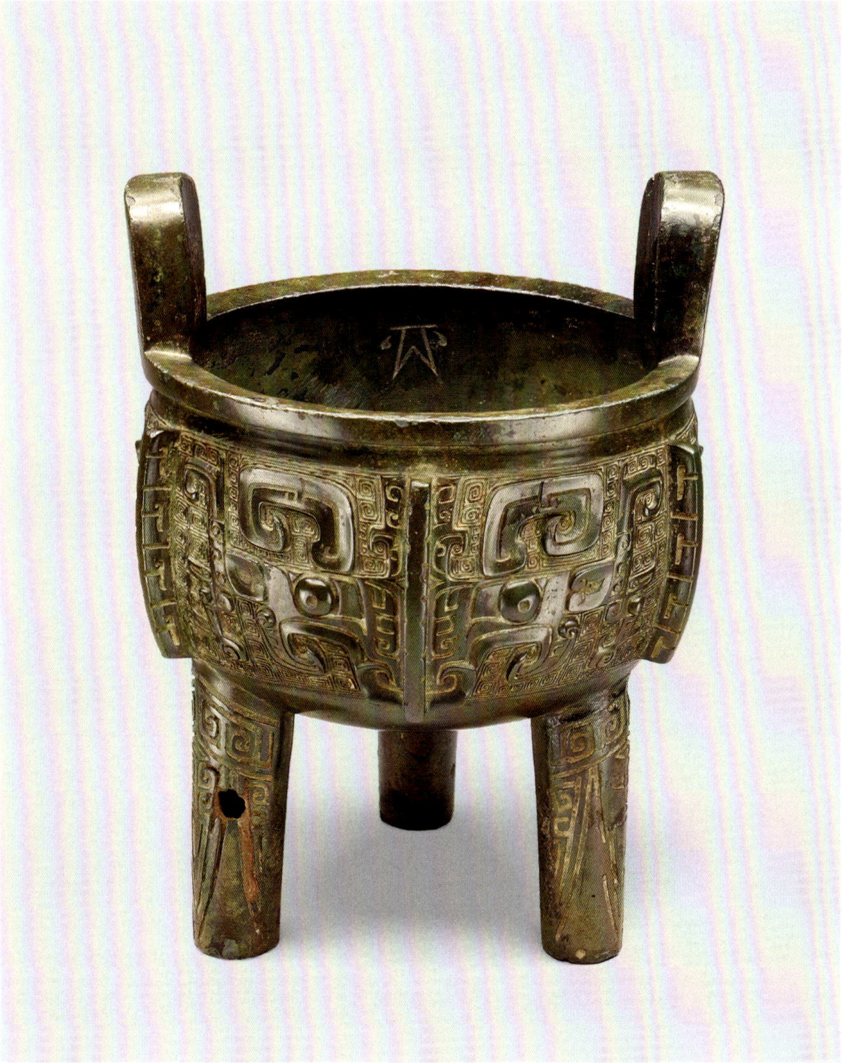

157 | TRIPOD CAULDRON OF RAN (*RAN DING*), late Shang dynasty (c. 1250–1046 BC)

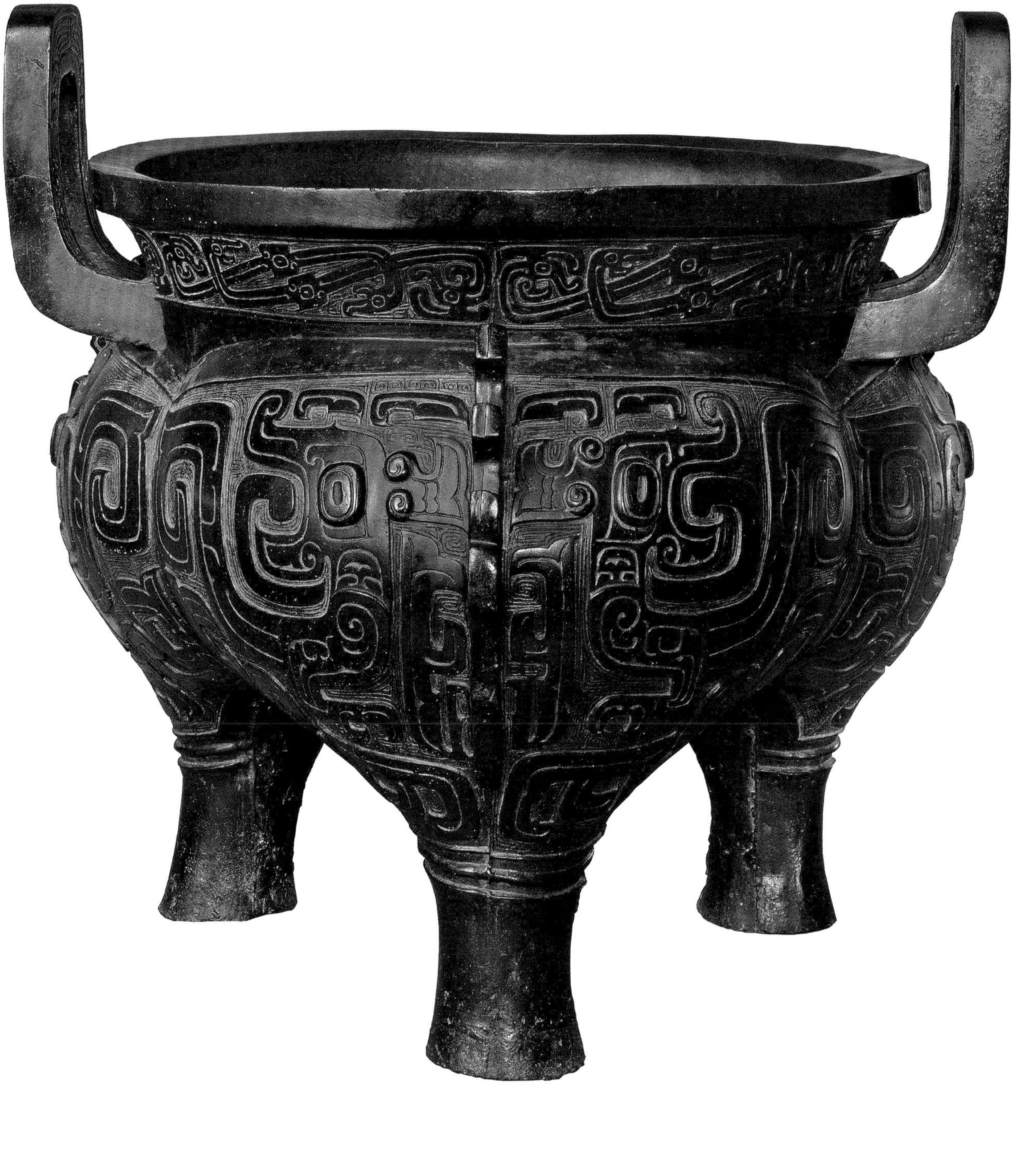

158 | LOBED TRIPOD CAULDRON OF OFFICER YIN (*SHI YIN LI*), Western Zhou dynasty (1046–771 BC)

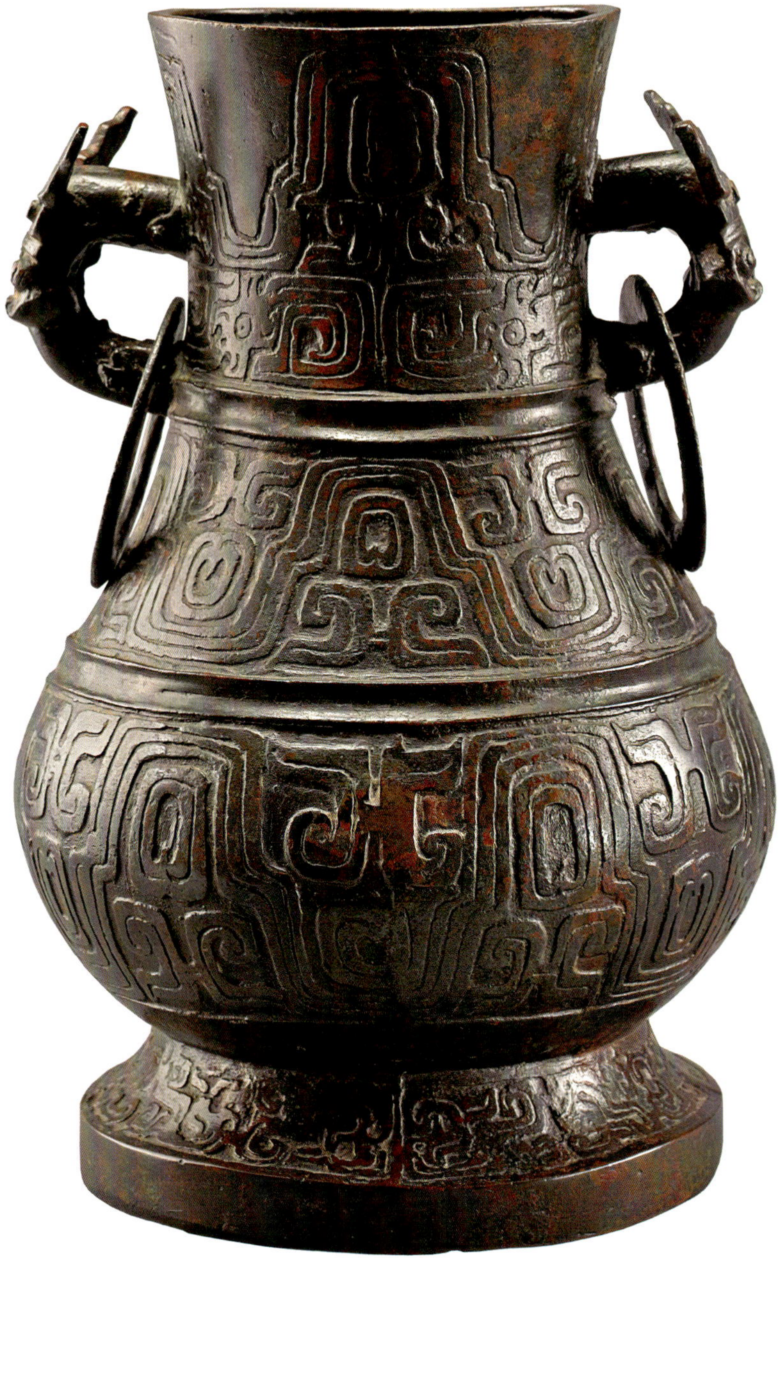

159 | JAR OF HUAN ZI MENG JIANG (*HUAN ZI MENG JIANG HU*), Spring and Autumn period (770–476 BC)

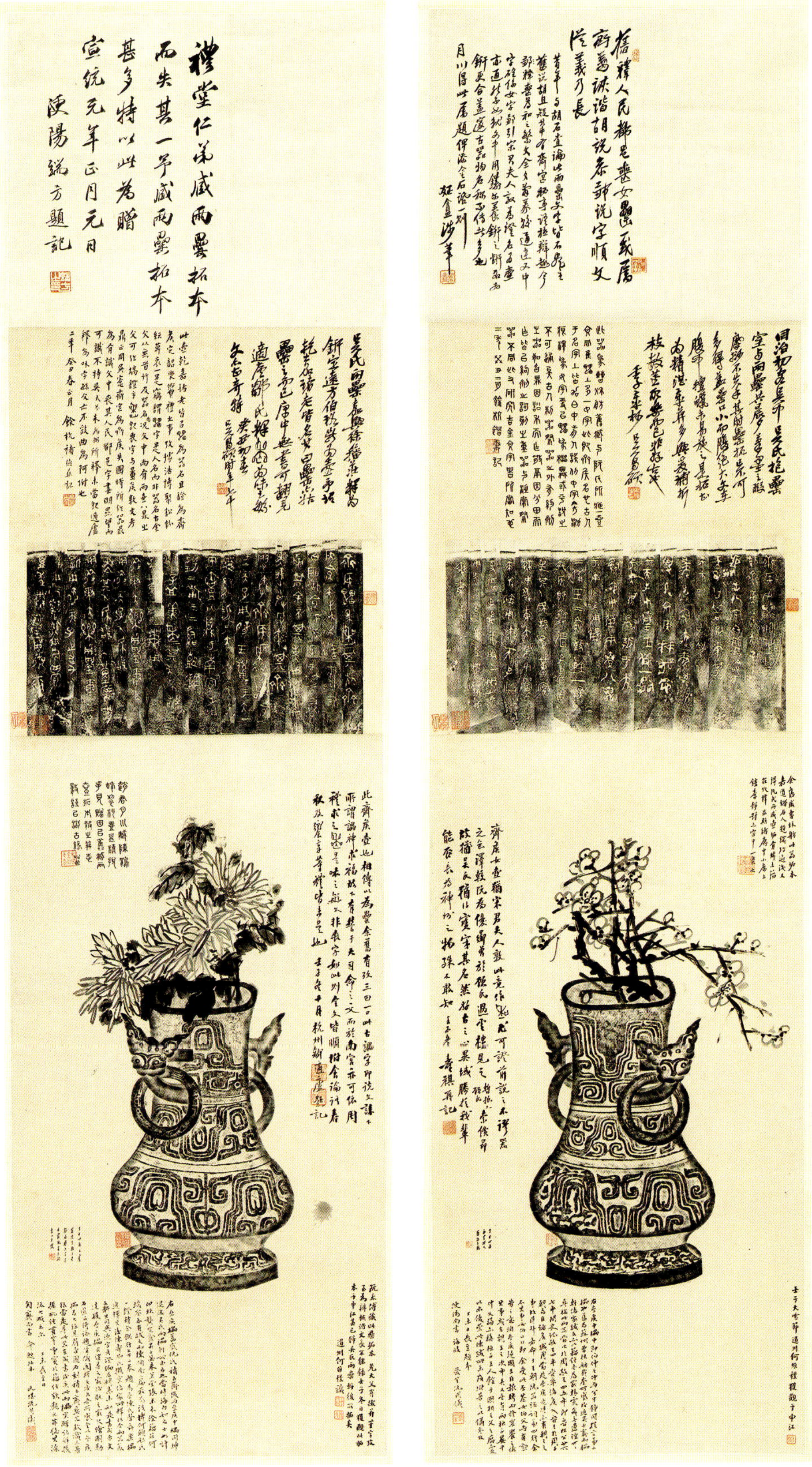

160–61 | Wu Changshi (Chinese, 1844–1927) and others. PAIR OF FULL-FORM RUBBINGS OF A BRONZE JAR, WITH PAINTED FLOWERS, late Qing dynasty (late 19th/early 20th century)

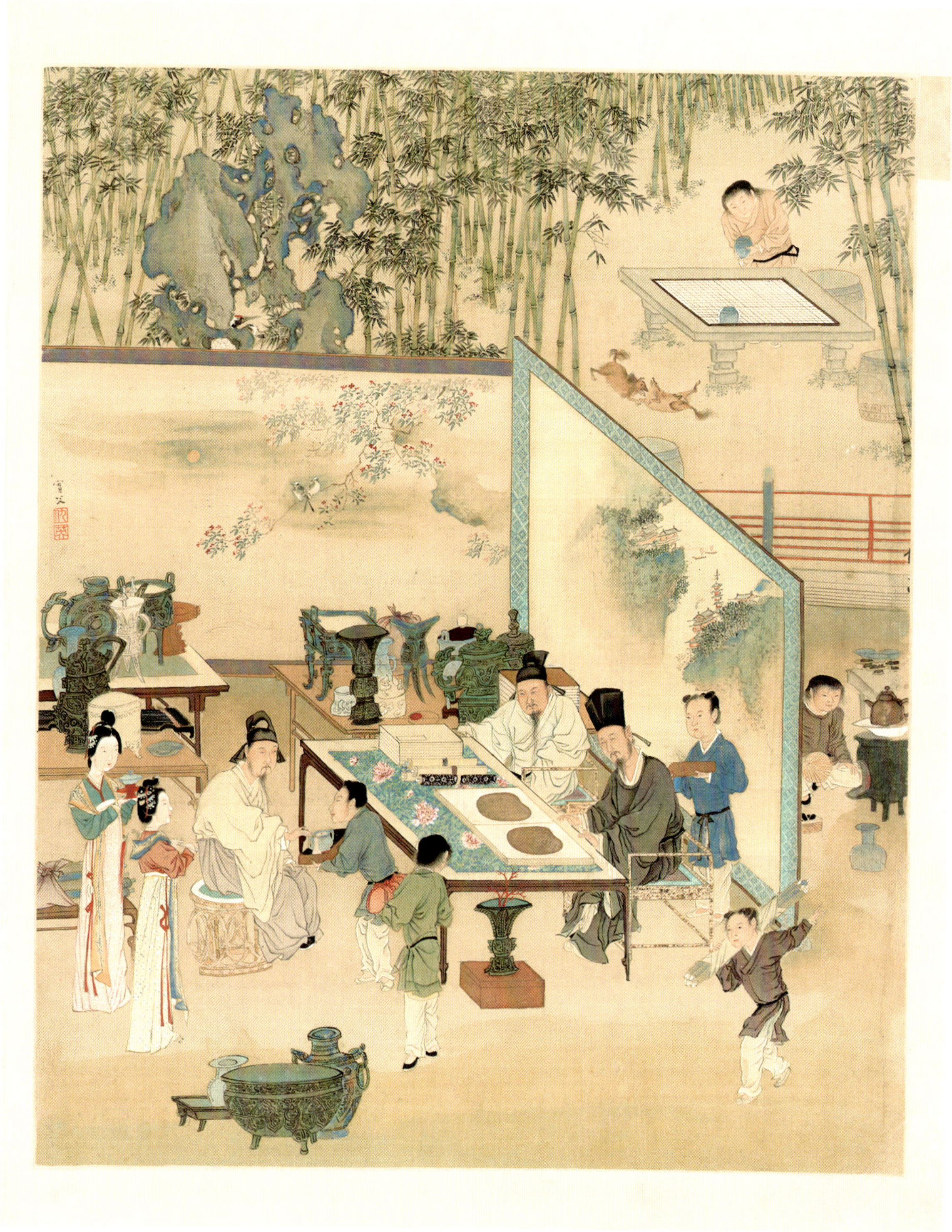

162 | Qiu Ying (Chinese, 1494–1552). APPRECIATING ANTIQUITIES IN THE BAMBOO GARDEN (*ZHUYUAN PINGU*), Ming dynasty (1368–1644)

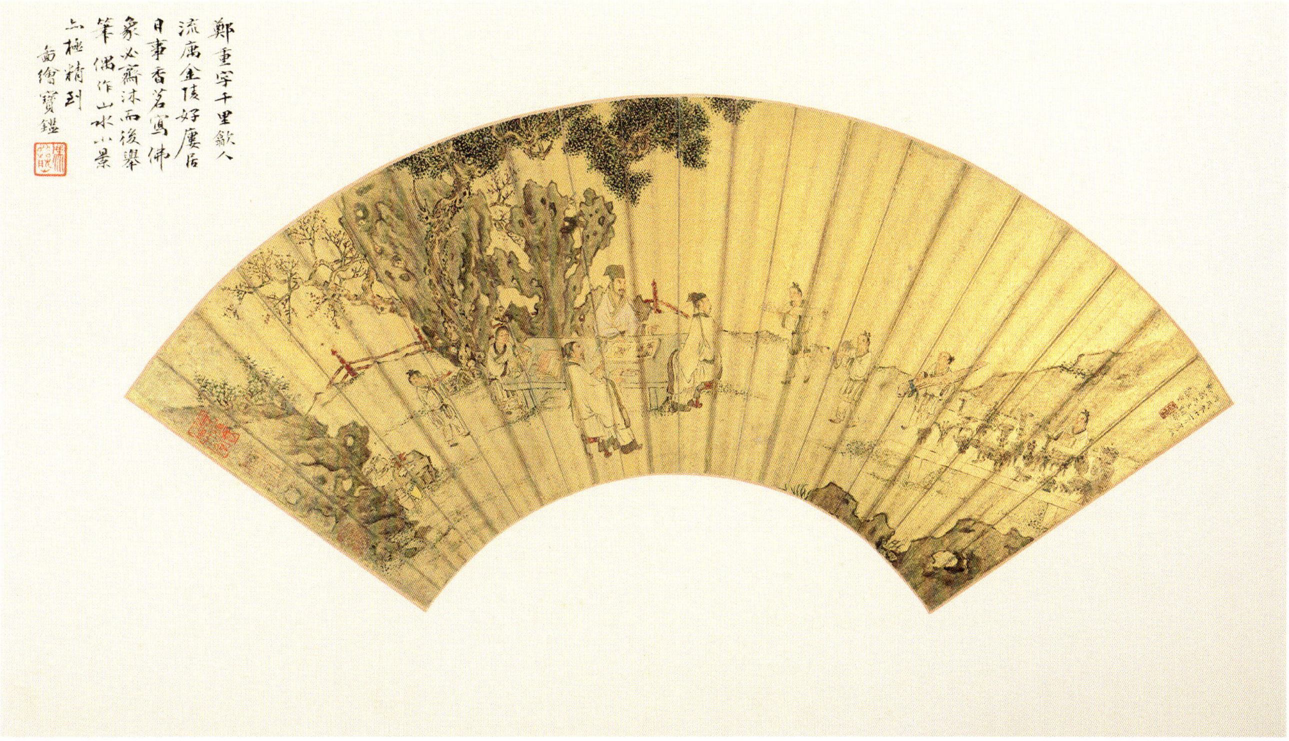

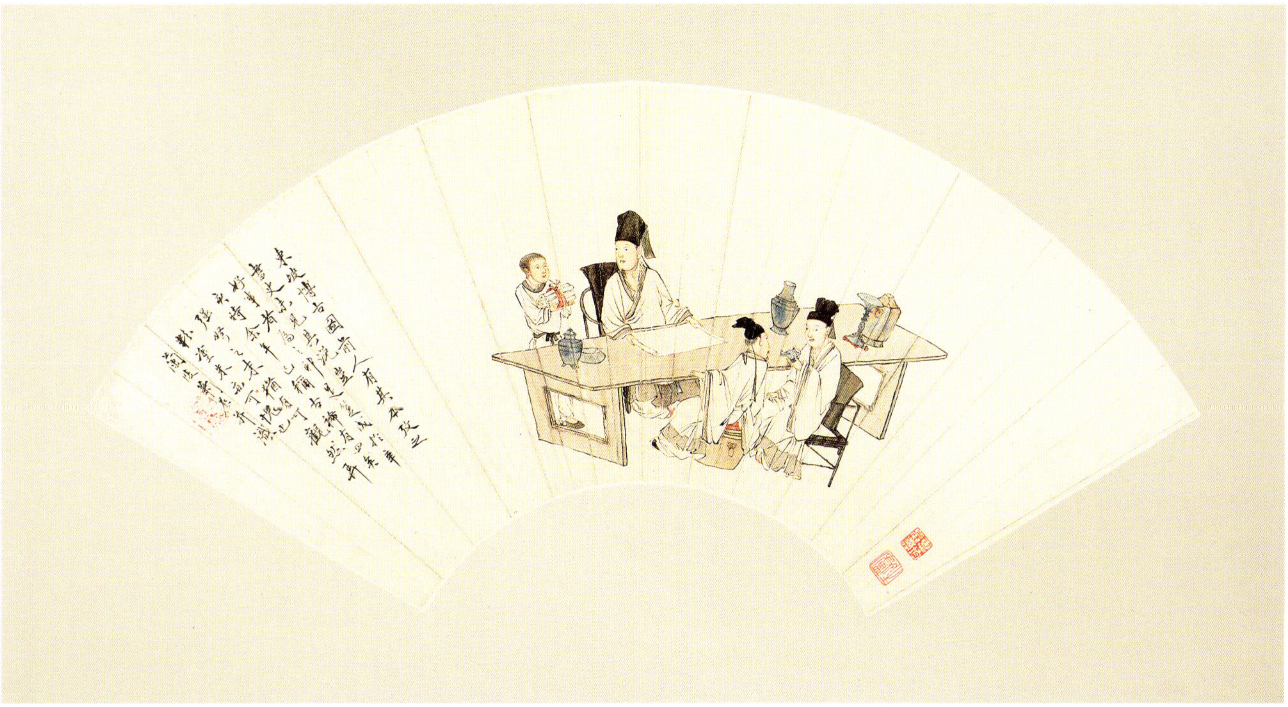

163 | Zheng Zhong (Chinese, active c. 1612–1648). APPRECIATING ANTIQUITIES (*PINGUTU*), Ming dynasty (1368–1644)

164 | Xiao Chen (Chinese, active late 17th–first half of 18th century). SU DONGPO EXAMINING ANTIQUITIES (*DONGPO BOGUTU*), Qing dynasty (1644–1911)

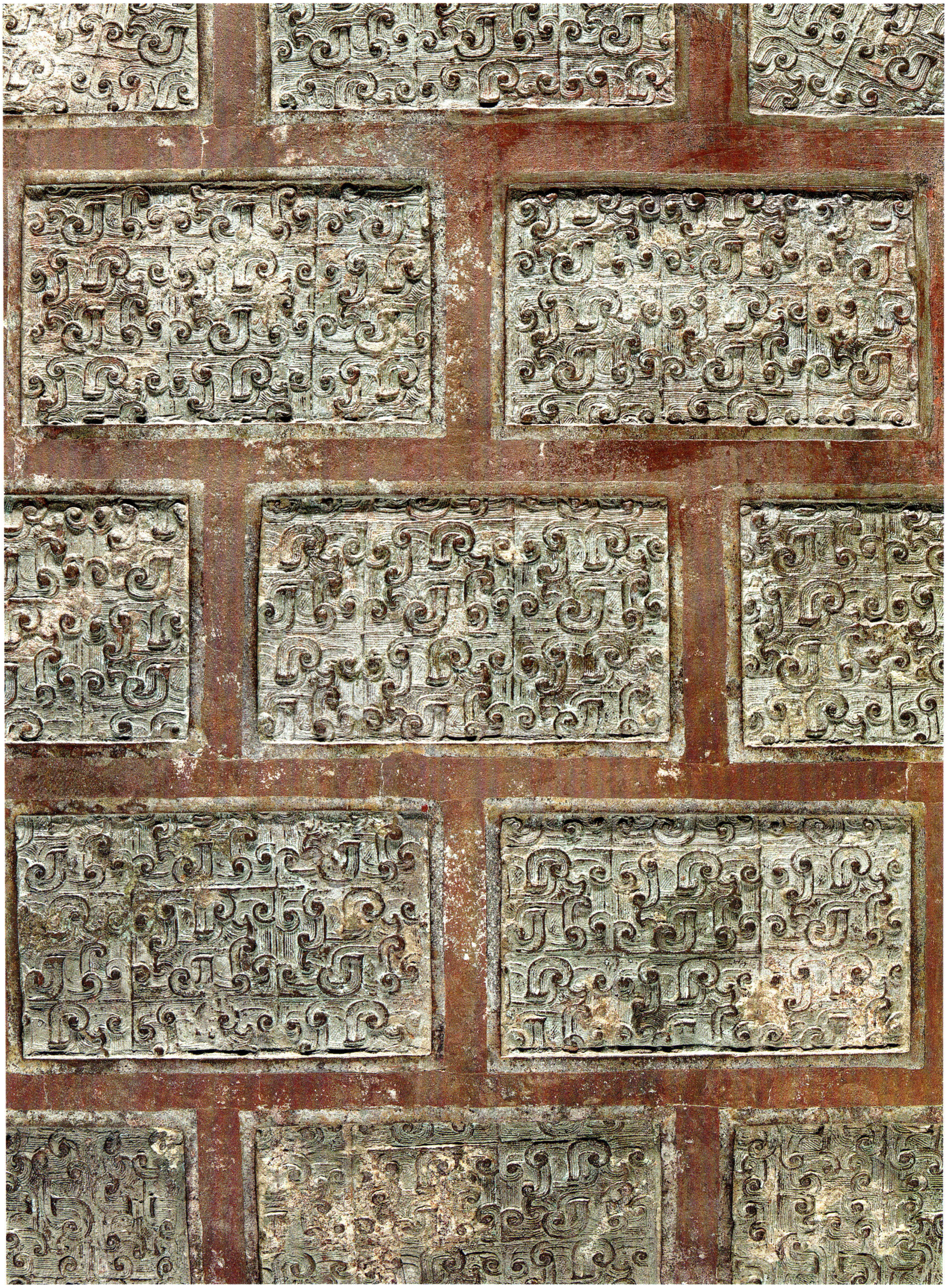

古今

THE PAST IN THE PRESENT

AN EPILOGUE

TAO WANG

Mirroring China's Past: Emperors, Scholars, and Their Bronzes offers a historical journey, traveling through time from one moment of inspiration to another, from one individual to a group of personalities, guided by ancient bronzes and a number of related objects. This project aims to investigate not only the context in which these remarkable pieces were originally created and used but also the different ways in which they were perceived, collected, and copied. On this fascinating but demanding trip, we have begun to comprehend the cultural impact of bronzes on China's emperors and scholars, as well as on society at large. The objects tell us intriguing stories about collectors and the relationship between art collecting and social development. Inevitably, questions arise: Are these ancient bronzes, created more than three thousand years ago, still revered today? What is the significance of antiquity in contemporary society?

In different forms, the past continues to live in the present. As David Lowenthal has argued, it provides us with guidance, identity, and enrichment, and sometimes it imposes preconditions under which the future develops.[1] Thus, our experience of the past is to a degree defined by the present, and the ways in which we engage with the past influence and determine the present and future. Today's China is no longer a traditional society; instead, it is a member of the modern and globalized world. Since the late nineteenth century, waves of Western dominance have challenged China's traditional material culture and ideology. More recently, particularly during the Cultural Revolution (1966–76), traditional art and literature were banned, and the vast legacy of China's past was temporarily erased. As the world moves increasingly toward a set of shared social, economic, and technological values, a knowledge of ancient societies may appear irrelevant, even useless. However, as this exhibition and publication show, in China the question of modernity is always tied to the past. "Return to the classics and trust the ancients," said the prominent antiquarian Luo Zhenyu, who played an important role in the transition from traditional *jinshixue* (study of bronze and stone) to modern archaeology.[2] In China's process of modernization, the study of the classics, as well as of ancient bronzes and stones, has survived because "the 'real' things or *realia* offer modern China an opportunity to invest its classics with a renewed materiality."[3]

As mentioned previously, many ancient bronzes that once were in imperial palaces and esteemed scholars' studios are now displayed prominently in museums in China and abroad. Distinctive landmarks in the history of world art, these exquisite works continue to captivate viewers, regardless of their cultural backgrounds. As Daniel Shapiro, an American collector of ancient Chinese bronzes, once wrote:

> The bronzes have brought me much. They have opened my eyes to another culture, helped me see the limits of my own, and allowed for growth and understanding that might not otherwise have been. Because of the bronzes I have come to better recognize and appreciate the importance of the past. They were a philosopher's stone for me,

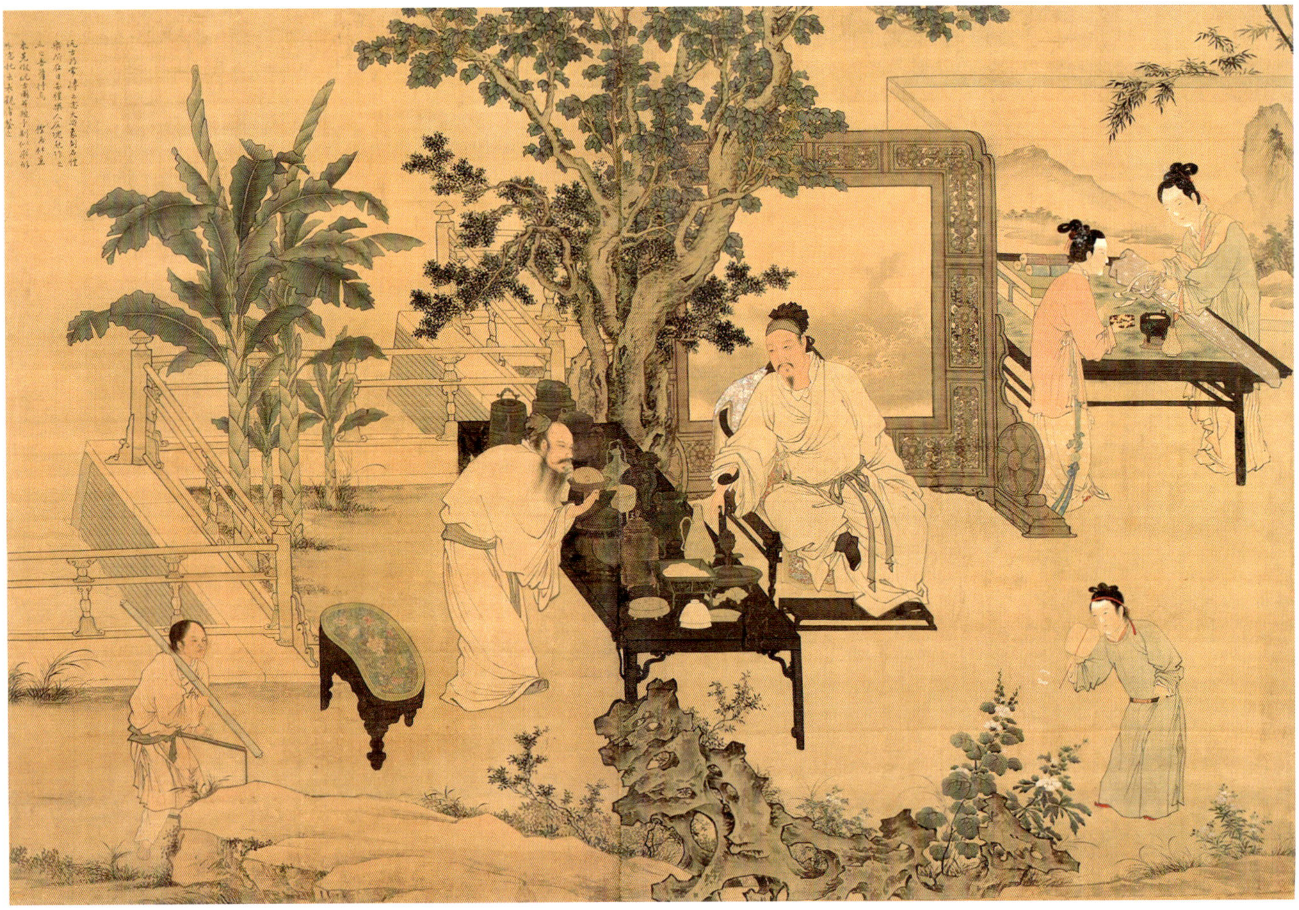

1 | Du Jin (Chinese, c. 1465–1487). *Enjoying Antiquities* (*Wangutu*), Ming dynasty (1368–1644). Ink and color on silk; 126.1 × 187 cm (49 5/8 × 73 5/8 in.). National Palace Museum, Taipei.

> capturing an otherwise unknown world, which, although little understood, has given me the sense that something foreign and strange is part of me. And they have provided me with rare and exquisite beauty, the musings here, and the pleasure to think that what I love and care for may be shared with others.[4]

History, as well as art, often repeats itself. Today's Chinese artists find themselves in a quandary when faced with the paradox of tradition. Many claim that contemporary art is born on the deathbed of tradition, but they find it difficult to distinguish between the contemporary and the traditional since no clear line exists. Indeed, many continue to use traditional motifs, methods, techniques, and media in their works. Although antiquities no longer perform their role as embodiments of heavenly mandate or symbols of orthodox ideology, they continue to fascinate and inspire us.

For these contemporary artists, this engagement with history is neither a lackadaisical recycling of old motifs and styles nor a revival of old traditions, but instead a self-reflective fusion of different elements. That is, using the traditional is not an act of stylistic borrowing but rather a way of asking an ontological question. This is certainly the case, for example, in Hong Hao's *Elegant Gathering* series (see pls. 165 and 167).[5] Taking up a long-standing theme and using traditional ink and paper, Hong and his assistants hand copied a number of famous classical paintings of the fifteenth and eighteenth centuries—when many *yaji* (Elegant Gathering) and *wangu* (Enjoying Antiquities) paintings were produced—and juxtaposed them with his digital photographs of people and objects. One of Hong's works was based on the Ming dynasty artist Du Jin's *Enjoying Antiquities* (*Wangutu*; fig. 1), in which two connoisseurs are depicted in a garden appreciating their collection of ancient bronzes, jades, and ceramics, with young maids unpacking boxes and a servant carrying a scroll painting. Du painted this work at the request of Jian Mian, a collector of antiquities, writing:

> It is commonplace to enjoy antiquities, but one's will is enriched when the scope of the interest is broadened. By studying images and providing names, ritual and music are found within them. People could regret and be ashamed if a day passes without ritual and music. To take them [ritual and music] as principle and adjust to them, this is what I have been waiting for. . . . My intention here goes far beyond depicting

physical form, and the meaning is thus expressed in words. May the viewer be aware of this.

Du's inscription, in a small, controlled hand and easily overlooked in the upper-left corner, expresses his objection to the fashion of treating antiquities as playthings. Instead, the artist's intention was to explore the more profound ritual meaning embedded in these objects.

In Hong's re-creation (pl. 165), however, the pictorial strategy is very different. He added several young visitors who either sit or stand, holding cameras. Their attention is obviously not on the objects but on the collectors. Nearby are more people in various groups, some chatting and one bending down to taste food. Three more figures, one in police uniform and the other in a casual jacket, have their backs turned so that their faces are concealed. Shopping bags are scattered on the ground, an empty beer bottle rests there as well, and a modern ashtray and cell phone sit among the antiquities. This work evokes the multiple relationships that connoisseurs and viewers, both past and present, have had with their objects.

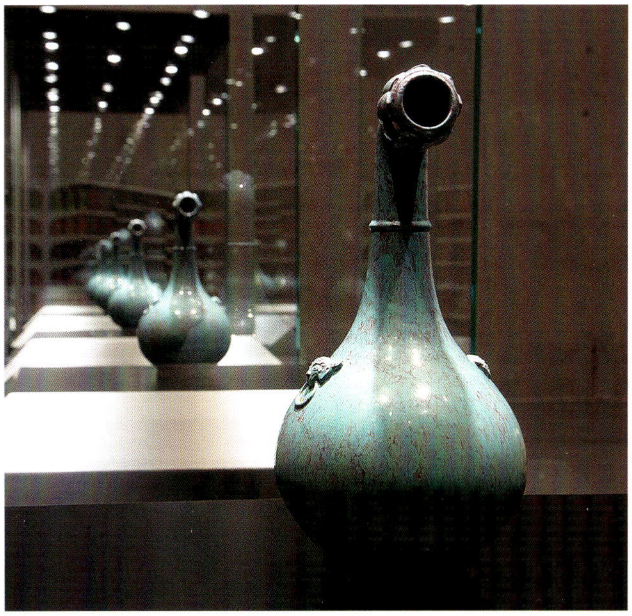

2 | Installation view of vases from the *Curved Vase* series at the Long Museum (West Bund Branch), Shanghai, 2014. Xu Zhen (Chinese, born 1977). For another example, see pl. 170.

In a second work (see pl. 167), which he based on an album painting titled *Yueman qingyou tu* (Outing under the Moon; see pl. 168) by the Qing dynasty court artist Chen Mei, Hong has increased the size of the composition and added a group of his own friends and acquaintances, including artists, collectors, curators, and scholars (both Chinese and foreign), to a scene depicting the inner quarters of the Forbidden City, where a group of court ladies are appreciating paintings and ancient bronzes. He integrates modern people with ancient ones; some look directly at the viewers and invite us to join in. By mixing different elements, the picture combines and contrasts the new and the old, representing a novel way of seeing. As Hong himself said:

> Painting and photography are two different artistic methods, as well as the past and the present two different systems. Yet I mix them on the same level. In fact there are many internal connections; for example, the photographs of people appeared on the *Yaji* [Elegant Gathering] paintings were taken by me at various exhibitions and parties, and the ancient paintings are about the elegant gathering of ancient literati. This is a cultural party, and I put cultural activities of different times into a single painting; thus, they depend on each other and create a new dynamic. It is like I am reproducing the ancient paintings, and the working process is like doing a restoration. I tried to make the picture perfect, confusing different time and space.[6]

In contemporary Chinese art, a good deal of humor, in particular irony, exists, and in this light modernity can be used as a tongue-in-cheek play against tradition. Reminiscent, in a similar way, of the La Pittura Colta artists' reinterpretations of the old masters in the 1980s, artists' social commentary is infused with a very contemporary sense of humor. Many current Chinese artists see themselves as new interpreters of traditions they received not only from Chinese history but also from Western art and philosophy. For example, Xu Zhen, one of the most vibrant and colorful young artists in China today, started with the international movement of conceptual art, paying little attention to his Chinese roots and focusing on popular culture and consumerism. In 2009 Xu established the MadeIn Company (paraphrasing *Made in China*), intentionally subsuming artistic individuality under a company, and then became a brand of the company himself. In his more recent works, Xu explores further the relationship between artist and artist-as-brand, challenging the idea of "originality." For instance, in 2013, he made the *MadeIn Curved Vase* series, which uses classical forms of porcelain vases from the Qing dynasty as models for high-quality reproductions (see fig. 2). The example included in this exhibition (see pl. 170) is a long-necked vase based on an eighteenth-century prototype (see pl. 169) that is itself an imitation of a Han dynasty bronze vase (see pl. 168). This reproduction replicates very closely the original shape and color, but its neck is folded down at a ninety-degree angle. By detaching the vase from its original function and context, Xu wants to illustrate what has been described as a "history that could have happened."[7]

Similarly, in twentieth-century European and American art and design, as Elizabeth Guffey has argued, the "retro" became trendy because it not only seemed avant-garde but also was capable of redefining the concept of the avant-garde.[8] For some artists, designers, and producers, retro is,

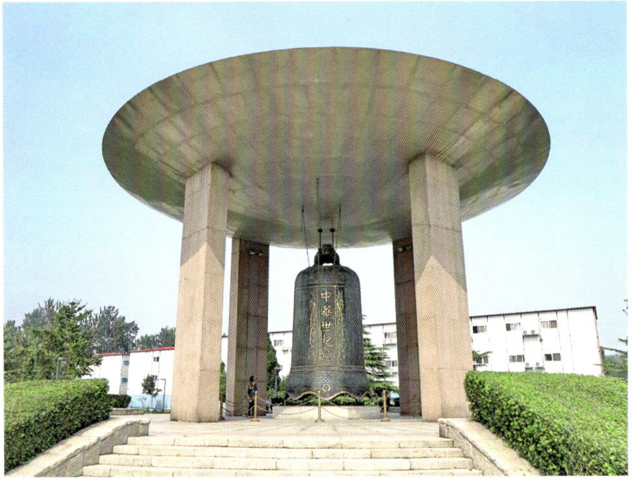

3 | The bell in the China Millenium Monument on West Chang'an Avenue in Beijing.

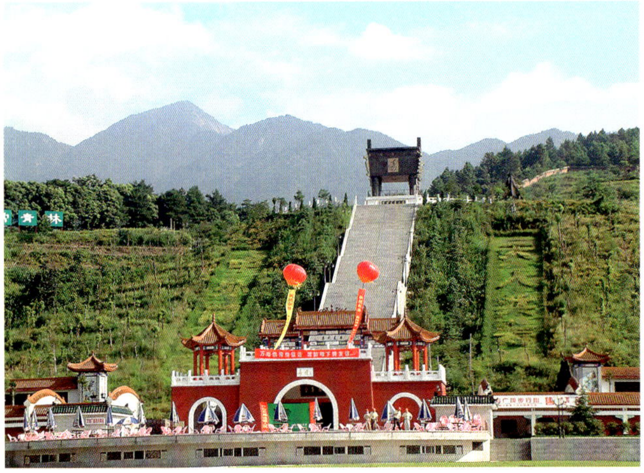

4 | The *ding* (cauldron) installed on Mount Hengshan in Hengyang, Hunan province, to celebrate the millennium.

as Guffey puts it, "a non-historical way of knowing the past" and provides "a new approach to understanding history itself."[9] This observation seems to ring true in contemporary Chinese art. Ancient iconography and artifacts serve as physical evidence of an important cultural heritage from which new generations can draw inspiration, offering the possibility of different perspectives and alternative discourses.

In China today, there is clearly a renewed focus on traditional culture. Antiquities, in particular ancient bronzes, still occupy a prominent position in the minds of many—they are perceived as historical or artistic objects, as well as commodities that can be traded on the market. We frequently hear of record-breaking sales of Chinese classical art at auctions and galleries, as private collectors compete fiercely for ownership of these precious antiquities. Museums in China, as well as those abroad, regularly exhibit China's treasures. But how has this changed the meanings of the bronzes?

To answer these questions, let us turn to two remarkable monuments built at the end of the last millennium, which relate to bronzes in tradition and legend, as well as to the concept of *zhong ding* (bells and cauldrons) that symbolize power and government. At the end of 1999, when China was preparing for the return of Macau—the last remaining Western colony to be restored to China—the Beijing municipal government built a very symbolic building, the China Millennium Monument. Located on West Chang'an Avenue, it consists of a museum, an altar, a bridge, and a square, all connected by a bronze passage measuring 263 meters long and 3 meters wide. At the eastern square hangs a bronze bell, 6.8 meters in height and weighing fifty tons, on which two dragons and fifty-six peonies are depicted (see fig. 3). All these elements are highly symbolic: Chang'an Avenue is the axis of the city, 1999 was the fiftieth anniversary of the People's Republic of China, two great rivers run through China—the Yangzi and Yellow rivers—and there are fifty-six ethnic groups in the country. In addition, a brief chronicle of the People's Republic of China, the score of the national anthem, and the Great Wall are inscribed on the body of the bell. The whole project was conceived and created with highly charged political motivations, as well as a reappropriation of traditional culture. On New Year's Eve 1999, President Jiang Zemin struck the bell.

Celebrations also took place far away from the capital. In August 2000, at Mount Hengshan (Hengyang, Hunan)—one of the five sacred peaks (the others include Taishan in Shandong, Songshan in Henan, Huashan in Shaanxi, Hengshan in Shanxi, and Hengshang in Hunan)—a new square bronze *ding* cauldron was installed to mark the new millennium (see fig. 4). Measuring 9.9 meters high and weighing fifty-six tons, the *ding* alludes to the unification of the country and the number of different ethnic groups living in China. Its surface decoration of the *ding* is also symbolic: the character *shou* (longevity) is written ten thousand times, expressing the wish that China and the Chinese people will last forever (*wanshou* [ten thousand years]). This is by far the largest bronze vessel ever made and, like the bronze bell in Beijing, it is embedded with the most explicit symbols of Chinese culture. During the installation ceremony, local media reported a marvelous spectacle: the sky suddenly turned dark, and thousands of cranes gathered, flying above the cauldron and taking part in the rituals (*wanhe laiyi*); this reminds us of the scene described in the *Shiji*, when the Han dynasty emperor Wudi (r. 140–87 BC) obtained the bronze cauldron from the region of Wei (see "Matter of Things," 17–31 in this catalogue). This could be easily dismissed as superstition or wishful thinking, but the people who wrote the story obviously thought that the bronze cauldron was a spiritual object, although their belief may differ greatly from that of the emperors. There, on the sacred peak, the old and new cultural and political symbolisms, the past and present, came together once again in a powerful way.

NOTES

1 | David Lowenthal, *The Past Is a Foreign Country* (Cambridge: Cambridge University Press, 1985).

2 | See Pai Shih-Ming, "'Returning to the Classics, Trusting the Ancient': Luo Zhenyu's Exploration of Traditional Chinese Identity in Modern China," in Yang Chia-Ling and Roderick Whitfield, eds., *Lost Generation: Luo Zhenyu, Qing Loyalists and the Formation of Modern Chinese Culture* (London: Saffron Books, 2012), 75–97; and Denis Thouard and Tao Wang, "Making New Classics: The Archaeology of Luo Zhenyu and Victor Segalen," in Sarah C. Humphrey and Rudolf G. Wagner, eds. *Modernity's Classics* (New York: Springer, 2013), 231–60.

3 | Thouard and Wang, "Making New Classics," 257.

4 | Daniel Shapiro, *Ancient Chinese Bronzes: A Personal Appreciation* (London: Sylph Edition, 2013), 26.

5 | Hong Hao and John Tancock, eds., *Elegant Gathering: Hong Hao's Opening, April 19–May 26, 2007*, exh. cat. (New York: Chambers Fine Art, 2007).

6 | Quoted from Cheng Xiaowei, "Jiedu yishujia Hong Hao de mima bianpai" [Decoding the Artist Hong Hao], *Sina*, http://collection.sina.com.cn/cjrw/20111129/ 143046971.shtml.

7 | Philip Tinari and Paula Tsai, eds., *Xu Zhen: A MadedIn Company Production* (Beijing: Ullens Center for Contemporary Art, 2016), 142.

8 | Elizabeth E. Guffey, *Retro: The Culture of Revival* (London: Reaktion Books, 2006).

9 | Ibid., 20, 85.

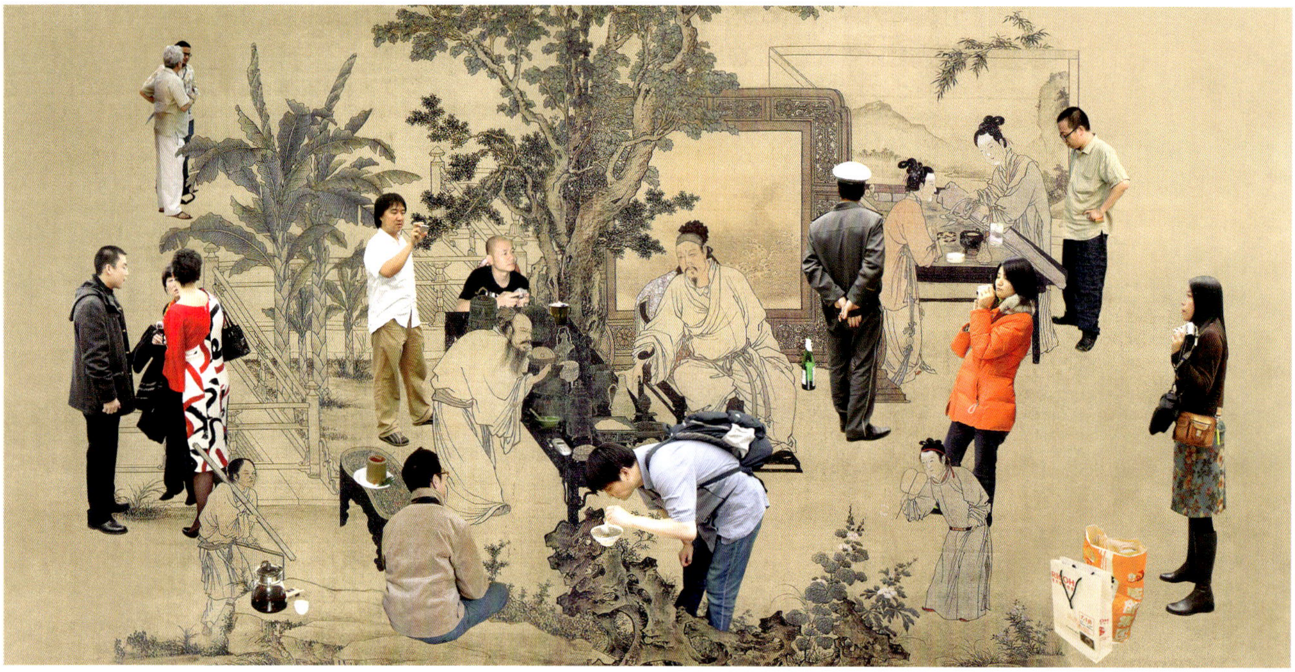

165 | Hong Hao (Chinese, born 1960). APPRECIATING ANTIQUES (*WANGUTU*) from ELEGANT GATHERING (*YAJI*), 2007

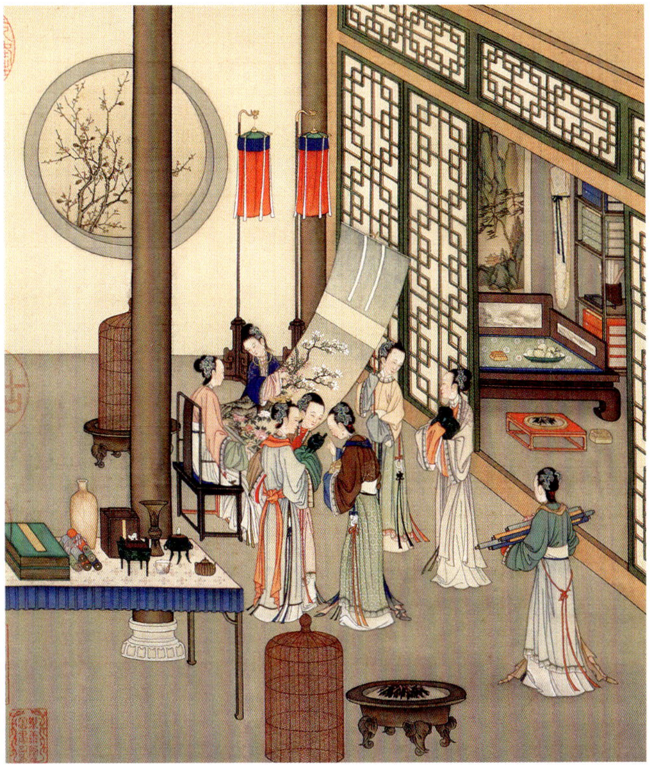

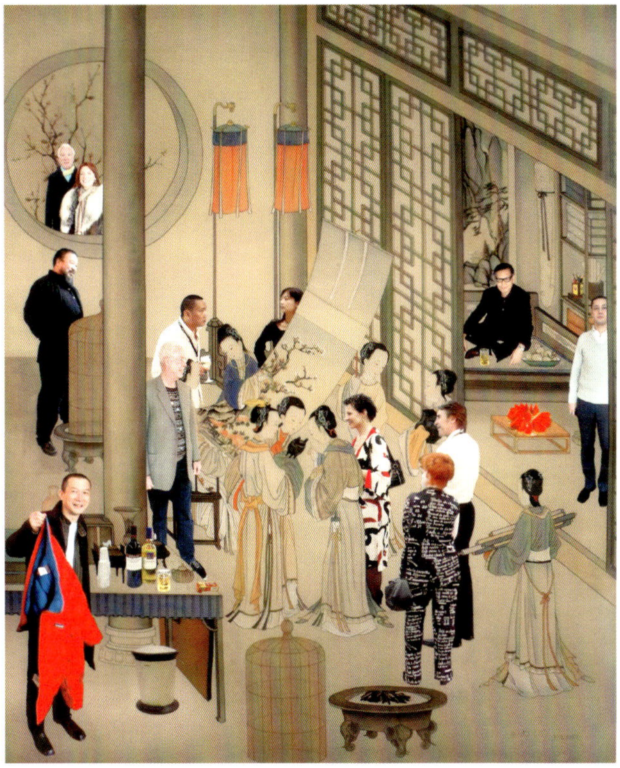

166 | Chen Mei (Chinese. 1694–1745), OUTING UNDER THE MOON (*YUEMAN QINGYOU TU*), Qing dynasty (1644–1911)

167 | Hong Hao (Chinese, born 1960). OUTING UNDER THE MOON (*YUEMAN QINGYOU TU*) from ELEGANT GATHERING (*YAJI*), 2007

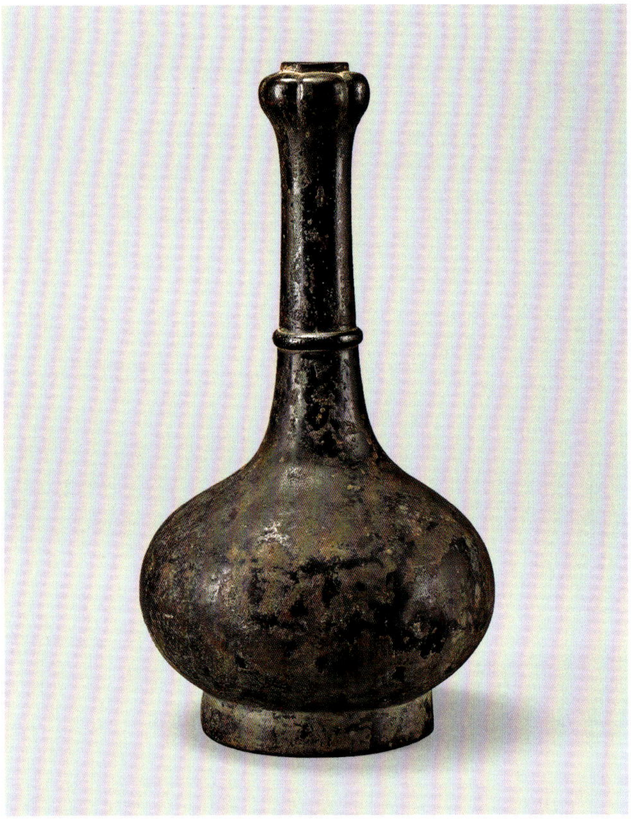

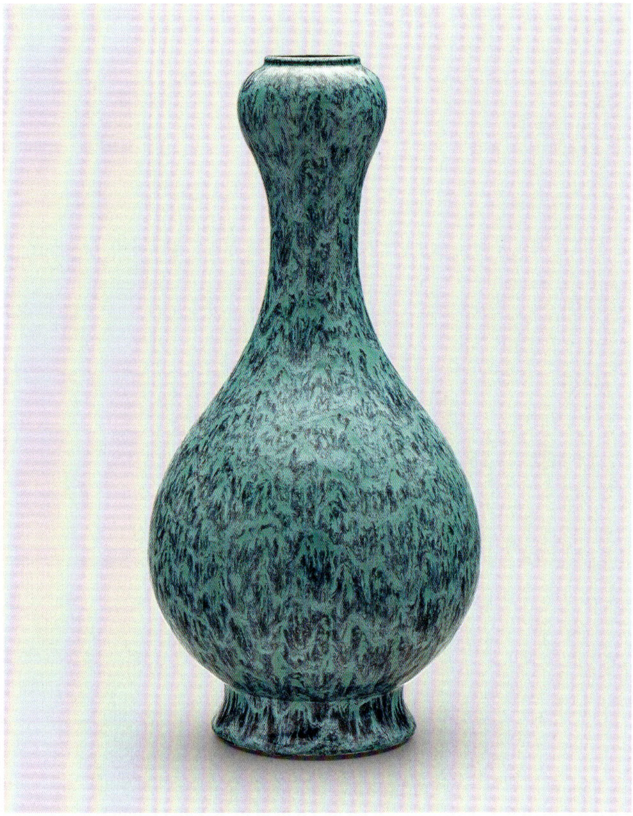

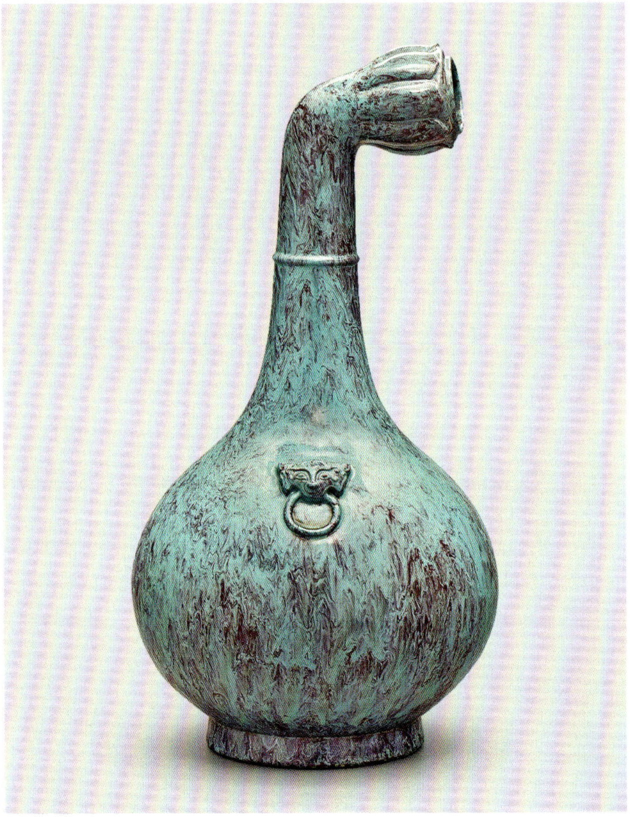

clockwise from top left

168 | BOTTLE WITH GARLIC BULB-SHAPED MOUTH, Western Han dynasty (206 BC–AD 9)

169 | BOTTLE WITH GARLIC BULB-SHAPED MOUTH, Qing dynasty (1644–1911), Qianlong reign (1735–96)

170 | Xu Zhen (Chinese, born 1977). BOTTLE IN THE FORM OF A PORCELAIN VESSEL MADE DURING QIANLONG'S REIGN, 2014

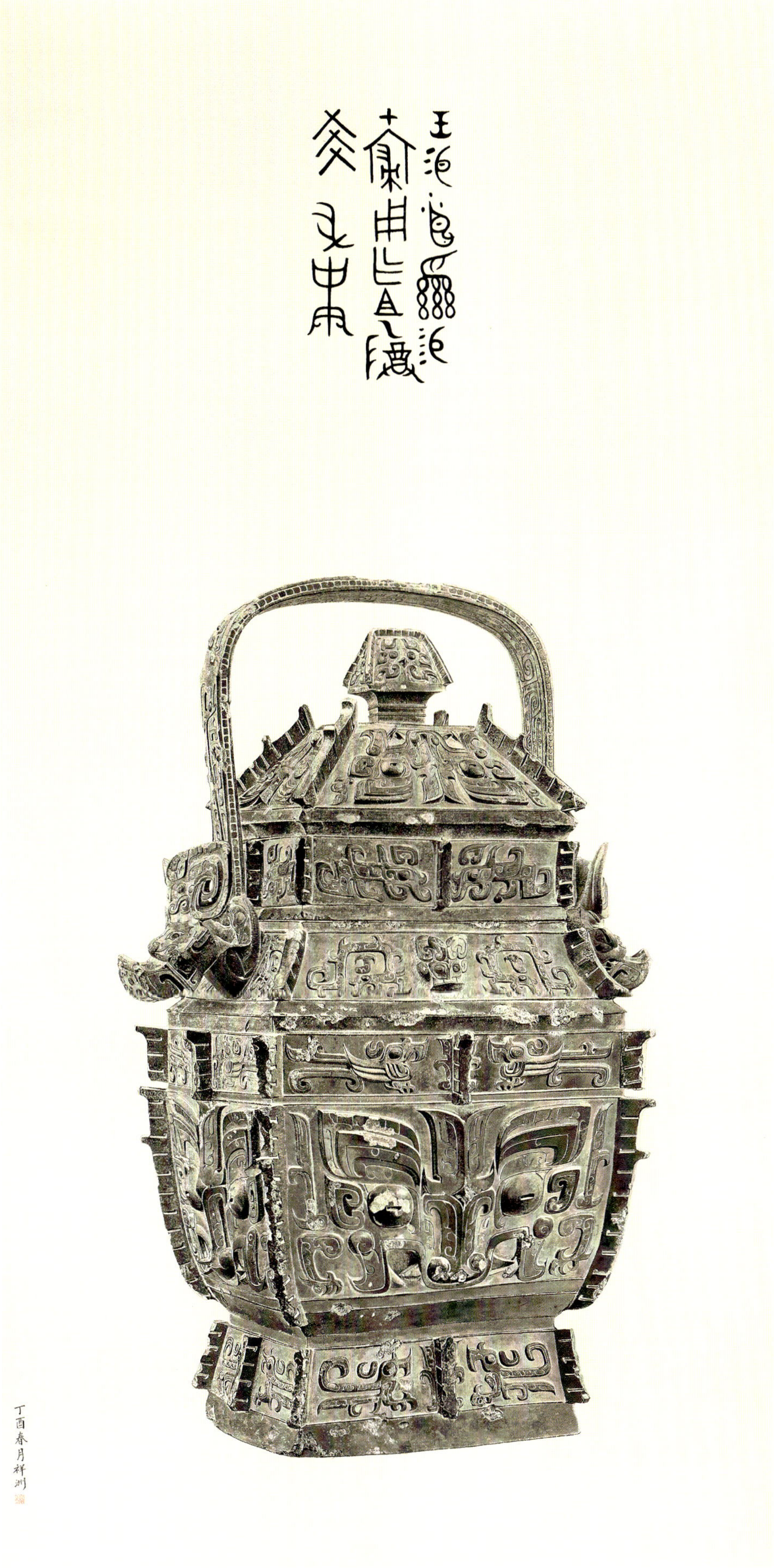

171 | Tai Xiangzhou (Chinese, born 1968). PAINTING OF THE "BUCKET OF MINISTER XI," 2017

CHECKLIST

This checklist includes all works reproduced in the plates sections of this book; if a given object did not also appear in the exhibition, this is noted at the end of the entry. Significant inscriptions on the works are reproduced here. In addition, if an object is known to have belonged to an important historical collection, the collector's name and life dates are also provided, followed by the source documenting that ownership. The following conventional abbreviations are used for citing those sources.

BG | *Bogutu* [Illustrated Broad Manifestation of Antiquity], *Yizhengtang* edition, 1753. Reprinted in JWWXJC 1:279–530; 2:1–342.

CA | Liu Xihai, *Chang'an huogubian* [Compilation of Antiquities Acquired in Chang'an], *juan* 1–3, 1905. Reprinted in *JWWXJC* 7:475–507.

FZ | Chen Jieqi and Deng Shi, *Fuzhai jijinlu* [Auspicious Metals Collected by Fuzhai], *juan* 1–8, 1918. Reprinted in *JWWXJC* 16:1–143.

GG | Gugong bowuyuan, *Gugong qingtongqi* [Bronzes from the Palace Museum] (Beijing: Zijincheng chubanshe, 1999).

GS | Chen Fangmei, *Gugong Shangdai qingtong liqi tulu* [Shang Ritual Bronzes in the National Palace Museum Collection] (Taipei: Guoli gugong bowuyuan, 1998).

HX | Wu Dacheng, *Hengxuan suojian suocang jijinlu* [Record of Auspicious Metals Collected and Examined at Hengxuan], *juan* 1–2, 1885. Reprinted in *JWWXJC*. 8:142–210.

JG | Wu Shifen, *Jungulu* [Record of Pursuing Antiquities], 1796–1875. Partially reprinted in *JWWXJC* 18:185–260.

JGJ | Wu Shifen, *Jungulu jinwen* [Bronze Inscriptions from the Record of Pursuing Antiquities], *juan* 1–3, 1895. Reprinted in *JWWXJC* 11:75–417.

JJ | Xiling yinshe, *Jijin liuying: Qingtongqi quanxing mota juncun* [Traces of Auspicious Metals: Full-Form Rubbings of Bronzes] (Shanghai: Shanghai shuhua chubanshe, 2014).

JS | Feng Yunpeng and Feng Yunyuan, *Jinshisuo* [Search for Metals and Stones], *juan* 1–12, 1821. Reprinted in *JWWXJC* 3:1–91.

JWWXJC | Liu Qingzhu, Duan Zhihong, and Feng Shi, eds., *Jinwen wenxian jicheng* [Compendium of Publications on Bronze Inscriptions] (Beijing: Xianzhuang shuju, 2005).

KT | Zhou Ya, *Kezhai jigutu jianzhu* [Illustrated Antiquities of Kezhai: An Annotation] (Shanghai: Shanghai guji chubanshe, 2012).

KZ | Wu Dacheng, *Kezhai jigulu* [Record of Antiquities Collected by Kezhai], vols. 1–26, 1918. Reprinted in *JWWXJC* 12:161–461.

LL | Wu Yun, *Liangleixuan yiqi tushi* [Illustrations and Annotations of the Ritual Vessels from Liangleixuan], *juan* 1–6, 1873. Reprinted in *JWWXJC* 8:1–142.

NS | Ningshou jiangu [Reflections on Antiquity from the Palace of Tranquil Longevity], *juan* 1–16, 1776–81. Reprinted in *JWWXJC* 7:1–413.

PG | Pan Zuyin, *Pangulou yiqi kuanzhi* [Inscriptions on the Ritual Vessel from Pangulou], *juan* 1–2, 1872. Reprinted in *JWWXJC* 7:559–611.

SD | Luo Zhenyu, Sandai jijin wencun [Bronze Inscriptions of Three Dynasties Auspicious Metals], *juan* 1–20, 1936. Reprinted Beijing: Zhonghua shuju, 1983, 3 vols.

TZ | Duanfang, *Taozhai jijinlu* [Records of Auspicious Bronzes from Taozhai], *juan* 1–8, 1908. Reprinted in *JWWXJC* 8:222–447.

XK | Zhao Jiucheng, *Xu Kaogutu* [A Supplement to Illustrated Catalogue for the Study of Antiquities], *Siku quanshu* edition, 1781. Reprinted in *JWWXJC* 1:248–78.

XJ | *Xiqing xujian jiabian* [Supplement A to the Ancient Mirror of Western Clarity], *juan* 1–20, 1793. Reprinted in *JWWXJC* 5:1–547.

XJJ | Liu Tizhi, *Xiaojiaojingge jinwen taben* [Rubbings of Bronze Inscriptions from Xiaojiaojingge], *juan* 1–18, 1935. Reprinted Taipei: Datong shuju, 1986.

XQ | *Xiqing gujian* [Ancient Mirror of Western Clarity], *juan* 1–40, 1751. Reprinted in *JWWXJC* 3:92–536; 4: –513.

XY | *Xiqing xujian yibian* [Supplement B to the Ancient Mirror of Western Clarity], *juan* 1–20, 1893. Reprinted in *JWWXJC* 6:1–511.

YQ | Wu Rongguang, *Yunqingguan jinwen* [Bronze Inscriptions from Yunqingguan], *juan* 1–5, 1842. Reprinted in *JWWXJC* 12:75–417.

ZJ | Zou An, *Zhoujin wencun* [Record of Inscribed Zhou Dynasty Bronzes], *juan* 1–6, 1916. Reprinted in *JWWXJC* 23:1–430.

ZY | Fang Junyi, *Zhuiyizhai yiqi kuanzhi kaoshi* [Studies of Inscriptions on Ritual Vessels from the Zhuiyizhai Studio], *juan* 1–30, 1935. Reprinted in *JWWXJC* 14:1–478.

1 | LOBED TRIPOD CAULDRON OF LADY QI (*QI FU LI*)

Late Shang dynasty (c. 1250–1046 BC). Bronze; h. 18.5 cm (7 1/4 in.), diam. of mouth 14.1 cm (5 9/16 in.). The Shanghai Museum, 47044. Yuan Baoheng (1827–1878), HX: 95.

2 | LOBED TRIPOD CAULDRON (*LI*)

Longshan culture (c. 2500–2000 BC). Earthenware; h. 20 cm (7 7/8 in.), max. diam. 16.5 cm (6 1/2 in.), diam. of mouth 12.4 cm (4 7/8 in.). The Art Institute of Chicago, gift of Mr. & Mrs. Potter Palmer, 1937.792.

3 | JAR OF LORD RUI (*RUI GONG HU*)

Western Zhou dynasty (1046–771 BC. Bronze; with lid: 37.6 × 25.1 cm (14 13/16 × 9 7/8 in.); lid: 14 × 11 × 6.8 cm (5 1/2 × 4 5/16 × 2 11/16 in.). The Palace Museum, Beijing, GU77462. Qing imperial collection, XQ: 19.5.

4 | CONTAINER IN THE FORM OF AN ANCIENT BRONZE JAR (*HU*)

Western Han dynasty (206 BC–AD 9). Earthenware; 44.0 × 20.5 × 20.5 cm (17 5/16 × 8 1/16 × 8 1/16 in.). The Art Institute of Chicago, gift of the Joseph and Helen Regenstein Foundation, 1962.588.

5 | JAR (*HU*)

Warring States period (475–221 BC). Bronze; h. 34.8 cm (13 11/16 in.), diam. of mouth 12.3 cm (4 13/16 in.). The Shanghai Museum, 75981.

6 | CONTAINER IN THE FORM OF AN ANCIENT BRONZE JAR (*HU*)

Warring States period (475–221 BC). Earthenware; h. 36.0 cm (14 in.), max diam. 21.6 cm (8 1/2 in.), diam. of mouth 8.3 cm (3 1/4 in.). The Art Institute of Chicago, bequest of Russell Tyson, 1964.723.

7 | CONTAINER (*LEI*)

Spring and Autumn period (770–476 BC). Bronze; h. 32.5 cm (12 13/16 in.), diam. of mouth 24.6 (9 11/16 in.), max. diam. 42 cm (16 1/2 in.). The Palace Museum, Beijing, GU77485. Qing imperial collection, XY: 16.32.

8 | JAR IN THE FORM OF AN ANCIENT BRONZE CONTAINER (*LEI*)

Eastern Zhou dynasty, Warring States Period (475–221 BC). Stoneware; h. 26.6 cm (10 5/8 in), max. diam. 34 cm (13 3/8 in.), diam. of mouth 16.5 cm (6 1/2 in.). The Art Institute of Chicago, bequest of Russell Tyson, 1964.999.

9 | LOBED TRIPOD CAULDRON (*LI*)

Late Shang dynasty (c. 1250–1046 BC). Bronze; 21 × 15.5 × 15.5 cm (8 1/4 × 6 1/8 × 6 1/8 in.), diam. 15.6 cm. Xiling Collection.

10 | TRIPOD CAULDRON (*DING*)

Late Shang dynasty (c. 1250–1046 BC). Bronze; h. 21.3 cm (8 3/8 in.), diam. 17 cm (6 3/4 in.). Anonymous loan.

11 | EWER OF FATHER YI (*FU YI HE*)

Late Shang dynasty (c. 1250–1046 BC). Bronze; 27.9 × 24.8 × 19 cm (11 × 9 3/4 × 7 1/2 in.), max. diam. 19.1 cm (7 1/2 in.). Asian Art Museum, San Francisco, The Avery Brundage Collection, B60B78. Qing imperial collection, XJ: 14.24.

12 | BUCKET OF FU CHENG (*FU CHENG YOU*)

Late Shang dynasty (c. 1250–1046 BC). Bronze; h. 25 cm (9 13/16 in.). Museum of Fine Arts, Boston, Anna Mitchell Richards Fund, 34.63a–6. Qing imperial collection, XQ: 15.24.

13 | PEDESTALED TUREEN OF DUKE JU (*BO JU GUI*)

Western Zhou dynasty (1046–771 BC). Bronze; 23.5 × 20 × 31 cm (9 1/4 × 7 7/8 × 12 3/16 in.). Xiling Collection. Pan Zuyin (1830–1890), HX: 31.

14 | PEDESTALED TUREEN OF DUKE HUAN (*JU BO HUAN GUI*)

Western Zhou dynasty (1046–771 BC). Bronze; 33 × 40.6 × 34.9 cm (13 × 16 × 13 3/4 in.). The Nelson-Atkins Museum of Art, Kansas City, Missouri, purchase: William Rockhill Nelson Trust, 47–26. Qing imperial collection, XJ: 12.39; Gu Zijia (late 19th century), KZ: 8.14.3 (inscription only).

15 | MASK

Western Zhou dynasty (1046–771 BC). Bronze; h. 26.1 cm (10 1/4 in.). Private collection.

16 | TUREEN OF OFFICER SHI (*YA SHI GUI*)

Late Shang dynasty (c. 1250–1046 BC). Bronze; h. 11.7 cm (4 5/8 in.), diam. of mouth 16.9 cm (6 5/8 in.). The Shanghai Museum, 25179.

17 | RECTANGULAR TUREEN (*FU*)

Spring and Autumn period (770–476 BC). Bronze; 18.6 × 33.3 × 21 cm (7 5/16 × 13 1/8 × 8 1/2 in.). The Art Institute of Chicago, Lucy Maud Buckingham Collection, 1924.242.

18 | JAR (*HU*)

Late Shang dynasty (c. 1250–1046 BC). Bronze; h. 36.8 cm (14 1/2 in.), diam. of mouth 19.2 cm (7 9/16 in.). MacLean Collection.

19 | JAR (*HU*)

Western Zhou dynasty (1046–771 BC). Bronze; 48.5 × 30 × 24.5 cm (19 1/4 × 11 3/4 × 9 5/8 in.). The Art Institute of Chicago, gift of Fred Eychaner and Tommy Yang Guo, 2008.702.

1

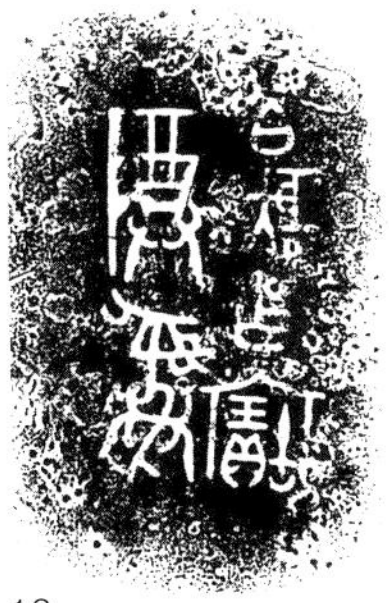

13

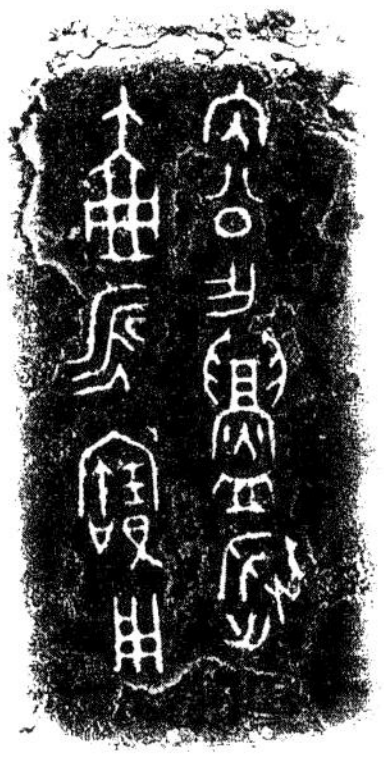

3

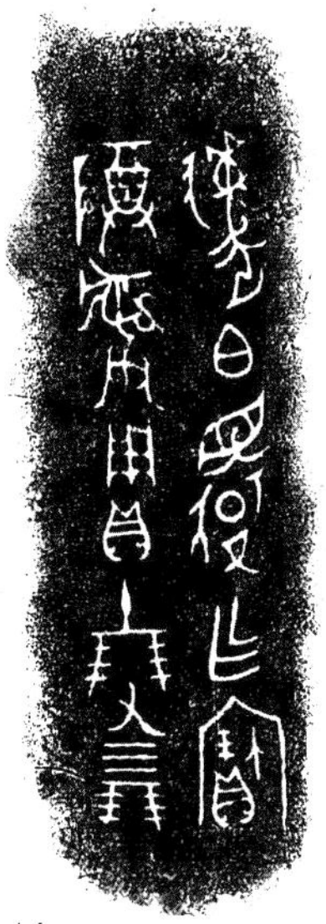

14

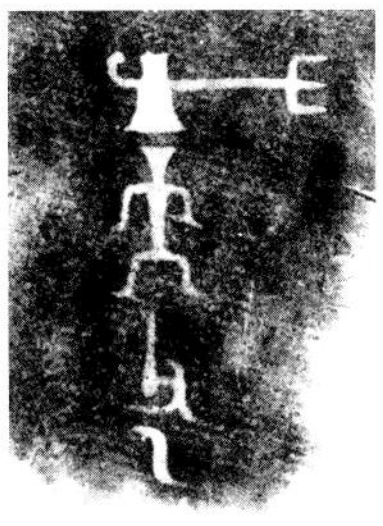

11

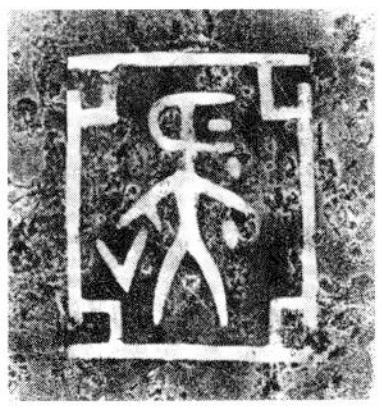

16

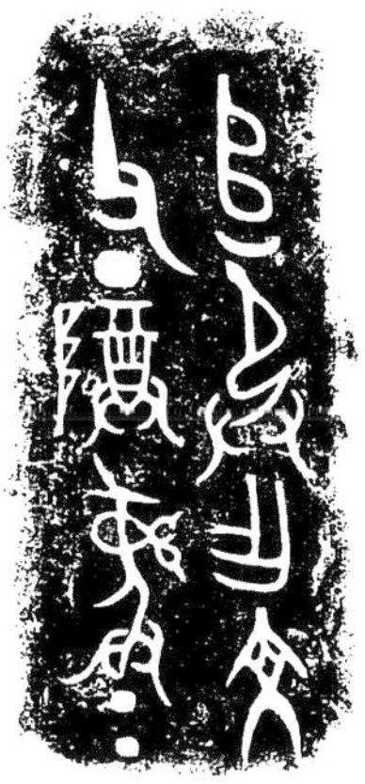

12

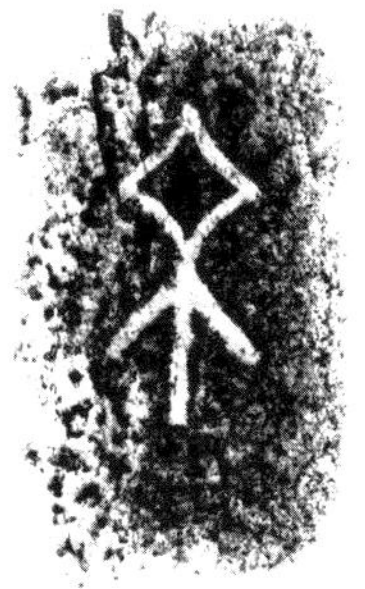

18

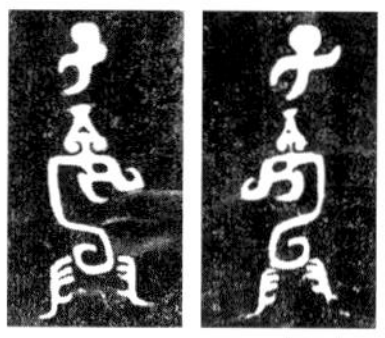

22–23

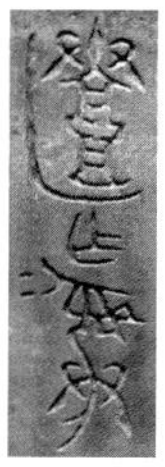

24

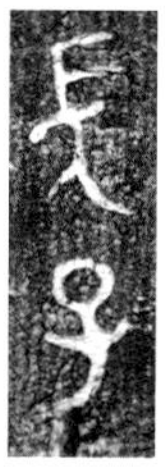

25

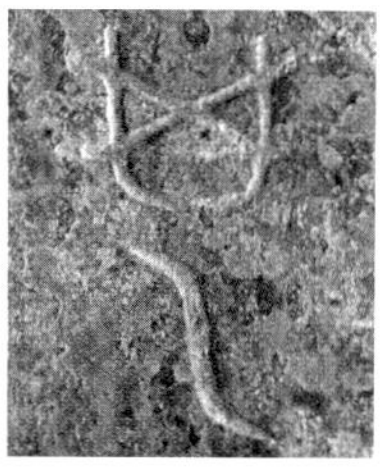

26

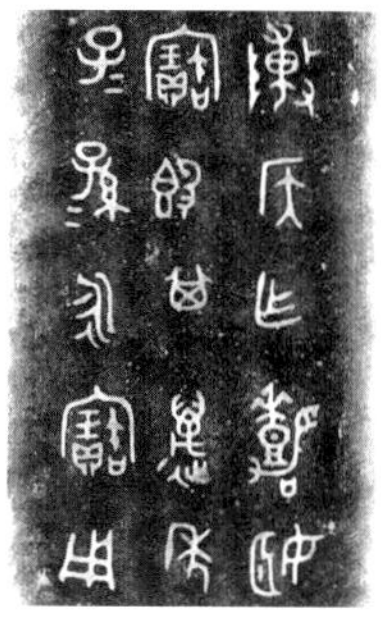

27

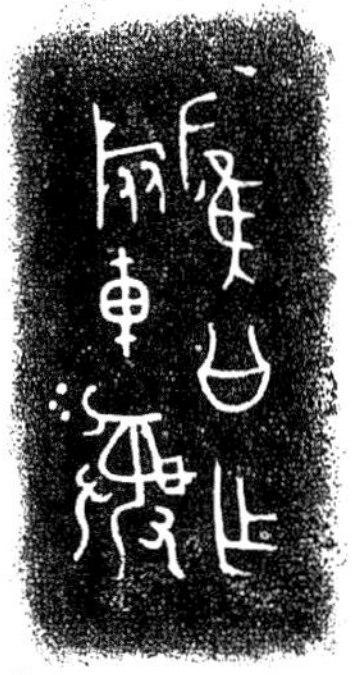

28

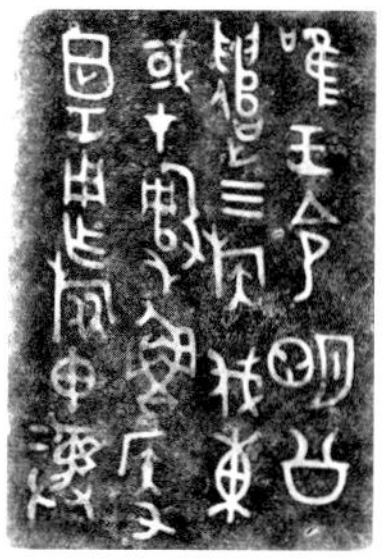

29

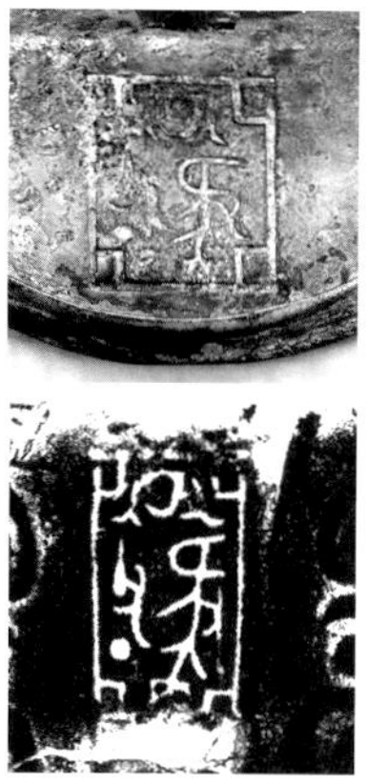

30 (top: lid, bottom: body)

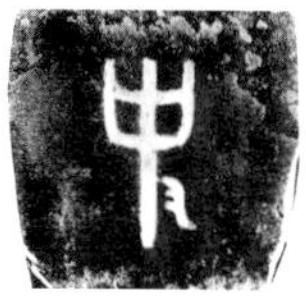

32

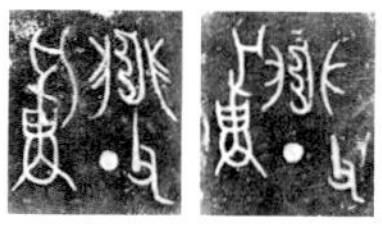

33

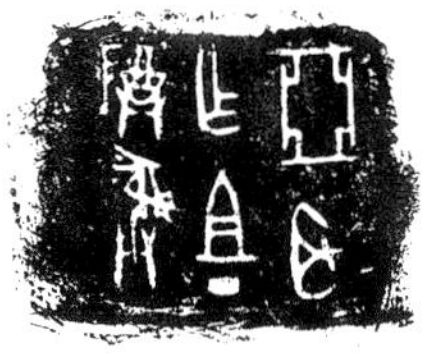

34

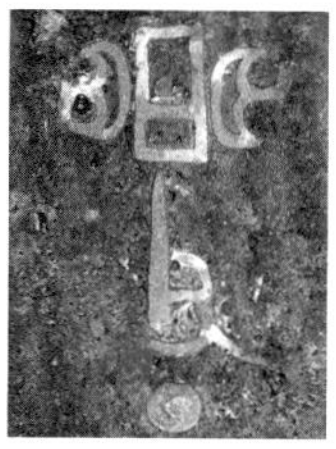

36

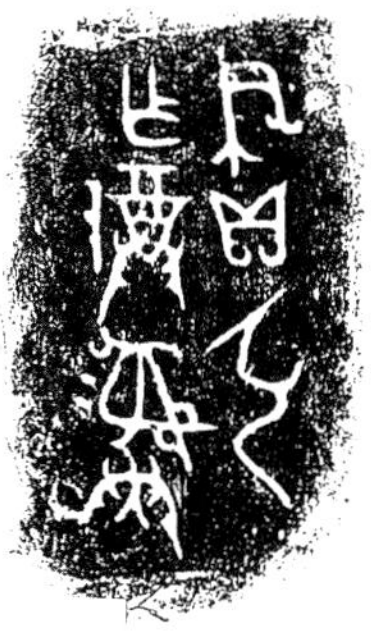

37

20 | BIPARTITE HEMISPHERICAL BOWL (*DUI*)

Warring States period (475–221 BC). Bronze with turquoise inlay; h. with handles 28.1 cm (11 in.), diam. without handles 16.5 cm (6 1/2 in.). The Shanghai Museum, 8758.

21 | JAR (*HU* OR *ZHONG*)

Western Han dynasty (206 BC–AD 9). Bronze with gilding; h. 46 (18 1/8 in.), max. diam. 36 cm (14 13/16 in.). The Art Institute of Chicago, Lucy Maud Buckingham Collection, 1927.315.

22–23 | PAIR OF TRIPOD CAULDRONS OF PRINCE GONG (*ZI GONG DING*)

Late Shang dynasty (c. 1250–1046 BC). Bronze; 22 (left): h. 16.5 cm (6 1/2 in.); 23 (right): h. 16.3 cm (6 7/16 in.). MacLean Collection.

24 | TRIPOD CAULDRON (*DING*)

Western Zhou dynasty (1046–771 BC). h. 29.9 cm (11 3/4 in.), diam. 25.5 cm (10 in.). Anonymous loan.

25 | SMALL TRIPOD CAULDRON OF CHANG ZI (*CHANG ZI DING*)

Western Zhou dynasty (1046–771 BC). Bronze; h. 7.4 cm (2 15/16 in.), diam. 12.6 cm (5 in.). The Art Institute of Chicago, Dr. Edith B. Farnsworth Collection, 1963.17.

26 | TUREEN (*GUI*)

Late Shang dynasty (c. 1250–1046 BC). Bronze; 12 × 22.5 cm (4 3/4 × 8 7/8 in.), diam. without handles 16.8 cm (6 5/8 in.). Anonymous loan.

27 | TUREEN OF MARQUIS CHEN (*CHEN HOU GUI*)

Western Zhou dynasty (1046–771 BC). Bronze; h. 12.4 cm (4 7/8 in), diam. without handles 20 cm (7 7/8 in). The Shanghai Museum, 23256. Qing imperial collection, XJ: 6.24; Wu Dacheng (1835–1902), JJ: 57.

28 | TUREEN OF LORD YING (*YING GONG GUI*)

Western Zhou dynasty (1046–771 BC). Bronze; w. with handles 23.5 cm (9 1/4 in.), w. of mouth 17.4 cm (6 7/8 in.), d. of mouth 18 cm (7 1/16 in.). The Palace Museum, Beijing, GU76926. Qing imperial collection, XQ: 13.19.

29 | PEDESTALED CONTAINER OF MARQUIS LU (*LU HOU ZUN*)

Western Zhou dynasty (1046–771 BC). Bronze; h. 22.2 cm (8 3/4 in.), diam. of mouth 20.7 cm (8 1/8 in.). The Shanghai Museum, 41562. Qing imperial collection, XQ: 13.8.

30 | GOBLET OF FATHER DING (*FU DING JUE* [OR *JIAO*])

Western Zhou dynasty (1046–771 BC). Bronze; goblet with lid: 24.7 × 17.6 × 11 cm (9 3/4 × 6 15/16 × 4 3/16 in.); lid: 6.7 × 16.8 × 8.7 cm (2 5/8 × 6 5/8 × 3 7/16 in.). Xiling Collection. Pan Shicheng (1804–1873), YQ: 1.26 (inscription only).

31 | GOBLET (*JIA*)

Late Shang dynasty (c. 1250–1046 BC). Bronze; h. 51.5 (20 1/4 in.), max. diam. 27.9 cm (11 in.), diam. of mouth 23.5 cm (9 1/4 in.). The Art Institute of Chicago, Lucy Maud Buckingham Collection, 1926.1599. Qing imperial collection, XQ: 23.11.

32 | CUP OF SHI (*SHI ZHI*)

Late Shang dynasty (c. 1250–1046 BC). Bronze; h. 13.9 cm (5 1/2 in), diam. of mouth: 7.4 cm (2 15/16 in). The Shanghai Museum, 43775. Qing imperial collection, XQ: 26.16.

33 | BUCKET OF FATHER DING (*FU DING YOU*)

Late Shang dynasty (c. 1250–1046 BC). Bronze; h. 32.2 cm (12 11/16 in.), w. of mouth 10.8 (4 1/4 in.), d. of mouth 14.3 cm (5 5/8 in.). The Shanghai Museum, 47054. Qing imperial collection, XQ: 15.2.

34 | BEAKER OF ER (*ER ZUN*)

Late Shang dynasty (c. 1250–1046 BC). Bronze; h. 23 cm (9 in.), diam. of mouth: 18.4 cm (7 1/4 in.). Private collection. Ye Zhishen (1779–1863), ZY: 17.16.1 (inscription only); Pan Zuyin (1830–1890), XJJ: 7.32.3 (inscription only).

35 | PITCHER (*GONG*)

Late Shang dynasty (c. 1250–1046 BC). Bronze; l. 20.3 cm (8 in.). Private collection. Qing imperial collection; XQ: 32.22.

36 | PITCHER OF FATHER DING (*FU DING GONG*)

Late Shang dynasty (c. 1250–1046 BC). Bronze; 18.7 × 24 × 12 cm (7 3/8 × 9 1/2 × 4 3/4 in.). Anonymous loan.

37 | PITCHER OF JIN YIN (*JIN YIN GONG*) AND LADLE

Western Zhou dynasty (1046–771 BC). Bronze; pitcher: 25.4 × 24.6 × 8.4 cm (10 × 9 11/16 × 3 5/16 in.); ladle: 21.7 × 4.4 cm (8 9/16 × 1 3/4 in.), diam. of bowl 3.2 cm (1 1/4 in.). The Shanghai Museum, 8242. Duanfang (1861–1911); TZ: 3.35.

38 | BIRD-SHAPED CONTAINER (*ZUN*)

Late Shang dynasty (c. 1250–1046 BC). Bronze; 15.9 × 13.3 × 5.7 cm (6 1/4 × 5 1/4 × 2 1/4 in.). The Art Institute of Chicago, Lucy Maud Buckingham Collection, 1936.139.

39 | OX-SHAPED CONTAINER (ZUN)

Shang dynasty (c. 1600–1046 BC). Bronze; l. 31.7 cm (12 1/2 in.). Private collection.

40 | RAM-SHAPED CONTAINER (*ZUN*)

Late Shang dynasty (c. 1250–1046 BC). Bronze; l. 22 cm (8 5/8 in.). Private collection.

41 | SQUARE CONTAINER OF OFFICER CHOU (*YA CHOU FANGLEI*)

Late Shang dynasty (c. 1250–1046 BC). Bronze; h. 62 cm (24 7/16 in.), max. w. 37.6 cm (14 13/16 in.), w. of mouth 16.9 cm (6 5/8 in.), d. of mouth 15.5 cm (6 1/8 in.). The Palace Museum, Beijing, GU77483. Qing imperial collection, GG: 81 (A very similar fanglei is illustrated in XQ: 10.5, but its description suggests it is more likely a late copy.)

42 | CONTAINER OF OFFICER CHOU (*YA CHOU LEI*)

Late Shang dynasty (c. 1250–1046 BC). Bronze; h. with lid 36.5 cm (14 5/16 in.), diam. of mouth 11.3 cm (4 7/16 in.). Lent by the Minneapolis Institute of Art, bequest of Alfred F. Pillsbury, 50.46.3a,b. Qing imperial collection, XQ: 12.6.

43 | SQUARE CONTAINER OF OFFICER RUO GUI (*YA RUO GUI FANGYI*)

Late Shang dynasty (c. 1250–1046 BC). Bronze; 29.2 × 19.1 cm (11 1/2 × 7 1/2 in.), max. diam. 15.6 cm (6 1/8 in.). Asian Art Museum, San Francisco, The Avery Brundage Collection, B60B767. Pan Zuyin (1830–1890), KZ: 13.3.1, 13.4.2 (inscription only).

44 | SQUARE CONTAINER OF OFFICER RUO GUI (*YA RUO GUI FANGYI*)

Late Shang dynasty (c. 1250–1046 BC). Bronze; 28.5 × 18 × 15.3 cm (11 1/4 × 7 × 6 in.). Anonymous loan. Qing imperial collection, XQ: 13.4.

45 | CONTAINER OF BO (*BO YU*)

Western Zhou dynasty (1046–771 BC). Bronze; h. 39.5 cm (15 9/16 in.), w. with handles 58 cm (22 13/16 in.), diam. of mouth 54 cm (21 1/4 in.). The Palace Museum, Beijing, GU77493. Qing imperial collection; XJ: 16.1.

46 | BASIN OF CONSORT YING OF QI (*QI YING JI PAN*)

Spring and Autumn period (770–476 BC). Bronze; h. 15 cm (5 15/16 in.), max. w. 55.5 cm (21 7/8 in.), w. of mouth 49.7 cm (19 9/16 in.), d. of mouth 50.2 cm (19 3/4 in.). The Palace Museum, Beijing, GU77492. Qing imperial collection; XQ: 32.37.

47 | EWER OF MARQUIS QI (*QI HOU YI*)

Western Zhou dynasty (1046–771 BC). Bronze; 24.7 × 48.1 cm (9 3/4 × 18 15/16 in.), The Shanghai Museum, 3924. Wu Yun (1811–1883); LL: 7.22.

48 | AXE (*YUE*)

Late Shang dynasty (c. 1250–1046 BC). Bronze with turquoise inlay; l. 19.6 cm (7 3/4 in.). Private collection.

49 | DAGGER-AXE (*GE*)

Late Shang dynasty (c. 1250–1046 BC). Bronze; 26.4 × 7.4 × 0.8 cm (10 3/8 × 2 15/16 × 5/16 in.). The Art Institute of Chicago, Samuel M. Nickerson Endowment, 1949.41.

50 | DAGGER-AXE (*GE*)

Warring States period (475–221 BC). Bronze inlaid with silver; 13 × 20 × 2 cm (5 1/8 × 7 7/8 × 3/4 in.). The Art Institute of Chicago, Gift of Russell Tyson, 1950.1627.

51 | JAR (*HU*)

Warring States period (475–221 BC). Bronze inlaid with copper; h. 44.7 (17 5/8 in.), max. diam. 30.6 cm (12 in.), diam. of mouth 12.4 cm (4 7/8 in.). The Art Institute of Chicago, Lucy Maud Buckingham Collection, 1928.143.

52 | JAR (*HU*)

Jar: Han dynasty (206 BC–AD 220); decoration: 20th century. Bronze with incised gilt decoration; h. 32.4 (13 1/16 in.), max. diam. 26.4 cm (10 7/8 in.), diam. of mouth 10.8 cm (4 1/4 in.). The Art Institute of Chicago, Lucy Maud Buckingham Collection, 1931.10.

53 | BIPARTITE HEMISPHERICAL BOWL (*DUI*)

Spring and Autumn period (770–476 BC). Bronze; h. 16.2 cm (6 3/8 in.), max. diam. 12.1 cm (4 3/4 in.). Private collection.

54 | CYLINDRICAL CONTAINER

Western Han dynasty (206 BC–AD 9). Bronze; h. 10.9 cm (4 5/16 in.), diam. 4.3 cm (1 3/4 in.). Anonymous loan.

55 | WEIGHT (*QUAN*)

Qin dynasty (221–206 BC). Bronze; h. 10.9 cm (4 5/16 in.), max. diam 15.2 cm (6 in.). The Shanghai Museum, 188050. For inscription, see pl. 55 on p. 83.

56 | BO BELL OF GREAT SPLENDOR (*DASHENG BOZHONG*)

Northern Song dynasty (960–1127). Bronze; 15 × 18 × 27.6 cm (5 15/16 × 7 1/16 ×10 7/8 in.). The Palace Museum, Beijing, XIN134359. Qing imperial collection, XQ: 26.1.

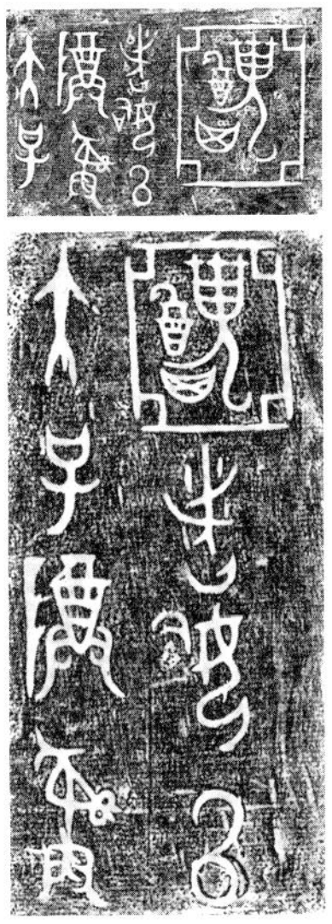

41

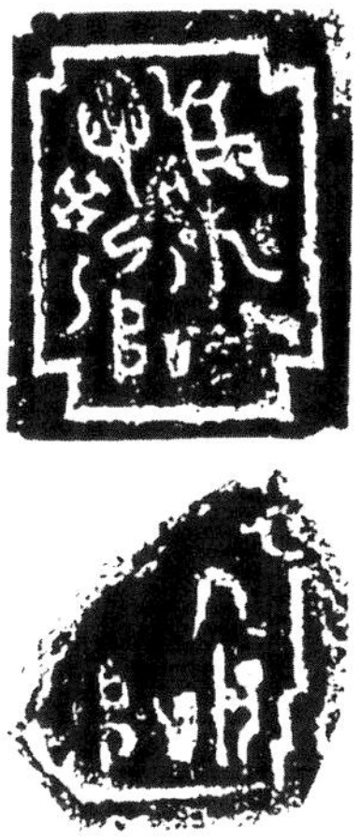

44

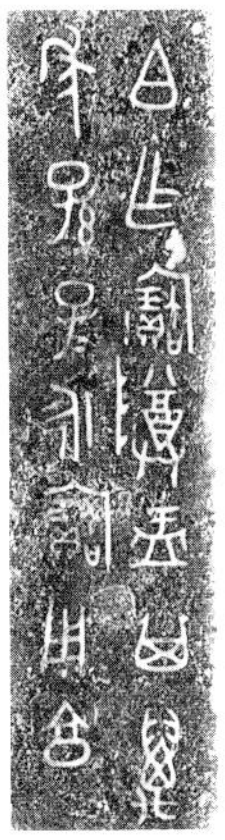

45

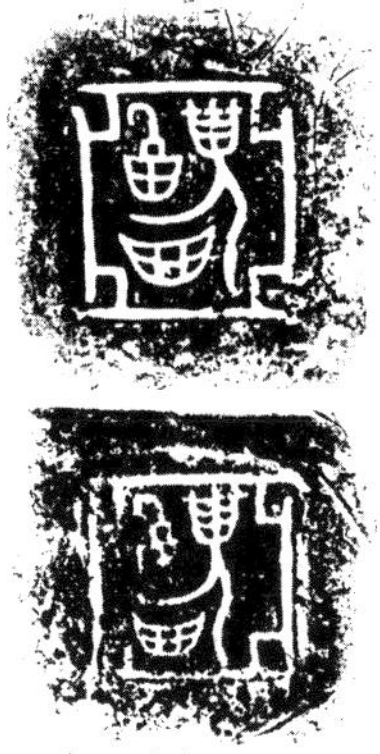

42 (top: lid, bottom: body)

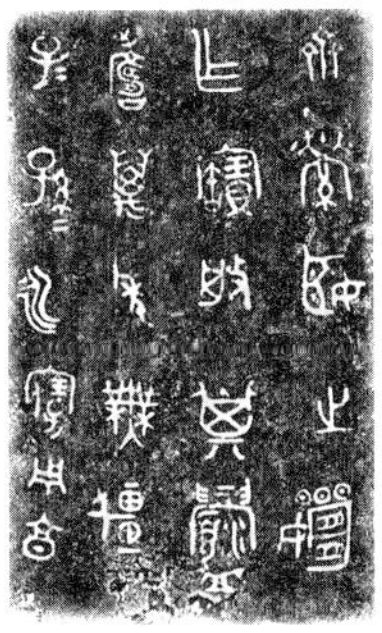

46

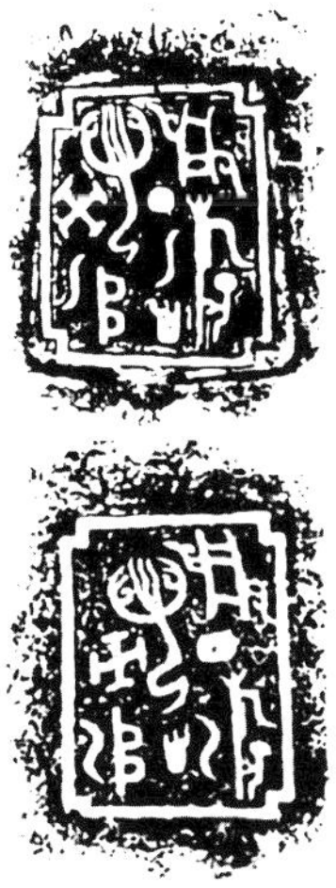

43 (top: lid, bottom: body)

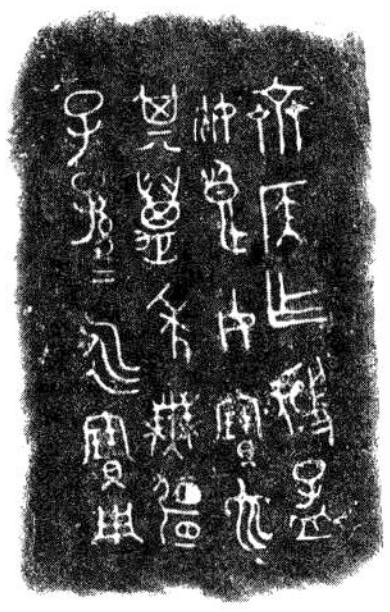

47

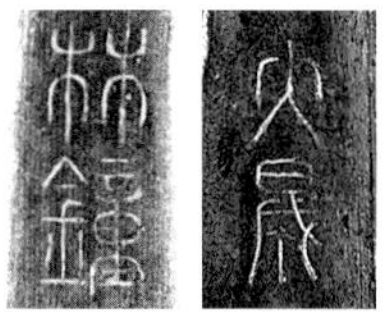

56 (left: lid, right: body)

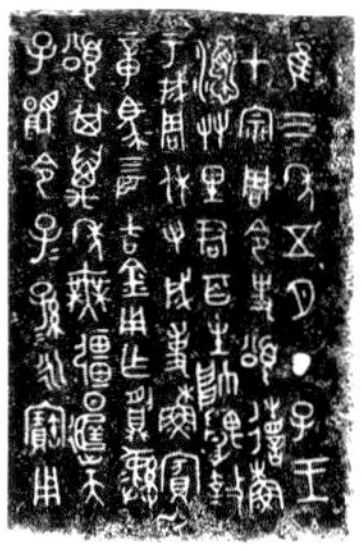

60

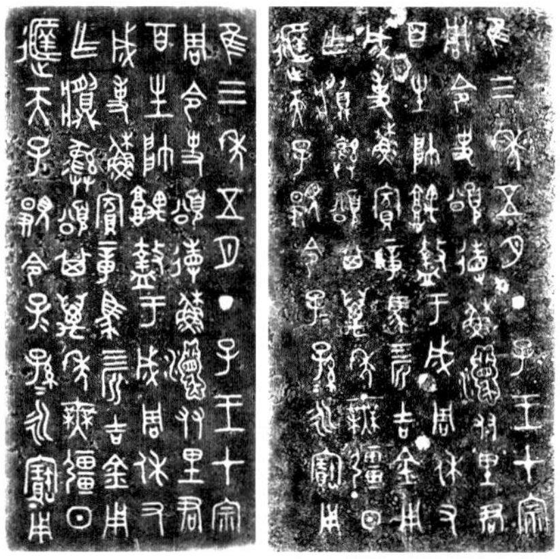

61 (left: lid, right: body)

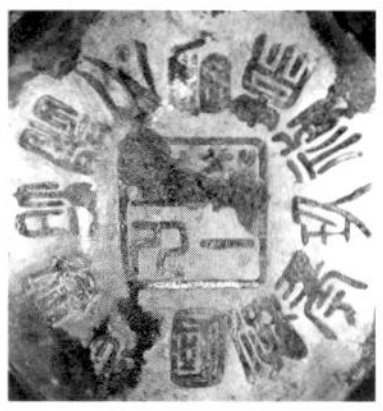

62

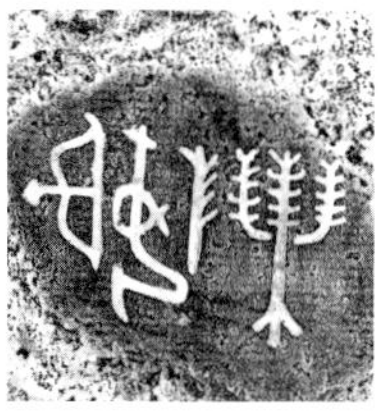

63

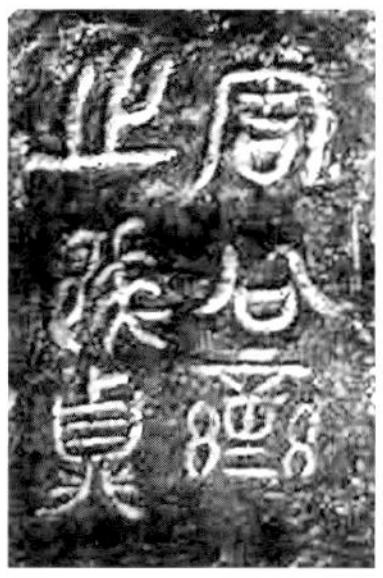

64

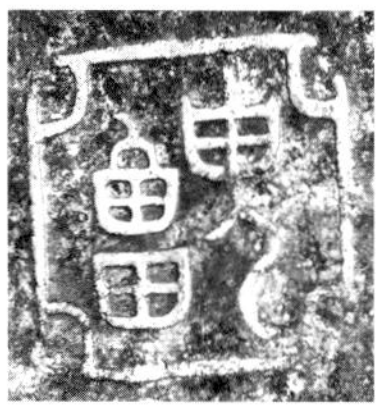

66

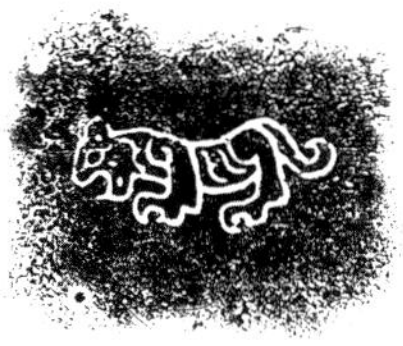

67

57 | BELL (*NAO*)

Zhou period (c. 10th–7th century BC). Bronze; h. 41.7 cm (16 1/2 in.), diam. 28.9 cm (11 3/8 in.). The Art Institute of Chicago, Lucy Maud Buckingham Collection, 1924.243. Possibly Song imperial collection, BG: 23.14.

58 | RECTANGULAR CAULDRON OF HOU CHUO (*HOU CHUO FANGDING*)

Western Zhou dynasty (1046–771 BC). Bronze; 21.3 × 17.4 × 13.3 cm (8 3/8 × 6 7/8 × 5 1/4 in.). The Shanghai Museum, 41544. Yao Yifu (12th century?), XK: 4.226–7 (inscription only); Chen Jieqi, FZ: ding.3 (inscription only). For inscription, see fig. 86 on p. 96.

59 | TRIPOD CAULDRON OF SONG (*SONG DING*)

Western Zhou period (1046–771 BC). Bronze; h. 38.4 cm (15 1/8 in.), diam. 30.3 cm (11 15/16 in.). The Palace Museum, Beijing, GU77390. Qing imperial collection; XJ: 1.31. For inscription, see fig. 2b on p. 102.

60 | TRIPOD CAULDRON OF SCRIBE SONG (*SHI SONG DING*)

Western Zhou dynasty (1046–771 BC). Bronze; h. with handles 29.4 cm (11 9/16 in.), diam. 28.7 cm (11 5/16 in.). The Shanghai Museum, 41558. Qing imperial collection, XQ: 3.21.

61 | TUREEN OF SCRIBE SONG (*SHI SONG GUI*)

Western Zhou dynasty (1046–771 BC). Bronze; h. 26.9 cm (10 9/16 in.), diam. of mouth: 22.7 cm (8 15/16 in.). The Shanghai Museum, 45688. Wu Dacheng, KZ: 15-6 (inscription only), KT: 73.

62 | CAULDRON MADE IN THE NINTH YEAR OF EMPEROR CHONGZHEN'S REIGN IN THE STATE OF LU (*CHONGZHEN JIUNIAN DING*)

Ming dynasty (1368–1644), Chongzhen reign (1628–44), 1636. Bronze; h. 21 cm (8 1/4 in.), max. w. 15 cm (5 15/16 in.), diam. of mouth 11.7 cm (4 5/8 in.). The Palace Museum, Beijing, GU77952. Qing imperial collection, NS: 1.46 (did not give the inscription).

63 | TRIPOD CAULDRON OF SHE NÜ (*SHE NÜ DING*)

Late Shang dynasty (c. 1250–1046 BC). Bronze; h. with handles 25.1 cm (9 7/8 in.), diam. of mouth 20.7 cm (8 1/8 in.). The Shanghai Museum, 43774. (An identical *ding* is illustrated in XQ: 3.13; it is now in the National Palace Museum Taipei, GS: 14).

64 | STEAMER (*YAN*)

Ming dynasty (1368–1644). Bronze; h. with handles 37.8 cm (14 7/8 in.), max. w. 22.9 cm (9 in.), diam. of mouth 21.6 cm (8 1/2 in.). The Palace Museum, Beijing, GU77911. Qing imperial collection, XJ: 13.21.

65 | STEAMER (*YAN*)

Late Shang dynasty (c. 1250–1046 BC). Bronze; 80.9 × 44.9 cm (31 7/8 × 17 11/16 in.). The Palace Museum, Beijing, GU76893. Qing imperial collection, XJ: 13.42.

66 | TUREEN WITH SQUARE PEDESTAL (*GUI*)

Song dynasty (960–1279). Bronze; h. 35 cm (13 3/4 in.), w. with handles 46 cm (18 1/8 in.), diam. 31.5 cm (12 3/8 in.). The Palace Museum, Beijing, GU78082.

67 | PEDESTALED TUREEN OF HU (*HU GUI*)

Western Zhou dynasty (1046–771 BC). Bronze; h. 34.7 cm (13 11/16 in), diam. of mouth 23.3 cm (9 3/16 in). The Shanghai Museum, 7234. The cover was once in Wu Dacheng's collection, KZ: 7.12 (inscription only).

68 | MINIATURE BOTTLE IN THE FORM OF AN ANCIENT BRONZE JAR (*HU*)

Ming dynasty (1368–1644). Rhinoceros horn; 13.3 × 4.2 × 4.7 cm (5 1/4 × 1 5/8 × 1 13/16 in.). The Art Institute of Chicago, gift of Homer E. Sargent, 1942.236. The prototype for this bottle is probably an illustration in *Bogutu*, BG: 7.12.

69 | GOURD-SHAPED JAR (*HU*)

Spring and Autumn period (770–476 BC). Bronze; h. 28.5 cm (11 1/4 in.), diam. of mouth 5.6 cm (2 3/16 in.). The Shanghai Museum, 18248.

70 | TAPIR-SHAPED CONTAINER (*XI ZUN*)

Song dynasty (960–1279) or Ming dynasty (1368–1644). Bronze inlaid with gold, silver, and turquoise; 24.5 × 35.2 × 11.7 cm (9 5/8 × 13 7/8 × 4 5/8 in.). Anonymous loan. Possibly Qing imperial collection, XQ: 9.33.

71 | TAPIR-SHAPED CONTAINER (*XI ZUN*)

Warring States period (475–221 BC). Bronze inlaid with gold, silver and turquoise; 26.7 × 16.5 × 41.9 cm (10 1/2 × 6 1/2 × 16 1/2 in.). Private collection.

72 | GOBLET (*JUE*)

Ming dynasty (1368–1644), Tianshun reign (1457–1464), 1464. Bronze; 20.5 × 19.1 × 8.4 cm (8 1/16 × 7 1/2 × 3 5/16 in.). The Art Institute of Chicago, gift of Mrs. H. R. Warner, 1933.1670. For inscription, see pl. 72 on p. 120.

73 | CENSER IN THE FORM OF AN ANCIENT BRONZE TUREEN (*GUI*)

Ming dynasty (1368–1644). Cloisonné; h. 10 cm (3 15/16 in.), w. with handles 20.3 cm (8 in.), max. diam. 14.6 cm (5 3/4 in.). Private collection.

74 | BEAKER IN THE FORM OF AN ANCIENT BRONZE CONTAINER (*ZUN*)

Ming dynasty (1368–1644). Cloisonné; h. 18.4 cm (7 1/4 in.), max. diam. 14.3 cm (5 5/8 in.). Private collection.

75 | CENSER IN THE FORM OF AN ANCIENT BRONZE TRIPOD CAULDRON (*DING*)

Qing dynasty (1644–1911). Porcelain; h. 25.1 (9 7/8 in.), diam. 15.9 cm (6 1/4 in.). The Art Institute of Chicago, bequest of Henry C. Schwab, 1941.531.

76 | CENSER IN THE FORM OF AN ANCIENT BRONZE TUREEN (*GUI*)

Qing dynasty (1644–1911). Porcelain; 8.4 × 20.4 × 16.1 cm (3 15/16 × 8 × 6 5/16 in.). The Art Institute of Chicago, Lucy Maud Buckingham Collection, 1924.391.

77 | BEAKER IN THE FORM OF AN ANCIENT BRONZE CONTAINER (*ZUN*)

Qing dynasty (1644–1911). Porcelain; h. 20.5 (8 1/16 in.), diam. 14.7 cm (5 13/16 in.). The Art Institute of Chicago, Lucy Maud Buckingham Collection, 1924.340.

78 | CENSER IN THE FORM OF AN ANCIENT BRONZE RECTANGULAR CAULDRON (*FANGDING*)

Qing dynasty (1644–1911). Dehua ware; 11.4 × 9.8 × 7.4 cm (4 1/2 × 3 7/8 × 2 15/16 in.). The Art Institute of Chicago, Lucy Maud Buckingham Collection, 1925.1482.

79–83 | DISHES INLAID WITH IMAGES OF ANCIENT BRONZES

Qing dynasty (1644–1911). Lacquer with inlay; each: 12.7 × 13.6 × 1.1 cm (5 × 5 3/8 × 7/16 in.). The Art Institute of Chicago, Gift of Mr. & Mrs. Philip Pinsof, 1961.60.1, 1961.60.3–6.

84–90 | MINIATURE VESSELS

Ming dynasty (1368–1644) or Qing dynasty (1644–1911). The Art Institute of Chicago, Lucy Maud Buckingham Collection, 1927.334–40.

84 | MINIATURE TUREEN (*GUI*)

Bronze with silver inlay; 3.9 × 5.3 × 3.3 cm (1 9/16 × 2 1/8 × 1 5/16 in.); lid: 2.1 × 3.1 × 2.6 cm (7/8 × 1 1/4 × 1 1/16 in.). 1927.334.

85 | MINIATURE BEAKER (*ZUN*)

Bronze with silver and copper inlay; h. 7.1 (2 13/16 in.), diam. 7 cm (1 7/8 in.). 1927.335.

86 | MINIATURE TUREEN (*GUI*)

Bronze with silver inlay; with lid: 6.7 × 6.1 × 3.5 cm (2 5/8 × 2 7/16 × 1 3/8 in.); lid: 2.7 × 3.8 × 3.1 cm (1 1/16 × 1 1/2 × 1 1/4 in.). 1927.336.

87 | MINIATURE BUCKET (*YOU*)

Bronze with silver inlay; with handle and lid: 7.7 × 4 × 3.8 cm (3 × 1 9/16 × 1 1/2 in.); lid: 1.8 × 2.4 × 2.2 cm (11/16 × 1 × 7/8 in.). 1927.337.

88 | MINIATURE BUCKET (*YOU*)

Bronze with silver inlay; with handles and lid: 9 × 5.9 × 4.4 cm (3 1/2 × 2 5/16 × 1 11/16 in.); lid: 2.4 × 3.5 × 2.4 cm (1 × 1 3/8 × 1 in.). 1927.338.

89 | MINIATURE TUREEN (*GUI*)

Bronze with gold and silver inlay; tureen, with handles and lid: 6 × 6.1 × 5 cm (2 3/8 × 2 3/8 × 2 in.); lid: 2.1 × 4.4 × 3.7 cm (13/16 × 1 11/16 × 1 7/16 in.). 1927.339.

90 | MINIATURE JAR (*HU*)

Bronze with silver inlay; 8.1 × 6 × 4.6 cm (3 3/16 × 2 3/8 × 1 13/16 in.). 1927.340.

91 | Feng Shu (Chinese, 1867–1948). BOOK OF RUBBINGS OF BRONZE INSCRIPTIONS ON INK STONES

1930. Bound volume of rubbings on paper; 41.5 × 32.5 cm (16 5/16 × 12 13/16 in.). Private collection.

92 | TABLE IN THE FORM OF AN ANCIENT BRONZE VESSEL

Qing dynasty (1644–1911). Wood; 85.7 × 161.6 × 49.5 cm (33 3/4 × 63 5/8 × 19 1/2 in.). Mr. and Mrs. Thomas J. Pritzker Collection.

93 | BRONZE MIRRORS WITH BOX, VOLUME ONE OF *ANCIENT MIRROR OF WESTERN CLARITY* (*XIQING GUJIAN*)

Mirrors: Han dynasty (206 BC–AD 220); box and paintings: Qing dynasty (1644–1911), Qianlong reign (1735–96). Mirrors: bronze; mirror on top: diam. 13 cm (5 1/8 in.); mirror on bottom: diam. 14 cm (5 1/2 in.). Box: wood, ink and color on paper, and silk; 44.9 × 32 × 6 cm (17 11/16 × 12 5/8 × 2 3/8 in.); The Palace Museum, Beijing, GU78252, GU78253.

94 | BRONZE MIRRORS WITH BOX, VOLUME EIGHT OF *ANCIENT MIRROR OF WESTERN CLARITY* (*XIQING GUJIAN*)

Mirror on top: Han dynasty (106 BC–AD 220); mirror on bottom: Tang dynasty (618–907); box and paintings: Qing dynasty (1644–1911), Qianlong reign (1735–96). Mirrors: bronze; mirror on top: diam. 12 cm (4 3/4 in.); mirror on bottom: diam. 22 cm (8 11/16 in.) Box: wood, ink and color on paper, and silk; 44.8 × 32 × 5.7 cm (17 5/8 × 12 5/8 × 2 1/4 in.). The Palace Museum, Beijing, GU78282, GU78561.

95 | BRONZE MIRRORS WITH BOX, VOLUME FORTY-TWO OF *ANCIENT MIRROR OF WESTERN CLARITY* (*XIQING GUJIAN*)

Mirror on top: Han dynasty (206 BC–AD 220); mirror on bottom: Tang dynasty (618–907); box and paintings: Qing dynasty, Qianlong reign (1735–96); Mirrors: bronze; mirror on top: diam. 11.3 cm (4 7/16 in.); mirror on bottom: diam. 15.7 cm (6 3/16 in.). Box: wood, ink and color on paper, and silk; 44.6 × 32.1 × 6.8 cm (17 9/16 × 12 5/8 × 2 11/16 in.). The Palace Museum, Beijing, GU78258, GU78281.

96 | SCREEN INLAID WITH BRONZE MIRROR

Mirror: Han dynasty (206 BC–AD 220); screen: Qing dynasty, Qianlong reign (1735–96), 1776. Mirror: bronze. Screen: wood; 92 × 69.5 cm (36 1/4 × 27 3/8 in.). The Palace Museum, Beijing, GU209652.

97 | Artist unknown. "COURT LADY LOOKING IN A MIRROR," FROM "TWELVE BEAUTIES"

Qing dynasty (1644–1911), late Kangxi reign (1709–22). Screen painting, remounted as a hanging scroll, ink and color on silk; 184 × 98.3 cm (72 7/16 × 38 11/16 in.). The Palace Museum, Beijing, GU6458-5/12.

98 | Liang Shizheng (Chinese, 1697–1763) and others. *ANCIENT MIRROR OF WESTERN CLARITY* (*XIQING GUJIAN*), *Wuyingdian* edition

Qing dynasty (1644–1911), Qianlong reign (1735–96). Book; 41.5 cm × 27.8 × 6.5 cm (16 5/16 × 10 15/16 × 2 9/16 in.). The Palace Museum, Beijing, Shu 00000723-1-6, 12-17, 23-32/42, Dian 17729-17734.

99 | STEMMED BOWL (*DOU*)

Eastern Zhou period (770–221 BC). Bronze; h. 21.4 cm (8 7/16 in.), diam. of mouth 18.5 cm (7 1/4 in.). The Palace Museum, Beijing, GU77557. Qing imperial collection, XQ: 29.26.

100 | VESSEL IN THE FORM OF AN ANCIENT BRONZE STEMMED BOWL (*DOU*)

Qing dynasty (1644–1911), Qianlong reign (1735–96). Nephrite jade; h. 20.9 cm (8 1/4 in.), diam. of mouth 15.5 cm (6 1/8 in.). The Palace Museum, Beijing, GU00103488.

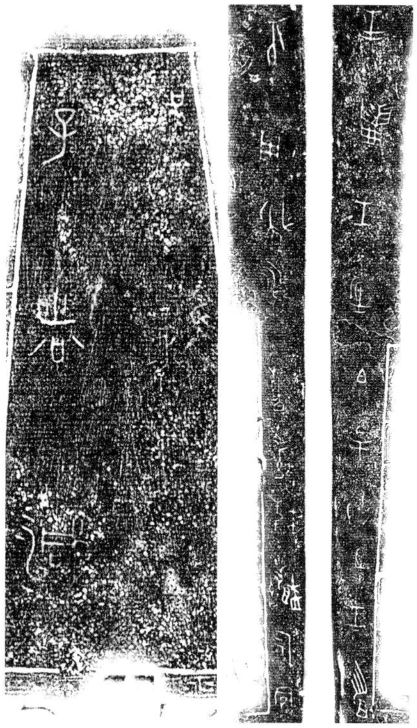

105

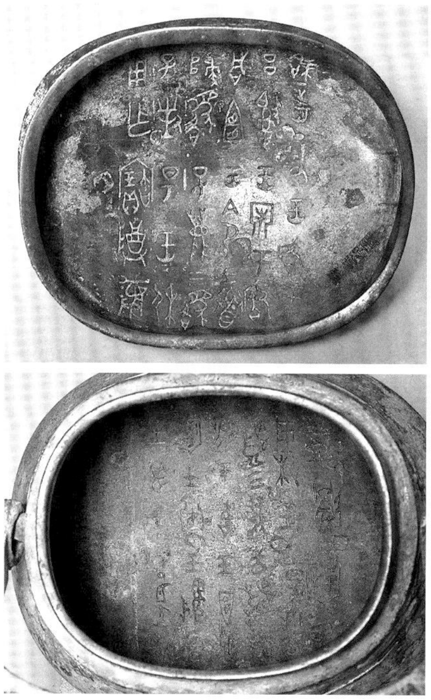

108 (top: lid, bottom: body)

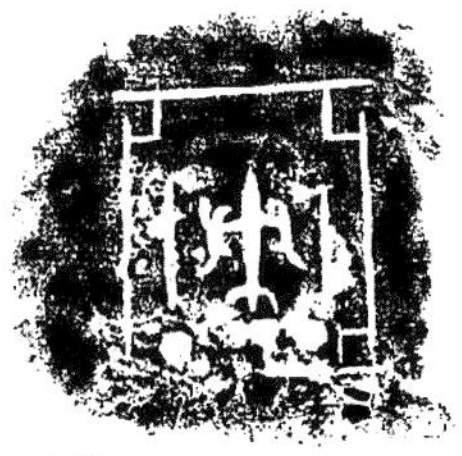

109

101 | EWER (*HE*)

Warring States period (475–221 BC). Bronze; 23.1 × 19.2 cm (9 1/16 × 7 9/16 in.). The Palace Museum, Beijing, GU78133. Qing imperial collection, XQ: 31.59.

102 | VESSEL IN THE FORM OF AN ANCIENT BRONZE EWER (*HE*)

Ming dynasty (1368–1644) or Qing dynasty (1644–1911). Bronze with inlays; 21.5 x 24 cm (8 7/16 × 9 7/16 in.). The Palace Museum, Beijing, GU78033.

103 | FLASK (*BIANHU*)

Warring States period (475–221 BC). Bronze inlaid with copper; 36.3 × 34.0 × 11 cm (14 5/16 × 13 3/8 × 4 5/16 in.). The Art Institute of Chicago, Lucy Maud Buckingham Collection, 1937.1.

104 | VESSEL IN THE FORM OF AN ANCIENT BRONZE FLASK (*BIANHU*)

Qing dynasty (1644–1911), Qianlong reign (1735–96). Copper decorated with cloisonné enamel with gilding; 8.5 × 23.3 × 21.9 cm (3 3/8 × 9 3/16 × 8 5/8 in.). The Palace Museum, Beijing, GU116412.

105 | *BO* BELL OF ZHE JIAN (*ZHE JIAN ZHONG*)

Eastern Zhou dynasty, Spring and Autumn period (770–476 BC). Bronze; 20.6 × 15 × 38.2 cm (8 1/8 × 5 15/16 ×15 1/16 in.). The Palace Museum, Beijing, XIN141957. Possibly Qing imperial collection, XJ: 17.16.

106 | BELL IN THE FORM OF AN ANCIENT BRONZE *BO* BELL

Qing dynasty (1644–1911), Qianlong reign (1735–96), 1761. Gilt bronze; 84.2 × 45.7 × 36 cm (33 1/8 × 18 × 14 3/16 in.). The Palace Museum, Beijing, GU00169493.

107 | LATE COPY OF THE BUCKET OF HEZI (*HEZI YOU*)

Possibly 18th century. Bronze; 13.3 × 13 × 11.3 cm (5 1/4 × 5 1/8 × 4 7/16 in.). The Shanghai Museum, 35707. Qing imperial collection, XQ: 15.9; Pan Zuyin (1830–1890), ZY: 12.12. For inscription, see fig. 5 on p. 151.

108 | BUCKET OF HEZI (*HEZI YOU*)

Western Zhou dynasty (1046–771 BC). Bronze; 21.8 × 21.1 × 14.3 cm (8 9/16 × 8 5/16 × 5 5/8 in.). Lent by the Minneapolis Institute of Art, bequest of Alfred F. Pillsbury, 50.46.941b. Qing imperial collection, XQ: 15.11; Li Shangnong (died 1896), ZY: 12.11.

109 | GOBLET (*JUE*)

Probably Ming dynasty (1368–1644). Bronze; h. with lid 25.7 cm. (10 1/8 in.), w. at spout 11.4 cm (4 1/2 in.). Lent by The Metropolitan Museum of Art, New York, Rogers Fund, 1943, 43.24.1a, b. Qing imperial collection, XQ: 26.46; Duanfang, TZ: 2.12.

110 | GOBLET (*JUE OR JIAO*)

Goblet: late Shang dynasty (c. 1250–1046 BC), lid: early 20th century. Bronze; with lid and handle 17.8 × 10.2 × 25.4 cm (7 × 4 × 10 in.). Lent by The Metropolitan Museum of Art, New York, Rogers Fund, 1943, 43.27.1a, b.

111 | VESSEL IN THE FORM OF AN ANCIENT BRONZE FLASK (*BIANHU*)

Ming dynasty (1368–1644) or Qing dynasty (1644–1911). Nephrite jade; with lid: 17.7 × 14.2 × 4 cm (6 15/16 × 5 9/16 × 1 9/16 in.); lid: 4 × 4.7 × 2.9 cm (1 9/16 × 1 13/16 × 1 1/8 in.). The Art Institute of Chicago, bequest of Russell Tyson, 1964.603.

112 | VESSEL IN THE FORM OF AN ANCIENT BRONZE PITCHER (*GONG*)

Qing dynasty (1644–1911). Nephrite jade; with lid: 15.0 × 12.3 × 6.6 cm (5 15/16 × 4 13/16 × 2 9/16 in.); lid: 4 × 11.6 × 7.4 cm (1 9/16 × 4 9/16 × 2 7/8 in.). The Art Institute of Chicago, bequest of Grace Brown Palmer, 1967.86 a–b.

113 | LIDDED VESSEL IN THE FORM OF AN ANCIENT BRONZE CONTAINER (*LEI*)

Qing dynasty (1644–1911), Qianlong reign (1735–96). Nephrite jade; with lid 20 × 10.1 × 6.5 cm (7 7/8 × 4 × 2 9/16 in.). The Palace Museum, Beijing, GU98298.

114 | CENSER IN THE FORM OF AN ANCIENT BRONZE TRIPOD CAULDRON (*DING*)

Qing dynasty (1644–1911). Nephrite jade; with lid 15.3 × 22.7 × 16.3 cm (6 × 8 15/16 × 6 3/8 in.). The Art Institute of Chicago, gift of Mr. and Mrs. Samuel M. Nickerson, 1900.843.

115 | CENSER IN THE FORM OF AN ANCIENT BRONZE RECTANGULAR CAULDRON (*FANGDING*)

Qing dynasty (1644–1911). Nephrite jade; with lid: 26.4 × 13.4 × 11.8 cm (10 3/8 × 5 1/4 × 4 5/8 in.); lid: 7.3 × 12.9 × 10.4 cm (2 7/8 × 5 1/16 × 4 1/16 in.); stand: 6.2 × 13.4 × 11.8 cm (2 7/16 × 5 1/4 × 4 5/8 in.). The Art Institute of Chicago, gift of Mrs. Morris Vehon, 1976.157 a–c.

116 | VESSEL IN THE FORM OF AN ANCIENT BRONZE JAR (*HU*)

Qing dynasty (1644–1911), Qianlong reign (1735–96. Porcelain; 21.8 × 25 cm (8 9/16 × 9 13/16 in.). The Palace Museum, Beijing, GU154810.

117 | VESSEL IN THE FORM OF AN ANCIENT BRONZE GOBLET (*GU*)

Qing dynasty (1644–1911), Qianlong reign (1735–96). Porcelain; h. 26.5 cm (10 7/16 in.), diam. of mouth 17.5 cm (6 7/8 in.). The Palace Museum, Beijing, GU154498.

118 | BIRD-SHAPED VESSEL IN THE FORM OF AN ANCIENT BRONZE CONTAINER (*ZUN*)

Qing dynasty (1644–1911), Qianlong reign (1735–96). Porcelain; 11 × 23.5 × 28.5 cm (4 5/16 × 9 1/4 × 11 1/4 in.). The Palace Museum, Beijing, GU00152627.

119 | VESSEL IN THE FORM OF AN ANCIENT BRONZE JAR (*HU*)

Qing dynasty (1644–1911), Qianlong reign (1735–96). Porcelain; h. 19.1 cm (7 1/2 in.), max. diam. 14 cm (5 1/2 in.). Private collection.

120 | VESSEL IN THE FORM OF AN ANCIENT BRONZE JAR (*HU*)

Qing dynasty (1644–1911), Qianlong reign (1735–96). Porcelain; 19.3 × 13.6 × 13.1 cm (7 5/8 × 5 3/8 × 5 3/16 in.). The Art Institute of Chicago, Lucy Maud Buckingham Collection, 1924.393.

121 | BIPARTITE VESSEL IN THE FORM OF AN ANCIENT BRONZE RECTANGULAR TUREEN (*XU*)

Qing dynasty (1644–1911), Qianlong reign (1735–96). Porcelain; h. 23.5 cm (9 1/4 in.). The Palace Museum, Beijing, GU00186476.

122 | BIPARTITE VESSEL IN THE FORM OF AN ANCIENT BRONZE RECTANGULAR TUREEN (*XU*)

Qing dynasty (1644–1911), Qianlong reign (1735–96). Porcelain; 25.2 × 20.3 × 23 cm (9 15/16 × 8 × 9 1/16 in.). The Palace Museum, Beijing, GU00186467.

123 | BIPARTITE VESSEL IN THE FORM OF AN ANCIENT BRONZE RECTANGULAR TUREEN (*XU*)

Qing dynasty (1644–1911), Jiaqing reign (1796–1820). Porcelain; 24.7 × 28 × 22.5 cm (9 3/4 × 11 × 8 7/8 in.). The Palace Museum, GU00186482.

124 | VESSEL IN THE FORM OF THE WESTERN ZHOU BRONZE TUREEN OF BAN (*BAN GUI*)

Qing dynasty (1644–1911), Qianlong reign (1735–96). Porcelain; h. 24 cm (9 7/16 in.), w. with handles 40 cm (15 3/4 in.), max. diam. 33 cm (13 in.). The Palace Museum, Beijing, GU160983. The original bronze was recorded in XQ: 13. 12 (*Maobo yi*).

125 | VESSEL IN THE FORM OF AN ANCIENT BRONZE BEAKER (*GU*)

Qing dynasty (1644–1911), Qianlong reign (1735–96). Porcelain; vase: h. 31 cm (12 3/16 in.), diam. of mouth 21.3 cm (8 3/8 in.); stand: 4.5 × 14.1 × 14 cm (1 3/4 × 5 9/16 × 5 1/2 in.). Private collection.

126 | VESSEL IN THE FORM OF AN ANCIENT BRONZE JAR (*HU*)

Qing dynasty (1644–1911), Qianlong reign (1735–96). Porcelain; h. 19.7 (7 3/4 in.), max. diam. 15.6 cm (6 1/8 in.), diam. of mouth 7.9 cm (3 1/8 in.). The Art Institute of Chicago, gift of Mr. & Mrs. Frank Flick, 1980.636.

127 | VESSEL IN THE FORM OF AN ANCIENT BRONZE STEMMED BOWL (*DOU*)

Qing dynasty (1644–1911). Porcelain; h. 16.3 (6 7/16 in.), max. diam. 14.4 cm (5 11/16 in.), diam. of mouth 14 cm (5 1/2 in.). The Art Institute of Chicago, Mrs. Siegfried G. Schmidt, 1966.440.

128 | WHEELED BIRD-SHAPED VESSEL (*ZUN*)

Qing dynasty (1644–1911), Qianlong reign (1735–96). Bronze with gilding; 32.6 × 18.1 cm (12 13/16 × 7 1/8 in.); diam. of wheels (each) 14.3 cm (5 5/8 in.). The Palace Museum, Beijing, GU77692.

129 | WATERPOT (*SHUICHENG*)

Qing dynasty (1644–1911), Qianlong reign (1735–96). Cloisonné enamel; 12.1 × 21 × 8.3 cm (4 3/4 × 8 1/4 × 3 1/4 in.). Private collection.

130 | RECTANGULAR CENSER IN THE FORM OF AN ANCIENT BRONZE CAULDRON (*FANGDING*)

Qing dynasty (1644–1911), Qianlong reign (1735–96). Bronze with gilding; 14.5 × 11.8 × 8.4 cm (5 11/16 × 4 5/8 × 3 5/16 in.). The Palace Museum, Beijing, GU78008.

131 | OX-SHAPED CONTAINER (*ZUN*)

Qing dynasty (1644–1911), Qianlong reign (1735–96). Bronze with champlevé enamels; 22 × 8 × 19 cm (8 11/16 × 3 1/8 × 7 1/2 in.). The Palace Museum, Beijing, GU116863. This object imitates an object recorded as a "Tang dynasty stand" in XQ: 38.29.

132 | VESSEL IN THE FORM OF AN ANCIENT BRONZE JAR (*HU*)

Qing dynasty (1644–1911), Qianlong reign (1735–96). Cloisonné enamel; 45.7 × 23.5 × 19.1 cm (18 × 9 1/4 × 7 1/2 in.). Private collection.

133 | VESSEL IN THE FORM OF AN ANCIENT BRONZE BUCKET (*YOU*)

Qing dynasty (1644–1911). Bamboo root; 17 × 14 cm (6 11/16 × 5 1/2 in.). The Palace Museum, Beijing, GU121155.

134 | CENSER IN THE FORM OF AN ANCIENT BRONZE RECTANGULAR CAULDRON (*FANGDING*)

Qing dynasty (1644–1911). Lacquer; 24.2 × 12.2 × 9.5 cm (9 1/2 × 14 13/16 in. × 3 3/4 in.). The Palace Museum, Beijing, GU114964.

135 | BOX SET IN THE FORM OF AN ANCIENT BRONZE JAR (*HU*)

Qing dynasty (1644–1911). Lacquer; 35 × 11.5 × 7.5 cm (13 3/4 × 4 1/2 × 3 in.). The Palace Museum, Beijing, GU110778.

136 | Artist unknown. "COURT LADY APPRECIATING ANTIQUITIES," FROM "TWELVE BEAUTIES"

Qing dynasty (1644–1911), late Kangxi reign (1709–22). Screen painting, remounted as a hanging scroll, ink and color on silk; painting: 184 × 97.8 cm (72 7/16 × 38 1/2 in.); overall with mount: 313 × 131 cm (123 1/4 × 51 9/16 in.). The Palace Museum, Beijing, GU6458.

137 | Ding Guanpeng (Chinese, 1708–1771). CHILDREN PLAYING

Qing dynasty (1644–1911), Qianlong reign (1735–96). Hanging scroll, ink and color on silk; 102.5 × 58.8 cm (40 3/8 × 23 1/8 in.). The Palace Museum, Beijing, GU4791.

138 | Artists unknown. ONE OR TWO? (*SHIYI SHIER TU*), MENTAL CULTIVATION HALL (*YANGXINDIAN*) VERSION

Qing dynasty (1644–1911), Qianlong reign (1735–96). Ink and color on paper; 230 × 168 cm (90 9/16 × 66 1/8 in.). The Palace Museum, Beijing, GU6493.

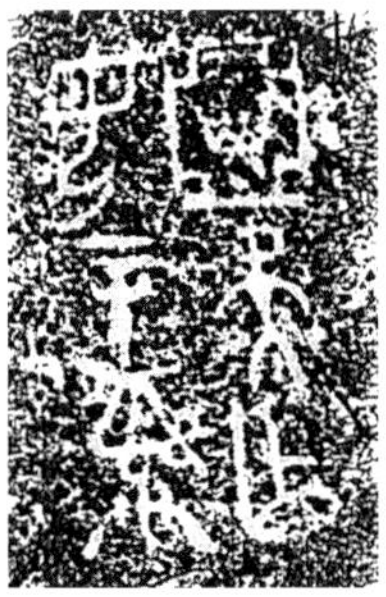

139

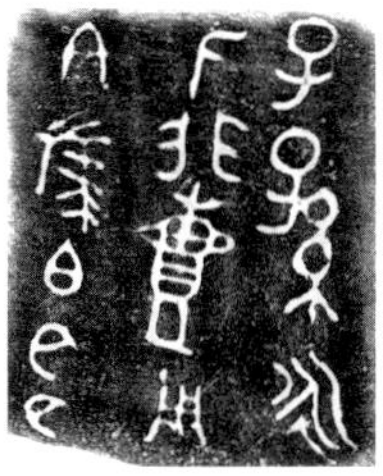

142

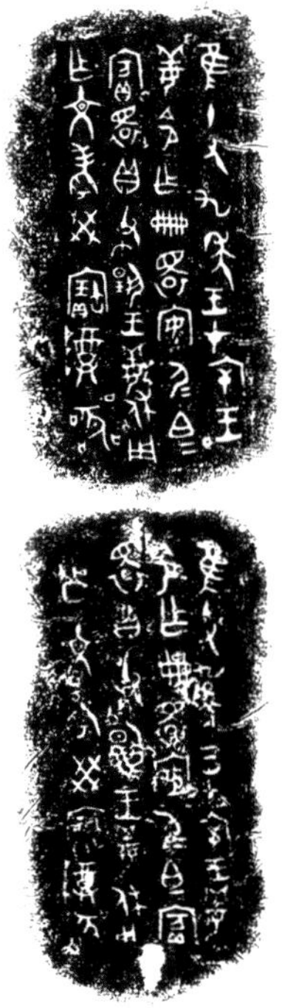

140 (top: lid, bottom: body)

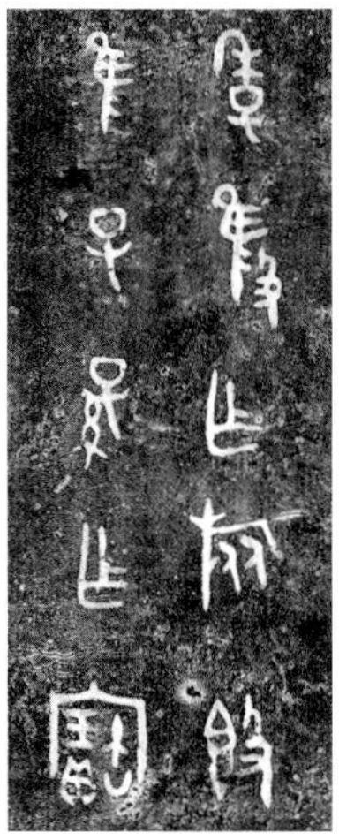

143

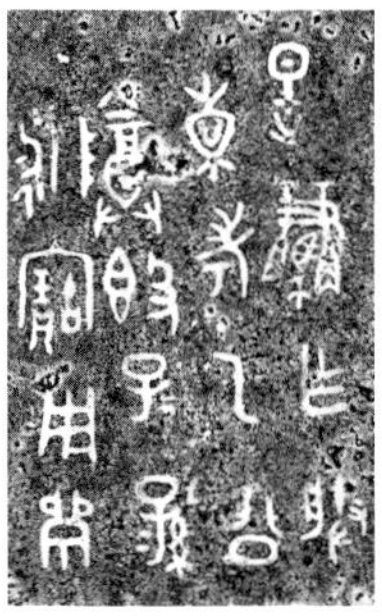

144

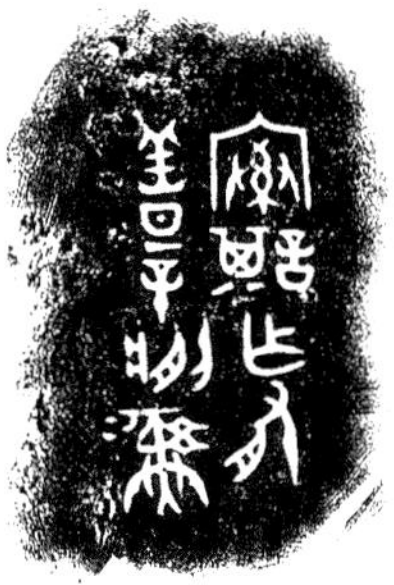

141

139 | BEAKER OF MOTHER XIN (*MU XIN ZUN*)

Western Zhou dynasty (1046–771 BC). Bronze; h. 25 cm (9 13/16 in.), diam. of mouth 22.5 cm (8 7/8 in.). Shang Shan Tang Collection. Pan Zuyin (1830–1890), XJJ: 5.21, SD: 11.28 (inscription only).

140 | BUCKET OF RECORDER HUAN (*ZUO CE HUAN YOU*)

Western Zhou dynasty (1046–771 BC). Bronze; h. 24.5 cm (9 5/8 in.). Private collection. Wu Shifen (1796–1856), JGJ: 2.3.86, JG: 2.55 (inscription only); Pan Zuyin (1830–1890), KZ: 19.22 (inscription only).

141 | GOBLET OF SUO QI (*SUO QI JUE*)

Western Zhou dynasty (1046–771 BC). Bronze; 24 × 18.3 cm (9 7/16 × 7 3/16 in.). The Shanghai Museum, 36041. Pan Zuyin (1830–1890), KZ: 21.17.3 (inscription only).

142 | JAR OF DUKE DUO FU (*BO DUO FU HU*)

Western Zhou dynasty (1046–771 BC). Bronze; h. 21.8 cm (8 9/16 in.), max. diam. 19.1 cm (7 1/2 in.), diam. of mouth 7.4 cm (2 15/16 in.). The Shanghai Museum, 21246. Qing imperial collection, XQ: 19.9; Pan Zuyin (1830–1890), XJJ: 4.79.2.

143 | TUREEN OF JI ZHI (*JI ZHI GUI*)

Western Zhou dynasty (1046–771 BC). Bronze; h. 20 cm (7 7/8 in.), diam. 18.4 (7 1/4 in.). The Shanghai Museum, 41563. Qing imperial collection, XQ: 28.5; Pan Zuyin (1830–1890), PG: 36.

144 | PEDESTALED TUREEN OF SHI XIE (*SHI XIE GUI*)

Western Zhou dynasty (1046–771 BC). Bronze; with handles and pedestal: h. 29.7 cm (11 11/16 in.); tureen: diam. 23.8 (9 3/8 in.); pedestal: diam. 28.3 cm (9 in.). The Shanghai Museum, 41550. Qing imperial collection, XQ: 27.13; Pan Zuyin (1830–1890), XJJ: 7.101.4.

145a–n | ALTAR SET (*JIN*)

Western Zhou dynasty (1046–771 BC). Bronze. Lent by The Metropolitan Museum of Art, New York, Munsey Fund, 1931, 24.72.1–14. Duanfang, TZ: 1.1.

145a | ALTAR STAND

Bronze; 18.1 × 89.9 × 46.4 cm (7 1/8 × 35 3/8 × 18 1/4 in.). 24.72.1. Duanfang, TZ: 1.2.

145b | BUCKET (*YOU*)

Bronze; container with lid: 31.8 × 24.1 × 22.9 cm (12 1/2 × 9 1/2 × 9 in.); pedestal: 14.6 × 21.6 × 17.5 cm (5 3/4 × 8 1/2 × 6 7/8 in.). 24.72.2 a–c. Duanfang, TZ: 1.4.

145c | BUCKET (*YOU*)

Bronze; max. h. with handle 47 cm (18 1/2 in.), w. 29.2 cm (11 1/2 in.). 24.72.3 a, b. Duanfang, TZ: 1.3.

145d | BEAKER (*ZUN*)

Bronze; h. 34.9 cm (13 3/4 in.), diam. of mouth 28.3 cm (11 1/8 in.), diam. of foot 17.5 cm (6 7/8 in.). 24.72.4. Duanfang, TZ: 1.6.

145e | EWER (*HE*)

Bronze; h. 28.6 cm (11 1/4 in.), w. with handle and spout 23.5 cm (9 1/4 in.). 24.72.5a, b. Duanfang, TZ: 1.7.

145f | CUP (*ZHI*)

Bronze; h. 14.6 cm (5 3/4 in.), w. at mouth 14.6 cm (5 3/4 in.), d. at mouth 12.4 cm (4 7/8 in.). 24.72.6. Duanfang, TZ: 1.10.

145g | GOBLET (*JIA*)

Bronze; max. h. with posts 33 cm (13 in.), w. with handle 26.7 cm (10 1/2 in.), d. 26.7 cm (10 1/2 in.). 24.72.7. Duanfang, TZ: 1.9.

145h | LADLE (*DOU*)

Bronze; 4.4 × 20.3 cm (1 3/4 × 8 in.), diam. of mouth of bowl 2.7 cm (1 1/16 in.). 24.72.8. Duanfang, TZ: 1.4 (together with bucket).

145i | GOBLET (*JUE*)

Bronze; max. h. with posts 25.1 cm (9 7/8 in.), w. at spout 22.9 cm (9 in.), d. 12.4 cm (4 7/8 in.). 24.72.9. Duanfang, TZ: 1.11.

145j | BEAKER (*GU*)

Bronze; h. 21 cm (8 1/4 in.), diam. of mouth 12.7 cm (5 in.), diam. of foot 7.1 cm (2 13/16 in.). 24.72.10. Duanfang, TZ: 1.8.

145k | CUP (*ZHI*)

Bronze; h. 14 cm (5 1/2 in.), max. diam. 7 cm (2 3/4 in.), diam. of mouth 6.2 cm (2 7/16 in.). 24.72.11. Duanfang, TZ: 1.13.

145l | CUP (*ZHI*)

Bronze; h. 14.6 cm (5 3/4 in.), max. diam. 7.9 cm (3 1/8 in.), diam. of mouth 7 cm (2 3/4 in.). 24.72.12. Duanfang, TZ: 1.14.

145m | GOBLET (*JUE*)

Bronze; h. 20 cm (7 7/8 in.), w. of mouth 14.6 cm (5 3/4 in.), d. 6.4 cm (2 1/2 in.). 24.72.13. Duanfang, TZ: 1.12.

145n | CUP (*ZHI*)

Bronze; h. 12.7 cm (5 in.), max. diam. 7.6 cm (3 in.), diam. of mouth 6.7 cm (2 5/8 in.). 24.72.14. Not in exhibition.

146 | Wu Dacheng (Chinese, 1835–1902) and others. COLLECTED ANTIQUITIES AT KEZHAI (*KEZHAI JIGUTU*)

Before 1892. Handscroll, ink and light colors on paper, rubbings; 41.5 × 1696 cm (16 5/16 × 667 3/4 in.). The Shanghai Museum, 64777.

147 | PEDESTALED TUREEN OF ZHUI (*ZHUI GUI*)

Western Zhou dynasty (1046–771 BC). Bronze; 35.6 × 40.6 cm (14 × 16 in.), max. diam. with handles 30.5 cm (12 in.). Asian Art Museum, San Francisco, The Avery Brundage Collection, B60B1056. Feng Yunpeng (1765–1835), JS: 1.27; Wu Dacheng, JJ: 45 (Two identical *gui* were recorded in XQ: 27.18 and 27.20, and are now in the National Palace Museum, Taipei, and the Palace Museum, Beijing, respectively.).

148 | TUREEN OF DUKE NAI (*BO NAI GUI*)

Western Zhou dynasty (1046–771 BC). Bronze; h. 17 cm (6 11/16 in.), diam. of mouth 21.3 cm (8 3/8 in.). The Shanghai Museum, 52098. Wu Dacheng, KZ: 9.6.2 (inscription only), KT: 53.

149 | OWL-SHAPED BUCKET OF XI (*XI YOU*)

Late Shang dynasty (c. 1250–1046 BC). Bronze; 18.5 × 12.4 × 9.9 cm (7 1/4 × 4 7/8 × 3 7/8 in.). The Shanghai Museum, 41119. Wu Dacheng, KZ: 14.8.2 (inscription only), KT: 55.

150 | TRIPOD CAULDRON OF PING AN (*PING AN JUN DING*)

Warring States period (475–221 BC). Bronze; h. 14 cm (5 1/2 in.), diam. of mouth 13.7 cm (5 3/8 in.). The Shanghai Museum, 25431. Pan Zuyin (1830–1890), HX: 21; Wu Dacheng, KZ: 6.19.2 (inscription only), KT: 60.

151 | EWER OF FATHER JI LIANG (*JI LIANG FU HE*)

Western Zhou dynasty (1046–771 BC). Bronze; 15.2 × 29.2 cm (6 × 11 1/2 in.). Asian Art Museum, San Francisco, The Avery Brundage Collection, B60B938. Qing imperial collection, XQ: 31.35; Pan Zuyin (1830–1890), HX: 93 (cover missing); Wu Dacheng, KT: 64.

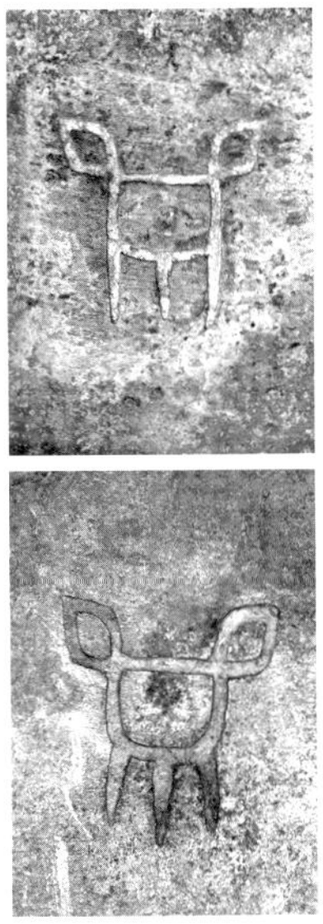

145b (top: lid, bottom: base)

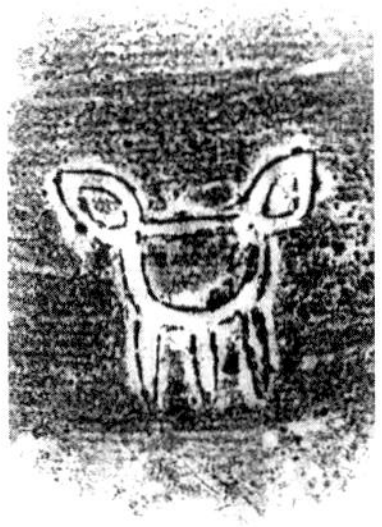

145d

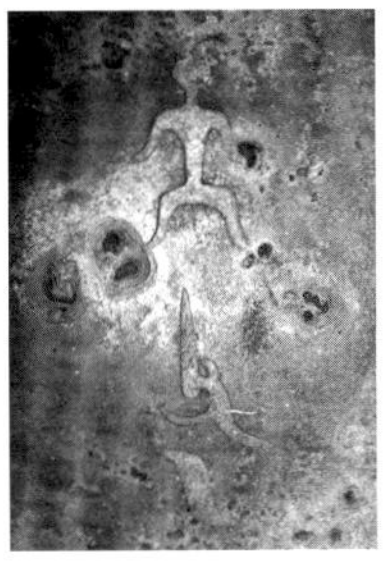

145f

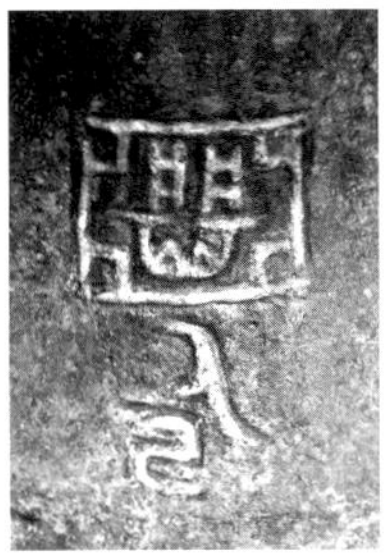

145j

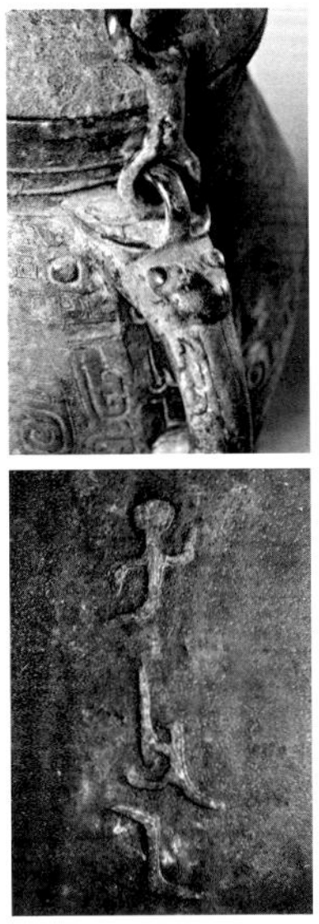

145e (top: lid, bottom: base)

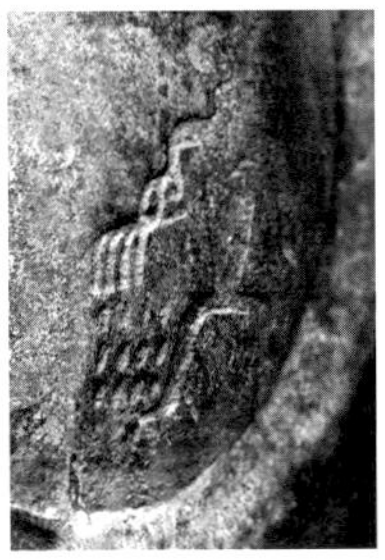

145g

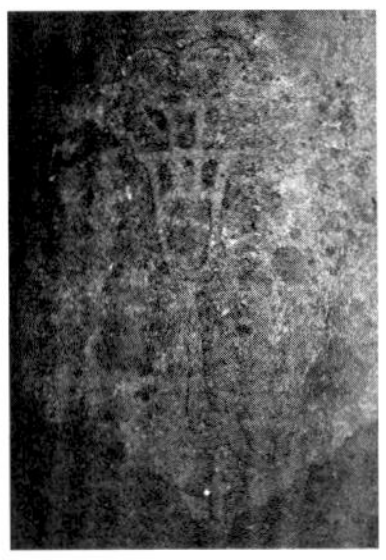

145l

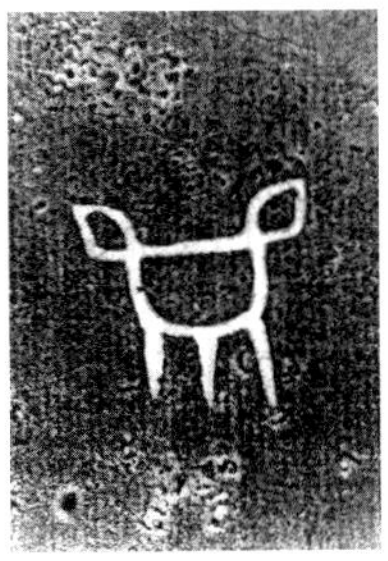

145c

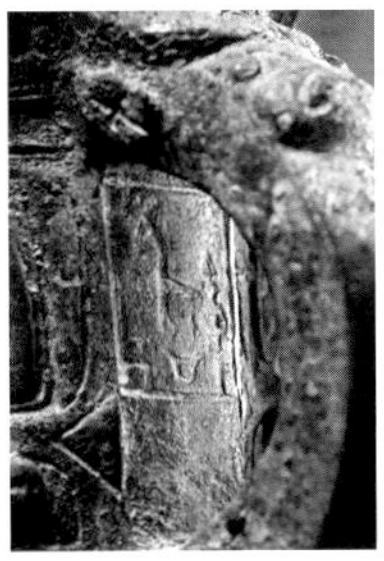

145i

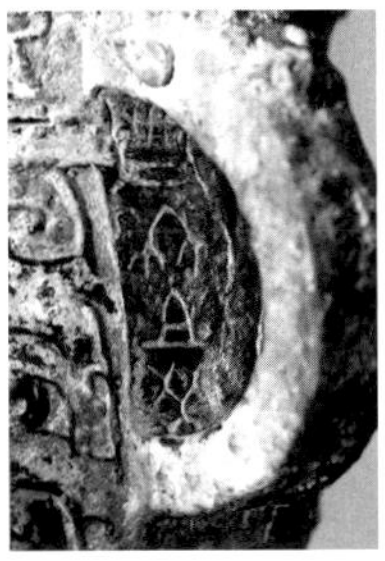

145m

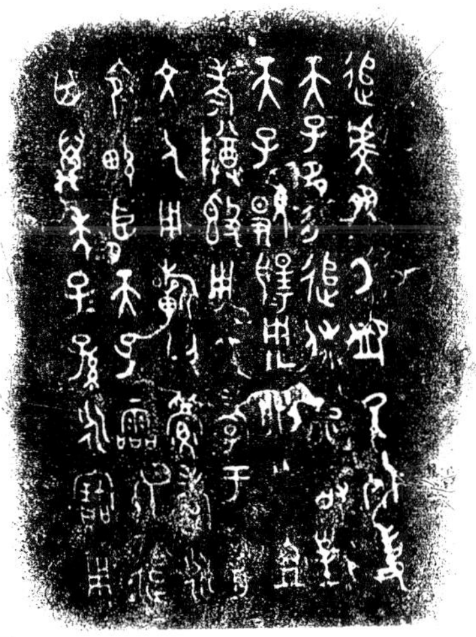

147

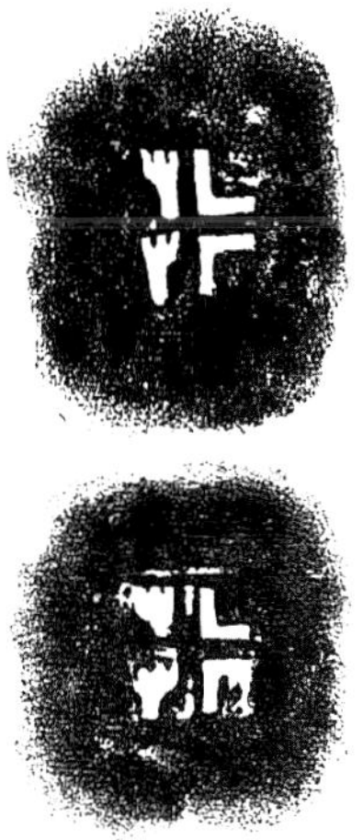

149

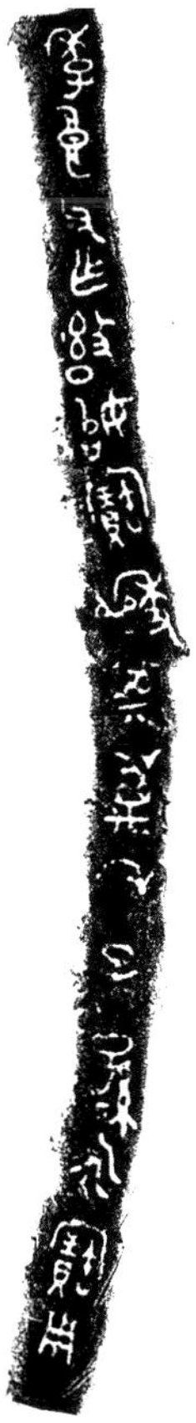

151

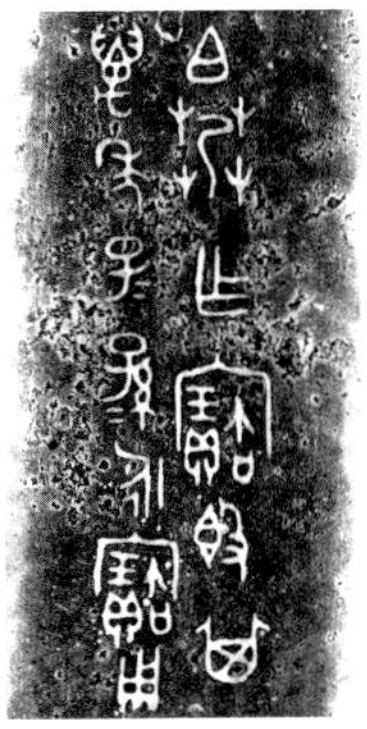

148

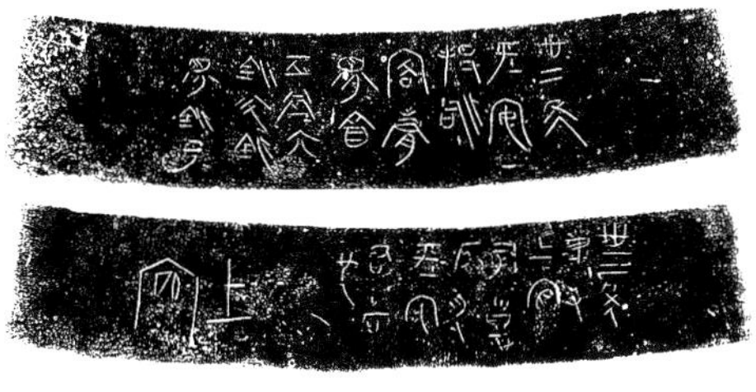

150

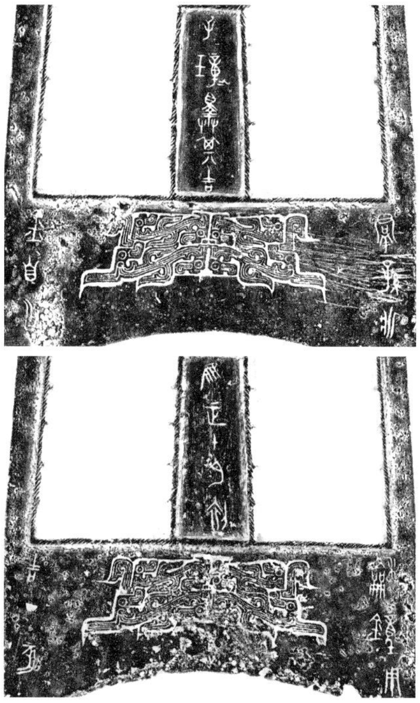

152

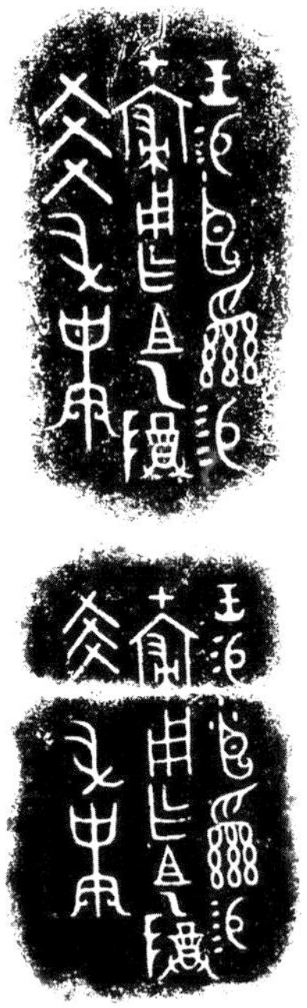

156 (top: lid, bottom: body)

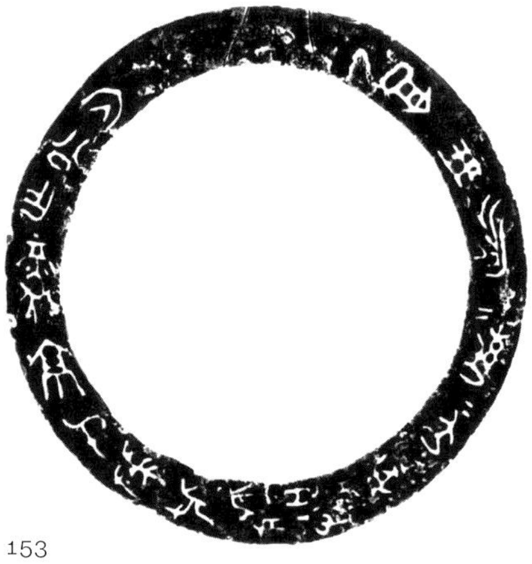

153

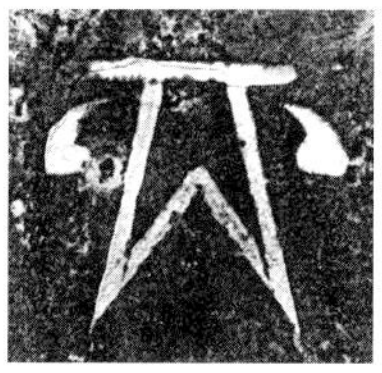

157

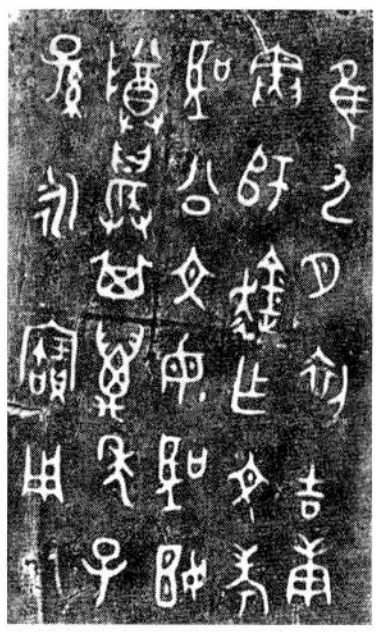

158

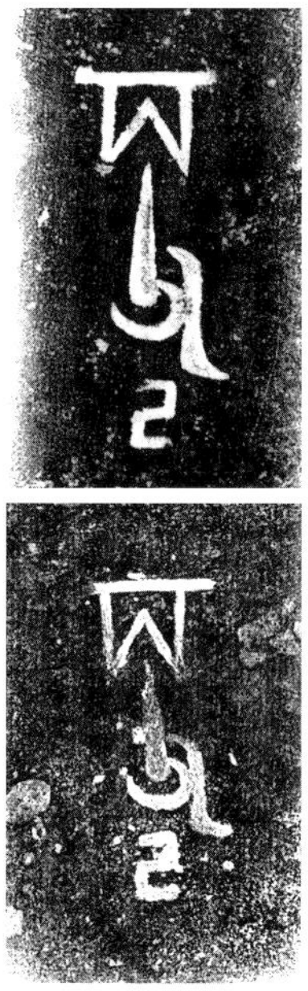

154 (top: lid, bottom: body)

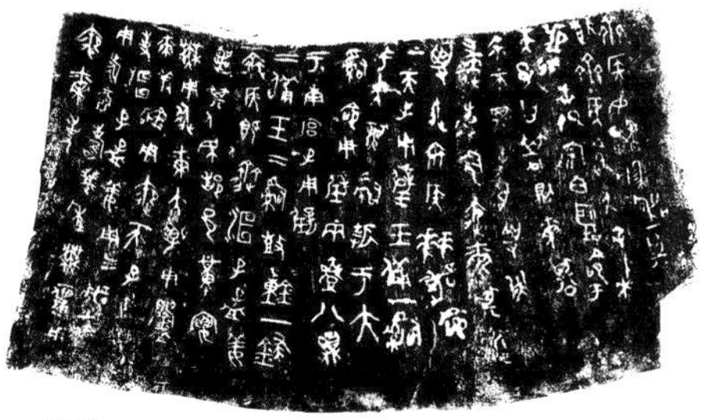

159

152 | BELL OF PRINCE ZHANG (*ZI ZHANG ZHONG*)

Eastern Zhou dynasty, Spring and Autumn period (770–476 BC). Bronze; 15.5 × 10 cm (6 1/8 × 3 15/16 in.). The Shanghai Museum, 38244. Qing imperial collection, XJ: 17.26–7; Wu Dacheng, KZ: 2.7 (inscription only), KT: 70.

153 | TRIPOD CAULDRON OF LORD RUI (*RUI GONG LI*)

Western Zhou dynasty (1046–771 BC). Bronze; 11.4 × 15.2 cm (4 1/2 × 6 in.), max. diam. 14.9 cm (5 7/8 in.). Asian Art Museum, San Francisco, The Avery Brundage Collection, B60B919. Wu Dacheng, KT: 76 (Pan Zuyin (1830–1890) had an identical one, HX: 96.).

154 | TWO RECTANGULAR CAULDRONS OF JU FU JI (*JU FU JI FANGDING*)

Late Shang dynasty (c. 1250–1046 BC). Bronze; 23.7 × 18.1 cm (9 5/16 × 7 1/8 in.). The Shanghai Museum, 25183, 25184. Wu Dacheng, XJJ: 2.16.8, 2.17.1 (inscription only), KT: 80.

155 | SQUARE CAULDRON WITH STOVE OF JI ZHEN (*JI ZHEN FANGLI*)

Western Zhou dynasty (1046–771 BC). Bronze; 17.9 × 15 × 12.3 cm (7 1/16 × 5 7/8 × 4 13/16 in.). Harvard Art Museums/Arthur M. Sackler Museum, Anonymous gift, 1944.57.18. Wu Dacheng, KT: 82.

156 | BUCKET OF MINISTER XI (*XIAO CHEN XI YOU*)

Late Shang dynasty (c. 1250–1046 BC). Bronze; 49.2 × 15.5 cm (19 3/8 × 6 1/8 in.). The Shanghai Museum, 83138. Wu Dacheng, KZ: 18.2.1–2 (inscription only), KT: 86.

157 | TRIPOD CAULDRON OF RAN (*RAN DING*)

Late Shang dynasty (c. 1250–1046 BC). Bronze; overall: h. 24.4 (9 5/8 in.), h. without handles 19.1 (7 1/2 in.), max. diam. 18.9 cm (7 7/16 in.), diam. of mouth 15.9 cm (6 1/4 in.) The Art Institute of Chicago, Lucy Maud Buckingham Collection, 1928.167. Duanfang, TZ: 1.18.

158 | LOBED TRIPOD CAULDRON OF OFFICER YIN (*SHI YIN LI*)

Western Zhou dynasty (1046–771 BC). Bronze; 50.8 × 54.6 cm (20 × 21 1/2 in.), diam. of mouth 47 cm (18 1/2 in.). The Palace Museum, Beijing, XIN142017. Fei Nianci (1855–1905), ZJ: 2.35.1 (inscription only).

159 | JAR OF HUAN ZI MENG JIANG (*HUAN ZI MENG JIANG HU*)

Spring and Autumn period (770–476 BC). Bronze; h. 22.1 cm (8 11/16 in.), diam. of mouth 13.4 cm (5 1/4 in.). The Shanghai Museum, 3672. Wu Yun, LL: 5.2.1, 5.3.1.

160–61 | Wu Changshi (Chinese, 1844–1927) and others. PAIR OF FULL-FORM RUBBINGS OF A BRONZE JAR, WITH PAINTED FLOWERS

Late Qing dynasty (late 19th/early 20th century). Hanging scrolls, rubbings on paper; each: mount: 230 × 55 cm (90 9/16 × 21 5/8 in.); painting: 166.5 × 44 cm (65 9/16 × 17 5/16 in.). Private collection. These scrolls depict cat. 161.

162 | Qiu Ying (Chinese, 1494–1552). APPRECIATING ANTIQUITIES IN THE BAMBOO GARDEN (*ZHUYUAN PINGU*)

Ming dynasty (1368–1644). Album leaf, painting on silk; 41.1 × 33.8 cm (16 3/16 × 13 5/16 in.). The Palace Museum, Beijing, XIN00119160–5/10.

163 | Zheng Zhong (Chinese, active c. 1612–1648). APPRECIATING ANTIQUITIES (*PINGUTU*)

Ming dynasty (1368–1644). Fan, ink and color on gold paper; 15.8 × 47.5 cm (6 1/4 × 18 11/16 in.). The Palace Museum, Beijing, XIN149033.

164 | Xiao Chen (Chinese, active late 17th–first half of 18th century). SU DONGPO EXAMINING ANTIQUITIES (*DONGPO BOGUTU*)

Qing dynasty (1644–1911). Fan, ink and color on paper; 18 × 51.6 cm (7 1/16 × 20 5/16 in.). The Palace Museum, Beijing, XIN00148779.

165 | Hong Hao (Chinese, born 1960). APPRECIATING ANTIQUES (*WANGUTU*) from ELEGANT GATHERING (*YAJI*)

2007. Ink, color, and digital images on paper; 86 × 172 cm (33 7/8 × 67 3/4 in.). Gay-Young Cho and Christopher Chiu.

166 | Chen Mei (Chinese, 1694–1745). OUTING UNDER THE MOON (*YUEMAN QINGYOU TU*)

Qing dynasty (1644–1911). Album leaf, ink and color on silk; 37 × 31.8 cm (14 9/16 × 12 1/2 in.). The Palace Museum, Beijing, GU9224–11/12.

167 | Hong Hao (Chinese, born 1960). OUTING UNDER THE MOON (*YUEMAN QINGYOU TU*) from ELEGANT GATHERING (*YAJI*)

2007. Ink, color, and digital images on paper; 126 × 105 cm (49 5/8 × 41 5/16 in.). Wu Hung and Judith Zeitlin.

168 | BOTTLE WITH GARLIC BULB–SHAPED MOUTH

Western Han dynasty (206 BC–AD 9). Bronze; 32.7 × 11.4 cm (12 7/8 × 4 1/2 in.), max. diam. 8.2 cm (3 1/4 in.). The Shanghai Museum, 5165.

169 | BOTTLE WITH GARLIC BULB–SHAPED MOUTH

Qing dynasty (1644–1911), Qianlong reign (1735–96). Porcelain; h. 28.7 cm (11 5/16 in.), max. diam. 14.5 cm (5 11/16 in.), diam. of mouth 3.2 cm (1 1/4 in.). The Art Institute of Chicago, gift of Dorothy Braude Edinburg to the Harry B. and Bessie K. Braude Memorial Collection, 1996.81.

170 | Xu Zhen (Chinese, born 1977). BOTTLE IN THE FORM OF A PORCELAIN VESSEL MADE DURING QIANLONG'S REIGN

2014. Porcelain; h. 31 cm (12 3/16 in.), diam. 17 cm (6 11/16 in.). The Art Institute of Chicago, 2017.91.

171 | Tai Xiangzhou (Chinese, born 1968). PAINTING OF THE "BUCKET OF MINISTER XI"

2017. Ink on paper; 357 × 140 cm (140 9/16 × 55 1/8 in.). Private collection. The object depicted is cat. 156 on this checklist.

SELECTED BIBLIOGRAPHY

Authors' names are given with surname first, followed by given name. For Chinese names and names in other Asian languages, no comma separates the surname from the given name, following standard practice in those languages, unless that author is equally well known in English-language scholarship or it is primarily their English-language publications that appear in this bibliography.

Allan, Sarah. "Erlitou and the Formation of Chinese Civilization: Toward a New Paradigm." *Journal of Asian Studies* 66:2 (March 2007): 461–96.

———. *The Shape of the Turtle: Myth, Art and Cosmos in Early China*. Albany: State University of New York Press, 1991.

———. "The *Taotie* Motif on Early Chinese Ritual Bronzes." In The *Zoomorphic Imagination in Chinese Art and Culture*, edited by Jerome Silbergeld and Eugene Wang, 21–66. Honolulu: University of Hawai'i University Press, 2016.

Alsop, Joseph. *The Rare Art Traditions: The History of Art Collecting and Its Linked Phenomena Wherever These Have Appeared*. Bollingen Series 35.27. New York: Harper and Row Publishers; Princeton, NJ: Princeton University Press, 1982.

Appadurai, Arjun, ed. *The Social Life of Things: Commodities in Cultural Perspective*. Cambridge: Cambridge University Press, 1988.

Bai Qianshen. "From Composite Rubbing to Picture of Antiques and Flowers (*Bogu huahui*): The Case of Wu Yun." *Orientations* 38:3 (April 2007): 52–60.

———. "Composite Rubbings in Nineteenth-Century China: The Case of Wu Dacheng (1835–1902) and His Friends." In *Reinventing the Past: Archaism and Antiquarianism in Chinese Art and Visual Culture*, edited by Wu Hung, 291–319. Chicago: Paragon Books, 2010.

Bagley, Robert. "Anyang Mold-Making and the Decorated Model." *Artibus Asiae* 69:1 (2009): 39–90.

———. "Changjiang Bronzes and Shang Archaeology." In *Proceedings, International Colloquium on Chinese Art History, 1991, Antiquities, Part 1, International Colloquium on Chinese Art History*, 209–55. Taipei: National Palace Museum, 1992.

———. "Ornament, Representation, and Imaginary Animals in Bronze Age China." *Arts Asiatiques* 61 (2006): 17–29.

———. "Shang Archaeology." In *The Cambridge History of Ancient China: From the Origins of Civilization to 221 B.C.*, edited by Michael Loewe and Edward L. Shaughnessy, 124–231. Cambridge: Cambridge University Press, 1999.

———. *Shang Ritual Bronzes in the Arthur M. Sackler Collections*. Cambridge: Harvard University Press, 1987.

Barnhart, Richard, Robert E. Harrist, and Hui-liang Chu. *Li Kung-Lin's "Classic of Filial Piety."* New York: Metropolitan Museum of Art, 1993. Exhibition catalogue.

Berger, Patricia. *Empire of Emptiness: Buddhist Art and Political Authority in Qing China*. Honolulu: University of Hawai'i Press, 2003.

Bickford, Maggie. "Huizong's Paintings: Art and the Art of Emperorship." In *Emperor Huizong and Late Northern Song China: The Politics of Culture and the Culture of Politics*, edited by Patricia B. Ebery and Maggie Bickford, 453–513. Cambridge: Harvard University Asia Center, 2006.

Bol, Peter K. "Emperors Can Claim Antiquity Too: Emperorship and Autocracy Under the New Policies." In *Emperor Huizong and Late Northern Song China: The Politics of Culture and the Culture of Politics*, edited by Patricia B. Ebery and Maggie Bickford, 173–205. Cambridge: Harvard University Asia Center, 2006.

———. *This Culture of Ours: Intellectual Transitions in T'ang and Sung China*. Stanford: Stanford University Press, 1992.

Boltz, William G. "Shuo wen chieh tzu." In *Early Chinese Texts: A Bibliographical Guide*, edited by Michael Loewe, 429–42. Berkeley: Society for the Study of Early China, 1993.

Brown, Bill. "Thing Theory." *Critical Inquiry* 28:1 (2001): 1–22

———, ed. *Things*. Chicago: University of Chicago Press, 2004.

Brown, Shana J. *Pastimes: From Art and Antiquarianism to Modern Chinese Historiography*. Honolulu: University of Hawai'i Press, 2001.

Bushell, Stephen W. *Chinese Art*. Vol. 1. London: Wyman and Sons, 1904.

Cahill, James. *An Index of Early Chinese Paintings and Paintings: T'ang, Sung, and Yuan*. Berkeley: University of California Press, 1980.

Chang, K. C. "Archaeology and Chinese Historiography." *World Archaeology* 13:2 (1981): 156–69.

———. "China on the Eve of the Historical Period." In *The Cambridge History of Ancient China: From the Origins of Civilization to 221 B.C.*, edited by Michael Loewe and Edward L. Shaughnessy, 37–73. Cambridge: Cambridge University Press, 1999.

Chang Lin-Sheng. "Li Gonglin yu Bei Song guqiwuxue de farren" [Li Gonglin and the Beginning of the Study of Ancient Objects in the Northern Song Dynasty]. In *Qianxi nian Songdai wenwu dazhan* [China at the Inception of the Second Millennium: Art and Culture of the Sung Dynasty, 960–1279], 19–46. Taipei: National Palace Museum, 2000. Exhibition catalogue.

———. "The National Palace Museum: A History of the Collection." In Fong and Watt, *Possessing the Past: Treasures from the National Palace Museum, Taipei*, 3–25.

Chang, Michael G. "Envisioning the Spectacles of Emperor Qianlong's Tours of Southern China: An Exercise in Historical Imagination." In *Visualizing Modern China: Image, History, and Memory, 1750–Present*, edited by James A. Cook, Joshua L. Goldstein, Matthew D. Johnson, and Sigrid Schmalzer, 25–46. New York: Lexington Books, 2014.

Chen Fangmei. *Gugong Shangdai qingtong liqi tulu* [Shang Ritual Bronzes in the National Palace Museum Collection]. Taipei: National Palace Museum, 1998. Exhibition catalogue.

———. *Qingtongqi yu Songdai wenhuashi* [Bronzes and the Cultural History of the Song Dynasty]. Taipei: Taiwan University Publication Center, 2016.

———. "Songdai guqiwuxue de xingqi yu Song fanggu tongqi" [The Rise of Studies of Antiquities and Archaic Bronzes in the Song Dynasty]. *Meishushi yanjiu jikan* 10 (2001): 37–160.

———. "Zaixian sandai: Cong Gugong Songdai fanggu tongqi shuoqi" [Representing the Three Dynasties: On the Song Archaistic Bronzes in the National Palace Museum]. In *Qianxinian Songdai wenwu dazhan* [China at the Inception of the Second Millennium: Art and Culture of the Sung Dynasty, 960–1279], edited by Lin Boting, 293–320. Taipei: National Palace Museum, 2000. Exhibition catalogue.

———. "Zhui sandai yu dingyi zhijian: Songdai cong 'kaogu' dao 'wangu' de zhuanbian" [Pursuit of the Three Dynasties through Ritual Bronzes: The Transition from 'Examining Antiquities' to 'Plaything' in the Song Period]. *Gugong xueshu jikan* 23:1 (2005): 267–332.

Chen Jieqi. *Chuangu bielu* [Separate Record on Transmitting Antiquity]. In *Pangxizhai congshu* edition, *juan* 28. Suzhou: privately printed, 1862–1908.

Chen Mengjia. *Chen Mengjia zhuzuoji: Xi Zhou tongqi duandai* [Collected Works of Chen Mengjia: Periodization of Western Zhou Bronzes]. Beijing: Zhonghua shuju, 2004.

———. *Meidi guozhuyi jielüe de woguo Yin Zhou tongqi jilu* [Collection of Yin Zhou Bronzes Plundered by American Imperialists]. Beijing: Kexue chubanshe, 1962. [Published under the name of the Institute of Archaeology, Chinese Academy of Sciences.]

———. "Song Dasheng bianzhong kaoshu" [Investigation of the Dasheng Bells]. In *Chen Mengjia xueshu lunwenji* [Academic Essays by Chen Mengjia], 528–33. Beijing: Zhonghua shuju, 2016.

Cheng Zhangcan. "Wanwu: Wan-Qing shifeng yu beita liutong" [Playthings: The Exchange of Rubbings as a Way of Living among Late Qing Scholar-Officials]. *Xueshu yanjiu* [Academic Research] (2015/12): 141–50.

Childs-Johnson, Elizabeth. "The *Jue* and Its Ceremonial Use in the Ancestor Cult of China." *Artibus Asiae* 48:3/4 (1987): 171–96.

———. "The Metamorphic Image: A Predominant Theme in the Ritual Art of Shang China." *Bulletin of the Museum of Far Eastern Antiquities* 70 (1998): 20–31.

Chuang Shen. "Archaeology in Late Qing Dynasty Painting." *Ars Orientalis* 24 (1994): 83–104.

Clifford, James. "On Collecting Art and Culture." In *The Predicament of Culture: Twentieth-Century Ethnography, Literature and Art*, 215–51. Cambridge: Harvard University Press, 1988.

Clunas, Craig. *Chinese Paintings and Its Audiences*. Princeton: Princeton University Press, 2017.

———. *Superfluous Things: Material Culture and Social Status in Early Modern China*. Urbana: University of Illinois Press, 1991.

Creel, Herrlee G. "Bronze Inscriptions of the Western Chou Dynasty as Historical Documents." *Journal of the American Oriental Society* 56 (1936): 335–49.

Dematte, Paola. "Emperors and Scholars: Collecting Culture and Late Imperial Antiquarianism." In *Collecting China: The World, China, and a History of Collecting*, edited by Vimalin Rujivacharakul, 165–75. Newark: University of Delaware Press, 2011.

Ebrey, Patricia B. *Accumulating Culture: The Collections of Emperor Huizong*. Seattle: University of Washington Press, 2008.

———. "Replicating Zhou Bells at the Northern Song Court." In *Reinventing the Past: Archaism and Antiquarianism in Chinese Art and Visual Culture*, edited by Wu Hung, 179–99. Chicago: Center for the Art of East Asia, University of Chicago, 2009.

Egan, Ronald. *The Problem of Beauty: Aesthetic Thought and Pursuits in Northern Song Dynasty China*. Harvard East Asian Monographs 271. Cambridge: Harvard University Asia Center, 2006.

Elliott, Mark C. *Emperor Qianlong: Son of Heaven, Man of the World*. Upper Saddle River, NJ: Pearson Education, 2009.

Elman, Benjamin A. *From Philosophy to Philology: Intellectual and Social Aspects of Change in Late Imperial China*. Cambridge: Harvard University Press, 1984.

Elsner, John, and Roger Cardinal, eds. *The Cultures of Collecting*. London: Reaktion Books, 1994.

Fong, Wen C., and James C. Y. Watt. *Possessing the Past: Treasures from the National Palace Museum, Taipei*. New York: Metropolitan Museum of Art; Taipei: National Palace Museum; New York: Harry N. Abrams, 1996. Exhibition catalogue.

Graham, A. C. *Disputers of the Tao: Philosophical Argument in Ancient China*. La Salle: Open Court, 1989.

———. *Two Chinese Philosophers: The Metaphysics of the Brothers Ch'eng*. La Salle: Open Court, 1992.

Guffey, Elizabeth E. Retro: *The Culture of Revival*. London: Reaktion Books, 2006.

Guy, R. Kent. *The Emperor's Four Treasuries: Scholars and the State in the Late Ch'ien-lung Era*. Cambridge: Harvard University Asia Center, 1987.

Harrist, Robert E. "The Artist as Antiquarian: Li Gonglin and His Study of Early Chinese Art." *Artibus Asiae* 55:3/4 (1995): 237–80.

Holzwarth, Gerald. "The Qianlong Emperor as Art Patron and the Formation of the Collections of the Palace Museum, Beijing." In *China: The Three Emperors 1662–1795*, edited by Evelyn S. Rawski and Jessica Rawson, 41–53. London: Royal Academy of Arts, 2005.

Hong Hao, and John Tancock, eds. *Elegant Gathering: Hong Hao's Opening, April 19–May 26, 2007*. New York: Chambers Fine Art, 2007. Exhibition catalogue.

Hsu Chin-hsiung. *Oracle Bones from the White and Other Collections*. Toronto: Royal Ontario Museum, 1979.

Hsu Ya-hwei (Xu Yahui). "Antiquaries and Politics: Antiquarian Culture of the Northern Song, 960–1127." In *World Antiquarianism*, edited by Alain Schnapp, Lothar von Falkenhausen, Peter N. Miller, and Tim Murray, 230–48. Los Angeles: Getty Research Institute, 2013.

———. "Antiquities, Ritual Reform, and the Shaping of New Taste at Huizong's Court." *Artibus Asiae* 73:1 (2013): 137–80.

———. "Guanyu Songdai guwuxue zhi yanjiu yu taolun" [Studies on Antiquarianism in the Song Dynasty]. *Zhongguo shixue* 21 (2011): 67–77.

———. "Reshaping Chinese Material Culture: The Revival of Antiquity in the Era of Print, 960–1729." PhD diss., Yale University, 2010.

———. "Zhida chongxiu Xuanhe bogu tulu de banyin tedian yu liuchuan."[Translation?] *Gujin lunheng* [Discourses on the Past and Present] 18 (October 2008): 76–96.

Hu Cangjian. "Liu Xihai nianpu" [Chronicle of Liu Xihai]. *Wenxian jikan* [Essays on Archival Documents] (2000/2): 133–51.

Hua Jueming, Feng Fugen, Wang Zhenjiang, and Bai Rongjin. "Fu Hao mu qingtongqi qun zhuzao jishu de yanjiu" [Study of the Casting Technology of Bronzes from the Fu Hao Tomb]. In Kaoguxue jikan [Essays on Archaeology] 1, edited by the Institute of Archaeology, Chinese Academy of Social Sciences, 244–72. Beijing: Kexue chubanshe, 1981.

———. "Shilafa de qiyuan he fazhan" [The Origin and Development of the Lost-Wax Techniques]. In *Kejishi wenji* [Papers on the History of Science and Technology] 13, edited by the Institute for the History of Natural Sciences, Chinese Academy of Sciences, 63–81. Shanghai: Shanghai kexue jishu chubanshe, 1985.

Institute of Archaeology, Chinese Academy of Social Sciences. *Yinxu Fu Hao mu* [Tomb of Fu Hao at Yinxu]. Beijing: Wenwu chubanshe, 1980.

Jacobson, Esther. "The Structure of Narrative in Early Chinese Pictorial Vessels." *Representations* 8 (1984): 61–83.

Jang, Scarlett. "The Culture of Art Collecting in Imperial China." In *A Companion to Chinese Art*, edited by Martin Powers and Katherine Tsiang, 47–72. Chichester: Wiley-Blackwell, 2015.

Kahn, Harold L. "A Master of Taste: The Monumental and Exotic in the Qianlong Reign." In *The Elegant Brush: Chinese Painting Under the Qianlong Emperor 1735–1795*, edited by Ju-hsi Chou and Claudia Brown, 288–302. Phoenix: Phoenix Art Museum, 1985. Exhibition catalogue.

Kane, Virginia C. "The Independent Bronze Industries in the South of China Contemporary with the Shang and Western Chou Dynasties." *Archives of Asian Art* 28 (1974/75): 77–107.

Karlgren, Berhard. "Marginalia on Some Bronze Albums." *Bulletin of the Museum of Far Eastern Antiquities* 31 (1959): 289–331.

———. "Marginalia on Some Bronze Albums II." *Bulletin of the Museum of Far Eastern Antiquities* 32 (1960): 1–24.

———. "Notes on the Grammar of Early Bronze Décor." *Bulletin of the Museum of Far Eastern Antiquities* 23 (1951): 1–37.

Kelley, Charles Fabens, and Ch'en Meng-chia. *Chinese Bronzes from the Buckingham Collection*. Chicago: Art Institute of Chicago, 1946.

Keightley, David. "The Religious Commitment: Shang Theology and the Genesis of Chinese Political Culture." *History of Religion* 17:3/4 (1978): 211–25.

———. "The 'Science' of Ancestors: Divination, Curing, and Bronze-Casting in Late Shang China." *Asia Major* 14:2 (2001): 143–87.

Kesner, Ladislav. "The *Taotie* Reconsidered: Meanings and Functions of the Shang Theriomorphic Imagery." *Artibus Asiae* 51:1/2 (1991): 29–53.

Kleutghen, Kristina. "One or Two, Repictured." *Archives of Asian Art* 62 (2012): 25–46.

———. "The Qianlong Emperor's Perspective: Illusionistic Painting in Eighteenth-Century China." PhD diss., Harvard University, 2010.

Kuhn, Dieter, and Helga Stahl, eds. *Perceptions of Antiquity in Chinese Civilization*. Heidelberg: Edition Forum, 2008.

Laing, Ellen. "Real or Ideal: The Problem of the 'Elegant Gathering in the Western Garden' in Chinese Historical and Art Historical Records." *Journal of the American Oriental Society* 88:3 (1968): 419–35.

Lawton, Thomas. "An Imperial Legacy Revisited: Bronze Vessels from the Qing Palace Collection." *Asian Art* 1:1 (1987/88): 51–79.

———. "Jin Futing: A 19th-Century Chinese Collector-Connoisseur." *Transactions of the Oriental Ceramic Society* 54 (1989–1990): 35–61.

———. "Rubbings of Chinese Bronzes." *Bulletin of the Museum of Far Eastern Antiquities* 67 (1995): 7–48.

———. *A Time of Transition: Two Collectors of Chinese Art*. Lawrence: Spencer Museum of Art, University of Kansas, 1991.

Ledderose, Lothar. "Rubbings in Art History." In *Catalogue of Chinese Rubbings from the Field Museum, Fieldiana Anthropology*, New Series 3, edited by Hartmut Walravens, 28–36. Chicago: Field Museum, 1981.

———. "Some Observations on the Imperial Art Collection in China." *Transactions of the Oriental Ceramic Society* 43 (1978–79): 33–46.

Lee, Thomas H. C. "Skepticist Reconstruction and Sagely Truth in Tension: Song Attempts to Draw the Boundaries of Historical Antiquity." In *Perceptions of Antiquity in Chinese Civilization*, edited by Dieter Kuhn and Helga Stahl, 253–89. Heidelberg: Edition Forum, 2008.

Lefebvre, Éric. "'L'Image des antiquités accumulées' de Ruan Yuan: La représentation d'une collection privée en Chine à l'époque pré-moderne." *Arts Asiatiques* 63 (2008): 61–72.

Liao Yaocheng. "The Epigraphy Studies of Li Gonglin and the Northern Song Literati." *Diancang* [Art and Collection] 14 (2015/5): 48–53.

Lin Wei-Cheng. "Replicating the Past: Ink Rubbing and Its Related Ideas in Contemporary Chinese Art." In *Reinventing the Past: Archaism and Antiquarianism in Chinese Art and Visual Culture*, edited by Wu Hung, 213–35. Chicago: Paragon Books, 2010.

Lin Yi-Hsin. "The Cultures and Collecting in Late Imperial China and Early Republican China: The Pan Family Collection in Suzhou." PhD diss., University of London, 2012.

Lin Zihui. "Qingmo cangshujia Liu Xihai" [The Late Qing Book Collector Liu Xihai]. *Shandong xingzheng xueyuan xuebao* [Bulletin of Shandong Administrative College], 8:135 (2014/8): 92–96.

Liscomb, Kathlyn Maureen. "Social Status and Art Collecting: The Collections of Shen Zhou and Wang Zhen." *Art Bulletin* 78:1 (1996): 111–36.

Liu, James T. C. *Ou-yang Hsiu: An Eleventh-Century Neo-Confucianist*. Stanford: Stanford University Press, 1967.

Liu Li. "Academic Freedom, Political Correctness, and Early Civilization in Chinese Archaeology: The Debate on Xia-Erlitou Relations." *Antiquity* 83:321 (2009): 832–43.

———. "'The Products of Minds as Well as of Hands': Production of Prestige Goods in the Neolithic and Early State Periods of China." *Asian Perspectives* 42:1 (2003): 1–40.

Liu Li, and Hong Xu. "Rethinking Erlitou: Legend, History and Chinese Archaeology." *Antiquity* 81:314 (2007): 886–901.

Liu Qingzhu, Zhihong Duan, and Shi Feng, eds. *Jinwen wenxian jicheng* [Compendium of Publications on Bronze Inscriptions], vols. 1–46. Beijing: Xian zhuang shuju, 2005.

Liu Yu. *Qianlong sijian zonglibiao* [Collation Tables of the Qianlong Emperor's Four Bronze Catalogues]. Beijing: Zhonghua shuju, 1989.

Liu Yuxia. "Anyang ye tong shu yanjiu [Studies on the Metallurgy of Anyang]." In *Anyang fajue baogao* [Excavation Reports of Anyang], no. 4, edited by Zhongyang yanjiuyuan lishi yuyan yanjiusuo [Institute of History and Philology, Academia Sinica], 681–96. Nanjing: Institute of History and Philology, Academia Sinica, 1933.

Liu Zheng. "Lidai jinwen jingdian zhuzuo yingyin congkan jieti" [Brief Introduction to the Reprinted Series of Important Publications on *Jinshixue*] 29. *Kyotosizumoto*, http://blog.sciencenet.cn/u/kyotosizumoto.

Loehr, Max. *Ritual Vessels of Bronze Age China*. New York: Asia Society, 1968.

Louis, François. *Design by the Book: Chinese Ritual Objects and the "Sanli tu."* New York: Bard Graduate Center, 2016.

Lowenthal, David. *The Past Is a Foreign Country*. Cambridge: Cambridge University Press, 1985.

Lu Liancheng, and Hu Zhisheng. *Baoji Yuguo mudi* [The Tombs of the Yu State in Baoji]. Beijing: Wenwu chubanshe, 1988.

Maryon, Herbert, and Harold J. Plenderleith. "Fine Metal Work." In *A History of Technology*, vol. 1, edited by Charles Singer and Trevor Illtyd Williams, 625–26. Oxford: Clarendon Press, 1954.

Masaaki Itakura. "Ba en 'Seien gashu zu kan' (Nerusan-Atokinzu Bijutsukan) no shi teki ichi-kyoko to shite no 'Seien gashu' to so no kaigaka o megutte [The Historical Position of Ma Yuan's 'Elegant Gathering in the Western Garden' (The Nelson-Atkins Museum of Art): Concerning the Pictorialization of This Theme as Fiction]. *Bijutsushi Ronso* [Studies in Art History] 16 (1999): 49–78.

McCausland, Shane. "The Emperor's Old Toys: Rethinking the Yongzheng (1723–35) Scroll of Antiquities in the Percival David Foundation." *Transactions of the Oriental Ceramic Society* 66 (2001–2): 65–75.

Miller, Peter N., and François Louis, eds. *Antiquarianism and Intellectual Life in Europe and China, 1500–1800*. Ann Arbor: University of Michigan Press, 2012.

Moser, Jeffery. "The Ethics of Immutable Things: Interpreting Lü Dalin's Illustrated Investigations of Antiquity." *Harvard Journal of Asiatic Studies* 72:2 (2012): 259–93.

———. "Recasting Antiquity: Ancient Bronzes and Ritual Hermeneutics in the Song Dynasty." PhD diss., Harvard University, 2010.

Mou Yongkang, and Wu Ruzuo. "A Discussion on the 'Jade Age.'" In *Exploration into China's Past*, edited by Roderick Whitfield and Tao Wang, 41–44. London: Saffron Books, 1999.

National Palace Museum. *Qianlong huangdi de wenhua daye* [Emperor Qianlong's Grand Cultural Enterprise]. Taipei: National Palace Museum, 2002. Exhibition catalogue.

———. *Shiquan Qianlong: Qing Gaozong de yishu pinwei* [The All Complete Qianlong: The Aesthetic Tastes of the Qing Emperor Gaozong]. Taipei: National Palace Museum, 2013. Exhibition catalogue.

Nickel, Lukas. "Imperfect Symmetry: Re-Thinking Bronze Casting Technology in Ancient China." *Artibus Asiae* 66:1 (2006): 5–39.

O'Neill, Timothy. "Xu Shen's Scholarly Agenda: A New Interpretation of the Postface of the *Shuowen jiezi*." *Journal of the American Oriental Society* 133:3 (2013): 413–40.

Owen, Stephen. *Remembrance: The Experience of the Past in Classical Chinese Literature*. Cambridge: Harvard University Press, 1986.

Pai Shih-Ming. "'Returning to the Classics, Trusting the Ancient': Luo Zhenyu's Exploration of Traditional Chinese Identity in Modern China." In *Lost Generation: Luo Zhenyu, Qing Loyalists and the Formation of Modern Chinese Culture*, edited by Yang Chia-Ling and Roderick Whitfield, 75–97. London: Saffron Books, 2012.

Pan Zuyin. "Shuowen guzhou bu xu" [Preface to "Shuowen guzhou"]. 1883. Reprinted in *Jinwen wenxian jicheng* [Compendium of Publications on Bronze Inscriptions], vol. 17, edited by Liu Qingzhu, Duan Zhihong, and Feng Shi, 203. Beijing: Xianzhuang shuju, 2005.

Paper, Jordan. "The Meaning of the 'T'ao-T'ieh.'" *History of Religions* 18:1 (1978): 18–41.

Pearce, David, and David Lewis Williams. *Inside the Neolithic Mind*. London: Thames and Hudson, 2005.

Pearce, Susan M. *Museum, Objects, and Collections: A Cultural Study*. Leicester: Leicester University Press, 1992.

Pomian, Krzysztof. *Collectors and Curiosities: Paris and Venice, 1500–1800*. Translated by Elizabeth Wiles-Portier. Cambridge: Polity Press, 1990.

Poor, Robert. "Notes on the Sung Dynasty Archaeological Catalogs." *Archives of the Chinese Art Society of America* 19 (1965): 33–44.

Powers, Martin J. "The Figure in the Carpet: Reflections on the Discourse of Ornament in Zhou China." *Monumenta Serica* 43 (1995): 211–33.

Radivojević, M., T. Rehren, J. Kuzmanović-Cvetković, M. Jovanović, and J. P. Northover. "Context Is Everything Indeed: A Response to Sljivar and Boric." *Antiquity* 88:342 (2014): 1315–19.

———. "Tainted Ores and the Rise of Tin Bronzes in Eurasia, c. 6500 Years Ago." *Antiquity* 87:338 (2013): 1030–45.

Rawski, Evelyn S. "Presidential Address: Re-envisioning the Qing: The Significance of the Qing Period in Chinese History." *Journal of Asian Studies* 55:4 (1996): 829–50.

Rawski, Evelyn S., and Jessica Rawson, eds. *China: The Three Emperors 1662–1795*. London: Royal Academy of Arts, 2005.

Rawson, Jessica. "Ancient Chinese Ritual Bronzes: The Evidence from Tombs and Hoards of the Shang (c. 1500–1050 BCE) and Western Zhou (c. 1050–771 BCE)." *Antiquity* 67:257 (1993): 805–23.

———. "Novelties in Antiquarian Revivals: The Case of the Chinese Bronzes." *National Palace Museum Research Quarterly* 22:1 (2004): 1–34.

Rong Geng. "Songdai jijin shuji shuping" [Review of Song Dynasty Publications on Bronzes and Stones]. In *Rong Geng xuanji* [Selected Writings of Rong Geng], edited by Zeng Xiantong, 1–66. Tianjin: Tianjin renmin chubanshe, 1994.

Rong Geng, and Weichi Zhang. *Yin Zhou qingtongqi tonglun* [A General Survey of Bronzes of the Shang and Zhou Periods]. Beijing: Kexue chubanshe, 1958.

Rudolph, R. C. "Dynastic Booty: An Altered Chinese Bronze." *Harvard Journal of Asiatic Studies* 11 (1948): 174–80.

———. "Preliminary Notes on Sung Archaeology." *Journal of Asian Studies* 22:2 (1963): 169–77.

Schnapp, Alain. "The Many Dimensions of the Antiquary's Practice." In *Antiquarianism and Intellectual Life in Europe and China, 1500–1800*, edited by Peter N. Miller and François Louis, 58–80. Ann Arbor: University of Michigan Press, 2012.

Schnapp, Alain, Lothar von Falkenhausen, Peter N. Miller, and Tim Murray, eds. *World Antiquarianism: Comparative Perspectives*. Los Angeles: Getty Research Institute, 2013.

Sena, Yun-Chiahn C. "Ouyang Xiu's Conceptual Collection of Antiquity." In *World Antiquarianism: Comparative Perspectives*, edited by Alain Schnapp, with Lothar von Falkenhausen, Peter N. Miller, and Tim Murray, 212–29. Los Angeles: Getty Research Institute, 2013.

———. "Cataloguing Antiquity: A Comparative Study of the *Kaogu tu* and *Bogu tu*." In *Reinventing the Past: Archaism and Antiquarianism in Chinese Art and Visual Culture*, edited by Wu Hung, 200–228. Chicago: Paragon Books, 2010.

Shapiro, Daniel. *Ancient Chinese Bronzes: A Personal Appreciation*. London: Sylph Edition, 2013.

Shen Huixing. "Cong 'Qingyige suocang guqiwu wen' kan Zhang Tingji de jinshi shenghuo" [Zhang Tingji's Antiquarian Life Reflected in His "Qingyige suocang guqiwu wen"]. *Sina*, May 20, 2014. blog.sina.com.cn/s/blog_4969983f-0101gect.html.

Shi Jiong, "'Dongpo bogu': 'Xiyuan yajitu de yige bianti'" ["Dongpo Appreciating Antiquities": A Variation of the "Paintings of Xiyuan Literati Gathering"]. *Xin Meishu* [New Art] (2016/3): 19–31.

Shi Zhangru. "Yinxu zuijinde zhongyao faxian, fulun Xiaotun diceng" [Recent Important Discoveries in Yinxu and the Question of the Stratification at the Xiaotun Site]. *Zhongguo kaogu xuebao* [*Reports of Chinese Archaeology*] 2 (1947): 25–100.

Shih Shou-Chien. "Qingshi shoucang de xiandai zhuanhua—Jianlun qi yu Zhongguo meishushi yanjiu fanzhan zhi guanxi" [The Modern Transformation of the Qing Imperial Collections, with a Discussion on Its Relationship to the Study of the History of Chinese Art]. *Gugong xueshu jikan* [Academic Journal of the National Palace Museum] 23:1 (2005): 1–33.

Sima Qian. *Records of the Grand Historian, Han Dynasty II*. Translated by Burton Watson. Revised ed. New York: Columbia University Press, 1993.

Siren, Osvald, trans. *A History of Early Chinese Painting*. London: Taylor and Francis, 1933.

Sljivar, Duško, and Dusan Boric. "Context Is Everything: Comments on Radivojević et al." *Antiquity* 88:342 (2014): 1310–15.

Spee, Clarissa von. "Wu Dacheng at 58: Two Handscrolls with Bronze Rubbings from the Shanghai Museum." *Orientations* 42:2 (2011): 124–30.

Starr, Kenneth. *Black Tiger: A Grammar of Chinese Rubbings*. Seattle: University of Washington Press, 2008.

Steuber, Jason. "Qing Dynasty Emperors Kangxi and Qianlong: Rule through Replication in Architecture and the Arts." In *Original Intentions: Essays on Production, Reproduction, and Interpretation in the Arts of China*, edited by Nick Pearce and Jason Steuber, 138–211. Florida: University of Florida Press, 2012.

Stuart, Jan. "Practices of Display: The Significance of Stands for Chinese Art Objects." In *Bridge to Heaven: Essays on East Asian Art in Honor of Professor Wen C. Fong*, edited by Jerome Silbergeld, Dora C. Y. Ching, Judith G. Smith, and Alfreda Murck, 693–711. Princeton: Princeton University Press, 2011.

Su Rongyu. "Anyang Yinxu qingtong jishu yuanyuan de shangdai nanfang yinsu: Yi zhumao jiegou wei anlie de chubu tantao jianji Quanwu bowuguan suocang fengzhujia de niandai he shuxing" [The Southern Elements in the Origin of Late Shang Bronze Technology: A Discussion of the *Jia* Goblet with Phoenix Poles in the Sen-oku Hakuko Kan, Based on Riveting Techniques]. In *Quanwu toushang: Quanwu bowuguan qingtongqi toushe saomiao jiexi* [Analysis of X-Rays and Scans of Bronzes in the Sen-oku Hakuko Kan], edited by Sen-oku Hakuko Kan and Kyushu National Museum, 352–86. Beijing: Kexue chubanshe, 2015.

———. "Erlitou wenhua yu Zhongguo zaoqi qingtongqi guojiaxing chutan: Jianlun nifan kuaifan fa zhuzao qingtongqi de youguan wenti" [The Erlitou Culture and the Development of the State in Early China: A Discussion on Related Questions of the Piece-Mold Casting of Bronzes]. In *Xia Shang duyi yu wenhua* [Urban Cultures of the Xia and Shang Periods], vol. 1, edited by Xu Hong, 342–72. Beijing: Zhongguo shehui kexue chubanshe, 2014.

———. "The Reception of 'Archaeology' and 'Prehistory' and the Founding of Archaeology in Late Imperial China." In *Mapping Meanings: The Field of New Learning in Late Qing China*, edited by Michael Lackner and Natascha Vittinghof, 423–49. Leiden: Brill, 2004.

Sun Zhenzhen. "Mingdai zhonghouqi 'Xiyuan yaji' ticai liuxing yuanyin tanxi" [An Analysis on the Popularity of the Theme of "Xiyuan Literati Gathering" in the Middle and Late Ming Dynasty]. *Wenxuejie* [Theory] (2012/5): 247–49.

Tang *Jianwei. Jinshi ru hua: Qingdai Dao-Xian shiqi jinshi shuhua yanjiu* [Painting Bronzes and Stones: Study on the Bronze-and-Stone Motif Painting and Calligraphy of Daoguang and Xianfeng Periods of Qing Dynasty]. Shanghai: Shanghai guji chubanshe, 2013.

Tang Jigen. "The Burial Ritual of the Shang Dynasty: A Reconstruction." In *Exploration into China's Past*, edited by Roderick Whitfield and Tao Wang, 173–81. London: Saffron Books, 1999.

Thorp, Robert L. *China in the Early Bronze Age: Shang Civilization*. Philadelphia: University of Pennsylvania Press, 2006.

———. "Erlitou and the Search for the Xia." *Early China* 16 (1991): 1–38.

Thote, Alain. "Intercultural Relations as Seen from Chinese Pictorial Bronzes of the Fifth Century B.C.E." *RES: Anthropology and Aesthetics* 35 (1999): 10–41.

Thouard, Denis, and Tao Wang. "Making New Classics: The Archaeology of Luo Zhenyu and Victor Segalen." In *Modernity's Classics*, edited by Sarah C. Humphrey and Rudolf G. Wagner, 231–60. Berlin: Springer, 2013.

Tinari, Philip, and Paul Tsai, eds. *Xu Zhen: A MadeIn Company Production*. Beijing: Ullens Center for Contemporary Art, 2016.

Tseng Yu-ho Ecke. "Emperor Hui Tsung, The Artist: 1082–1136." PhD diss., New York University, 1972.

———. "The Importance of Ink-Imprints." In *Catalogue of Chinese Rubbings from the Field Museum*, Fieldiana Anthropology, New Series 3, edited by Hartmut Walravens, 24–27. Chicago: Field Museum of Natural History, 1981.

Underhill, Anne P. "Changing Patterns of Pottery Production during the Longshan Period of Northern China, c. 2500–2000 B.C." PhD diss., University of British Columbia, 1990.

———. *Craft Production and Social Change in Northern China*. New York: Springer, 2002.

Vanderstappen, Harrie A. "Shang Ceremonial Bronzes and Their Décor." In *Ritual and Reverence: Chinese Art at the University of Chicago*, edited by Harrie A. Vanderstappen, Richard A. Born, and Sue Taylor, 27–36. Chicago: David and Arthur Smart Gallery, University of Chicago, 1989.

Wagner, Donald B. *Iron and Steel in Ancient China*. Leiden: Brill, 1993.

Wan Jiabao. "Anyang chutu qingtong sanzuqi de yanbian—Xianqin jishushi de ge'an kaocha zhiyi" [The Development of Bronze Tripods Excavated at Anyang: A Case Study of History of Technology in Early China]. *Dalu zazhi* [Journal of Mainland] 45:4 (1972): 201–12.

Wang, Eugene Yuejin. "Afterlife Entertainment: The Cauldron and Bare-Torso Figures at the First Emperor's Tomb." In *Beyond the First Emperor's Mausoleum: New Perspectives on Qin Art*, edited by Liu Yang, 59–96. Minneapolis: Minneapolis Institute of Arts, 2014.

———. "Mirror, Death, and Rhetoric: Reading Later Han Chinese Bronze Artifacts." *Art Bulletin* 76:3 (1994): 511–34.

Wang Guowei. "Songdai zhi jinshixue." *Guoxue lunheng* 1:3/4 (1927): 45–59. Translated by Liu Chongxiong as "Archaeology in the Sung Dynasty." *China Journal* 6:5 (1927): 222–31.

Wang, Q. Edward. "Beyond East and West: Antiquarianism, Evidential Learning, and Global Trends in Historical Study." *Journal of World History* 19:4 (2008): 489–519.

Wang, Tao. "'Hu gui' mingwen zhong de 'chijin' jiqi xiangguan wenti" [The Term 'Red Metal' in the Inscription of the Hu gui Vessel, and Other Related Questions]. In *Yanse yu jisi: Zhongguo gudai wenhua zhong yanse hanyi tanyou* [Color and Ritual: An Exploration of Meanings of Color in Early Chinese Culture], 280–96. Shanghai: Shanghai guji chubanshe, 2013.

———. "Pottery to Bronze: A Cultural and Technological Transition in Early China." *Transactions of the Oriental Ceramics Society* 72:8 (2007): 25–34.

———. "A Textual Investigation of the Taotie." In *The Problem of Meaning in Early Chinese Ritual Bronzes, Colloquies on Art and Archaeology in Asia*, edited by Roderick Whitfield, 102–18. London: Percival David Foundation of Chinese Art, School of Oriental and African Studies, 1992.

Wang Zilin. *Ming Qing huanggong chenshe* [Interior of the Imperial Palaces in the Ming and Qing Dynasties]. Beijing: Zijincheng chubanshe, 2011.

Watson, William. *Cultural Frontiers in Ancient East Asia*. Edinburgh: Edinburgh University Press, 1971.

Weber, Charles D. *Chinese Pictorial Bronze Vessels of the Late Chou Period*. Ascona: Artibus Asiae, 1968.

Wei, Betty Peh-T'i. *Ruan Yuan, 1764–1849: The Life and Work of a Major Scholar-Official in Nineteenth-Century China Before the Opium War*. Hong Kong: Hong Kong University Press, 2006.

Wei Xinying. "Qinggong cang qingtongqi pulu: 'Qianlong sijian' xiangguan wenti tanxi" [The Bronze Records of the Qing Palace: Analysis of Relevant Issues on 'Qianlong sijian']. *Gugong xuekan* [Academic Journal of the Palace Museum] (2015/1): 340–54.

White, William Charles. *Bone Culture of Ancient China*. Toronto: University of Toronto Press, 1945.

Wu Hsiao-yun, ed. *Qianlong huangdi de jingzi: Qinggong jingjian wenhua yu diancang* [Reflections of the Emperor: The Collection and Culture of Mirrors at the Qing Court]. Taipei: National Palace Museum, 2015. Exhibition catalogue.

Wu Hung. *The Double Screen: Medium and Representation in Chinese Painting*. Chicago: University of Chicago Press, 1996.

———. "Emperor's Masquerade: 'Costume Portraits' of Yongzheng and Qianlong." *Orientations* 26:7 (1995): 25–41.

———. *Monumentality in Early Chinese Art and Architecture*. Stanford: Stanford University Press, 1995.

———. "On Rubbings: Their Materiality and Historicity." In *Writing and Materiality in China*, edited by Judith T. Zeitlin and Lydia H. Liu, 29–72. Cambridge: Harvard University Press, 2003.

———, ed. *Reinventing the Past: Archaism and Antiquarianism in Chinese Art and Visual Culture*. Chicago: Paragon Books, 2010.

Wu Zhenfeng. *Shang Zhou qingtongqi mingwen ji tuxiang jicheng* [Collected Inscriptions and Illustrations of Shang and Zhou Bronzes]. Shanghai: Shanghai guji chubanshe, 2012.

Xia Nai. "Shen Kuo yu kaoguxue" [Shen Kuo and Archaeology]. In *Xia Nai wenji* [Collected Writings of Xia Nai], edited by Institute of Archaeology, Chinese Academy of Social Sciences, 465–80. Beijing: Shehui kexue wenxian chubanshe, 2000.

Xin Deyong. *Jianyuan yu gaiyuan: Xi Han Xinmang nianhao yanjiu* [Using and Changing the Reign Names: A Study of the Reign Names of the Western Han and the Xinmang Period]. Beijing: Zhonghua shuju, 2013.

Xu, Jay. "Art Collecting at the Dawn of Modern China: The Case of Wu Dacheng (1835–1902)." *Lotus Leaves: Society for Asian Art* 12:2 (2010): 1–7.

Xu Lianggao. "Cong Shang Zhou renxiang yishu kan Zhongguo gudai wu ouxiang chongbai chuantong" [There is No Idol Worship in Ancient China as Reflected in the Figurative Art of the Shang and Zhou Periods]. In *Kaogu qiuzhiji* [Seeking Knowledge in Archeology], edited by Institute of Archaeology, Chinese Academy of Social Sciences, 334–52. Beijing: Zhongguo shehuikexue chubanshe, 1997.

Ya Zuo. "Capricious Destiny: Shen Gua (1031–1085) and His Age." PhD diss., Princeton University, 2011.

Yan Yun [Lin Yun, pseud.]. "Shangdai buci zhong de yezhu shiliao" [Metallurgical Evidence in Shang Oracle Bone Inscriptions]. *Kaogu* [Archaeology] (1973/5): 299.

Yang Xin. "Quwei chunzhen, huaiyuan lishi: Qiu Ying kuan 'Xiyuan Yajitu' yanjiu" [A Study on the "Xiyuan yajitu" attributed to Qiu Ying]. *Zhongguo lishi wenwu* [Journal of National Museum of Chinese History] (2008/2): 2, 6–11.

———. *"Yinzhen weiping meiren tu tanmi"* [Research on the Set of Paintings *Yinzhen Weiping meiren tu*]. *Gugong bowuyuan yuankan* [Bulletin of the Palace Museum] 154 (2011/2): 6–23.

Ye Guoliang. *Songdai jinshixue yanjiu* [Study of Song Antiquarianism]. Taipei: Taiwan shuju chubanshe, 2011.

Yetts, W. Perceval. *The George Eumorfopoulos Collection: Catalogue of the Chinese and Corean Bronzes, Sculpture, Jades, Jewellery, and Miscellaneous Objects*. Vol. 1. London: E. Benn, 1929.

Yu Hui-chun. "Bronzes from Afar: Ch'ien-lung's 'Hsi-ch'ing Hsu-chien Chia-pien Fu-lu." *Meishushi yanjiu jikan* 31 (2011): 151–96.

———. "The Intersection of Past and Present: The Qianlong Emperor and His Ancient Bronzes." PhD diss., Princeton University, 2007.

Yu Weichao, and Gao Ming. "Zhoudai yong ding zhidu yanjiu" [A Study of the Use of *Ding* Cauldrons during the Zhou Dynasty]. *Beijing daxue xuebao (Shehui kexue ban)* [Bulletin of Beijing University (Social Sciences)] (1978/1): 84–98; (1978/2): 83–96; and (1979/1): 83–96.

Yue Hongbin and Zhanwei Yue. "Shilun Yinxu Xiaomintun daxing zhufan de zhuzao gongyi he qixing; Jianlun Shangdai guanxi liyi" [Preliminary Discussion on Casting Techniques and Forms of the Large Mold Found at Xiaomintun in Yinxu, and the Related Question of Ritual Bath in the Shang Dynasty]. *Kaogu* [Archaeology] (2009/6): 72–76.

Yue Zhanwei, Zhichun Jing, Yu Liu, James B. Stoltman, and Jonathan Mark Kenoyer. "Yinxu qingtongqi zhuzao jishu xiangguan wenti" [Relevant Questions on the Casting Technique of Shang Dynasty Bronzes from Yinxu]. *Gugong wenwu yuekan* [National Palace Museum Monthly of Chinese Art] (2012/10): 47–54.

Zhang, Hongxing. *The Qianlong Emperor: Treasures from the Forbidden City*. Edinburgh: National Museums of Scotland, 2002. Exhibition catalogue.

Zhou Ya. *Kezhai jigutu jianzhu* [Illustrated Antiquities of Kezhai. An Annotation]. Shanghai: Shanghai guji chubanshe, 2012.

Zhu Jianxin. *Jinshixue* [Studies of Bronzes and Steles]. Hong Kong: Shangwu yinshuguan, 1964.

Zhu Shuai. *"Xiqing gujian yanjiu"* [Study of *Xiqing gujian*]. MA thesis, Zhongguo meishu xueyuan [China Central Academy of Fine Arts], Beijing, 2013.

INDEX

Page numbers in **bold** refer to illustrations. Dynasty names follow object names if needed to distinguish objects with identical descriptive titles.

PHOTOGRAPHY CREDITS

Unless otherwise noted, photographs of artworks in the collection of the Art Institute of Chicago are by the Department of Imaging at the Art Institute of Chicago, Director of Photography Christopher Gallagher, Robert Hashimoto, Jonathan Mathias, Aidan Fitzpatrick, and Craig Stillwell, with postproduction by Jonathan Mathias and Shelby Silvernell, and are copyrighted by the Art Institute of Chicago; photographs of artworks in the collection of the Palace Museum, Beijing, are by Hu Chui, Jin Yueping, Li Fan, Liu Mingjie, Liu Zhigang, Tian Mingjie, Wang Jin, Yu Ningchuan, and Zhao Shan and are copyrighted by the Palace Museum, Beijing; and photographs of artworks in the collection of the Shanghai Museum are by Zhang Xudong and others and are copyrighted by the Shanghai Museum.

Every effort has been made to identify, contact, and acknowledge copyright holders for all reproductions; additional rights holders are encouraged to contact the Art Institute of Chicago Department of Publishing. The following credits apply to all images that appear in this catalogue for which acknowledgment is due.

P. 16; p. 50, pl. 12: Photograph © 2018 Museum of Fine Arts, Boston.

P. 49, pl. 11; p. 75, pl. 43; p. 214, pl. 147; p. 218, pl. 151; p. 220, pl. 153: Photograph © Asian Art Museum of San Francisco.

P. 52, pl. 14 (top and bottom): Photography by Jamison Miller.

P. 53, pl. 15; p. 66, pl. 35; p. 67, pl. 36; p. 70, pl. 39; p. 78, pl. 48; p. 81, pl. 53: Photo Studio Roger Asselberghs—Frédéric Dehaen.

P. 65, pl. 34: Courtesy of J. J. Lally & Co., New York. Photograph by Oren Eckhaus.

P. 71, pl. 40: Photo © Christie's Images / Bridgeman Images.

P. 73, pl. 42; p. 164, pl. 108: Bridgeman Images.

P. 119, pl. 71: Littleton & Hennessy Asian Art.

P. 120, pls. 73 and 74; p. 126; p. 169, pl. 117; p. 170, pl. 119; p. 176, pl. 129; p. 179, pl. 132: Photography by David Stansbury.

P. 130, fig. 3: © 2017 Trustees of the British Museum.

P. 188, fig. 1: Photography by John Lamberton.

P. 189, fig. 2b; p. 215, pl. 148: Sotheby's.

P. 200, fig. 3: LC-USZ62-94188.

P. 222, pl. 155: Imaging Department © President and Fellows of Harvard College.

P. 236, pl. 165; p. 237, pl. 167: Photography by Jamie Stukenberg, Professional Graphics, Inc.